MATTHEW PARIS ON THE MONGOL INVASION IN EUROPE

CULTURAL ENCOUNTERS IN LATE ANTIQUITY AND THE MIDDLE AGES

VOLUME 38

General Editor
Yitzhak Hen, *The Hebrew University of Jerusalem*

Editorial Board
Barbara Bombi, *University of Kent*
Paul M. Cobb, *University of Pennsylvania*
Adam S. Cohen, *University of Toronto*
Kate Cooper, *Royal Holloway, University of London*
Maria Mavroudi, *University of California, Berkeley*
Judith Olszowy-Schlanger, *University of Oxford and École Pratique des Hautes Études*
Carine van Rhijn, *Universiteit Utrecht*
Peter Sarris, *University of Cambridge*
Daniel Lord Smail, *Harvard University*

Volumes published in this series are listed at the back of this book.

Matthew Paris on the Mongol Invasion in Europe

by
ZSUZSANNA PAPP REED

BREPOLS

British Library Cataloguing in Publication Data
A catalogue record for this book is available from the British Library.

© 2022, Brepols Publishers n.v., Turnhout, Belgium.

All rights reserved. No part of this publication may
be reproduced, stored in a retrieval system, or
transmitted, in any form or by any means, electronic,
mechanical, photocopying, recording, or otherwise
without the prior permission of the publisher.

D/2022/0095/113
ISBN 978-2-503-59552-8
eISBN 978-2-503-59553-5
DOI 10.1484/M.CELAMA-EB.5.124466
ISSN 1378-8779
eISSN 2294-8511

Printed in the EU on acid-free paper.

For C. & J.
Familia omnia.

Table of Contents

List of Illustrations	9
Abbreviations	11
Introduction	15
Chapter 1. Inside the Book	25
Mise-en-abîme Within and Without	27
The North by the North-west	42
Chapter 2. Outside the Book	55
The Book in the Scriptorium	56
The Scriptorium in England	63
England in the European Networks	89
Northern Connections	91
The Council of Lyon in 1245	107
Chapter 3. Fright. Mongols in the North and East (1237–1240)	123
1237: Chaldeans, Medes, Persians, and Armenians	126
1238: Northbound to *Hungaria major*	132
1239: Dacia, Gothia, Frisia	148
1240: False Alarm and Irruption	155
Chapter 4. Fight. Mongols in the Middle (1241)	159
Holy War on the Mongols	162
The First 1241 Cluster	172
Henry Raspe's Letter	175
Frederick II's Letter	188
The Second 1241 Cluster	214
Chapter 5. Flight. Rivalling Stories of Retreat (1243–1248)	225
1243: The Tartar Khan's Englishman	227
1244: Frederick's Triumph	256
1244: The Man from Russia	264
1245–1248: Endgame	272

8   TABLE OF CONTENTS

Chapter 6. Letters from the Afflicted Lands in the *Additamenta*   281

Chapter 7. The Afterlife of Matthew's Mongol Story   313
    Chronicles and their Afterlife   316
        The *Flores historiarum*   318
        An Elizabethan Bestseller   335
    Back to the Future: Modern Historiography   352
    Loco prologi   364

Appendix 1. Alternating Storylines: Europe, Britain, and the Holy Land in 1237   369

Appendix 2. Comparison of Phrases   373

Appendix 3. Alternating Frederick's Story   377

Appendix 4. Mongol-Related Entries and Clusters: 1241   379

Appendix 5. Events and Rumours: 1241 vs 1244   383

Appendix 6. List of Manuscripts   387

Bibliography   409

Index   453

List of Illustrations

Figures

Figure 1.	Matthew Paris on his deathbed, *Historia Anglorum*, MS R, fol. 218^v.	35
Figure 2.	Example for headings and initials, MS B, fol. 145^r.	40
Figure 3.	*Terra habitabilis* in MS A, fol. vii^v.	46
Figure 4.	*Terra habitabilis* in MS C, fol. 1^v.	47
Figure 5.	The narrative structure of the first 1241 cluster.	174
Figure 6.	Mongol warrior, MS B, fol. 145^r.	197
Figure 7.	Cannibal feast, MS B, fol. 167^r.	234
Figure 8.	News of the episcopal election of Otto of Montferrat, MS B, fol. 166^v.	248
Figure 9.	Drawing of the Pisan and Genoese galleys, MS B, fol. 147^r.	249
Figure 10.	'Impertinens' notation on the margin and arrows in the gutter between columns in MS B, fol. 170^v.	260
Figure 11.	Matthew Paris, 'Self-Portrait with the Virgin Mary', *Historia Anglorum*, MS R, fol. 6^r.	315
Figure 12.	Archbishop Parker's (?) note at the bottom of a page in the *Chronica majora*. MS B, fol. 106^v, col. b. The next leaf is torn from MS B.	341
Figure 13.	The Croatian-Hungarian Count Nicholas Zrinyi's victories over the Ottomans were transformed into curious Tartar-themed materials, such as this printed sheet.	351

Tables

Table 1.	Correlation between references to Legate Otto and Mongol-related entries in the *Chronica majora*.	106
Table 2.	The structure of Ivo of Narbonne's letter with Matthew Paris's preface and commentary	229

Abbreviations

BAV	Biblioteca Apostolica Vaticana
BL	British Library
CM	Matthew Paris, *Matthæi Parisiensis, monachi Sancti Albani, Chronica majora*, ed. by Henry Richards Luard, RS, 57, 7 vols (London: Longman, 1872–1883)
EH	Matthew Paris, *Matthew Paris's English History, from 1235 to 1273*, trans. by J. A. Giles, 3 vols (London: Henry G. Bohn, 1852)
FH	Matthew Paris, *Flores historiarum*, ed. by Henry Richards Luard, RS, 95, 3 vols (London: HMSO, 1890): not identical with the *Flores historiarum* by Roger of Wendover
FOH	Matthew of Westminster, *Flowers of History*, trans. by C. D. Yonge, 2 vols (London: Henry G. Bohn, 1853)
HA	Matthew Paris, *Matthæi Parisiensis, monachi Sancti Albani: Historia Anglorum, sive, ut vulgo dicitur, Historia Minor*, ed. by Frederick Madden, RS, 44, 3 vols (London: Longmans, Green, Reader, and Dyer, 1866–1869)
HM (1571) and HM (1589)	Matthew Paris, *Matthaei Paris, monachi Albanensis, Angli, historia maior à Guilielmo Conquaestore, ad vltimum annum Henrici tertij*, ed. by Matthew Parker (London: Reginaldum Vuolfium [Reyner Wolfe], 1571) and (Zurich [Tiguri]: Christoffel Froschauer, 1589), respectively
HM (1640), HM (1644), and HM (1684)	Matthew Paris, William Rishanger, and Roger of Wendover, *Matthæi Paris monachi Albanensis Angli, historia major: Juxta exemplar Londinense 1571, verbatim recusa; et cum Rogeri Wendoveri, Willielmi Rishangeri, authorisque majori minorique historiis chronicisque MSS, in Bibliotheca Regia, Collegii Corporis Christi Cantabrigiæ, Cottoniaque, fideliter collata*, ed. by William Watts (London: Richard Hodgkinson, 1640), (Paris: Guillelmus Pele, 1644), and (London: A. Mearne, T. Dring, B. Tooke, T. Sawbridge, & G. Wells., 1684), respectively
MGH	Monumenta Germaniae Historica
	Const. — Constitutiones
	Epp. — Epistolae
	SS — Scriptores (in folio)
	SS. rer. Germ. — Scriptores rerum Germanicarum
MS A	Cambridge, Corpus Christi College, MS 26

ABBREVIATIONS

MS *AC*	London, BL, MS Cotton Claudius D VI
MS *Ad*	Oxford, Bodleian Library, MS Add. C. 22 [SC 28782]
MS *Ar*	London, BL, MS Arundel 96
MS *As*	Oxford, All Souls College, MS 37
MS *B*	Cambridge, Corpus Christi College, MS 16II
MS *BA*	London, BL, MS Cotton Vespasian E III
MS *Bd*	Oxford, Bodleian Library, MS Bodley 912 [SC 30434]
MS *Be*	New Haven, Yale University, Beinecke Rare Book and Manuscript Library, MS 426
MS *BI*	Cambridge, Corpus Christi College, MS 16I
MS *C*	London, BL, MS Cotton Nero D V
MS *Ca*	London, BL, MS Cotton Cleopatra A XVI
MS *CC*	Copenhagen, Det Kongelige Bibliotek, Acc. 2011/5 (Courtenay Compendium)
MS *Ch*	Manchester, Chetham Library, MS 6712 [A.6.89]
MS *Cl*	London, BL, MS Cotton Claudius E VIII
MS *CO*	Oxford, Corpus Christi College, MS 2*
MS *E*	Eton College Library, MS 123
MS *F*	Oxford, Bodleian Library, MS Fairfax 20 [SC 3900]
MS *GC*	Cambridge, Gonville and Caius College, MS 162/83
MS *H*	Oxford, Bodleian Library, MS Hatton 53 [SC 4122]
MS *Hr*	London, BL, MS Harley 641
MS *Hu*	San Marino, Huntington Library, MS HM30319
MS *J*	London, BL, MS Cotton Julius D VII
MS *L*	Linz, Oberösterreichische Landesbibliothek (formerly the Studienbibliothek), MS 446
MS *LA*	London, BL, MS Cotton Nero D I
MS *Ld*	Oxford, Bodleian Library, MS Laud 572
MS *Lm*	London, Lambeth Palace Library, MS 188
MS *Lp*	London, Lambeth Palace Library, MS 1106
MS *Lt*	Oxford, Bodleian Library, MS Lat. hist. D IV (formerly Phillipps MS 11257)
MS *M*	Oxford, Bodleian Library, MS e. Musaeo 149 [SC 3659]
MS *N*	London, BL, MS Cotton Nero D II
MS *O*	London, BL, MS Cotton Otho C II
MS *OB*	Innsbruck, Universitäts- und Landesbibliothek Tirol, MS 187 (Ottobeuren Collection)
MS *Ow*	London, BL, MS Cotton Otho B V
MS *P*	Paris, Bibliothèque nationale de France, MS Latin 6045
MS *R*	London, BL, MS Royal 14 C VII
MS *Ra*	Oxford, Bodleian Library, MS Rawlinson B 186 [SC 11547]
MS *Re*	London, BL, MS Royal 14 C VI
MS *Rf*	Oxford, Bodleian Library, MS Rawlinson B 177
MS *T*	Cambridge, Trinity College, MS R.4.2 (James no. 635)

MS *U*	Unknown private collection (formerly A. Chester Beatty, MS W 70, sold Sotheby's lot 18, 3 December 1968)
MS *W*	Oxford, Bodleian Library, MS Douce 207
MS *Wf*	Westminster, Library of the Dean and Chapter, MS 24
MW (1567) and *MW (1570)*	Matthew of Westminster, *Flores historiarum Matthaei Westmonasteriensis monachi*, ed. by Matthew Parker (London, 1567) and (London: Ex officina Thomæ Marshij, 1570), respectively
PRO	Public Record Office
RS	*Rerum Britannicarum Medii Aevi Scriptores* (Rolls Series)
s.a.	*sub anno*

Introduction

> The one duty we owe to history is to rewrite it.
>
> *Oscar Wilde, The Critic as Artist (1891)*

Hearing the din of the army, a mother hid her two children in the oven and climbed in after them. Her feet did not fit as she held them, but that was not their undoing: the Mongol troops did not stop to look for them, they simply set the home on fire before riding on, turning the village near Cegléd into smouldering ruins.[1]

After their homes and crops had been burnt, their animals driven away, the survivors of the Mongol attack at Kiskunmajsa were starving. They sliced the flesh off the shanks of a young boy, using the same knife and precision they had used for their cattle back in the years of peace and prosperity.[2]

The bodies of over thirty people, mostly children and women, were hacked to pieces and thrown over the last hiding place of a family, two infants and two adults whose skeletons were found in a cavity in a storage pit. Judging from their position, 'they hid in the pit and later also died there'.[3]

Another lady in Szank hid her gold and crystal headdress, wrapped in two distinct types of fabric, before she was killed with thirty-three others, mostly women and children.[4]

---

1 Gulyás, 'Egy elpusztult falu Cegléd határában (Pest M.)'; Gulyás, 'Egy elpusztult tatárjáráskori ház Cegléd határában'.

2 'From the Kiskunmajsa-Jonathermál site, the remains of at least thirty-three individuals, mainly juveniles and females, were recovered from two buildings. Both burnt and unburnt bones occurred. Numerous bones revealed sharp force trauma that had not healed; however, based on discolouration of the cut marks and the bones, they might have happened around the time of death. The characteristics of the parallel cuts resemble the marks of meat and sinew removal found on the bones of domestic animals'. Buzár and Bernert, 'Bugac–Felsőmonostor-Csitári Tanya és Kiskunmajsa-Jonathermál tatárjárás kori lelőhelyek'.

3 Szilágyi, 'Perished Árpádian-Age Village at Dunaföldvár'.

4 Sz. Wilhelm, '"Akiket nem akartak karddal elpusztítani, tűzben elégették"'; Paja, 'Tatárjárás kori leletek vizsgálati lehetőségei'.

16 INTRODUCTION

A man whose body was left unburied with many others near Bugac was almost certainly left-handed.[5]

The archaeological detail attests to cruel ravaging, looting, devastation, starvation; the charter evidence to reconstruction and rewards for the defenders. But they would be less likely to gel into a coherent story had we no access to the memory of the Mongol invasion via precious written evidence perpetuating it in narrative form.[6] It is the written memory that this volume is about. Layers of evidence — texts written, copied, annotated, used, and reused — easily lend themselves to the metaphor of archaeological layers attesting to continued life, rebuilt homes, and the accumulating remains of new life growing over the blackened ruins.[7] However, this cursory visual metaphor, although it aptly reflects on the diachronicity of the matter, detracts attention from the complexity of the evidence at hand. Transference, intertextuality, translation, irretrievable loss and fragmentation, forgetting and not knowing, delay and mishearing, misunderstanding, and manipulation complicate the textual memory of any given event in the time before now.[8]

---

5 The man's body was found holding the bronze sheath of a dagger in his right hand, which suggests that he was fighting with his left hand. His right arm shows the signs of two healed pre-mortem fractures, which may have been the reason for his left-handedness. Szabolcs Rosta's findings explained in Sebestyén, 'A tatár népirtás nyomai a Kiskunságon'. More on the excavation in Rosta, 'Pétermonostora pusztulása'.

6 For example, juxtaposing the Kiskunmajsa find above and the line 'homines in Ungaria se mutuo comederunt, ita ut nec filii a parentibus nec parentes a filiis abstinerent' (in Hungary the people ate each other, so that neither parents abstained from their children, nor children from their parents) from the *Annales S. Rudberti Salisburgensis* speaks of unthinkable horrors, where the archaeological conclusion which underpins the text's validity would perhaps remain undetected without the memory preserved in written sources. 'Annales Sancti Rudberti Salisburgenses a. 1–1286', p. 788.

7 The phenomenon of obliterating evidence of destruction either by rebuilding the ruins or building upon them is particularly important in the archaeology of the Mongol invasion of Hungary. For decades, the excavated finds seemed inexplicably scanty considering the scale of devastation described in written sources. As József Laszlovszky had argued in an essay written shortly before the above-mentioned finds were discovered and published, 'the reason for the apparent absence [of evidence of destruction] does not lie in the unsuccessful excavations or their insufficient number. Intact finds attesting to such extent of devastation are unearthed by the archaeologists' spades only where the annihilation was not followed by reconstruction and rebirth. In all those places where the population was not entirely eradicated, or where the ruined settlement was in a particularly propitious location — even if entirely depopulated — new settlers moved in: it is normal that they clean the ruins as best as they can, and rebuild and repair the damaged buildings'. Laszlovszky, 'Tatárjárás és régészet', p. 458.

8 Not to mention the fact that the conventional division of textual and artefactual/material evidence has recently become interoperable in more ways than this meagre simile suggests — there is more to this nexus than simple similarities. Disrupting the conventional archaeology-text connection (or separation) has been necessary to reach new depths and is ongoing. For example, the Foucauldian idea of the archaeology of knowledge; the concept of

While at a glance the present volume is an attempt to deconstruct and reconstruct the textual memory of the 1241–1242 Mongol invasion in Hungary, it is, admittedly, not really that — it cannot be that. A multidimensional, multilayered mass of interconnected memory and written record envelopes the 'kernel of truth' rather than describes it: probing into it from various angles yields cross sections and surprising connections, and what is more, valuable information about the individuals who created it. So, this study is but a mere slice out of it all: a very specific probe driven into the available body of evidence to inform us about the English material as well as its makers and users across time.

The place is St Albans, Hertfordshire, England. The time is the first half of the thirteenth century — the world was about to end in the middle anyway.[9] The protagonist: Matthew Paris, chronicler, Benedictine monk. It is uncertain when Matthew was born (probably around 1200), but many details of his later life and career in St Albans have survived.[10] He is doubtless one of the best-informed chroniclers and historians of thirteenth-century England, and the author of a large number of works. His awe-inspiring *Chronica majora* is often seen as the apex of the St Albans historiographical tradition. As will be detailed in Chapter 2, the *Chronica majora*, the narrative which contains the Mongol story, is itself part of a bigger, loosely connected body of texts: diverse manuscripts repeatedly amended, abridged, edited, and cut, often illustrated by tinted drawings, marginal illustrations, and maps, mostly in his own hand.

How do we read a text so challenging in both volume and complexity as Matthew's *Chronica majora*? It is inevitable to call on modern discourses and debates surrounding the so-called linguistic (or discursive) turn in twentieth-century historiography,[11] for example, Hayden White's by now well-known observation that 'the historical narrative was an historian's

---

text being extended to include material evidence (among others, in Donald, 'Metropolis'); or devoting more attention to the medium of texts as artefacts (White, 'The Historical Text as Literary Artifact', or more recently, the studies in Hansen, ed., *The Book as Artefact, Text and Border*); and Eleine Treharne's recent forays into the phenomenon that is the medieval book as an object-in-the-world, in Treharne, *Perceptions of Medieval Manuscripts*.

9 It did not. But as Matthew Paris records, too, prophecies circulated in England at the time, forecasting that the world would end in 1250 or 1260: 'Cum fuerint anni transacti mille ducenti, | Et quinquaginta post partum Virginis Almae, | Tunc Antichristus nascetur daemone plenus'. *CM*, VI, p. 80. 'When twice six hundred years and fifty more | Are gone, since blessed Mary's son was born, | Then Antichrist shall come full of the devil'. Translation in *EH*, III, p. 454. More on his attitudes to prophecies in Lerner, *The Powers of Prophecy*; Weiler, 'History, Prophecy and the Apocalypse in the Chronicles of Matthew Paris'.

10 His life and career were described by Luard in *CM*, I; and Vaughan, *Matthew Paris*. The best introductions, however, are found in more topical publications such as Lewis, *The Art of Matthew Paris*; Weiler, 'Matthew Paris on the Writing of History'; Weiler, 'Historical Writing and the Experience of Europeanization'.

11 Rorty, *The Linguistic Turn*.

attempt to mediate between the historical field, the unprocessed historical record, other historical accounts, and an audience' and had to be analysed as such.[12] While White's insights into the narrativity of historiography were crucial in choosing my subject, the post-postmodern anxieties about the knowability of the past and the reliability of texts stimulated a more nuanced analysis in the present book. As Roger Chartier formulates, 'without doubt this book [White's *Metahistory*] liberated historiography from the inflexible boundaries of a classical approach totally insensible to the modalities and figures of discourse. It should be congratulated and thanked for doing so. Still, is it possible [...] to pass over the question of the text's "honesty", its "objectivity"? Isn't it the very object of the history of history to understand how, in each particular historical configuration, historians put into operation research techniques and critical procedures that give their discourses (in unequal measure) just such an "honesty" and "objectivity"?'[13]

The present work combines textual hyperfocus with a vast historical panorama, which makes epistemology — both that of my study and of the *Chronica majora* — a central concern. *What* can we know about Matthew's Mongol story? Striving for a realistic interpretation of the birth and the life of a heavily layered historical text, built on tradition governing both its received content and the resulting structure, is acknowledging its complexity. This at once complicates the task and relieves the burden of the historian. Interpreting in this multifocal frame what we may know about the inception and the use of Matthew's chronicle reveals a finely enmeshed and fluid system of chance and intention in the fabric of the text, leading us to appreciate the intended and unintentional aspects of the resulting narrative as equal. The subject of this book, thus, is an 'event' in the past — not the event of the Mongol invasion of Eastern Europe but that of Matthew Paris writing his version of the story.

As for *how* we can mobilize and connect the key factors in the making of the text: while the subject of the Mongol military campaign always looms on the horizon, the volume primarily concerns the methods of the chronicler and the movement of texts between the site of the event and that of capturing it in writing. The methodology is based on mixed methods of metahistory and history. While historical biography and prosopography, history of communication and international relations contextualize the inception and transmission of Matthew's text in the lived world,

---

12 White, *Metahistory*, p. 5. As Edward Soja summarizes the implications of this paradigm-shift, 'White opens historiography and the narrative discourse to "fictionalization", to a poetics of interpretation that draws from literature and literary criticism to represent a real world that is simultaneously real and imagined'. Soja, *Thirdspace*, p. 174; cited in Westphal, *Geocriticism*, p. 90.

13 Chartier, *On the Edge of the Cliff*, p. 38. Citing White, *The Content of the Form*, p. 192.

reception and memory studies, as well as narratology (or narratologies rooted in *Erzähltheorie*), have proven to be fertile and inspiring domains to speculate about the historical transmission of information.[14] Anchoring in reality the convoluted chain of 'the metahistory of the historiography of a story', I must touch upon the reality of the author(s) and audience of the invasion, so the process of reading and writing — both material and intangible — also constitutes a sliver of my study. As for the material aspects, at times the volume also enlists methods of codicology and book history to track the movement of text and information across written sources.

While acknowledging the immense differences between 'particular historical configurations' across the seven hundred years that this volume (however patchily) spans, this present metahistory sidesteps the alterity of medieval historiography and emancipates the medieval historian from his eternal role of 'primary source'. Making his texts (or rather, the texts that we know through him) the subject of my inquiry, I wish to depict Matthew Paris as an equal of his predecessors and not so different from later historians who used his text as 'primary source' to reconstruct the reality which he himself was busy reconstructing out of textual evidence available to him. Arthur Smith wryly notes that 'the modern historian is often faced by the demoralising alternative, whether he will be critical, cautious and dull; or will accept Matthew Paris and make a good story'.[15] Neither sounds fair or appealing. Understanding the text as a historical narrative perhaps avoids this double trap. The *Chronica majora* is perceived as a work of history by both the author and his audience, but at the same time it is a narrative — even fictitious at times. In this in-between place, the narratological investigation provides a framework for historiography too.

Narratology, operating with various distinctions, and obviously with the caveat of the fundamental difference between fiction and historiography, can grapple with these questions.[16] As Dan Shen and Dejin Xu

---

14 More specifically, 'postclassical interdisciplinary narrative theories' rather than the original structuralist discipline. See Ansgar Nünning's categorization, whereby he lists the amalgamation of the theory of historiography and narrative theory (represented by scholars such as Arthur Danto, Lionel Gossman, Dominick La Capra, Paul Ricoeur, Hayden White, Robert F. Berkhofer, Philippe Carrad, Ann Rigney, Dorrit Cohn, and Gerard Genette) in this domain: Nünning, 'Narratology or Narratologies?', p. 251.

15 Smith, *Church and State in the Middle Ages*, p. 170.

16 Tzvetan Todorov's 'histoire' and 'discours' in Todorov, 'Les catégories du récit littéraire', and Seymour Chatman's similarly dichotomous 'story' and 'discourse' in Chatman, *Story and Discourse*. More multidimensional distinctions include Genette's 'story', 'narrative', and 'narrating' in Genette, *Narrative Discourse*, and Genette, *Narrative Discourse Revisited*; as well as Shlomith Rimmon-Kenan's 'story', 'text', and 'narration' in Rimmon-Kenan, *Narrative Fiction*; and Mieke Bal's 'fabula', 'story', and 'text' in Bal, *Narratology*.

summarize, 'in fiction, we are only concerned with how the narrator rearranges the textual story within the boundary of the text', whereas in historiography 'the narratological discussion of (among other elements) order, duration, and frequency may involve both the textual and the extra-textual worlds'.[17] In this vein, as all historical narratives, Matthew Paris's Mongol story comes with baggage: it is a text shaped by practices and strategies that often go beyond the author's field of vision, competence, or understanding — both prior to and after its completion. As will be amply demonstrated, Matthew constructed his 'narrative' out of received material, so tracing his process of creating an original narrative out of sec-ondhand passages is essentially an intrabibliographical investigation of the text to establish the typological relationships between episodes, both on the macro- and microstructural levels. Intuitively but not entirely uninten-tionally, the structure of the book resembles Matthew's modus operandi in framing and interpreting received materials: the in-depth exploration of Matthew's chronicle world through the text itself is preceded and followed by shorter chapters describing the text's physical and temporal context to provide a referential frame to the textual analysis of the Mongol story.

Regarding the scope of the present study, two important premises determine my personal ecology of sources and methods, enabling me to pack such an expansive and multifarious discussion into a single volume, preferably without losing the plot, pun intended. First, the source base is narrow: Matthew Paris's *Chronica majora*. This is not due to unmotivated research or choosing to operate with the lowest common denominator. The body of English sources about the cataclysm in Hungary, first and foremost Matthew's oeuvre, is truly unique, and subsequently crossed the Channel to become an integral part of our present-day knowledge and memory on a grand scale. Second, the timeframe is long because knowledge transfer never really stops — the very fact that a historian wrote this book about Matthew's text, and you are now reading it, adequately illustrates this point.[18]

The spatial significance of Matthew's historical project is not to be glossed over. To set the scene, the first chapter begins with a look into Matthew's chronicle world. Two main themes are explored through these intrabibliographical wanderings: the concepts, conventions, and practices of writing historiography that shaped the *Chronica majora*, and the spatial

---

17 Shen and Xu discuss this question in relation to autobiography as a subset of historiography in Shen and Xu, 'Intratextuality, Extratextuality, Intertextuality', p. 46. Order, duration, and frequency are Genette's narratological categories.

18 In its scope it resembles Norman Garnett's recent work (first volume published to date), which traces the tentacular historiography of a single event, an impressive example of the sheer size of such an undertaking when not restricted to a single scriptorium. Garnett, *The Norman Conquest in English History*.

context of Matthew's Mongol story in his own geographical conception. Both these frames are revisited time and again in the subsequent analytical chapters. The latter, Matthew Paris's medieval geographical conception, not only situates the Eastern European plot within the chronicle world, but is also inherently connected to Matthew's lived experience, writing his chronicles in a connected, busy scriptorium deeply embedded in the networks of power and literacy in the English realm. Therefore, lifting our eyes from the text, we also look around in the scriptorium: the second chapter contextualizes the production of Matthew's book through an exploration of the immediate reality surrounding Matthew Paris, the ego-network that supplied his narrative with information, and the European networks which provided him with original documents and a fairly coherent sense of the significance of the Mongol invasion for Christian Europe.

For the purposes of this analysis, Matthew's 'Mongol story' is understood as the totality of all Mongol-related entries and correspondence copied into the main text of the *Chronica majora* and the *Additamenta*.[19] Chapters 3, 4, 5, and 6 focus on this very text, the earliest and fullest surviving body of written evidence about the Mongol invasion which survived in England. Examining Matthew's ways of pooling and structuring received materials, on the one hand, it will be studied as a literary product, focusing on authorial and editorial decisions that shaped the story within the larger context of the whole chronicle. On the other hand, various phases of the Mongol story will be seen as a 'transnational' creation written in one periphery (the North-west) about another (the North) out of materials mediated by an international network of information, which is the subject of the second part of the respective chapters.

In these chapters, the Mongol story is discussed in four parts — distinct phases informed by different networks at different times. First, the information about the eastern and northern ravages of the Mongols in 1237–1240 in Chapter 3, in which two discrete bodies of material are entwined: the Mongols harassing the Saracens in the Outremer and beyond, and the same happening in the *Urheimat* of the Hungarians, *Hungaria major* somewhere beyond the north-eastern steppe. Establishing that the text was written much later and identifying indirect evidence, the chapter unveils the text's remarkably close ties with documents from the First Council of Lyon in 1245. As an early counterpart of the 'Lyon entries' discussed in Chapter 5, the nuanced examination of both the text and the circumstances of its creation lead to important observations about Matthew's sources and the historian's craft in his self-authored portion of the *Chronica majora*, specifically the way he ordered material in chronological order in hindsight.

---

19 For a tabulated list of all the entries, see Appendix 7, available online at <https://brepols.figshare.com>, from the link <https://doi.org/10.1484/A.14453112>.

Chapter 4 examines the peak year of the story of the Mongol invasion in the chronicle, a complex body of text that contains a wealth of 'original' letters incorporated into the chronicle — those by Henry Raspe (containing another one by Frederick II). Entries that make up this complex story-within-a-story are dated to the height of the European invasion and are often seen as containing the most authentic information about the Mongol invasion in Europe, even though none of them come directly from the afflicted region. While they show a good understanding of the situation, more detailed than the previous group indeed, they are less informative regarding events on the Eastern European front (especially places and people) than the missives preserved in the *Additamenta* somewhat later (Chapter 6). In addition to a thorough narratological examination of the structure of embedded and alternating entries which Matthew uses to construct a complicated dynamic of texts, unravelling the potential chain of Matthew's informants and sources takes us to unexpected locations in Europe.

Chapter 5 continues to reveal surprising European entanglements of information and power networks, which connect various materials arriving to England from both mortal adversaries: the papacy and the empire. Perhaps the best known of all of Matthew's 'Mongol story', the eyewitness reports contained under the years 1243 to 1248 show Matthew's skilful (though at times seemingly irrational) configuration of post-invasion materials, by which the narrative not only leaves behind Eastern Europe but also ushers in the next phase of the Mongol story: the threat in the Holy Land. Similar to the beginning of the Mongol story, the role of the pope's Lyon court, and of the delegates and prelates working on the First Council of Lyon, are explored through careful examination of the textual context of and references within the passages concerned. Chapter 6 is devoted to the *Additamenta*, an appendix of original documents. Examining the links and the discontinuities between main text and appendix, the chapter delves into questions of travelling compendia and letter collections within the European information exchange about the Mongol threat before and after their Eastern European campaign. Finally, it is here where apocalyptic prophecies are addressed again, after a brief excursion into the field in Chapter 3.

Placing Matthew's Mongol story into historical perspective, the last chapter looks into some of the milestones of the afterlife of one of these western texts, leading to scholarship of the recent past. Matthew Paris's Mongol matter is contextualized within texts written by his contemporaries, which is followed by its afterlife in the later Middle Ages and beyond. This is largely based on the use of 'contemporary' historiography in later works, with special emphasis on the process of falling out of use. Following the history of 'Matthew's Mongol story' in England and its journey back to the afflicted lands, the chapter demonstrates that Matthew

Paris's narrative did not penetrate national historiographies until the nineteenth century, and in certain cases not even then. In contrast with the relative silence in Czech and Polish scholarship, a very specific branch of modern historiography, the study of Anglo-Hungarian relations across history, is briefly examined in relation with the Hungarian reception of Matthew Paris.

The various intersecting methodologies deployed, the diversity of perspectives and scale interrogated, and the exponential growth of materials to cover (especially towards the end) no doubt make this an ambitious project, inevitably patchy and perhaps uneven at times — following in the footsteps of the protagonist in more ways than one. The consistency of the study lies in its sympathetic approach, plumbing the depths of a truly pre-modern (and somehow uncannily modern) text with an unwavering attention to the historiographical thinking and practice of the interconnected network that was involved in producing it. And plumbing the depths is not a mere figure of speech here. As will be explained, and the title also suggests, Matthew Paris's oeuvre — and the Mongol story in it — bears out the truly medieval concept of mise-en-abîme copiously and in various ways. The depths of textual recursivity built into the *Chronica majora* are not only detected and analysed in the text but are also shown to continue both in other texts and in historiographical practice. Reframing, interpreting, and commenting on the *Chronica majora*'s Mongol story, the present study is another mirror in the endless line of infinite mirrors. On the one hand, understanding this recursivity of historiography emancipates Matthew's history, elevating it from the role of simple repository of primary sources to that of historical scholarship. In this vein, the medieval chronicler's 'bias and agenda' is repositioned as a historian's interpretive frame to narrate the recent past. On the other hand, it also carries the promise that the students and scholars using the present study will use this work in their own interpretation and their own stories — whether about the Mongols or Matthew Paris, or something completely different.

One of the aims of this study, thus, is to establish the factors that conceived, shaped, and sometimes deleted the story of the Mongol invasion in the past. The longitudinal approach reveals how surviving sources had been copiously mediated already by the time they hit the desk in the scriptorium at St Albans, and how they continued to split, merge, and change in multiple ways until they hit my desk and yours. At the same time, responding to the unsurprising lack of in-depth dialogue between scholarship about English historiography and about the Mongol invasion in Europe, the volume is also intended to be a fount of resources, providing ample footnotes, comprehensive appendices, and consistent, extensive references to texts for scholars interested in either (or both) field. Meeting in the middle, at the intersection of methodologies of history, literature, and manuscript studies, the book is hoped to bring together and connect readers from different backgrounds and foster new dialogues and interdisciplinary research.

Finally, in more generic terms, the primary aim of the study is to shed light on processes of knowledge transfer, the physical mobility of information in the Middle Ages and beyond, as well as the individuals who knowingly or unknowingly participated in this longue durée enterprise across nearly eight centuries. Yes, we can see the Mongol invasion of Eastern Europe through a glass darkly — probably a good thing, considering the horrors of the original subject matter. But while we cannot venture beyond the looking glass, this work takes a gander at the mirror and its makers, as well as its endless reflections throughout the history of history writing.

CHAPTER 1

Inside the Book

> 'Let's pretend there's a way of getting through into it, somehow, Kitty. Let's pretend the glass has got all soft like gauze, so that we can get through. Why, it's turning into a sort of a mist now, I declare! It'll be easy enough to get through —' She was up on the chimney-piece while she said this though she hardly knew how she had got there. And certainly the glass *was* beginning to melt away, just like a bright silvery mist. In another moment Alice was through the glass, and had jumped lightly into the Looking-glass room.[1]

The Introduction above began with the description of unspeakable horrors in 1241–1242 and ended with a suggestion that nearly eight hundred years later we (thankfully) cannot fully reconstruct the events that took place, let alone conceive the real scale of devastation or the fear and suffering of the individuals involved. Besides the temporal distance, physical distance is of the essence here, too: the book is about the perceptions or knowledge gathered at one place about events happening at another, over 1800 kilometres away as the crow flies.[2]

In the main text of the *Chronica majora*, the events themselves span across two decades and forty entries between 1237 and 1257, which mention the Mongols in various contexts — some fleeting tangential mentions, some monolithic accounts going into military-precision detail. Based on these, the chronology of the Mongol invasion(s) in Matthew's rendering can be reconstructed as a timeline of increasingly startling events, which then fizzles out by the end. First, he presents the first major milestones of the Mongol campaign, recording the Mongol ravaging in remote lands but increasingly close to the frontier of Christian Europe. The Mongols emerging from the northern mountains laid waste to *Hungaria major* (1238), then turned against Russia and Poland and eventually Hungary.

---

1 Carroll, *Through the Looking-Glass*, pp. 11–12.
2 Approximate distance between the village of Muhi in Hungary and St Albans in England.

The core of the Mongol story in Eastern Europe is recorded in a number of entries under 1241. The king of Hungary was either too inept or simply left to his own failing devices in defending his country. After receiving threatening letters from the khan and frightful news from the Dominicans and Franciscans he had sent out to explore, he tried to move into the more fortified areas of the country. The events leading up to the irruption and the most horrendous atrocities run their course by 1241, when the Mongols eventually arrived at the Hungarian border with devastating force and speed and killed everyone they found. The king managed to flee to Illyria and pleaded for help from Emperor Frederick II and the pope. Even though the Mongol invasion in Hungary took place in 1241–1242, there are no Mongol-related entries under the year 1242 in the body of the chronicle.

After a year's silence about the Mongol operations, Matthew returns to the story in entries dated 1243 and 1244 suggesting a more extended occupation than the abruptly ending year-long blitzkrieg of 1241. Following a rambling personal account in a letter dated to 1243, in an entry under 1244 the Holy Roman emperor, Frederick II, is finally reported to have embraced the wretched kingdom and brought peace in return for doing homage to him. Following this, as Matthew writes, 'the Mongols, being persecuted and no longer able to withstand the imperial attacks, abandoned the northern parts and quickly travelled to the eastern parts': the number of entries decreases, and Matthew relocates the Mongol presence to the Holy Land. The last wave is more evenly distributed in the text: the sequence of entries about the Mongols in the Holy Land runs between the years 1244 and 1257.

Matthew's immediate empirical world, the monastery he inhabited, was situated in the thirteenth-century realities of England, the northwestern edge of Christian Europe.[3] It was within the confines of his monastery where Matthew and his helpers conceived his chronicle world, primarily the massive *Chronica majora*, built out of a dazzling array of texts. The political, social, military, and religious events, vicariously experienced by the chronicler through his informers' oral accounts and written information, were configured into a chronicle world that is far from being static and knowable — it is a fluid reflection of the lived world as the chronicler(s) perceived it across a rather long period of time. The aim of the present chapter is to examine some of the most important factors that affected the construction of the Mongol story over time. Exploring the chronicle world, I introduce two important facets of situating Matthew's Mongol story in his conception of time and space: first, the

---

3 On the implications of England's peripheral geographical location, see Thomas, *A Blessed Shore*; Bullón-Fernández, 'Introduction: Not All Roads Lead to Rome'; Mittman, *Maps and Monsters in Medieval England*; Saul, 'England and Europe'.

concept of mise-en-abîme as a pervasive idea detectable on various levels of Matthew's historiography; followed by textual clues about Matthew's conception of the geographical location and movement of the Mongol theatres of war.

Mise-en-abîme Within and Without

The *Chronica majora*, this giant receptacle which — among a myriad of other narrative strands and stories — contains Matthew Paris's Mongol story, is no doubt what is commonly called a work of history. Understanding why and how it was written at large is essential for understanding the making of the Mongol story, the process I call configuring in this present discussion. Many modern scholarly studies on medieval chronicles and historiography begin with the near-impossible mission of defining what 'history' is. Elizabeth Tyler and Ross Balzaretti's definition, for example, sums up the complexity of the modern understanding: 'Our term "history" is an exceptionally polyvalent term simultaneously encompassing the past itself, in the sense of what actually happened, sustained writing about the past (including both accounts from the past and the accounts we produce ourselves about the past), and the discipline of history as practiced by scholars in the modern academy'.[4] The polyvalence of the term roots in Antiquity where 'the Ciceronian rhetorical tradition which divides narrative into three kinds, *fabula*, *argumentum*, and *historia*, leaves the third of these terms to cover a huge variety of literary forms: […] all writing about actual events of real life and factual matters in past and present has to be thought of as *historia*'.[5] *Historia* is, thus, a type of narrative, no doubt written as such by any self-respecting medieval historiographer, regardless their familiarity with Cicero or Isidore of Seville on the matter. Out of the 'huge variety of literary forms', the chronicle is perhaps the most engaged with narrative devices and conventions.[6]

---

4 Tyler and Balzaretti, eds, *Narrative and History in the Early Medieval West*, p. 3.

5 Davenport, *Medieval Narrative*, p. 92. In Isidore of Seville's more elegant prose: 'Historia est narratio rei gestae, per quam ea, quae in praeterito facta sunt, dinoscuntur'. Isidore of Seville, *Etymologiarum*, p. 41.

6 I will not distinguish between 'contemporary' chronicles and those dealing with the distant past here, primarily because the dynamic of the *Chronica majora*, especially its intensive afterlife, makes such a categorization methodologically unwieldy. For a discussion of this 'genre' — 'contemporary history', 'history of recent events', 'eyewitness history', or 'modern history' — see Staunton, *The Historians of Angevin England*, pp. 20–21. Also note the unpicking of dichotomies between literature and history along the axis of the medieval understanding of fictionality in works such as Otter, *Inventiones*; Agapētos and Mortensen, eds, *Medieval Narratives between History and Fiction*. As the latter conclude (p. 22), 'the tension between referentiality and imagination is never ultimately released or resolved in discourses about the past'.

Based on the modern scholarly distinction between chronicles as narrative histories on the one hand, and annals as enumerative records on the other, Alastair Matthews states that chronicles 'should be structured according to chronological order and provide a coherent narrative; have some form of closure; and be written by a single, named author'.[7] Matthew Paris's chronicle certainly obeys this mild imperative. Here, two of these criteria will be examined: the interrelated concepts of chronology and coherent narrative. In medieval chronicle writing, chronology and narrative cohesion are not simply two individual criteria: chronology is one of the organizing principles that overwrites other aspects and devices of narrative cohesion, but the latter is what helps communicate that chronology and its significance for readers. The view that chronicle writing grew out of annalistic record-keeping throughout the development of medieval historiography has been superseded, but it does highlight the existence of an intrinsic link between the two. This nexus does not concern the development of the genre, but the actual practice of preserving and producing historical knowledge. Annalistic work and archiving contemporary records played an immensely important role in the physical construction of a chronicle.[8] Annalistic drafts and records or contemporary continuations of older chronicles were necessary to write history through a process of 'the self-conscious construction (emplotment) of cogent stories, made meaningful by selection, omission and careful interpretation'.[9]

While the process of information migrating from contemporary records (or letters and letter collections received from elsewhere) into the historical narrative of chronicles is a relatively rarely explored area,[10] the concept of emplotment — the cognitive side of the same process — going back to Hayden White's (originally Ricoeurian) understanding of the historical text as literary artefact, has become an increasingly widely

---

7 Matthews, *The Kaiserchronik*, p. 10. Coining this definition, Matthews used Poole, *Chronicles and Annals*; Dumville, 'What Is a Chronicle?'.

8 Rosamond McKitterick cautions scholars against the traditional understanding of the development of historical forms, which considers the expansive annal as a mature form of the paschal annal, and the chronicle as the former's direct descendant. In Foot, 'Finding the Meaning of Form', p. 93. It is now commonly accepted that historical writing in England existed in two main modes side by side: the annalistic record of contemporary and near contemporary events, and the chronicle, distinguished 'by a unifying theme and a moral purpose, expressed in a polished literary style'. Martin and Thomson, 'History and History Books', p. 399.

9 Foot, 'Finding the Meaning of Form', p. 102. See also Stafford, 'Noting Relations and Tracking Relationships in English Vernacular Chronicles', p. 26.

10 The question has been addressed in a number of ways. For example, as general observation in Davenport, *Medieval Narrative*, or in specific studies, for example, Coleman, 'Lombard City Annals and the Social and Cultural History of Northern Italy'; Broun, 'Creating and Maintaining a Year-by-Year Chronicle'.

used approach to historiographical texts.[11] In very brief terms, emplotment operates with reducing the phenomena of reality, and making sense of the evidence about the same phenomena by ordering, connecting, and explaining them in a singular perceived framework, primarily guided by chronology. 'Like a novel, history simplifies, organizes, fits a century into a page'.[12] Much like in Lewis Carroll's fictional map that had 'the scale of a mile to the mile', writing a complete universal history is an impossible undertaking.[13] But what may be literally impossible is possible literarily. The phenomena of the real lived world — selected by the availability of information and the intention of the author (which, in turn, are contingent upon multifarious factors throughout the history of any text) — are collated arbitrarily, then abridged, rearranged, copied, damaged. At every turn, reality is edited consciously or unconsciously to produce a 'chronicle' as we know it.[14]

Besides reduction and loss of real-world phenomena in the process of 'fitting a century into a page', emplotment involves the opposite too: added content and significance. As Eviatar Zerubavel summarizes emplotment in the context of historical memory: 'The most remarkable feature of human memory is our ability to mentally transform essentially unstructured series of events into seemingly coherent historical narratives [...]. In order for historical events to form storylike narratives, we need to be able to envision some connection between them. Establishing such unmistakably contrived connectedness is the very essence of the inevitably retrospective mental process of emplotment'. So, where there is reduction, there is always addition in emplotment, and of special importance here is the authorial and editorial additions that pervade a text whether in the form of (re)structuring and connecting, or of adding and collating supplementary material or authorial insights.[15] In practice this takes many forms; as Kathryn Gerry formulates it about Matthew Paris's *Gesta Abbatum*, for example, it 'reveals Matthew Paris's attempts both to engage with an

---

11 Of note here is Tom Kindt and Hans-Harald Müller's remark about the 'wholesale import' of variations of this specific term in the 'narrativist turn' of theology, psychology, sociology, history, and law, which first raised the need of going beyond structuralism and towards contextualist interpretation. Kindt and Müller, eds, *What Is Narratology?*, p. vi.

12 Marrou, 'Comment comprendre le Métier d'historien', cited in Veyne, *Writing History*, p. 4.

13 Carroll, *Sylvie and Bruno Concluded*, p. 169. The same idea appears in Jorge Luis Borges's 'Of Exactitude in Science', in *A Universal History of Infamy*, p. 131.

14 In White's words: 'There is nothing natural about chronologically ordered registrations of events. Not only is the chronological code in terms of which the events are ordered culture-specific and conventional but the events included in the chronicle must be selected by the chronicler and placed there to the exclusion of other events that might have been included if the time of their occurrence had been the only operative consideration'. White, *The Content of the Form*, p. 176.

15 Zerubavel, *Time Maps*, p. 13.

existing historical document and to make sense of the material remains inherited by the monks of St Albans in the mid thirteenth century'.[16]

The author's attempt to 'make sense' of previous texts and other evidence in the course of writing is attained through a diversity of literary devices on the micro- and macro-level of the text. This also concerns the question of the historian's authority as an omniscient narrator. As Peter Cosgrove (writing about Gibbon) states 'one of the functions of the omniscient narrator of history is to reprise the qualities of the perfect reader, the reader for whom the document holds no secrets. Historians make narratives by translating other texts into texts of their own [...]. Another function of the omniscient narrator is to display the power of method as collection, arrangement, taxonomy'.[17] Just like Gibbon and many others before and after him, Matthew Paris was literally making history as he wrote; consequently his approach to using sources is as important a part of his history as the content he captures.

How did Matthew craft his narrative? As Matthew Fisher notes, derivative textuality such as that preserved in the *Chronica majora*, 'obscures the underlying bricolage and presents to the reader a largely seamless surface', which often makes it difficult to unpack the nuanced shifts in register and perspective which show the scribe and chronicler at work.[18] The appearance of parataxis smooths the texture even more. In Suzanne Lewis's words, Matthew used a narrative technique which created 'a text in which the essential components are juxtaposed as equal, without causal, subordinating, or even temporal relationships. Paris's great chronicle must be deciphered as if it were a palimpsest of different histories superimposed in both transparent and opaque layers of disjunctive episodes, in which the ubiquitous conjunction *et* serves simultaneously to link and to separate'.[19] Michael Gaudio continues Lewis's thought about grammatical *et* linking one historical episode to the next, suggesting a paratactic mode of writing history — a model that creates its 'narrative' at the level of the signifier but not at the level of the signified.[20] While this certainly rings true while reading Matthew's relentlessly flowing narrative sequentially, the following chapters demonstrate that probing the *Chronica majora*'s Mongol story on both the intertextual and the intratextual levels reveals a more complex relationship between various components making up the entries themselves. Showing the importance of Lewis's thinking about Matthew's art in the widest possible sense of the word and in more fields than art history, Asa Simon Mittman also uses Lewis's description of Matthew's

---

16 Gerry, 'Artistic Patronage and the Early Anglo-Norman Abbots of St Albans', p. 169.

17 Cosgrove, *Impartial Stranger*, p. 16.

18 Fisher, *Scribal Authorship*, p. 60.

19 Lewis, *The Art of Matthew Paris*, p. 51.

20 Gaudio, 'Matthew Paris and the Cartography of the Margins', p. 54.

historiographical practice as a starting point for his own conceptualization of Matthew's strip maps. Using Jorge Luis Borges's imagined metaphor of a story as the Labyrinth, Mittman likens the maps in the *Chronica majora* to the fictional book of a Chinese scholar invented by Borges suggesting that they are both 'productively linked by the labyrinthine constructs they contain': made up of forking paths but essentially unidirectional.[21]

Forking paths in the chronicle text are essentially subplots running parallel to the main thrust of the historical narrative. The stops and starts, back loops, repetition, and stories that go nowhere add to rather than detract from the *historia* they are part of. How can we describe the productive process that is at work in such a complex and often seemingly chaotic text? In this complex endeavour, both Louis Mink's and economic historian Mary S. Morgan's terminology provides useful handles on this unwieldy topic. On the one hand, Louis Mink stresses the role of subjectivity, the point of view of the narrator to shape every element of the narrative through the processes of event selection and event sequencing.[22] On the other hand — while dismissing the chronicle as the opposite of narratives, which is certainly at odds with my approach here — Morgan distinguishes further processes in what she calls 'configuring' or creating a productive order, borrowing the terms 'colligation' and 'juxtaposition' from art history.[23] In this vein, and as will be shown, the rhythm of the *Chronica majora* as well as the entries' relationship with their immediate neighbours within the sequence are especially important in constructing the story of the Mongol invasion and incorporating it into the body of the chronicle.

The way in which the Mongol story is written into the main narrative flow of the chronicle bears out at every juncture that Matthew's conscious attempt to order his narrative went beyond chronology being the single organizing principle. While it is no doubt the primary principle in ordering his material, Matthew did have some room and possessed the tools to navigate multiple narrative spaces by interlacing various storylines. Carpenter cites Matthew stating that 'Sed quae simul contigerunt, simul minime poterunt enarrari' (Those things which are connected together can by no means be narrated together).[24] While this statement does underpin Carpenter's suggestion that Matthew believed 'passionately that events in

---

21 Mittman, 'Forking Paths?', pp. 135–36. See also the same idea by Borges discussed by Bertrand Westphal, where the 'lines' — so clearly separable into strands in Matthew Paris's chronicle — become 'points' in the conceptualization of time and space in postmodern history. Westphal, *Geocriticism*, pp. 18–23.

22 Mink, 'Narrative Form as a Cognitive Instrument'.

23 Morgan, 'Narrative Ordering and Explanation', pp. 88–93.

24 MS *B*, fol. 237ʳ, col. b; *CM*, v, p. 136; cited in Carpenter, 'Chronology and Truth'. Giles translates it as 'But all that happened at the same time cannot be related at once'. *EH*, II, p. 357.

history must be put in their proper "order" or "time",[25] it is not to say that he did not attempt to create a coherent narrative wrought out of parallel and overlapping strands in the *Chronica majora*. One nuance to point out: 'minime poterunt' ('can by no means') does not necessarily refer to prohibition, but the lack of ability. Here Matthew seems to simply state the fact that the format of a linear chronicle does not allow narrating things that happened at the same time in a parallel fashion, so the reader will have to do the connecting sometimes.[26] The reason why he sticks to the linear narrative — as opposed to the format of some contemporary parallel histories — is given by Carpenter: he inherited the format from Wendover's *Flores historiarum*, which the *Chronica majora* contained and continued.[27]

All these concerns go back to the original question: What is history and how did Matthew view his duty as a historian? Conversely, the answer to this general question is particularly important for specific practices and narrative techniques he employed in constructing his history. In a profoundly medieval way, the concept of mise-en-abîme is helpful in revealing some of the dynamic behind Matthew's text.[28] Originally a heraldic device, the concept comes from a medieval practice.[29] In literature, André Gide identified this phenomenon in *Hamlet*, *Wilhelm Meister*, and, of course, in his own works, for example, *Cahiers d'André Walter*, *Le traité du Narcise*, and *La tentative amoureuse*.[30] Gide's observation opened the way for a multitude of works analysing the definition, structure, and function of

---

25 Carpenter, 'Chronology and Truth'.

26 This preoccupation with recording parallel events in a more satisfactory manner gave rise to the format of parallel histories, most eminently in the twelfth century, for example, Martinus Polonus, 'Chronicon pontificum et imperatorum'.

27 Carpenter, 'Chronology and Truth'. Chroniclers acknowledged and addressed this problem in different ways. See, for example, the parallel columns in Martinus Polonus's *Chronicle of the Popes and Emperors*.

28 In a personal journal entry, André Gide uses examples of heraldic images to describe his insight into the depth of certain literary narratives, including his own. Finding a visual metaphor in medieval culture, he coined the phrase *mise-en-abime*, based on '*blazon dans le blazon*', that is, old shields and coats of arms mimicking the double mirror effect: a smaller shield would appear in the larger shield, sometimes more than once in the image. Gide, *Journal (1889–1939)*, p. 41. Gide's reference to mirrors was further dissected and extrapolated in Dällenbach, *Le récit spéculaire*, pp. 52–53; Dällenbach, *The Mirror in the Text*, pp. 12–15. Described as the double-mirror effect in Hollahan, 'Reviews: Dällenbach, *The Mirror in the Text*', p. 358.

29 'When somebody receives a blazon, he obtains the pre-established blazon of arms to which the recipient belongs, it is to say, when somebody receives a blazon, he has the chance to insert his personal emblem into the blazon of his lineage. Over time, these modify the totality of the emblem, creating a recursive space, which represents linearly the evolution of a family, fiefdom, etc.' Duarte, *Fractal Narrative*, p. 95.

30 Gide, *Journal (1889–1939)*, p. 41.

mise-en-abîme, eminently Lucien Dällenbach, Mieke Bal, Moshe Ron, and more recently, Iddo Dickmann.[31]

The role of mise-en-abîme in narratives has been amply discussed and will be judiciously used in my own discussion of Matthew Paris's narrative below. Before examining this device in the narrative inside Matthew's chronicle world — specifically how it shaped the Mongol story — an image of his likeness draws attention to how it pertains to the bigger picture: the medieval understanding of the relationship of history and *historia*. It is impossible to ignore the fact that Matthew joined a living tradition when he began to copy Roger of Wendover's *Flores historiarum*, which was at the time nearly new — can we even imagine these books as crisp and fresh, nearly unread, and bravely facing a future, probably long and definitely uncertain? Matthew's *Chronica majora* cannibalizing and continuing the *Flores* was nothing out of the ordinary, an act of preservation by reproduction and enrichment, the scribe's rite of passage to grow into his own and to place his tome in the historiographical continuum to be carried on by subsequent generations. This can be continued ad infinitum — the double-mirror effect — if we continue with the image of a modern scholar writing about Matthew's *historia* and the next researcher reading and using the former scholar's work.

The infinite regress created by embedding and framing stories within stories is a mirror image — even continuation — of the relationship of the book as an artefact and text existing in the empirical world. In addition to the textual depth, the mise-en-abîme continues outside the physical book too. As will be revisited in the last chapter, the image of Matthew on his deathbed in the third volume of the *Chronica majora*, albeit not executed

---

31 Dällenbach, *Le récit spéculaire*; Bal, 'Mise en abyme et iconicité'; Ron, 'The Restricted Abyss'; Dickmann, *The Little Crystalline Seed*. Perhaps the most intellectually entertaining way a medievalist ever embraced this concept is Carlo Ginzburg's, who, of course, turns it inside out and places the historian's craft and potential to generalize in the centre of a scholarly mise-en-abîme: 'If I'm not mistaken, both essays, Franco Moretti's and mine, imply the device known as mise en abyme: since clues, as a topic, are analysed by means of an approach based on clues, the details replicate the whole. But clues require first-hand reading: the person responsible for the final synthesis cannot delegate this task to others. Moreover, a close, analytic reading is compatible with an enormous amount of evidence. Those familiar with archival research know that one can go on leafing through innumerable files and quickly inspecting the contents of countless boxes before coming to a sudden halt, arrested by a document which could be scrutinized for years. Likewise, a chicken (I hope that nobody will be upset by such a comparison) walks back and forth, glancing around, before abruptly snatching up a worm until then concealed in the ground. Once again, we come back to *Ansatzpunkte*: the specific points which, as Auerbach argues, can provide the seeds for a detailed research programme provided with a generalizing potential — in other words, a case. Anomalous cases are especially promising, since anomalies, as Kierkegaard once noted, are richer, from a cognitive point of view, than norms, insofar as the former invariably includes the latter — but not the other way round'. Ginzburg, 'Our Words, and Theirs', p. 114.

by his own hand, shows the chronicler with his own book (Fig. 1). The way in which his book appears in the selfsame book, so does his *historia* appear in history. His book is part of the reality he is writing about.[32]

Within the chronicle world and on the textual level, mise-en-abîme manifests in embedded narratives, that is, moving between levels on different diegetic scale. In the *Chronica majora*'s narrative, there are two distinct, albeit often overlapping, sequencing techniques — embedding and alternation — which he deploys at every structural level of his chronicle.[33] And it is not all Matthew's doing. Due to the fact that he often relied on *rescripta* of letters, which, in turn, often contained further letters, the nature of the material available to him also creates the impression of recursivity. From passages embedded in entries, entries making up clusters, to clusters loosely constituting subplots, and so on, by using the same narrative structure on each level — consciously or not — Matthew creates a fractal-like narrative that is holistically pleasing.[34]

Gide's mise-en-abîme, the infinite regress of stories within stories within stories that are characterized by a relation of homology, is a textual fractal. Matthew's chronicle world is a recursive space by the self-similarity of its components on every level. Of course, the number of the narrative levels of the *Chronica majora* is finite, and the principle does not always work out flawlessly in a project subordinated to real-life events and their contingencies. Still, entries, subplots, plots, and strands being governed by

---

32 Miriam Weiss, in her analysis of this image as *Repräsentationsbild*, alludes to the monk's body being one with his book, ending at the same time, and the deathbed becoming a grave memorial. Weiss, 'M[athaeus] Parisiensis, hujus scriptor libelli', p. 196.

33 Dällenbach states that a text may integrate mise-en-abîme by presenting it 'en bloc', by breaking it down so that it alternates with the narrative that frames it, or by submitting it to diverse occurrences. Dällenbach, *Le récit spéculaire*, p. 82. As will be shown below, the structure of the *Chronica majora* relies on alternating episodes of different diegetic levels. About scale and depth, Gransden also offers two fascinating examples of recursivity similarly detectable in the *Chronica majora*, which gives an insight into the world of a Benedictine monk historian: On the one hand, in his understanding of the lived world, 'He regarded the ideas he had as a Benedictine as equally applicable to all parts of this hierarchic system. A kingdom therefore was a macrocosm of a monastery, and, conversely, a monastery was a microcosm of a kingdom. This attitude helps explain Matthew's political views because he believed that monastery, kingdom and papacy represented the same static pattern of government on a progressively large scale'. On the other hand, closely related to this, about the scale of his representations of this world: 'Matthew's historical method in the *Chronica* is reproduced in miniature in the *Gesta Abbatum*'. Gransden, *Historical Writing in England*, 1, pp. 373, 374.

34 Many of nature's objects are fractals, featuring patterns that repeat at an increasingly fine resolution, such as trees, fern leaves, clouds, rivers, coastlines, and mountains. While nature abounds in fractals, from the humble cauliflower to the canopy of an oak tree, the best-known man-made fractal, the Fibonacci spiral, approximates the golden spiral by circular arcs being drawn in smaller and smaller squares arranged in an infinite ratio. See more on nature's fractals in Mandelbrot, *The Fractal Geometry of Nature*.

Figure 1. Matthew Paris on his deathbed, *Historia Anglorum*, MS R, fol. 218ᵛ. By permission of the British Library.

similar architecture create a pleasing pattern and satisfy self-similarity as one of the criteria of a fractal structure: the relationship between the items at the top, or largest resolution, carries down and repeats through each and every level of the model.

Matthew Paris's narrative is not unique; fractals are indeed everywhere, and their presence does not necessarily signify intention, planning, or design.[35] Similarly, due to the nature of work in a scriptorium as well as to the fact that he had to juggle way too many variables, Matthew was not in the position to structure his narrative by careful planning before and revising his structure after writing the text, like a novelist. Accumulating materials and configuring (writing and story-building) were near parallel processes across a rather long period of time, constantly churning out materials that were difficult to reorganize or move around at later stages. Borrowing concepts from the field of information processing and knowledge ordering, Matthew's approach to creating his chronicle was thus 'bottom-up', since the scriptorium's agile working methods meant that the patterns used in the smallest unit were extended to higher and higher levels of organization as the amount of text grew, which, in turn, created the impression of fractals.[36]

Within this hierarchical structure, labelling a relatively disjointed body of chronicle entries and clusters of entries as a 'story', especially when it is but one of the many stories making up a grand narrative, may sound tenuous at first. However, while the Mongol events within Matthew's chronicle are certainly not written up in the form of a coherent and contiguous narrative, they can be perceived to emerge as one of the subplots within the 'proto-narrative discourse' of the *Chronica majora*.[37] Eberhard Lämmert's early concept of narrative strands (*Handlungsstränge*),[38] and Gérard Genette's similar ideas about narrative discourse help define what makes the Mongol story (and other similar subplots) stand out in the nar-

---

35 As Moshe Ron unpacks Mieke Bal's discussion of iconicity of the mise-en-abîme, Bal rejects that the author's intention would be a criterion for identifying mise-en-abîme in a text. Ron, 'The Restricted Abyss', p. 422.

36 To borrow an accessible definition of bottom-up strategy from Wikipedia: 'piecing together of systems to give rise to more complex systems, thus making the original systems subsystems of the emergent system'.

37 Hayden White points out that 'a chronicle is not a narrative by Ricoeur's reasoning because it does not possess the kind of structure with which a plot alone could endow it. But that does not mean that it is not a mode of symbolic discourse [...]. While the value of the chronicle considered as a list of facts is undeniable, its value as an instance of proto-narrative discourse is equally great. In fact, Ricoeur argues, the chronicle is the symbolic mode in which the human experience of "within-time-ness" achieves expression in discourse'. White, *The Content of the Form*, p. 176.

38 Lämmert, *Bauformen des Erzählens*, p. 44; Kindt and Müller, eds, *What Is Narratology?* More on the later application of this in Suerbaum, '"Entrelacement"?', pp. 7–8.

rative.[39] Lämmert was one of the first scholars to define narrative strands, which according to his definition must differ in at least one of three categories: 'Verschiedene Handlungszeit — verschiedener Schauplatz — verschiedene Personen'. The most obvious strands in the *Chronica majora* take place in different places (*verschiedener Schauplatz*) and involve different personages (*verschiedene Personen*), but they run parallel to the other strands chronologically. The main strands comprise the history of England and the English dynasty, of the Holy Land, and of Europe.[40] Occasionally, certain individuals cross over from one strand to another, for example, Richard, earl of Cornwall, who is active in all three. Similarly, the Mongol story crosses over from one strand to another as the chronicle time progresses. The strands are not presented side by side, but by alternating the place of events told.

Björn Weiler writes that 'neither Matthew nor his audience were limiting their reading of the *Chronica Maiora* to those sections which modern historians may find relevant. Instead, they perused and conceived the text as a whole, where individual passages echoed what had gone before and foreshadowed what was yet to come'.[41] This observation about medieval reading practice not only stands as caution for modern historians to avoid plundering Matthew's text for passages stripped off of their context, but also reveals the medieval historian's understanding of their readers' expectations about historical prose: on the whole, making sense was key. One way of presenting compelling historical connections was constructing a mise-en-abîme narrative in which the strands contain plots and subplots, which is a way of interpretation, placing certain events in the context of other, greater concerns. For example, as will be explained in detail, the Mongol story of the early 1240s is a subplot within the plot that concerns Emperor Frederick II's deeds in a number of war-torn fronts across Europe. This, in turn, is interlaced into narrative strands in the form of singular entries or clusters of entries.[42]

Embedding and alternation are detectable in the Mongol story on the level of one of the major subplots. The broad preliminary outline summed up at the beginning of this chapter shows that one of the most conspicuous characteristics of the Mongol story at large is its transfer

---

39 Genette, *Narrative Discourse Revisited.*

40 As opposed to Martinus Polonus's parallel histories of popes and emperors, in Matthew's chronicle of the recent past there is one history of pope and emperor: the history of their conflict, to which other subplots are subordinated, such as Frederick's military manoeuvres in northern Italy, the Mongol invasion, etc.

41 Weiler, 'Matthew Paris, Richard of Cornwall's Candidacy for the German Throne, and the Sicilian Business', p. 81.

42 I refer to the Mongol plot as the 'Mongol story' here, in order to distinguish it from the episode referred to as the 'Jewish-Mongol Plot' in scholarship; see, for example, Menache, 'Tartars, Jews, Saracens and the Jewish-Mongol "Plot" of 1241'.

from the East to the North and then back to the East again.[43] This tripartite structure is a simplified and somewhat distorted account of the immense and varied Mongol campaign which had, in reality, started long before it entered Matthew's field of vision and lasted beyond his chronicle and lifetime. Matthew embeds the 1241 story of the Mongols in Europe between sequences about the Mongols ravaging lands outside the Christian oecumene. Although the image of the assailants changes across time, the theatres of war do not overlap, so Matthew's account creates the impression that one single Mongol horde was swarming from one heathen end of the world to another, thwarted by Christendom (and Frederick II) in the middle — thousands of miles traversed and devastated by seemingly timeless and indefatigable horsemen for over a decade.

On the level of single entries (and contiguous clusters thereof), it is conspicuous that these are generally not singular and isolated in the *Chronica majora*: they normally form part of a subplot in one way or another. Inserted into the flow of narrative, they are connected by their shared location and recurring characters, and this invisible thread strings them together to form a subplot. They emerge and re-emerge in the narrative with variable frequency determined both by the amount of received material and by Matthew's authorial decision to intensify or slacken the pace of the story, rather than the actual pace of the sequence of pertinent events. As will be discussed below, clusters may have been created by Matthew himself by drawing together disparate pieces of news and other texts which seemed relevant to him, but also by receiving them in bundles, which he then edited and contextualized by his own explanation or linking phrases. Clusters are easily distinguishable and clearly signposted in the flow of the main narrative.[44] Matthew clarifies their logical connection to their immediate surroundings in the chronicle, with either linking phrases ('Dierum autem ipsorum curriculo', 'Eodemque tempore anni', etc.) or a longer explanation. Creating a mise-en-abîme structure, the tripartite form observed in the Mongol subplot at large can also be detected on this

---

43 More on the geographical placement of the events in Matthew's chronicle world later in the present chapter.

44 As Bal explains how this works in a text, 'Ils ne signifient autre chose que l'appartenance de l'énoncé réflexif à l'univers de la diégèse. Sont exclus par exemple les interventions d'auteur(s), les invocations à la muse etc. La mise en abyme sera de ce fait toujours *interruption*, de la narration relayée au personnage, souvent aussi, mais pas nécessairement, relais de la focalisation et/ou interruption de la diégèse. La mise en abyme est réflexive et ("méta-") diégétique, objet de la narration au deuxième degré'. Bal, 'Mise en abyme et iconicité', p. 119. That this structure was embraced but was not Matthew's invention is briefly pointed out by Karl Schnith: 'Die Gliederung der materia in zahlreiche mittlere, kleine und sogar kleinste Einheiten, deren Kern jeweils ein Ereignis oder eine Gruppe ähnlicher Vorkommnisse bildet, war schon dem späten 12. Jahrhundert geläufig, wie das Beispiel der *Historia Scholastica* des Petrus Comestor zeigt'. Schnith, *England in einer sich wandelnden Welt*, p. 204.

INSIDE THE BOOK 39

narrative level: the main text of a cluster, a string of conjoined entries, is framed by shorter introductory and concluding entries or passages in Matthew's own voice. This is the simplest form of providing entries with background information or cohesive power, which prop up and frame entries that would otherwise seem disjointed and incongruent.[45]

But even entries are further divisible. Individual entries are the easiest to delineate in Matthew's manuscripts, as they visually extend from heading to heading. Headings are written in red ink on the right-hand side of the column (in-filled graphemes), and never occupy the full length of a line.[46] Where the length necessitates, they are written across several lines forming a triangle or trapeze flush right, in which every line is shorter than the previous one.[47] The entry itself (not the heading) starts with a large initial on the left, alternating between red and blue ink, and decorated with lines of flourish in the opposite colour (Fig. 2). The spatial relationship between headings and text shows that entries were written continuously, with the next heading in mind. While he had a fairly good idea how much of his text will fit the page and was obviously concerned with orphan lines — there are no orphans in MS *B* at all — widows were clearly acceptable.[48]

---

45 'Bracketing' clusters or even larger narrative units in this way results in a triad of two thematically related pieces of text flanking a longer passage in the middle. Recursive bracketing creates the impression of mise-en-abîme. Moshe Ron discusses frames and framing as the visual equivalent of bracketing: a painting may be isolatable, for example, by a 'frame marking it off from the contiguous context'. Ron, 'The Restricted Abyss', p. 428. While, as amply demonstrated in this book, this structure is detectable in many of Matthew's entries, and on a higher level, in subplots even, writing and revising a chronicle of this size across a considerable amount of time forgoes the possibility (and quite probably even the intention) that such a structure would be followed rigidly at all cost. The loose, intuitive use of this form of configuring the story, however, helps maintain coherence and control the various levels of detail within the individual strands.

46 While Matthew Paris's mise-en-page clearly operates with headings, they are still written in a semi-contiguous way whereby the units are not separated by space, retaining to some extent the tradition of *scriptura continua* — possibly out of economic considerations. See more on this, discussed in relation to silent reading, in Saenger, *Space between Words*. Years often start with a more richly decorated initial: the 'A' in the 'Anno gratie' normally has a sweeping train decorated with flowers and flourishes in tan, red, dark blue, and Matthew's characteristic pale green. The alternating red and blue initials are not unique; see, for example, the non-historiated small initials in a 1240s Psalter (potentially associated with the Augustinian priory of St Frideswide, Oxford, preceded by a prayer from St Albans) in London, BL, MS Arundel 157, fols 3–131.

47 There are pages where the headers are not arranged in this way and simply run the full length of the lines. Future palaeographical studies of Matthew's handwriting may consider the fluctuation of this practice when identifying different hands across the manuscripts.

48 A widow is a lone word or short group of words that appears at the bottom of a paragraph, column, or page. An orphan describes words that appear at the top of a page. Widows longer than a word or two were written on the left as usual, and the line continued with the first words of the red header filling out the rest of the space until the margin.

Figure 2. Example for headings and initials, MS *B*, fol. 145ʳ. By permission of the Parker Library, Corpus Christi College, Cambridge.

If the entry ended in a widow line of one word, it was written on the right. The fact that the red headers accommodate these, as well as their elegant, unconstricted form never squeezed into any predefined shape, both suggest that headers were written after finishing the previous entry and before starting the new one. Nothing suggests that he would write the text and embellish it in colours afterwards: Matthew had at least three pens at hand and alternated them while writing. Besides the black ink used for the text, he used red for headings and flourishes, and he also had blue ink at hand which was used for page headers (e.g. *De — tem — pore — // — regis — Henrici —* stretched across the open verso and recto) and flourishes. The blue ink was also at hand for the carefully alternating red and blue inline initials Matthew used to separate passages within entries that comprise more than one element. This is where palaeography meets narratology: these delineable passages often mark the alternation of Matthew's own voice, reported speech, original letters, or linking passages within one entry.

These graphic divisions are often helpful in identifying discreet components that make up seemingly homogeneous entries. Although they are not always consistently applied, they often mark the concatenated nature of Matthew's entries, which were frequently arranged in metadiegetic layers rather than being written in a sequence. As several examples from the Mongol story will bear this out in later chapters, recursive embedding within single entries further enhanced the depth of his narrative. This was not always Matthew's sole creation. Letters and letter collections in this period — his raw material — were in themselves mini narratives of recursive depth, composed self-consciously and deploying familiar images and models in new contexts. As will be copiously discussed in Matthew's adoption of letters and *rescripta* collections, the organizing principle is a key factor. Wim Verbaal, adopting the literary concept of macrotext for letters and letter collections, emphasizes that 'whereas each single text is a unit of meaning in itself, the macro-text derives its meaning from the interaction between its constituents. It constitutes a new "storyline" by which it has to be understood'.[49] In this sense, the complexity derives from the fact that Matthew Paris's macrotext is made up of both heavily edited fragments and collections preserving the hallmark of their original creators, which are macrotexts in their own right.

---

49 Verbaal explains that a letter collection 'does not limit itself to a conservation of singular documents but rearranges them into new significant, meaningful composite units, that in their turn can be rearranged into a more overarching significant body. The individual letters thus become immersed in larger units that derive their significance from their composing elements but that, in their turn, redefine the significance of each of their single constituents'. Verbaal, 'Epistolary Voices and the Fiction of History', p. 14.

42   CHAPTER 1

In the resulting mise-en-abîme Matthew concatenated passages in his own voice with those of illustrious guest performers, ranging from reporting the message of powerful Saracens and other Others relayed by their exotic emissaries, to quoting the words of the crowned heads of Europe. This technique is frequently deployed to break out of the chronological restriction of linearity. The epistolary sources and reported speech embedded into the narrative give Matthew a chance to disrupt the two-dimensional linearity of and enlarge upon various aspects of the 'chronological bulletins'.[50] This kind of recursive embedding — creating a complex fabric of extradiegetic, intradiegetic, and metadiegetic layers — not only sets apart different types of sources Matthew used in order to construct his story of the Mongol campaign in Europe but also adds extratextual authority and human depth to the accounts which would otherwise remain distant and formulaic.[51]

The North by the North-west

The idea and perception of distance is of importance in any account as exotic as that of the Mongols' Eastern European exploits in an English chronicle. But it is important to see that the space in which the Mongol story takes place is not exactly simply a distant location in the world Matthew Paris lived in but one that exists in the chronicle world.[52] But can they be pinpointed in delineated spaces in Matthew's chronicle world? As Brett Whalen observes, the 'continued uncertainty over the whereabouts of the Tartars' was palpable in Europe even as late as the mid-1240s, even at as well-connected a place as the papal court buzzing with travelling royals, envoys, legates, prelates, supplicants, and mendicants.[53] In the first couple of instances, the Mongols are shown to break forth from a generic barbarian and hostile landscape in the north, and harass the 'Saracens' of the East. In the European leg of the invasion, the theatre of war is certainly the Kingdom of Hungary. In the *Chronica majora*, all Eastern Europe–related entries concern Hungary. Bohemia and Poland never appear

---

50 David Carpenter's terminology to describe the *Chronica majora* as a chronological sequence of disconnected events. Carpenter, 'Chronology and Truth'.

51 Alastair Matthews provides an excellent overview of a current theory of strands and embedding, in the context of the German rhymed *Kaiserchronik*, a medieval work of historiography, which is particularly relevant here. Matthews, *The Kaiserchronik*, p. 120.

52 Yi-Fu Tuan's theory presenting space as an area of freedom and mobility, and place as an enclosed and humanized space, can be used to frame Matthew's distance from the location of the events he wrote about. Tuan's notion that 'compared to space, place is a calm center of established values' separates Matthew's regulated and orderly lived place from the vast, directionless expanse of the chronicle world. Tuan, *Space and Place*, p. 54.

53 Whalen, *The Two Powers*, p. 132.

independently from Hungary (except for the 1257 entry on their rulers as electors of the king of Germany), and both receive five mentions each.[54] The Rus' is mentioned three times altogether, always in relation with the Mongol invasion devastating Hungary. It is also notable that all mentions of *Ruscia* (also as *Ruthenia*) come from passages that Matthew Paris copies from 'original sources'.[55] Other Eastern European nomenclature, such as Moravia or Sclavonia, is not mentioned.

The *Chronica majora*'s narrative space, and within it the location of the Mongol story, can also be seen in the context of other texts and images that constitute the universe Matthew Paris created within the confines of the St Albans scriptorium. As is noted by his biographers, Matthew is known to have travelled outside St Albans once in his lifetime, when he travelled to Norway upon a papal mandate, landing in the port of Bergen sometime around 10 June 1248 when a great fire was ravaging the city, followed by a violent thunderstorm.[56] He did travel in England as well; for example, he was at the royal court at Westminster in 1247, and with the king at Winchester in July 1251.[57] The seemingly limited personal experience of distance and physical travel is, however, undetectable in Matthew's works. He is not only acutely aware of the vast size and diversity of the oecumene but is also committed to providing visual aids for his readers, mostly in the form of individual maps bound together with various historical texts.

Matthew Paris was, thus, not only a historian and archivist, but also an artist. His artwork, which includes cartographic images too, was probably initially drawn on loose sheets of vellum and later bound together with his own and others' works according to relevance.[58] He is well known for creating itineraries of routes from London to Palestine, a real treat for armchair pilgrims; the first known views and plans of London penned in the margins to illustrate the events he described; no less than four detailed

---

54 Bohemia in the *Chronica majora*: CM, IV, pp. 109, 109–12, 112–19 (1241), 270–77 (1243); V, pp. 438–39 (1254), 604 (1257). Poland: IV, pp. 109, 109–12, 112–19 (1241), 386–89 (1245); V, 438–39 (1254), 604 (1257).

55 Ruscia/Ruthenia in the *Chronica majora*: CM, IV, pp. 112–19 (1241), 386–89 (1245), 634–35 (1247).

56 Vaughan, *Matthew Paris*, p. 6; Weiler, 'Historical Writing and the Experience of Europeanization', p. 208; Weiler, 'Matthew Paris in Norway'. See also Chapter 2, note 47.

57 Vaughan, *Chronicles of Matthew Paris*, p. 2.

58 Lewis, *The Art of Matthew Paris*, pp. 471–72. As Robert T. Tally notes, 'the literary representation of a seemingly real place is never the purely mimetic image of that space. In a sense, all writing partakes in a form of cartography, since even the most realistic map does not truly depict the space, but, like literature, figures it forth in a complex skein of imaginary relations'. Tally, 'Review of Bertrand Westphal, *La Géocritique*'. What we have in Matthew's oeuvre is an interconnected corpus of texts and maps together, which certainly complicates the skein beyond the possibilities of the present chapter, but, at the same time, also informs the present analysis with the dimension of coexisting, overlapping, and sometimes conflicting imagination(s) of space in genres traditionally considered as mimetic.

44   CHAPTER 1

maps of Great Britain, intended to complement his shorter chronicle of English history; and two versions of a *mappa mundi*, that is, maps of the known world.[59] The so-called Acre maps are decorated with drawings of various modes of transport from camels to oxcarts and boats. Castles and churches mark the built environment, and the traveller can travel across space as well as time: biblical scenes of Noah's ark in Armenia, and Jonah and the whale next to Nineveh position the geographical places in Christian history. Lengthy passages also put the beginning and the end on the same page: the miraculous events in the life of Christ are juxtaposed with the looming end of the world to be brought about by the Mongols in the Holy Land.

Positioning the Mongol story within Matthew Paris's universe — featuring an army that is characterized by being on the move at all times — is informative regarding his sources, but also reveals Matthew's own distance from the events. On the one hand, through the entries constituting the Mongol story in the *Chronica majora*, East, North, and West meet in intricate ways. While the Mongols, for example, were described to have broken forth from the northern mountains, Hungary, the place within Christian Europe that was afflicted by the Mongols, was also more or less in the north. Understanding that the story was situated in the north puts its sources and framing in a slightly different light and adds another layer to what we know about Matthew's connectedness with the actual North.[60] For modern readers the Mongol cataclysm in Hungary looks like a frontier clash between the nomads from the east and the easternmost bastion of Western Christianity. But the story seen from Matthew Paris's scriptorium, situated near the westernmost ends of Christendom, reflected different geographical realities. On the other hand, Matthew Paris's chronicle does not shape the place and space where the Mongol invasion takes place, which is not at all a genre specificity. In the German *Kaiserchronik*, for example, as Alastair Matthews suggests, the author 'defines places within it or movement through it to relate to exemplary roles of pope and emperor'.[61]

---

59 Maps of the inhabited world: MSS *A*, fol. vii^v; *C*, fol. 1^v. Matthew Paris produced other maps: each volume of the *Chronica majora* was originally prefaced with preliminary matter including a copy of the itinerary, a map of Palestine, and a map of England and Scotland in MSS *A*, *BI*, *R*. Maps of England and Scotland: *BI*, fol. v^v (incomplete); *R*, fol. 5^v; *AC*, fol. 12^v; *J*, fols 50^v–53^r; *LA*, fol. 187^v, the latter being a sketch of Roman routes. Maps of Palestine: *A*, fols iii^v–iv^r; *BI*, fol. iii^v (incomplete); *R*, fols 4^v–5^r (and its medieval copy in London, BL, MS Cotton Tiberius E VI, fols 3^v–4^r); and in the St Albans Bible: MS *CO*, fol. 2^v. Itineraries: *A*, fols i^r–iv^r; *BI*, fol. iii^r (incomplete), iv^r; *R*, fols 2^r–4^r; *LA*, fols 183^v–184^r. John of Wallingford, Matthew Paris's contemporary and fellow monk at St Albans (d. 1258), is also known to have collected a small manuscript of miscellaneous materials (MS *J*), which includes a schematic tripartite map of the world on fol. 46^r and the above-mentioned map of Britain on fols 50^v–53^r, now separately bound.

60 Weiler, 'Historical Writing and the Experience of Europeanization', pp. 208–09.

61 Matthews, *The Kaiserchronik*, p. 57.

Despite the clear indication that he had an idea about the geography of the region, in Matthew's chronicle the Mongol invasion takes place on a space-less, placeless level.

Where the events took place, thus, can be sought outside the narrative that describes them, for example, the *mappae mundi* now associated with Matthew Paris, which comprise a set of rather unique cartographic works. Based on their nomenclature, they show similarities with the Anglo-French tradition of maps with detailed coastlines, for example the Hereford Mappa Mundi.[62] Two slightly different versions survive, both from *c.* 1250. Both the map in MS *A* (Fig. 3) and its copy in *C* (Fig. 4) have the same place names and the same arrangement.

According to Matthew Paris's own rubric, his autograph map is 'Summatim facta est dispositio mappa mundi magistri Roberti de Melckelea et mappamundi de Waltham. Mappamundi [*D* adds: dum] regis quod est in camera sua apud Westmonasterium figuratur in ordinali [*D* has ordine] Matthaei de Parisio' (a reduced copy of the world maps of Master Robert Melkeley and Waltham [Abbey]. The king's world map, which is in his chamber at Westminster, is most accurately copied in Matthew Paris's ordinal).[63] Vaughan, concurring with Beazley before him, maintains that Paris's world maps are the least interesting among his other cartographic works.[64] Even though Lewis maintains these opinions about the 'cartographic value' of Paris's *mappae mundi*, she is the first modern scholar to recognize the importance of depicting consistently contemporary material, even if the layout of the maps is but a distorted version of an earlier tradition.[65] More recently they have been increasingly recognized as important medieval works.[66] They are in fact unique maps that reveal a great deal about the mapmaker's concept of European regions and provinces.

As opposed to the famous Hereford Mappa Mundi, for example, Matthew Paris's map does not present parallel histories at different stages, and there are no ethnic names, biblical references, Solinian monstrous

---

62 Lewis, admitting that the extent to which Matthew Paris was the original cartographer of his maps remains a conjecture due to a lack of sources, establishes a tenuous link between the encyclopaedic map tradition of the Ebstorf Map and related maps in search of Matthew Paris's sources. Lewis, *The Art of Matthew Paris*, p. 376.

63 Translation from Vaughan, *Matthew Paris*, p. 247. Note that Vaughan's siglum *D* denotes MS *C* in the present work to avoid confusion with Luard's sigla.

64 Vaughan, *Matthew Paris*, p. 247; Beazley, *The Dawn of Modern Geography*, p. 586.

65 'In their insistence on contemporary material and modernization of nomenclature, the *Chronica Majora* maps are landmarks in the history of cartography. While Matthew Paris never surmounted the limitations of a medieval bookman's geography, his constant reworking and updating of information, his wide-ranging curiosity, and concern for accurate details are nonetheless remarkable albeit distant harbingers of modern scientific mapmaking'. Lewis, *The Art of Matthew Paris*, p. 323.

66 Kim, 'Matthew Paris, Visual Exegesis, and Apocalyptic Birds'; Connolly, *The Maps of Matthew Paris*.

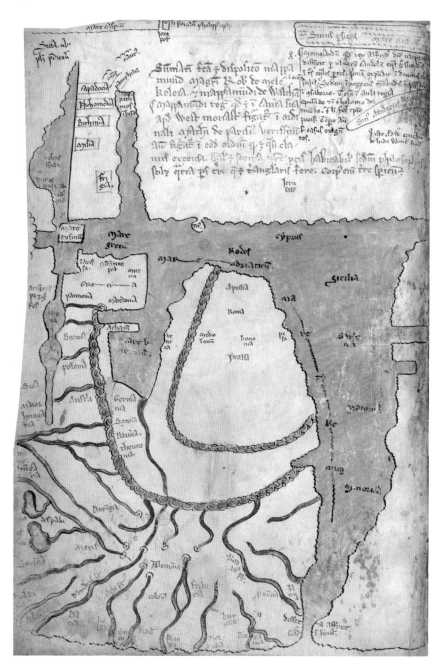

Figure 3. *Terra habitabilis* in MS A, fol. vii[v]. By permission of the Parker Library, Corpus Christi College, Cambridge.

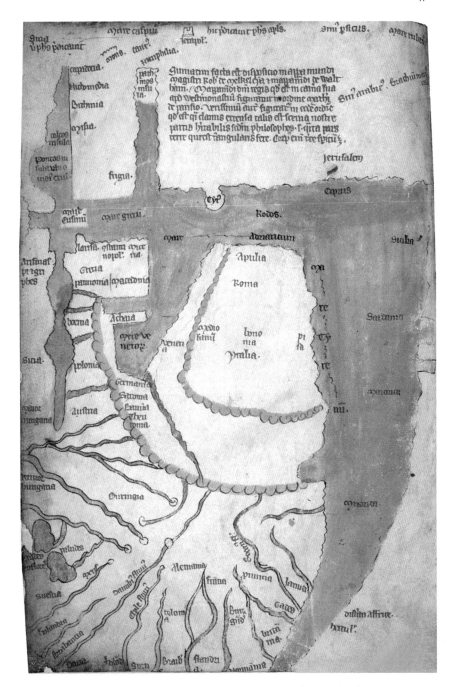

Figure 4. *Terra habitabilis* in MS C, fol. 1ᵛ. By permission of the British Library.

48   CHAPTER 1

races and curiosities, or pictorial representations of cities.[67] Instead, similarly to Lambert of St Omer's twelfth-century map of Europe,[68] the place names are almost entirely contemporary, and the nomenclature is consistent: apart from names of provinces and kingdoms only a few selected geographical features are spelled out.[69] There are only three waterways marked in Europe: the Danube, the Elbe (?), and the Maeotian Marshes. The geographical features (mountains, waterways) and the names of islands and cities are written in black ink and thus are clearly distinguished from names of provinces written in red. The provinces of the Greek peninsula and Asia Minor are also in black (the ones in Asia Minor also in red frames). This creates an image dominated by red provinces in Central, Western, and Northern Europe, and less emphatic black legends in the territories east of Bohemia and the Adriatic Sea. Whatever Matthew Paris used the distinction of red and black ink for, the copier (himself?) in MS C did not deem it relevant and all the inscriptions there are uniform and red.

Eastern Europe occupies the north-eastern corner of the densely labelled large European peninsula, which occupies approximately three quarters of the map. The Eastern European region, especially the provinces of the Holy Roman Empire, is clearly marked and detailed. The place names here are gathered in two major groups. The transalpine cluster of *Aust[ri]a*, *Polonia*, and *Boemia* is north of *Germania*, *Saxo[n]ia*, *Bau[ar]ia*, and *Theutonia*, and south of a long narrow gulf separating it from Scythia. This gulf is a westward projection of the Black Sea.[70] Perhaps the most interesting and novel feature in the map is the distinction between an eastern Greater Hungary (*Hungaria major*) and a western Lesser Hungary (*Hungaria minor*), which will be an important subject in the next chapter. On the very margin, the most extreme north of Europe, Scythia's (*Sicia*) immediate neighbours to the west are *Maior Hungaria*, *Minor Hungaria*,

---

67 Kline, *Maps of Medieval Thought*.

68 Lambert, canon of St Omer, was a French Benedictine monk (*c.* 1061–1150); his *Liber floridus*, an encyclopaedia of biblical, theological, geographical, natural historical, and musical themes, was completed around 1120. The earliest Ghent manuscript is Lambert's autograph, and ten copies survive with three main redactions. Each copy contains about ten different maps, the hand-shaped (probably for easy mnemonics) map of Europe is in Ghent, Universiteitsbibliotheek, MS 92, fol. 241ʳ. See Beazley, *The Dawn of Modern Geography*, pp. 570–73, 621–24.

69 Suzanne Lewis also notes that Paris's maps 'are remarkably free of the medieval tendency toward symmetry and stereotype, and contain surprisingly few biblical, classical and legendary features'. Lewis, *The Art of Matthew Paris*, p. 323. The only notable exceptions to this are the legend 'arimaspi et grifes' on the European shores of the Black Sea, and the use of the antiquated province name 'Pannonia', alongside the contemporary 'Hungaria', both situated in vastly different locations on the map despite the fact that they should more or less denote the same geographical area.

70 The name of this gulf is illegible on MS A. It was probably illegible already at the time of copying, because MS C omits it altogether.

and the legend *Meodes paludes inferiores* in the proximity of two lakes. In other maps and geographies, the Maeotian Marshes (Sea of Azov) are usually attached to the *Tanais* (Don), the border between Europe and Asia.[71]

The mapmaker clearly distorted the map to fit a rectangular leaf, and the northern edge is crowded into a very small space. This is a very similar manoeuvre to what Matthew himself describes in a brief caption scribbled on another map: near the bottom of the page on his Map of Britain, a sentence, interrupted halfway through by a small image of city walls indicating London, reads 'Si pagina pateretur, hec totalis insula longior esse deberet' (if the page had allowed it, this whole island would have been longer).[72] Due to a similar distortion of the northern European region in his *mappa mundi*, whereupon the contemporary nomenclature and the spatial relationship of places to one another were stretched into a rectangular shape, certain features end up in unexpected places.[73] The River Danube, for example, is marked as springing forth in the middle of Alemannia and flowing into the northern ocean near Brabantia. The eastern character of the Maeotian Marshes is ignored. Thus, Hungary, positioned in relation to the location of the marshes, ended up on the northern edge of the map along with Scythia and, further westward, *Suescia*, *Holandia*, and *Brabantia*. Pannonia province, similarly to the Hereford Map, is separate from Hungary, and it appears as one of the provinces of the peninsular Greece next to Macedonia.

Besides his *mappae mundi*, there is further sporadic evidence for Matthew Paris's familiarity with elements of contemporary Eastern European geography, for example, notes found in proximity to the Map of Palestine found in the St Albans Bible.[74] One of these notes states that, 'in parte boreali est Ruscia et Cumania et Wlakania, et superius uersus Antiokhiam est Yconium'.[75] Although Vaughan suggests (and Edson concurs)

---

71 In *Getica* 24. 123–24, Jordanes tells how the Huns, following a hind in hunt, crossed these impassable swamps, which divided their own lands from Scythia. On the Hereford Map, it is depicted as a river running from north to south, marked as *paludes* at the easternmost corner of Northern Europe.

72 MS R, fol. 5ᵛ. See more in Gaudio, 'Matthew Paris and the Cartography of the Margins', p. 50.

73 This is why the otherwise familiar map has a layout that does not seem to correspond to other extant examples of *mappae mundi*. Consequently, while Woodward's nomenclature-based typology classifies them along maps like the Anglo-Saxon, Sawley, and Hereford Maps as Orosian, Matthew Paris's maps defy Leonid Chekin's layout-based typology, where they constitute their own category. This rigid dependence on layout makes it difficult to identify patterns of similarity and shared sources for Paris's maps within the wider context of English cartographic works.

74 *Map of Palestine*, MS CO, fol. 2ᵛ.

75 What Vaughan transcribes as 'Rumania' and 'B…lakania' is more likely *Cumania et Wlakania* (Cumania and Valachia). Vaughan, *Matthew Paris*, p. 240. Imre Boba suggests that in the thirteenth century there were two political organizations of the Vlachs (Valachians), one

CHAPTER 1

that these notes 'seem to show him [Matthew Paris] in the very act of collecting cartographical material', it is notable that they do not actually feature in any of his maps as legends.[76] However, although neither Cumania nor Russia appears on any of Matthew's maps, their north-eastern location and the fact that they were neighbouring areas were known to Matthew. This is evident, for example, from the passage that suggests that a 'populosa Cumanorum colonia' is neighboured by the Rutheni,[77] as well as the more verbose description of the geographical locations involved using the concepts and nomenclature in contemporary understanding of Macrobian zonal geography:

> Redargiutur enim epistola, quasi continens falsitatem. Dicitur enim in ea, gentem ipsam ignotam Tartarorum ab Australibus mundi, quae sub torrida zona sunt, partibus erupisse, quod evidenter apparet fictitium. Non enim audivimus eos Australes vel etiam Orientales partes peragrasse. [...] Et cum sint in totius mundi capacitate septem climata, videlicet Indorum, Ethiopum vel Maurorum, Egiptiorum, Jerosolimitanorum, Graecorum, Romanorum, et Francorum, nec sint tam remoti in tota nostra habitabili, quos mercatores navigando non rimentur, unde poeta Oratius, 'Impiger extremos curris mercator ad Indos', [Hor. 1 Epist. i.] ubi tot et tales hactenus latuerunt? ut quid tam fraudulenta inter eos et tam occulta conjuratio? Sunt igitur, ut inquiunt, Hircani et Sicii, humanam caedem avide sitientes, montes et salebras Boreales inhabitantes, qui feralem vitam ducentes, deos colunt montium, et praevisa in die; qui etiam cum Cumanis sibi conterminis et jam confoederatis, machinante imperatore, regem Hungariae cum quibusdam aliis magnatibus expugnarunt.

> (The letter, too, was proved to contain falsehoods; for it was stated in it, that this unknown race of Tartars had burst forth from the southern parts of the world, under the torrid zone, which plainly

---

south of the Carpathians along the Lower Danube and Moldavia, and one east of the Carpathians, towards the Seret River. Boba, 'Vlachs in the History of Central Europe', p. 102. Valachian tribes, however, were dwelling in large areas from Bulgaria to Transylvania. Their presence near Belgrade is attested by sources such as an eleventh-century letter by Emperor Basileios II, mentioning Vlachs 'living all over Bulgaria and belonging to the archbishopric Ochrid'. Miron, 'Die rumänische Sprachgemeinschaft', p. 185, cited in Boba, 'Vlachs in the History of Central Europe', p. 101.

76 Scholars do not raise the possibility that these notes were by a hand different than that of Matthew. Vaughan, *Matthew Paris*, p. 240. Evelyn Edson even suggests that these notes were collected from travellers to guide Matthew in his future productions. Edson, *Mapping Time and Space*, p. 124.

77 'dum ad populosam Cumanorum coloniam pervenissent dicti Tartari [...]. Quorum vicinitas Ruthenos ab eis non multum distantes, vix cautos efficit et munitos [...] intenderent praecavere'. *CM*, IV, p. 113. This description is found in a letter attributed to Frederick II; more on this letter and its sources in Chapter 4 below.

appears to be a falsehood; for we have not heard that they passed through the southern or even the eastern countries.[78] [...] And as there are only seven climes in the whole extent of the world; namely, those of the Indians, Ethiopians or Moors, Egyptians, Jerusalemites, Greeks, Romans, and French, and there are none so remotely situated in the whole of the habitable part of the world, that merchants will not find their way amongst them, as the poet says:

'To India far the merchant finds his way'.

Where have such people, who are so numerous, till now lain concealed? Why is there now such a crafty and secret conspiracy amongst them? There are, also, as they say, Hyrcanians and Scythians, who thirst eagerly for human blood, inhabiting the mountainous and rugged regions of the north, leading the life of wild beasts, worshipping the gods of the mountains on appointed days; and these people, by the machinations of the emperor, have, together with their neighbours, the Cumanians, who have now entered into an alliance with them, made war on the king of Hungary and some other nobles.)[79]

Although the reference to Cumans and Valachians seems contemporaneous and related to the Mongol invasion of Eastern Europe, the fact that the note is scribbled next to the Map of Palestine may suggest that this piece of information arrived together with information about the Holy Land, perhaps from an older crusader account.[80] While the source of these notes is untraceable, perhaps oral communication, they reflect some information received of the ethnic composition of the south-eastern ends

---

78 This is an interesting negative statement — argumentum ad ignorantiam — especially in light of another text copied into the *Additamenta*, echoing many others from this time: 'How innumerable nations, hateful to other men, and of unbounded wickedness, treading the earth in disdain, *from the east even to the frontiers of our dominion, have utterly destroyed the whole earth*'. Henry Raspe's letter in the *Additamenta*: MS *LA*, fol. 86ʳ, col. a; *CM*, VI, p. 77; *EH*, III, p. 451 (my italics).

79 MS *B*, fol. 146ᵛ, col. a; *CM*, IV, pp. 119–20; *EH*, I, pp. 347–48.

80 Regarding 'Wlakania', Paris's note also reflects similar information to Gervase of Tilbury's who says 'illinc uersus septentrionem sunt Cumani, adorantes quicquid illis mane occurrit primo [...] a diuisione Danubii usque Constantinopolim sunt uiginti quatuor diete uersus eurum. Primo enim occurrit desertum Bulgarie, quod est terra Blacti (Blaca)'. (North of there [Brandiz] are the Cumani, who worship the first thing that meets them in the morning. [...] From the division of the Danube to Constantinople it is twenty-four days' journey to the south-east. First one comes to the wilderness of Bulgaria, which is the territory of Blactum.) Book II, Chapter 7 in Gervase of Tilbury, *Otia Imperialia*, p. 241. Editors S. E. Banks and J. W. Binns suggest that Blacti/Blaca refers to Blactum, which they interpret as Belgrade. Though people of similar names were found near Belgrade at the time (see note 75 above), it is more likely, however, that Gervase referred to the Valachian people settled in north-east Bulgaria rather than the city.

of Christendom.[81] Similarly to the bulk of the Eastern European material in Matthew's historiography being relegated into the volume of the *Additamenta*, these notes also remain liminal: they are on the verge of being incorporated into the main narrative but remain contained in obscure personal notes.

The concept of liminality raised by these notes takes us back to the second issue regarding Matthew Paris's maps in relation to the Mongol story in the chronicle's text. The doubly liminal position of this content within the chronicle indicates the author's distance from the notes and legends. They are indeed doubly liminal: on the one hand because of the maps' peripheral positioning of the actual geographical regions and peoples on maps, and on the other hand because factual information about them regularly appears outside the main body of the narrative, often in one-off notes and rubrics. The former is a simple and (since Michael Camille's works) well-known phenomenon, which is clearly observable in Matthew Paris's maps. Gaudio, drawing on Michael Camille's work on natural images on the margins of manuscripts and how they construct authority, recalls Camille's concept that 'the dialectic of center and margin offers a particularly appropriate model for interpreting Matthew's cartography', and argues that the position of such images at or around the edges of the page reproduces the hierarchical status of nature in the Middle Ages.[82] Citing Jacques Le Goff's classic observation, Gaudio restates that 'nature — associated with the forest, the desert, and solitary living — was in every way held to be the antithesis of civilized Christian society'.[83] Within the world of the *Chronica majora*, the latter is substantiated by the fact that these are spaces where Matthew Paris merely records information received where appropriate but chooses not to carry them over into his own narrative.

Lastly, but importantly: while the peripherality of the region(s) involved in the Mongol story is manifest in many ways within and without the *Chronica majora*, the geographical peripherality of Matthew Paris's England is also worth noting. Even the most cursory glance at Matthew's

---

81 The phrase 'information received' must be used and understood consciously and carefully to avoid jumping to broad generalizations about Matthew Paris's 'knowledge', especially in instances such as this, where pieces of information appear only once and in a liminal position.

82 Gaudio, 'Matthew Paris and the Cartography of the Margins', p. 52. Referring to Camille, *Image on the Edge*. Notably, Dorothy Kim uses this model to disprove Gaudio's suggestions about the positioning of certain figures on the margin, by presenting a more nuanced interpretation that takes into consideration revisions and changes made to the illustration in question — an approach not dissimilar to that of the present volume. Kim, 'Matthew Paris, Visual Exegesis, and Apocalyptic Birds', p. 26.

83 Gaudio, 'Matthew Paris and the Cartography of the Margins', p. 50; citing Le Goff, *The Medieval Imagination*, p. 58.

world map, let alone his telling rubric near London on another map,[84] reveals Matthew's awareness of his own geographical peripherality in a European context. Alfred Thomas suggests (in comparison with Bohemia specifically) that 'England was geographically and politically marginal for most of the premodern period while English was by no means the international language today'.[85] This may seem exaggerated for this period when the English royals were demonstrably active and highly mobile members of the Angevin power network on a European scale. But it was hard work on the ground, especially for a historian: what Weiler terms as the *experience* of Europeanization was both the process and the product of keeping England abreast with European expansion and dynastic developments.[86] Informing English historical narratives about continental events and their intimate ties to the English monarch and aristocracy can be seen as a response to this perceived peripherality. Instead of an overall centre/periphery-based view, it steers the present discussion to the lived experience of the agents of networks connecting England and the Continent. For example, Hugh M. Thomas's suggestion about a multifocal Europe, that is, 'a model of Catholic Europe as an intellectual free trade zone with personnel and resources flowing from place to place and with certain centers of particularly intensive activity emerging as a result'. In this framework, medieval England was an important hinterland that provided resources to several continental centres of intellectual and cultural development.[87] This is the subject of the following discussion about the world surrounding Matthew Paris, in which the mobility of English secular clerics and intellectuals between centres of learning gains special importance.[88]

---

84 See note 72 in this chapter.

85 Thomas, *A Blessed Shore*, p. 7.

86 Weiler, 'Historical Writing and the Experience of Europeanization'. This reciprocal process is similar to the so-called structural theory of action, which postulates that 'on the one hand, the structure of a social network influences the objectives and options for action of the players involved, while on the other hand, the concrete actions of the players reproduce and modify the network structure itself'. As Robert Gramsch-Stehfest summarizes in a network science context, 'historical events can therefore be described as a continual network transformation process'. Gramsch-Stehfest, 'Entangled Powers', p. 371.

87 Thomas, *The Secular Clergy in England*, p. 239.

88 This mobility varied: there were countries where it was higher than in others; for example, Julia Barrow demonstrates that secular clerics in France and England were more likely to participate in the international schools than were their German counterparts. Barrow, 'Education and the Recruitment of Cathedral Canons', pp. 126–29, 131–37. Interestingly, Hungarian students were also highly mobile from the mid-twelfth century onwards, and what is more, they seemingly ran in the same circles, even the same university *nations* — as if to replicate their geographical proximity suggested by medieval maps, especially those of Matthew Paris. Bauer, 'Picturing and Promoting New Identities', p. 122.

CHAPTER 2

Outside the Book

> Kublai asks Marco, 'When you return to the West, will
> you repeat to your people the same tales you tell me?'
> 'I speak and speak', Marco says, 'but the listener retains
> only the words he is expecting'.[1]

Matthew Paris often diligently named his informants when it came to domestic affairs, but he is somewhat less forthcoming about his sources when
it comes to international events such as the Mongol invasion. Mapping
his ego-network and what we know about his primary informants reveals
that while these individuals have travelled a great deal and are also known
to have been in direct contact with each other and St Albans, the idea
that Matthew Paris and his team were — and had to be — in personal
contact with their informants is misleading and simplistic. Especially in
diplomacy and politics overseas, the information exchange in which the
St Albans scriptorium participated relied on more professional ways of
moving texts and intelligence. Political players needed letters, circulars,
and documents for their future decisions, and historiographers needed
them for recording the past and present. Many people whose day-to-day
operation involved travelling and working abroad made it their business to
be part of this process by creating and moving documents about the news
and intelligence that they gathered. The minutiae of disseminating and
accumulating the Mongol materials in the *Chronica majora* show that the
St Albans scriptorium had access to a much larger number of documents
through less personal connections than previous Matthew Paris studies
suggest. Starting from named sources, this chapter will reveal their overlapping and complex European networks, prominent connecting hubs, and
their importance in relaying Mongol-related documents to England.

---

1 Calvino, *Invisible Cities*, p. 135.

The Book in the Scriptorium

Scholarship on Matthew Paris's life and work is staggering, but having been produced by a large number of people, some armed with typewriters and computers, across many lifetimes, it seems to be dwarfed by the work produced by Matthew himself. According to Weiler's estimate, in modern printed editions his writings number nearly seven thousand pages, his *Chronica majora* alone containing over one million words.[2] While it is no doubt his magnum opus, Matthew Paris's historical oeuvre was not limited to the narrative of the *Chronica majora*. He wrote shorter historical works as well, mostly abridged versions of his monumental *Chronica majora*, such as the *Flores historiarum* (different from that of Roger of Wendover).[3] The *Flores historiarum*, whose popularity and long afterlife will be discussed in detail in Chapter 7, is a redaction of the *Chronica majora*, which was for long attributed to a Matthew of Westminster in earlier scholarship.[4] Vaughan later established that this work is the *Flores historiarum* by Matthew Paris created out of MSS *AB* of the *Chronica majora*.[5]

And that is not all. The London, BL, MS Royal 14 C VII codex (MS *R*) contains the *Historia Anglorum* (probably written between 1250 and 1259), the last volume of the *Chronica majora*, and various other well-known items.[6] The *Abbreviatio chronicorum* (or *Historia minor*, MS *AC*) is based for the most part on the *Historia Anglorum* and mainly covers the years from 1067 to 1253. It is illustrated with such often studied drawings by Matthew as the genealogy of English kings and the map of the British Isles. Cambridge University Library, MS Ee III 59 contains Paris's

---

2 Weiler, 'Historical Writing and the Experience of Europeanization', p. 210; Weiler, 'History, Prophecy and the Apocalypse in the Chronicles of Matthew Paris', p. 253. For a comprehensive overview of Matthew Paris's works, only perfunctorily listed below, see 'Matthew Paris and the St Albans School of Historiography' in Gransden, *Historical Writing in England*, I, pp. 356–79.

3 Autograph copy in Manchester, Chetham Library, MS 6712, fols 7–298 (MS *Ch*). See the full List of Manuscripts in Appendix 6.

4 Matthew Parker published this text as Matthew of Westminster's work in Matthew of Westminster, *Flores historiarum*. C. D. Yonge maintained the same argument of authorship in his translation three hundred years later: Matthew of Westminster, *Flowers of History*.

5 Vaughan suggests that Matthew Paris wrote MSS *A* and *B* as one book (*AB*), which was the earliest and original manuscript of the *Chronica majora*. This was also the manuscript in which he made his first revisions of Roger of Wendover's *Flores Historiarum*. Vaughan, *Matthew Paris*, pp. 59, 97. More on the *Flores* tradition and its editorial history in Chapter 7.

6 These include maps of the Holy Land and the British Isles, an itinerary from London to Apulia, a full-page painting of the Virgin and Child with a monk kneeling before them (often said to be Matthew Paris himself), and a portrait of Matthew Paris on his deathbed (by another scribe). See Figs 11 and 1, respectively.

Life of King Edward the Confessor.[7] Other biographical works attributed to Matthew Paris include the French verse *Life of St Alban* written sometime between 1230 and 1250.[8] The *Becket Leaves* are four surviving folios from a French verse *vita* of Thomas Becket with large illuminations. Matthew is also said to have produced Latin biographies of Stephen Langton and Edmund Rich. Finally, some fortune-telling tracts in Oxford, Bodleian Library, MS Ashmole 304 were almost entirely copied and illustrated by Matthew Paris around 1250.[9]

Matthew Paris's historical oeuvre was, thus, not limited to the narrative of the *Chronica majora*. And even the *Chronica majora* is not limited to the *Chronica majora*. On the one hand, London, BL, MS Cotton Nero D I (MS *LA*), contains the *Additamenta* (also known as the *Liber Additamentorum*), which is an integral part of the *Chronica majora* corpus, and also contains a variety of other works.[10] On the other hand, there are several autograph manuscripts of the *Chronica majora*, parts of which are sometimes bound together with other works by Matthew, but separately from one another. Cambridge, Corpus Christi College, MS 26 (MS *A*) is a history from the beginning of the world to 1188, which was copied by Matthew Paris but hardly contains any text written by him.[11] Cambridge, Corpus Christi College, MS 16II (MS *B*), also Matthew's autograph, covers the years between 1189 and 1253.[12] After Matthew's death, this volume was copied as London, BL, MS Cotton Nero D V (MS *C*), and

---

7 This is the only surviving copy of this work but is believed to be a slightly later copy made in London, probably by court artists, based on Paris's own autograph text and illustrations. In Vaughan, *Matthew Paris*, pp. 173–76.

8 Dublin, Trinity College, TCD MS 177 (formerly MS E I 40), a manuscript also containing a *Life of St Amphibalus* and various other works relating to the history of St Albans Abbey.

9 This manuscript has been recently studied in Iafrate, 'The Workshop of Fortune'. This is the codex that contains the illustration famously analysed by Michael Camille in 'The Dissenting Image'. See note 156 in Chapter 7 below.

10 These include maps, biographical works such as the illustrated *Vitae Offarum* and the *Gesta abbatum*, the lives of the first twenty-three abbots of St Albans with a miniature portrait of each, coats of arms, as well as copies of original documents.

11 In his edition of the *Chronica majora*, Luard says, 'the St Albans compilation, used by Roger of Wendover and Matthew Paris as the basis of their histories, and popularized by some other compiler under the name of Matthew of Westminster'. *CM*, I, p. lxxvi. Luard's argument is based on simple internal evidence such as the fact that in the case of those portions which are different in Paris and Wendover (such as the history down to 231 and between 1012 and 1065), the 'Westminster manuscripts' follow MS *A*. *CM*, I, p. xv. Sigla as in Luard's edition: MSS *A*, *B*, and *C* (the 'fair copy'). Luard's printed edition is based on MSS *A* (up to 1188) and *B* (from 1189 to 1253).

12 Recently, in 2003, the prefatory section to MS *B*, fols i[r]–v[v], containing lists and genealogies of kings, a diagram of the winds, itineraries, maps, and the picture of the elephant given by Louis IX to Henry III, has been bound separately as MS 16I. The part containing the chronicle text itself, fols 1[v]–282[r], has been rebound as MS 16II.

London, BL, MS Harley 1620 (MS *D*).[13] In *C*, known as the 'fair copy', the text is framed by the *Mappa terrae habitabilis* at the beginning, and the historical account *Quaedam gesta de rege Arthuro* on four leaves at the end, taken from Geoffrey of Monmouth's *Historia regum Britannniae*.[14] The last parts of the *Chronica majora* from 1254 to 1259, as well as the whole of the *Historia Anglorum*, are contained in MS *R*. This volume also includes a fourteenth-century continuation (fols 219^r–231^r).

Within Matthew's immense oeuvre, the *Chronica majora* cannot be seen as a discreet, self-contained text. It is an accumulated/accumulating work, a stage in a continuous tradition of narratives.[15] As Broun summarizes: 'The usual first step for anyone wishing to begin a chronicle was to copy another chronicle and so create a text sufficiently long to fill a manuscript book. [...] A record of recent events might be added at this initial stage. As time went by, the chronicle would be updated with a record of events in subsequent years'.[16] Manuel Muñoz Garcia's newest findings, based on digital palaeography; Miriam Weiss's reconsideration of the modes of collaboration at St Albans, highlighting such important aspects as the role of the library and new conclusions about producing the so-called 'clean copy'; as well as Greasley's thoughtful reconstruction of the time of writing various portions based on internal textual evidence further nuance our present understanding of the chronology of production.[17] Firstly, as Muñoz Garcia stresses, manuscripts were written in a variable number of years, and Matthew's contribution — written in stints — in

---

13 *CM*, VII, p. xi.

14 This fragment is examined in Stallcup, 'An Arthurian Excerpt from the "Historia Regum Britanniae"'.

15 As Matthew Fisher, in his description of 'derivative textuality' explains, Matthew Paris's works as examples of derivative texts are 'the sites of extensive textual transformation. The authors of derivative texts use the words of others in order to create a new textual whole, using old sources in the service of a new textual agenda. [...] These texts, neither compilations nor translations, but rather assemblages, do not fit neatly with conventional definitions of composition and creation'. Fisher, *Scribal Authorship*, p. 7.

16 Broun, 'Creating and Maintaining a Year-by-Year Chronicle', p. 142. Matthew was certainly trained in this technique in the scriptorium, perhaps by his predecessor, Roger of Wendover. It is important to see Matthew as part of a 'self-perpetuating' historiographical tradition at St Albans. As Gransden summarizes 'Once a tradition of chronicle writing was established in a monastery it tended to be self-perpetuating; one chronicle provided a model, and also the foundation stone, or at least a quarry, for another'. Gransden, 'The Chronicles of Medieval England and Scotland: Part 2', p. 134.

17 According to Vaughan, the *Chronica majora* was written in two stages. Matthew first began working on it in or around 1245 and completed the portion from the Creation to 1250 by about 1251. Then he took up writing again in 1253 and continued the chronicle until his death in 1259. Vaughan, *Matthew Paris*, pp. 59–71, 75–77. This has been since further studied and elaborated in Muñoz García, 'The Script of Matthew Paris and his Collaborators', Weiss, *Die 'Chronica maiora' des Matthaeus Parisiensis*, and Greasley, 'Revisiting the Compilation of Matthew Paris's *Chronica majora*'.

each manuscript could have been made at different stages throughout his active working life.[18] Greasley argues that 'the compositional process of the *Chronica majora* was more complex than previously thought'. In his chronological reconstruction, some time after Matthew and the other monks of the St Albans' scriptorium had decided to produce a copy of Wendover's *Flores historiarum*, Matthew's attentions next turned to compiling the first part of the *Gesta abbatum*, which was originally bound into the same book as the *Flores* revision. It was not until 1247 that the work began on expanding Wendover's work into a lengthier chronicle, and Matthew completed the second part of the *Chronica* sometime in early 1251. Later, he decided to continue, and the chronicle was then extended to Matthew's death in 1259.[19]

According to Muñoz García's (admittedly highly hypothetical) calculations, it seems that the net time consumed by Matthew's copying stints was about two and a half years altogether, which is at odds with Luard's assumption that Matthew Paris could not have written everything attributed to him in his lifetime.[20] Admittedly, this net calculation does not include life outside copying such as festivities, travel, and periods of inactivity. What is more important in light of the present discussion is the time spent with all the other activities taking place before, after, and during the physical act of committing the histories to parchment: the 'gathering of information, drafting, illuminating, and editing' which significantly extended the overall production time. The most obvious example for a manuscript that was being written over a number of years is the *Liber Additamentorum*, which shows obvious palaeographical signs of teamwork, and a rather laborious process of accumulating texts parallel to other work in the scriptorium.[21]

This is exactly what happened in the case of the *Chronica majora*, so its text is layered: the first part of the chronicle was almost entirely taken over from Roger of Wendover.[22] Manuscripts *A* and *B* incorporate both parts of Wendover's *Flores historiarum* (i.e. the 'received' history from Creation

---

18 Muñoz García, 'The Script of Matthew Paris and his Collaborators', p. 137. For the variety of hands changing even within one page, see the bottom of the columns above the drawing on MS *B*, fol. 147[r], Fig. 9 below.

19 Greasley, 'Revisiting the Compilation of Matthew Paris's *Chronica majora*'.

20 Muñoz García, 'The Script of Matthew Paris and his Collaborators', p. 142.

21 Muñoz García, 'The Script of Matthew Paris and his Collaborators', p. 141.

22 Roger of Wendover, *Flores Historiarum*; Roger of Wendover, *Liber qui dicitur Flores historiarum*. Coxe's edition covers the chronicle from the year 447 as opposed to Luard's which starts with the death of King Stephen in 1154. Even though Coxe's edition is founded entirely on Oxford, Bodleian Library, MS Douce 207 (MS *W*), and is ignorant of variant readings, references before 1154 will be quoted from his edition. As for references earlier than the years Coxe's edition covers, the only published material available of Wendover's text is the *Chronica majora*. This *Flores historiarum* should not be confused with that of Matthew Paris published in Matthew Paris, *Flores historiarum*, ed. by Luard.

to 1202, and Roger's continuation from 1202 to 1235).[23] The full text was edited by Matthew Paris: he revised it and added his own material, but he did not perform substantial changes or use fundamentally different or new sources in his additions. Thus, the structure of the chronological accumulation of the text is (1) the earliest portions (the first part of the *Flores* up to 1202) have the most editorial layers; (2) Wendover's own material (1202–1235) somewhat less; and (3) the last (Matthew Paris's own chronicle and the *Additamenta*) has only one, namely Matthew Paris's original, re-edited by himself only. His editing work entailed both stylistic amendments and factual corrections and insertions. While in the inherited part Matthew Paris's work was restricted to alterations of barely more significance than scribal modifications, his efforts to chronicle near-contemporary events allowed a much richer material into the fabric of the *Chronica majora*. Muñoz Garcia's palaeographic study of the chronology of the production of the *Chronica majora* and the *Liber Additamentorum* more or less corresponds to Vaughan's assumptions: MSS *A*, *B*, belonging to MS Group I (*c.* 1240–1250), and MS *LA* in MS Group III (*c.* 1255–1259) were all written several decades after the events they record.[24]

The physical process of chronological ordering, editing, and repeated polishing undertaken by Matthew Paris and his team is an important practical dimension of understanding the resulting narrative. Describing the perceived chaos of Matthew's working style, Vaughan levels harsh criticism against his craft as a historian. In his words, 'if Matthew's work is careless, it is also undisciplined and unsystematic. Not one of his manuscripts is a final fair copy; in all of them marginal additions and corrections show that he went back constantly to re-read, revise, and amplify what he had already written.[25] This, however, was a necessity in an information hub where news arrived with various lengths of delay, in various formats, and

---

23 Two manuscripts of Roger of Wendover's *Flores* have come down to us, both late copies: MS *W*, written *c.* 1300, and MS *Ow*, written *c.* 1350. The authorship of this *Flores historiarum* is debated. Vaughan summarizes the debate in Vaughan, *Matthew Paris*, pp. 22–25. Also see Kay, 'Wendover's Last Annal'.

24 Figure 3.39 in Muñoz García, 'The Script of Matthew Paris and his Collaborators', p. 142.

25 Vaughan, *Matthew Paris*, pp. 120–31. Elsewhere: 'it cannot be denied that Matthew Paris was an extremely unsystematic worker'; 'Of Matthew's failings, as a chronicler, one of the most obvious is his carelessness'. Vaughan, *Matthew Paris*, pp. 117, 130. Similarly condemning views can be found in other scholarly works, too: 'Matthew Paris, for example, several of whose autographs have survived, has been shown to have been exceptionally careless, leaving out verbs, repeating passages through homoeotopy, substituting wrong words. Much of his time he was copying or abridging, he worked in haste, and, apparently, never revised what he had written. In the *Chronica Majora* and the *Liber Additamentorum* he preserved copies of some 350 miscellaneous documents. He was not a good editor, it is a clumsy interpolation of a phrase of his own into the narrative of the earlier St Albans chronicle for AD 1119, which accounts for the verbless first paragraph'. Colledge, 'The Capgrave Autographs', p. 138.

of highly uneven quality. As David Carpenter's more recent re-evaluation of Matthew Paris's chronology suggests, 'it was probably written on a series of separate leaves and it was from these, shuffled into chronological order, that the *Chronica majora* itself was ultimately copied'.[26]

This method of the physical construction of historical works that were being written in monastic scriptoria is best summarized in the preamble of the *Worcester Annals* as follows. 'It will be your business to see that there is always a sheet [*scedula*] attached to the book, on which may be noted in pencil deaths of illustrious men and anything in the state of the kingdom which is worth remembering, whenever the news comes to hand. But at the end of the year let a man appointed to the task — write out briefly and succinctly, in the body of the book, what he thinks truest and best to be passed down to the notice of posterity'.[27] As Broun comments on this process, the scribes entering fresh material into the chronicle were 'working from anything between a complete draft of the text and a few notes'.[28] Importantly, Carpenter adds that the process of moving the notes to final draft was of varied length, and at times it was relatively short. Matthew needed an agile system whereby the clean copy was produced in the last minute, to be revised at some point, if necessary.

As opposed to what Powicke surmised, positing a lost original from which the present text was copied, Carpenter confirms Vaughan's reconstruction of the process whereby Matthew Paris produced very full drafts soon after the events they recorded, and the present text (sans the final revisions, pastedowns, and deletions) is 'the lost original'.[29] As the *scedulae* themselves are no longer available for study, it is unknown how much material and what type of material Matthew rejected in the editorial process.[30] Vaughan's statement, 'it seems that Matthew considered no information irrelevant', can only be read as a hyperbole: I find it untenable to assume that Matthew inserted every single piece of information he acquired through his channels.[31] The editorial process is more transparent in abridged works: comparing the *Chronica majora* with the *Flores historiarum*, for

---

26 Carpenter, 'Chronology and Truth'.

27 'Annales de Prioratus de Wigornia', p. 355. Translation in Cheney, 'Notes on the Making of the Dunstable Annals', p. 92. Also cited in Hilpert, *Kaiser- und Papstbriefe*, p. 37.

28 Broun, 'Creating and Maintaining a Year-by-Year Chronicle', p. 147.

29 Carpenter citing Powicke, 'Review of *Matthew Paris* by Richard Vaughan' in Carpenter, 'Chronology and Truth'. Similarly important questions of draft and final copy arise in other works by Matthew Paris; see, for example, the discussion of the multilayered edition process in his *Vie de St Auban*, and of the suggestion that the surviving copy is a 'maquette', in Slater, 'Matthew Paris, Cecilia de Sanford and the Early Readership of the Vie de Seint Auban', p. 190.

30 For a closer examination of what may seem to be a *scedula* bound in one of the Matthew Paris autographs, see Papp Reed, 'Post It'.

31 Vaughan, *Matthew Paris*, p. 126.

example, is particularly informative about Matthew's conscious effort to maintain his plot by removing whole strands altogether.

Vaughan observes that 'Matthew made no attempt to organize his chronicle, as for instance, did William of Malmesbury, in the form of a coherent narrative covering a period of years. Instead, he collected all the information he could obtain, and recorded it in rough chronological order'.[32] However, the very fact that he repeatedly revised, reworded, complemented, and probably even rearranged his material shows that Matthew's intention was indeed to produce a narrative. For one, he is known to have 'tampered with' his sources and revised and edited them thoroughly to suit his general purpose.[33] Björn Weiler underlines the importance of examining the chronicler's methods and technique, and adds a further plane by emphasizing that the question is not whether certain passages are genuine or not, but that they have to be observed in the context of the whole to be meaningful.[34] The *Chronica majora* is not simply a series of isolated entries, but a literary composition, a narrative wrought along the trajectory of a universal history with a specifically English focus. Matthew himself repeatedly refers to his own chronicle as *historia regni Angliae*, even though he maintains a growing interest in continental matters.[35]

The *Chronica majora* was intended to be a self-contained, finite composition, which is demonstrated by Matthew Paris's own explicit statement suggesting that, at least for a long time, he was writing a work that was going to be completed at the end of 1250: a definitive chronicle of the history of England (in the world) from Genesis to 1250, a literary product with a beginning and an end.[36] He obviously changed his mind and continued accumulating and sorting materials and working on the continuation until his death nearly a decade later.

> Hic quoque proposuit frater Matheus Cronica sua terminare, propter imminentia quaedam pericula. Si enim de potentibus vera dicantur et scripturae commendentur, bella parantur ei; si taceantur, vel bona

---

32 Vaughan, *Matthew Paris*, p. 143.

33 Vaughan was the one of the first scholars to point this out, although in his work, the question of 'inaccuracy and occasional deceit or wilful misrepresentation' is discussed in the analysis of Paris's personality and his 'trustworthiness and veracity as a chronicler', rather than the content he produced. Vaughan, *Matthew Paris*, pp. 134, 136. Also emphasized in Sweeney, 'Thomas of Spalato and the Mongols'.

34 Weiler, 'Matthew Paris, Richard of Cornwall's Candidacy for the German Throne, and the Sicilian Business'; Weiler, 'Historical Writing and the Experience of Europeanization'.

35 Vaughan gives several examples for apologizing for digression into inapposite matters: *CM*, IV, p. 316; V, pp. 92, 438, 440. In Vaughan, *Matthew Paris*, pp. 111, 126. More on his international perspective in Weiler, 'Historical Writing and the Experience of Europeanization'; Weiler, 'How Unusual Was Matthew Paris?', pp. 202–03.

36 About ending the chronicle, see *CM*, V, p. 300; Vaughan, *Matthew Paris*, pp. 60–61.

OUTSIDE THE BOOK   63

pro malis annotentur, mutilabitur, et de blandimentis, adulationibus et falsitatibus graviter opus totale comdempnabitur et redarguetur.[37]

> (Here brother Matthew proposed to terminate his Chronicles on account of certain imminent dangers. For if true things are said of the powerful and commended to writing, wars are bred for him; if things are passed over in silence, or good things are written for bad, the whole work will be mutilated, and vehemently condemned and discarded as flatteries, adulation, and falsities.)

It is unknown whether he had a similar vision for the continuation, but the realization that the chronicle was written in stints points to important issues regarding the narrative of the chronicle. In the present volume, I repeatedly point out that his history is authored and edited prose, in which Matthew consciously controlled the frequency and alternation of various storyline elements in hindsight, purposefully using various elements and discarding others to create a coherent and contiguous history that 'makes sense'. At the same time, it is clear that he could not see and plan the whole narrative ahead: besides the uneven availability of sources, the practicalities of managing the stints, and the sheer foreseeable length of the chronicle, Matthew, who no doubt headed the historiographical project, was in control of the narrative thrust of only a given portion of the text at a time.[38] On the whole, the narrative strands give the impression that working on various stints may have overlapped, but they were probably not completely parallel: Matthew more or less proceeded chronologically. Once one was written up, the next portion consumed his attention, and if new material arrived about something they had already entered in the chronicle, it may have been revised but sometimes not: this accounts for the occasional inconsistencies in various parts of the same story. And new material seems to have been continuously arriving on and off from various sources. The differences between Matthew's main sources are clearly visible in the different perspectives and agenda detectable in the various phases of the Mongol story as well.

The Scriptorium in England

Besides the practicalities of turning news into historiography at St Albans, the Mongol story in the *Chronica majora* was shaped by a large number of factors in the world outside Matthew's scriptorium. The primary determinant of the scope and depth of any historical work is the availability

---

37 *HA*, III, pp. xxx, 319.
38 For a discussion of the dilemma of historical progress in literary criticism, see Jauss, *Toward an Aesthetic of Reception*, pp. 7–9.

of sources: the pool of documents and information that comprise the raw material for the historiographer. Matthew is known to have travelled outside St Albans, even outside the kingdom, across the sea. Dedicated to his profession, he met people, took notes, and received documents for his chronicle during his journeying. However, the haul from these personal trips contributed a tiny sliver of all the raw material he needed for his vast chronicle, so — as any omniscient narrator of world history would — he had to rely on intelligence, documents, and texts relayed to him through chains and networks of information. Matthew's text contains a good number of references to his direct informants but also attests to the fact that the original sources of his materials — especially in the case of the Mongol story — passed through many hands before they reached his desk at St Albans. The length of the information chains and number of mediators connecting the original source to St Albans varies. In many cases even the two endpoints — continental source and Matthew's direct informants — are impossible to determine with complete certainty, let alone the middlemen. As will be discussed in more detail in the relevant sections of Chapters 3 to 6, the original continental sources of information had a profound impact on the coverage of overseas events such as the Mongol invasion — and ultimately, their memorialization in scholarship. However, tracing the connections converging at St Albans, Matthew Paris's so-called 'ego-network' helps situate his place in contemporary society and reveals the channels through which continental sources may have arrived in England.[39]

Judging from the contemporary parts of the *Chronica majora* and his other works, Matthew Paris, working in St Albans, was one of the well-appointed English chroniclers of his time, if not the single best-appointed one.[40] As attested by his chronicle, his sources for the present and recent past ranged from current rumours, strange anecdotes and tales, and oral reports of visitors and travellers he met at St Albans, to circulars, letters,

---

39 In a so-called ego-network of the *Chronica majora*, for example, the *alteri* (or nodes connected to the ego node) would yield visually stunning hubs (nodes with a degree far higher than the average in a network) and communities (a set of nodes which are relatively more connected to each other than to the rest of the graph). However, the scope and research questions of the present volume take to heart Marten Düring's wise words, 'it might be just fine to describe your network verbally and to read up on network theory for further inspiration', and leave big data for future research. Düring, 'Should I Do Social Network Analysis?'.

40 Seb Falk reminds the reader that St Albans was an extremely busy monastery, not least for the fame of its shrine of St Alban, 'visited day and night by pilgrims who left gifts in the niches of the richly painted marble tomb'. Matthew Paris once records a charter from 1258, in which the abbot appoints 'five men from Westwick (and manure from St Albans)' whose task was to boost the supplies of bread and beer for the monks and guests. A hundred years after Matthew Paris, the community had to install a two-story watching loft to keep an eye on the pilgrims coming and going. Falk, *The Light Ages*. Citing *CM*, v, p. 669.

OUTSIDE THE BOOK   65

charters, documents, newsletters, prophecies, theological treatises, and all sorts of written materials he could lay his hands on. As noted, there are many tiny clues about Matthew's far-reaching activities to accumulate his material. Some scholars examined the availability and use of books; for example, autograph annotations testify that at least one copy of the widely circulated *Gesta regum Anglorum* by William of Malmesbury is known to have been read and used by him.[41] Other research established an impressive list of direct informants based on Matthew's textual references.[42] The connection with Alexander Swereford's *Red Book of the Exchequer* has been noted by several scholars.[43] However, as Mark Hagger observes, 'neither of these alternatives — a specific request for information or a more generalized rummage through the royal archives — was likely to result in a systematic interrogation of the records'.[44] This point raises an interesting question about Matthew's agency in accumulating his materials.

J. C. Holt says that Matthew Paris was 'a seeker of sources' with the instincts of a magpie, who actively employed the 'rag-bag of assorted documents' sent to religious houses, also carefully 'examining the contents of the sacks, chests and presses at St Albans'.[45] The operative word here, however, is not 'seeker' but 'sent'. As Nathan Greasley points out in his study of the role of the Lincoln diocesan chancery and Oxford University as content providers, 'a large bulk of reliable source of documentary material was [...] sent to St Albans, and Matthew did not have to set up newsgathering channels of his own', and his 'methods of newsgathering were rather more typical than his readers might expect when they see the *Chronica majora*'s remarkable size'.[46]

---

41 Weiler, 'How Unusual Was Matthew Paris?', p. 212.

42 A summary list of named sources can be found in Vaughan, *Matthew Paris*, pp. 13–17; *HA*, III, pp. xxvii–xxix; and 'Matthew Paris and the St Albans School of Historiography' in Gransden, *Historical Writing in England*, I, pp. 356–79. Sophia Menache also provides a handlist of specific references to informants in the *Chronica majora* in Appendix 2 of Menache, 'Written and Oral Testimonies in Medieval Chronicles', pp. 21–22.

43 Vaughan, *Matthew Paris*, pp. 17–18; Hagger, 'A Pipe Roll for 25 Henry I', pp. 137–38; Lewis, *The Art of Matthew Paris*, p. 13; Hilpert, *Kaiser- und Papstbriefe*, pp. 44–89; Weiler, 'Matthew Paris on the Writing of History', p. 265. More recently Nathan Greasley has argued that the Red Book material probably came to Matthew as part of a much larger body of documents and that far from gaining it as a result of his friendship with Swereford, the abbey probably did not receive it until after the latter's death. Greasley, 'Revisiting the Compilation of Matthew Paris's *Chronica majora*'.

44 Hagger, 'A Pipe Roll for 25 Henry I', p. 138.

45 Holt, 'The St Albans Chroniclers and Magna Carta', pp. 85, 87.

46 Greasley, 'Matthew Paris's Networks of Information'. I am grateful to Nathan Greasley for providing me with several chapters from his work in progress at the 2018 International Medieval Congress at Leeds. Hans-Eberhard Hilpert also discussed the circulation of documents in his study of the *Chronica Majora*'s papal and imperial letters. Hilpert, *Kaiser- und Papstbriefe*. It is notable that episcopal registers and acta typically preserved materials about the spiritual and temporal issues and jurisdiction of the bishop; the kind

66   CHAPTER 2

Seeker or recipient? Of course, it is not unimportant how much agency one attributes to Matthew in the selection of his materials. By looking into the sources and vestiges of 'bundles' or 'dossiers' received, as well as Matthew's historiographers' practice and sources, the evolution of the Mongol story in the *Chronica majora* is a Petri dish showing historiography in action. Another, often neglected factor in this process is that Matthew Paris did not produce his works alone: Vaughan identified at least fifteen scribes who helped in copying out his various works and also helped with the collection of information.[47] Vaughan's work was further nuanced by Manuel Muñoz García's analysis of the palaeographic characteristics of Matthew's handwriting across a large corpus of autographs, using the digital framework Archetype.[48]

Besides the preselected nature of his incoming sources, the prominent standing of some of his informants, bringing him oral reports and written documents, is also important: the documents that made it into works by Matthew Paris and others were deliberately shaped by the highest power circles of contemporary England. While some of the more anecdotal entries give the impression that Matthew was a keen interviewer who captured accounts of faraway adventures after discussions with visitors at his abbey, in reality he was not informed by happenstance. Written sources sent to and circulating between religious houses — not just St Albans — constitute a much larger part of Matthew's sources. Copies of important letters and newsletters probably reached the chronicler without asking. Efforts to distribute newsletters to religious houses, for example, have been shown to have commenced as early as Richard I's reign, and this no doubt multiplied by the time of Matthew's career as a historian.[49] His named sources range from fellow clerics to powerful contemporary figures who knew why it was important to carry or send their news to St Albans, and their decisions what to disseminate were the first filters of reality before they even reached the monastic scriptoria.[50]

---

of correspondence and reports that Matthew and other religious houses may have received were probably sent onwards to be preserved and not entered into official archives.

47 Carpenter, 'Chronology and Truth', points out that this was manifestly true for at least one period, when Matthew Paris spent a considerable amount of time in Norway in the second half of 1248, appointed to reform the monastery of Nidarholm. The number of hands assisting Matthew in the manuscript is discussed in Vaughan, *Matthew Paris*, p. 384; Vaughan, 'The Handwriting of Matthew Paris'. For the work of one of his named assistants, John of Wallingford, himself a chronicler, see John of Wallingford, *The Chronicle*; Vaughan, 'The Chronicle of John of Wallingford'.

48 Muñoz García, 'The Script of Matthew Paris and his Collaborators'.

49 Gillingham, 'Royal Newsletters, Forgeries and English Historians'.

50 Weiler arrives at the same conclusion about Matthew's Danish informants: 'This does not, of course, mean that Odo, John and Nicholas were simply passive informants — they clearly chose to share the information they possessed. But then Matthew still had to be willing to accept their testimony, had to be willing to tap into it repeatedly, and about a whole range of

OUTSIDE THE BOOK 67

Accumulating information, thus, was not entirely under Matthew's control. For one, the arduous physical process and the management of assistants and scribes (especially in the earlier stages of gathering and organizing material) was probably encumbered by the uneven distribution and level of detail of incoming news.[51] In addition, the networks of information, channels of exchange available and accessible for him, were at the mercy of his informants, who in turn were also affected by various factors on their end. Subscribing to the theory that he was more or less supplied with precurated information to feed his chronicle, as is obliquely suggested by Greasley, may, at a glance, seem to undermine the argument that he was actively and consciously constructing his own narrative. However, neither the proven involvement of a number of scribes nor receiving preselected materials detracts from Matthew's skill and authorship. Appreciating the physicality of archiving, ordering, and writing, as well as the number of people involved, nuances our understanding of his role in the process, but it does not take away from the fact that the *Chronica majora* is a narrative, more specifically, that it is Matthew Paris's narrative. His creativity was the fullest when it came to ordering and juxtaposing received material, and his most adroit skill as a historiographer was his ability to hold the continuously evolving narrative together, despite the fact that the process from drafts to fair copy (accumulation to configuring) was neither continuous nor fast and even paced. In this vein (and for simplicity's sake) the subsequent analysis in the present volume will continue to refer to Matthew Paris as the author at work — although it is understood and acknowledged that it is a not undeserved shorthand for the authorship of a team of scribes and other helpers whose identity remains unknown.

Stepping outside Matthew's scriptorium, the next question is who his informants were and what connected them besides Matthew's person. An interconnected network of known and unknown individuals glimmers

---

matters that went well beyond the piece of news they had initially been willing to share with him'. Weiler, 'Historical Writing and the Experience of Europeanization', p. 224.

51 As for Matthew's 'team', M. B. Parkes's words about monastic scriptoria must be noted: 'Some communities hired scribes (laymen or secular clergy) to supplement the efforts of the monks, as at St Albans, and, later, at Abingdon where hired scribes produced copies of patristic texts whilst the monks copied books for the *opus Dei*. Monks also compiled and maintained the records required for running a monastery and protecting its privileges. Organized copying by members of a community usually lasted only for short periods: once a community had built up its collection of texts, organized copying was abandoned, and with it some of the distinctive features in local handwriting'. Parkes, 'Handwriting in English Books', p. 111. Although the present work is hoped to contribute insights into knowledge organization in the St Albans scriptorium, more systematic interdisciplinary research is necessary to understand the logistics of managing training, human resources, physical supplies, and — most importantly — the receipt, processing, output, and storage of texts in medieval English chronicle production. The roles of potential hired scribes, the St Albans *almarius*, and other personnel also need to be clarified.

through both Matthew's own text and passages he quotes from elsewhere. The source text and the methodology used in the present volume is strictly limited to Matthew's Mongol story, so I expressly avoid the impression of attempting to perform network analysis of the probable sources of the *Chronica majora*. The terminology of network science, however, may prove useful in emphasizing the networked nature of the information channels that aggregated the news of the world for Matthew, with hubs such as the Lincoln Cathedral, the First Council of Lyon, and Matthew's scriptorium itself.

Björn Weiler observed about Matthew's historiographical practice in the context of other similar works that 'the genre [of universal history] experienced something of a revival, but the texts produced were also fundamentally different from earlier examples. Much of the difference resided in a more extensive thematic and geographical coverage'.[52] This extensive thematic coverage was possible partly due to a more consciously built network of news and knowledge exchange, whereby many of the actors (or nodes) understood their role as hubs and information carriers, ultimately contributing to historiography. As will be shown in later chapters, the afterlife and use of these productions give another lease of life to these relational connections across centuries to come. Besides the more immediate contemporary position and power games, this longevity — the ability to reach out to posterity — was one of the motivations behind the efforts of both powerful individuals and the increasingly institutionalizing information hubs for disseminating news and documents to chroniclers.

Looking through Matthew's own text for names of primary informants, out of all the English personages whom Matthew mentions as sources, various people (and their overlapping networks) emerge. Though not named in direct connection with the Mongol material, Chapters 3 to 6 below will reveal that their continental connections and interests may be detectable behind some of the passages. First, the people who are named as primary informants and were known not only to travel extensively but also to participate in collecting and disseminating documents and letters to which they had access through their connections: Richard of Cornwall, Simon de Montfort, John Mansel, and, to a more limited extent, a certain John of Schipton, prior of Newburgh. The former three were powerful, wealthy, well connected, and very much plugged into continental politics. Richard of Cornwall, the king's younger brother, was one of the most influential, mobile, and internationally embedded personages in the realm at the time.[53] Similarly to the so-called 'Dominican Dossier' that he is

---

52 Weiler, 'Historical Writing and the Experience of Europeanization', p. 212.

53 Matthew Paris alludes to his wealth, for example, in an entry under 1251: 'Mihi autem Mathaeo Parisiensi super hoc edoceri cupienti, ne falsa huic libro insererem, sub indubitata certitudine comes significavit quod, omnibus sumptibus computatis, in ipsius ecclesiae

suspected to have acquired and transmitted to Matthew Paris in the late 1230s, Richard of Cornwall or his chancery may have contributed to Matthew's Mongol story, too.[54] His involvement in imperial politics and papal crusades made him criss-cross the continent and the Middle East, and he is known to have stayed in St Albans several times. Even more, he is verifiably known to have periodically supplied Matthew Paris with information about continental matters and events of local importance. Some of Richard's information for Matthew Paris concerned his own person such as his expenses at Hailes and his crusade participation.[55]

He is also known to have travelled with documents that he obtained on his travels.[56] And travel he did. Richard of Cornwall's itinerary often involves personages whom Matthew Paris cites as sources or mentions in relation with the Mongol issues, including Frederick II, Louis IX of France and Queen Blanche, the pope, and members of the German aristocracy. Firstly, in 1235 Richard took an active part in promoting the marriage of his sister Isabella to Emperor Frederick II, with whom he personally exchanged many letters and presents, for example, the ones Matthew

---

constructione decem milia marcas exposuerat, addens quoddam verbum memorabile, immo et commendabile; "Utinam Deo complaceret ut omnia quae in castro de Walingeford expendi tam sapienter et tam salubriter expendissem". (When I Matthew Paris, desired to be informed upon the matter, in order that I might not insert falsities in this book, the earl with unhesitating certainty informed me that, when all expenses were reckoned, he had laid out ten thousand marks in the building of that church; adding this remarkable and praiseworthy speech: 'Would that it had pleased God that I had expended all that I have laid out in the castle of Wallingford in as wise and salutary manner'.) *CM*, v, p. 262; *EH*, ii, p. 464. Further mentions listed in Vaughan, *Matthew Paris*, p. 13. Richard's contributions to the *Chronica majora* are more recently summarized in Greasley, 'Revisiting the Compilation of Matthew Paris's *Chronica majora*', pp. 235–36.

54 See more on Richard's purported role in bringing the 'Dominican Dossier' to St Albans in note 152 in this chapter.

55 See the account of the dedication of the church at Hailes in note 53, above. Crusader account: *CM*, vi, pp. 43–47, 71, 144–48, 166–67; *EH*, i, pp. 287–90, 308, 362–71, 385–86. Vaughan attributes these crusading passages to Richard himself in Vaughan, *Matthew Paris*, p. 13. A similar hint at Richard conveying information to Matthew about French matters is that about the imprisonment of the French king in 1251: 'Hoc mihi haec scribenti idem comes assertive narravit' (This circumstance was related to me, the writer of these pages, by the earl himself). In *CM*, v, p. 347; *EH*, ii, p. 538.

56 Communication did not rely solely on Richard's own person; it involved professionals in both Germany and England. Richard's involvement in German politics meant that he was extremely well connected with chanceries there. This was true throughout his highly mobile international career but especially later, during his time as king of the Romans, when he also exercised his power through issuing charters and arbitrating among his German subjects in absentia when 'he retained the company of his royal chancellor, and was regularly visited by envoys and princes from Germany'. Weiler, 'Image and Reality in Richard of Cornwall's German Career', p. 1118.

70 CHAPTER 2

copied in the *Chronica majora* under 1239 and 1244.[57] In 1240, Richard visited St Albans on his way to Jerusalem.[58] In June in the same year, Richard went to Paris, where Louis of France and his mother, Queen Blanche, gave him a hearty welcome.[59] If Koch's interpretation is to be believed, after he crossed the Channel and met the royals, he headed to Lyon before continuing his journey to the Holy Land (he arrived at Acre in October 1240).[60] His communications were not limited to the French relatives: 'Richard had taken good care on his journey overland through France and the kingdom of Arles to remain in touch with his imperial brother-in-law'.[61] However, Matthew also records that the Curia was interfering with Richard's itinerary rather heavy-handedly: though he originally planned to meet the emperor in 1240, the papal legate and the archbishop of Arles forbade him to leave St Giles to meet Frederick, so instead of meeting in person, he only sent a messenger from La Roque.[62] Matthew Paris does record that in 1241 he is once again in St Albans, on

---

57 *S.a.* 1239, *CM*, III, pp. 575–89; *EH*, I, p. 201. Despite this marriage alliance, Matthew Paris notes that Frederick II complained that Richard was in the hands of the papal party: *CM*, IV, p. 577; *EH*, II, p. 189. Details of the five imperial letters Matthew obtained from Richard of Cornwall: Hilpert, *Kaiser- und Papstbriefe*, pp. 97–114. In November 1234, Frederick's envoy, Peter de Vinea, was the one who conveyed the imperial request for the hand of Henry's sister Isabella and an accompanying dowry of thirty thousand marks. On 15 July 1235 Frederick's third wedding was celebrated with great pomp at Worms. Isabella died in 1241. Bayley, 'The Diplomatic Preliminaries of the Double Election', p. 458; Huffman, *The Social Politics of Medieval Diplomacy*, pp. 249–53.

58 Much of Richard's itinerary, in fact, is reconstructed on the basis of Matthew's account, which, especially for the year 1240, is very detailed concerning his movements, as well as letters exchanged between Henry III and Frederick II, which Richard may have carried. Richard visited St Albans on his way to London, and then Dover where he set sail to France: 'Eodem anno, comes Ricardus, paratis omnibus quae ad iter Jerosolimitanum necessaria videbantur, venit ad abbatiam Sancti Albani, ubi ingressus capitulum, a conventu suffragia petiit orationum. Et postea Londonias veniens, circa dies inter Ascensionem et Pentecosten, fratri suo regi et legato et aliis magnatibus valedicens, versus Doveram gressus maturavit'. (In this year [1240] Earl Richard, having made all the necessary preparations for his journey to Jerusalem, went to the abbey of St Albans, and entering the chapter house, begged the assistance of the prayers of the brotherhood; from thence he went to London, between Ascension Day and Whit Sunday, and bade farewell to the king, his brother, the legate, and the rest of the nobles; after which he hastened his steps towards Dover.) *CM*, IV, pp. 43–44; *EH*, I, p. 287. Also in Koch, *Richard von Cornwall*, p. 50, citing *HA*, II, p. 437.

59 *S.a.* 1240, *CM*, IV, p. 45; *EH*, I, p. 288. Blanche was half English, the daughter of Alfonso VIII of Castile and Eleanor of England, queen consort of Alfonso VIII. Blanche's mother and Henry III's aunt, Eleanor, was daughter of Eleanor of Aquitaine and King Henry II of England, so Blanche and Henry III were cousins once removed. Queen Blanche was Richard's aunt twice removed.

60 Koch, *Richard von Cornwall*, p. 51.

61 Jackson, 'The Crusades of 1239–41 and their Aftermath', p. 46. Jackson cites *CM*, IV, p. 47 (*EH*, I, p. 289); 'Annales de Prioratus Dunstaplia', p. 152.

62 *CM*, IV, pp. 46–47; *EH*, I, p. 289. Cited in Huffman, *The Social Politics of Medieval Diplomacy*, p. 265.

his way to see both the emperor and then the pope in 1241 to try and negotiate peace between them.[63]

After his return, he visited his sister Isabella, the empress of Frederick II. Assisting Henry III's attempt to recruit German military support in his war against the French king, Richard is known to have been at Saintes in 1242 where he signed an agreement with the German princes: the coalition involved princes of the Rhineland and the Low Countries, with the counts of March, Flanders, and Hainault agreeing, while the archbishop of Cologne blatantly chose to give a wide berth to the German pact.[64] Richard visited Louis IX and Blanche again in 1247 and in 1250.[65] In 1250 Richard proceeded to Lyon, where Innocent IV still held his court. The pope received him with respect, and they talked at length behind closed doors — no doubt discussing Richard's potential involvement in the fight against Frederick II, who also happened to be his brother-in-law. After some travels in France, he returned to England on 25 April 1250.[66] The so-called Sicilian business was beginning to unfold, and finally, in January 1257 Richard of Cornwall was crowned as king of the Romans, which did not go down particularly well in history, but that is a story which — albeit not wholly irrelevant — goes beyond the timeframe of my subject here.[67]

Literacy, exchange of written information, and the collection and distribution of texts were not hinged upon Richard's person single-handedly: as Noël Denholm-Young notes, 'the large and highly organised household of Earl Richard of Cornwall included a secretarial staff at whose head was a prothonotary, and the earl's letters frequently betray the expert touch'.[68] This is further attested by an interesting snippet which proves that some

---

63 Richard in St Albans: *CM*, IV, p. 145; *EH*, I, p. 369. The negotiations: *CM*, IV, p. 147; *EH*, I, pp. 369–71.

64 Huffman, *The Social Politics of Medieval Diplomacy*, p. 266.

65 Tout, 'Richard of Cornwall', p. 169. Matthew Paris records Richard's meeting with Queen Blanche in 1250 in *CM*, V, pp. 96–97. See also in Koch, *Richard von Cornwall*, pp. 104–05.

66 Koch, *Richard von Cornwall*, pp. 104–06.

67 Weiler, 'Image and Reality in Richard of Cornwall's German Career'; Weiler, 'Matthew Paris, Richard of Cornwall's Candidacy for the German Throne, and the Sicilian Business'; Weiler, 'Henry III and the Sicilian Business'; Weiler, *Henry III of England and the Staufen Empire*, pp. 170–97.

68 Denholm-Young, 'The Cursus in England', p. 84. That Richard's clerks were powerful people, albeit not particularly nice or popular, is attested to by an incident Matthew records under 1247: 'Nicholas Danne (may he not be "damned") also, the clerk, treasurer, and confidential adviser of Earl Richard, who, together with his associate John Bretasche, a knight (who was struck by a similar vengeance), had made a practice of seizing on money in all directions, and heaping it up for the use of the earl, one dark night as, surfeited with wine, and puffed up with feasting, he was carelessly riding a restive horse, fell to the ground drunk, and, striking against the trunk of a tree in the road, he broke his neck, and lying on his back vomited forth his life, with the wine of which he had drunk too much'. *CM*, IV, p. 588; *EH*, II, p. 198.

72   CHAPTER 2

of his letters were drafted either by ecclesiastical clerks or even by foreign
clerks, while the role of the chancery as a place of authentication was
commonly accepted: a letter sent from Lewes on 14 May 1264 was drafted
and written by Master Arnold of Holland, Richard's chancellor, 'without
the advice and consent of any chancery clerk'.[69] Besides the previously
mentioned chancellor and envoys between Germany and England, the
fact that he employed a busy secretarial staff outside England, too, is also
evidenced by a surprising congruence of letters, including one Mongol-
related one. Three of Frederick II's letters addressed to Henry III and
Richard of Cornwall, copied into the *Chronica majora*,[70] are also contained
in two Austrian manuscripts from the late thirteenth century.[71] Hilpert
suggests that they were probably already present in Richard's chancery in
the form of a letter collection (or a number of smaller bundles of letters),
and he may have taken the material to Germany himself some time later.[72]

Richard clearly took it upon himself and his team to serve as a hub of
information, both pulling and pushing texts about events on his itinerary
and beyond. His networks of information exchange are difficult to disentangle, but it is reasonable to suggest that Richard was also a transmitter of
texts of both French and Cistercian origin — networks which, of course,
often overlap.[73] A telling entry about these entanglements in Richard's life
is the brief 1246 report about the dedication of the Cistercian Beaulieu
Abbey, attended by the king and queen, Richard, as well as prelates and
nobles of the kingdom. He then took thirteen monks from Beaulieu to

---

69 *Foedera, conventiones, litterae*, I.1, p. 440. Cited in Chaplais, *English Diplomatic Practice in the Middle Ages*, p. 122.

70 One *s.a.* 1240 and two *s.a.* 1241 in *CM*, IV, pp. 16–19, 112–19, 175–76. Also nos 2531, 3216, 3264, in *Regesta Imperii*, V.1, pp. 505, 567, 575.

71 Wilhering, Stiftsbibliothek, MS 60 in the Cistercian Abbey of Wilhering; see Grillnberger, 'Die Handschriften der Stiftsbibliothek zu Wilhering', p. 26. Hilpert also notes another formulary in Vienna, Österreichische Nationalbibliothek, MS 590. About the letters and Richard's chancery Hilpert says: 'Zudem treten die aus England bekannten Kaiserbriefe — teilweise sogar durch die Adresse nach England verweisend — in den beiden Österreichischen MSS nahezu zusammenhängend auf, so daß die Parallelüberlieferung bei Matthaeus Paris und in diesen MSS nicht ohne weiteres mit einem Zufall in den Irrungen und Wirrungen des verästelten Komplexes der "Vinea"-Überlieferung erklärt werden kann. Die einzig plausible Möglichkeit, diesen Sachverhalt zu erklären, besteht in der Annahme, daß auf dem Wege über Richard von Cornwall diese Briefe aus England in die deutsche Reichskanzlei Richards gekommen sind und dort — wohl erst zur Zeit Rudolfs von Habsburg — zur Zusammenstellung eines Formelbuches mitverwandt wurden, auf welches die heute vorhandenen MSS der Klasse B zurückgehen'. Hilpert, *Kaiser- und Papstbriefe*, pp. 125–26.

72 Further, Hilpert eliminates the possibility that the letters would have been copied from Matthew Paris. Hilpert, *Kaiser- und Papstbriefe*, p. 125. As opposed to these, the imperial letter in *CM*, IV, pp. 26–29 (no. 3019, in *Regesta Imperii*, V.1, pp. 541–42) is not found in these manuscripts.

73 See note 108 in this chapter.

settle at the above-mentioned Hailes, a Cistercian monastery he founded near Winchcombe in the same year.[74] There is no room here to go into all the Cistercian entries in the *Chronica majora*, but regarding Richard's connections with them it is notable that Louis IX and Queen Blanche, his personal acquaintances and possibly informants, are also known to have had strong ties with the Cistercian Order. For example, in 1244, the *Chronica majora* reports that Louis IX, the duke of Burgundy, and Queen Blanche, 'who had obtained from the pope the privilege of being allowed to go into the religious houses of the Cistercian order', all attended the General Chapter of the order together to confirm their mutual support against 'the son of Satan', Frederick II.[75]

The renowned figure of Simon de Montfort, the earl of Leicester — a literate political figure with his own dense and busy web of correspondence — was another connection between Lincoln and Oxford, and many other people, including nodes in Matthew's ego-network. Simon was yet to become the notorious Lewes rabble rouser at this time but was already a highly mobile and influential baron, second only to his brother-in-law, Richard of Cornwall, in prestige and power in the English realm.[76] Similar to Richard, Simon's connections also cast light on the intense entanglement of many familiar figures in Matthew's ego-network. For example, under the year 1240 (MS *B*, fol. 137^{r}), Matthew Paris describes the English troops' expedition to the Outremer, and at the bottom of the account, he (or a later hand) adds information about Simon de Montfort's route as well as the names of the knights led by Simon and Richard of Cornwall. Simon's closest friends were Lincoln's Robert Grosseteste and Richard Gravesend, Robert's second-in-command.[77] His 'spiritual director' was Adam Marsh (Adam de Marisco, Bishop Robert Grosseteste's close associate), who in

---

74 *CM*, IV, p. 86; *EH*, II, p. 177.

75 *CM*, IV, pp. 391–93; *EH*, II, pp. 32–34. Giles incorrectly places this event at Chichester, instead of Citeaux. Further connections with her Cistercian foundations in Grant, 'The Queen and the Abbots'.

76 Son of a French aristocrat and an English lady of noble origins, Simon went to England for the first time in 1230 and, forging strong ties to Peter des Roches and Ranulf of Chester, and later to the powerful Grosseteste, bishop of Lincoln, he rose to prominence in Henry III's realm — 'going places', as Maddicott puts it — surprisingly fast. Maddicott, *Simon de Montfort*, pp. 8–37.

77 So close were they to Simon, in fact, that he remembered them in his will. Beyond his immediate family, five further figures are prominent in his will. The first two are Adam Marsh, a close friend of long standing who had counselled Simon through his travails in Gascony, and Richard Gravesend, Robert of Grosseteste's familiar who was finally consecrated as the bishop of Lincoln in 1258. The others were Peter of Montfort, Hugh Despenser, and Ernaut du Bois. Ambler, *The Song of Simon de Montfort*, p. 210. Matthew Paris himself writes about the friendship between Robert and Simon, who regarded the bishop as a father confessor and was on terms of most intimate friendship with him: 'cui comes tanquam patri confessori extitit familiarissimus' in *CM*, V, p. 416.

1238 became the lecturer of the Franciscan house at Oxford and within a few years was regarded by the English province of that order as an intellectual and spiritual leader.[78] But having literate friends is not enough: as Rishanger, chronicler at St Albans, suggests, Simon was 'commendably endowed with the knowledge of letters' and was able to maintain a frequent and fecund epistolary exchange with Bishop Grosseteste and Adam Marsh in the Latin language.[79] The close connections also included Simon's wife Eleanor (Henry III's sister, married to Simon in 1238), an agile, independent, and influential woman who was also a prolific letter writer and who also maintained very close and good rapport with Grosseteste.[80] Finally, Simon was directly connected with St Albans,[81] and, as will be discussed below, he displayed keen interest in writings about the Mongols.[82]

Another well-appointed person to consider as the potential transmitter of 1240s Mongol-related letters and texts is an often overlooked person in Matthew's network, John Mansel, the wealthy and powerful councillor of Henry III.[83] A later entry *s.a.* 1264 in a continuation of the *Chronica majora* describes him as the king's and the queen's 'special clerk and counsellor' and 'the richest man in the world'.[84] Hui Liu, writing about Mansel's relationship with Matthew Paris, draws attention to the fact that, although he did not care very much for him as a person, Matthew saw Mansel as an

---

78 Maddicott suggests that the two men were probably brought together by Robert Grosseteste, first lector of the Oxford Franciscans from about 1230 to 1235 and a friend of Marsh from an earlier time. Maddicott, *Simon de Montfort*.

79 Maddicott, *Simon de Montfort*, p. 94.

80 'The Montforts were closely connected to Robert Grosseteste, bishop of Lincoln [...]. Both Simon and Eleanor de Montfort were literate and closely associated with the thirteenth-century movement for moral and spiritual reform and are likely to have been familiar with the ideals found in them. A later chronicler described Simon de Montfort as a "pleasant and courteous" (*jocundi facetiae*) speaker and informs us that he had been instructed in all good teaching by Grosseteste. Contemporary letters show that household servants were transferred between Grosseteste and Eleanor's household and that she and her husband sent two of their sons to Grosseteste to learn their letters and "be trained in good manners" (*morum disciplina*)'. Kjær, 'Food, Drink and Ritualised Communication', p. 76.

81 For example, he made a confraternity agreement with the monastery in which he made arrangements for the feeding of the poor and posthumous Masses for himself and his wife. Maddicott, *Simon de Montfort*, p. 104. A copy of the charter can be found in Paris, Bibliothèque nationale de France, MS Clairambault 1021, fol. 42ʳ, available online at <https://gallica.bnf.fr/ark:/12148/btv1b90008692/f.38.image>.

82 Maddicott, *Simon de Montfort*, p. 98. See more on Simon's interest in Mongol matters in Chapter 6.

83 Hilpert's comprehensive overview of papal and imperial correspondence in the *Chronica majora*, for example, does not mention him. Hilpert, *Kaiser- und Papstbriefe*. More on his life and career: Baylen, 'John Maunsell and the Castilian Treaty of 1254'; Baylen, 'John Maunsell: The Royal Clerk'.

84 Though Matthew does note Mansel's immense revenues in the *Chronica majora*, these particular epithets are found in a continuation. *EH*, III, p. 341.

important informant.[85] Mansel spent two years in Italy fighting alongside King Henry III's army sent in response to Frederick II's call for assistance with his northern Italian campaign.[86] He returned in 1240, but his travels across the Channel did not end there. Besides sporadic reports about disputes surrounding John's royal appointment to the prebend of the church of Thame,[87] Matthew also records a secret foreign mission of Mansel's in 1247.[88] Other trips abroad on royal mission included negotiations with the king of Scotland, visiting Louis IX of France, and later becoming one of the ambassadors to France.[89] There are records outside the chronicle that attest to Mansel's continued embeddedness in continental diplomacy: on 30 January 1256, Henry III apologized to Alfonso X 'for sending as envoys the prior of Hurley and Drew de Barentin instead of the bishop of Hereford and John Mansel […]: the bishop was too ill, and Mansel too busy with difficult royal business'.[90]

Although he takes pains to stress the secrecy surrounding Mansel's mission in 1247, Matthew reveals that the clerk was off to negotiate a marriage alliance between Henry's son, Edward, and the daughter of the duke of Brabant, and even exposes the messenger's own thoughts on the outcome of their mission.[91] Liu suggests that Matthew's wording betrays his pleasure at being so well informed, presumably by Mansel himself. This secret mission is important as Matthew's self-congratulatory record of it allows a glimpse into an otherwise undocumented connection with the duke of Brabant — an important person mentioned in connection with Mongol-related intelligence from the Continent.[92] In addition, John

---

85 Liu, 'Matthew Paris and John Mansel', p. 164; *CM*, IV, pp. 623, 645; *EH*, III, pp. 210, 224.

86 His valiance praised in 1238, in *CM*, III, p. 485; *EH*, I, p. 129.

87 This royal appointment particularly angered Robert Grosseteste whose ire eventually made Mansel relinquish his position of his own accord. *CM*, IV, pp. 152–54; *EH*, I, pp. 373–76.

88 1247, MS *B*, fols 214ʳ, cols a–b, and 216ᵛ, col. b; *CM*, IV, pp. 623, 645; *EH*, II, pp. 226, 243. The second entry is written on the margin in MS *C*.

89 In 1255, 1255–1256, and 1259, respectively. *CM*, V, pp. 505, 516 and 548, 741; *EH*, III, pp. 138, 164, 324.

90 'actam arduis dictus J. nostris absoluitur negociis' in *Close Rolls of the Reign of Henry III, 1254–1256*, p. 391, cited in Chaplais, *English Diplomatic Practice in the Middle Ages*, p. 90, n. 64. Mansel's Castilian mission in 1256 is recorded in the copy of a letter by Henry III: *CM*, VI, p. 284; *EH*, III, p. 473.

91 This is Henry II, duke of Brabant, who at this time was married to Sophie of Thuringia (1224–1275), daughter of Ludwig IV of Thuringia and St Elizabeth of Hungary by whom he had two children, Henry and Elizabeth. His second daughter with Mary of Swabia (Hohenstaufen), Beatrix (1225–1288) was married to Henry Raspe, landgrave of Thuringia, at Creuzburg on 10 March 1241. The 1247 marriage proposal carried by John Mansel, however, probably concerned his third daughter, Mary, who afterwards became wife of Ludwig II, duke of Upper Bavaria and count palatine of the Rhine. Edward, the future king of England, married Eleanor of Castile. See more in Chapter 4.

92 Besides this chronicle entry, no letters to the duke nor any instructions to the messengers were enrolled. Liu states that the only evidence from the government records was the

is found in Germany again in 1257, when, together with the earl of Gloucester, he is sent to Germany on behalf of Richard of Cornwall, freshly elected as the king of the Romans by Conrad of Hochstaden, archbishop of Cologne, the duke of Brabant, the landgrave of Thuringia, and many others: 'Et invenerunt omnia prospera, et primatum terrae corda ita domino comiti devota et inclinata, ut jurarent ei fidelitatem; et nonnulli civitatum et castrorum suorum claves nuntiis resignarunt' (He found all things favourable, and the hearts of the chief men of the country so well disposed and devoted to the earl, that they at once swore allegiance and fealty to him, and the keys of some of the cities and castles were delivered to these messengers).[93]

Mansel was 'busy with difficult royal [and personal] business' while at home in England, too. Although it is not known whether he ever enjoyed the hospitality of the monks, he was definitely not unknown in St Albans. As a result of long-standing hostilities, under the year 1251, Matthew recounts one of the probable reasons why Mansel was unpopular in St Albans circles: a knight, a certain Geoffrey (Rufus) de Childewick, took by force a horse loaded with presents from a servant of the church of St Albans 'quasi praedo violentus' (like a highway robber).[94] Since Geoffrey happened to be the brother-in-law of John Mansel, *domini regis clericus specialis* — the king's special adviser — the wheels of justice were particularly reluctant to grind and the perpetrator got off scot-free despite the abbot's protest and Matthew Paris's own indignant complaint made to the king in person.[95] Besides the unfortunate incident with John Mansel's brother-in-law, the powerful 'clerk' can be seen to play a part in

---

expenses given to Mansel after his return to England. In December 1247 to January 1248, a Jewish debt of over sixty marks was granted to Mansel, for the king had sent him to the duke of Brabant (PRO C 60/45, m. 11), while the abbot of Deulacresse delivered fifty marks which he owed the king to Mansel as the king's gift: PRO C 60/45, m. 10 and *Calendar of Patent Rolls, Henry III*, p. 7. Liu, 'Matthew Paris and John Mansel', p. 164, n. 34.

93 *CM*, V, p. 604; *EH*, III, p. 210. See also in Bayley, 'The Diplomatic Preliminaries of the Double Election', p. 467.

94 *CM*, V, p. 234; *EH*, II, p. 441. Also discussed in Carpenter, 'King, Magnates, and Society', p. 47. Perhaps to appease the monks, Mansel brought from Spain a rare work dealing with the life of St Alban. Baylen, 'John Maunsell and the Castilian Treaty of 1254', p. 490, n. 71.

95 Geoffrey de Childewick married John Mansel's 'malicious' sister, Claricia, in 1250. Matthew also intimates that John, the special clerk of the king 'whose wealth equalled that of a bishop', was of common birth, probably born into the family of a simple country priest — if he was born to the same father as Claricia. *CM*, V, pp. 129, 234; *EH*, II, pp. 352, 441. In a passage written in his hand, an irate Matthew speaks of his own futile attempt to bring the knight to justice: 'When the writer of this book, namely brother Matthew Paris, reproached the king for these proceedings, undismayed, the latter said "Does not the pope act in the same way, subjoining in his letters, notwithstanding any privilege or indulgence?" However, at length speaking more modestly, he added "Wait awhile, wait; we will think on the matter". But all recollection of his words and promises passed away with the sound of his voice'. MS *B*, fol. 236ʳ, col. b; *CM*, VI, pp. 129–30; *EH*, II, pp. 352–53.

St Albans's life again in 1258, when (alongside Simon de Montfort and many others) he signed the royal confirmation of the charter of St Albans in Westminster.[96]

Mansel's missions bear out that the connection between England and the duchy of Brabant had always been steady and continued well into the end of the century.[97] Pierre Chaplais notes that a few decades later than the period under study here, on 2 August 1297, the great seal of the English monarch was used to close up *a whole group of letters* written to various foreign addressees, one of them the duke of Brabant.[98] This late example not only shows the duke of Brabant's involvement in wholesale international diplomatic correspondence, but also the way in which these letters moved across Europe and England: a bundle of letters sealed with a single royal seal, to be opened, processed, and disseminated by the primary addressee.[99] A letter in the *Additamenta* makes it clear that the duke was in contact with the mendicant orders: the friars' letters originally addressed to the duke, copied together with a letter by Henry Raspe to the same, suggest the mendicants' important role in this network.[100]

John Mansel's former chaplain, John of Schipton, prior of Newburgh, is perhaps less known in scholarship than the others, even though in

---

96 *CM*, v, p. 672; *EH*, iii, p. 264.

97 Earlier, the duke of Brabant, Henry I, was the leader of the German party sent to England to ensure Henry III's sister Isabella's safe passage to her continental wedding with Frederick II. As Benjamin Wild points out, 'he had long been a contact of the English and played a significant role in the anti-Staufen alliances of King John'. Wild, 'A Gift Inventory from the Reign of Henry III', p. 546.

98 *Treaty Rolls*, nos 458–65. Cited in Chaplais, *English Diplomatic Practice in the Middle Ages*, p. 97. Elsewhere Chaplais also cites a similar batch of letters moving between countries, with a professional pitstop in between: 'When Master Bertrand de Got and Master Raoul Allaman, Boniface VIII's envoys to England, took their leave of Edward I at Conway on 6 April 1295, *they were given a whole batch of letters* to take to the chancellor, then at Chester. With one exception, all these letters, addressed to cardinals and others in the Curia, were in the form of drafts, apparently in French; the chancellor was to have them translated into Latin and sealed with the great seal before handing them over to the envoys for delivery'. Chaplais, *English Diplomatic Practice in the Middle Ages*, p. 132. The duke of Brabant at this time was John II the Peaceful, who was Edward I of England's son-in-law through his marriage to Margaret of England.

99 Bundles, seals, movement, preservation, and loss: the materiality of correspondence is a fascinating question which remains to be explored in a more nuanced way in the future — especially in terms of its role in chronicle writing. This is necessary, on the one hand, because of the obvious dependence of chronicle writing on correspondence and reports; on the other hand, because our current knowledge of this correspondence partly relies on letter collections of texts *that were meant to be preserved*, and on chronicles like Matthew Paris's — doubly so. This takes us to the question of what was discarded — an issue also raised in Chapter 6 in the present volume. Mary Garrison's study of the chasm between the world of medieval correspondence seen through letters that were meant to be preserved as opposed to archaeological material is particularly inspiring. Garrison, '"Send More Socks"', pp. 70–71.

100 See more on this in Chapter 6.

the later years of the *Chronica majora* there is a considerable amount of information that he brought over to England, particularly about the Flemish/Brabantian affairs in the 1250s. While his relationship and connections to St Albans are not clear, he, like Mansel, ran errands for Henry III abroad, and the intelligence he gathered made it into the chronicle somehow. The year 1253 finds him in Gascony where he was sent by the king to gather supplies to bring over to England, and in 1254 he is in Flanders appointed as a special councillor to keep the English Crown informed about the war in Flanders.[101] His efforts were rewarded by 'intimacy with the king' that Matthew notes on the occasion of commemorating his death:

> Obiit insuper prior de Neuburgo Johannes canonicus, qui prius domini Johannis capellanus, ad tantam provectus est excellentiam, ut non tantum prior de Neuburg et consiliarius archanus et nuntius ad principes conterminos efficeretur, sed ad praesulatuum culmina suspiraret.

> > (Also died John the canon, prior of Newbury [Giles's error, correctly: the Augustinian priory of Newburgh, North Yorkshire], who was formerly chaplain to John [Mansel], and was promoted to such, a high position, that not only was he prior of Newbury [Newburgh], a secret adviser of the king, and a messenger to neighbouring princes, but he now aspired to episcopal dignities.)[102]

As is clear by now, these individuals were both directly and indirectly associated and regularly corresponding with one another. The last, and perhaps most important person who connects them all is Robert Grosseteste, the bishop of Lincoln (bp 1235–1253), who crops up in a variety of contexts. As Greasley (and Hilpert before him) demonstrates, the diocese of Lincoln, spearheaded at this time by Matthew's personal acquaintance, the indomitable and versatile Robert Grosseteste, was an important informant for his chronicle.[103] The *Chronica Majora* and *Liber*

---

101 *CM*, v, pp. 409, 437; *EH*, III, pp. 51, 72.

102 *CM*, v, pp. 610–11; *EH*, III, p. 215. In fact, Matthew repeated the news twice, see also: 'Obiit quoque eodem tempore prior de Neuburgo, Johannes canonicus; qui sicut episcopus Elyensis W[illelmus], de quo predictum est, domino regi familiaris et consiliarius extitit specialis' (And at the same time, also, died John the canon, prior of Newbury [...], who, as well as William, bishop of Ely, of whom we have spoken above, was a familiar and special adviser of the king). *CM*, v, p. 588; *EH*, III, p. 197. William of Kilkenny, Lord Chancellor of England and bishop of Ely in 1255–1256, is known to have travelled to Rome several times in the 1230s and died on a diplomatic mission to Spain. Stacey, 'Kilkenny, William of'.

103 Although exempt from episcopal visitation, it is notable that St Albans belonged to the Lincoln diocese. Cheney, *Episcopal Visitation of Monasteries*, p. 39. Bishop Robert Grosseteste was not only an informer but also a subject of the *Chronica majora*. As a result, Matthew Paris's chronicle has been used to (re)construct Robert Grosseteste's image as a churchman and scholar in later historiography. Similar to the method

Additamentorum contain five letters addressed to Robert Grosseteste, and eight letters sent by Robert.[104] Elsewhere, a note appears, indubitably referring to Robert, at the very end of Matthew Paris's copy of the tract on the Virgin Mary saying 'Hoc quoque scriptum adquisivit frater Matthaeus Parisiensis ab episcopo memorato et ad usus claustralium manu sua scripsit; cujus anima in pace requiescat. Amen' (Brother Matthew Paris acquired this text from the aforementioned bishop and he wrote it out with his own hand for his cloister's use).[105] Connections of learned discourse did not stop at Matthew's desk in St Albans: his fellow monk, a certain Nicholas Grecus, helped Grosseteste translate Greek texts.[106] Importantly, Robert was present and very active at the First Council of Lyon where Matthew's fellow monks certainly consulted him, and Matthew himself also certifiably met him on occasions when he stayed at St Albans on his way to and from London.[107] As will be shown below, Grosseteste's Lincoln chancery was a hub of communications, connecting disparate networks of information exchange through active correspondence, as well as collecting and disseminating materials in the diocese and beyond.

Regarding the Mongol-related texts incorporated into the *Chronica majora*, a great deal of interconnected and overlapping networks of information can be detected behind the unnamed sources. Nathan Greasley discusses separately the various institutions which disseminated material in Matthew Paris's England — the diocese of Lincoln, the Cistercians, and the Dominicans centring on the University of Oxford — which helps understand the multitude of Matthew's sources. However, these channels were, in reality, both enmeshed with and independent of one another

---

employed in the present volume, understanding the narrative about one of Matthew Paris's well-known subjects, the bishop's recent biographer, James McEvoy, states that 'the historiographical examination of the growth of this myth shows how, upon a medieval substrate contemporary with Grosseteste himself (the chronicle of Matthew Paris, essentially), layer after layer of significance was in succeeding centuries heaped upon his *Memorandum* of 1250 and his Letter to Master Innocent (Ep. 128; 1253). These overlaid meanings can be peeled off again one by one, by the application of the historian's tools, in the interests of an unbiased assessment of what Grosseteste actually thought, said, wrote, and did'. McEvoy, *Robert Grosseteste*, p. 62. This double role in the *Chronica majora* raises important questions about Robert's literary activities of self-fashioning by proxy, a point that is hoped to elicit more scholarly attention in future Matthew Paris studies.

104 Greasley, 'Matthew Paris's Networks of Information'. Admittedly, Robert Grosseteste as sender was not necessarily Matthew Paris's direct source for these letters.

105 London, BL, MS Royal 4 D VII, fol. 248ʳ. Cited by Greasley, 'Matthew Paris's Networks of Information'.

106 *CM*, IV, p. 233; *EH*, I, p. 438.

107 McEvoy, *Robert Grosseteste*, p. 64. More detail on his participation in Lyon on p. 119 below. Although St Albans was exempt from episcopal visitations, Robert Grosseteste was passionate about his personal involvement in monastic affairs in his diocese (an agenda certainly unpopular in monastic circles at the time) and is known to have visited St Albans several times. Hoskin, *Robert Grosseteste and the 13ᵗʰ-Century Diocese of Lincoln*, pp. 116–23.

at the same time. While these networks may each have had their own separate channels of information, they were connected by a number of eminent personalities affiliated with a multitude of different networks throughout their careers, across time and space.

Institutionally, Lincoln, Oxford, and Paris emerge as prominent hubs connected by professional and academic ties, ecclesiastic, monastic, and mendicant administration and exchange. Contemporary realities in these complex urban and social spaces, as well as the degree of mobility and literacy of the people moving between them, further complicate the task of identifying probable connections. Suggesting that these networks of influence and information exchange overlapped when they cooperated, one also needs to bear in mind that their cooperation was far from idyllic, their rapport often poisoned by prejudice or manipulation. The different understanding of the religious way of life and authority sparked and kept alive relentless hostilities, conflicts of interest, and venomous libel between secular and regular canons, between chapters and their bishops, between secular canons and Cistercians, and so on.[108] At the same time, they depended on one another. One of the prominent hubs of information exchange in Matthew's ego-network, Bishop Grosseteste, for example, was unpopular for his obsession with and relentless pursuit of episcopal visitations, but his communications were always welcome additions to the *Chronica majora*.[109]

Starting from Matthew's ego-network, one of the closest and busiest sites of information exchange and a clearing house of news was very likely Grosseteste's Lincoln, home of the Cathedral of Lincoln, the cathedral school, and a very active body of secular clergy.[110] It is important to go beyond Grosseteste's personal contributions to the chronicle and see his cathedral close as an active, internationally networked community whose activities and connections can be detected in the text, even where no source is identified. Spearheaded by Robert Grosseteste, of course, the Lincoln literates provided an indispensable background to the bishop's far-reaching activities. Besides their ties with a dense network of connections

---

108 The differences at the root of their bitter rivalry as well as strategies of cooperation are discussed in 'The War against the Monks' chapter in Thomas, *The Secular Clergy in England*, pp. 345–64. Not to mention conflicts on a larger scale, for example, those between king and bishops, and between king and barons: 'instances of forceful resistance survive from Lincoln (St Hugh and Robert Grosseteste), Chichester (Richard), Dublin (Lawrence), or Hereford (Thomas Cantilupe), as well as Canterbury (Stephen Langton and Edmund Rich). Just how widespread a stance this had become is further illustrated by the broad episcopal backing for the rebel barons in 1258, who sought to impose baronial control over the king's government'. Weiler, 'Bishops and Kings in England, c. 1066–c. 1215', p. 196.

109 Hoskin, *Robert Grosseteste and the 13th-Century Diocese of Lincoln*, p. 117.

110 The importance of the Lincoln cathedral chancery in disseminating papal letters, in Hilpert, *Kaiser- und Papstbriefe*, pp. 178–79.

both in England and overseas, secular clergy (i.e. priests and other clerics outside of monastic orders), especially cathedral canons, were increasingly coming from university-educated circles, which explains their strong friendship ties as alumni and former fellow students going back to shared personal history and education at Paris, Bologna, or Oxford.[111]

The connections and erudition of secular clergy account for their exceptional role in producing and disseminating texts from the twelfth century onwards. On the one hand, they 'produced and preserved records for their own purposes' — as instructed by Alexander Neckam in his *Sacerdos ad Altarem* — in order to 'preserve their privileges, instruments, charters, chirographs, and muniments, either as originals or copies' to the extent of accumulating small private archives, which often survived because they were bequeathed to the cathedral archives.[112] The fact that they were involved in producing and copying documents is further attested by the fact that they often employed their own scribes.[113] On the other hand, secular clerics probably had a major role in the dissemination of texts. Hugh Thomas mentions the prestige of the art of letter writing among these intellectuals.[114] Although Thomas does not mention news exchange or disseminating international correspondence among the genres circulated by canons and secular clergy, there is no reason to dismiss the possibility of this type of activity.[115]

Thus, cathedral canons and other secular clergy in the thirteenth century were a force to be reckoned with, especially in matters of communication and literacy. As opposed to cloistered monks, cathedral canons,

---

111 Julia Barrow argues that approximately one third to half of canons at cathedrals, including Wells, Hereford, and Lincoln, were university magistri by the first quarter of the thirteenth century. Barrow, 'Education and the Recruitment of Cathedral Canons', pp. 134, 138.

112 Thomas, *The Secular Clergy in England*, p. 131. More on Alexander Neckam's ties with Paris, Oxford, and his native St Albans as well as various other stops during his career in the Augustinian Order, in Dunning, 'St Frideswide's Priory as a Centre of Learning in Early Oxford', n. 103.

113 Thomas, *The Secular Clergy in England*, p. 263. A certain Peter of Hungary, for example, is known to have employed a clerk of the name William, who appears alongside Peter's brother, Henry, among the witnesses to a charter from *c.* 1230. No. 2174 in *The Registrum Antiquissimum of the Cathedral Church of Lincoln*, VII, pp. 191–92. More on Peter in note 122 in this chapter.

114 'Modern scholars do not generally assign as much aesthetic value to letter collections as to plays or poems, but for medieval scholars letter writing was the equivalent of an art form as well as being an important practical task. Gerald of Wales preserved a number of his letters, partly to illustrate his various travails but clearly also to enhance his literary status, since he included them in the same work as his poetry, speeches, and prologues'. Thomas, *The Secular Clergy in England*, p. 273. Elsewhere he mentions epistolary collections, for example, that of William of Potterne, a canon and important royal bureaucrat, who had given a '"beautiful epistolary with excellent letters", that began with "a thoroughly beautiful golden letter", clearly an initial with gold leaf'. Thomas, *The Secular Clergy in England*, p. 311.

115 Thomas, *The Secular Clergy in England*, p. 262.

for example, had houses round the close but resided part of the year in the country parishes attached to their prebends. Even more 'often, they instituted a vicar or a "curatus", took the balance of their prebendial income, and resided at the court, the papal curia, or one of the universities'.[116] Besides canons, secular clergy also included unbeneficed clerks; Robert Grosseteste, for example, started his career working as a clerk under Hugh of Lincoln's episcopate. Regarding Lincoln in particular, for example, Adam of Eynsham's biography of St Hugh of Lincoln (Hugh of Avalon, bishop of Lincoln between 1186 and 1200) describes the canons at Lincoln as being 'heavily involved in royal government, prominent in worldly affairs, and excelling in both learning and wealth'.[117] Many were born into aristocratic families, but some were upwardly mobile intellectuals who entered the networks of the elite and the relative comfort of benefices through mobilizing their connections.[118] They depended on their prebends and estates for income, and to get lucrative benefices they had to be able to manoeuvre an impressive network of influence.[119]

The international embeddedness of Lincoln Cathedral was ensured not only by the connections of English secular canons but also by the fact that some of them were of foreign origin. Adam of Eynsham describes how Hugh of Lincoln, a Frenchman himself, for example, recruited learned clerics from schools both in England and overseas to assist him.[120] It has been suggested that in 1193, when Gerald of Wales and other English students at the University of Paris could not return to the city due to the conflict flaring up between Philip II and Richard I, students studying in the same *natio* left for England with them.[121] At around the time of Gerald's arrival in Lincoln in 1196, a *magister* Peter of Hungary, and later his

---

116 Deanesly, *A History of the Medieval Church*, p. 189.

117 Thomas, *The Secular Clergy in England*, p. 41; Adam of Eynsham, *The Life of St Hugh of Lincoln*, I, pp. 92–93.

118 Hugh M. Thomas repeatedly frames the role of secular clergy in the Twelfth-Century Renaissance of England in terms of networks — networks of kinship, friendship, and aristocratic patronage. More about the mutual codependence of bishops and secular clerks through service and patronage in Burger, *Bishops, Clerks, and Diocesan Governance*.

119 Thomas, *The Secular Clergy in England*, p. 108.

120 Thomas, *The Secular Clergy in England*, p. 137; Adam of Eynsham, *The Life of St Hugh of Lincoln*, I, pp. 110–13.

121 Gerald of Wales, *The Autobiography*, p. 127; Bárány, Laszlovszky, and Papp, *Angol-magyar kapcsolatok a középkorban*, p. 192; Catto, *The Early Oxford Schools*, p. 21. A hundred years before them, another Anglo-Hungarian clerical connection made it into history: Lucas of Hungary, later archbishop of Esztergom, maintained a friendship with Walter Map, also intricately connected with the Cathedral of Lincoln. Map first held a prebend in the diocese of Lincoln and was chancellor of the diocese by 1186. He later became precentor of Lincoln before moving on to London, Hereford, and Oxford. Map, *De nugis curialium*, pp. 142–45. See more in Bárány, Laszlovszky, and Papp, *Angol-magyar kapcsolatok a középkorban*, pp. 145–46.

brother Henry, also begin to crop up in the *Registrum antiquissimum* of the Cathedral of Lincoln, first as witnesses to various charters, then as canons gradually deepening their involvement in the life of the cathedral.[122]

How exactly the literate community surrounding the Lincoln cathedral operated is debated. Rodney Thomson, in his analysis of surviving medieval book lists and catalogues from Lincoln, argues that Xenia Muratova's suggestion about a busy 'cathedral scriptorium' is untenable, suggesting instead the possibility that the cathedral hired in scribes and decorators for individual book commissions.[123] Thomson's analysis points out that the book lists show a less than impressive book-production activity, and a surprisingly (even disappointingly) jejune collection of classics and reference works at the disposal of the cathedral community. The absence of this type of literary and scribal activity, however, does not preclude the possibility that a busy scriptorium, or more precisely, scriptoria, did in fact exist and had a role in disseminating various other types of texts in their networks.

First, as Greasley points out, certain aspects of Lincoln's role in preserving and forwarding documents have been attested.[124] Here, especially members of the secular clergy were the highly mobile, literate members of society, who had excellent connections to the movers and shakers of their time. While direct evidence is scarce for links between surviving epistolary collections by secular clergy and chronicles written in monastic settings such as St Albans, the cooperation between these two communities (despite their documented hostilities and rivalry) must have extended to this domain of literacy. As Hugh Thomas concludes about the role of secular clergy in general, 'the accomplishments of the secular clergy reveal the limitations that claustration placed on the influence of the regular clergy', which can by all means be extended to information networks feeding cloistered historians.[125] Somewhat separated from Lincoln, Greasley also highlights the existence of other networks that may have pushed information in Matthew's direction: the University of Paris, the University

---

122 Among others, he is mentioned as the executor of a will in the early 1220s in *Testamenta vetusta*, I, pp. 45–47. In 1223 or 1224, he is recorded as a canon of Lincoln, ordaining a chantry at the altar of Saint Nicholas in the church of Lincoln. *The Registrum Antiquissimum of the Cathedral Church of Lincoln*, IV, no. 1135. This endowment as well as the management of his obit assigned to his brother, Henry, are also discussed in Kay, 'Living Stones'. It is also of note that a canon named Hugo d'Hungeri is mentioned once in the statutes of Lincoln Cathedral as early as *c.* 1184, but nothing else is known about his life. *Statutes of Lincoln Cathedral*, III, p. 793.

123 Thomson, *Catalogue of the Manuscripts of Lincoln Cathedral Chapter Library*, pp. viii–ix; Muratova, 'Bestiaries', pp. 131–34.

124 For example, David Carpenter highlighted the role played by Bishop Hugh of Wells's chancery in initial copying, publication, and distribution of the Magna Carta. Carpenter, *Magna Carta*, pp. 373–79. Previously, Hans-Eberhard Hilpert drew attention to the Lincoln connection in Hilpert, *Kaiser- und Papstbriefe*, pp. 174–200.

125 Thomas, *The Secular Clergy in England*, p. 369.

84   CHAPTER 2

of Oxford, and the mendicant orders, but indirect evidence suggests that these significantly overlapped with (and through) Lincoln's network of exchange of news and information.

First of all, university ties and networks cannot be separated from the secular clergy of Lincoln or from mendicant networks. On the one hand, Lincoln's catchment area was enormous. The medieval diocese of Lincoln stretched right across the centre of England and included the University of Oxford, but their bond went beyond the ecclesiastical administration, and the literate layers of the two cities were connected by hundreds of personal ties.[126] On the other hand, university life from the 1220s onwards was imbued with the increasing influence of mendicant scholarship, primarily in centres like Paris, Cologne, Oxford, and later, Cambridge. At this time Oxford was firmly established as an academic centre, with houses founded by the Dominicans (Blackfriars 1221) and the Franciscans (1224), which were later followed by foundations by the Carmelites (1256) and the Augustinians (1267).[127] Finally, university folks were extremely diverse and mobile at the time. For example, as Patrick Zutshi explains about the so-called 'dispersal of Oxford' in *c.* 1208–1210, 'the university did not need to own buildings or to dispose of endowments. This lack of an institutional infrastructure was in fact one of the main strengths of early universities, since it gave their members the flexibility to depart with relative ease when circumstances in the host town or city so dictated'.[128] The few personages named in the present overview demonstrate this exceptional mobility and connections during and beyond their university years, all connected through multiple ties, being associated to more than one institutional network at a time or across time.

At the highest educational level, the far-reaching alumni networks of the University of Paris were also connected to both Lincoln and Oxford through the mobility of students and scholars. Famous canon lawyers Simon of Sywell, working under Hugh of Lincoln until 1195, and John of Tynemouth, who may have served as a canon of Lincoln Cathedral during the 1190s, are both known to have lectured at Oxford (Simon also

---

126 Deanesly, *A History of the Medieval Church*, p. 188. 'Oxford was quite well placed as a centre of higher learning; it lay at the junction of two principal routes, and was frequently chosen for the hearing of legal cases, including ecclesiastical ones — the diocese of Lincoln, to which it belonged, was so large that the inhabitants of the southern part of it required a nearer centre than Lincoln to travel to'. Barrow, *The Clergy in the Medieval World*, p. 206.

127 University halls founded and governed by Christian denominations are called permanent private halls. Some of these, for example, Greyfriars, are now defunct. There are now six permanent private halls at Oxford.

128 Zutshi, 'The Dispersal of Scholars from Oxford', p. 1060. Matthew Paris himself copies Wendover's entry about this incident into the received part of his chronicle, *CM*, II, pp. 525–26.

OUTSIDE THE BOOK   85

taught in Paris and Bologna).[129] As noted before, it is speculative but not impossible that Peter of Hungary, the Lincoln canon who is known to have been active in the cathedral close in the 1220s, was a Hungarian cleric who had studied at the University of Paris.[130] Grosseteste and Edmund Rich (Edmund of Abingdon) were colleagues at Oxford for some time during the years between 1214 and 1222, and they both knew one another from Paris.[131] Another one of Matthew's known informants, the Dominican Robert Bacon (d. 1248), studied in both Oxford and Paris.[132] Even closer to Matthew's Mongol material, an oblique reference can be found to a very similar connection in one of the letters discussed in Chapter 6 below: a Hungarian bishop's letter addressed to William of Auvergne, bishop of Paris, where the bishop's attribute as an alumnus of Paris, *qui erat scholaris Parisius*, was noted for a reason.[133]

---

129 The 'two famous archdeacons', Gerald of Wales and Walter Map, maintained their connection, even friendship, throughout their life, but it all began in Oxford. Bate, 'Walter Map and Giraldus Cambrensis'. Gerald of Wales spent two years in Oxford before travelling to Lincoln to study under William de Montibus there, William himself being an Oxford alumnus and friend of Walter Map, archdeacon of Oxford from 1197. Gerald of Wales, *The Autobiography*, pp. 127, 139; Bárány, Laszlovszky, and Papp, *Angol-magyar kapcsolatok a középkorban*, p. 192.

130 See note 113 in this chapter.

131 McEvoy, *Robert Grosseteste*, p. 33. More on Grosseteste's time in Paris, in Russell, 'Some Notes upon the Career of Robert Grosseteste', p. 203. St Edmund of Abingdon (*c.* 1174–1240), archbishop of Canterbury, was a respected lecturer in mathematics, dialectics, and theology at the Universities of Paris and Oxford. He died in France in 1240 and was canonized in 1246. More on Matthew Paris's authorship of and sources for a biography of Edmund Rich in Davis, 'An Unpublished Life of Edmund Rich'. It is notable that based on a late source, Grosseteste is sometimes connected to Cambridge as well: 'Richard of Bardney's verse life of Robert Grosseteste, bishop of Lincoln, states that Grosseteste studied logic and rhetoric at Cambridge before 1199. But this source is very late (it dates from 1502), and R. W. Southern's ingenious attempt to rehabilitate it has found little resonance'. Zutshi, 'The Dispersal of Scholars from Oxford', p. 1058.

132 Not to be confused with the Franciscan Roger Bacon, who was much younger than Matthew Paris, and flourished mostly in the second half of the century, after Paris's death. The confusion recurs in contemporary sources, even Matthew Paris himself. For example, Robert Grosseteste, in a letter to William de Raleigh, refusing to appoint the latter's nephew, W. de Grana, calls Robert Bacon to witness that he is willing to allow the lad ten marks a year out of his private purse. The manuscript refers to him as 'Rogerus Bacun' but the date (1235?) clearly suggests that Grosseteste meant Robert. Grosseteste, *Letters*, p. 96. Matthew also copies a passage about Robert Bacon from Roger of Wendover's chronicle with some emendations, where he erroneously refers to Robert as Roger. *CM*, II, pp. 244–45.

133 It is notable though that sender and addressee were not fellow students as suggested in earlier literature. See the discussion of this question in Chapter 6, esp. n. 32. Once again, Robert Grosseteste is known to have corresponded with the prelate associated with a Mongol-related document in Matthew Paris. A letter addressed to William of Auvergne in which he writes 'What I am to give as compensation for your affection I do not know, because I am ignorant of how to love you back with a love that is equal to yours, and there

86   CHAPTER 2

John of Toledo's close connections to Lincoln also demonstrate the impossibility of separating information networks: across his life, he was actively connected not only to Lincoln and Oxford but also to the international network of papal legates, discussed below. John was a widely travelled English-born Cistercian, the personal physician of the pope in Rome. Although at this time he was not yet a cardinal (he was created cardinal priest of S. Lorenzo in Lucina in the consistory of 28 May 1244), he was one of the clerics abducted by Frederick II's troops, along with cardinals James of Pecorari, Gerard of Malemort, and Legate Otto of Montferrat.[134] Another tangentially connected secular prelate is Richard of Gravesend, who was tied to ecclesiastic posts across Lincoln (dean), Hereford (archdeacon), and Oxford (treasurer).[135] Although Richard was appointed as chaplain to John of Toledo only in 1254 and became bishop of Lincoln in 1258, Attila Bárány suggests that John maintained close contact with Lincoln through Richard.[136] John of Toledo is interesting here, as he was part of the circles who were actively preoccupied with the Mongol question: after the death of James of Pecorari in 1244, Master Roger of Várad entered John's service, and they probably travelled to the Council of Lyon together.[137]

Robert Grosseteste's personal ties connected his chancery to letters and documents disseminated through mendicant channels. On the one

---

is no other way for me to repay you', which attests to personal acquaintance and sustained friendship. No. 78 in Grosseteste, *Letters*, pp. 270–71.

134 See notes 214 and 242 in this chapter. For his impassioned speech recorded in the *Chronica majora*, see Chapter 6. The highly mobile Cistercians were often transmitting delicate messages between pope and legates. For example, when Pope Gregory IX wrote to his chaplain, Gregory of Romagna, on 13 October 1240, to prepare the ill-fated fleet that would carry the prelates to his council in Rome, his 'commands were that the legate with the assistance of the bearer of the letter, a Cistercian monk, should make what arrangements he could at Genoa for the hire of an armed fleet [...] taking care above all that no news of it should reach the ears of the emperor or his adherents. Letters were sent also to the podesta of Genoa to facilitate the negotiations, and to the legates in France and England, James, cardinal-bishop of Preneste, and Otho, cardinal-deacon of S. Nicholas in carcere Tulliano, to bid them make the required payments out of the large sums which they had collected against the emperor. The instructions of the Cistercian monk were that he should use all diligence to induce the Genoese to accept a moderate sum of money'. Macaulay, 'The Capture of a General Council', pp. 6–7.

135 Sayers, 'Center and Locality', p. 119.

136 Bárány, 'A Tatárjárás híre Nyugat-Európában', p. 514.

137 Bárány, 'A Tatárjárás híre Nyugat-Európában', p. 514. A similarly connected Cistercian moving in several networks at once is Stephen of Lexington, and his brothers John and Robert of Lexington, both royal officials. His oldest brother, Henry of Lexington, was treasurer of Salisbury, from 1246 dean of Lincoln, and from 1253 bishop of Lincoln. Stephen was one of the prelates captured along with James of Pecorari and Legate Otto of Montferrat in the Battle of Giglio in 1241. John was also travelling on the ill-fated boat. See Chapter 4 ('The Second 1241 Cluster'). Vaughan lists him as one of Matthew's named 'friends and informants', Vaughan, *Matthew Paris*, p. 14.

hand, the close association between Adam of Marsh (to be detailed below) and Grosseteste bears out this important nexus.[138] On the other hand, a perhaps lesser-known connection to John of St Giles may have equipped Grosseteste with more continental information than his letters reveal. John, whom Matthew Paris — reporting about the bishop's grave illness — described as an 'elegant scholar and teacher, skilled in medicine and theology', was the physician of choice of crowned heads and important prelates such as Grosseteste.[139] The Dominican John of St Giles was already master of theology in Paris in 1228, and five years later succeeded Orlando of Cremona as lecturer in theology at Toulouse University.[140] In the summer of 1235, he went to Mainz, where, according to Matthew Paris, he formed part of the suite of Isabella of England at her wedding with Frederick II.[141] He returned to England after 14 September 1235, to announce Isabella's pregnancy to the royal household.[142]

As for his rapport with Robert Grosseteste, we know that the bishop was keen to summon him in 1235 to help him ease the burden of his pastoral responsibilities in Lincoln.[143] In 1237 he petitions Friar Jordan of Saxony to allow John of St Giles to come to his aid: 'hear my petition with ears of compassion and be willing to permit, or rather instruct, Brother John to have the kindness to remain constantly at my side as a support for my weakness, an aid to my inadequacy, a stimulus to my laziness, a pillar of strength when I waver, a prod for my hesitancy, and a consolation in times of trial'.[144] In another letter, Grosseteste begs Alard, the English Dominican provincial, to allow John of St Giles, who was coming to England at Michaelmas, to be with him for a year.[145]

Francis Stevenson may have touched upon an important connection in his description of the close relationship between the two men. Dominican *magistri* were at this time involved in teaching theology in Paris, Oxford, Cambridge, and Cologne (the latter particularly famous for Al-

---

138 For more on their relationship and correspondence, see notes 78 and 151 in this chapter.
139 '[1253] About the same time, whilst the dog-days were exercising their evil influence, Robert, bishop of Lincoln, lay seriously ill at a manor of his called Buckdon; he therefore called in Master John of St Giles, a brother of the order of Preachers, one who was skilled in medicinal art, and a learned lecturer in theology, in order that he might obtain from him consolation, both in body and mind'. *CM*, v, p. 400; *EH*, III, p. 44.
140 Also known as Johannes Anglicus, Joannes Ægidius de Sancto Albano, and Joannes de Sancto Ægidio. He is not to be confused with the John of St Giles who was rector of Banbury and a member of Grosseteste's household. Grosseteste, *Letters*, p. 91, n. 2.
141 Jacquart, 'St Giles, John of (d. 1259/60), Dominican Friar and Physician'.
142 Hinnebusch, *The Early English Friars Preachers*, pp. 358–59.
143 Letter no. 16, in Grosseteste, *Letters*, p. 93.
144 Letter no. 40, in Grosseteste, *Letters*, pp. 159–60.
145 Letter no. 14, in Grosseteste, *Letters*, p. 91.

CHAPTER 2

bertus Magnus, and later John Duns Scotus).[146] John of St Giles stayed in Cologne,[147] and then from July to September 1235, Mainz, where he established connections.[148] Although no direct evidence exists to support any exchange between John and Grosseteste about continental affairs, this trip to Cologne may be pertinent, since copies of letters about the Mongol invasion in Eastern Europe, inserted in a self-contained cluster in the *Additamenta*, are all markedly associated with the Franciscan and Dominican Orders, and connections with Cologne are also detectable.[149]

As these examples may already suggest, by this time another similarly highly mobile layer of ecclesiastic society emerged and entered the information exchange: the pervasive networks of mendicants who were also active in higher education in Oxford, Paris, and Cologne. Friars were often famously chastised by cloistered monks, including Matthew Paris;[150] nevertheless their mobility, erudition, and illustrious patrons destined them to become the legs, eyes, and ears of both high clergy and cloistered clerics and monks such as Matthew. It is telling that Bishop Grosseteste, in his efforts to be informed about everything happening in his diocese, also relied on itinerant friars to report to him about local issues that archdeacons and rural deans were not willing or able to communicate.[151] The reliance on friars for information was not Grosseteste's invention: their activities as travelling informants and communicators pervaded the whole of Christendom and were intimately intertwined with other major news networks, such as episcopal sees, papal legates, universities, as well as royal and aristocratic chancelleries.

---

146 More on Dominicans in Cologne, especially English students, in Huffman, *Family, Commerce, and Religion*, pp. 231–32.

147 Stevenson, *Robert Grosseteste, Bishop of Lincoln*, p. 183. Alistair Crombie also suggests that John met Albertus Magnus in Cologne: Crombie, *Robert Grosseteste and the Origins of Experimental Science*, p. 191.

148 Stevenson, *Robert Grosseteste, Bishop of Lincoln*, p. 183. William Hinnebusch suggests that John of St Giles was a very close friend of Grosseteste, and attended to the bishop on his deathbed. Hinnebusch, *The Early English Friars Preachers*, pp. 358–60, 449–51, 459–61.

149 See Chapter 6.

150 Collard, 'Matthew Paris, Brother William and the Franciscans'.

151 'Grosseteste was, then, aware, through Adam [of Marsh]'s letters and messengers he sent that there was important information about pastoral needs and issues within his parishes, which he was not able to obtain through the diocesan administrative systems in place. Marsh pointed out some of the problems of communication. [...] The archdeacons and rural deans were not able, or perhaps not willing, to tell the bishop everything happening in the parishes. The friars provided more detail. Additionally, the bishop made use of the friars' opinion of those seeking ordination or institution, an opinion based on their travels through Lincoln parishes and which Grosseteste, like Marsh, may have considered more reliable than the local inquisitions required before the institution of each new clergyman'. Hoskin, *Robert Grosseteste and the 13th-Century Diocese of Lincoln*, p. 114.

The mendicant networks' direct influence is palpable when it comes to identifiable clusters of information in the *Chronica majora*. For example, James M. Powell and Hans-Eberhart Hilpert, and more recently Nathan Greasley, all identified such groups of documents integrated into the chronicle by Matthew. Besides Mongol-related letters, the most impressive mendicant contribution to the St Albans history is what Powell terms the 'Dominican Dossier', a bundle of documents that seems to have arrived at Matthew's desk together and then were copied into various parts of the *Chronica majora*.[152] While such bundles are indeed identifiable and significant, the immense interconnectedness of the networks discussed above serve as a caveat that neither reconstructing Matthew's ego-network on the basis of his own source references, nor pinpointing the influence of various networks on unattributed passages provides the full picture. As noted at the beginning of this chapter, the entries that make up Matthew's story of the Mongol invasion are nearly all unmarked, their source unknown. But as the analysis and contextualization of the relevant entries in subsequent chapters will show, going beyond Matthew's authorship, and even beyond the influence of his direct informants, the material was shaped by larger scale factors: the accessibility and original purpose of preselected materials circulating in European channels, as well as Matthew's own narrative and historiographical methods and his very own vision for the key plots that make up his chronicle.

England in the European Networks

Studies focusing on Matthew Paris's information networks are based on references within his text and extend to the circles of Matthew's direct informants, much like the previous overview of his so-called ego-network.[153] But how to connect Mongol news on the Continent with Matthew's ego-network and the complex and interconnected communities to which

---

152 Powell, 'Matthew Paris, the Lives of Muhammad, and the Dominicans'. The contents of this dossier, according to Powell, were as follows: (1) A letter purportedly from Patriarch Gerold of Jerusalem to Pope Gregory IX found under the year 1229; *CM*, III, pp. 179–84 (elsewhere Powell suggests that this is a forgery: Powell, 'Patriarch Gerold and Frederick II'). (2) A part of the Lives of Muhammad *s.a.* 1236, *CM*, III, pp. 343–61. (3) A passage immediately following these lives concerning the heretical nature of the Patarenes and the Bulgarians, *CM*, III, p. 361. (Powell believed that Matthew had based this very brief entry upon a much more substantial report which he abbreviated on his own accord. Powell, 'Matthew Paris, the Lives of Muhammad, and the Dominicans', p. 68. Continuing and further corroborating the argument therein, he also suggests that the Dominican Dossier was brought to St Albans by Richard, earl of Cornwall, one of Matthew's most important and influential named sources. Powell, 'Patriarch Gerold and Frederick II', p. 25.) (4) Rumours about Emperor Frederick's faith inserted under 1238, *CM*, III, pp. 520–21.
153 Vaughan, *Matthew Paris*; Hilpert, *Kaiser- und Papstbriefe*.

90   CHAPTER 2

it was so repletely connected? Concerning the continental sources, the Eastern European rulers' rapid and efficient communication of the Mongol onslaught to the West and the apparent lack of response, let alone military aid, gave rise to detailed studies in the field, which all touch upon Matthew Paris's records too.[154] Karl Rudolf, for example, reconstructs the chronology of the impact of the Mongols in Hungary in 1241/42, analysing and comparing with each other and with the parallel tradition three groups of epistolary sources covering contemporary events: the authentic appeals of the king and the population of Hungary, sent from the afflicted region and kept in copy either in the pontifical archive or at intermediate stages; original letters preserved in the Baumgartenberg formulary and a Carinthian or Aquileian *ars dictaminis* written at the beginning of the fourteenth century;[155] and pro-imperial letters in the *Chronica majora*, whose survival he attributes to contacts with the English court and oral information based on authentic documents.[156]

As noted, Matthew Paris's narrative was impacted by the sources he had access to, and these can shed light on the time of writing. For example, Nathan Greasley found a methodical shift in composition occurring at exactly the point during 1247 that the *Liber Additamentorum* is introduced: 'Suddenly, Matthew needed to seek out fresh information to fill the final annals of the second part'.[157] Due to the above-described interconnectedness of the information networks in England and across the Channel, the chain of transmission between Matthew's direct informants and the ultimate source of the information relayed by them is rarely possible to reconstruct with certainty, but through the analysis of the Mongol entries several influential continental hubs emerge that may have acted as places of mediation. In the following, two centres of the most important networks will be introduced, specifically their role in transmitting information about the Mongols: information networks in the Holy Roman Empire and the information hub of Pope Innocent IV's court in Lyon. To put it simply, at the height of their rivalry, both had their reasons to gather information about the Mongol threat: while the former focused on self-defence and polishing the Hohenstaufen image at the time of the invasion, the latter was preoccupied with questions of expansion and conversion after the attacks on Eastern Europe.[158]

---

154 Rudolf, 'Die Tartaren 1241/1242'. Felicitas Schmieder has devoted more excellent articles to the topic, including Schmieder, *Europa und die Fremden*; Schmieder, 'Der Einfall der Mongolen nach Polen und Schlesien'. More recently, Veszprémy, 'A Tatárjárás'; Bárány, 'A Tatárjárás híre Nyugat-Európában'.

155 Oxford, Bodleian Library, MS Lat. 68, fol. 53ʳ. See Rudolf, 'Untersuchungen zur summa dictaminis "de scartabello fratris Hermanni"'.

156 Rudolf, 'Die Tartaren 1241/1242', p. 83.

157 Greasley, 'Revisiting the Compilation of Matthew Paris's *Chronica majora*', p. 250.

158 Rudolf, 'Die Tartaren 1241/1242', p. 83.

As demonstrated through Matthew's direct informants above, England's tight connections with the royals and regional rulers in the Holy Roman Empire meant that he was in constant regular contact with individuals who were not only informed of, but directly involved in imperial politics both in and outside the empire.[159] And he had a few surprising connections of his own, too. If this chapter seems chaotic it is, again, because of the many intimately interrelated participants who not only inform Matthew's chronicle but also repeatedly appear as characters in the plot. Small clues found hidden in Matthew's texts show multifarious correspondence and reports about dynastic marriages, archiepiscopal and papal intrigue, deep personal friendship, and coronation politics — of and by people who also happened to know a great deal about the Mongol threat in Europe.

Northern Connections

The title 'northern connections' refers to a network of communication in the northern parts of the empire and beyond. On the one hand the importance of information circulating about the Mongols in various parts of the Holy Roman Empire will be examined through three information hubs that glimmer through the Mongol-related letters of the *Chronica majora*: Thuringia, Brabant, and the closely related city of Cologne. Lacking direct evidence to the ways in which these continental hubs may have relayed Mongol-related information to St Albans (despite the certifiable connections of Earl Richard and John Mansel), the importance of letter collections and circulars will be shown through the example of surviving similar documents from other parts of the empire. On the other hand, this is where Matthew's personal contacts and their networks must be mentioned, as they are also detectable behind some of the Mongol-related material in the *Chronica majora*: through his own trip to Norway Matthew will be shown to be personally connected to important and mobile prelates.

Even though Matthew's pro-Hohenstaufen narrative places the emperor himself on a pedestal when it comes to the Mongol threat, the prominence of Henry Raspe, and Henry, the duke of Brabant and Lower

---

159 These certainly did not include the king's chancery: as Hilpert notes, a series of imperial letters, which were demonstrably sent to England, remained unknown to Matthew and although he occasionally mentions Henry III's answer to the emperor, not a single letter of the English king to the emperor was copied in the *Chronica majora*. None of the letters addressed to Henry III in the *Chronica majora* (*CM*, IV, pp. 16–19, 26–29, 112–19, 175) are known elsewhere; Matthew's text is the only textual witness. Hilpert thus infers that Matthew had no access to the political correspondence of the king himself. Hilpert, *Kaiser- und Papstbriefe*, p. 125.

Lorraine, as his sources for the Mongol story points to the North (discussed in Chapter 4), where the emperor himself spent hardly any time. In the period under study here, he was mostly sojourning (and waging bloody war) in the Italian peninsula.[160] Northern perceptions of the proximity of the Mongol threat to their regions also increased their communications about it: Frederick II's inactivity is in stark contrast with the concern and activity of territorial authorities in his empire. Communications, diplomacy, and trade between England and the empire were also not hinged upon the emperor's person. Not only were the empire's issues in the hands of kings (and their assigned regents), powerful dukes and archbishops also created a complex and fluid system of regional powers.

Eschewing traditional views about German princes somehow 'usurping' royal prerogatives in this period, Huffman echoes Benjamin Arnold stating that 'because the imperial court lacked sufficient personnel for a central government, the emperors actually encouraged such regionalism as a form of shared rule'.[161] In the framework of what Huffman terms 'creative regionalism', the Anglo-imperial diplomacy was a multifarious business with many stakeholders on both sides of the Channel.[162] The ducal and comital courts of local dynasties were powerful players in papal and imperial matters, crusading efforts, and trade, and their courts were also busy hubs of information. Thuringia and Brabant (and their own interregional kinship and communication ties even beyond the borders of Frederick's empire) were particularly important for Matthew Paris's communication networks, and this left its mark on the Mongol story, too.[163]

Thuringia at the time was under the jurisdiction of Henry Raspe. Although a historian once said that it 'would not be worthwhile, even if it were possible, to write a life of Henry Raspe', Henry Raspe's person is doubtlessly important in the *Chronica majora*.[164] He is certainly a slippery figure, but far from uninteresting. When Sigfried, archbishop of Mainz and regent for the emperor's young son Conrad, suddenly changed sides and turned against the Staufens, Frederick II appointed Henry Raspe and Wenceslas of Bohemia as co-regents (*Reichsgubernator*) in 1242. Changing sides, however, was part of the game: Henry Raspe himself ended up

---

160 In fact, he died in his hunting lodge of Castel Fiorentino in the south of Italy, which was part of his kingdom of Sicily. He is buried in the cathedral in Palermo.

161 Huffman, *The Social Politics of Medieval Diplomacy*, pp. 262–63.

162 Huffman, *The Social Politics of Medieval Diplomacy*, p. 263.

163 Notably, as Piet Avonds succinctly states, the medieval history of the duchy of Brabant 'at least until the beginning of Burgundian rule, should henceforth be linked with German history', with strong ecclesiastical connections and a merchant capital on important trade routes connecting Brabantine cities with the heart of the empire. Avonds, 'The Duchy of Brabant', p. 75.

164 Stacey, 'Review: Receipt Rolls'. One of the bold scholarly enterprises which defy Stacey's words is Werner, *Heinrich Raspe, Landgraf von Thüringen und römischer König*.

as an anti-king elected in opposition of Frederick II. After Frederick's 1245 excommunication by Pope Innocent IV, the pope — with the support of Archbishop Sigfried III of Mainz and Conrad of Hochstaden, archbishop of Cologne — made a group of German princes elect him as king on 22 May 1246, in Veitshöchheim near Würzburg.[165] While Henry Raspe's double-cross probably affected Matthew's channels of information exchange somewhat, Matthew remains informed about continental affairs after Henry's election, and even after his death.

Besides some of the Mongol-related entries, the entries about Ludwig IV of Thuringia and his wife, St Elizabeth *filia regis Hungariae, uxor landegravii*, are definitely tied to him. The news of Elizabeth's canonization reached St Albans in Paris's lifetime, but her story had begun before he started his own narrative around 1238. Closer in time to his own portion of the chronicle, Matthew began to add longer and longer interpolated materials to Wendover's narrative. Among these additions by Matthew Paris, the first entry on St Elizabeth is one of the longest insertions made into the text of Wendover's *Flores*.[166]

Although St Elizabeth's son, Hermann II of Thuringia, was the landgrave at the time, his tender age and his forceful uncle's overpowering regency leave no doubt that the youth was inconsequential for Matthew Paris.[167] Although it has nothing to do with Henry's person, it is also

---

165 Henry Raspe was known as *rex clericorum* or *Pfaffenkönig* (priests' king) because of this election and receiving donations from Rome.

166 It appears *s.a.* 1219, in relation to an anecdote about Pope Innocent III's ambiguous instruction regarding the murder of Gertrude of Meran: 'Reginam interficere nolite[,] timere bonum est: et si omnes consenserint, ego non[,] contradico', *CM*, III, p. 51. Already referring to her as a saint, the entry obviously dates from later than 1235, the year of her canonization. The fact that Ludwig died of the plague is not recorded, but it may have been known to Matthew, which explains why the chronicler inserted this item directly preceding Wendover's passage about the 1219 pestilence in Damietta. To fit the bill, the chronicler places Ludwig's death in Damietta in 1218 (and in another instance, in 1219), instead of Otranto in 1227. He inserts another short reference to St Elizabeth at the end of the entry of the Damietta siege (1218) in Wendover's part of the chronicle. *CM*, III, p. 37. Luard connects the passage to that in Alberic of Trois-Fontaines's *Chronica*, inserted under the year 1213, but Alberic does not mention St Elizabeth in his account and their wording differs significantly too. Alberic of Trois-Fontaines, 'Chronica', p. 898.

167 Hermann was actually closer to the St Albans network of information exchange than one would think. Jean de Joinville reminisces that during a magnificent feast given by Louis in Saumur in 1241 (Jean himself was not yet eighteen at the time), Hermann II of Thuringia was waiting at table on the Queen Mother, Blanche of Castile, along with two other young noblemen, the count of Boulogne and the count of St Pol. Queen Blanche is said to kiss him on the forehead out of devotion, because she had heard that his mother had kissed him there many times. Joinville, *Memoires*, p. 32. Alexandra Gajewski describes Blanche's kiss as the conscious display of humility of a woman in an 'exceptional position of power, which attached special meaning to her actions'. Gajewski, 'The Patronage Question under Review', pp. 243–44.

notable that a Mongol-related footnote appears one page before the entry about his election as king of the Romans *s.a.* 1246, which — besides Henry's connection with Mongol news in Matthew's eyes — otherwise has no bearing to the rest of the text on the folio.[168] In other texts, Matthew reveals familiarity with Henry Raspe's life and career at various junctures, ranging from notes such as 'He was a refined man of an illustrious family, and a close kin of the most saintly Elizabeth, and for that reason the German magnates, particularly the bishops, gladly pledged him their homage',[169] to the report of Frederick's sons and allies rebelling against the pope in 1251.[170]

The other Henry, Duke Henry II of Brabant, is also a recurring character in the *Chronica majora*, at least as frequently mentioned — if not more — as Henry Raspe.[171] It is hard to know whether Matthew knew about Henry of Brabant through his networks connecting him to Henry Raspe's circles or the other way round because the two Henries were seemingly both prolific letter writers and also connected by marriage: Henry of Brabant at the time was newly married to Sophie of Thuringia, Henry Raspe's niece, which explains their exchanges in letters. Attila Bárány also notes an often ignored aspect of the Brabantian dynastic ties, which explains how they were indirectly affected by and probably well-informed about Hungary's devastation by the Mongols: besides being Henry Raspe's niece, Sophie was also the daughter of St Elizabeth of Hungary and niece of Béla IV of Hungary. His connection may explain why the king of Hungary (and the king of the Rus') allegedly sent the 'testimony of a Tartar' to the duke of Brabant, which survives in an unfinished French historical and prophetic compilation from 1244.[172] But, besides keeping in touch

---

168 MS *B*, fol. 202^v, bottom left corner. Red rubric: 'Nota hic incomparabilem stragem'. Framed note: '.xii. hominum interfecti sunt a Chorosminis Jerusalem. Rex Turcorum impugnatur et expugnatur a Tartaris. Soldanus Babiloniae restitit Tartaris stipatus .ccc. armatis'. *CM*, IV, p. 544.

169 'vir elegans et genere preclarus et sanctissime Elizabeth sanguine propinquus. Unde libencius fecerunt ei homagium magnates Alemannie, et maxime prelati', Paris, 'Ex Abbreviatione cronicorum Angliae', p. 449. Cited in translation in Klaniczay, *Holy Rulers and Blessed Princesses*, p. 217.

170 'The recollection of past misfortunes, too, was as it were a thorn in the eye of those who sided with the pope; for Henry Raspe, the landgrave of Thuringia, whom he [the loathsome Pope Innocent IV] had purposed to raise to the imperial dignity, and whose promotion he had expended an immense sum of money, perished by an ignominious death; after whose decease, Henry, count of Gueldres, was elected; but on reflecting on the disgraceful death of the former, he rejected this elevation'. *CM*, v, p. 201; *EH*, II, pp. 414–15.

171 *CM*, IV, pp. 21, 109, 111, 490, 623, 645, 654; VI, pp. 76–78.

172 Sophie was very active politically, and participated in the Thuringian throne controversy on behalf of her son, Henry. Bárány, 'A Tatárjárás híre Nyugat-Európában', p. 509. See also in Chapter 6 below. The *Livre* by a Moses ben Abraham is in The Hague, Koninklijke Bibliotheek, MS 131 A 3, in which the testimony occupies fols 36^r–37^r. Rachetta points out that according to Moses, the Tartar spoke before the duke of Brabant after April 1241 (the

with family, the court of the duke of Brabant was also a kind of clearing house for correspondence, in which John Mansel was one of the English connections. As will be shown, his name crops up next to not only Henry Raspe in the *Chronica majora*, but also the bishop of Paris and others, and even after his death Brabant news continue to feature in the European strand in the last decade of Matthew's narrative.

The territory of the duchy of Brabant was largely situated within the boundaries of the diocese of Liège in the archbishopric of Cologne; the remaining part resided in the diocese of Cambrai in the archbishopric of Reims. So, besides the ties to the ducal court of Brabant, the region was also in Matthew's field of vision through the connections between the English royal court and the Cologne archbishop, Conrad of Hochstaden (Hochstadt or Hostade). The Cologne archbishop, *armipotens et belliger archiepiscopus*, was an extremely powerful figure at the time.[173] As prince-bishop he was one of the seven electors of the emperor, and (from 1238) the arch-chancellor of Italy as well.[174] Conrad, acutely aware of the Mongol threat, is reported to have assumed the cross himself.[175] The archiepiscopal court was also an important node of political power in Anglo-imperial matters.

Similarly to the role of the archiepiscopal see in Lincoln, Cologne's role as a power centre went hand in hand with its role as hub of information exchange as well.[176] As Joseph Huffman points out, the close connections of England and Cologne began to weaken only by the appointment of Conrad of Hochstaden, who 'concentrated on strengthening a grip on his territorial principality and therefore wanted little to do with the schemes of either the emperor or the English king'.[177] This was apparently mutual, as Henry III consistently avoided associating himself with Conrad.[178] Yet, the archbishop evidently had many ties with England through other channels. Benjamin Wild, for example, notes that Henry I of Müllenark (Molenark), archbishop of Cologne prior to Conrad (1225–1237), is known to have acted as an intermediary between the English and imperial courts, and

---

date of the Battle of Legnica, alluded to in the testimony) and before 1244 (the date of the *Livre*) in 'Herke', i.e. the modern Herk-de-Stad in Limburg. Rachetta, 'Paris 1244', p. 255.

173 *CM*, V, p. 74; *EH*, II, p. 310.

174 Historically, the archiepiscopal office of Cologne was also very much connected to local aristocratic families such as the Berg, Altena, Hochstaden, Falkenburg, and others.

175 'Annales Sancti Pantaleonis Coloniensis', p. 535.

176 Seminal works on the entanglement of political power and communications in the earlier Middle Ages include Leyser, *Communications and Power in Medieval Europe: The Carolingian and Ottonian Centuries*; and Leyser, *Communications and Power in Medieval Europe: The Gregorian Revolution and Beyond*.

177 Huffman, *The Social Politics of Medieval Diplomacy*, p. 269. See also Huffman's monograph on the connections of England and Cologne: Huffman, *Family, Commerce, and Religion*.

178 Weiler, *Henry III of England and the Staufen Empire*, p. 108.

96   CHAPTER 2

(according to Henry III's gift inventory) even appears to have received a belt as a gift.[179] His *ministerialis*, Henry Zundendorp (Heinrich von Sudendorf, also mentioned in this source), established links with England as early as the reign of King John.[180] This Henry, a Cologne clerk, entered the English king's service to assist him in maintaining diplomatic contacts. Like many similar knights and clerks, his 'double loyalties and linguistic capabilities' were probably invaluable in teenage Henry III's copious attempts at Anglo-imperial marriage negotiations at the time.[181] Matthew Paris himself mentions Archbishop Henry in the *Chronica majora*; for example, he is named as the source who informed Henry III of England about the Mongol threat in a letter.[182]

The annals of Cologne, written at the Benedictine monastery of St Pantaleon, recorded with much less of a time lag than chronicles, were actively reporting the progress of the Mongol army. As they also stressed, they received first-hand information about the onslaught from refugees from the afflicted region, who then participated both in disseminating the news and in the crusade preparations that ensued:

> Rex itaque profugus ad ducem Austrie se contulit et postmodum per Waciensem episcopum ab imperatore auxilium postulavit, sponsa illi perpetua subiectione, si per operam suam contingeret ipsum regnum recuperare. Ex hoc conflictu et ante conflictum tam Polonie quam Hungarie multi fratres Predicatores et Minores evaserunt, qui signo crucis per totam fere Teuthoniam clericos et laicos adversus predictos barbaros armaverunt. Imperator etiam scripsit magnatibus Teuthonie, ut se in adiutorium ipsius prepararent, eo quod ipse vellet afferre auxilium populo Christiano contra truculentiam barbarorum. Ipse etiam rex, filius imperatoris, archiepiscopus Coloniensis et plurimi nobiles Teuthonie signum crucis vivifice assumpserunt. Timor non modicus eiusdem barbare gentis remotiores etiam partes, non solum Galliam, sed et Burgundiam et Hispaniam invasit, quibus nomen Tartarorum antea incognitum fuit. Multa quidem de ortu, ritu et victu

---

179 Wild, 'A Gift Inventory from the Reign of Henry III', p. 546. Huffman, noting the presence of his envoys in Westminster in 1227, also notes his willingness to continue the traditional intermediary role that Cologne's archbishop played with the English court. Huffman, *The Social Politics of Medieval Diplomacy*, p. 243.

180 Wild, 'A Gift Inventory from the Reign of Henry III', p. 546.

181 Chaplais, *English Diplomatic Practice in the Middle Ages*, p. 172. For more detail about how subsequent Anglo-imperial diplomacy was at this time subordinated to the territorial interests of the Cologne archbishop, Conrad of Hochstaden (1238–1261), see Huffman, *The Social Politics of Medieval Diplomacy*, p. 262; Wand, 'Die Englandpolitik der Stadt Köln'.

182 'Simili modo scriptum est regi Anglorum ex parte archiepiscopi Coloniensis'. *CM*, IV, p. 111. Further mentions, often referring to his correspondence and contact with Henry III and Richard of Cornwall: *CM*, IV, pp. 188, 495, 545, 548, 624, 634, 658; V, pp. 17, 25–26, 74, 601, 624–27, 640–41, 657; VI, pp. 253, 341, 368–69.

predicte barbare gentis audimus incredibilia et omnino inhumana, que nondum nobis plene cognita supersedimus hic scribenda, donec nobis super hoc mera veritas illucescat, quam loco congruo ducemus ponendam.

> (The fleeing king [of Hungary] ran to the duke of Austria, then through the bishop of Vác requested help from the emperor, promising his eternal submission, should he be able to recover his country with his assistance. Many Dominican and Minorite brothers fled from this danger, and even beforehand, who recruited clerics and laypeople against the aforementioned barbarians in nearly all of Germany. The emperor also wrote to the nobles of Germany to prepare themselves to help him, because he also wants to bring assistance to the Christian people against the cruelty of the barbarians. The son of the emperor, the king, as well as the archbishop of Cologne and many German nobles rapidly took the sign of the cross. Because this barbarian people evoked no little fear in remoter parts too, and reached not only Gallia but also Burgundy and Spain, where the name of the Tartars was unknown before. We have heard many incredible and thoroughly inhumane things about the origins, rites, and life of the aforementioned barbarians, but since these are not entirely clear for us yet, we shall forgo describing these until the clear truth enlighten us, then we shall present it where appropriate.)[183]

Little is known about the dissemination of the originals in the Continent and even less about how they jumped the English Channel.[184] Matthew's Mongol-related letters are only the tip of the iceberg of Mongol-related correspondence moving between these centres and beyond, but even they show the intensity of exchange and main directions in his networks. Copying diplomatic missives was an immense undertaking, for which trained clerks were employed in every ruler's court — be they settled or itinerant. Matthew had no access to the English royal rolls; his coverage of international events shows that he evidently received various documents originating in and circulated by European and English chanceries. Pierre Chaplais brings abundant evidence for the staggering work of copyists and messengers involved in sending, copying, and disseminating diplomatic

---

183 'Annales Monasterii Sancti Pantaleonis Coloniae: 1238–1249', pp. 476–77 (my translation).

184 Concerning royal letters, Chaplais explains that 'the English royal departments responsible for the issue of diplomatic letters did keep a record of them before dispatch. Some of the great seal letters were enrolled in one of the series of chancery enrolments (Almain, Close, French, Gascon, or Roman Rolls); others were enrolled elsewhere [...] or their drafts were filed. For privy seal letters similar files or drafts were kept by the wardrobe'. Chaplais, *English Diplomatic Practice in the Middle Ages*, p. 98.

98   CHAPTER 2

letters and other information. To appreciate the business of clerks engaged in correspondence and the amount of copying involved, it is also notable that copying did not only take place for archival reasons in chanceries sending or receiving them. Sometimes two exemplars were sent by two different routes to cope with the problem of interception (*propter viarum pericula*). The number of exemplars of various letters, especially those intended to be circulated among religious houses too, was surprisingly high.[185]

Matthew's more complex entries on the Mongols place a special emphasis on the chain of information transfer which informed the original authors, but this only reveals the beginning of the long chain of transmission. It is here that the so-called letter collections (*rescripta*) must be mentioned, since they show that letters could travel without the participation of sender and addressee. First and foremost, the Ottobeuren letter collection, originally copied in the Benedictine monastery of Ottobeuren in Bavaria, and now held in the University Library of Innsbruck.[186] Other such letter collections which are known to have circulated Mongol-related information in Europe include the *Baumgartenberger Formelbuch*, which contained a single letter from King Béla of Hungary,[187] a fourteenth-century Carinthian-Aquileian *ars dictaminis*,[188] as well as the collection of Peter of Vinea, which contained some letters by Frederick and was known in England through Richard of Cornwall's mediation.[189] A lesser known, shorter collection was probably not collected by addressees or diligent chancery clerks but written and carried together by Hungarian clerics with the intention of dissemination. It never made it into collections because it

---

185 Chaplais, *English Diplomatic Practice in the Middle Ages*, p. 95.

186 Documentary contents of MS *OB*: Fol. 1^v: King Béla IV of Hungary to Conrad IV; 2^r: Vision about the Mongol invasion of 1241; 'Anno ab incarnatione verbi M°CC°XL°I° gens Tartarorum in multitudine gravi totam Ungariam in desolationem redegit generalem, omnem intendens delere christianitatem. Qualiter autem venerint epistola docet subscripta'; 2^r–4^r: Iulianus Hungarus: Epistola de vita Tartarorum; 4^r: Letter from Wenceslas I about the Mongols in Poland in 1241; 4^r–5^v: Letter by Frederick to the Swabians about the Mongol attack; 5^v–6^r: Wenceslas to Conrad IV; 6$^{r–v}$: Frederick III to Conrad IV; 6^v–7^r: Bartholomaeus Tridentinus OP to the Bishop of Brixen; 7^r: Frederick III to Henry of Tanne, bishop of Constance; 7$^{r–v}$: Conrad I to Bishop Siboto of Augsburg; 7^v: Otto II to Bishop Siboto of Augsburg; 8$^{r–v}$: Prophecy in the dialogue of Aristotle and Alexander. Manuscript description at *Manuscripta: Mittelalterliche Handschriften in Österreich*, <https://manuscripta.at/hs_detail.php?ID = 7768> [accessed 9 April 2020].

187 *Das Baumgartenberger Formelbuch*. Manuscripts in: Polak, *Medieval and Renaissance Letter Treatises and Form Letters*.

188 Rudolf, 'Untersuchungen zur summa dictaminis "de scartabello fratris Hermanni"'.

189 Huillard-Bréholles, *Vie et correspondence de Pierre de la Vigne*. On the Mongol-related sections and Richard of Cornwall, see Hilpert, *Kaiser- und Papstbriefe*, pp. 125–27. The collections sometimes overlapped; e.g. Letter 4 in the Ottobeuren manuscript is also found in Peter of Vinea's collection. More on formularies and letter collections in Grévin, 'Writing Techniques in Thirteenth- and Fourteenth-Century England'.

OUTSIDE THE BOOK   99

remained undelivered and stayed in Siena. Only one of the letters survived in an eighteenth-century copy.[190]

Matthew Coulter emphasizes the role of ecclesiastical institutions in the forwarding and preserving of letters collections, such as that kept in Ottobeuren. Similarly to my argument about Matthew's story of the Mongols in the *Chronica majora*, he also points out that the collection serves as a salient reminder that it is also 'a piece of monastic history writing in which meaning is imparted through the conscious arrangement of material'.[191] The curated nature of the *rescriptum*-collection is also telling: the Ottobeuren manuscript is certainly a prime example for thematically collated documents that travelled together and is probably very similar to the type of materials that reached Matthew at St Albans.[192] Besides attesting

---

190 According to an eighteenth-century inventory, four letters on the Mongol invasion were kept in the archives of the Dominican monastery of Siena; however, when the archive was transferred to the State Archives these were lost. The full text of one of the four letters survived in a copy from 1702 held at the city library at Siena, which was published by Fedor Schneider in 1915. Little is known about the lost letters; Schneider suggests that they were sent at the same time and that they all conveyed the same message, only the addressees and partly the senders were different. The preserved letter is from the chapters of Székesfehérvár, Győr, Buda, Veszprém, and Pécs, from the Cistercians, Premonstratensians, Augustinians, Benedictines, Dominicans, Franciscans, Hospitallers, Templars, and brothers of other orders, as well as counts, knights, and citizens, addressed to the pope (and to the clergy and the secular authorities, to all communities and all of Christianity, especially to the monks at the Roman Curia), carried by the canon and provost Magister Solomon from Székesfehérvár to the clergy and the secular authorities, to all communities and all of Christianity. Schneider, 'Ein Schreiben der Ungarn an die Kurie'. On the dispersal of the documents of Tuscany's oldest Dominican convent, see Lisini, *Inventario generale del R. Archivio di Stato in Siena*, p. 18.

191 Coulter, 'Patterns of Communication during the 1241 Mongol Invasion'. Borrowing a literary concept originally describing short story collections by Mara Santi, Wim Verbaal suggests that this particular aspect of letter collections can be analysed as 'macrotext', designed to tell something in itself, as a collection: 'a macrotext is a sign in its own right generated by independent texts, whose meaning does not correspond to the mere sum of the meanings of the individual texts. [...] the core element of a macrotext is its composite character, its being made up of autonomous texts [...]. Although the collected texts compose a new and broader semiotic entity, in turn autonomous and independent, they do not lose their original autonomy. In fact, the single components are interlinked but do not merge in the process of semanticization that generates a broader semiotic unit'. Verbaal, 'Epistolary Voices and the Fiction of History', p. 13; citing Santi, 'Performative Perspectives on Short Story Collections', p. 147. Bainton's analysis of Roger of Howden, Ralph de Diceto, and Stephen of Rouen raises particularly salient points about integrating such material in historiography. Bainton, 'Epistolary Documents in High-Medieval History Writing'.

192 As Garrison explains, 'letter collections are the most important vehicle of the transmission of letters. Letter collections could be assembled either from the sender's drafts or from the receiver's copies; the two processes are known as *Absenderüberlieferung* or "sender transmission" and *Empfängerüberlieferung* or "receiver transmission"'. Garrison, '"Send More Socks"', pp. 74–75. This particular collection, however, seems to conform to neither: it is a

to the interoperability of aristocratic chanceries and monastic scriptoria, the Ottobeuren manuscript is also an example for the movement of these compilations between monasteries, even between those belonging to different orders. The manuscript originating from the Benedictine Abbey of Ottobeuren, for example, is known to have moved to the Cistercian abbey of Stams in Tyrol at some point, and some passages (namely the Cedar of Lebanon prophecy on fol. 2^r) are known to have ended up in Cistercian and Benedictine manuscripts, too.

As noted at the beginning, separate from these continental circulars and their mediators, Matthew also had more direct access to Mongol-related material through his own ego-network in the North. In fact, some of the *Chronica majora*'s Mongol-related entries take us even further north, beyond the borders of Frederick's empire, pointing to Matthew's contacts with Scandinavian courts. Matthew identifies a number of St Albans citizens, Odo, John of St Albans and his son, Nicholas, as well as a priest, Edward, and his uncle, as his sources who had spent several years in the Danish king's court and were his primary informants.

> Quam etiam accepi a viris fidelibus et discretis, et fidedignis, qui Daciam, in famulatu Domini Regis Daciae, multis annis inhabitarunt, qui de pago Beati Albani erant oriundi vel educandi; Odone, videlicet, ejusdem regis thesaurario et trapezita, Magistro Johanne de Sancto Albano, aurifabro incomparabili; qui etiam, amator Martyris devotus et specialis, exterius feretrum, quod 'capsidem' vocamus, fabricavit, solemne ejusdem Martyris domicilium; filio quoque ejusdem Johannis, Nicolao de Sancto Albano, qui quandoque cuneum et monetam dicti regis Daciae triginta annis custodivit; qui Rex, dictus 'Aldemarus', plus quam quadraginta annis regnavit. Ipse Nicolaus etiam Domini Regis Anglorum postea monetam et cuneum custodivit. Domino quoque Edwardo clerico, Domini Regis Anglorum speciali consiliario; et filio ejus patruo primogenito. Talium virorum testimonio fidem indubitatam arbitror adhibendam.

> (Also I was informed about these events by certain reliable and trustworthy men, who had been born or brought up in the district of the blessed Alban, and who had lived for many years in Denmark in the service of the Danish king. They were Odo, the treasurer and mint-master of the king, Master John of St Albans, an incomparable goldsmith who was also a devoted and fervent lover of the martyr and who had made the outer part of the bier which we call the casket, the solemn dwelling place of the martyr; also John's son, Nicholas of St Albans, who looked after the mint and coinage of the

---

thematic collection, which — as the letters in Matthew Paris's *Additamenta* suggest too — was probably not one of its kind when it came to Mongol affairs.

king of Denmark for as long as thirty years (this king whose name was Valdemar, reigned for more than forty years), and Nicholas himself was also later in charge of the coinage and mint for the lord king of England, also master Edward, a priest, and a special counsellor of the lord king of England; also Edward's uncle, the firstborn son. I think we can believe the testimony of such men as these without having any doubts.)[193]

This contact will be particularly relevant in the discussion of the curious references to Dacia in entries under 1238 and 1239.[194] While the Danish titbits remain more or less isolated in the early parts of the Mongol story, another more intricately connected northern network can be detected behind some later Mongol entries. Matthew's Norwegian trip and his direct informants there are the bridge between the previously described web of informants and information from Thuringia and the legatine networks discussed in the next section.

The role of Richard of Cornwall and John Mansel in bringing news from the Continent — specifically the northern regions of the empire — seems to be rather straightforward. However, less direct evidence suggests that Matthew had more personal (and at the same time more roundabout) ways to collect information about continental affairs, including those of Henry Raspe, Håkon, king of Norway, and William, the papal legate to Norway whose information about the empire Matthew may have carried across the Channel himself. While their (especially William's) involvement in Matthew's information gathering cannot be certified with explicit references from the chronicle, their real-life relationship with other individuals featured in the relevant passages indirectly confirms the existence of an interconnected circle of agile and politically active clerics, who were moving around international news, including that of the Mongol invasion.

The clue is a report of how Frederick's sons and allies (including Henry Raspe and the duke of Brabant) rebelled against the pope in 1251, in which Matthew explicitly names his source: 'Et hoc idem protestatus est idem rex mihi ipsi Mathaeo, qui et haec scripsi, sub magni juramenti attestatione' (and this the said king [Håkon, king of Norway] declared to me, Matthew, who wrote these pages, and attested it with a great oath).[195] Håkon IV of Norway (r. 1217–1263) was becoming an important figure

---

193 Walsingham and Paris, *Gesta abbatum monasterii Sancti Albani*, p. 19; Walsingham, *Deeds of the Abbots of St Albans*, p. 67. Björn Weiler, examining Matthew's 'Scandinavian' material in the *Chronica majora* and elsewhere, also suggests that three St Albans men were involved in bringing information to Matthew. Weiler, 'Historical Writing and the Experience of Europeanization', pp. 208–09.

194 See the discussion of these entries in the next chapter.

195 Based on Håkon's testimony, Matthew relates Raspe's 'ignominious death'; see note 170, above. *CM*, v, p. 201; *EH*, II, pp. 414–15.

in European politics around 1240, and his struggle to be acknowledged as a legitimate Christian king by the pope pulled him in the middle of the preparations for the crusade against the Mongols. Besides the busy exchange between the Curia and his court in Bergen, primarily through papal commissions sent to investigate his claims, he also attempted to strengthen his ties with the papacy by issuing a vow of crusade.[196] Later, however, he commuted this vow into warfare against pagan peoples in the North in light of the Mongol invasion of Europe.[197] The pope offered the imperial crown to Håkon as early as 1246, but the king refused it as he had vested interests in Castile and a potential trade alliance with Alfonso X, an ally and relative of the Hohenstaufens.[198] Importantly, Matthew Paris met Håkon in person when he travelled to Bergen to present the king with letters from King Louis IX of France who sought Håkon's support for his next crusade and offered him safe conduct across his own land should he decide to come.[199]

As for Håkon's embeddedness in European written exchange, David Brégaint suggests that the Norwegian court was keen to exploit foreign visitors to recruit skilled intellectuals to their court. Though the main reason for Matthew's visit in Håkon's court was to bear messages from Louis IX of France, it is suggested that his brief sojourn had major literary consequences for the court and king; Knut Helle, for example, identifies possible connections between Matthew's history and *Hákonar saga* — especially with respect to one of the main subjects of the present volume: the use of letters and documents in the historical narrative.[200] Literacy thus seemed to be in demand at Håkon's court, he himself being an educated man, 'vir discretus et modestus atque bene literatus', interested in history and political correspondence, though with limited understanding of Latin.[201] As a man carrying important documents, Matthew no doubt used this opportunity to obtain texts that may have found their way into his chronicle.

It is notable that Håkon sought to be crowned not by his own arch-bishop but by Cardinal William of Sabina (also known as William of

---

196 Jackson, ed., *The Seventh Crusade, 1244–1254*, p. 23.

197 2 August 1243, no. 27, in *Diplomatarium Norvegicum*, I, pp. 21–22.

198 Gelsinger, 'A Thirteenth-Century Norwegian-Castilian Alliance'. Bayley interprets Matthew's informant, 'idem rex', as Richard of Cornwall, but this seems illogical in the text. Bayley, 'The Diplomatic Preliminaries of the Double Election', p. 460.

199 Vaughan, *Matthew Paris*, pp. 6–7. More on his close and personal connections with Håkon in Vaughan, *Matthew Paris*, p. 18.

200 Brégaint, *Vox Regis*, p. 235, citing Helle, 'Anglo-Norwegian Relations', pp. 110–11.

201 'Et qui cum eo loquebatur, videlicet scriptor praesentis libelli, has literas patentes eidem porrexit [...]' (When the letter containing this message, of which the writer of this book was the bearer, reached the king of Norway, [...]). *CM*, IV, p. 652; *EH*, II, p. 248; Brégaint, *Vox Regis*, p. 216.

Modena, Guglielmo de Chartreaux, or Guglielmus de Sabaudia (Savoy)), papal legate, who came to perform his coronation.[202] William arrived in Norway in 1247, a year before Matthew Paris, but before his trip, he is known to have spent several months in England.[203] In Henry Leach's colourful early twentieth-century paraphrase of Matthew's account, 'he assured the English, who thought he had come to rob them, that he wished merely to proceed from Dover to Lynn. At Lynn, however, he stayed three months, secretly enriching himself, and departed in a veritable Noah's Ark, laden with all the good things of England'.[204] Whether he was still in Bergen when Matthew arrived there is unclear. Based on Håkon's saga, which states that the tragic fire that welcomed Matthew upon his arrival took place 'fourteen nights before St John's eve' (9 June), and the thunderstorm followed 'a few days later', Leach establishes that Matthew reached Bergen about 10 June 1248, on board a trading ship.[205] Their trips so close in time suggest that they came into contact either in England or in Bergen, which probably enriched Matthew's collection of letters and documents. The above-mentioned 1251 entry confirms that Matthew remained in touch with the Norwegian king even after his trip to the Bergen court.[206]

Finally, while on the subject of papal legates, it must be noted here that William of Sabina was a close associate and very good friend of Otto, legate to England, who is a recurring character in Matthew's English history. In fact, Otto is such a frequently recurring person in the *Chronica majora* that the list of references pertaining to him takes up nearly four pages in Luard's index.[207] A key figure in the negotiations between pope and emperor, as

---

202 See saga evidence discussed in Brégaint, *Vox Regis*, p. 308.

203 *CM*, IV, p. 626; *EH*, II, pp. 228–29.

204 Leach, 'The Relations of the Norwegian with the English Church', p. 551.

205 'The saga apparently also describes the accident which happened to the very ship of Matthew Paris, for the lightning, Sturla says, "flew out afterwards into the voe and struck a mast on a ship which floated off the town, and dashed the mast asunder into such small chips that they could scarcely be seen anywhere. One bit of the mast did hurt a man who had got on board the ship from the town to buy finery; but there was no harm done to anyone else who was on board"'. Leach, 'The Relations of the Norwegian with the English Church', p. 553. More on this trip: Weiler, 'Matthew Paris in Norway'. According to Prestwich 'the chronicler, in contrast to his normal style, was regrettably reticent about his experiences, from recording the great thunderstorm and fire which struck when he arrived'. Prestwich, 'Edward I and the Maid of Norway', p. 160.

206 Greasley also notes this trip as a watershed event in acquiring sources for the chronicle: 'The annals after the introduction of the *Liber* were certainly written after Matthew's return from Norway, as the annal for 1247 references a conversation between him and Håkon IV'. Greasley, 'Revisiting the Compilation of Matthew Paris's *Chronica majora*', p. 250. See note 195 in this chapter.

207 *CM*, VII, pp. 438–41. Matthew even records a touching vision of him by his friend, William: 'episcopus Sabinensis Willelmus, vir quidem sanctus Romanaeque ecclesiae cardinalis, qui in Suescia et Norwegia paucis ante elapsis annis existens legatus, regem Haconem

well as a figurehead of the pope's avarice and nepotism in his dealings with England, his story is bound to be intertwined with that of Frederick's war efforts to curb the Mongol onslaught in Europe.

Surprisingly little is known about the person of Legate Otto who worked and travelled in England between 1237 and 1241. Our key primary source about his life is the *Chronica majora*. He is Otto of Montferrat, also known as Ottone Candido or Oddone da Tonengo (Tonengo is a locality in Montferrat / Italian: Monferrato, which is part of the Piedmont region in northern Italy) who was created cardinal deacon of S. Nicola in Carcere in 1227. At one point Matthew notes that he formerly served as legate to Denmark.[208] He was appointed as the papal legate in England, Wales, and Ireland on 12 February 1237, at King Henry III's request made towards the end of 1236. He celebrated a synod in London in 1237, in which he solved the controversy between the archbishops of York and Canterbury concerning the primacy.[209] Considering the relative dearth of information elsewhere, it is all the more surprising how much Matthew knows about Legate Otto even after the legate had left the British Isles. It is perhaps pertinent here that in May 1245, right before the First Council of Lyon, Innocent dispatched him to Germany to negotiate peace with Frederick II and to regularize the *umiliati*.[210] The mission was unsuccessful. Together with William of Sabina and others, he accompanied Pope Innocent IV

Norwagiae, ut praedictum, coronaverat, cum quadam nocte sanus et incolumis in stratu suo dormiret, vidit in visione nocturna, quod Otto cardinalis, qui paulo ante obierat, sedit in quodam concilio generali populoso nimis, et cum supervenisset Willelmus, nec aliquis ei assurrexisset nec daret locum sessionis, solus Otto assurgens ei palam dixit ipsi, "Amice, ascende superius; locum tibi sessuro reservavi". Erant nempe ipsi duo re vera dum viverent amicissimi. Willelmus autem, cum evigilaret, commotus est vehementer. Et datum est ei desuper scire, quoniam infra tertium diem ab hoc saeculo foret migraturus'. (William, bishop of Sabina, a holy man and a cardinal of the Roman church who had been some few years back legate in Sweden and Norway, and had crowned Haco king of that country, whilst sleeping one night safe and sound in his bed, saw a vision, in which Cardinal Otto, who had died a short time previously, appeared sitting in a sort of general council densely crowded with people, and he the said William went thither, but no one rose on his entrance, or offered him a seat, excepting only the said Otto, who, raising him from his seat, publicly said to him, 'My friend, come up higher: I have reserved place for you to sit in'. These two men had, in fact, been the greatest friends when Otto was living. William, when he awoke, was much disturbed, and it was intimated to him from above that he would depart this life within three days.) *CM*, V, p. 230; *EH*, II, p. 437. The visionary was the very same William of Sabina, papal legate to Sweden and Norway, who advised the abbot and the prior of the monastery of Nidarholm to petition the pope for help to reform the monastery. The prior had been in personal correspondence with Matthew Paris previously, which was one of the reasons why they suggested the pope assign Matthew for the task. *CM*, V, pp. 42–44; *EH*, II, pp. 283–85.

208 *CM*, IV, p. 121; *EH*, I, p. 196.

209 Fletcher, *The Popes and Britain*, p. 47. See more in Williamson, 'Some Aspects of the Legation of Cardinal Otto'.

210 Tiraboschi, *Vetera Humiliatorum Monumenta*, II, pp. 198–200.

to France in November 1244 and remained with him in Lyon. Less is known about his life after the council, but he seems to have worked as an *auditor* in Lyon and he is last mentioned there in Innocent IV's archives in February 1249.[211]

As will be discussed below, the legate's story in England and the Continent is intimately intertwined with the Mongol story at places, which may serve as indirect evidence for the existence of a complicated network of legatine exchange, to which Matthew was privy to some extent. His adventures in England are meticulously covered in the *Chronica majora*, and he is a recurring character in the chronicle in a variety of settings, including many Mongol-related entries.[212] In fact, the correlation between the occurrence of references to Legate Otto and Mongol-related material is remarkable. As will be shown time and again in the present volume, between the years 1237 and 1250, but most strikingly between 1240 and 1244, Mongol entries often follow or are embraced by two entries about Legate Otto (see Table 1).[213]

Otto is also featured in an illustration next to the bishop of Palestrina and the archbishop of Bordeaux.[214] And this, again, is not without significance when it comes to the transmission of news about the Mongols. The former was James of Pecorari, who came to Hungary as Pope Gregory IX's legate in the early 1200s together with Master Roger, bishop of Várad

---

211 More on his life and career: Williamson, 'Some Aspects of the Legation of Cardinal Otto'; Davies, 'The Appointment of Cardinal-Deacon Otto as Legate'; Silanos, 'Ottone da Tonengo'.

212 See more in Chapter 4.

213 The complete list of all entries containing references to Legate Otto: *CM*, III, pp. 97–98, 102–03, 103, 105, 109, 395–96, 403, 403–04, 412, 413, 413–14, 415, 416–20, 420–41 (Otto's statutes), 444–46, 469–70, 473, 475–78, 480, 481–84, 484–86, 487, 499, 517, 524, 525–26, 530–31, 539–40, 567, 568, 568–69, 613–14, 616; IV, pp. 6, 6–7, 10–11, 32–33, 34–35, 35–36, 37–38, 38–43, 49, 55, 60, 60–61, 68–70, 72–73, 74, 74–75, 81–82, 83–84, 84–85, 109, 120–21, 125, 126–29, 129–30, 137, 164–65, 170, 240, 250–52, 269, 291–94, 332–36, 336–37, 381–82, 383–85, 393; V, pp. 191–97, 228, 230, 414; VI, pp. 119, 145–46. The proximity of entries in the current order of the *Additamenta* is irrelevant due to the many rearrangement projects throughout its history.

214 As the rubric describes the illustrious but ill-fated passengers of the Genoese boat: 'Rothomagensis, Burdegalensis, Rothomagensis [*sic*] et alii·archiepiscopi et episcopi; [Jacobus] Praenestinus episcopus, Otto cardinalis, Gregorius de Romagna, legati; Cluniacensis, Cisterciensis, Clerevallensis, Pontiniacensis et alii abbates capti' (Archbishops and bishops of Rouen [Peter II of Colmieu], Bordeaux [Gerard of Malemort], Rouen [an error, probably Amanevus de Grisinhac, archbishop of Auch], and of others, the bishop of Palestrina [James Pecorari], legates Cardinal Otto [Montferrat] and Gregory of Romagna, as well as abbots of Cluny, Citeaux, Clairvaux, Pontigny, and others). MS B, fol. 147ʳ; *CM*, IV, p. 125; *EH*, I, p. 352.

106 CHAPTER 2

Table 1. Correlation between references to Legate Otto and Mongol-related entries in the *Chronica majora*.

YEAR	REFERENCE TO LEGATE OTTO	MONGOL-RELATED ENTRY
1237	III, 395–96	III, 397
1238	III, 487	III, 488–89
1240	IV, 6–7; 10–11	IV, 9
1240	IV, 72–73, 74, 74–75; 81–82, 83–84, 84–85	IV, 76–78
1241	IV, 109; 120–21	IV, 106–07; 109–20
1241	IV, 125, 126–29, 129–30; 137	IV, 131–33
1243	IV, 269	IV, 270–78
1244	IV, 291–94	IV, 298, 299–300
1244	IV, 336–37	IV, 337–47
1244	IV, 383–85; 393	IV, 386–90
1250	V, 193	V, 191

Note: The correlation and proximity between Otto and Mongol entries can be demonstrated by the page numbers of the printed edition. Page numbers are to the Rolls Series edition, *CM*, I–VI.

(Oradea).[215] The latter was Gerald of Malemort, the very archbishop who was the addressee of one of the most important Mongol-related letters inserted into the *Chronica majora*.[216]

While it would be tempting to connect Matthew Paris to Legate Otto through the person of William of Sabina, it is more pertinent that Otto, embroiled in the most complex issues of the British realm during his stay there, regularly corresponded with Robert Grosseteste of Lincoln about a large variety of subjects.[217] The proximity of entries about Otto and Grosseteste can be detected, for example, in the description of Legate Otto's arrival in 1237, which is directly preceded by a brief note about

---

215 In fact, Master Roger dedicated to James the well-known *Carmen miserabile*, one of the most important surviving narratives about the Mongol invasion. Roger of Várad [Master Roger], 'Epistle to the Sorrowful Lament'. It must be noted here that Master Roger's work is not known to have been disseminated beyond the borders of the Kingdom of Hungary in the thirteenth century. Almási, 'Egy rogeriusi motívumegyezés értelmezési lehetőségei'; Almási, 'Forrásadatok és feltevések Rogerius életrajzi vázlatához'.

216 Ivo of Narbonne's letter to the archbishop of Bordeaux: MS *B*, fols 166ᵛ, col. b–167ᵛ, col. b; *CM*, IV, pp. 270–77; *EH*, I, pp. 467–73.

217 See his letters addressed to Legate Otto of Montferrat (Tonengo): nos 74, 76, 79, 82, 104, 105, 110, in Grosseteste, *Letters*, pp. 262, 266, 271, 281, 329, 330, 341.

an attempt on the life of Grosseteste.[218] The 1238 Oxford disturbances that involved Legate Otto were chronicled by Matthew Paris who was no doubt informed through Lincoln, since Robert Grosseteste used his past connections to the university and got himself involved in the reconciliation between students and legate.[219] After tracing Matthew's ego-network and indirect sources across the width and breadth of the empire and even Northern European courts, we are back to Lincoln. Matthew's sources were known to him through various different networks and through their mutual interconnectedness, and the subject of the next section is Lyon, an important hub that shows the same agents at work. Lyon at the time of the First Council in 1245 was more than a place. It was the temporary home to many of the members of the above described networks, and as such it brought together and connected an unprecedented number of people from all walks of life, including many of those who were already in close contact: prelates, legates, monks, friars, and barons. What they had in common, in the spirit of the council, is that they all knew a great deal about the Mongol invasion that had shaken their world a couple of years before.

The Council of Lyon in 1245

What makes the Council of Lyon so important for an English chronicle's account of the Mongol invasion of Eastern Europe? Primarily, the unparalleled degree of literacy and intensive exchange of information by both the organizers and the delegates, as well as its highly thematic agenda. The First Council of Lyon in 1245 was a major Western European event at which a great deal of information and intelligence was explicitly gathered and disseminated about the threats to Christendom, which included the Mongols. Although not by much, the first shock of the Mongol invasion was largely over in Eastern Europe by the time of the council. But just as John of Plano Carpini still comes across mounds of dead bodies outside Kiev, the memory of the onslaught was still clear in the minds of the afflicted peoples.[220] Eastern European rulers were still on guard in case of a repeated attack.[221] Independent of the local memory of the attacks, the Mongol threat was very much an issue in the forefront at the pope's court

---

218 'Et eodem pestis genere episcopus Lincolniensis seditiose praeventus, a portis mortis vix est revocatus' (The life of the bishop of Lincoln, too, was also attempted by the same means, and he was with difficulty recalled from the gates of death). *CM*, III, p. 394; *EH*, I, p. 54. See Appendix 6.

219 Stevenson, *Robert Grosseteste, Bishop of Lincoln*, pp. 283–84.

220 See Chapter 3.

221 In 1254 Béla is still pleading for help 'Rumores enim de Tartaris de die in diem nobis adueniunt [...] firmiter in breui proposuerunt, contra totam Europam suum innumerabilem exercitum destinare'. *Codex diplomaticus Hungariae ecclesiasticus ac civilis*, IV.2, pp. 219–20.

108   CHAPTER 2

in Lyon as well, particularly because news from the Holy Land indicated that Christendom's foes were now threatening them in the East. The hope of the 'Saracens' and the 'Tartars' happily annihilating each other, making the holy warriors the laughing third, gave way to various conjectures about possible alliances.[222] 'Know thy enemy' — now called 'threat intelligence' — was at the heart of the pope's communications in Lyon: alliance must be preceded by reconnaissance.

The evidence for documents received in England confirms the existence of lively communications from and about this momentous international event. Matthew Paris's detailed accounts about the synod itself — all received material — are testimony to the influx of news from Lyon to England. Interspersed with the occasional swashbuckling stories of bloodshed and assassins, Matthew's account of the event itself is formal and detailed, and it remains one of the most important and comprehensive surviving records of the council. It is in many ways similar to the anonymous *Brevis nota eorum quae in primo concilio Lugdunensi generali gesta sunt*, now in Bologna, and other 'official' sources.[223] Reiterating the pentafecta of the synod's agenda, Matthew gives an account of the sermon which the pope delivered at the second session on 5 July 1245:

> Et satis eleganter sermonem continuans, comparavit quinque dolores suos maximos quinque plagis Crucifixi. Unum, de inhumanis et feraliter Christianitatem vastantibus Tartaris. Alium, quem pro schismate Romaniae, id est, Graecae ecclesiae, quae nostris temporibus et paucis evolutis annis a gremio matris suae, velut novercae, insolenter et insolerter decisa est et aversa. Alium, pro serpigine novarum haeresum, scilicet Paterinorum, Bugarorum, Jovinianorum, et aliorum scismatum, sectarum, et errorum, quae jam multas civitates Christianitatis, praecipue tamen Lumbardiae, subrependo maculavit. Alium, de Terra Sancta, in qua Corosmini detestabiles domos Templi et Hospitalis, civitatem quoque Jerusalem, et alias multas Christianorum civitates, cum magno Christiani sanguinis profluvio, usque ad internecionem, solo tenus diruendo, destruxerunt. Alium

---

222 In the *Chronica majora*, this scenario was prognosticated by the bishop of Winchester in 1238. See Chapter 3. Karl Rudolf argues against Gian Andri Bezzola's thesis that inserting the Mongols into the European 'world order' could not have happened until after the 1260s and stresses the extraordinary speed of the leap from the first encounters with the Mongols to a fully developed mission concept in 1245. Rudolf, 'Die Tartaren 1241/1242', p. 81; Bezzola, *Die Mongolen in abendländischer Sicht*, p. 9.

223 MS B, fols 187ᵛ, col. a–193ʳ, col. b; *CM*, IV, pp. 430–73; *EH*, II, pp. 64–103.
Bologna, Colegio de España, MS 275, fols 83–85. Manuscript available online at <http://irnerio.cirsfid.unibo.it/browser/275/001/> [accessed 13 February 2020]. Published by Ludwig Weiland as 'Appendix 1: Relatio de concilio Lugdunensi'. Weiland based his edition of the text on this particular manuscript as well as BAV, MS Ottobon. Lat. 2520 and MS Vat. Lat. 4734.

vero, de principe, id est, imperatore, qui, cum esse teneretur summus saecularium yconomus et protector ecclesiae, hostis factus familiaris, ecclesiae Christi efficax et validus factus est inimicus, et ministrorum ejus adversarius jam manifestus.

> (He then proceeded with an eloquent sermon, in which he compared his five principal griefs to the five wounds of the Crucified One. One of these griefs was the cruelty of the inhuman Tartars, who were devastating Christendom; another was the schism of the church of Romania that is, the Greek church, which had, in our times, only a few years back, been torn away from the bosom of its mother, as if she were a stepmother; another grief was caused by the creeping in of new heresies, namely, those of the Paterins, Bugarians, Jovinians, and other schismatic and erroneous sects, which had by degrees polluted many cities of Christendom, and especially of Lombardy. Another cause of grief originated with the Holy Land, where the detestable Chorosmins had levelled to the ground and utterly destroyed the houses of the Templars and Hospitallers, the city of Jerusalem, and many other Christian cities, and caused a great effusion of Christian blood, even to a general massacre. And another grief was caused by the prince, that is, the emperor, who, although he was bound to be the chief manager of secular affairs and protector of the Church, was now become an active and powerful enemy of the Church of Christ, indeed its chief one, and an open opposer of its ministers.)[224]

In a slightly different order, the *Brevis nota* exposes the same 'five pains' threatening the Church: the first was the indignity of the prelates and their subordinates, the second the arrogance of the Saracens, the third the schism with the Greeks, the fourth the cruelty of the Tartars, the fifth the persecution by Emperor Frederick.[225]

Judging from accounts hinting at various types of written communications, the surviving material from and about the council (an impressive amount of which was preserved in the *Chronica majora*) is just the tip of the iceberg. The encounters with the Mongols on various fronts was one of the fervently discussed 'pains' of the Church, and as such it elicited a great deal of intelligence, research, and reporting across the royal courts

---

224 MS *B*, fol. 188ʳ, col. a; *CM*, IV, pp. 434–35; *EH*, II, pp. 67–68.

225 'Primus erat de deformitate prelatorum et subditorum, secundus de insolentia Sarracenorum, tertius de scismate Grecorum, quartus de sevitia Tartarorum, quintus de persecutione Frederici imperatoris'. *Brevis nota*, Bologna, Colegio de España, MS 275, fol. 83ʳ; 'Appendix 1: Relatio de concilio Lugdunensi', p. 514. Tangl suggests that the record was made by a papal notary chiefly for the purpose of preserving a precedent for conciliar procedure. Tangl, 'Die sogenannte Brevis nota'.

of Europe and the Curia. Mongol-related intelligence can be found in all kinds of texts produced for or at the council, ranging from papal correspondence to friars' letters and eyewitness reports about both the Mongol ravages in Eastern Europe and the Mongols themselves. After a brief overview of the type of material that came together in Lyon in the summer of 1245, the present chapter concludes with a summary of Matthew's potential access points to this enormous pool of information.

About the pope's flight to Lyon, Matthew writes, 'leaving his papal ornaments, and again becoming Senebald [referring to Innocent's original name Sinibaldus], and but lightly armed, he mounted a swift horse, and with a well-filled purse, and almost without the knowledge of his attendants, suddenly and secretly took his departure; nor did he spare his horse's sides'.[226] With Frederick II's imperial forces surrounding Rome, air was running out for the pope who finally evacuated the eternal city at the end of 1244. This move, although a large-scale logistical operation, did not seem to hamper the Curia's ability to attend to business as usual, including matters of foreign policy. Innocent first travelled to his birthplace, Genoa, where he was met with a warm welcome by a jubilant crowd.[227] Far from the lone horseman painted by Matthew Paris, the magnitude of the flight is indicated by the fact that the pope's Genoese allies diverted twenty-two galleys for the pope's rescue operation.[228]

Regarding portable texts and archives, the move from Rome to Lyon was an undertaking of massive proportions making sure that the pope did not arrive at his new office empty-handed and uninformed.[229] His

---

226 'Relictis Papalibus ornamentis, veterem inuit Senebaldum, et levitar armatus, equum ascendit velocissimum, manu non vacua, et vix cubiculariis consciis, clam subitoque discedens, non equinis pepercit lateribus'. MS B, fol. 178ʳ; CM, IV, pp. 354–55; EH, II, p. 2. The image at the bottom of the page shows the pope spurring his galloping horse in flight. The side of the horse is bleeding, and its nostrils are steaming with exhaustion. Innocent has only a sceptre to indicate his standing, his common cloth cap suggesting what Matthew wrote about him in his text. This account refers to the first leg of Innocent's journey from Sutri where he first stayed with his cardinals after leaving Rome.

227 Matthew's version is different: under the year 1245, he inserts a letter which relates that some cardinals — upon the pope's treacherous plan — tried to persuade Henry III to invite Innocent to his court, but he, wisely, followed the counsel to keep a wide berth from the pope and ban his entrance to the kingdom, the same way as in France and Aragon, 'infamia enim curiae Papalis id promeruerat, cujus foetor usque ad nubes fumum teterrimum exhalabat' (for the evil name of the papal court, the stench of which exhaled its foul smoke even to the clouds, deserved that such a result should ensue); MS B, fol. 185ʳ, col. a; CM, IV, p. 410; EH, II, p. 48. The last phrase 'cujus foetor [...] exhalabat' is erased from MS B. They have been rewritten in a hand of Parker's time from MS C, where Matthew's occasionally harsh discourse about the pope was not tempered by such erasures.

228 For the adventurous story of the pope's progress from Rome to Lyon, including the role of the Genoese podestà and his maritime assistance, see Whalen, The Two Powers, pp. 146–49.

229 It is notable that residence outside Rome was not unusual for the peripatetic popes of the thirteenth century: 'Many popes spent time in their native cities, where their landed

court, well prepared for the transplant, travelled with the most essential letters and archival materials. The pope had official copies of ninety-one documents made and sealed by high-ranking prelates to vouchsafe for their authenticity. This was later known as *Transsumpta de Lyon*, whose purpose, in Giulio Battelli's words, was to serve as a 'white paper' for the future and which was still in use at the time of the Council of Constance (1414–1418).[230] The *Transsumpta de Lyon* was described in a *Summarium* composed at the end of the thirteenth century (BAV, MS Ottobon. Lat. 2546, fols 1^r–10^v). A copy was immediately handed over to the monks of Cluny for safekeeping. This Cluny version of the *Transsumpta* was partially copied at Cluny in 1413, which is now in the Vatican Archives, specifically in the Diplomatic Archives formerly kept at Castel Sant'Angelo: the *Archivum Arcis* (A.A.). Finally, the Cluny version was once again copied and described between 1773 and 1774 in sets of loose sheets and booklets shortly before almost all of them were lost in the revolution; these (the so-called de Barive copy) are now kept in Paris.[231]

Battelli suggests that the whole of the *Transsumpta* were indeed collated with one agenda in mind: the condemnation of Frederick II and his world.[232] MS A.A., Arm. C. 398 is particularly important here as it contains *Transsumpta XVII* (numbered as such in the *Summarium*; = no. 3 in the de Barive MS, Paris, BnF, MS Latin 8990, fol. 105^r), which contains documents concerning the Kingdom of Hungary, specifically organized along the axis of the 'five pains' of the Church. The notarized transcripts of six documents expressly commissioned by Innocent IV for the purpose of taking them to the Council of Lyon are royal missives informing the pope about various foreign affairs of Hungary or concerning the pope's intercession in such affairs.[233] And nearly all of them could be used for

---

influence provided stability: Innocent IV at Genoa, for example, and Boniface VIII at Anagni. The two French popes, Urban IV (1261–4) and Clement IV (1265–8), never entered the papal city of Rome. Of the thirteenth-century popes, Gregory spent much time at Anagni, Innocent IV at Genoa and Lyons, Clement IV at Perugia and Viterbo, and Gregory X at Orvieto and Lyons'. Sayers, 'Center and Locality', p. 115.

230 Battelli, 'I Transunti di Lione del 1245', p. 336.

231 Paris, Bibliothèque nationale de France, MS Latin 8990. The seventeen Cluny *rotuli* are copied on fols 1–14 and 19–46.

232 'Infatti la sentenza che si stava per pronunciare non era diretta a colpire soltanto l'uomo; essa doveva condannare tutta una concezione politica e perciò i documenti, cominciando con i diplomi di Ottone I (962) e di Enrico II (1020), comprendevano atti d'imperatori, di re d'Inghilterra e Irlanda, d'Aragona, d'Ungheria e di Boemia, di senatori di Roma, di principi tedeschi, di giudici di Sardegna'. Battelli, 'I Transunti di Lione del 1245', p. 336.

233 The transcripts are headed by the following preamble: 'Sex documenta ex diversis temporibus et variarum materiarum ex decreto Innocentii papae IV. Occasione concilii generalis Lugduni transscripta, quae transscriptio iterata fuit anno 1413 — more Gallicano 1412 — procurantibus notariis publicis Cluniacensibus'. Printed in Artner and others, eds, *Magyarország mint a nyugati keresztény művelődés védőbástyája*, p. 28.

112   CHAPTER 2

research or evidence at the papal court in preparation for drawing up and arguing papal policy concerning the very 'five pains' the synod was convoked about.

Just to show the scope of the collection — people and events grievously upsetting the harmony and unity of the Church, ranging from Mongols, through unruly prelates and Frederick II, to crusading and heresy — the miscellaneous transcripts include (1) a letter to the pope from Béla IV petitioning him to call a crusade against the Mongols (written in Csázma, 19 January 1242),[234] (2) an 1199 letter by King Emerich asking the pope to exonerate him from the slanderous accusations of the bishop of Vác, (3) Andrew III of Hungary's letter of gratitude to Honorius III for allowing his son's coronation as king of Halych, (4) Béla IV's letter to Gregory IX, urging him to stop hampering Frederick II's campaign in Lombardy, (5) Emerich of Hungary thanking the pope for his intercession against the crusaders at Zara and asking that Archbishop Job of Esztergom would not be appointed as papal legate on account of his hostility towards the Hungarian monarch, and (6) a 1238 letter to Gregory IX in which Béla IV promises to wage war against the Bulgarians and confirms that he is sending the bishop of Győr as an emissary to negotiate this issue at the Curia.[235]

Even more so than the missives of foreign affairs assiduously collected and organized at the papal archives, the role of personal mobility and communication was paramount in informing the court of the most recent status of the Mongol threat. This includes information both from Eastern Europe and from the Far East. The latest and longest of the aforementioned transcribed letters, the one concerning the Mongols in Hungary, for example, also contains information about Hungarian prelates sent to the pope to discuss and promote the matter of a crusade: 'we first sent to the Apostolic See the venerable father, the bishop of Vác, [...] for the tribulations of Hungary and those of the churches of Christ existing there. Second, [we sent] Lucas, provost of Győr, and Archdeacon Stephen, who, as we understand, were capsized in the waves of the sea. Now, for the third time, we commit to your fatherly care our much-loved Dominican friars.'[236] In the *Chronica majora*, a letter confirms the mission of the bishop of Vác, too.[237] Importantly, these previous emissaries — whether they made it to

---

234 This letter is discussed in relation to the Hungarian clerics' 1242 letter carried (but never delivered) by Master Solomon in Schneider, 'Ein Schreiben der Ungarn an die Kurie', p. 664. For Solomon's letters, see note 190 in this chapter.

235 Artner and others, eds, *Magyarország mint a nyugati keresztény művelődés védőbástyája*, pp. 28–37.

236 Artner and others, eds, *Magyarország mint a nyugati keresztény művelődés védőbástyája*, p. 30. This letter can also be found in *Historia diplomatica Friderici Secundi*, VI.2, p. 903.

237 'per venerabilem Vatiensem episcopum, dicti Hungariae regis legatum, ad nostram curiam, postea ad Romanam didicimus destinatum' (as we have been informed by the venerable

Rome or not — all carried letters and documents for the papal court's use. Although the visits of envoys despatched at the time of the Mongol attacks preceded the move to Lyon, written records of them either travelled to the pope's new home like the transcribed collection above, or were delivered to the court at the time of the council.[238]

As for personal accounts disseminated and recorded at the synod, Matthew states that 'from the kingdom of Hungary, however, which had, to a great extent, been laid waste by the Tartars, none came'. This, however, may have been only partially correct as there is some evidence attesting to the availability of personal accounts by Hungarians and other Eastern Europeans in Lyon. For one, Matthew's own reference to the bishop of Vác, in the 'emperor's letter' under 1241, contradicts this statement.[239] Indeed, István (Stephen) Báncsa, travelling a great deal on papal commission, is known to have continued his successful ecclesiastical career, and though no direct evidence for his synodal participation exists, the network of his remarkably extended and powerful *familia* ensured his virtual presence in the papal court and beyond.[240] As another potential representative from Transylvania, Bak and Rady suggest that it is possible that Master Roger of Várad was also present at the council.[241] Attila Bárány, citing Babinger, goes further and suggests that he also carried the text of his *Carmen miserabile* to the synod, which he attended in the company of his patron, the English cardinal John of Toledo.[242] Finally, a certain Theodoric, parish priest of

---

bishop of Vatzen [Vác], the said king of Hungary's ambassador to our court). MS *B*, fol. 145ᵛ, col. b; *CM*, IV, p. 114; *EH*, I, p. 343.

238 If the date is to be accepted, the transcripts were produced or filed on 13 July 1245, so right between the second and third session of the First Council of Lyon, held on 5 and 17 July respectively.

239 MS *B*, fol. 145ᵛ, col. b; *CM*, IV, p. 114; *EH*, I, p. 343.

240 Peripatetic as they were, this high-ranking cleric was actually in Hungary at the time of the Mongol invasion. For István's extended family, including *nepotes* in York and *familia* in Aragon, see Bácsatyai, 'Személyi összeköttetések a Curia Romana és a magyar egyház között'. Bácsatyai identifies Dénes (Dyonisius), *comes de Ungaria*, as István's brother, and father of various *nepotes* that István is known to have patronized. He also explains the large number of Spanish clergy in István's *familia*: after the death of Cardinal Gil Torres in 1253, István inherited his *familia*. Dániel Bácsatyai citing Linehan, 'La carrera del obispo Abril de Urgel', pp. 161–62. István's *familia* is mapped comprehensively in Kiss, *Dél-Magyarországtól Itáliáig*. Interestingly, István is known to have dealt with English matters as cardinal; in 1262, for example, one of the addressees of his cardinal's orders was John Mansel. Kiss, *Dél-Magyarországtól Itáliáig*, p. 170.

241 Anonymus and Master Roger, *The Deeds of the Hungarians and Epistle to the Sorrowful Lament*, p. xliv.

242 Bárány, 'A Tatárjárás híre Nyugat-Európában', p. 514. Citing Babinger, 'Maestro Ruggiero delle Puglie relatore prepoliano sui Tartari', p. 58. Tibor Almásy and László Veszprémy argue that the *Carmen* was not known outside Hungary at the time; see note 215. About John of Toledo, see notes 136, 137 in this chapter, and Chapter 5 ('1245–1248: Endgame').

114   CHAPTER 2

'Malembach' (i.e. Mühlbach/Sebeş, in Transylvania), is also known to have been in Lyon in February 1245.[243]

Besides itinerant prelates and clergy, personal relations from the afflicted lands were also likely brought by mendicant friars who were in Lyon prior to and during the council. These unnamed Franciscan and Dominican travellers, who quickly became the pope's ears and eyes on the ground, provided the bulk of the Mongol intelligence from beyond the confines of the Christian oecumene. Importantly, a number of them are known to have been present in Lyon at this time, probably carrying their confreres' previous missives and reports with them. For example, John of Plano Carpini, who embarked on his journey to the Mongols from Lyon on 16 April 1245, acknowledges in his prologue that he travelled with his associate Benedictus Polonus.[244] Their departure took place two months before the council, and John chose Polish and Czech Minorites to accompany him on his journey. Besides Benedictus Polonus, we know that John's original companion also included Stephen of Bohemia, who was left at Kaniov (or Kaniev) on the lower Dnieper on 19 February 1246, not being able to travel further because of illness. It is also pertinent here that under the year 1244, Matthew Paris inserts an entry about Archbishop

---

243 Sebeş was one of the cities in the bishopric of Alba, Transylvania, in the territory of the Hungarian kingdom from the second half of the twelfth century. After the Mongol invasion, its city walls were fortified. Theodoric appealed for a licence to hold multiple benefices: 'Dilecto filio Theodoro Plebano de Malembach, canonico Cibiniensi, Ultrasilvane diocesis, salutem, etc. Cum beneficia, que in partibus Ungarie obtines, per Tartarorum rabiem sint distructa, et nichil aut modicum percipias ex eisdem, nos devotionis tue precibus inclinati, ut preter eadem beneficia aliud, etiamsi curam animarum habet, recipere licite, si tibi canonice offeratur, ac una cum eis retinere libere, non obstante Constitutione Generalis concilii, valeas, auctoritate tibi presentium indulgemus. Nulli ergo, etc. nostre concessionis, etc. Si quis autem, etc. Datum Lugduni VIII. Kal. Martii Anno Secundo'. *Vetera monumenta historica Hungariam Sacram illustrantia*, I, p. 192, no. 358; *Urkundenbuch zur Geschichte der Deutschen in Siebenbürgen*, pp. 71–72, no. 80. Romanian translation in *Documente privind istoria României, C, Transilvania*, p. 326.

244 'Mandatum enim a summo pontifice habebamus, ut cuncta perscrutaremur et videremus omnia diligenter. Quod tam nos quam frater Benedictus Polonus eiusdem Ordinis, qui nostre tribulationis fuit socius et interpres, fecimus studiose'. Gießauf, *Die Mongolengeschichte des Johannes von Piano Carpine*, p. 86. As a note here, there exists an odd manuscript in the Bibliothèque nationale de Luxembourg, MS 110, which needs further research, pertaining to its information about and from Plano Carpini, which says 'Anno dominice incarnationis M°.CC°.XLVI°. Bele rex Hungarie audiens nuntios domini pape sibi per omnia manifestantes vitam et mores, ut superius dictum est, Thartarorum, nec mora et ecce nuntii sui aulam intrantes, quos ad eosdem Thartaros direxerat eorum gesta et secreta scrutando, qui per omnia, ut frater Johannes [de Plano Carpini?] regi nuntiaverat, enucleaverunt in hunc modum'. Istványi, 'XIII. századi följegyzés IV Bélának'. Fascicle IV of the codex is written in the same hand probably in northern France, and contains a version of Plano Carpini's report starting on fol. 175, a hitherto unpublished text about the Huns on fols 187ʳ, col. b–190ʳ, col. a, and this note on fol. 187ʳ, cols a–b.

Peter of Russia's account of the deadly sweep of the Mongol army, which may have been recorded at the Council of Lyon.[245]

Despite the relatively tacit and non-committal conciliar resolutions regarding the Mongol threat, Lyon was buzzing with Mongol-related information from the afflicted region that has been accumulated, duly processed, and preserved from the first news arriving at the pope's court from the 1230s onwards.[246] The buzz in Lyon did not stay in Lyon. On the one hand, the Curia was busy creating newsletters and 'official' communications to be disseminated across Christendom. It was during Innocent IV's papacy when the practice began of grouping some letters together at the end of each year as 'curial letters' of special importance for the Curia and Roman Church as a whole.[247] While the pope's direct correspondence may have been jeopardized by hostile imperial and royal policies to block papal communications, the council served as an information hub in alternative ways.[248] One of the secondary purposes of synods, for example, was for the delegates to obtain and exchange as much current information about the expansion of Christendom as possible. Much of this information was gathered and transported home in the form of copies prepared at the synod.[249]

Despite the large amount of documents and other information crossing the Channel, it is important to note that the dissemination of papal intelligence or synodal materials was not always as uncomplicated as it may seem. As attested to by Matthew's narrative, the importance of written materials, charters, reports, and letters was inflated to a point of hysteria. Moving and rehousing the papal court, including the archive and chancery, from Rome to Lyon was not without drama, as Matthew Paris himself recounts — openly expressing his disapproval about the riches brought into Lyon by visiting prelates, favour seekers, and papal agents.[250] The city at this point was a veritable chaos of travellers arriving with precious cargo, and met with suspicion and hostility by both locals and visitors.

---

245 MS B, fol. 182ʳ, cols a–b; *CM*, IV, pp. 386–89; *EH*, II, pp. 28–31. Matthew Paris inserted the account under 1244, but other evidence suggests that it was probably connected to the Council of Lyon a year later. See Chapter 5.

246 For the council resolutions about the Mongol threat, see Chapter 5.

247 Whalen, *The Two Powers*, p. 263, n. 3.

248 See note 255 in this chapter.

249 Albeit regarding a later synod, Enikő Csukovits's study on the Council of Constance functioning as a book fair and scientific forum, based on Cardinal Fillastre's well-annotated book lists, provides an excellent insight into the intense scribal activity that can be associated with local and ecumenical synods. Csukovits, 'A konstanzi zsinat mint könyvvásár'. The book-fair function of the same synod was also investigated by Daniel Hobbins, who studied the publishing and distribution of works by Jean Gerson, introducing the notion of 'distribution circles' through which Gerson could reach international audiences. Hobbins, *Authorship and Publicity before Print*, p. 186.

250 *CM*, IV, p. 418; *EH*, II, p. 54; *HA*, I, p. 501.

116   CHAPTER 2

At the height of preparations for the council in May, as Matthew relates, a fire broke out in Innocent's chambers, and Matthew suggests that the pope started the fire deliberately, hoping to use the losses as an excuse to extort money from visitors to Lyon, but the blaze got out of hand.[251] Obviously the fire consumed more than just valuables; it affected archival materials too: for example, Matthew notes that King John's 'detestable' charter concerning the English tribute to the pope also disappeared in the flames.[252]

Matthew Paris's unusual treatment of this particular entry across various versions of his chronicles is indicative of its importance.[253] These severely edited passages, along with later accounts of 'papal militia' as well as the military orders hired to protect the papal party and their possessions, both show that the turmoil in Lyon was indeed great and the influx of foreigners into the city was such that it caused concerns reverberating as far as St Albans — where, as usual, the quandary was thought to be the pope's own fault.[254] Besides the noticeably high importance attached to the relocation of the pope's chancery, the fact that the pervasive imperial conflict with the pope was fought also in ink and parchment is aptly illustrated by Matthew's note that upon England's near impoverishment due to the papal taxes,

> Urgente igitur necessitate, praeceptum est ipso tempore ex parte aliquorum magnatum, pro multiformi oppressione regni dolentium, ut custoditis portubus, *papales literae*, quae cotidie ad emungendum pecuniam portabantur, *caperentur*.
>
> (an order was given by some of the nobles, who lamented and compassionated [*sic*] the manifold and ceaseless oppression and pillage of the kingdom, that all the seaports should be diligently and closely watched, *in order that the pope's letters*, which were daily brought to England to extort money, *might be seized on*.)[255]

---

251 Also noted in *Les registres d'Innocent IV*, p. vi; Whalen, *The Two Powers*, p. 157.

252 *CM*, IV, p. 417; *EH*, II, p. 54.

253 Whalen points out that the text relating the suspicions about the pope was originally nearly the same in the *Chronica majora* and the *Historia Anglorum*, but later Matthew amended the latter (London, BL, MS Royal 14 C VIII, fol. 138ʳ), where a modified account of the fire was subsequently inserted, on a small piece of parchment sewn over the original folio. Here Matthew claims that one of the pope's ministers in the chancery caused the fire by neglect and then blamed it on 'secret arsonists' sent by the emperor to kill the pope. Whalen suggests that Matthew heard rumours about the fire later and changed his account accordingly. Whalen, *The Two Powers*, p. 267, n. 15.

254 *CM*, IV, pp. 417–18; *EH*, II, pp. 53–54; 'Appendix 1: Relatio de concilio Lugdunensi', p. 515.

255 *CM*, IV, p. 417; *EH*, II, p. 53 (my italics). Similar measures are known to have been taken to block and intercept papal communication by the excommunicated Emperor Otto IV. As Dick de Boer notes, he laid roadblocks with garrisons all over the Appenine roads, and clerics carrying letters from the Curia were robbed in order to prevent messages of

Although the pope's direct mediation of the Mongol material to English circles was hampered by mutual hostility and distrust, the blockade of papal communications on the English shore evidently did not stop the information flow between the pontiff's Lyon court and various literate destinations in England. Directly or indirectly, the intelligence amassed at the Curia was no doubt the fountainhead for most of the Mongol material that made it across the Channel in the second half of the 1240s.

The synod attracted considerable interest in England — not so much because of the kingdom's direct stake in 'the five pains' of Christendom, as for the papal policies regarding Church matters ranging from episcopal visitations (Robert Grosseteste's hobby horse) to legal resolutions, crusades, and excommunication. The official documents produced at the council (or right afterwards), although probably widely disseminated across the Christian world, are now no less difficult to trace than missives and reports by representatives. Had Matthew not taken it upon himself to copy these in his chronicle, the council would be much lesser known than it is now. The reason why the synodal documentation, moving together with a wealth of Mongol-related texts, made it into the *Chronica majora* lies in their role of underpinning one of Matthew's main narratives therein. The council is a prominent subject in the *Chronica majora* mostly because of the papal-imperial conflict which constitutes the backbone of the chronicle's European strand. By the time Matthew was writing the entries, it was clear that the Mongol subplot within his Frederick-centred European strand was documented extensively enough to furnish a relatively coherent story that not only framed Frederick's exploits but also smoothly fed into the story of the crusades towards the end of the decade.

Although imperial news and the materials associated with the pope's court in Lyon are discussed somewhat separately in this volume, it must be noted that the division was far from being that straightforward. Changing sides was very much part of the imperial game, which often disrupted the lines of information exchange and sometimes connected unlikely sources. For example, the aforementioned Conrad of Hochstaden, archbishop of Cologne, was one such connector. Seemingly an 'imperial source' for Matthew and discussed as such above, he was not pro-Hohenstaufen. In fact, lobbying for the second deposition of Frederick II, Conrad and Archbishop Sigfried of Mainz visited Innocent IV's new court at Lyon right

---

support being delivered to Otto's opponents north of the Alps. Boer, '"He Proved to Be an Inseparable Travel Companion"', p. 61. Léon Blin's summary and map of the continental routes to Lyon give a very good idea about the roads leading to and away from the council. Blin, 'Du Brabant à Lyon et en Italie'.

118   CHAPTER 2

before the pope announced the call for the Council of Lyon in December 1244.[256]

As for the mediators of the conciliar material that found its way to the *Chronica majora*, whence Matthew Paris received the documents and accounts of events related to the council is uncertain, but the difference in register and the placement of the entries do suggest that he acquired the relevant texts from different informants at different times. Some individuals will be familiar from the overview of Matthew's ego-network above; some are less prominent people. For example, without reference to the Mongol-related materials, Matthew's account of the synod gives an insight into the composition of the English party. He names three representatives from St Albans, who were sent in place of the abbot, an aged and obese man no longer fit to travel: 'Inter quos abbas Sancti Albani, corpore gravis et jam ad senilem declinans aetatem, magistro Martino, qui tunc temporis in Anglia prospere commorabatur, testimonium veritati super hoc perhibente, rationabiliter per quendam monachum suum, Johannem videlicet de Bulum, et quendam clericum suum, magistrum Rogerum de Holderne, suam excusavit absentiam; et sic indempnis et quietus remansit, domino Papa per ipsos civiliter salutato' (the abbot of St Alban's, who was a corpulent man and now verging on old age, sent reasonable excuses for his absence by a monk of his convent, named John de Bulum, and Master Roger de Holden, a clerk, and to the truth of his statements in this matter, Master Martin, who was at the time dwelling in England, gave this testimony, and thus he remained indemnified and peaceable, sending civil greetings to the pope by the said messengers of his).[257] Further, we also know from the *Chronica majora* that Matthew received information about the council from the Augustinian prior of Westacre, *qui est monachus Cluniacensis*, who told him of various gifts made to the pope at the Council of Lyon.[258] According to Matthew's account of the synod, an English contingent of procurators led by William of Powic (Powicke) was present, reading out a memorandum of protest against King John's privilege placing his kingdom in vassalage to the Apostolic See without baronial consent,

---

256 For their possible impact on materials included *s.a.* 1243, see also Chapter 5 ('1243: The Tartar Khan's Englishman').

257 *CM*, IV, p. 430; *EH*, II, p. 64.

258 *CM*, IV, p. 428; *EH*, II, p. 62. Noted in Vaughan, *Matthew Paris*, p. 16. This can be either Robert de Alenzun or a certain Simon. Robert de Alenzun: first mentioned between October 1231 and October 1232, last mentioned between October 1256 and October 1257 (Norfolk F (Rye), 49, 94; PRO E40/2871;/2954). Simon: mentioned ab anno 1249 (no primary source indicated), in Blomefield, *An Essay towards a Topographical History of the County of Norfolk*, IX, p. 160. Both cited in Smith and London, *The Heads of Religious Houses*, p. 483.

with special import placed on the financial grievance caused by benefices awarded to foreigners and taxes levied.[259]

Besides these straightforward, seemingly direct connections, Robert Grosseteste, bishop of Lincoln, and his scribes are strong contenders for moving information between Lyon and St Albans. As briefly noted above,[260] Robert Grosseteste, who was certifiably Matthew's informant at various points in time, was an active participant at the synod.[261] He arrived in Lyon some time before the council, and he was definitely in attendance there.[262] He was one of the English party who came to propose the canonization of Edmund of Abingdon (d. 1240), archbishop of Canterbury and Grosseteste's former colleague at Oxford, which was the third point on the agenda. While most English bishops were represented by procurators, Grosseteste took it upon himself to attend in person with Adam Marsh as his advisor.[263] It is notable that setting off from Lincoln in November 1244, he was already on his way to Rome when Innocent's bull convoking the Lyon synod (issued on 3 January 1245) reached him, and once there he stayed in Lyon long after the council, returning to England only in October 1245. Although personally on a different mission altogether, it is not unlikely that the Lincoln prelate had access to and took home reports and texts that concerned issues beyond the immediate purview of his mission. Both Hans-Eberhard Hilpert's and, more recently, Nathan Greasley's studies have demonstrated the wide circulation of Grosseteste's correspondence and its availability to Matthew Paris.[264] Greasley argues that the fact that they all contain papal correspondence suggests that the

---

259 *CM*, IV, pp. 440–45; *EH*, II, pp. 73–77.

260 The connection between Lincoln and Matthew Paris is discussed in the section on 'The Scriptorium in England' above.

261 See note 107 in this chapter. He returned to Lyon in 1250, to further his arguments against centralized Church appointments in a memorandum handed over to Innocent IV. McEvoy, *Robert Grosseteste*, p. 30.

262 McEvoy shows that Robert Grosseteste's name (Robt Lincolniensis) appears on the first folio of the *Transsumpta of Lyons*. Another source seems to suggest that he delivered a sermon there: London, Lambeth Palace Library, MS 499, a source of much diverse and worthwhile material on Grosseteste, some of which appears to have emanated from his own household, says 'These new constitutions which follow were made law by Pope Innocent IV at Lyons in the General Council. Robert Grosseteste bishop of Lincoln was present and preached there, taking his theme from the Gospel verse, "A very great multitude spread their garments in the way" [Mt 21. 8]'. McEvoy, *Robert Grosseteste*, pp. 2, 37. More on the Lambeth MS in Goering, '"Notus in Iudea Deus"'.

263 McEvoy, *Robert Grosseteste*, p. 33.

264 Hilpert, *Kaiser- und Papstbriefe*, pp. 174–200. There is one letter by Grosseteste in the *Chronica majora* (*CM*, IV, pp. 506–07), which also contains a letter from Pope Innocent IV, and two in the *Additamenta* (*CM*, VI, pp. 137–38, 213–17), which also contain letters from the pope's commissioners and the pope himself, respectively. Two further letters addressed to him can be found in the *Additamenta* (*CM*, VI, pp. 148–50, 186–87).

120   CHAPTER 2

letters were intended for wide circulation from their inception, and that Matthew received it along with many other clerics across England.[265]

Naturally for such an important political event, the synod was not merely an ecclesiastical affair, and English royal circles were also involved in collecting and forwarding information about the proceedings. Matthew records the attendance of Earl Roger Bigod with some of his fellow nobles.[266] This must be the same delegation that appears in the *Chester Annals* which relates that King Henry III received a report in 1245 from his representatives sent to the council: 'and whilst he was tarrying there [Gannoch, Wales] there came to him Richard [de Clare], earl of Gloucester, and William de Vesci, with a great band of soldiers and armed men, and very soon after came Roger Bigod, earl of Norfolk, and William de Cantelupe, and others on their return from the Council of Lyons, to confer with the king concerning the council'.[267]

Although no direct textual evidence can be detected, it is highly likely that Henry III, a regular visitor at St Albans, and his networks mediated some of the information. Despite the fact that in 1244 the king was originally appointed to participate by Frederick II, he was not actually present at the council in 1245.[268] However, he had access to reports and letters through his proxies and is known to have visited St Albans several times. A remarkable document using the trope of Jesus's five wounds to describe the synod, for example, appears as the first entry in a roll entitled 'Articuli et petitiones praelatorum Angliae, et responsiones ad ipsos factae et alii diversi articuli in concilio generali dunensi et alibi, cum supplicationibus factis Domino Papae regno Angliae, temporibus Henrici tertii et Edwardi

---

265 Greasley, 'Matthew Paris's Networks of Information'. He further corroborates this suggestion by citing Franciscan scholar Adam Marsh (Adam de Marisco, *c.* 1200–1259) to shed more light on the actual process of disseminating correspondence at the time. 'As I requested elsewhere, I wish the transcripts of the letters of the lord king of France and the lord of Tusculum to be returned to me, if you please, when you have had them read or even transcribed'. Marsh, *The Letters*, I, p. 45.

266 'Electi sunt igitur, et ad hoc ad curiam missi, comes Rogerus Bigod [Roger Bigod, earl of Norfolk], Johannes filius Galfridi, Willelmus de Cantelupo [William Cantilupe, Henry's regent and steward], Philippus Basset [Philip Basset], Radulphus filius Nicholai [Ralph FitzNicholas], magister Willelmus de Powic clericus [William Powicke, added in a rubric on the margin]'. MS *B*, fol. 186ʳ, col. b; *CM*, IV, p. 420; *EH*, II, p. 56. Bigod's proxy is mentioned again in *CM*, IV, p. 478; *EH*, II, p. 65. See also Weiler, *Henry III of England and the Staufen Empire*, p. 111.

267 *Annales Cestrienses*, p. 64. Lunt asserts that they delivered a written report, but — although this is highly probable — the actual text does not contain any references to a written document. Lunt, 'The Sources for the First Council of Lyons', p. 74.

268 Henry III as a source is mentioned by Matthew Paris in *HA*, II, p. 455, III, p. 8; cited in Vaughan, *Matthew Paris*, p. 13. For Henry III's appointment to represent the emperor at Lyon, see Weiler, *Henry III of England and the Staufen Empire*, p. 112.

filii eiusdem', which was possibly written later than Matthew's chronicle but may have had the same exemplar.[269]

Finally, the king's brother, the emperor's brother-in-law: Richard, earl of Cornwall. Plenty of evidence has been shown to attest to his St Albans connections, and he and his circles are definitely connected to Lyon as well. While it is certain that Richard was informed about the proceedings of the first Lyon council through his extensive information network, and his chancery was ready to serve as a clearing house of news, he was not personally present at the synod in 1245. He was, however, in Lyon in 1250 when he personally met the pope.[270] Nathan Greasley, tapping into the immense importance of the councils of Lyon in disseminating materials in the direction of St Albans — among others — suggests that a bundle of materials from Lyon came to Matthew as part of a third large donation of material besides similarly large parcels received from Richard of Cornwall, and through some mediation from the exchequer. Nathan Greasley's suggestion about the methodical shift of 1247, detectable through the increase of incoming material in the second part of the chronicle, fits the timeframe: this volume of newly acquired sources no doubt entails texts associated with the Council of Lyon, which probably reached English scriptoria in around 1247.[271]

After Chapter 1, focusing on Matthew's chronicle world, the aim of this chapter was to examine the accumulation of the materials for the chronicle in the empirical world surrounding Matthew Paris, gradually opening the angle from contextualizing the book within the scriptorium, the scriptorium in England, and England in the web of continental networks of power and information. Looking through the lens of Matthew Paris's sources for

---

269 Lunt, 'The Sources for the First Council of Lyons', p. 73.

270 More about his itinerary on p. 71 in this chapter.

271 'Aside from the probability that the production of the *Gesta* intervened between the *Chronica*'s first and second parts, a lengthy pause between the two is also to be inferred from the sudden availability of certain documents as soon as the second part began, an abrupt shift in the prominence given to Richard of Cornwall and certain manuscript evidence. In 1247, work finally began on expanding this particular rendition of Roger of Wendover's work into a lengthier chronicle. Such an extension was possible in part because of the donation of at least two significant batches of documents. Much of this was probably not given to Matthew by Alexander of Swereford, but was instead taken from a set of rolls attributed to the exchequer clerk. Matthew also received original correspondence from Richard of Cornwall, and both these donations were used to enliven the chronicle's narrative'. Greasley, 'Revisiting the Compilation of Matthew Paris's *Chronica majora*', p. 254. Another interesting milestone is also noted to have occurred in 1247 when Matthew met the king, which Weiss interprets in the context of redactions motivated by sudden royal patronage. Weiss, *Die 'Chronica maiora' des Matthaeus Parisiensis*, pp. 176–77. More on this 'Schlüsselmoment' in light of Matthew's self-fashioning in Weiss, 'M[athaeus] Parisiensis, hujus scriptor libelli', p. 195.

international affairs, primarily the Mongol invasion of Europe, the opposing poles of contemporary European powers emerge, connected by the patterns of communication of both conflict and cooperation between the hundreds of individuals whose literacy and personal connections played an important part in the papal-imperial power struggle.

The recurrence of the same people connecting different networks points to a densely interrelated, populous, but essentially finite pool of people — both known and unnamed — who were providing Matthew's ego-network with materials about the cataclysm. This snapshot of literates collecting, preserving, and forwarding information about the Mongols in various parts of Europe, as well as of their aims and priorities to do so, is only one half of the equation that defined Matthew's Mongol story. The other half is Matthew himself: the way he and his team selected and configured the available material producing a text with a perceptible narrative structure and reasonable authenticity — producing, against the odds, a rather reliable *historia* of the Mongol invasion within the greater frames of the conflict between the papacy and the emperor. This is the subject the next four chapters, focusing on the components, structure, and plot(s) of the Mongol story in the *Chronica majora*.

CHAPTER 3

Fright

Mongols in the North and East (1237–1240)

> As when a Vultur on Imaus bred,
> Whose snowie ridge the roving Tartar bounds,
> Dislodging from a Region scarce of prey
> To gorge the flesh of Lambs or yeanling Kids
> On Hills where Flocks are fed, flies toward the
> Springs.[1]

Franciscan traveller John of Plano Carpini's 1245 *Ystoria Mongalorum*, an eyewitness account circulated in Western Europe after 1247, suggests that the memory of the devastation lingered, not only on the page, but very palpably in real life too.[2]

[Ch. 5.27] Quam devincentes, iverunt contra Rusciam, et fecerunt magnam stragem in terra Ruscie, civitates et castra destruxerunt et homines occiderunt, et Kioviam, que est metropolis Ruscie, obsederunt; et cum diu obsedissent illam ceperunt et occiderunt homines civitatis. Unde quando per terram illam ibamus, inveniebamus innumerabilia capita et ossa hominum mortuorum super campum iacere. Fuerat enim civitas valde magna et nimium populosa, et nunc quasi in nichilum redacta est. Vix enim ducente domus sunt ibi modo, et illi homines tenentur in maxima servitute. Inde procedentes pugnando, destruxerunt totam Rusciam. [Ch. 5.28] De Ruscia autem et de Comania processerunt duces predicti, et pugnaverunt contra Hungaros et Polonos, ex quibus Tartari in Polonia et in Hungaria plures interfecti fuerunt; et si non fugissent, et viriliter restitissent Hungari, exivissent Tartari de finibus suis, quia Tartari habuerunt talem timorem, quod omnes fugere attentabant.

([Ch. 5.27] Which [the destruction of the city of Orna] once complete, they set forth against Russia and wreaked havoc there, destroying cities and castles, and murdering people. They laid siege

---

1 Milton, *Paradise Lost*, Bk III, ll. 431–35.

2 Also known as John of Pian del Carpine but will be referred to by his more widely used name, Plano Carpini, in this book.

unto Kiev, the capital of Rus', and at length they took it and killed the townspeople. Whereupon, travelling through that country, we found innumerable skulls and bones lying on the ground. Once a very large and populous city, it is now reduced to nothing: for there are scarcely two hundred houses there, whose inhabitants are kept in the harshest servitude. The Tartars then continued their campaign and destroyed all of Russia. [Ch. 5.28] Moreover, the aforementioned leaders marched out of Russia and Comania, and fought against the Hungarians and the Polish, many of whom were slain in Poland and Hungary, and had the Hungarians not fled but withstood them manfully, the Tartars would have been driven from their territory, because the Tartars were so frightened that they were all about to flee.)[3]

Plano Carpini's report demonstrates the living memory of the Mongol destruction ten years after, and the perspective afforded by the knowledge of the whole story, which contextualized the ravages in Kiev in relation to the Mongols' subsequent progress into and retreat from Poland and Hungary.[4] Similar to John's physical encounter with the traces of the Mongol attacks, Matthew Paris's earliest chronicle entries regarding the Mongols were recorded several years after their dust settled in the Christian kingdoms of Central and Eastern Europe. Matthew recorded sporadic reports about their progress back in the late 1230s when the conquest of Hungary was just a glimmer in the great khan's eye. As will be discussed in this chapter, internal evidence indicates that the Mongol material was inserted into the chronicle in hindsight, especially the early reports between 1237 and 1240.

Anton Chekhov allegedly said that 'if in Act I you have a pistol hanging on the wall, then it must fire in the last act'.[5] Retracing the narrative thrust of the series of events in the *Chronica majora* reveals that the onset of the Mongol invasion was inserted primarily because the outcome was known by the time of writing. In the same vein, the chronicle had to include the outcome of the Eastern European leg of the Mongol military campaign because of the uncertainty surrounding their whereabouts and prospects of future encounters which were an urgent matter in and after the mid-1240s. The rulers and military leaders of the West shifted their tentative gaze to the Holy Land, exploring the events of the recent past for

---

3 Gießauf, *Die Mongolengeschichte des Johannes von Piano Carpine*, p. 100 (my translation).

4 The wording and the interpretation found in John's report, often at variance with Matthew Paris's Mongol-related passages, suggest that there are no intertextual connections between them.

5 The dramatic principle Chekhov's gun is known from various sources. Besides various published texts, his biographer Donald Rayfield suggests that Chekhov formulated the principle in a conversation in 1889, recorded in the notes of a certain Ilia Gurliand. Rayfield, *Anton Chekhov*, p. 203.

knowledge either to overcome or to build alliance with the erstwhile foe in another theatre of war.

The Mongols, appearing from behind forbidding northern mountains in the 1230s, are like Chekhov's gun in the story, a gun that is finally fired in 1241 when they 'struck no little fear and terror into all Christendom' and elicited both fear and valiant opposition on behalf of the chronicle's recurring protagonists.[6] The complexity of the physical and conceptual process of writing history was a more intricate task than simply obtaining and copying pertinent texts. The process of making sense of the past by selection and organization, then channelling the events into the narrative framework of the chronicle, was a multifarious undertaking. The Mongol story in the *Chronica majora* was majorly impacted by extratextual factors such as the sources and the time of receipt of incoming news. But this was closely intertwined with Matthew Paris's own process of 'configuring' the story and the narrative techniques that he used to embed it in the greater historical narrative of his chronicle.

Under the year 1238, the same as Matthew's start of the Mongol story, the chronicler of the Cistercian monastery of Melrose, Scotland, writes 'Hic primo auditur in terra nostra, quod nefandus exercitus Tartareorum multas terras vastavit, quod utrum verum fit, in subsequentibus apparebit' (At this time, it is first heard in our country that the infamous army of the Tartars laid waste many lands; whether this is true will turn out in what follows).[7] It may have been the time when the English public 'first heard of' the Mongol mobilization, but it certainly was not the time when the chroniclers recorded it.[8] It is obvious that the lag between the events recorded and the time of writing was significant. Small clues have been found to prove this; for example, although Hans-Eberhard Hilpert suggests that these early Mongol entries were indeed written early, that is, before 1241, elsewhere he brings an example for a 1239 entry that had to come from the Council of Lyon.[9] Vaughan (citing Plehn's observation) also draws attention to the fact that one of the 1239 entries alludes to the death

---

6 'toti Christianitati non mediocrem timorem et horrorem incusserunt'. *CM*, IV, p. 109; *EH*, I, p. 339.

7 *Chronica de Mailros*, p. 149.

8 Similar to my argument here, this sentence was used to unpack the stratification of the material in the Melrose chronicle based on a small textual clue: 'More precision is possible for item (iii), which ends with a comment that the veracity of reports of Tartar devastation will become apparent below: this is likely to have been written after Stratum 23, which includes a copy of Innocent IV's letter containing a reference to a Tartar invasion of the Holy Land'. Broun and Harrison, *The Chronicle of Melrose Abbey*, p. 155.

9 He argues that the perfect infinitive in the phrase 'et a culmini imperiali abjudicasse Fredericum dictum imperatorem' in this particular papal letter fragment suggests that it can not have been written in this form before the Council of Lyon in 1245. Hilpert, *Kaiser- und Papstbriefe*, p. 32.

126   CHAPTER 3

of Gilbert and Walter Marshall, which happened in November 1245, thus making that year the terminus post quem for the time of writing.[10]

The year 1245 seems to be an important milestone indeed, but there are other reasons why there must be a great deal said about the texts' possible connections with the Council of Lyon that took place in that year. Besides the fascinating details of the synod that Matthew himself chronicled using original documents, the following overview of the communications exchanged and disseminated at Lyon also serves as a prelude to Chapter 5 below, since Matthew's post-invasion reporting about the end of the Mongol military operations in Eastern Europe are also associated with the pope's court and council.[11] Upon closer examination, they have a lot in common with later entries: not only the names that crop up in the vicinity (for example, Legate Otto and his circles) but also the themes that they are associated with in the chronicle, such as heterodoxy and conversion. The Mongol references entered under these early years make sense in the context of the political and ecclesiastic concerns prevailing in the mid-1240s. Understanding that both the beginning and the end of the Mongol story may have mostly come from Lyon puts the clusters inserted under 1241 (Chapter 4) in a new light too, and the differences between the phases emerge sharper than before.

Nuancing the overview of the dissemination of information in the extratextual world surrounding St Albans in the previous chapter, here the impact of Matthew's ultimate continental sources on his text will also be explored. Instead of questioning Matthew's credibility as a historian or tracing his immediate informants who themselves often had little to do with the documents they relayed, the probable origin of the texts is in the limelight: the continental flow of information about the Mongol attacks that Matthew was able to tap into through a diversity of access points.

1237: Chaldeans, Medes, Persians, and Armenians

To revisit Chekhov's gun once more, perhaps the most important point in any discussion of Matthew Paris's sources for the pre-1240 entries concerning the Mongol advance is the time lag between receiving the information and inserting the texts in the narrative of the chronicle. While this seems straightforward enough, it is not without contention.

---

10 'Nec postea ipse vel frater ejus Walterus sincero corde regem, ut prius; dilexit; nec fortunato casu prosperabantur'. *CM*, III, p. 524; *EH*, I, p. 160. Vaughan cites Plehn's argument: Vaughan, *Matthew Paris*, pp. 59–60; Plehn, *Der politische Charakter von Matheus Parisiensis*, p. 135.

11 A bundle of Mongol-related letters in the *Additamenta*, to be discussed in Chapter 6 below, will also be shown to have some ties with the council.

For example, despite earlier scholarly suggestions of a significant time lag, Hans-Eberhard Hilpert considers the 1239 mention of Christian victories as evidence that these entries cannot have come from after 1241, the year when the Christian forces were outnumbered and crushed at Liegnitz (Legnica).[12] However, this statement must be nuanced in view of Matthew's constantly evolving process, his penchant for merging information from different sources, and the likely origin of these particular entries, and of those inserted later.

The events described take place in faraway lands, but the menace is palpable despite the lack of references to subsequent stages of the invasion. Both the wording and the ominous phrasing indicate that Matthew inserted them once he was aware of the enormity of the Mongol impact in Christian Europe and the invasion of Hungary: this is a mere introduction of the 'genus hominum monstruosum'; the mother lode is to be discovered a few years on. Though the lack of prolepsis — references to future events, implying an omniscient narrator — is certainly odd, it is not sufficient grounds to reject the probability of constructing the Mongol story in retrospective.[13] The probable reason for avoiding prolepsis is literary: like similar chronicle narratives (and unlike the *Chronicle of Melrose* mentioned above), by doing so Matthew avoided the 'tension between the knowledge on the part of the reader that has accumulated as the narrative progresses and the lack of knowledge on the part of some characters', and allowed his readers to make their own conclusions as they progress in the text.[14]

So, the Mongol story had to begin somehow, and Matthew Paris made sure to prepare the ground with a few preliminary mentions where appropriate. The first time the avid chronicle reader hears about the Mongols

---

12 Although he does accept that Matthew projected the 1241 Mongol threat onto 1238 ('Hier interpretiert Matthaeus Paris eindeutig eine 1241 für Europa bestehende Gefahr in das Jahr 1238 hinein'), Hilpert partially dismisses Vaughan's and Hans Plehn's earlier suggestions that Matthew wrote his earliest Mongol news only after the Mongol invasion: 'Doch ist letzteres [the 1239 entry] gerade der Nachweis dafür, daß die Nachricht aus der Zeit vor 1241 stammt, später wären solche Übertreibungen unmöglich gewesen'. Hilpert, *Kaiser- und Papstbriefe*, p. 158.

13 As Carpenter notes (citing a number of examples), Matthew 'was perfectly aware that he was telling stories in stages and frequently informed readers that there would be further installment in due course'. Carpenter, 'Chronology and Truth'. There are references to later portions in the chronicle, for example, in Merlin's prophecies (AD 465), 'Hoc reperies in ultimo folio hujus voluminis ad mortem Henrici II. in hoc libro', or in the entry on the death of Muhammad under the year 622, 'Haec autem in anno gratiae MCCXXXVI. quae de Machometo vera sunt plenius dicuntur'. *CM*, I, pp. 206, 271. It is important, though, that the latter is a marginal comment, not part of the narrative per se. None of the Mongol-related entries have explicit evidence for prolepsis in this form, but the content and voice of entries can sometimes provide circumstantial evidence for Matthew's knowledge of later stages of the same theme or story.

14 Matthews describes this style in his study of the narrative of the German *Kaiserchronik*: Matthews, *The Kaiserchronik*, p. 92.

128   CHAPTER 3

is the 1237 letter to Pope Gregory IX, sent by Philip, prior of the Dominican province of Terra Sancta, mainly concerning the conversion of the patriarchs of Jerusalem.[15] As Amanda Power sums up, 'Between 1239 and 1245 the existing papal mandate to the friars for preaching in the lands of Muslims and pagans was extended to include Greeks, Bulgarians, Cumans, Georgians, Jacobites, Nestorians, Armenians, Maronites, Ethiopians, Syrians, Russians, Iberians, Alans, Ziqui, Khazars, Indians, and Nubians. This enterprise was cast in apocalyptic terms by Honorius III and Gregory IX, who both declared that "since the eleventh hour has come in the day given to humanity [...] it is necessary that spiritual men [possessing] purity of life and the gift of intelligence should go forth with John [the Baptist] again to all men".[16] At this point, the Mongols are associated with the story of the 'Saracens' and appear in the context of conversion and heterodoxy, connecting a number of themes that received increasingly intensive attention in the 1240s.

> Ipse praeest Caldaeis, Medis, et Persis, et Armeniis, quas terras Tartari pro magna parte jam vastaverunt; et in aliis regnis in tantum dilatatur ejus praelatio, quod septuaginta provinciae ei obediunt, in quibus habitant innumerabiles Christiani, servi tamen et tributarii Sarracenis, exceptis monachis, quos liberos dimittunt a tributo.

> (This man [probably Ignatius III David, patriarch of Antioch, and head of the Syriac Orthodox Church 1222–1252][17] is chief over the Chaldeans, Medes, Persians, and Armenians, whose territories the Tartars have now ravaged to a great extent; and his prelateship extends so far in other kingdoms, that seventy provinces are under his subjection, in which numberless Christians dwell as slaves, and tributary to the Saracens, with the exception of the monks whom they exempt from tribute.)[18]

---

15 The Dominicans appear to have been established in Jerusalem by the late 1220s, but this ended when the Khwarezmians sacked the city in August 1244. *Letters from the East*, p. 133.

16 Power, *Roger Bacon and the Defence of Christendom*, p. 234. Citing the bull *Cum una hora undecima*, first issued by Gregory IX in 1235, and reissued by Innocent IV ten years later, listing eighteen peoples in addition to 'Saracens and Pagans'.

17 For Ignatius III's relationship with Rome, see Weltecke, 'Contacts between Syriac Orthodox and Latin Military Orders', p. 69, esp. n. 84. The pope congratulates the patriarch on his decision in a letter issued on 28 July 1237. Potthast, *Regesta Pontificum Romanorum*, p. 884. 'The rejoicing, however, was premature, as the reconciliations had been prompted by fear of a Tartar invasion, and they later returned to heresy. About the year 1247, the patriarch Ignatius III admitted the supremacy of the Apostolic See, and the mafrian bar Ma'dan spoke of Rome as "the mother and the head of all churches". King, *The Rites of Eastern Christendom*, p. 70. More on this episode in Allen, ed., *Eastward Bound*, p. 98.

18 MS B, fol. 106ᵛ; *CM*, III, p. 397; *EH*, I, pp. 56–57. The folio after fol. 106 is missing in MS B; Luard printed the text from fols 264ᵛ–265ʳ in MS C.

As is the case in other (more directly) Mongol-related letters, Matthew's version is the only known copy of this letter. In a brief preface, Matthew explains that Brother Godfrey, the papal penitentiary, had distributed copies to the Dominicans in France and England, having himself received the letter from Brother Philip.[19] The presentation of the letter is an apt example of Matthew Paris's way of wrapping original letters in his own narrative and other received texts in order to create a complex narrative item. Matthew frequently uses alternation as a method of weaving a narrative out of more than one strand of history taking place in different geographical locations. Nuancing Suzanne Lewis's and Michael Gaudio's previously cited thoughts about Matthew's 'paratactic' narrative technique — operating with 'essential components juxtaposed as equal, without causal, subordinating, or even temporal relationships', the elements of the disparate stories indeed seem to be loosely tied together by phrases expressing the contemporaneity of various events taking place in spatially compartmentalized narrative units.[20] While the alternating entries are often left without conjunction, Matthew is ready to provide phrases or sentences of cohesion when he can. 'Anno quoque eodem' (In the same year; i.e. 1237), writes Matthew right after Legate Otto's procession from the white cliffs to Westminster,[21] 'venit jocundus rumor de Terra Sancta' (pleasing news arrived from the Holy Land), which is how he prefaces the letter of Godfrey — and ultimately Friar Philip's letter to the pope.[22] After the letter, Matthew again connects the entries by explaining the rationale of their juxtaposition: he introduces his description of the heresy of the Nestorians, probably received from the same source as Philip's letter, with a backward reference: 'Quia de Nestorianis mentio superius facta est, dignum duximus huic libro eorum inserere superstitionem' (As mention has been made above of the Nestorians, we have thought proper to insert in this book an account of their superstitions).[23]

Matthew selected and ordered adjacent entries one after the other with a keen editorial eye. The alternation of the episodes that comprise parallel

---

19 *CM*, III, pp. 396–99. Translation in *EH*, I, pp. 55–58, more recently *Letters from the East*, pp. 133–35. This letter is the second entry in which Matthew mentions Prester John in relation with the region, but the famous priest-king's later amalgamation with the Mongol story was not known for Matthew. For the discussion of a later Dominican chronicle, that of Nicholas Trivet, referring to the Mongols in relation to Prester John (called *Sacerdotus Johannes, rex Indiae* in this entry), see Chapter 7 ('Chronicles and their Afterlife').

20 See Chapter 1 ('Mise-en-abime Within and Without').

21 See more about the calamities of Legate Otto in this chapter below, as well as in Chapter 4, where I point out that his person crops up in the vicinity of further Mongol-related entries: Ivo of Narbonne's letter to the archbishop of Bordeaux and the news of the Mongols' 'dispersal to the East' under the years 1243 and 1244.

22 MS *B*, fol. 106ᵛ; *CM*, III, p. 396; *EH*, I, p. 55.

23 MS *B*, fol. 106ᵛ; *CM*, III, p. 399; *EH*, I, p. 58.

strands is clearly visible in the wider context of the Dominican letter. Going back a couple of entries, following Frederick II's invitation to an assembly at Vaucouleurs — and explaining in detail why the king and the bishop of Winchester declined it — Matthew continues with local news from the English countryside and the arrival of Legate Otto to England.[24] The English nobles are grumbling:

> Omnia rex pervertit, jura, fidem, promissa, in omnibus transgreditur. Nunc enim matrimonio se sine suorum amicorum et hominum naturalium [consilio] alienigenae copulavit; nunc legatum, regni totius immutatorem, clam vocavit; nunc sua dat, nunc data cupit revocare.
>
> > (The king perverts all laws, breaks his faith and promises, and transgresses in everything he does: he a little while ago united himself in marriage to a foreigner without consulting his friends and natural subjects; and now he has secretly summoned a legate to make alterations throughout the whole kingdom at one time he gives away his own, and then endeavours to recall what he has given.)[25]

Describing the carnivalesque pomp and circumstance and Otto's surprisingly deferential reception of all the riches showered upon him by the king, obviously a pawn of foreign interests, Matthew expressly moves the narrative space from the shore to the heart of his kingdom: 'Rex autem ei usque ad confinium maris occurrit, et inclinato ad genua ejus capite, usque ad interiora regni deduxit officiose' (The king himself met him at the seaside, and bowed his head to his knees; after which he officiously conducted him to the interior of the country).[26] Then, alternating the Eastern heresies with domestic affairs, he returns to Legate Otto who, again, surprises the English with his humility and tact.[27] After this, Matthew

---

24 The rubrics marking the entries are as follows: 'Quomodo imperator vocavit omnes magnates Christianitatis'; 'Confectum est crisma in ecclesia Sancti Albani'; 'De morte J[ohannis] comitis Cestriae'; 'De quodam mirabili grandine et pluvia diuturna'; 'De adventu O[ttonis] legati in Anglia' (how the emperor summoned all the princes of Christendom; the holy unction is consecrated in the church of St Albans (not a separate rubric in *EH*); about the death of J, earl of Chester (not a separate rubric in *EH*); about the remarkable rain and hail continued (not a separate rubric in *EH*); about the arrival of Legate O. in England). MS *B*, fol. 106^{r-v}; *CM*, III, pp. 393–95; *EH*, I, pp. 53–54.

25 MS *B*, fol. 106^v, col. a; *CM*, III, p. 395; *EH*, I, pp. 54–55. In 1236, Henry III married Eleanor of Savoy and promoted his new wife's uncle, William of Savoy, bishop-elect of Valence, which was met with hostility on the part of the majority of the English baronage, especially Henry's brother, Richard of Cornwall.

26 MS *B*, fol. 106^v, cols a–b; *CM*, III, p. 396; *EH*, I, p. 55.

27 'Dominus autem Otho legatus, de quo superius mentio facta est, prudenter ac modeste se gerens, munera pretiosissima sibi oblata in magna parte respuens, contra consuetudinem Romanorum, indignationem in toto regno conceptam tam clero quam militia, citra opinionem multorum, per gestum suum ordinatum temperavit' (The legate Otto, of whom

turns to the slaughter of the Templars near Damietta, introducing the new topic with a phrase to indicate the parallel nature of the events described: 'Circa idem tempus, increbuerunt rumores lamentabiles, totam Terram Sanctam confusione perfundentes' (About this time, lamentable rumours prevailed, spreading confusion [Giles has 'dismay'] throughout the Holy Land).[28] At the end of the entry he also adds that 'Facta est autem ista congressio detestanda mense Junio' (This hateful conflict occurred in the month of June), and continues with the Hospitallers' arrival to assist their brethren in the Holy Land.[29] The episodes concerning the legate and the foreigner-friendly English king alternate neatly with news from the Holy Land, in which the Mongol reference is but a passing detail.[30]

When Matthew inserts original documents in the narrative flow, the entries (sometimes two consecutive entries about the same event or topic) wrought out of texts from different sources are often bracketed by the chronicler's own text. For example, here instead of a straightforward descriptive or narrative entry, the conversion issue is explained in a rather long original letter inserted between brackets of interpretation and explanation in Matthew's own voice. The Mongol story, composed out of received material by default, is replete with such complex entries. Philip's letter to the pope embedded in Godfrey's letter is a case in point: the greetings and the explanation of the sources function as preface; the long interpolation of the Nestorian faith is a quasi-footnote to provide background to the letter about the conversion. And the whole unit is wedged between two entries about Legate Otto — the one about his arrival accompanied by the sound of bells and whistles, and the one about his quiet moderation and tact. It is also remarkable that the whole letter is visibly placed in brackets by a frequently used peritextual tool placed in the margin: a key symbol marking the beginning and the end of a passage deemed 'impertinens', that is, irrelevant.[31]

---

mention has been before made, by conducting himself prudently and with moderation, and refusing, in a great measure, the valuable presents offered to him, contrary to the usual custom of the Romans, calmed by his well-ordered conduct the angry feelings which had been conceived against him, as well by the clergy as the nobles, falling short of the opinion of many). MS C, fol. 265^v; *CM*, III, p. 403; *EH*, I, pp. 61–62.

28 *CM*, III, p. 404; *EH*, I, p. 62.

29 *CM*, III, p. 406; *EH*, I, p. 63.

30 The rest, although it takes us far from our subject, remains interesting as Matthew continues to construct a masterful narrative by bringing in Frederick II's campaign in Italy and revisiting the growing hostility surrounding the increasingly difficult English king 'cum haec ita in transalpinis partibus agerentur' (whilst these events were passing in the transalpine provinces). *CM*, III, p. 410; *EH*, I, p. 66. Finally, the Eastern digression is over: Matthew returns to Legate Otto's sojourn in England, where he enjoys hospitality and riches offered to him, despite his humble protest, and carries on with English domestic matters. *CM*, III, p. 412; *EH*, I, pp. 68–69.

31 See more in Chapters 5 and 6, esp. pp. 259–62 and 310, Fig. 10.

132   CHAPTER 3

While the two strands of the story, swinging the focus from the Holy Land to England and back, seem to be entirely unrelated, Otto's person is the link that connects them. Besides the fact that Prior Philip's letter was inserted into the narrative by alternating matters of the Holy Land with Legate Otto's travels in England (see Appendix 1), Otto's connections can be detected in the letter itself, too: it is highly probable that the Willelmo de Monte Ferrato cited in Philip's letter was related to the large and powerful Montferrat family, and a kin of Legate Otto.[32]

As the instalments of the goings-on in the Holy Land alternate with accounts of domestic affairs, this narrative context of these early Mongol entries is similar to those towards end of the chronicle: the 1237 letter is not part of the Mongol story but of a different, equally complex, equally 'foreign' story in the *Chronica majora* — that of the Holy Land.[33] It is unclear whether the peoples afflicted by the Mongol attacks are only the Armenians or all the patriarch's subjects including the Chaldeans, Medes, and Persians (*praeest Caldaeis, Medis, et Persis, et Armeniis,* **quas terras Tartari pro magna parte jam vastaverunt**), but it is clear that the Mongol reference is just a brief note in a longer account that is essentially about conversion, going hand in hand with the succeeding entry about the Nestorians' error. Whether intentionally or not, the very beginning of the Mongol story is characterized by its distance from Latin Christianity, taking place in a region known to the chronicler primarily through descriptions of heathens and heresies.

1238: Northbound to *Hungaria major*

Subsequent Mongol entries slowly approach the main setting of the plot. After the fleeting mention of the Mongols in the Holy Land in 1237, their first substantial appearance in the story is situated in the heathen North, more precisely, in *Hungaria major*, Greater Hungary. The entry consists of three different stories. First, faithful to the title, a description of the northern ravages of the Mongols, then a brief excursion to Gothland and Frisia, ending in a curious anecdote about the bishop of Winchester's

---

32 'jam plures recepimus literas; quod fratri Willelmo de Monte Ferrato, qui cum aliis duobus fratribus linguam illam scientibus apud eum aliquandiu commemoratus est, promisit quod velit obedire et redire ad gremium ecclesiasticae unitatis' (we have already received several letters, informing us that he [Prester John] promised brother William de Montferrat, who with two other brothers learning that language stayed some time with him, that he would be obedient and return to the bosom of the united Church). MS *B*, fol. 106ᵛ, col. b; *CM*, III, p. 398; *EH*, I, p. 57. William is known mainly because he is mentioned more than once in the lives of St Dominic; see his testimony, for example, in the 'Appendix' of Mamachi and Ferretti, *Annales ordinis Praedicatorum*, I, cols 107–10.

33 See text at note 18 in this chapter.

interjection at the meeting between the Saracen legates and Henry III of England. This is the first description of the Mongols as a people in the *Chronica majora*, and it is not without extra- and intratextual echoes. At this point it is worth reading the whole entry in one piece:[34]

De Tartaris prorumpentibus de locis suis terras septentrionales devastantibus. In diebus illis missi sunt Sarracenorum legati solennes ad regem Francorum, nuntiantes et veraciter explicantes, principaliter ex parte Veteris de Monte, quoddam genus hominum monstruosum et inhumanum ex montibus borealibus prorupisse, et spatiosas terras et opulentas Orientis occupasse, Hungariam Majorem depopulasse, literasque comminatorias cum legationibus terribilibus destinasse. Quorum dux se nuntium Dei excelsi affirmat, ad e[do]mandas gentes sibi rebelles.

Hi quoque capita habentes, magna nimis et nequaquam corporibus proportionata, carnibus crudis et etiam humanis vescuntur; sagittarii incomparabiles, flumina quaevis cimbis de corio factis et portatilibus transeuntes, robusti viribus, corporibus propagati, impii, inexorabiles, quorum lingua incognita omnibus quos nostra attingit notitia; gregibus, armentis, et equitiis abundantes, equos vero habentes velocissimos, potentes iter trium dierum uno conficere; ante, non retro, bene armati, ne fugam ineant; ducem habentes ferocissimum, nomine Caan. Hi borealem plagam inhabitantes, vel ex Caspiis montibus vel ex vicinis, dicti Tartari, a Tar flumine, numerosi nimis, in pestem hominum creduntur ebullire, et hoc anno, licet aliis vicibus exierint, solito immanius debacchari.

Unde Gothiam et Frisiam inhabitantes, impetus eorum pertimentes, in Angliam, ut moris est eorum, apud Gernemue, tempore allecis capiendi, quo suas naves solebant onerare, non venerunt. Hinc erat quod allec eo anno in Anglia quasi pro nihilo prae abundantia habitum, sub quadragenario vel quinquagenario numero, licet optimum esset, pro uno argento in partibus a mari etiam longinquis, vendebantur.

Ille igitur nuntius Sarracenus potens et genere praeclarius, qui ad regem Galliae venerat, ex parte universitatis Orientalium destinatus nuntiare talia, et petens auxilium ab Occidentalibus, ut possint melius furorem Tartarorum reprimere, unum a latere suo nuntium ad regem Angliae direxit Sarracenum, qui haec omnia venerat regi nuntiare, et qui diceret, quod si ipsi talium impetus non possent sustinere, quid restat, nisi ut et partes devastent Occidentalium, juxta illud poeticum, 'Nam tua res agitur, paries cum proximus ardet'. Postulavit igitur ille

---

34 I inserted line breaks to show the caesurae between component parts. The text is contiguous in the manuscript and all printed versions.

nuntius auxilium in tam generali et urgenti articulo, ut ipsi Sarraceni, freti auxilio Christianorum, injurias talium propulsarent. Cui, cum tum praesens forte fuerat, jocose verbum suscipiens, respondit episcopus Wintoniensis, qui cruce quidem signatus erat; 'Sinamus canes hos illos devorare ad invicem, ut consumpti pereant. Nos cum ad Christi inimicos, qui residui remanebunt, venerimus, trucidabimus, et mundabimus terrae superficiem; ut universus mundus uni catholicae ecclesiae subdatur, et fiat unus pastor et unum ovile'.

(The Tartars ravage the northern countries. About this time, special ambassadors were sent by the Saracens, chiefly on behalf of the old man of the mountain, to the French king, telling him that a monstrous and inhuman race of men had burst forth from the northern mountains, and had taken possession of the extensive, rich lands of the East; that they had depopulated Hungary Major, and had sent threatening letters, with dreadful embassies; the chief of whom declared, that he was the messenger of God on high, sent to subdue the nations who rebelled against him.

These people have very large heads, by no means proportionate to their bodies, and feed on raw flesh, and even on human beings; they are incomparable archers, and cross over any rivers in portable boats, made of hides; of robust strength, and large in their bodies, impious and inexorable men; and their language is unknown to all within reach, of our knowledge. They abound in flocks, herds, and breeds of horses; the horses are very swift, and able to perform a journey of three days in one; the men are well armed in front, but not behind, that they may not take to flight; and their chief is a most ferocious man, named Khan. These people inhabit the northern region, either the Caspian mountains, or the adjacent places, and are called 'Tartari', from the river Tar; they are very numerous, and are believed to have been sent as a plague on mankind, and although they had sallied forth on other occasions, they seemed this year to rage more fiercely than usual.

The inhabitants of Gothland and Friesland, dreading their attacks, did not, as was their custom, come to Yarmouth, in England, at the time of the herring-fisheries at which place their ships usually loaded; and, owing to this, herrings in that year were considered of no value, on account of their abundance, and about forty or fifty, although very good, were sold for one piece of silver, even in places at a great distance from the sea.

This powerful and noble Saracen messenger, who had come to the French king, was sent on behalf of the whole of the people of the East to tell these things; and he had assistance from the western nations, the better to be able to repress the fury of the Tartars; he also sent a Saracen messenger from his own company to the king of England, who had arrived in England, to tell these events, and to say, that if they themselves could not withstand the attacks of such people, nothing remained to prevent their devastating the countries of the West: according to the saying of the poet, 'For when your neighbour's house doth burn, The fire will seize on yours in turn'. He therefore asked assistance in this urgent and general emergency, that the Saracens, with the assistance of the Christians, might resist the attacks of these people. The bishop of Winchester, who happened to be then present, and wearing the sign of the cross, interrupted his speech, and replied jocosely, 'Let us leave these dogs to devour one another, that they may all be consumed, and perish; and we, when we proceed against the enemies of Christ who remain, will slay them, and cleanse the face of the earth, so that all the world will be subject to the one Catholic church, and there will be one shepherd and one fold'.)[35]

The appearance of the Mongols in the chronicle and the way in which they are shown to progress towards Europe show an acute literary sense of building suspense. It is here that Matthew Paris sows the seeds of the Mongol story emerging through increasingly frequent entries in the year 1241 and thereafter. While it is unknown whether medieval readers, including Matthew Paris himself, were aware of the immense distance between Armenia (in the previous entry) and the northern mountains (whatever they may be), or between the Old Man of the Mountain and *Hungaria major*, the Mongol threat is described as covering vast areas, rapidly moving towards one goal: Christian Europe. That the Mongols materialize in Greater Hungary and cause concern in the North suggests that they were at this time still depicted as a faraway menace, and the situation was rendered increasingly uneasy by association: If they take Greater Hungary, what is next? Hungary?

Besides the maps discussed in Chapter 1, it is clear that Matthew Paris was aware of the existence of *Hungaria major* and the prevailing ideas about its whereabouts, which is also attested by these entries.[36] The idea

---

35 MS *B*, fols 116ᵛ, col. b–117ʳ, col. a; *CM*, III, pp. 488–89; *EH*, I, p. 131. As will be shown, the Mongols appear in the same geographical space in the next Mongol-related entry from 1239; see the discussion in the next section ('1239: Dacia, Gothia, Frisia'): MS *B*, fol. 132ʳ, col. b; *CM*, III, p. 639; *EH*, I, p. 253.

36 As was discussed Chapter 1, in Matthew Paris's *mappa mundi Hungaria maior* is marked on the northern edge of the map, separate from *Hungaria minor*. See Figs 3 and 4. Notably, there is also a fleeting reference to 'et utramque Hungariam' (both Hungaries) in Matthew's preface to a letter by the duke of Brabant dated to 1241. MS *B*, fol. 145ʳ, col. a; *CM*, IV, p. 109; *EH*, I, p. 339.

136   CHAPTER 3

of an 'older' Hungary was not unknown in the Middle Ages. Eleventh- and twelfth-century Hungarians, safely tucked away from the prying eyes of Latin literacy,[37] may have known about Eurasian Hungarians, and surviving references are said to suggest that they had maintained some contact with them.[38] The first paragraph of the so-called Riccardus report, for example, continues to puzzle scholars looking for the lost sources which he refers to, but these suggestions remain highly speculative:

> Inventum fuit in gestis Ungarorum christianorum, quod esset alia Ungaria Maior, de qua septem duces cum populis suis egressi fuerant, ut habitandi quererent sibi locum; eo quod terra ipsorum multitudinem inhabitantium sustinere non posset, qui cum multa regna pertransissent, et destruxissent, tandem venerunt in terram que nunc Ungaria dicitur.

> (It was found in a Christian *Gesta Ungarorum* that there is another, Greater Hungary which the seven chiefs and their peoples had left in order to find a place to settle in because their lands were no longer able to sustain the multitudes of their people, who crossed and devastated many countries until they reached the land which is now called Hungary.)[39]

As opposed to the purported centuries-long living contact, Latin chronicles did not begin noting the original homeland of the Hungarians until the late twelfth century.[40] But Matthew Paris's information certainly came from more recent Western sources.

Both the story of the Saracen mission to the French king and that of the depopulation of the north-east contain tantalizing clues that may cast more light on the network that brought the information to St Albans. As for the time of receiving the *Hungaria major* information, Matthew's word use indeed indicates that he had access to a description earlier than

---

37 Of course, medieval Hungarian literacy, especially the first chronicles, have a vast literature of their own; for a very brief overview of Hungarian national historiography in the context of twelfth- and thirteenth-century European developments, see Kersken, 'High and Late Medieval National Historiography', pp. 195, 200.

38 György Györffy suggests that Muslim writers as late as the twelfth century reported how the Hungarian court kept in touch with the other branches of the Hungarian people; unfortunately he does not support this statement with citations. Györffy, *Julianus barát és a napkelet fölfedezése*, p. 16.

39 Bendefy, *Magna Hungaria és a Liber Censuum*, p. 209. Gyula Kristó posits that it is now lost and should not be identified with the extant *Gesta Ungarorum* by Béla III's anonymous notary. Kristó, 'Egy 1235 körüli Gesta Ungarorum körvonalairól'.

40 For example, Godfrey of Viterbo at the end of the twelfth century wrote 'Ungarorum regna duo esse legimus, unum antiquum aput Meotidas paludes in finibus Asie et Europe, et alterum quasi novum a primo regno in Pannonia derivatur, quam Pannoniam nonnulli novam Ungariam vocant'. Godfrey of Viterbo, 'Memoria saeculorum', p. 102.

Plano Carpini's account and later reports, which unfailingly refer to the region using various Latin forms of 'Bashkiria'. William of Rubruck's later information, for example, calls the homeland of the Eastern Hungarians *Paskatir* (cf. Baschart in Plano Carpini),[41] and Roger Bacon also refers to the ancient homeland of the Hungarians as Pascatyr.[42]

Scholars are understandably cautious about Matthew's sources of the information about *Hungaria major*.[43] The journey of this unique piece of information to St Albans is indeed a complex issue, and albeit not scarce, the surviving evidence is disjointed. To date, I have not been able to find direct intertextual connections between the passages in the *Chronica majora* and other contemporaneous continental historiographies written about the early advance of the Mongols. Rather than contemporary chronicles and books, the movement of shorter, less fixed texts is more likely to have disseminated the Mongol information, in this case either some version of the Riccardus report or the Julian report, or any similar document now lost, not excluding oral communications.[44]

---

41 Rockhill, *The Journey of William of Rubruck*, pp. 130–31. Dienes suggests that Rubruck knew about Julian's travels, and does not exclude the possibility that the two travellers met during Julian's sojourn in Rome. Dienes, 'Eastern Missions of the Hungarian Dominicans'.

42 'Post eam ad orientem est terra Pascatyr quae est magna Hungaria, a qua exiverunt Huni, qui postea Hungri, modo dicuntur Hungari; qui colligentes secum Bulgaros et alias nationes aquilonares ruperunt, sicut dicit Isidorus, claustra Alexandri. Et solvebatur eis tributum usque in Aegyptum, et destruxerunt terras omnes usque in Franciam; unde majoris potentiae fuerunt quam adhuc sunt Tartari; et magna pars eorum resedit in terra quae nunc vocatur Hungaria, ultra Bohemiam et Austriam, quae est modo apud Latinos regnum Hungariae'. (To the east from here [i.e. Ethylia] is Pascatyr, which is Greater Hungary. Huns came from here, who later became Hungri, later called Hungari, who, uniting with the Bulgars and other northern peoples, broke down the walls of Alexander, so says Isidore. And tribes as far as Egypt were scattered by them, and they destroyed every land up to France, and from there till now they were greater powers than the Tartars; and a large part of them settled in the land that is now called Hungary, beyond Bohemia and Austria, which is called the Kingdom of Hungary in Latin authorities.) Bacon, *Opus majus*, I, p. 367. Jackson suggests that Roger Bacon read Rubruck's report since he met him probably during a visit to Paris in 1256–1257 and had the opportunity to collate his own text of the *Itinerarium* with the friar's oral statements. Jackson, *The Mongols and the West*, p. 138.

43 As far as I know, besides Nathan Greasley discussing the Julian intelligence in the context of the information network of the Oxford Dominicans, no research attempted to identify the chain of transmission of the report to England. Greasley, 'Matthew Paris's Networks of Information'.

44 The dissemination of these reports was probably more multifarious than the surviving manuscripts suggest. As Peter Jackson points out about John of Plano Carpini's account, his 'party halted in Cologne during their return journey in 1247, when Benedict dictated his relatively sober account to an anonymous cleric of the city. Incomplete versions of his report were circulating even before the party rejoined Pope Innocent at Lyons in October 1247. Salimbene, who subsequently met Carpini at Sens in 1248, gives the impression that he was then virtually engaged on a lecture tour. Thereafter, it is possible that his report would have slid into obscurity had not Vincent of Beauvais incorporated sizeable extracts in his *Speculum historiale* (c. 1253), one of the most popular works of the Middle Ages.

138   CHAPTER 3

Friar Julian, Hungary's celebrated Dominican traveller on a mission from Béla IV of Hungary, was the one who first brought the news of the Mongol threat to the Hungarian court. The first exploratory journey recorded in medieval Latin sources was that of four Dominican friars led by Otho, whose aim was to find 'priores Ungaris'.[45] However, Julian and his companions were the first explorers to actually reach what they described as *Hungaria major* — and lived to tell the tale.[46] Two primary sources attest directly to his travels, during which he also located the Hungarians who remained in *Hungaria major*: Friar Riccardus's report about the first journey (*De facto Ungarie Magne*) and Julian's own *Epistolae* about the second one. Regardless of their reliability, the contents of both reports were quickly becoming common knowledge across Christian Europe, their text was widely disseminated and cited, and their contents and message reverberated in the farthest corners of Latin literacy through chains of transmission that are now impossible to untangle.

Friar Riccardus's report is addressed to the Holy See.[47] It begins with the vague description of the initial journey by the aforementioned Friar Otho, who met Eastern Hungarians but did not reach their homeland. After a three-year-long expedition, Otho returned to Hungary just days

---

Vincent did the same with Simon of Saint-Quentin's *Historia* (which has not survived in its original form), thus ensuring that the material the two reports contained was transmitted over time to an extensive readership'. Jackson, *The Mongols and the West*, p. 147. In Bk IX, ch. 44 of his *History of the Mongols*, John recounts that when his servants 'in habitu tartarico' (wearing Tartar garb) went to visit the papal legate to Germany (Hugh of St Cher) 'they were almost stoned by the Germans on the way, and they were therefore forced to take off their clothes'. Gießauf notes that the *Annales Sancti Pantaleonis* records that the papal legate and the retinue of the newly elected king arrived in Cologne at the same time as John and Benedict. Gießauf, *Die Mongolengeschichte des Johannes von Piano Carpine*, pp. 121, 224, n. 653.

45 The reliability of the Riccardus report is often questioned. Denis Sinor, for example, rejects the idea that Julian actually made the journey described in Riccardus's report, and concludes that no reliable account survives of Western Hungarians ever finding such a country. Sinor, 'Le rapport du Dominicain Julien', p. 1162. For comprehensive historiographical criticism of scholarship regarding the question, primarily Sinor's arguments, see Rimányi, 'Closing the Steppe Highway'.

46 György Györffy suggests that it was the Julian report that disseminated Hungarian geographical knowledge about this Asian region in Christian Europe. Györffy, *Julianus barát és a napkelet fölfedezése*, p. 36. Balogh also argues that the reason why Latin sources refer to the people living in the region as Hungarians and not as Bulgarians is the dissemination of Julian's Hungarian-oriented viewpoint. Balogh, 'A mongol támadások a Volga-vidéki népek ellen', p. 14.

47 Manuscript descriptions can be found in the somewhat outdated but useful Bendefy, *Magna Hungaria és a Liber Censuum*. Latin text in Dörrie, 'Drei Texte zur Geschichte der Ungarn und Mongolen', pp. 151–61. English translation in Dienes, 'Eastern Missions of the Hungarian Dominicans', pp. 237–40; German translation as 'Bericht des frater Riccardus' in Göckenjan and Sweeney, eds, *Der Mongolensturm*, pp. 67–92.

before his death to inform his fellow friars of the discovery.[48] The rest of Riccardus's report outlines Julian's journey, who set out with three companions across the Balkans to Constantinople and from there across the Black Sea to Tmutarakan, where they were informed that their kinsmen live further north. Two friars turned back and one died, but Friar Julian reached *Hungaria major*, where he was celebrated by the locals and was able to communicate with them in his native Hungarian. The Hungarians warned him about the impending Mongol invasion of Europe, and Julian successfully returned home with the news.

The earliest text of the aforementioned Riccardus report about *Hungaria major* and the Mongol threat is found in an edition of the *Liber Censuum*, the indispensable list of papal tax revenues to be extracted from the ecclesiastical provinces.[49] The text of the codex — and the Riccardus report in it — was subsequently copied many times over several centuries, and copies of this report may well have travelled together with those of the frequently used *Liber Censuum*, readily accessible at the pope's court: first Gregory IX in Rome, then Innocent IV in Lyon.[50] Even though no copies of the Riccardus report are known to have existed in England, it is important to note that versions of similar papal registries survived

---

48 Dörrie dates this trip to 1234–1235: Dörrie, 'Drei Texte zur Geschichte der Ungarn und Mongolen', pp. 137–39. Bendefy gives a more detailed argument for 1235–1236: Bendefy, *Az ismeretlen Juliánusz*, pp. 65–72. Dienes agrees with a start date of 1235: Dienes, 'Eastern Missions of the Hungarian Dominicans', p. 227.

49 Riccardus's report was copied into Censius's *Liber Censuum*, the official tax list of the Curia. *Liber censualis Romanae curiae*: Florence, Biblioteca Riccardiana, Riccardiano, MS Ricc. 228, fols 17ʳ–367ᵛ, printed in Fabre and Duchesne, *Le Liber censuum de l'Église romaine*. *De facto Ungarie Magne a frater Riccardo invente* is on fols 328ʳ–329ʳ. Bendefy dates the addition of the Riccardus report to this codex (originally composed *c.* 1228) to sometime between 1254 and 1279, so it is probably a copy of earlier exemplars that are now lost. Bendefy, *Magna Hungaria és a Liber Censuum*, p. 66. Some of its later copies also contain Riccardus's report, e.g. Vatican, Archivio Apostolico Vaticano, MS Miscell. Arm. XV. T. 1; BAV, MS Vat. Lat. 6223, and Vat. Lat. 1437, fol. 191ᵛ (*c.* 1327–1368, <https://digi.vatlib.it/view/MSS_Vat.lat.1437>); Vatican, Archivio Apostolico Vaticano, MS Miscell. Arm. XV, T. 2, fol. 416ʳ; and the eighteenth-century BAV, MS Barb. Lat. 2514, fol. 389ʳ, etc. The report also survived in codices which did not contain the *Liber Censuum*, for example, the aforementioned *Diversa ad historiam pertinentia* (originally from the Kirschgarten Monastery) in BAV, MS Pal. Lat. 965, fols 201ʳ–203ᵛ (*c.* 1360, <https://digi.ub.uni-heidelberg.de/diglit/bav_pal_lat_965/0407>); Budapest, Egyetemi Könyvtár, Coll. Hevenesi Kaprinay Pray, MS 10831, <https://edit.elte.hu/xmlui/handle/10831/24454>. For the report in the *Liber Censuum*, see more in Schmieder, 'Der Einfall der Mongolen nach Polen und Schlesien', p. 85, n. 61. Battelli, 'I Transunti di Lione del 1245', pp. 351, 364.

50 Fabre and Duchesne, *Le Liber censuum de l'Église romaine*, pp. 43–56. Gregory IX died on 22 August 1241. His successor, Celestin, died on 10 November 1241. Innocent IV was only elected in 1243, and from 29 November 1244 onwards resided in Lyon.

140   CHAPTER 3

in numerous copies; even St Albans had access to a copy of the *Liber provincialis*, which was copied in the *Additamenta*.[51]

While elements of the Riccardus report may suggest that the unique information in the 1238 entry may be rooted in some version of it, the path of this information is more likely to be sought in the other document, Julian's own report, the *Epistolae*, in which he summarizes his second journey undertaken in 1237.[52] The report records that a threatening letter by the Mongol Khan was intercepted by Grand Duke Yuri Vsevolodovich of Vladimir-Suzdal, who, in turn, informed Julian about the Mongol military plans to attack Hungary. Julian copied the Latin translation of the Mongol letter in his report, the wording of which makes Matthew's words in the 1238 entry very suggestive indeed:

> literasque comminatorias cum legationibus terribilibus destinasse. Quorum dux se *nuntium Dei excelsi* affirmat, ad e[do]mandas gentes sibi rebelles.
>
> Ego, Chayn, *nuncius regis celestis*, cui dedit potentiam super terram subicientes mihi se exaltare et deprimere adversantes, miror de te, rex Ungarie, quod cum miserim ad te iam tricesima vice legatos, quare ad me nullum remittis ex eisdem; sed nec nuntios tuos vel litteras mihi remittis. [...] Intellexi insuper quod Cumanos servos meos sub tua protectione detineas. Unde mando tibi quod eos de cetero apud te non teneas, et me adversarium tibi non habeas propter ipsos! Facilius est enim eis evadere quam tibi, quia illi sine domibus cum tentoriis ambulantes possunt forsitan evadere. Tu autem in domibus habitans, habens castra et civitates, qualiter effugies manus meas?
>
> (and had sent threatening letters, with dreadful embassies; the chief of whom declared, that he was the *messenger of God on high*, sent to subdue the nations who rebelled against him.)[53]

---

51 MS *LA*, fols 163ᵛ–166ᵛ; *CM*, VI, pp. 446–53. Both the *Liber Censuum* and the *Liber provincialis* serve as a catalogue of archbishoprics and other jurisdictions of the Church and contain the *Provinciale Romanum*. In thirteenth-century England, copies similar to Matthew's are often found in historiographical miscellanies, probably based on Bologna, Colegio de España, MS 275 or its derivative. It normally has no narrative elements; it is simply a list of all papal provinces, enumerating their archbishoprics and then the archbishoprics' suffragan bishoprics using the formula 'Archiepiscopatus *xy* hos h[abe]t suffraganeos'. Tangl, *Die päpstlichen Kanzleiordnungen*.

52 Julian's reports are published in Julian of Hungary, 'Epistula de vita Tartarorum', in Dörrie, 'Drei Texte zur Geschichte der Ungarn und Mongolen', pp. 165–82; Hautala, *Ot 'Davida, carja Indij' do 'nenavistnogo plebsa satany'*, pp. 374–81. German translation in Göckenjan and Sweeney, eds, *Der Mongolensturm*, pp. 101–10. More on Hungarian Dominicans and the Mongol threat in Dienes, 'Eastern Missions of the Hungarian Dominicans'; Göckenjan, 'Das Bild der Völker Osteuropas'.

53 MS *B*, fol. 116ᵛ, col. b; *CM*, III, p. 488; *EH*, I, p. 131 (my italics).

> (I, Chaym, *messenger of the heavenly king*, to whom he has given
> on earth to exalt those who submit to him and to cast down his
> adversaries, I wonder at you, king of Hungary, that although I have
> sent you messengers thirty times, you have sent me back none of
> them, nor did you send me messengers of your own or letters. [...]
> Further, I have learned that you keep the Cumans, my slaves, under
> your protection. Whence I charge you that henceforward you do
> not keep them with you, and that you do not make me your
> enemy on their account. For it is easier for them to escape than
> for you. Since they, having no houses and continually on the move
> with their tents may possibly escape. But you, living in houses and
> possessing fortresses and cities, how can you flee from my grasp?)[54]

The European dissemination of Julian's report was fast and efficient, but
despite the probably intensive afterlife of the text, only three manuscripts
survive.[55] As soon as it was put in writing, it was handed over to Salvius de
Salvis, at the beginning of 1238 at the latest. Salvius was at the Hungarian
court at the time and forwarded a copy to Rome. Julian also sent a copy
to Berthold, patriarch of Aquileia, who forwarded it to Henry IV, bishop
of Brixen, as well as Meinhard, count of Tyrol, which is known because
in 1241 it was also copied into the Ottobeuren Collection.[56] This version
contains a paragraph about the contemporary circulation of the report.[57]

Matthew's references to *Hungaria major* in a Mongol context, also
alluding to the khan's threatening letters, naturally raise the suspicion that
one of the reports somehow reached St Albans. Documentary sources
other than the reports themselves are, of course, also potential informants,

---

54 Hautala, *Ot 'Davida, carja Indij' do 'nenavistnogo plebsa satany'*, pp. 380–81. Translation in
   Sinor, 'The Mongols in the West', p. 9. (My italics.)
55 Dörrie, 'Drei Texte zur Geschichte der Ungarn und Mongolen', pp. 163–64. The
   three manuscripts: BAV, MS Pal. Lat. 443, <https://digi.ub.uni-heidelberg.de/diglit/
   bav_pal_lat_443>, and MS Vat. Lat. 4161, <https://digi.vatlib.it/mss/detail/Vat.lat.4161>,
   as well as the Ottobeuren manuscript published in Hormayr zu Hortenburg, *Die goldene
   Chronik von Hohenschwangau*, which was thought by Dörrie to be lost but is in fact MS *OB*.
   For the latter, see Lerner, *The Powers of Prophecy*, p. 11.
56 This is the Ottobeuren Collection described in the previous chapter.
57 MS *OB*, fols 3ᵛ–4ʳ: 'Notum sit omnibus Christi fidelibus quod hoc scriptum rex Hungarie
   delegavit patriarche Aquilegensi et patriarcha transmisit episcopo Brixiensi et comiti
   Tyrolensi, ut de ipsi universis Christi fidelibus transmittant admonendo eos, ut deum
   pro ecclesia exorare studeant. Preterea scire desideramus omnes ad quos presens scriptum
   pervenerit quod lator presentium justus et verdicus sit'. Dörrie, 'Drei Texte zur Geschichte
   der Ungarn und Mongolen', p. 163. More recently Matthew Coulter examined the
   Ottobeuren manuscript and its place in the European circulation of similar letters. See the
   conference paper, Coulter, 'Patterns of Communication during the 1241 Mongol Invasion'.

142   CHAPTER 3

but the mention of the threatening letters may point to the actual reports.[58] Though without supplying hard evidence, Veszprémy and Szovák in their edition of the Julian reports suggest that they probably reached Matthew Paris, as well as Rubruck and Plano Carpini.[59] Peter Jackson, also without going into detail, writes that 'although the earliest reports outlining the Mongol threat, produced by the friars Richardus in *c.* 1235 and Julian in 1237–8, seem to have been known to Matthew Paris within a few years, it was the Franciscan and Dominican envoys of Pope Innocent IV, returning in 1247–8, who made available a significant corpus of more or less accurate information on Mongol society and its customs, in the reports of Carpini and of Simon of Saint-Quentin'.[60]

While there is no evidence for its onward journey to England, the Julian report seems to be a likely candidate for the source of the 1238 entry: addressed to the pope, expressly written with the aim of wide dissemination, and sufficiently menacing in content and tone. And there is another intriguing connection between the *Chronica majora* and the content of Julian's report: the so-called Cedar of Lebanon prophecy, a text he copied into his chronicle, is known to have been 'travelling together' with the report in other documents. There are nine known manuscripts of this prophecy, six of them, including Matthew's version in the *Chronica majora*, coming from England,[61] but it is certain that the prophecy did not originate there.[62] Besides the English copies, one copy of the prophecy was found in the aforementioned Ottobeuren manuscript, one

---

58 For example, Béla IV's letter to Conrad IV: 'velut locuste ex heremo prodeuntes maiore Ungaria, Bulgaria, Cumania, Ruscia, nec non Polonia et Moravia'. Hormayr zu Hortenburg, *Die goldene Chronik von Hohenschwangau*, p. 65.

59 Veszprémy and Szovák, 'Pótlás 1999-ben', p. 798.

60 *CM*, III, p. 488; *EH*, I, p. 131; Jackson, *The Mongols and the West*, p. 137; Dörrie, 'Drei Texte zur Geschichte der Ungarn und Mongolen', pp. 158–59, 166, 172, 179; Bezzola, *Die Mongolen in abendländischer Sicht*, pp. 37–53; Göckenjan and Sweeney, eds, *Der Mongolensturm*, pp. 71–96.

61 Versions were copied into the *Annals of Dunstable* and the *Chronica majora*. Two other copies can be found in London, BL, MS Royal 13 E IX, fol. 27ᵛ, and Cambridge, St John's College, MS 239, back flyleaf. Lerner knows of these four. In addition, Greasley notes that the *Annals of Lewes Priory* also contains the text (agreeing with the Dunstable version), and the *Lanercost Chronicle*, too, in a much-altered version under the year 1207. The former is noted in 'The Annals of Lewes Priory'. The latter is discussed in Vincent, '"Corruent Nobiles!"'. I am grateful to Nathan Greasley for bringing this detail to my attention.

62 Lerner, *The Powers of Prophecy*, p. 12. As opposed to the versions of Alberic, the Ottobeuren scribe, and another English copy, the prophecy is not dated to 1240 in the *Chronica majora*, but a year before that. Cf. Cambridge, St John's College, MS 239, back flyleaf: 'Anno Domini M⁰C⁰C quadrgesimo [*sic*] pervenit ad nos hec scriptura'. Cited in Lerner, *The Powers of Prophecy*, p. 14.

in a late thirteenth-century Italian manuscript, and one in Alberic of Trois-Fontaines's chronicle.[63]

Matthew Paris felt that it was within the remit of his history to preserve widely circulated theories about the world's end.[64] The Cedar of Lebanon vision, found under 1239 in the *Chronica*, is one of these. According to Matthew's version, the prophecy resulted from a miracle that transpired in a Cistercian cloister, emulating the biblical Belshazzar's Feast (Daniel 5. 24–28): a monk celebrating Mass saw a hand spelling out a prophetic message on the wall. The text of the prophecy is as follows:

> Eodem tempore cuidam monacho Cisterciensi apparuit manus candida scribens in corporali haec verba. Cedrus alta Libani succidetur; Mars praevalebit Saturno et Jovi. Saturnus vero in omnibus insidiabitur Jovi. Erit unus deus, id est, monarcha. Secundus deus adiit. Filii Israel liberabuntur a captivitate infra undecim annos. Gens quaedam sine capite reputata vagans veniet. Vae clero, viget ordo novus; si ceciderit. Vae, ecclesiae. Fidei, legum, et regnorum mutationes erunt, et tota terra Sarracenorum subvertetur.

> (In the same year there appeared to a certain monk of the Cistercian order, a white hand writing bodily the following words: 'The lofty cedar of Lebanon shall be cut down. Mars shall prevail over Saturn and Jupiter, and Saturn shall lay snares for Jupiter in all things. There shall be one God, that is a monarch. The second God has come. The sons of Israel shall be released from captivity within eleven years. A certain people, considered to be without a leader [lit. 'without head'], shall come in their wanderings. Alas for the clergy; if it should fall, a new order flourishes; alas for the faith of the church, of laws, and of kingdoms. Changes shall occur, and the whole Saracen nation [lit. 'land'] shall be subverted'.)[65]

---

63 McGinn located a version of the text in BAV, MS Vat. Lat. 3822, fol. 6ᵛ. McGinn, *Visions of the End*, p. 318, n. 5. This is a short addition appended at the end of a handful of folios containing the Sibylline prophecies and other texts written in different ink and hands throughout. The description of the miracle is missing; only the text of the prophecy is copied. Alberic's version of the prophecy: Alberic of Trois-Fontaines, 'Chronica', p. 949.

64 For a nuanced analysis of prognostic texts and prophecies in Matthew Paris, see Weiler, 'History, Prophecy and the Apocalypse in the Chronicles of Matthew Paris'.

65 MS B, fols 121ᵛ–122ʳ; *CM*, III, p. 538; *EH*, I, p. 171. Lerner's composite translation based on all manuscripts of the prophecy: 'The high Cedar of Lebanon will be felled. Mars will prevail over Saturn and Jupiter. Saturn will waylay Jupiter in all things. Within eleven years there will be one God and one monarchy. The second god has gone. The sons of Israel will be liberated from captivity. A certain people called "without a head" or reputed to be wanderers, will come. Woe to the clergy! A new order thrives: if it should fall, woe to the Church! There will be many battles in the world. There will be mutations of faith, of laws, and of kingdoms. The land of the Saracens will be destroyed'. Lerner, *The Powers of Prophecy*, p. 16.

144   CHAPTER 3

While Matthew records that the monk was Cistercian, the Ottobeuren manuscript locates the miracle 'apud Snusnyacum monasterium cysterciensis ordinis'.[66] The Ottobeuren version — the earliest surviving copy — does not leave it to chance that the reader realizes who the people 'without a head' may be: the brief introduction 'Anno ab incarnatione verbi M°CC°XL°I° gens Tartarorum in multitudine gravi totam Ungariam in desolationem redegit generalem, omnem intendens delere christianitatem. Qualiter autem venerint epistola docet subscripta' (In the 1241st year of the incarnation of the Word, the people of the Tartars in overwhelming numbers rendered all of Hungary into general desolation, intending to annihilate the whole of Christendom. However, the letter below explains how they arrived) is followed by Julian's *Epistola*. Another commonality is the dialogue between Aristotle and Alexander (fol. 8^{r-v}), which will be discussed in relation to later parts of the *Chronica majora* in Chapters 5 and 6 below. Judging from the textual differences and the absence of the rest of the Ottobeuren Collection in Matthew's chronicle, a direct connection between the two texts seems unlikely. But as Matthew Coulter noted in his analysis of Letter 10, 'the fact that both the Ottobeuren scribe and Matthew Paris, two monks working hundreds of kilometres apart with no knowledge of each other, both recorded information originating ultimately from the same source is indicative of the importance of forwarding letters as a means of passing on information and shows how both compilers drew their source material from wider communication networks'.[67]

Similarly inconclusive but perhaps suggesting some distant connection is the tradition of associating the Old Man of the Mountain with Hungary, *Hungaria major*, and the Mongols. The Cistercian Alberic of Trois-Fontaines (d. *c.* 1252) knew about the region and even connects the Old Man of the Mountain with Hungary in two curious early entries:

> [1231] Dux Bavarie Ludovicus a quodam sicario Assacino occiditur, a veteri de Montana transmisso. Quod audiens rex Hungrie eidem veteri

---

66 MS *OB*, fol. 2^r: 'Anno domini M°CC°XLmo apud Snusnyacum monasterium cysterciensis ordinis hec visio facta est cuidam monacho celebranti presentibus abbate et ministro. Apparuit quedam manus scribens in corporali verba hec'. Lerner suggests that *Snusnyacum monasterium* is an imaginary monastery: Lerner, *The Powers of Prophecy*, p. 42. Sylvain Piron, after Lerner, also says that 'le nom exotique de l'improbable monastère' may have played a role in the initial success of the Cedar prophecy; but when the context of the Mongol invasion was replaced by that of the fall of the Latin kingdom of the East, the same text was reworded as the vision in versions after 1300 occurred in Tripoli. Piron, 'La parole prophétique', p. 277. It is, however, possible that the name, exotic as it may sound, is a corrupted version of *Fusniacum*, that is Foigny, the third daughter house of Clairvaux, in the diocese of Laon in Picardy (founded in 1121). For evidence of literary networks between Hungarian and Transylvanian Cistercian houses, some destroyed in the Mongol invasion, see Papahagi, 'Lost Libraries and Surviving Manuscripts'.

67 Coulter, 'Patterns of Communication during the 1241 Mongol Invasion'.

multa transmisit in auro et argento exenia et eius gratiam impetravit et optinuit.

[1237] Igitur rumor erat, hunc populum Tartarorum in Comaniam et Hungariam velle venire; sed utrum hoc verum sit, missi sunt de Hungaria quatuor fratres Predicatores, qui usque ad veterem Hungariam per 100 dies iverunt. Qui reversi nunciaverunt, quod Tartari veterem Hungariam iam occupaverant et sue ditioni subiecerant.

> (Louis, duke of Bavaria was killed by an assassin sent by the Old Man of the Mountain. Hearing this, the king of Hungary sent to the same Old Man gifts of gold and silver, and obtained and held his friendship.)[68]
>
> (Therefore, there was a rumour that this people of the Tartars wanted to come to Cumania and Hungary, but [to find out] whether this was true, four Brothers Preachers were sent from Hungary, who travelled for a hundred days to Old Hungary. When they returned, they brought the news that the Tartars had already occupied Old Hungary and subjected it under their power.)[69]

The Cistercian textual connections are wafer-thin and lead us no closer to Matthew's sources, but this opaque layer of commonalities can certainly be used to suggest that both Alberic and his Cistercian network and Matthew Paris had access to a version of a source (or source compilation) that associated the beginning of the Mongol story with *Hungaria major* and the Assassins, which may or may not have contained a description of Julian's travels and the Cedar prophecy on the wall.

In addition to the references to *Hungaria major*, the 1238 entry is a mixed bag of all things foreign — yet familiar. The various viewpoints assumed by each component show the diversity of sources Matthew had at his disposal. Enveloped in the Saracen mission, Matthew interpolates a description of the 'inhuman race' and a short passage about herring fisheries in Yarmouth. The Saracen mission, originally dispatched to the French king, is also given a profoundly English context at the end: the legates cross the Channel to meet the king, but the punchline puts the

---

68 Alberic of Trois-Fontaines, 'Chronica', p. 929.

69 Alberic of Trois-Fontaines, 'Chronica', p. 942. Under the year 1239, Alberic refers his readers to the report of John of Plano Carpini. Stressing the efficiency of the Cistercian network connecting houses such as Alberic's in Champagne, Heiligenkreuz, Waverley in England, and Cikádor in Hungary, Attila Bárány also notes the geographical proximity of Alberic's monastery to the Lotharingian border of the empire. Bárány, 'A Tatárjárás híre Nyugat-Európában', p. 489. For indirect connections between Matthew Paris and Alberic of Trois-Fontaines, see the discussion of the Cedar of Lebanon prophecy (notes 62, 65, and 66 above), which they both inserted in their respective histories.

146 CHAPTER 3

bishop of Winchester in the limelight.[70] His figure also anchors the faraway events to English history by the fact that his witticism directly precedes the entry reporting his death.[71] Sophia Menache says, 'If the words attributed to the prelate are indeed genuine, and perhaps they were, we have here an additional example of the close link between Matthew Paris and thirteenth-century society, the idioms, symbols, and attitudes of which the *Chronica Majora* portrays so well'.[72] Indeed, this entry is more about the English court than its exotic subject. Similar to the 1237 controversies concerning Legate Otto and the foreigner-loving Henry III, Bishop Peter's controversial figure is similarly intertwined with the theme of the king's attitude towards foreigners.

The bishop was one of the foreigners who frequently feature in Matthew's narrative endowing English positions and benefices to their own kindred.[73] For example, in 1234 Henry III dismissed Peter des Roches, the man who crowned him, from favour and Peter's favourite (or nephew, as Roger of Wendover — or Matthew? — suggests), Peter des Rivaux, from office.[74] In this context, he is the figurehead of alienness with all its glories and hazards at court, a person closely associated with Henry III in more ways than one, and a mouthpiece whose words can be interpreted as witty or glib, depending on the reader's own persuasion. If the reaction of Peter des Roches who interrupted the Saracens' speech was intended to be droll (*jocose*), the episode puts the famous Poitevin 'Butterfly Bishop' in a fairly positive light.[75] At the same time, in hindsight (at the

---

70 Peter des Roches, though a foreigner, is close to home: before becoming bishop in 1205, he was precentor in Lincoln. *Fasti Ecclesiae Anglicanae*, pp. 12–15. Commenting on a different prelate but just as apposite here, Schnith observes that Matthew Paris occasionally compares unworthy clergymen to buffoons, and more importantly, their speech and gestures are elements of action that drive the plot and highlight problems: 'Das Bild des Zischenden, Schielenden, die Nase Rümpfenden ist vielleicht dem histrio nachgeformt, und es dürfte kein Zufall sein, daß Matthäus Paris gelegentlich einen unwürdigen Geistlichen einem Possenreißer vergleicht. Rede und Gebärde sind das Geschehen vorantreibende, Probleme aufweisende und Knoten lösende Handlungselemente, die der Enählung oft dramatisches Gepräge verleihen und über den einzelnen Abschnitt hinausdrängen'. Schnith, *England in einer sich wandelnden Welt*, p. 204.

71 MS B, fol. 117ʳ, col. a; *CM*, III, p. 489; *EH*, I, p. 132. The red title 'De morte episcopi Wintoniensis, Petri scilicet de Rupibus' is accompanied by an upside-down mitre and episcopal staff drawn in the gutter between the two columns. The entry is dated to 9 June: 'Anno quoque eodem, quinto idus Junii, obiit episcopus Wintoniensis, Petrus scilicet de Rupibus'.

72 Menache, 'Written and Oral Testimonies in Medieval Chronicles', p. 10.

73 *CM*, III, pp. 220, 240, 245, 252, 265.

74 *CM*, III, p. 240; Vincent, *Peter des Roches*, pp. 429–30.

75 According to the *Lanercost Chronicle*, s.a. 1216, the bishop once encountered King Arthur and dined with him. When he asked for a token of their meeting, Arthur told him to close his hand, then open it, and a butterfly flew out. For the rest of his life the bishop was able to repeat this miracle, and 'multi eum Episcopum de Papilione vocitarent' (many people called

time of writing) Matthew knew that the bishop was to be proven wrong. Unwise and shallow, and one line later, dead. *De mortuis nil nisi bonum*: this ambiguous episode says more about Matthew's cautiously formulated opinion about Peter (and the king!) than the subsequent obituary about the 'irreparable loss' that the English kingdom incurred upon his death.[76]

The complex 1238 entry also contains the first description of the Mongols in a series of many where they are described in terms of their body shape, their language, and their mores. As seen above, the second paragraph of the entry deals with the barbarians as fellow humans, albeit horrible ones, and is written in the anthropological template used in later accounts.[77] Time and again these features recur in the chronicle, some of them clearly illustrated in detailed marginal illustrations. Although not following the wording exactly, the thematic of this short description echoes another similar passage under 1240, Frederick's letter (1241),[78] as well as a longer one found both in the *Additamenta*,[79] and in the *Waverley Annals*.[80] The wording and the order of features are nearly always different despite the obvious correspondence between the themes addressed.[81]

While the 1238 entry still appears in a 'Saracen' context, it contains the first passage that presents the Mongols using phraseology that becomes commonplace in the course of the post-invasion pieces of the Mongol story. The description is clearly interpolated in between pre-invasion events, and, in turn, inserted into the flow of the narrative oscillating between the Holy Land and Matthew's homeland. The pre-invasion events are interrelated in the text but take place in three very distinct geographical locations. The threat is still only encroaching upon the periphery from nearly all cardinal directions visible from St Albans: the East afflicting various groups of 'Saracens', *Hungaria major* in the mysterious North-east, and finally, in a few odd remarks, the Scandinavian North. The former two

---

him the 'bishop of butterflies'). *Chronicon de Lanercost*, p. 23. According to Matthew Paris, the bishop was Poitevin, although this is now debated.

76 On Matthew Paris editing some of his condemning views about Peter des Roches in the *Chronica majora*, see Vincent, *Peter des Roches*, p. 293.

77 Large heads, disproportionate bodies; feed on raw meat, even human; incomparable archers; cross rivers in portable leather boats; strong and large; impious and inexorable; speak an unknown language; have many swift horses; can cover vast distances with speed; armed in front, but not behind; their chief is a ferocious man, named khan; they come from the north; named after the River Tar; they are numerous; and they have been sent as a scourge on mankind. See descriptors aggregated from different descriptions in Appendix 8, available online at <https://brepols.figshare.com>, from the link <https://doi.org/10.1484/A.14453112>.

78 MS *B*, fols 145ʳ, col. b–146ʳ, col. b; *CM*, IV, pp. 112–19; *EH*, I, pp. 341–47.

79 MS *LA*, fols 85ᵛ, col. b–86ʳ, col. a; *CM*, VI, pp. 75–76; *EH*, III, pp. 449–50.

80 'Annales de Waverleia', p. 324.

81 This is demonstrated in the comparative table in Appendix 8, available online, <https://doi.org/10.1484/A.14453112>.

148   CHAPTER 3

are intimately connected in the text and can be seen as an organic part of the Mongol story that continues in subsequent parts of the chronicle, but the latter is a story that never really joined the Mongol story. The unwieldy note about Gothland and Friesland, wedged between the Mongol khan and the Saracen legates, belongs to a handful of distinct pieces of information that can be associated with Danish informants, and as will be discussed shortly, the northern information dries up after the Danish king Valdemar's death.

The case of Philip's letter and subsequent pre-invasion entries amply demonstrate that Matthew had an effective way to construct a flowing narrative out of parallel events taking place in various places at a time. This technique continues in the building of the Mongol story in later parts of the chronicle. The way in which the Mongol references are interspersed among events unfolding in the East is precisely the way he inserts entries making up a new subplot about the Mongols emerging among the events of 1241. The packaging is, however, different; at this point, the Mongol plot is only just beginning. Despite the pointedly northern orientation of the passages, the context expressly appears in relation with the East: when the thundering Mongol army appears on the north-eastern horizon, the Christian kings and prelates can be seen cavorting with Saracens and conjecturing about the signs of the approaching Mongol threat, in the safety of their own homes.

1239: Dacia, Gothia, Frisia

While most of the previously mentioned pre-invasion entries were connected to materials circulating in Europe in the mid-1240s, a small part of these early sections probably arrived in Matthew's scriptorium before the others. Even though they seem to be an integral part of the surrounding passages, their tone and focus make them outliers in the Mongol story.[82] A handful of Mongol-related entries (a sentence in 1238, and longer entries in 1239 and 1240) discuss the atrocities in a markedly northern context. The place of the onslaught is defined as the north in the previously discussed passage *s.a.* 1238: the Mongols break forth from the north (*terras septentrionales, montibus borealibus, borealem plagam inhabitantes*),

---

82 As will be shown below, the 1239 entry is more hopeful in tone than later reports: 'Tartari, [...] victi recesserunt. Maxima autem pars eorum in manu fortitudinis et ore gladii cecidit trucidata, obviantibus eis in virtute Spiritus Sancti quinque regibus Christianis et Sarracenis ad hoc confoederatis' (the Tartars, [...] were defeated and forced to retreat; the greatest portion of these, however, were slain at the sword's point, and fell before the hand of power, having been attacked by five Christian and Saracen kings, who were united for this purpose by the grace of God's holy spirit). MS B, fol. 132ʳ, col. b; *CM*, III, p. 639; *EH*, I, p. 253.

and irrupt into *Hungaria major*, which — as demonstrated above — was also thought to be situated in the north.[83]

The northern preoccupation with the Mongol threat, and even actual Mongol threat to the north, appears in scattered European sources. Early in the history of the Mongol conquests, in the 1220s, the fall of Kiev does seem to have had a fallout effect on northern areas, though not yet as palpable as the subsequent Mongol tribute as was the case of Novgorod and Smolensk later.[84] Henry of Livonia's chronicle, for example, suggests the Russians' northern (Baltic) orientation after the onslaught — the Mongol disaster brought peace elsewhere:

> Bisdecimus quartus iam presulis affuit annus / Et nondum terra tranquilla pace quievit. / Eodem anno fuerunt Tatari in terra Valvorum paganorum, qui Parthi a quibusdam dicuntur, qui panem non comedunt, sed carnibus crudis pecorum suorum vescuntur. Et pugnaverunt Tatari cum eis et debellaverunt eos et percusserunt omnes in ore gladii, et alii fugerunt ad Ruthenos, petentes auxilium ab eis. Et pervenit verbum per universam Rusciam, ut pugnarent cum Tataris, et exiverunt reges de tota Ruscia contra Tataros et non valuerunt pugnare cum eis et fugerunt coram eis. Et cecidit rex magnus Misteslawe de Kywa cum quadraginta milibus virorum, qui astabant ei. Sed et alter rex Galacie, Misteslawe per fugam evasit. Et de regibus aliis ceciderunt in eodem bello circiter quinquaginta. Et persecuti sunt eos sex diebus et interfecerunt ex eis plures quam centum milia virorum, quorum numerum Deus solus novit, et ceteri fugerunt. Et misit rex de Smalenceka et rex de Plosceke et quidam alii reges de Ruscia nuncios suos in Rigam, petentes ea que pacis sunt. Et renovata est pax per omnia, que iam dudum ante facta fuerat.
>
> > (It was now the prelate's twenty-fourth year [1222], and the land did not rest in tranquil peace. In that same year the Tartars (who are said by some to be Parthians and who do not eat bread, but feed

---

83 MS *B*, fol. 116ᵛ, col. b; *CM*, III, p. 488; *EH*, I, p. 131. 'Tartaris prorumpentibus de locis suis terras septentrionales', 'genus hominum monstruosum et inhumanum ex montibus borealibus prorupisse'. It is perhaps telling that the word 'orientis' was inserted in the sentence 'et spatiosas terras et opulentas Orientis occupasse' above the line in Matthew's hand. The original sentence was 'et spatiosas terras et opulentas occupasse', *Hungaria major* being mentioned in the next sentence, separately from the opulent Saracen east. Neither passage expressly states that *Hungaria major* was thought to be situated in the north, but it is certain that it was implicitly understood. For the discussion of Matthew's concept of this region as evidenced in other manuscripts, see Chapter 1.

84 Out of the northern Russian territories, Smolensk and Novgorod had to pay tribute, but Pskov and Polotsk were never directly affected by the tax collection. Selart and Robb, *Livonia, Rus' and the Baltic Crusades*, p. 279.

on raw flesh of their flocks) were in the land of the Valvus pagans.[85] The Tartars warred upon them and defeated them and slew them all with the edge of the sword and others fled to the Russians, seeking aid from them. Word went out through all of Russia that they should fight with the Tartars, and the kings of all Russia went out against the Tartars. The Russians were not strong enough to fight with them and fled before them. Mstislav, the great king of Kiev, fell, together with forty thousand men who stood by him. The other King Mstislav, of Galicia, escaped by flight. About fifty of the other kings fell in the same battle [the Battle of Kalka]. The Tartars pursued the Russians for six days and killed more than a thousand men, whose numbers God alone knows; the rest fled. The king of Smolensk, the king of Polozk, and certain other Russian kings sent their emissaries to Riga seeking terms of peace. Peace was renewed throughout all the areas as it had prevailed in earlier times.)[86]

An equally odd reference can be found in the Ottobeuren Collection, which contains the letter Otto II, duke of Bavaria, sent to Bishop Siboto of Augsburg.[87] Similar to other letters circulating about the ongoing invasion in Europe, for example, the 'emperor's letter' in the *Chronica majora*, Otto describes a three-pronged attack.[88] However, instead of listing Polonia, Bohemia, and Hungary as destinations, he (or whoever copied his letter) says, 'Exercitus autem hostium antedictorum protenditur in tres partes; primus videlicet versus Norwagiam, secundus Boemiam, tercius in Hungariam'. While this is incorrect, perceivably so even for most contemporaries, at some point it was obviously conceivable enough for someone to write down and was disseminated this way.

Finally, the *Hákonar Saga Gamla* (ch. 333), composed in 1264/65, records that a number of 'Byarmians' came as refugees to Håkon IV of Norway, because they had been assailed by the Mongols.[89] The king had them baptized and then settled them north of the Malangerfjord — no

---

85 The *valvi* are the Cumans whom the Mongols drove towards Hungary after their victories in the Rus'. The term is probably a corrupted Latin version of the German *falones*, cf. Otto of Freising and Rahewinus, *The Deeds of Frederick Barbarossa*, p. 66. Jüri Kivimäe suggests that the description 'Parthians who do not eat bread, but feed on raw flesh of their flocks' refers to the pagan *valvi*, rather than the Mongols in the passage. Kivimäe, '"Henricus" the Ethnographer', p. 103.

86 Henry of Livonia, *The Chronicle*, p. 205; Henry of Livonia, *Chronik*, pp. 186–87.

87 MS *OB*, fol. 7ᵛ. More on this collection in Chapter 2 ('Northern Connections'). Calendared as no. 11325 in *Regesta Imperii*, v.1, p. 71; *Árpádkori új okmánytár*, p. 139.

88 The idea of a three-pronged attack also appears in 'the emperor's letter' (Chapter 4, 'The First 1241 Cluster') and the report of the 'Russian archbishop' (Chapter 5, '1244: The Man from Russia').

89 'Byarmians' probably refers to people living in northern Russia, east of the White Sea. See for example, 1.8.16, 3.2.8, 5.13.1–2, 6.5.10, 8.8.9, 8.14.6, 9.4.22–25 in Saxo Grammaticus,

doubt to please the pope in his continued efforts to legitimize his kingship.[90] However, in the Western European context, closer to Matthew, less is noted about fears in the North. The concern about the Mongol threat is due to their alliances rather than actual Mongol threat: for example, when writing to the archbishop of Trondheim in 1243, Innocent IV approves the Norwegian king's request to transfer his crusade vow for the Holy Land into one against the Mongols, should they return within the year.[91]

Matthew Paris's references to Mongol threat or related concerns in the north are completely independent and oblivious of these texts. But, as noted above, they also seem separate and disjointed within his own Mongol story, which also results in these odd passages awkwardly inserted. They are out of place not just in the context of the passage itself, but in the context of being inserted into the typically more organically flowing narrative. First, an obviously inorganically embedded passage within the previously discussed 1238 entry notes that 'the inhabitants of Gothland and Friesland, dreading their attacks, did not, as was their custom, come to Yarmouth, in England'.[92] Then, in 1239, Matthew reports that

> Sub illius temporis spatio Tartari, gentes inhumanae, qui stragem magnam exercuerant et Christianorum jam fines in manu hostili invaserant, in majori Hungaria discurrendo, victi recesserunt. Maxima autem pars eorum in manu fortitudinis et ore gladii cecidit trucidata, obviantibus eis in virtute Spiritus Sancti quinque regibus Christianis et Sarracenis ad hoc confoederatis. Post quorum internecionem rex Daciae et rex Hungariae fines per praedictos Tartaros quasi in desertum redactos fecerunt Christianis populis, quos illuc miserant, inhabitari. De quibus ex sola Dacia naves plusquam quadraginta exierunt. Eodem anno, mons Cassinus inexpugnabilis captus est a fidelibus imperatoris.

> > (About this time the Tartars, a barbarous race of people, who had invaded the Christian countries and committed great slaughter, wandering here and there in Greater Hungary, were defeated and forced to retreat; the greatest portion of these, however, were slain at the sword's point, and fell before the hand of power, having been attacked by five Christian and Saracen kings, who were united for this purpose by the grace of God's holy spirit. After the slaughter of these barbarians, the kings of Dacia and Hungary sent some

---

Gesta Danorum. For Matthew Paris's personal connections with Håkon, see Chapter 2 ('Northern Connections').

90 Aalto, 'Swells of the Mongol-Storm around the Baltic', p. 9; Helle, Lillehammer, and Omre, *Aschehougs Norgeshistorie*, p. 198.

91 Knut, Norwegian prince, also received his *commutatio* from the pope on 2 August 1243, no. 27, in *Diplomatarium Norvegicum*, I, pp. 21–22; *Codex diplomaticus Hungariae ecclesiasticus ac civilis*, IV.1, p. 303.

92 MS B, fol. 117[r], col. a; *CM*, III, p. 488; *EH*, I, pp. 131–32.

Christians to inhabit the provinces, which had been reduced, as it were, to a desert by the said Tartars; and more than forty ships went from Dacia alone filled with them. In the same year Mount Casino, an impregnable place, was taken by the emperor's army, as has been more fully related above.)[93]

The commonality of these entries is that they appear in a very specific geographical context: *Gothia*, *Frisia*, and *Dacia*. These seemingly straightforward place names, specifically *Gothia*, stand for a rather confusing territory in medieval cartography and geography, after one of the most powerful geographical interpretive frames, Isidore's *Etymologiae*, stated that *Dacia, ubi et Gothia*. It seems justifiable to argue that *Gothia* in the 1238 passage indeed referred to Denmark.[94] Other notes, explicitly about Valdemar, confirm that Matthew understood *Dacia* as Denmark, too. Because of the other prevalent meanings of Dacia outside Matthew's chronicle, it is not impossible that he misunderstood some news that he received about either Hungarian or Russian resettlement campaigns and co-opted them for his story of the Danish boats. But since neither Danish nor Eastern European repopulation drives can be substantiated with historical evidence at this point, the only solid information we are left with is that, for Matthew, these events took place in Denmark and the North.

The connection between Gothland/Friesland (1238), *Dacia/Hungaria* (1239), and *Daci* (1240) in these Mongol-related passages may be detected in the collocation of toponyms used in the *Chronica majora*. The odd 1238 passage about the herrings in Yarmouth is one of the two instances when Matthew refers to a *Gothia*, and there is but a handful of mentions of *Frisia*, and they appear together in Mongol-related entries.[95]

---

93 MS *B*, fol. 132ʳ, col. b; *CM*, III, p. 639; *EH*, I, p. 253.

94 This was further complicated by the confusion about 'Dacia' (Denmark *vs* Roman province south-east of Pannonia, encompassing some of the contemporary territory of the Kingdom of Hungary), as well as the fact that by this time many well-known English maps also identified Dacia with Russia. On the Hereford Mappa Mundi, for example, rubric no. 471 is *Dacia, hec et Rusia*. As Westrem explains: 'Roman Dacia comprised much of modern Romania and Bulgaria. (The name was also used, alternating with "Dania", for Denmark [see Honorius Augustodunensis 1.22 and 24 n. 1; Denmark is "Dacia" on the Gough Map].) "Dacia" and "Russia" are linked in a single legend on the Sawley Map. The wording in this legend makes the two toponyms refer to the same territory, but it does so less precisely than Isidore's reference to "Dacia, ubi et Gothia" (14.4.3) or the reading in E[xpositio] M[appe] M[undi] ("Dacia que et Ruscia"), in which this territory is situated between the Alanus and Tisza rivers, (III.173–74). The description on the Map closely follows this location'. *The Hereford Map*, pp. 198–99.

95 For example, a terrifying portent appearing over the country, from 1217 — inserted in the portion authored by Wendover. These early passages echo the *Historia Damiatina* by Oliver of Cologne (also known as Oliverus scholasticus and Oliver of Paderborn), placed directly after relating the passage of the withdrawal of the first contingents of the Fifth Crusade, led by King Andrew II of Hungary and Duke Leopold of Austria. *CM*, III, pp. 13–14.

To leap forward a little, Matthew mentions them side by side in his preface to a 1241 letter by the duke of Brabant about the Mongol ravages in Christian Europe:

> De horribili vastatione inhumanae gentis quae Tartari nuncupantur. [...] Jamjam Frisiam, Guthiam, Poloniam, Boemiam, et utramque Hungariam pro majori parte inaudita tyrannide, principibus, praelatis, civibus, et colonis effugatis et trucidatis, quasi in eremum redegerunt.
>
>> (Of the dreadful ravages committed by the Tartars. [...] Already had they, with unheard-of tyranny, in a great measure reduced to a desert the countries of Friesland, Gothland, Poland, Bohemia, and both divisions of Hungary, slaying or putting to flight princes, prelates, citizens, and rustics.)[96]

Besides the repeated proximity of mentions of *Gothia/Dacia* and *Frisia* to references to the Mongols in Hungary, the Frisian affairs in this portion of the chronicle are attached to the Danish king Valdemar's figure. A few entries prior to involving Frisia in the Mongol affairs, in the entry about King Valdemar's death in 1241, Matthew notes that the king, 'who had presumptuously threatened to invade England',[97] 'had reigned over the Danes for forty years, and during his whole life, from the time when he was capable of bearing arms, continued to persecute the infidels in Scythia, Friesland, and Russia'.[98]

As noted in the overview of Matthew's northern connections in Chapter 2 above, the Norwegian king, another confirmed northern connection of Matthew Paris, can be seen as an active contributor of information for Mongol-related entries — albeit not much to do with Scandinavia — inserted under the late 1240s. However, these odd early references to the northern preoccupation with the Mongol attack on Europe come from across the Skagerrak. The 1239 entry about the repopulation of lands devastated by Mongols is only one half of the story about the ships sent by the Danish and Hungarian kings. As will be shown, it is revisited under the year 1240 in the context of false rumours about a potential Danish

---

96 MS *B*, fol. 145ʳ, col. a; *CM*, IV, p. 109; *EH*, I, pp. 338–39. See the detailed discussion of this entry in Chapter 4.

97 MS *B*, fol. 133ʳ, col. b; *CM*, IV, p. 9; *EH*, I, p. 260.

98 Matthew Paris, 'Regnavit autem in Dacia quadraginta annis et amplius. Ipse fere omnibus diebus vitas suae, postquam aptus fuit armis, infideles persequebatur, scilicet in Sithia, et in Frisia et Ruscia'. This particular sentence is written separately in a rubric at the bottom of the page, which concerns the civil war that ensued after the death of Valdemar and his heir, which suggests that it was added in hindsight after finishing the page. Waldemar (referred to as such in the main text) is called Aethelmar here. The main entry itself is marked by an inverted crown for Waldemar II, and an inverted coronet for his son. MS *B*, fol. 142ᵛ, col. b; *CM*, IV, p. 92; *EH*, I, p. 325.

invasion of England.[99] Matthew's fears of a Danish invasion reflected very real concerns at the court. As Lars Kjær explains, 'in 1240, King Henry III of England sent two separate missions to acquire more intelligence about the situation in Denmark. They must have brought back reassuring news, for English sources give no indication of preparations against invasion in the following years'.[100]

In view of the 'Danish threat', the entry seems to be an amalgamation of English court intelligence and the information of the previous entry about Danish boats, including some direct connections provided by fellow St Albans denizens.[101] However, although Matthew seems to have had some direct access to information coming from the Danish court, this is not necessarily where he received information about Valdemar II and his realm.[102] The Danish king's connections in the greater European dynastic scene explain the unique geographical context in which he appears in Matthew's chronicle. Denmark at the time was an emerging power with potential. From Valdemar I's time onwards, the kingdom was carefully negotiating with the empire, regional authorities, and England, too. As early as in 1187, for example, 'the Emperor Frederick Barbarossa wrote to his son Henry warning him about the friendship between the archbishop of Cologne, the kings of England and Denmark and the count of Flanders', and in Frederick II's time, the so-called 'Golden Bull' of 1214 set out that the Holy Roman emperor concluded a 'perpetual friendship' for the preservation of peace with Valdemar II.[103] Through his engagements and marriages, he was intimately connected to the ruling houses of Saxony, Bavaria, Bohemia, and Flanders.[104] The usual suspects disseminating European news in chanceries of Cologne and Brabant or St Albans travellers

---

99 MS *B*, fol. 133ʳ, col. b; *CM*, IV, p. 9; *EH*, I, p. 260. See the next section ('1240: False Alarm and Irruption').

100 Abstract in English in Kjær, 'Valdemar 2. Sejr, Matthew Paris og den engelske invasionsfrygt'.

101 For Matthew Paris naming as his sources a handful of St Albans citizens who had spent several years in the Danish king's court (Odo and John of St Albans, John's son, Nicholas, as well as a priest, Edward, and his uncle), see Chapter 2 ('Northern Connections').

102 See Chapter 2 ('Northern Connections').

103 Benham, *Peacemaking in the Middle Ages*, p. 183.

104 His dynastic connections include his first marriage to Dagmar (Margaret) of Bohemia, daughter of King Ottokar I of Bohemia; and his second marriage to Bengerd (Berengaria) of Portugal, daughter of King Sancho I of Portugal, and a sister of Ferdinand, count of Flanders. Valdemar was also connected to England with many ties; for example, his sister, Helen, was married to William of Winchester (William of Lunenburg or William Longsword), who, as the nephew of King Richard I, was even a candidate for the English throne at one point. William died young and his issue, Otto the Child, had less contact with his English heritage after he became duke of Brunswick-Lüneburg (1235–1252). Although focusing on the generation of Valdemar I and Henry II of England, Jenny Benham's monograph provides valuable background to the similarities and connections between Denmark and England, and also discusses the type of embassies and envoys negotiating between them. Benham, *Peacemaking in the Middle Ages*.

connected Matthew Paris's ego-network directly to Mongol news: due to the dense web of alliances and communications surrounding Valdemar II's court, pieces of news about Danish ships and Mongols could reach St Albans in various configurations and through various channels.

Compared to Matthew's usual entries that at least can name the kingdoms involved, if not the king by name, the victory of 'five Christian and Saracen kings' back in 1239 sounds foggy. The first part of the entry is still not more than the description of events far far away, though not so far away that they would be outside the purview of Europeans. They are rulers on the edge of Christian Europe, but rulers all the same. And the entry ends in even more familiar lands. If it was not for the curvature of the Earth, with a pair of military-grade binoculars Denmark would be visible from the herring-filled port of Yarmouth. What is striking about the mentions of Denmark in a Mongol context is not their proximity or veracity (or lack thereof), a feature all three of them share: they are stuck into the text very awkwardly. They probably arrived in St Albans together, and Matthew added the passages to his text where he deemed fit. Whether they were random pieces of news that were inserted into the flow of the nascent Mongol story opportunistically or Matthew used them by some more deliberate design, the overall effect in the raising arc of the plotline is clear: overlooking the clumsy phrasing, the reader can gather their relentless north-western progress and its fallout in familiar lands on the horizon.

1240: False Alarm and Irruption

There are two 1240 entries about the Mongols, the last two Mongol passages before the attack on Hungary. The first is a false report of a Danish invasion due to Danish plans to repopulate lands devastated by the Mongols:

> Percrebuerunt enim illo tempore rumores in Anglia quod Daci disponebant ipsam hostiliter invadere. Quod tamen nihil aliud erat, nisi quod, navibus oneratis hominibus utriusque sexus, terras a Tartaris vastatas disposuerunt colere et inhabitare et populis restaurare.

> (At this time, too, there were frequent reports in England, that the Dacians were making preparations to invade England; but this arose, from nothing else than that they were preparing, in ships laden with people of both sexes, to inhabit and cultivate the territory which had been devastated by the Tartars, and to restore it to the use of human beings.)[105]

---

105 MS *B*, fol. 133ʳ, col. b; *CM*, IV, p. 9; *EH*, I, p. 260.

Although it is entered under 1240 it seems little more than the repetition, but in fact is a continuation, of the aforementioned 1239 entry with the added twist that the Mongol threat in the North indirectly caused false alarm about Danish threat in England. In this year, Matthew presents a seemingly relentless string of various oppressions and foreign threat that befell the people of England, so it is perhaps not irrelevant that it is awkwardly interjected at the end of an entry that was supposed to relate the how the king caused the citizens of London swear fealty to his son, Edward.[106]

As usual, the Mongol snippet is inserted into an entry in the flow of domestic affairs, this time the absolution of crusader vows and extorting monies. And as usual, Legate Otto is not far from the scandalous events; a few entries up, his letter about the pope's instructions concerning the crusader vows is copied in full, and in the entry right after the Danish report, another one continues the absolution thread: friars selling waivers 'accepta tamen pecunia quanta sufficere videbatur unicuique ad viaticum ultramarinum. Et factum est in populo scandalum cum scismate' (on receipt from each of as much money as seemed to be sufficient for him to procure necessaries for his voyage, and a great scandal and schism arose amongst the people).[107] As noted before, the logic of previous alternating entries is there, but it is, for some reason, more fragmented, less elegantly fused into the narrative than elsewhere. More importantly, these short passages remain isolated within the narrative. After this, the 'Danish strand' of the Mongol story is discontinued for good, and Matthew does not refer to Danish issues again until 1251.[108]

The last entry prior to the invasion is a long description of the irruption of the Tartars, as well as their description, and conjectures about their origins.[109] Similar to the compact version in 1239, and many others after it, including Matthew's illustrations, this is a generic description of the Mongols: a barbaric, strong, ugly, and heathen people from the back of beyond. Although Matthew is known for his penchant for *mirabilia*, portents, and exotic animals, no other peoples are described in such detail by Matthew. The descriptions were included because many such texts travelled together with the type of sources Matthew was working with.

As noted above, there is a wealth of commonalities between the themes addressed in various versions of the descriptions in the *Chronica majora* as well as other similar known texts. Besides a few notable exceptions, the

---

106 MS *B*, fol. 133ʳ, col. b; *CM*, IV, p. 9; *EH*, I, p. 260.
107 MS *B*, fol. 133ʳ, col. b; *CM*, IV, p. 9; *EH*, I, p. 261.
108 MS *B*, fols 249ᵛ, col. b–250ʳ, col. a; *CM*, V, p. 221; *EH*, II, pp. 430–31.
109 MS *B*, fols 140ᵛ, col. b–141ʳ, col. a; *CM*, IV, pp. 76–78; *EH*, I, pp. 312–13. See text (in comparison with similar passages) in Appendix 8, available online, <https://doi.org/10.1484/A.14453112>.

recurring features — disproportionate bodies, repulsive diet (even canni-balism), strength and skills in archery, means of transport such as horses and boats, their armour and weaponry, origin and prehistory, as well as nefarious plans to subjugate the world — are all similar, yet formulated in different order and using different phrases. The most tantalizing aspect of these descriptions is that despite the number of similar texts, no two are close enough to build a stemma of any sort, let alone reconstruct their path to St Albans. No doubt, the large number and variety of such descriptions in the *Chronica majora* and elsewhere (for example, Thomas of Spalato) is indicative of one thing: descriptions of Mongols were popular texts, and despite a formulaic content, they circulated in many forms, enriching each other with both transference and direct borrowing. Just to show how similar yet different these descriptions are: the 1238 passage,[110] the 1240 entry,[111] and the relatively self-contained description of the Mongols in Frederick's letter under 1241,[112] contain strikingly similar word use (e.g. 'sagittarii incomparabiles', 'impii' and 'gens impia', 'equos velocissimos', 'Tartari a Tar/quodam flumine'). But as Appendix 2 shows, though the descriptions are unmistakeably similar, they rarely correspond verbatim.[113]

Citing Karl Schnith's analysis, Karl Rudolf attributes more authorial intervention to Matthew Paris than simple copy-paste of various versions. He suggests that Matthew used information found in letters to rephrase various snippets in his own contributions to the same topic elsewhere in the chronicle; for example, he identifies parts of Frederick II's letter rephrased in the 1240 entry about the 'Irruption of the Mongols' attrib-uted to Matthew's own pen.[114] This thinking is important here as it is based on the implicit understanding that Matthew's historiographical practice was more far-sighted than an annalistic ordering of incoming information. The suggestion that Matthew composed self-authored passages out of received material, which in the final version preceded their source, also tacitly confirms the time lag and hindsight that allowed such writing processes, as well as the chronicler's narrative control over his text.

---

110 MS *B*, fol. 116ᵛ, col. b; *CM*, III, pp. 488–89; *EH*, I, pp. 131–32.
111 MS *B*, fols 140ᵛ, col. b–141ʳ, col. a; *CM*, IV, pp. 75–78; *EH*, I, pp. 312–13.
112 MS *B*, fol. 145ᵛ, col. b; *CM*, IV, p. 115; *EH*, I, p. 342.
113 See the full comparative table of descriptors in Appendix 8, available online, <https://doi.org/10.1484/A.144531112>.
114 Rudolf, 'Die Tartaren 1241/1242', p. 93.

The title of the 1240 entry itself, *Quomodo Tartari resumptis viribus de montibus suis prorumpentes, Orientalium multis finibus vastatis, etiam Christianos jam perterruerunt,* is a quasi summary of all that was written about the Mongols before. Between 1237 and 1240, the Mongols are shown to move from the East to the North, where the kingdoms on the edges of the mental map of the Christen oecumene were the first ones to tackle them. Compared to what was coming in the next year, they are few and far between, all written in Matthew's voice but already using tropes that arrived in England after the onslaught. They are also different because of their eastern/north-eastern placement beyond or at the gates of Christendom. Finally, their frequency, tone, and integration into the narrative strands sets them apart from the main body of the Mongol story. The fact that these early passages are so different in nature and content from the rest of the Mongol narrative in the *Chronica majora* shows all the more how the core of the story is surprisingly consistent.

The composition and origin of the sources that reached Matthew, as well as the time when he received and inserted them in his chronicle, were both determining factors in the shaping of his Mongol story. The confluence of East and North in the story of the Mongol threat is the result of Matthew marrying two very distinct pools of sources. The more disjointed short insertions about northern affairs — short-lived among the other strands — remain isolated, while the main plotline continues and is clearly connected to other portions of the Mongol story with a number of invisible threads. On the one hand, it was demonstrated that pre-1241 entries were written long after the events they describe, and with most of the 1241 materials already at Matthew's disposal. On the other hand, they have much in common with the entries in the last phase of the Mongol story. Mirroring on a larger scale Matthew's usual narrative structure of placing original documents between passages written in his own voice, together these entries comprise Matthew's prelude to the immense central body of the Mongol story, stitched together from a large number of letters, documents, and reports, under the year 1241.

CHAPTER 4

Fight

Mongols in the Middle (1241)

> But, alas! for our misdeed,
> Anger rose within Thy breast,
> And Thy lightnings Thou did'st speed
> From Thy thundering sky with zest.
> Now the Mongol arrow flew
> Over our devoted heads;
> Or the Turkish yoke we knew,
> Which a free-born nation dreads.[1]

It was a heavy burden that Pope Gregory IX passed on to his successors when he died in August 1241, and uncertainties and anxieties of the two years between his death and Innocent IV's election were not easing off with the renewed and seemingly relentless conflict between the papacy and the Holy Roman Empire. Matthew Paris at this time was already hard at work gathering materials that would make sense in and of the tumultuous years of the mid-1240s. As Whalen puts it, the conflict of pope and emperor permeated all walks of life of the European public, and it seeped deeply into the chronicles of the age: 'Chroniclers with their own stakes in the outcome memorialized the clash between the papacy and empire in their historical writings, leaving traces of wider reactions to the turmoil disrupting their society: the circulation of wild rumors, the clamoring of the people, and the awe caused by apocalyptic signs of a world in crisis. Nothing less than the fate of Christendom seemed to hang in the balance between the discordant two powers'.[2] And, as this chapter will show, this concerned not only the chronicles' account of the history of the conflict between emperor and pope, but everything else around and in between.

It is by now obvious that Matthew's story of the Mongols was woven out of materials received from various sources, and configuring them into a narrative was primarily dictated by external factors such as the time of their

---

1 The national anthem of the Republic of Hungary: Ferenc Kölcsey, 'Himnusz' [Anthem], in *Gems from Petofi and Other Hungarian Poets*, pp. 101–03.
2 Whalen, *The Two Powers*, p. 3.

160 CHAPTER 4

receipt at the St Albans scriptorium and the nature of the received material, often acquired in bundles already collated according to theme. While the *Chronica majora*'s pre-invasion entries, inserted on a one-per-year basis, were associated with faraway territories of 'Saracens', *Hungaria major*, and (oddly) Denmark, the second detectable phase in the Mongol story comes from people closer to the issues preoccupying European powers. The previously mentioned entry bearing the title *Quomodo Tartari resumptis viribus de montibus suis prorumpentes, Orientalium multis finibus vastatis, etiam Christianos jam perterruerunt* (How the Tartars breaking forth from their mountains, having regained their strength and having destroyed many regions, now alarmed even Christians) marks both the diabolical enemy crossing the Christian borders and the beginning of a new sequence in the chronicle building from sources and a different perspective.[3]

The entry itself is a lengthy description of the savagery of the Mongols, after which the story progresses in a rapid succession of complex units. These entries are now some of the best-known and most frequently cited sources about the Mongol invasion. What they have in common is that most of them appear in an imperial context. Matthew's sources and informants for these entries are different than the previous and the following sections, which results in a distinctive tone and content. Between 1240 and 1244 Matthew inserts a string of entries about the Mongols, peaking in 1241. In that year he created a double cluster out of disparate materials such as Henry Raspe's letter to the duke of Brabant concerning the Mongols, containing a dialogue between Louis IX and his mother; a letter of Frederick II to Henry III, and an illustration of a Mongol warrior on horseback;[4] an odd segue about suspicions of Frederick II's plot to bring on the Mongol invasion;[5] an entry about Henry sent to assist his brother Conrad against the Tartars;[6] and another entry about the Jews' involvement with the Mongols.[7] After this busy year, containing no fewer than five long and complicated Mongol-related entries, nothing is inserted in the main text of the chronicle under 1242, the actual year when most of the Mongol destruction took place in the Kingdom of Hungary. Returning to the one Mongol-related entry per year ratio, 'Frederick's Mongol story' is closed by

---

3 MS *B*, fols 140ᵛ, col. b–141ʳ, col. a; *CM*, IV, pp. 76–78; *EH*, I, pp. 312–13. See text in Appendix 8, available online at <https://brepols.figshare.com>, from the link <https://doi.org/10.1484/A.14453112>.

4 MS *B*, fols 145ʳ, col. a–146ᵛ, col. a; *CM*, IV, pp. 109–19; *EH*, I, pp. 339–47.

5 MS *B*, fol. 146ᵛ, col. a; *CM*, IV, pp. 119–20; *EH*, I, pp. 347–48.

6 MS *B*, fol. 148ʳ, col. a; *CM*, IV, p. 131; *EH*, I, pp. 356–57. Cf. 'Annales de Theokesberia', p. 118.

7 MS *B*, fol. 148ʳ, cols a–b; *CM*, IV, pp. 131–33; *EH*, I, pp. 357–59.

a brief notice that the king of Hungary asked for Frederick II's help against the Mongols, and his country was freed sometime in the middle of 1244.[8]

Man weiß nur das, was man sieht, one knows only what one sees, but the *Chronica majora*'s Mongol story at this point is written by men who were not there. Despite the vivid detail, neither Matthew nor his sources were in the thick of the events. Whether it was John Mansel or Richard of Cornwall and his secretarial staff who placed Mongol-related texts within Matthew's reach, or they came from the pope's court through ecclesiastic channels, looking at the probable origin of the letters one by one, their German focus is immediately apparent.[9] How and why Matthew Paris integrated this specific body of material into the *Chronica majora* is the subject of the following narrative analysis.

The drama unfolding on various fronts in 1241 is woven out of a number of interrelated strands. Chris Given-Wilson, discussing Henry Knighton's approach to constructing the narrative of his chronicle, explains that his preferred method of composition was to weave his sources, 'or extracts from them, into his narrative, sometimes breaking them up into a number of sections interspersed with his own comments or with information derived from another source. It is from this method of composition that the idea of a "text" derives'.[10] While Given-Wilson identifies a number of fourteenth-century chroniclers who employed this method, for example, Adam Murimuth and Thomas Walsingham, the following analysis of the two Mongol clusters of 1241 in the *Chronica majora* demonstrates that it was, in fact, dexterously deployed already in the mid-thirteenth century.

About the use of documents in the *Chronica majora*, Karl Schnith points out that their purpose for Matthew was on the one hand to provide gravitas (through *historischen Beweiskraft*, historical evidential value); on the other hand, they drove the plot forward (*Handlung*), validated the opinions expressed, and thus took on the role of notes in modern historiography.[11] In the following, a closer look at how Matthew Paris configured his story of the Mongols out of various sources will underpin how he

---

8 MS *B*, fol. 170ᵛ, cols a–b; *CM*, IV, p. 298; *EH*, I, pp. 489–90. Ivo of Narbonne's eyewitness account (illustrated by a well-known drawing of a cannibal feast), an outlier in this sequence, is inserted under 1243. MS *B*, fols 166ᵛ, col. b–167ᵛ, col. b; *CM*, IV, pp. 270–77; *EH*, I, pp. 467–73. Illustration on 167ʳ. Due to its perspective and probable sources, this letter belongs in the next sequence of Mongol entries and will be discussed in Chapter 5 below.

9 As noted elsewhere, papal correspondence was not always particularly welcome on the English shore. See more about the blockade against papal communication in the discussion of the Council of Lyon in Chapter 2 ('England in the European Networks').

10 Given-Wilson, *Chronicles*, p. 15.

11 Schnith, *England in einer sich wandelnden Welt*, pp. 120, 200: 'der auf die Bedeutung des Briefes bei Matthaeus hinwies; dieser "ist sich der historischen Beweiskraft von Dokumenten bewußt", sie trieben die Handlung voran, dienten als Bekräftigung vorgetragener Meinungen "und übernehmen so die Rolle der Anmerkungen in der neueren Geschichtsschreibung"'. As cited in Rudolf, 'Die Tartaren 1241/1242', p. 92, n. 57.

162   CHAPTER 4

managed to negotiate various angles within single entries or thematic blocks. As Appendix 3 shows, the Mongol-related material in 1241 is all written in relation to Frederick II's manoeuvres on the Continent, which, in turn, are embedded in the larger frame of the much-condemned papal policies. Before entering the chronicle world, thus, a potted history of pertinent Mongol-related events will be useful, especially from the angle of German participation. Matthew Paris's first entries report immense continental armies, bloody battles, and Christian victory over the Mongols. While they are at odds with the reports and letters inserted later in the chronicle, they are not completely spurious. In fact, they all fit the narrative of the 1241 crusade preparations against the Mongols, an aspect of the Mongol invasion in Europe which is often overshadowed by narratives of destruction and lack of defences in Eastern Europe.

Holy War on the Mongols

As Peter Jackson suggests, 1241 was indeed the 'year of the crusades'. Similar to Matthew's lists about Frederick's armies, Jackson lists the theatres of holy war, which indeed show a remarkably dispersed and disjointed military effort fought on way too many fronts in defence of the Church — Frederick was only one of them. The remnants of Theobald of Navarre's troops were joined by Richard of Cornwall on the Palestinian coast; contingents were on the way to reinforce Baldwin II of Courtenay's army in Constantinople; the Swedes and Teutonic Knights, responding to the pope's crusading call, were marching against the Orthodox Russians; and the pope authorized commuting vows made for a crusade in Syria to defend the papacy against the new enemy, Frederick II.[12] It was amid all these operations and preparations that King Béla's pleas for help elicited the first official response from the pope. After some correspondence with the Hungarians as well as prelates in Germany, on 16 June, Pope Gregory promised Béla, his brother Coloman, and all others who took up the cross for the defence of Hungary the same privileges and the same indulgence as had been granted to those who crusaded in the Holy Land. A holy war was proclaimed against the Mongols in Europe.[13]

---

12 Jackson, 'The Crusade against the Mongols (1241)', p. 5. Later on in the *Chronica majora*, Matthew himself refers to the crusader zeal once again: 'Ut quid igitur cruce signati has insanias negligentes intendunt sulcare lacerto vel brachiis flumina, vel maria transmeare ad expugnandos Sarracenos vel Tartaros longe furentes, quorum crudelitas his inferior longe censetur?' (Why, then, did the crusaders, paying no heed to these insane acts, plough the rivers with their arms, or cross the sea to attack the Saracens or Tartars, who vent their fury at a distance, when their cruelty is considered much less than these proceedings of his?). MS B, fol. 227ʳ, col. a; *CM*, V, p. 66; *EH*, II, p. 303.

13 Letter no. 822 in *Epistolae saeculi XIII e regestis pontificum Romanorum selectae*, I, pp. 722–23.

But the situation was complex. Mikolaj Gladysz's account of the crusade calls and the 'soi disant "crusade"' (Gladysz's scare quotes), frames the crusading conundrum in the context of the larger-scale implications of the conflict between pope and emperor. Matthew Paris could not have done it better. First of all, it is clear that the pope's bulls allowing Hungarian defence troops to act as 'crusaders', then ordering the Cistercian abbot of Heiligenkreuz and the Viennese mendicants to proclaim the crusade, are barely more than exercises in morale-boosting.[14] Gladysz confirms that there is nothing to show that this in fact resulted in any armed action being taken against the invaders.[15] After relegating the Mongol problem to the bottom of his priority list, Gregory IX's death in August 1241 rendered void any papal plans for an anti-Mongol crusade in the end. So what is Matthew Paris talking about? As Gladysz explains, 'under the influence of the appeal for help from the countries invaded and damaged by the Mongol invasion, and then the rapidly spreading news of the defeats at Legnica and Muhi, there was a spontaneous campaign of preaching the cross at the bidding of certain members of the ecclesiastical and secular elites, though not authorised by the pope'.[16] This was not entirely spontaneous and driven by Christian charity. The unauthorized German crusaders' 'usurpation of papal prerogatives' exploited the crisis of papal authority and at the same time responded to the panic among the general populace. The crusader troops may never have marched across their borders, but the European conflicts which engendered and promoted their initiative bought them a prestigious plot in an important chronicle.

Matthew's entry suggests that Conrad mobilized an immense army who 'were prepared to fight to the death against the said Tartars', and then, joined by his brother Henry, he achieved victory in 'a most bloody battle [...] near the banks of the river Delpheos, not far from the Danube'. Both the name of Henry and the Delpheos River are obviously incorrect, and the timing seems off, but the account is, nevertheless, an important testament to Central European military plans and propaganda.[17] Heavily

---

14 I have not been able to find the papal order to the Viennese mendicants. Both Maier and Gladysz mention it (Gladysz citing Maier), but Maier points to the *Annales Wormatienses* which does not contain any reference to this letter. Maier, *Preaching the Crusades*, p. 60. Citing 'Annales Wormatienses: 873–1360', p. 47.

15 Gladysz, *The Forgotten Crusaders*, p. 261.

16 Gladysz, *The Forgotten Crusaders*, p. 260.

17 For older speculations about the mysterious Delpheos (Dnepr, Denvir = Theben): Strakosch-Grassmann, *Der Einfall der Mongolen in Mitteleuropa*, p. 142; Strakosch-Grassmann viewed the report as unfounded, pp. 135, 147. On such 'victories', see also the comments in Sinor, 'X: Les relations entre les Mongols et l'Europe', p. 45. More recently, Stephen Pow studied this mysterious reference in the context of military reality and non-Latin sources. He proposes that the 'Delpheos River, not far from the Danube' may refer to Develtos (Debeltos, Develt, etc.) in Thrace near the Sredetska River, also mentioned by Idrisi, a probable place where the Latin Empire would try to block Mongols approaching

mediated and possibly somewhat confused from the beginning, the text forms the core of the *Chronica majora*'s accounts of Christian response to the Mongol threat: the emperor's Christian response, that is. The protagonists are the imperial offspring: Henry, identified with Frederick's 'natural' son Enzio, and the child Conrad.[18]

King Béla's complaint 'nichil consolacionis vel subsidii recepimus nisi verba' stands in stark contrast with Matthew's record, and the actual preparations seem to have been limited to the defence of German lands.[19] At some point before 25 April 1241, thirteen-year-old King Conrad, the emperor's son, did institute a *Landfrieden* (territorial peace) throughout the kingdom so that forces could be concentrated against the Mongols, and appointed 1 July as the date for the crusading army to assemble at Nuremberg.[20] Within two weeks or so, he arrived at Weiden, some fifty

---

from the north. Delvetos was the border fortress between Bulgaria and the Latin Empire, in possession of the Latins. It was on the route to Constantinople, which implies that the Mongols at least entertained the possibility of sacking the city for its wealth. This, of course, means that the emperor referred to in the entry is not Frederick II. Based on narrative sources, Pow surmises that in 1240 or 1239 a substantial army of crusaders came to aid the Latins; Baldwin, for example, gathered troops from France, Flanders, and elsewhere, and returned through Germany in 1240. In any case, muddling the facts about the river was almost certainly not Matthew's doing: he probably received the story already aligned to fit Frederick's story. Pow, 'Conquest, Withdrawal, and Diplomatic Overture'.

18 The error probably stems from the fact that Enzio's name was also spelled Henthius sometimes; for example, his residence in Sassari, Sardinia, is known as the *domus domini regis Henthii*. Although not entirely erroneous (Enzio is the Italian version of Heinz, the diminutive of Heinrich), Schwammel argues that Matthew incorrectly referred to Frederick's 'natural' son Enzio of Sardinia as Henry. Schwammel, *Der Antheil des österreichischen Herzogs Friedrich des Streitbaren*, p. 18. Luard's edition also corrects the name to Enzio. This interpretation appears without comment in modern historical accounts: e.g. Rudolf, 'Die Tartaren 1241/1242', p. 95, or Jackson, 'The Crusade against the Mongols (1241)', p. 8. However, the question of when and how he could be fighting bloody battles in Central Europe seems to remain unprobed: It is known from several certifiable sources that on 3 May 1241 he attacked the Pisan fleet at the island of Giglio, capturing almost all the cardinals, a hundred high prelates, and a rich booty. See note 192, and Fig. 9 below. Matthew explains that the two deeds happened one after another: 'sent his son Henry, who had, as has been stated, conquered the prelates and their convoy, to join his brother Conrad' and his army, which may suggest that he travelled to help command Conrad's army, rather than marched with his own. MS *B*, fol. 148r, col. a; *CM*, IV, p. 130; *EH*, I, p. 356. More research is needed to find evidence for this trip outside the *Chronica majora*.

19 Rudolf, 'Die Tartaren 1241/1242', p. 88.

20 The pertinent *Military Instructions (Praecepta bellica)* were drawn up in Conrad IV's court at Esslingen on 19 May 1241: 'Principes non ineant campestre bellum cum Tartaris, sed terminos suos defendant, ne si contigeret eos succumbere, quod Deus avertat, non possent vires suas de cetero congregare. 2. Habeant balistarios. 3. Non fiat cervisia, sed frumentum servetur. 4. Non ducantur victualia ad renum, sed tantum ad loca defensionis. 5. Item habens tres marcas in redditibus habeta scutum quod dicitur setzschilt. 6. Item prohibeatur continua taberna, item vestes preciosae'. *Constitutiones et acta publica imperatorum et regum*, p. 445. This also appears as an addendum to 'Frederick II's letter to the magnates of

or more miles to the east, so it seems that the crusade was actually set in motion.[21] On 13 June, however, he was probably still busy putting his ducks in a row, since Frederick II, duke of Austria, sent him a letter from Vienna about the progress of the Mongols, in which he requests him to send troops but to kindly refrain from ravaging his lands on the way to meet the Mongols ('sine lesione terre nostre'). Frederick II of Austria also suggests sending envoys and letters to the kings of France, England, and Spain and urging them to send assistance.[22] As an incentive, he adds that the Mongols have collected booty in over forty countries by that time, so annihilating them promises to be a lucrative affair for the victors.[23] In the meantime, in Saxony, a number of princes took the cross at Merseburg.[24] Jackson, based on letters copied into the *Chronica majora*, suggests that since Henry Raspe, landgrave of Thuringia, was arranging for the preaching of the crusade in his territories at an early date, it is likely that he himself was among the *crucesignati*.[25] In reality, probably for the reasons discussed above, the zealous crusader spirit seems to have been diverted when the pope died in August 1241. In Rome, instead of

---

Swabia', in MS *OB*, fol. 5ʳ. Although the pragmatic defence instructions even concerned beer brewing, little is known about the actual preparations. Frederick's imperial order to mobilize, the 'Encyclica contra Tartaros', followed Conrad's *mandata* on 20 June. *Constitutiones et acta publica imperatorum et regum*, p. 445. Both are also in *Historia diplomatica Friderici Secundi*, v.2, pp. 1214–18.

21 Jackson, *The Mongols and the West*, p. 66. A summary of the Erfurt council by the bishop of Constance, written on 25 April, in *Historia diplomatica Friderici Secundi*, v.2, pp. 1209–14.

22 'mittendo solempnes nuncios atque scripta Franciae, Hispaniae et Angliae Regibus et ceteris nobilibus universis, qui censentur nomine christiano': no. 80 in *Árpádkori új okmánytár*, pp. 136–37.

23 'Denique tantis sciat ipsos vestra Serenitas divitiis habundare occasione quadraginta Regnorum, que per ipsos exterminium sunt experta, quod per interitum eorundem viginti Regna exaltari possunt divitiis et honore': no. 80 in *Árpádkori új okmánytár*, pp. 136–37. This is certainly at odds with the later Western descriptions, painting a picture of the Mongols as poor and living off of meagre resources. Jackson, 'Medieval Christendom's Encounter with the Alien', p. 48. Money was also a factor in proclaiming a crusade itself: 'the vows of those who were incapable of fighting could be redeemed for money payment', probably not an insignificant sum if the call indeed met with an outstanding response from all and sundry across Christian Europe. Jackson, 'The Crusade against the Mongols (1241)', pp. 7–8. With reference to the Holy Land, Matthew also mentions the possibility of redeeming crusader vows for money, in *CM*, IV, p. 133; *EH*, I, p. 359.

24 Jackson, 'The Crusade against the Mongols (1241)', p. 7. A letter from Hungarian Dominicans and Franciscans to their confreres also mentions the Merseburg gathering: 'Conuenerunt autem in Ciuitate Merseburg; ibi audierant, quod rex Hungariae scripserat Regi Boemiae, quod viribus receptis, et maximo exercitu congregato, occurrere voluisset'. *Codex diplomaticus Hungariae ecclesiasticus ac civilis*, IV.1, pp. 212–13. See Chapter 6.

25 Jackson, 'The Crusade against the Mongols (1241)', p. 7; *CM*, IV, p. 110; VI, p. 78; *EH*, I, p. 340. A Thuringian lord, the bailiff of the church of Breitungen, Thuringia, also seems to have taken the cross in 1241, in letter no. 1015: Dobenecker, ed., *Regesta diplomatica necnon epistolaria historiae Thuringiae*, p. 170.

166   CHAPTER 4

fighting the Mongols, the resources gathered were used to lead a crusade against Frederick II after the German barons revolted against Conrad in September 1241.

News of the crusade (either or both) against the Mongols in Europe reverberated in contemporary continental sources, but none describe actual military victory over them. Some sources, primarily German annals, suggest that the Hungarian and Polish defeat mobilized enthusiastic crowds to fight the intruders.[26] The Bavarian *Annales Scheftlarienses maiores* (1092–1248) report in vivid detail the fear and subsequent call for crusade in response to the news of the death of one king of Hungary and the flight of the other (Coloman and Béla IV, respectively). According to this source, the Mongols did not penetrate *ad fines nostros* ('our borders', presumably Bavaria), since they were defended by the 'right hand of God'.[27] The Swabian *Annales S. Trudperti*, composed somewhat later, also states that people, young and old alike, were enthusiastically taking the sign of the cross after the defeat of their eastern neighbours in Poland and Hungary.[28] However, not all continental sources share Matthew Paris's enthusiasm for the crusaders' victory over the Mongols. In the *Annales Garstenses (Continuatio Garstensis)*, written in Upper Austria, the annalist records that the number and variety of crusaders was overwhelming, including children and women, and reflects on the popeless crusade, explicitly stating that the crusaders lacked a leader ('quia ducem exercitus non habebant') so the military effort achieved next to nothing.[29] Instead, the Mongols withdrew either on account of their own free will or because God made them do so.[30]

---

26 Most recently summarized in Pow, 'Conquest, Withdrawal, and Diplomatic Overture'.

27 'Quorum timore omnis ecclesia turbatur et verbum crucis publice in omnibus ecclesiis predicatur, et multitudo hominum in universis mundi partibus signatur ad resistendum ipsis; sed dextra Dei nos defendente ad fines nostros non pervenerunt'. In 'Annales Scheftlarienses maiores, a. 1092–1247', p. 341.

28 'Tam iuvenes quam senes cruce signati sunt contra Tartaros'. In 'Annales Sancti Trudperti', p. 297.

29 'Continuatio Garstenses, a. 1182–1257', p. 597.

30 'Tartaris proprie voluntatis motu sive Domino disponente retroversis'. In 'Continuatio Garstenses, a. 1182–1257', p. 597. As for contemporary views on their sudden withdrawal, Stephen Pow also cites Bartholomew of Lucca (c. 1236–1327), a Dominican friar, historian, and pupil of Thomas Aquinas, who saw God's will behind events. Pow, 'Conquest, Withdrawal, and Diplomatic Overture'. 'Ut in Gestis Germanorum habetur et Martinus etiam scripsit', in Bartholomew of Lucca [Ptolemaeus], *Die Annalen*, p. 124. Also 'Tartari transeuntes montes Riffeos, qui dividunt Asiam maiorem ab Europa, ut habes in nostra Tripartita libro II, marchias Ungarorum perforant, quas ipsi Silvas vocant, totam Ungariam quasi vastant nemini parcentes sive sexui sive etati, *ut historie Germanorum tradunt*': Bartholomew of Lucca [Ptolomaeus], *Historia ecclesiastica nova*, p. 531; Bartholomew of Lucca [Ptolemaeus], *Die Annalen*, p. 110 (my italics). Although his chronicle comes from a generation after the invasion, his text probably contains vestiges of a certain *Gesta Germanorum*, which Bartholomew claims to have used as a source for his account.

Rather than explaining the seemingly rapidly evaporating Mongol threat by divine providence, Matthew Paris's narrative about Christian resistance in this phase of the Mongol military campaign certainly echoes those in the former group. Evidently using local sources from the empire for his Mongol story — not the annals, of course — Matthew could at this point refer to various accounts suggesting that the Mongols abandoned Europe on account of the threat by the emperor, who ultimately orchestrated the crusade effort by appointing his son to lead the holy troops to victory.[31] By cleverly organizing his patchwork material regarding the invasion, Matthew was able to control a fairly coherent narrative even when a story like this was at variance with other Mongol-related entries constituting the story in the *Chronica majora*.

An overview of the folios between 142[v] and 144[v], right before the Mongol clusters in 1241, reveals the rhythm that Matthew created by alternating his focus between England (the oppression by the pope) and the Continent (the conflict between pope and emperor).[32] The sufferings of the English Church under the avaricious pope (and sometimes under their own king, too) and Frederick's north Italian exploits in 1241 are woven together to create a story of conflict and resistance, in which Frederick's strife as the antithesis of the Holy See seems to vindicate and amplify the righteous dismay of the English against the pope. Despite the exciting title, for example, the entry 'De quadam visione cuidam presbytero facta Londoniis mirabili' is in fact a rather sordid story of money extortion, first by the mayor of London and then by the king himself.[33] This is then followed by six consecutive entries regarding Frederick's anti-papal campaign, supported by quoting (embedding) various speeches and letters, constructed similarly to the Mongol clusters later.[34]

---

31 MS *B*, fol. 170[v], cols a–b; *CM*, IV, pp. 298–99; *EH*, I, pp. 489–90.
32 See Appendix 3. For easier visualization, events of the imperial-papal history (last column) are shaded grey.
33 MS *B*, fol. 142[v], col. b; *CM*, IV, p. 93; *EH*, I, p. 326.
34 First, Matthew relates that the emperor forbade his prelates to assemble at the council that Gregory IX convoked: 'Quomodo imperator mutato consilio praelatos praemunivit ne ad concilium celebrandum convenirent' in MS *B*, fol. 143[r], col. b; *CM*, IV, p. 95; *EH*, I, p. 327; then he inserts a moving speech by Frederick and closes the entry by adding that the pope confirmed Frederick's excommunication. The same story continues with the pope's letter to Frederick: 'Epistola consolatoria Papae admonens praelatos, ut spretis minis imperialibus ad concilium properare minime formidarent' in MS *B*, fol. 143[r], col. b; *CM*, IV, p. 96; *EH*, I, p. 329. Although it is referred to as an 'epistola consolatoria', known as a type of diplomatic missive at the time (also known as *littere consolatorie* or *deploratorie*), this letter dissents from the usual formulary. See more on this type of diplomatic correspondence in Chaplais, *English Diplomatic Practice in the Middle Ages*, pp. 83–85. In a brief 'Continuatio', the outcome of the exchange is explained, with special emphasis on the bishop of Norwich. MS *B*, fol. 143[v], col. a; *CM*, IV, p. 98; *EH*, I, p. 330. The passage spills over to the bottom margin. The bishop of Norwich features again not long after this; see note 45 below.

168   CHAPTER 4

Frederick's story begins in earnest when he is described reaching Faenza, in a dramatic entry whereby Matthew recounts a speech by Frederick given to the women of the city who come begging him to let the city go unharmed. Note the phrase 'dignitati regiae, vel saltem sexui non parcentes', used by Matthew to describe cruelty inflicted upon civilians, all too familiar in the story of the Mongols that is about to start.[35] Juxtaposing Frederick's questionable but larger-than-life deeds and the pope's even more questionable and clearly miserly conduct, Matthew continues with the sufferings of the city of Faenza followed by the Roman court likened to a harlot on account of 'Romanae ecclesiae insatiabilis cupiditas'.[36] This, again, is followed by an entry in which Matthew takes the thread about papal avarice back to England: the pope demands a revenue of a hundred marks from the monks of Peterborough.[37] After the pope's demands imposed on Peterborough, Matthew steers the story to Canterbury, where the next two entries take place.[38]

With a short note about Richard of Cornwall's successful efforts to bring peace to Provence, Matthew's narrative leaves the shores of England again for another couple of entries about Frederick's movement in Europe and beyond.[39] The first one relates the 'intense and obstinate attacks' of the

---

35 See the same phrase used to describe the Mongols repeatedly in Appendix 8, available online, <https://doi.org/10.1484/A.14453112>.

36 'De miseria Foegiae civitatis Ytalicae jam diu obsessae'. MS *B*, fol. 143ᵛ, col. b; *CM*, IV, p. 98; *EH*, I, p. 331. 'Quam venalis facta est eo tempore curia Romana, et inhians et confidens in pecunia consimilis facta est meretrici prostanti'. *CM*, IV, p. 100; *EH*, I, p. 332.

37 'Dominus Papa petiit a monachis de Burgo annuum redditum centum marcarum de aliqua ecclesia'. MS *B*, fol. 144ʳ, col. a; *CM*, IV, p. 101; *EH*, I, p. 332. It is notable that Matthew (or his collaborator) erased the harsh criticism about the Roman court on this folio and the original text survived only in MS *C*. In MS *B*, however, no one filled the scrubbed page with text until a passage was written over the erasure by a hand from Matthew Parker's time. For Matthew Parker's interventions, see Chapter 7 below.

38 St Edmund becomes distinguished by miracles: 'De gloriosa fama signipotentissimi Aedmundi Cantuariensis archiepiscopi et confessoris'. MS *B*, fol. 144ʳ, col. a; *CM*, IV, p. 102; *EH*, I, p. 334. The monks of Canterbury obtain absolution from the pope and elect Boniface as their archbishop, who was 'totally incompetent, compared with the archbishops his predecessors, for such a dignified station': 'Quomodo monachi Cantuariae beneficium absolutionis a domino Papa impetrarunt, et quomodo Bonefacium electum Ballay avunculum reginae secundum regis desiderium et preces elegerunt'. MS *B*, fol. 144ʳ, col. b; *CM*, IV, p. 103; *EH*, I, p. 334. This entry is severely edited; see Luard's edition providing both versions of the text: *CM*, IV, pp. 104–05. Manuel Muñoz Garcia attributes the writing over the erasures to a separate hand, identified as Hand 5, the scribe of stints ranging from a few lines to a number of leaves between fols 144ʳ and 236ʳ in the manuscript. Muñoz García also found the same hand in three other manuscripts, MSS *LA*, *AC*, and *B*. Muñoz García, 'The Script of Matthew Paris and his Collaborators', pp. 191, 241.

39 'De oppressione comitis Provinciae'. MS *B*, fol. 144ᵛ, col. a; *CM*, IV, p. 105; *EH*, I, p. 336. It is notable that this piece of information is also closely connected to Frederick, as Matthew describes that it was upon his exhortations that the count of Toulouse (Raymond VII, r. 1222–1249) was raiding the lands of Ramon Berenguer IV, count of Provence. Raymond

Venetians on Frederick,[40] and the second one enumerates the previously noted 'six wars' in which Frederick is embroiled in one way or another.[41] This is where Matthew Paris begins dovetailing his Mongol material with Frederick's other exploits, alternating his deeds in Italy (Faenza and his conflict with the pope) with his remote commitment to and involvement by proxy in the Mongol cataclysm threatening his empire and Christendom at large.

Within this oscillating narrative wrought out of two strands, the Mongol story in 1241 is introduced in the form of two contiguous clusters of entries. These entries are all part of Frederick's story: the imperial strand. On the one hand, Matthew proves to be adept at the art of relevance, not only making sense of the Mongol story in the European framework this way, but also using the episodes to enrich, underpin, and illustrate the imperial story — alternating with the not entirely unrelated domestic story of England's dealings with the pope. On the other hand, regarding the selection of topics within the imperial-papal strand, it is notable that Matthew often worked from ready material, pre-selected and arranged bundles that were already associated by the time they landed in his hands. The German origin of the news about the Mongol campaign's progress renders the perspective consistent. The motives and consequences of the stakeholders in the Mongol story were coded into the received material.

As Appendix 4 shows, the first long cluster about the Mongol threat is presaged in a catalogue of Frederick's six theatres of war, some of which are described in detail in subsequent entries relating parallel events.[42] Zooming in on the two clusters of Mongol-related texts between fols 144^v and 148^r, all under the year 1241, the deconstruction of the complex patchwork of colligated texts that helps to disentangle Matthew's use of vicarious information can also be used to reveal layers of sources, perspectives, and networks that supplied St Albans with continental news in the second half of the 1240s.

---

of Provence (r. 1217 or 1220–1245) was the father of all queens of consequence at the time: Margaret, Eleanor, and Beatrice were the respective wives of Louis IX of France, Henry III of England, and Charles I of Sicily. The entry is dated under 1241, and Matthew — probably to avoid prolepsis — does not mention that Sanchia was originally engaged to Raymond VII of Toulouse but married Richard, earl of Cornwall, on 23 November 1242.

40 'Veneti pro nece Potestatis Mediolanensis filii ducis Venetorum guerram continuant contra imperatorem.' MS B, fol. 144^v, col. a; CM, IV, p. 106; EH, I, p. 336.

41 'De captione Foegiae civitatis Ytaliae et de multiformi sollicitudine imperatoris ut se defenderet contra multos rebelles.' MS B, fol. 144^v, col. a; CM, IV, p. 106; EH, I, p. 336.

42 MS B, fol. 144^v, cols a–b; CM, IV, pp. 106–07; EH, I, pp. 336–37.

170   CHAPTER 4

As explained in the above-mentioned 'summary entry' about Frederick's various military fronts, 'de multiformi sollicitudine imperatoris ut se defenderet contra multos rebelles', the Mongol subplot is merely one of the many elements that make up Frederick's story at this point. The juxtaposition — or to revisit Morgan's term, 'colligation' — of entries about events taking place in various geographical locations and the Mongol clusters comprise the narrative of Frederick II's exploits across a large swathe of Christendom:[43]

> tertium, cum Conrado filio suo, haerede Jerusalem, qui secum traxit exercitum inaestimabilem et innumerabilem ex tota Alemannia et finibus adjacentibus et imperiali potestati pertinentibus, contra Tartaros, ipso eodem Conrado existente capitali, concomitantibus ducibus Austriae, Saxoniae, Baivariae, et aliis magnatibus, tam praelatis quam aliis, quos longum est numerare, cum populari multitudine cujus non erat numerus, qui omnes uno humero, et alacri voluntate crucesignati contra dictos Tartaros, pro universali ecclesia dimicaturi, pro capitibus communiter parabantur.

> > (a third army, under his son, Conrad, heir to the kingdom of Jerusalem, who had collected under him an innumerable army from the whole of Germany and adjacent provinces under the imperial dominion, he had sent against the Tartars, his son Conrad being the commander-in-chief, but accompanied by the dukes of Austria, Saxony, and Bavaria, and other nobles, prelates, and others, too numerous to mention, and followed by an innumerable host of people, who had all with one accord voluntarily and eagerly assumed the cross, and were prepared to fight to the death against the said Tartars on behalf of the Church universal.)[44]

Right before the first Mongol cluster Matthew briefly revisits England to recount the king's act of might in the repercussions of the election of the bishop of Winchester ('De constantia et oppressionibus monachorum Wintoniensium'),[45] but after this brief digression, Frederick II takes over

---

43 Colligation is not simply positioning various elements together to make up a whole but bringing (isolated facts) together by an explanation or hypothesis that applies to them all — in this case, Frederick's rebellion against the avarice of the papal court. Morgan, 'Narrative Ordering and Explanation'; for more on using the term 'colligation', see Chapter 1 ('Mise-en-abîme Within and Without').

44 This passage is highlighted by a marginal rubric 'Vel Faventiae imperatoris' in red ink, on MS B, fol. 144ᵛ, cols a–b; CM, IV, pp. 106–07; EH, I, pp. 336–37.

45 MS B, fol. 144ᵛ, col. b; CM, IV, pp. 107–08; EH, I, pp. 337–38. William de Raleigh, bishop of Norwich (formerly the treasurer of Exeter Cathedral), was translated to the see of Winchester on 1 September 1242, but Henry III objected and appealed to Pope Innocent IV, who rejected the appeal. More on William and his network in Vincent, 'The Politics of Church and State as Reflected in the Winchester Pipe Rolls'.

the stage nearly singlehandedly — the story alternating between the Italian theatre of war and the fight against the Mongols. The Mongol episodes serve to illustrate Frederick's valiant efforts to defend Christendom, and at the same time, they draw attention to the raw power of Frederick, the *stupor mundi*, whose force (commanding his sons) is equal to the Mongol onslaught. First, the emperor takes the city of Faenza. Drawing up a not so subtle parallel between his vengeful speech to the women of Faenza in a previous entry, and of the Mongols' barbarian mercilessness described thereafter, Frederick finally emerges as a figure of forgiveness. He spares the inhabitants this time: 'Tunc enim demum sanguis generosus cum se viderit de rebellibus triumphasse' (seeing that he had triumphed over the rebels, his generous blood inclined to mercy).[46]

The complex series of entries that follows (referred to as the first Mongol cluster here) is wrought out of at least four different sources and glued together by the narrator's own voice reporting about the escalating Mongol offensive in the context of receiving and disseminating news by Christian rulers. As can be seen in Appendix 4, between the two Mongol clusters of Frederick's story, the chronicler revisits the matters of Gregory IX's council in the usual form of back-and-forth exchange of verbal and physical atrocities. This is followed by the story of Enzio's capture of the legates and prelates on the Tyrrhenian Sea: the emperor orders the prelates to be captured, and his son, Enzio, hijacks them at sea.

The plot of the prelates and their capture concludes with an imperial letter sent to the English king from Faenza, followed by the second, much shorter cluster of Mongol-related episodes consisting of two entries — the one where Henry (Enzio) is sent to assist his brother Conrad against the Mongols,[47] and the one about the 'enormous wickedness of the Jews'.[48] This cluster marks the end of Frederick's story for now. The narrative returns to English affairs, for instance, relating how people were absolved from their vow of assuming the cross and fighting in the Holy Land, on

---

46 In the entry entitled 'Quomodo capta civitate Foegiae imperator civibus pepercit'. MS *B*, fol. 144ᵛ, col. b; *CM*, IV, pp. 108–09; *EH*, I, p. 338.

47 'Quomodo captis et incarceratis legatis et praelatis ei qui cum ipsis fuerunt, Henricus filius imperatoris ad Conradum mittitur in adjutorium contra Tartaros et Cumanos'. MS *B*, fol. 148ʳ, col. a; *CM*, IV, p. 131; *EH*, I, pp. 356–57. The framed marginal rubric, 'Et cito post, dominus Praenestinus, obediens domino Papae usque ad mortem, a nequam saeculo transivit ad requiem', next to the heading of this entry is in fact the last sentence of the previous one about the hijacked prelates. Together with the two previous bas-de-page rubrics about the captives' misery, its presence suggests that Matthew revisited the prelates' story at least once and added texts that he clearly had no room for because the Mongol/ Cuman entry was already written contiguously afterwards.

48 'De quodam immani scelere Judaeorum'. MS *B*, fol. 148ʳ, cols a–b; *CM*, IV, p. 131; *EH*, I, pp. 357–58.

172   CHAPTER 4

payment of a sum of money;[49] and events important on the national scale, such as the confirmation of Master Nicholas of Farnham in the bishopric of Durham,[50] and the death of Earl Gilbert, marshal.[51]

Alternating Mongol-related material and episodes of Frederick's anti-papal campaign in the Italian peninsula thus forms the backbone of Frederick's story. In turn, the resulting plot of the emperor's exploits is alternated with entries of English relevance. The recursive use of alternation creates a rhythm and maintains a relatively tight control over the scope of the material entered in this part of the chronicle. The same dynamic is detectable inside the entries, lending them depth and a sense of authenticity by serial embedding of reported and direct speech, and by framing the entries by Matthew's own cohesive passages — thus creating the pleasing impression of mise-en-abîme.[52] Recursivity can be detected in the internal structure of the individual entries too. The following detailed examination of the dizzying narrative layers of the first cluster allows a glimpse into how Matthew's consistent (or is it orthodox and uninspired?) use of a handful of narrative devices carries to the configuration of the smallest units and the lowest narrative levels.

The First 1241 Cluster

Under the year 1241, the Mongol material is thus inserted into the story of the emperor and the pope in the form of two self-contained units: a longer and a shorter cluster of contiguous and conjoined entries. Even though the script and the layout reveals no segmentation, they certainly do not come from a single source: nearly all of Matthew's storylines reveal a complex

---

49 'Quomodo de cruce accipienda praedicabatur. Et statim votum pro pecunia data remittebatur'. MS B, fol. 148^r, col. b; CM, IV, p. 133; EH, I, p. 359.

50 'De confirmatione magistri N. de Fernham in episcopi Dunelmensem'. MS B, fol. 148^v, col. a; CM, IV, p. 134; EH, I, p. 359.

51 'De miserabili morte comitis Gileberti Marescalli'. MS B, fol. 148^v, col. a; CM, IV, p. 135; EH, I, p. 360. These events are not only marked in the usual way on the margin — mitre and staff for the episcopal election (previous note); reversed shield, sword, and spear for Marshall's death — but there is also an unframed illustration of Gilbert's fall from his horse at the bottom of the folio. The next English entry once again underpins the perennial complaint, the pope's avarice: how two of the pope's clerks exacted money throughout the whole of England and in Ireland for the use of his holiness. 'Quomodo colligebatur pecunia per totam Angliam ad opus Papae iterum ad expugnandum imperatorem per Petrum Rubeum et Petrum de Supino'. MS B, fol. 148^v, col. b; CM, IV, p. 137; EH, I, p. 361. This concerns Frederick indirectly, since the money extorted was supposed to go for the fight against him ('ad expugnandum imperatorem'), although this is only stated in the heading, not in the entry itself.

52 See the discussion of mise-en-abîme framing the analytical chapters in the present book, in Chapters 1 and 7.

system of various viewpoints, not always synchronized to create a homogeneous focus.[53] Besides simply ordering the entries in a particular sequence (colligation), Matthew often adds more detail and depth by embedding episodes or material from diverse sources into contiguous texts conceived as an entry. Perhaps the most complex embedding out of all the entries constituting the Mongol story is the first self-contained Mongol cluster under the year 1241. This first cluster is a long build-up to the second: the ravages described, as well as the consternation and increasingly zealous exchanges between crowned monarchs and lesser players in European politics comprise a lengthy and detailed introduction to the second, more reticent report about how 'the hostile army, although almost innumerable, was repulsed'.[54]

As shown in Figure 5, the first cluster is actually composed out of five separate but contiguous entries connected by the narrators' linking sentences explaining the logical link between them (marked as MP): (a) Matthew's brief description of the 'dreadful ravages committed by the Tartars' serves as preface to (b) Henry Raspe's letter to the duke of Brabant on the same subject (*super praedictis*).[55] The letter itself is followed by Matthew's own words and the embedded exchange of Louis IX and his mother, Queen Blanche, also *super praedictis* as part of the same entry.[56] Next, (c) the emperor's letter concerning the approach of the Mongols is followed by (d) a brief report about the dissemination of the letter, written in two separate entries.[57] Still very much about the subject of Frederick's involvement with the Mongol threat, (e) fake news about the 'the machinations of the emperor' closes the sequence.[58]

---

53 Cf. the merciful Frederick II in 'demum sanguis generosus cum se viderit de rebellibus triumphasse' and the very same person as 'dominus Sathanae': MS *B*, fol. 144ᵛ, col. b, and fol. 146ᵛ, col. b; *CM*, IV, pp. 108, 121; *EH*, I, pp. 338, 349, respectively. This is often attributed to uncritical handling of sources in modern scholarship, e.g. 'But although Matthew realized the value of documents in substantiating his narrative, he had little critical sense about them. [...] In fact, Matthew's critical powers are less remarkable than his wide range of interests and almost unlimited curiosity'. Gransden, *Historical Writing in England*, I, p. 361.

54 MS *B*, fol. 148ʳ, col. a; *CM*, IV, p. 131; *EH*, I, pp. 356–57.

55 'De horribili vastatione inhumanae gentis quae Tartari nuncupantur'. MS *B*, fol. 145ʳ, col. a; *CM*, IV, p. 109; *EH*, I, pp. 338–39; followed by 'Literae transmissae ad ducem Braibanniae super praedictis'. MS *B*, fol. 145ʳ, cols a–b; *CM*, IV, pp. 109–12; *EH*, I, pp. 339–41.

56 The French king's exchange is written contiguously as part of the entry containing the Brabant letter but a red rubric, 'Dictum regis Francorum notabile', on the margin guides the reader to the French king's words.

57 'Epistola imperatoris de adventu Tartarorum' MS *B*, fols 145ʳ, col. b–146ʳ, col. b; *CM*, IV, pp. 112–19; *EH*, I, pp. 341–47. 'Publicatur haec epistola missa pluribus principibus'. MS *B*, fol. 146ᵛ, col. a; *CM*, IV, p. 119; *EH*, I, p. 347.

58 'Oritur mala super his suspicio'. MS *B*, fol. 146ᵛ, col. a; *CM*, IV, pp. 119–20; *EH*, I, pp. 347–48.

174 CHAPTER 4

Entry	No.	Narrative components (reading left → right)
(a) Of the dreadful ravages committed by the Tartars	1	MP: 'northern' description + intro to next entry
(b) The letter to the duke of Brabant concerning the Mongols, and a dialogue between Louis IX and his mother	1	Henry Raspe's letter
	2	Henry: Mongols in Bohemia — Henry: chain backward — Henry (reported speech): Wenceslas's story about Bohemia — Henry: exhortation to crusade — Henry: Mongols in Hungary — MP: chain forward — MP: linking passage — MP: Blanche and Louis / MP (direct speech): Exchange of Blanche and Louis — MP: comment on Louis's speech — MP: chain forward + link to next entry
	3	
(c) The letter of the emperor	1	Frederick: intro — Frederick: chain backward (Stephen Báncsa) — Frederick: chain backward (Conrad and others) — Frederick: description of Mongols — Frederick: exhortatio — Frederick: date and place of issue
	2	Account of Mongol sweep — Account of three-pronged campaign — Frederick: 'Länderkatalog' from the Saladin Letter
	3	Frederick: Emergence of Mongols, campaign from Cumania to Hungary — Frederick: Three-pronged campaign — Frederick: exhortatio
(d) The publication of the foregoing letter	1	MP: chain forward + intro. to Frederick's letter — Frederick: addition to the letter addressed to the French king
(e) Suspicions of Frederick II's plot to bring on the Mongol invasion	1	MP: commentary on opinions about Frederick's letter

First cluster of contiguous entries: Frederick and the Mongols s.a. 1241

Figure 5. The narrative structure of the first 1241 cluster.

Treating the whole sequence as a unit, it starts with a generic reminder about the Mongols and ends with a similar, albeit more detailed, description in the context of the 'Mongol-Jewish Plot'.[59] Between these two, Matthew provides the reader with a vivid report of the European response to the threat, in which he has the opportunity to quote near-witnesses and authorities in order to illustrate the depravity of the 'impious hordes'. Nevertheless, this sequence is primarily about the 'telephone tree', an emergency chain of communication, of European monarchs and the Church.

Henry Raspe's Letter

At the heart of the first cluster stands an oddly constructed, long entry, disguised as a simple letter by its header, 'Literae transmissae ad ducem Braibanniae super praedictis'. The microcosm of this 'letter' is made up of various pieces of embedded texts, a small-scale model of higher levels of the chronicle narrative. The first 1241 cluster of Mongol-related entries operates on many levels, quoting or embedding passages in various ways. In fiction, these can be labelled as the extradiegetic, intradiegetic, and metadiegetic narrative levels. In a serially embedded text, the metadiegetic narrative level is one embedded within the intradiegetic level, which is likewise embedded within the extradiegetic level.[60] Thus, a metadiegetic narrative is essentially a story within a story within a story, and in this vein, the first cluster is organized in a way which roughly resembles embedded fiction. Borrowing terminology from the world of fictional narratives, Matthew's account may thus be seen as the 'extradiegetic narrative': it is the voice of the author who narrates a story from outside the fictional universe of a particular text (marked as Level 1 in Figure 5). For example, the first entry is told in the narrator's voice, recapping some of the previous information in a short summary:

> Dierum autem ipsorum curriculo, gens ilia inhumana et feralis, exlex, barbara, et indomita, quae Tartari nuncupantur, temerario ac violento impetu terras Boreales et Aquilonares Christianorum horribili exterminio devastantes, toti Christianitati non mediocrem timorem et horrorem incusserunt. Jamjam Frisiam, Guthiam, Poloniam, Boemiam, et utramque Hungariam pro majori parte inaudita tyrannide, principibus, praelatis, civibus, et colonis effugatis et trucidatis, quasi in eremum redegerunt. Cujus rei eventui testimonium literarum ad

---

59 The term used in Menache, 'Tartars, Jews, Saracens and the Jewish-Mongol "Plot" of 1241'.

60 'Genette explains that metadiegetic (or second-degree) narrative bears either an explanatory, a thematic or an enunciative (rather than content-based) relation to the primary narrative'. Pier, 'Metalepsis', p. 191; citing Genette, *Narrative Discourse*, pp. 232–34.

176   CHAPTER 4

citeriores partes transmissarum evidens testimonium perhibebat, sub hac forma.

> (During all this time that inhuman and brutal, outlawed, barbarous, and untameable people, the Tartars, in their rash and cruel violence, visited the northern provinces of the Christians with dreadful devastation and destruction, and struck great fear and terror into all Christendom. Already had they, with unheard-of tyranny, in a great measure reduced to a desert the countries of Friesland, Gothland, Poland, Bohemia, and both divisions of Hungary, slaying or putting to flight princes, prelates, citizens, and rustics. This occurrence is evidently testified by the following letter, which was sent into these parts.)[61]

Within the story of the Mongols as told by Matthew — based on received material but related in the voice of an omniscient narrator who is not part of his narration — there is an embedded story: Henry Raspe's letter, which may be considered the intradiegetic layer (marked as Level 2 in Figure 5). It is related by an intradiegetic narrator who exists within the storyworld of a particular text (he features in the chronicle as a character in his own right) and transmits a story that is framed by the extradiegetic narrative level. Although the epistolic form of Raspe's account of the Mongol advance does not lend itself to further embedding easily, Raspe expressly quotes his 'cousin' Wenceslas using indirect speech, offering the reader his story even closer to the fire (metadiegetic level).[62] Wenceslas's information is wrapped in Henry's letter, inside Matthew's Mongol story. Letters containing copies of other letters were not Matthew's invention.[63] Rather, he exploited and multiplied the embedded structure of received

---

61 MS B, fol. 145ᵣ, col. a; CM, IV, p. 109; EH, I, pp. 338–39.

62 Wenceslas I of Bohemia, though distantly related on the maternal line through Philip of Swabia, was not Henry Raspe's cousin. Later, in 1242, they were, however, politically paired by Frederick II to act as co-regents for his underaged son, Conrad — the very same Conrad who, in the *Chronica majora*, is shown to organize armed response to imminent Mongol attacks in Germany.

63 For example, Henry Bainton's comprehensive overview of epistolary documents in the chronicle texts of Roger of Howden, Ralph de Diceto, and Stephen of Rouen describes how epistolary documents functioned as 'narrative intertexts'; that is, not simply 'evidence' or truth claims deployed to authenticate a history writer's own narrative but complex and self-conscious texts that negotiate the potentially fictive nature of documentary intertexts, within the potentially fictive nature of the historiographical discourse that frames them. Bainton explains in detail how his approach to the embedding of epistolary documents is indebted to approaches growing out of the works of Ricoeur, Barthes, and White. Bainton, 'Epistolary Documents in High-Medieval History Writing'.

materials in his own narrative, which resulted in at least one additional narrative layer.[64]

While Matthew's preface harkens back to the previously discussed pre-invasion Mongol entries, especially the (last) mention of Friesland, Gothland, and *both divisions* of Hungary (i.e. major and minor), here the story gets closer and closer to the afflicted lands through embedding or moving through narrative layers.

> Dilecto ac semper diligendo domino et socero suo, illustri principi duci Braibanniae H[enricus] Dei gratia Longrathungiae comes, palatinus Saxonum, paratam ad beneplacita serviendi voluntatem. Pericula antiquitus in scripturis sanctis praedicta, peccatis nostris exigentibus, nunc pullulant et erumpunt. Quaedam enim gens crudelis et innumerabilis, exlex et effera, vicinos nobis terminos invadit et occupat, et jam usque ad terram Polonorum pervenit, terris multis aliis peragratis et populis exterminatis. Super quibus tam per nuntios proprios, quam per regis Boemiae dilecti consanguinei nostri plenius certificati et vocati sumus, ut in ipsius succursum et fidelium defesionem festinanter accingamur. Veraciter enim et plene nobis constat, quod eadem gens Tartarorum circiter octavas Paschae terras Boemiorum crudeliter et impetuose invadet, quibus si non subveniatur tempestive, stragem facient inauditam. Et quia jam paries nobis proximus succenditur, et terra vicina patet vastationi, et aliquae jam vastantur, auxilium et consilium Dei et fratrum vicinorum pro universali ecclesia anxie et flebiliter invocantes postulamus.

> > (Henry, by the grace of God, count of Thuringia,[65] palatine of Saxony, to his well-beloved and always to be beloved lord and father-in-law, the illustrious duke of Brabant, good-will in his service whenever he shall demand it. The dangers foretold in the

---

64 A similar case was examined in relation with the first mention of the Mongol threat in the *Chronica majora, s.a.* 1237, where Matthew's entry contains Godfrey's letter, which, in turn, quotes Prior Philip's letter. See Chapter 3 ('1237: Chaldeans, Medes, Persians, and Armenians'). The examination of these *rescripta* in the *Chronica majora*, as epistolary and rhetorical production, is not within the purview of the present volume, but since Matthew's historiographical practice relied on them to a great extent, and contemporary *ars dictaminis* strongly affected — if not shaped — the narrative of Matthew's chronicle, this kind of research is necessary in the future to explore themes such as '"intertextuality", "discourse", "genre", the "author" and the "public", "plot", "intrigue" and "narrative structure", "self-identification" and "representation" or the use of irony, topoi, figures of speech, rhythmical clausulae and arithmetic rhythms' of the original letters and their influence on the *Chronica majora*. The potential aspects of such a 'letter-oriented' approach are summarized as above in Ysebaert, 'Medieval Letters and Letter Collections as Historical Sources', p. 37.

65 The original text's 'Longrathungiae comes' refers to Thuringia rather than Lotharingia (Lorraine) suggested both by Luard's transcription and J. A. Giles's translation, taken over by many scholars uncritically. See note 71.

Scriptures in times of old, are now, owing to our sins, springing up and breaking out; for a cruel and countless horde of people, outlawed and wild, is now invading and taking possession of the territories adjoining ours, and has now, after roving through many other countries, and exterminating the inhabitants, extended their incursions as far as the Polish territory. Of these matters we have been fully informed, as well by our own messengers as by the letters of our beloved cousin, the king of Bohemia, and have been called on to prepare ourselves with all haste to proceed to his assistance, and to the defence of the Christians. For we are truly and plainly informed by him that this said race of people, the Tartars, will, about the octaves of Easter, cruelly and impetuously invade the Bohemian territory, and if seasonable assistance be not given to the Bohemians, an unheard of slaughter will take place.[66] And as the house adjoining our own is already on fire, and as the neighbouring country is open to devastation, whilst some countries are even now being ravaged, we, on behalf of the Church universal, anxiously invoke and beg assistance and advice from God and our neighbouring brother princes.)[67]

Stepping out of Wenceslas's metadiegetic story world, Henry continues with his own plea, looking at the threat from his own standpoint. As will be shown in the discussion of the next entry below (Frederick's letter), exhortation to join a cause as an ally or to offer auxiliary troops was an established letter type at the time, which adhered to its own rhetorical conventions.[68] Henry Raspe's brief exhortation informs the addressee(s) about his own efforts, helped by the Church and the mendicant orders, to raise the banner of a crusade against the Mongols:

Et quia mora plena est periculo, omni vos qua possumus rogamus diligentia, ut in nostrum succursum tam pro vestra quam nostra

---

66 Duke Henry II (the Pious) of Silesia, Wenceslas's brother-in-law, initially asked his help in fighting off the Mongols but did not wait for his troops which resulted in the devastating Battle of Legnica on 9 April 1241. Wenceslas, at the time in the vicinity of Dresden, returned to his own kingdom apparently bringing reinforcement from Thuringia and Saxony. Wenceslas's call to arms is what this passage may refer to. After the battle, the army marched through Moravia without attacking fortified places until they entered Hungary at *Trenčín*. More on the Battle of Legnica in Schmilewski, ed., *Wahlstatt 1241*. The charter evidence to reconstruct Wenceslas's itinerary or the extent of the damage is very scanty, only two charters (7 May 1241 and 3 May 1247) contain any references to the Mongols' double-time march in Wenceslas's territories. *Codex diplomaticus et epistolaris regni Bohemiae*, IV.1. Summarized in Somer, 'Sources on the Mongol Invasion of the Kingdom of Bohemia in 1241'.

67 MS *B*, fol. 145ʳ, col. a; *CM*, IV, pp. 109–10; *EH*, I, p. 339.

68 See note 139. Ivo of Narbonne's letter also contains a similar section, see Chapter 5, esp. Table 2.

liberatione vos quantocius ad arma properetis, strenue praeparantes militiam copiosam, nobiles, potentes, et audaces, cum sibi subjectis populis, non segniter excitando, promptos et paratos eos, cum vobis nostros nuntios iterato direxerimus. Nos autem ministerio praelatorum nostrorum, Praedicatorum, ac Minorum, crucem facimus, quia Crucifixi res agitur, generaliter praedicari, orationes et jejunia indici, et ad bellum Jesu Christi communiter terras nostras evocari. His etiam adicimus, quod magna pars ejusdem detestabilis gentis, cum exercitu alio illis adjecto, Hungariam inaudita vastat tyrannide; adeo quod rex dicitur vix sibi partem modicam observasse. Et ut multa paucis perstringamus, adeo opprimitur et tantis et tot pressuris coangustatur ecclesia et populus Borealis et Septentrionalis, quod talibus nunquam ab initio mundi fuerit unquam flagellatus. Datum anno gratiae MCCXLL., die qua cantatur Laetare Jerusalem.

> (And as delay is pregnant with danger, we beg of you, with all possible diligence, to take arms and to hasten to our succour, as well for the sake of our freedom as for that of your own, and to use strenuous endeavours to prepare a powerful force, by arousing the powerful and brave nobles with the people subject to them, and to hold them ready and prepared till we again send our messengers to you. We are now, by the instrumentality of our prelates, and Preacher and Minorite brethren, causing a general crusade (for it is a matter connected with Christ) to be preached, prayer and fasting to be enjoined, and our territory in general to be roused to war for the sake of Jesus Christ.
>
> To this we may add, that a large horde of this detestable race of people, in conjunction with another army which is allied with them,[69] is ravaging Hungary with unheard of cruelty, to such an extent that the king is said to retain only a very small portion for himself. To sum up the matter in a few words, the Church and the people in the northern countries are so oppressed and overwhelmed with so many and such great troubles and difficulties, that they have never suffered so severely from any scourge since the

---

69 When a Mongol vanguard assaulted the fortified town of the Moravian Olmütz (according to some historians at least), already at Kłodzko/Glatz in Lower Silesia, e.g. Hartog, *Genghis Khan*, p. 173; Chambers, *The Devil's Horsemen*, p. 99. If this indeed took place, Wenceslas's Bohemian cavalry managed to ward them off, and the Mongols rode southward across Moravia to reunite with the other branch of the Mongol army. The latter was led by Batu, who had by this time annihilated the Hungarian defence in the Battle of Muhi. Jackson, *The Mongols and the West*, p. 63. This quite old hypothesis is recounted in detail and citing sources (including the *Chronica majora*) in D'Ohsson, *Histoire des Mongols*, pp. 127–31. The ultimate source, however, is Dalimil's chronicle, a fourteenth-century rhyming chronicle in Old Czech. Tomáš Somer posits that the otherwise unreliable chronicle may actually relate a real event. Somer, 'Forging the Past', p. 239.

180   CHAPTER 4

beginning of the world. Given in the year of grace 1241, on the day when is chanted, 'Let Jerusalem rejoice'.)[70]

Looking at the letter as a whole, a great deal of detail corresponds to real-world events and persons, as described in the previous section. According to Matthew, the letter was written by 'H[enricus] Dei gratia Longrathungiae comes, palatinus Saxonum', who is identical with Henry Raspe, rather than the count of Lorraine, although this may not have been obvious for Matthew.[71] Until 1241, the landgrave of Thuringia was Hermann II (28 March 1222–3 January 1241), the young son of landgrave Ludwig IV of Thuringia and St Elizabeth of Hungary, who never officially ruled without Henry Raspe during his short life. Assuming that he did not appropriate this title prematurely, the terminus post quem of this letter is 1241 when Henry Raspe officially seized the throne of Thuringia and married Beatrix of Brabant on 10 March, thus becoming formally authorized to call himself the landgrave of Thuringia in diplomatic correspondence. In fact, the very letter to his brand new father-in-law is dated to 10 March, apparently the day of his wedding.[72] This one is not the only letter associated with Henry Raspe that Matthew had access to: a full letter from Henry II of Brabant addressed to Henry Raspe is copied into the *Additamenta*, in which he recounts the invasion of 'all Russia and Poland as far as the confines of the kingdom of Bohemia, and the middle part of Hungary'.[73]

Henry Raspe's letter is emphatically written about the affliction 'in the north' ('populus Borealis et Septentrionalis')[74] spreading like wildfire towards the lands of the German aristocracy and effecting a call for crusade:

---

70 MS B, fol. 145ʳ, cols a–b; CM, IV, pp. 109–11; EH, I, pp. 339–40.

71 Henry Raspe was Ludwig IV's brother, thus Hermann's uncle. He assumed the regency when Hermann was four, and some claim that he poisoned his nephew to fully seize the reign over Thuringia in 1241 (see, e.g. Döring, *Der Thüringer Chronik*, p. 285). The letter is addressed to the sender's father-in-law, Henry II, duke of Brabant. In 1241, Henry Raspe married his third wife, sixteen-year-old Beatrix (1225–1288), one of the daughters of Henry II of Brabant. Even though scholars, for example, Karl Rudolf and Hans-Eberhard Hilpert, have long corrected the sender's mistaken identity, some publications using only English-language sources still gloss over this important point. Rudolf, 'Die Tartaren 1241/1242', p. 97. Although without explanation, Hilpert also identifies the sender as Henry Raspe. Hilpert, *Kaiser- und Papstbriefe*, p. 156. Although probably not the case, it must be noted that letter collections compiled to assist in practising the *ars dictamini* quite liberally modified or truncated the names in the *salutatio*.

72 Laetare Sunday, the fourth Sunday of Lent, fell on 10 March in 1241. It was a busy day for Henry: Rudolf also quotes charters that confirm that he gave a castle and two cities to his new wife on this day. Rudolf, 'Die Tartaren 1241/1242', p. 97.

73 MS LA, fol. 86ʳ, cols a–b; CM, VI, pp. 76–78; EH, III, pp. 450–51. More on this letter in Chapter 6 below.

74 'et septentrionalis' is added separately on the margin. It is unlikely that Henry Raspe, with his court in Thuringia, would refer to the progress of the Mongols to Bohemia as the north, but it makes sense in Matthew Paris's chronicle world; see Chapter 1.

'causing a general crusade [...], prayer and fasting to be enjoined, and our territory in general to be roused to war for the sake of Jesus Christ'. This probably refers to Conrad IV's armies marching towards Nuremberg in July 1241 and may be in reference to Raspe's own intention to take the cross against the Mongols.[75] The communication chain, which is of special importance for the report, started with the king of Bohemia, who notified his co-regent Henry Raspe. Wenceslas, the king of Bohemia, did in fact send missives about the Mongol threat to the Holy Roman Empire. One of these, written to Conrad IV, whose regent was Henry Raspe at the time, survives from 1241, but later than the letter alluded to in Raspe's.[76] The chain is continued by a brief note reporting that the duke of Brabant informed in this way further important persons, including the king of England. In this linking passage Matthew switches to his own extradiegetic voice and closes the letter with a sentence set apart by a blue initial *S* (although not starting in a new line or new paragraph): 'et is [sic] fuit [tenor] literarum transmissarum ad episcopum Parisiensem ex parte ducis Braibantiae. Simili modo scriptum est regi Anglorum ex parte archiepiscopi Coloniensis' (Letters of similar purport were also sent by the duke of Brabant to the bishop of Paris; and the archbishop of Cologne also wrote to the king of England to the like effect).[77] This sentence also bears out Hilpert's suggestion that Matthew had no access to Henry III's correspondence, so he sought his material about the king's involvement in various events elsewhere.[78] Legate Otto is explicitly named as the source for Matthew's Mongol information in 1241 on the margin of folio 145[r]

---

75 See note 25 above, as well as the discussion of Henry Raspe's other letter in the *Additamenta*, in Chapter 6.

76 Later dating is suggested by the fact that it refers to the death of the Polish duke and the Mongols' return to Hungary: 'que interfecto Duce Poloniense reversa est in Hungariam ad exercitum sue gentis copiosum et fortem' as well as noting that since Easter ('a tempore paschali') he has learned the cruel ways of the Mongols, seeing their ravages on the borders of Poland, Moravia, and Hungary, as well as Austria. In this later letter, Wenceslas also says that he is about to set off to fight in Hungary and will be back with more news after his return, if God wills. 'Cum autem jam procedamus in Ungariam et vestram forte moram trahere contigerit Excellentiam, si vestre placuerit Celsitudini reditum nostrum exspectabitis, ut si sani per Dei graciam reversi fuerimus, nos possimus et sciamus de singulis plenius expedire'. *Árpádkori új okmánytár*, pp. 134–35. This, however, is not known to have taken place.

77 Starting with a blue initial *S*. MS *B*, fol. 145[r], col. b; *CM*, IV, p. 111; *EH*, I, p. 340. Also note that the destination of the 'Tartar hostage' allegedly sent to the duke of Brabant by the Hungarian king was Paris, although no other documents survive concerning this person and his trip westwards. Rachetta, 'Paris, 1244', p. 254.

78 See more on Matthew's ego-network in Chapter 2 ('England in the European Networks'). More recently, albeit in a study only tangentially touching upon the issue of Matthew's sources, Heather Blurton suggests that Matthew must have obtained the letters from his association with the royal chancery. Blurton, *Cannibalism in High Medieval English Literature*, p. 82.

182 CHAPTER 4

containing Henry Raspe's first letter, but it is a later addition to the page.[79] This description of the communication chain in the letter points to the circles of the archbishop of Cologne and the duke of Brabant, rather than channels connecting Matthew to Henry Raspe.

Besides the actual letter by Henry Raspe and the closing note about its dissemination, the entry encloses various additional elements and is made up of three distinct parts. The individual blocks are not only separated from the rest of the entry in tone and focus but are also expressly marked by red and blue initials within the entry.[80] The letter itself is closed by a brief paragraph in Matthew's voice echoing the previously discussed passages about the emperor's labours to keep Europe safe from the Mongols, which is in keeping with Henry's words about calling a crusade. Placing the Mongol threat in the context of the conflict between pope and emperor, Matthew's five lines take the readers back to the theme of the previous entries, while connecting to the crusade mentioned in Henry Raspe's letter:

> Pro hac igitur immani tribulatione, et ecclesiae dampnosa, quae inter dominum Papam et dominum imperatorem orta est, discordia, indicuntur jejunia et orationes cum elemosinis largioribus diversis regionibus, ut Dominus complacatus super populum, qui magnificus hostium triumphator aeque dimicat in paucis ut multis, superbiam conterat Tartarorum.

> > (Wherefore, to heal this severe infliction, and to settle the disputes which had arisen between the pope and the emperor, fastings and prayer, with bountiful almsgiving, were enjoined on the people of the various countries, that the Lord, the mighty subduer of his enemies, who fights with few or with many, might become pacified towards his people, and crush the pride of these Tartars.)[81]

Following this brief extradiegetic linking paragraph by the historian, the third part of the entry is an exchange between Blanche and Louis IX about the necessity of crusade to thwart the Mongol advance in Europe under 1241:

> Hujus igitur Dominici furoris flagellum formidabile cum immineret populis, certificata ait mater regis Francorum, venerabilis ac Deo dilecta matrona, regina Blanchia; 'Ubi es, fili mi, rex Lodowice?' At ipse accedens, ait; 'Quid hoc, mater?' At ipsa profunda trahens suspiria in lacrimas prorupit aduberes, et licet mulier, non tamen

---

79 See text in the discussion of 'Frederick II's Letter' below, and note 121.

80 Note the alternating red and blue initials marked in the transcriptions given in notes 77, 81, 82.

81 Starting with a red initial P. MS B, fol. 145ʳ, col. b; CM, IV, p. 111; EH, I, p. 340.

muliebriter haec imminentia librans pericula, dixit; 'Quid agendum, fili carissime, super tam lugubri eventu, cujus rumor terrificus fines nostros pervolavit? Imminet nostrum omnium et sacrosanctae ecclesiae nostris temporibus exterminium generale, ex impetuoso super nos adventu Tartarorum'. Quo audito, rex voce flebili, sed non sine divino spiramine, respondit; 'Erigat nos, mater, caeleste solatium. Quia si superveniant ipsi, vel nos ipsos, quos vocamus Tartaros, ad suas Tartareas sedes unde exierunt, retrudemus, vel ipsi nos omnes ad caelum subvebent'. Ac si diceret, 'vel nos ipsos repellemus, vel si contingat nos vinci, Christi confessores vel martires ad Deum migrabimus'. Et hoc verbum nobabile atque laudabile non tantum Francorum nobilitatem, sed adjacentium finium habitatores crexit et animavit.

> (When that venerable and well-beloved servant of the Lord, Blanche, mother of the French king, was informed of this scourge of God's wrath, which was impending over the nations, she called her son to her, saying, 'King Louis, where are you, my son?' On which he approached her and said, 'What want you, mother?' She then sighed deeply and burst into tears, but, although a woman, she pondered on these imminent perils not as a woman, and said to him, 'What, my dear son, is to be done concerning these lamentable events, a frightful report of which has flown to our territories? A general destruction of us all and of the holy Church is imminent in our time, owing to the impetuous incursions of the Tartars amongst us'. The king, on hearing this, with a mournful voice, but as if by divine inspiration, replied, 'May comfort from heaven raise us up, my mother. And if these people, whom we call Tartars, should come upon us, either we will thrust them back into the regions of Tartarus, whence they emanated, or else they shall send all of us to heaven'. As though he would say, 'Either we will repulse them, or if we should happen to be conquered, we shall depart to the Lord as confessors of Christ or martyrs'. This remarkable and praiseworthy speech inspired and raised the courage, not only of the French nobility, but also of the inhabitants of the adjacent countries.)[82]

The source of this emotional vignette could be anyone in the various overlapping networks, ranging from Richard of Cornwall to the Cistercian Order. Regardless of the source, however, this piece of text further emphasizes that at this point the Mongol threat, no doubt brought on either by the pope or by the emperor (more likely, the pope), was a problem to be

---

82 Starting with a blue initial *H*. MS *B*, fol. 145ʳ, col. b; *CM*, ɪᴠ, pp. 111–12; *EH*, ɪ, p. 340.

184   CHAPTER 4

solved by the crowned heads of Christendom. If the *Chronica majora* was a movie, this entry would be read out to a montage of European rulers becoming concerned, passing on the word, and rousing their spirit to a new crusade.

It is notable that in comparison with the pathos of this conversation, Matthew's sporadic reports about Queen Blanche's attitude towards crusading efforts show ebbing enthusiasm, which probably mirrored reality. The Pastoreaux movement (1251), which Blanche initially supported but which soon went badly wrong, as well as the disappointment over Louis's defeat in the Seventh Crusade (1248–1254) were great blows to Blanche.[83] Her proceedings against the French knights who took the cross against Conrad also bear this out: she ordered the lands of all those who left France to fight the emperor to be confiscated. All these were reported by Matthew Paris,[84] showing Blanche's ever-eroding faith in the power of crusades, especially against the backdrop of Christian dissent between pope, emperor, and their complicated and changeable networks of political allies. Blanche's figure and Matthew's frequent reports about her regency are important here, as they highlight the existence of intersectional passages and entries, which belong to more than one storyline in the chronicle. Due to its placement and context, this episode is clearly part of the Mongol subplot but can also be seen as the first of many references to Blanche's indirect involvement in and commentary on various crusading efforts.[85]

Although the narrative frame in this particular entry is created around the figure of Louis, the most Christian king, the protagonist in the anecdotal episode is clearly his mother, Blanche, a relative of the English king, whose pious deeds Matthew regularly relates in the chronicle. Similar to her changing attitudes towards crusading, Minois suggests that Blanche herself appears as an ambiguous character in the *Chronica majora*.[86] It is true that in 1236, Matthew quotes the barons' slander about her: 'They were indignant', he says, 'that the kingdom of kingdoms, France, was

---

83 As Robert Lerner points out, she was further embittered by Pope Innocent's attitude towards Louis's effort. Lerner, 'The Uses of Heterodoxy', p. 201.

84 The progress of the Pastoureaux movement led by James of Hungary; Blanche's action against French knights, both under 1251: *CM*, v, pp. 246–54, 260–61, respectively.

85 Peter Jackson observes the juxtaposition of the Mongol invasion with signs of heterodoxy such as the Pastoreaux movement in contemporary chronicles which often linked the two, from the 1250s, explicitly or otherwise. While this is not found in the *Chronica majora*, two writers, in fact, suggestively move on to the Pastoureaux directly after their account of the Mongol invasion, which in the case of the *Deeds of the Bishops of Le Mans* was even removed from its chronological context to fit this logic. Jackson, *The Mongols and the West*, p. 143, citing 'Richeri Gesta Senoniensis ecclesiae', pp. 310–11, and 'Gesta Domni Gaufridi de Loduno Episcopi', pp. 499–500.

86 Minois, *Blanche de Castille*, p. 17. For more on this powerful royal woman, see also Grant, *Blanche of Castile, Queen of France*.

governed by the advice of a woman',[87] and what is more, a debauched woman, 'who, it was said, was spotted by the seed of both count [of Champagne] and legate [of the pope] and who transgressed the boundaries of modesty of widowhood'.[88] However, it is notable that these are all written in reported speech, carefully avoiding the impression that they reflect Matthew's own opinions.

Later, breaking away from these initial reports, the descriptions turn into the genuine admiration of how she runs the kingdom during the crusade of Saint Louis: 'Blanche was therefore magnanimous, woman by sex, but male by character, a new Semiramis, a blessing for the century, and she left the kingdom of France without consolation'.[89] This later sentence unpacks the brief epithet 'et licet mulier, non tamen muliebriter' in her dialogue with Louis IX, and in this context Blanche's manliness appears unquestionably positive. Interestingly, this particular line in the manuscript is written over an erasure, now illegible, which suggests that this description of the queen may be a later development, probably overwriting a previous line in a subsequent phase of revision.[90] If her 'manly' counsel in this particular passage is also interpreted as admiration, it further corroborates the theory that the passage was added at a much later date than 1241, once Matthew's sources assumed more positive overtones — probably after the queen's involvement in the crusade in the Holy Land, her warm welcome of Richard of Cornwall, and her abundant support of the Cistercian Order.

As for the intimacy of the exchange, the copious tears and the mournful voice that contradict the closing sentence about the appeal of the French royals' words are not left in there by accident. According to Sophia Menache, 'Matthew's appeal to dialogues or oral delivery also functioned as a rhetorical tool, the main purpose of which was to enrich the historical

---

87 'Indignabantur enim quod regnum regnorum, scilicet Gallia, consilio muliebri regebatur'. *CM*, III, p. 366.

88 [1230] 'Indignabantur enim talem habere dominam, quae ut dicebatur, tam dicti comitis quam legati Romani semine polluta, metas transgressa fuerat pudicitae vidualis'. *CM*, III, p. 196. This is a reiteration of earlier mentions of the scandal, e.g. [1226] 'Oriebatur interim rumor irrecitabilis ac sinister; scilicet, quod dominus legatus secus quam deceret se habebat adversus dominam Blancam. Sed impium est hoc credere, quia aemuli ejus hoc disseminaverunt. Benignus autem animus dubia in melius interpretatur'. *CM*, III, p. 119. Later Matthew quotes a couplet written about the rumoured dalliance at the university of Paris (*s.a.* 1229 in *CM*, III, p. 169), which also appears as a rumour started by the scholars of the university in Matthew's abbreviated history of England: 'Orta tunc temporis, secus quam deceret, falsa infamia de pudicitiae laesione inter legatum et reginam Blanchiam, dispersa est Parisiensum scolarium universitas'. *HA*, III, p. 254.

89 'Magnanima igitur Blanchia, sexu femina, consilio mascula, Semirami merito comparanda, valedicens saeculo, regnum Francorum omni solatio reliquit destitutum'. *CM*, V, p. 354; *EH*, III, p. 7.

90 MS *B*, fol. 145ʳ, col. b, *CM*, IV, p. 111; *EH*, I, p. 340.

narrative and further attract the reader's attention'.[91] In addition, she also points out that reported speech in medieval chronicles also had a role to 'enhance narrative reliability'.[92] While both are important aspects in employing this form of dialogue in historical writing, this particular exchange brings to mind another one regarding the Mongols: Matthew quoting an epic solution for the Mongol problem by the bishop of Winchester in 1238. As was pointed out in Chapter 3, in passages quoting direct speech, the Mongols — used by God to exact punishment on humankind — are used for character assassination committed by the person omnipotent in his own chronicle world: the author. The wisecrack of the bishop of Winchester has been shown to gain significance in view of the later stages of the Mongol story already known by Matthew Paris at the time of writing — which was to prove the bishop's theory wrong as the story unfolded. In contrast, the words of the French king are left open: since he is not the real target of the prophecy inserted in hindsight, his either/or prediction is left double-ended on purpose.

The exchange, however, looks less flattering for the 'French nobility' (*Francorum nobilitas*) in view of an entry under the year 1249. The deeds of the haughty count of Artois, mentioned in relation to the Mongols — this time in the Holy Land — makes it obvious that the 'courage raised' among the French nobility did not amount to much in the end.[93] Readers who persevered to read later years in the chronicle, or to find later references to the Mongols therein, could reach the point at which the French king receives a letter from the king of the Tartars in the Holy Land. The new setting brings together various themes repeatedly discussed in the context of the Mongol story, and uses prolepsis ('Quod veraciter evenit, sicut sequens sermo plenius elucidabit'), which is relatively rare

---

91 Menache, 'Written and Oral Testimonies in Medieval Chronicles', p. 8. She later reiterates this thought, saying 'The oral addresses or dialogues quoted by both Matthew Paris and Giovanni Villani often appear just as a subterfuge, a literary means, among others, to captivate the audiences and impart more authenticity to their reports, which remain in the main, completely imaginary. To sum up, oral addresses mainly served to manipulate existing feelings, whether hatred, latent antagonism, or unlimited support'. Menache, 'Written and Oral Testimonies in Medieval Chronicles', p. 17.

92 Menache, 'Written and Oral Testimonies in Medieval Chronicles', p. 17.

93 Originally a county of Flanders until the twelfth century, Artois belonged to the French crown at this time, the first count of Artois, Robert (I) the Good (1216–1250), prince of France, being a son of Louis VIII and Blanche of Castile. Robert died in the Seventh Crusade while leading an attack on Al-Mansurah, without the knowledge of Louis IX. Matthew reports about his exploits with little sympathy, for example, how his pride caused the massacre of his army, *CM*, v, pp. 154–65. Notably, Robert was very much part of the aristocratic network from which Matthew occasionally received information: he was married to Matilda, daughter of Henry II of Brabant and Marie of Hohenstaufen; see more on the Brabant connections in Chapter 2.

in the *Chronica majora*.[94] What is more important here is that bringing in Louis and Blanche as early as 1241 — somewhat tenuously linked to Frederick's person by Matthew's contrived postscript about the emperor's counsel to the French king — foreshadows the next stage in the Mongol story. Although cleverly juxtaposed to the German crusaders' initiative and Frederick's involvement in this instance, the French royals' crusading zeal remains oddly out of place until Matthew reintroduces the Mongol threat facing Christians in the Holy Land as the trials and tribulations of Louis IX towards the end of the decade.

The exchange between king and queen mother is not created by embedding an intradiegetic passage proper, as the narrator remains Matthew. But the exchange written in direct quotes provides a glimpse into a seemingly private conversation between the French royals, containing unusually emotive language. The last sentence, however, makes it clear that it — if not entirely the work of Matthew himself — was either meant to be public or was disseminated publicly.[95] The placement of the entry right before the emperor's letter is not a coincidence. Despite the lack of a heading to separate it from the letter of Henry Raspe, the conversation belongs with the emperor's letter, which is thus both preceded and followed by entries about Louis IX. The French king's contagious Christian zeal makes way to Frederick's sobering account not only about the Mongols but about the worrying discord among Western nations, which, as will be shown later, is then closed by Frederick addressing and advising Louis IX about the necessity of reconsidering his allegiance to the pope. These brackets around the imperial letter turn it into a dialogue between French and imperial thinking about the state of contemporary affairs.

---

94 In the entry relating how the count of Artois, in his greed, turned down the Saracens' offer to retain Damietta and demanded Alexandria to boot, Matthew writes 'Non enim debuerunt Christiani alia intentione transfretasse, nisi ut Christi adquirerent haereditatem. Sarraceni igitur ad invicem colloquentes dicebant; "Sinite modo, sinite. Superbia et avaritia, quas Christus Jesus Deus eorum maxime odit, ipsos omnes exterminabit". Quod veraciter evenit, sicut sequens sermo plenius elucidabit'. (Wherefore we believe that the Lord was offended; for the Christians crossed the sea for no other purpose than to gain possession of Christ's inheritance. The Saracens, conversing amongst themselves, said, 'Wait awhile, wait; this pride and avarice, which are especially hateful to Jesus Christ their God, will destroy them all'; and so it turned out, as the following history will fully show.) *CM*, v, p. 88; *EH*, ii, p. 320. The destruction of the count's army takes place one year later.

95 As Karl Schnith summarizes the function of such dialogues, they are motif-bound and they encapsulate the desired image of human behaviour: 'Aus der Situationsschilderung geht ein Typ des motivgebundenen Zwiegesprächs hervor, der das erstrebte Bild menschlicher Verhaltensweise in aktuelle Zeitkritik einfaßt. Politisches und Persönliches mischen sich'. Schnith, *England in einer sich wandelnden Welt*, p. 200. For more on 'eavesdropping' and the 'fiction-making' of historians incorporating letters and documents in their narratives, see Bainton, 'Epistolary Documents in High-Medieval History Writing', pp. 24–25.

188   CHAPTER 4

Matthew writes the last sentence about the king's 'remarkable and praiseworthy speech' which 'inspired and raised the courage, not only of the French nobility, but also of the inhabitants of the adjacent countries' using his own historian's voice. This is important for the narrative not only because of the omniscient historian's criticism to be rendered meaningful in retrospective, but also because it propels the chain of communication onwards. The whole entry, no more than a column and a half in the manuscript, thus merges three passages from three different sources: news from Thuringia, news about a generic European crusade, and news from the circles of the French king and his mother. These are glued to one another within the entry, as well as to the next one, by Matthew's own linking sentences which invariably stress the existence of a highly efficient information chain in Frederick's empire and beyond.[96]

As a result of being constructed out of chains of letters and *rescripta*, in Matthew's narrative, the wildfire of the Mongol threat met its match in the efficient communication of Christian princes and royals, also bolstered by 'the instrumentality of our prelates and Preacher and Minorite brethren'.[97] In this vein, he closes the entry with a final push: 'The emperor then, on hearing of these things, wrote to the Christian princes, and especially to the king of England, as follows'.[98] The news about the Mongols and the crusading zeal of those whose hearts were touched by their apocalyptic appearance is shown to spread from kingdom to kingdom faster than the Mongol threat itself — the Mongol story seems to be moving towards a tipping point. Even though Frederick's figure has been heavily looming over the narrative of the events of 1241, inserting his letter as the heart of the cluster is the first occasion when Matthew introduces Frederick II into the Mongol story — or rather, the other way round: finally slots the Mongol story into that of the emperor.

Frederick II's Letter

Henry Raspe's letter, even together with the passages added by Matthew Paris, is dwarfed by the uninterrupted monolith of the next entry in this Mongol cluster, entitled 'Epistola imperatoris de adventu Tartarorum'.

---

96 Karl Rudolf also detects Matthew's intention to use this passage to connect the story to Frederick's person: 'Das Beispiel Ludwigs IX. von Frankreich "erexit et animavit" nicht nur den französischen Adel, sondern auch die Bevölkerung der angrenzenden Länder. Als entscheidender Mann sieht der englische Chronist nur den Kaiser, der das ganze Abendland gegen die Tartaren zu mobilisieren sucht'. Rudolf, 'Die Tartaren 1241/1242', p. 94.

97 'ministerio praelatorum nostrorum, Praedicatorum, ac Minorum'. MS B, fol. 145^r, col. a; *CM*, IV, p. 110; *EH*, I, p. 340.

98 'Dominus imperator super his certificatus, principibus Christianis, praecipue regi Anglorum, scripsit sub hac forma'. MS B, fol. 145^r, col. b; *CM*, IV, p. 112; *EH*, I, p. 341.

Besides detailed eyewitness accounts such as that of Roger of Várad's *Carmen miserabile* or Thomas of Spalato's *Historia Salonitanorum*, Frederick's letter — through Matthew's transmission — has become part and parcel of the modern understanding of the events of the Battle of Muhi and its aftermath.[99] Despite the fact that it only survived in Matthew Paris's English chronicle and is obviously not the original imperial version of the letter (if such a thing ever existed), it is never not one of the sources cited in studies or source collections concerning the Mongols in Hungary.[100]

Although not as diverse as the hotchpotch of passages in Henry's letter, the missive attributed to Frederick II also reveals some of Matthew's editorial decisions as well as traces of interfering with the original text(s). While the Mongol story is entirely made up of received material, the treatment of the component texts varies in Matthew's practice. Commenting on Henry Knighton's fourteenth-century Leicester chronicle, Chris Given-Wilson notes that Knighton 'viewed newsletters as dissoluble texts, to be abridged, rearranged or epitomized in whatever fashion best suited his narrative, [and] he treated official documents such as statutes, treaties or royal letters patent as fixed texts, to be reproduced faithfully and with due acknowledgement'.[101] Similarly, Matthew's obvious precision with which he recounted statutes — for instance, the resolutions of the First Council of Lyon — seems to be a little more lax when it comes to letters, although it would be an exaggeration to accuse him of downright forgery. What he did to received material was 'contributing little more than stitches which provided continuity' and, more importantly, coherence and relevance to the rest of his narrative.[102]

The authenticity of Frederick's letter has been the subject of debate both in modern source criticism and — in a different way — in the Middle Ages, too. In a subsequent entry, a kind of postscript after Frederick's text, Matthew himself notes that the imperial letter was thought by many — admittedly not by Matthew himself — to have been written under false pretences, as part of Frederick's ploy to conceal his wicked machinations with the Mongols.[103] This accusation is clearly the opinion of the pope's

---

99 Roger of Várad [Master Roger], 'Epistle to the Sorrowful Lament'; Thomas of Spalato, *Historia Salonitanorum atque Spalatinorum pontificum*.

100 E.g. the comprehensive Hungarian collection of documentary sources about the Mongol invasion: Nagy, ed., *Tatárjárás*, pp. 50–52. A recent reappraisal of sources of and approaches to the battle also mentions it as a key document: Laszlovszky, Pow, and Pusztai, 'Reconstructing the Battle of Muhi', p. 32. It also appears as an imperial letter in nearly all national *monumenta*-type collections of medieval documents pertaining to national histories.

101 Given-Wilson, *Chronicles*, p. 16.

102 Given-Wilson, *Chronicles*, p. 16.

103 'Fuerunt namque qui dicerent, imperatorem hanc Tartarorum pestem sponte fuisse machinatum, et per hanc elegantem epistolam scelus tam nepharium nequiter palliasse'

party, which is quoted without mentioning the pope himself. Matthew goes on to say that the 'letter, too, was proved to contain falsehoods', which does not necessarily negate Frederick's authorship but allows for the possibility that the letter was written by someone lesser informed than the emperor should be.[104] Importantly, while Matthew's words cannot help certify the emperor's authorship, they indirectly indicate that he himself was not the author. The question, then, is the extent of Matthew's 'contribution' to this unique document.

Echoing Matthew's concern about the letter's authenticity, the absence of this particular letter in *regestas* and chancery collections as well as its patchwork nature have raised suspicions among modern scholars. The *Chronica majora* may well be the only source where it is preserved; however, that is insufficient grounds to suppose that the missive was completely made up by Matthew, as it has been suggested by Lewis.[105] Tampering, of course, is never altogether out of the question in the *Chronica majora*, but in this case it is probably limited to two (perhaps three) passages. First, both Luard and Liebermann note that the last part of the letter is taken from the alleged letter of Frederick I to Saladin from the year 1188, which is in the part of the chronicle that Matthew copied from Wendover.[106] Secondly, Hilpert — admitting that stylistics alone is insufficient to judge the authenticity of the passages — more recently confirmed that the text does not appear to be tampered with besides the passage from the Saladin-letter and possibly one further passage criticizing the Church.[107] Third, I propose that the sentence about 'thrusting the Tartars back into Tartarus' — wordplay very much in line with Matthew's taste — repeating the words of the French king in the previous entry is a cohesive device authored by Matthew to create a dialogue between king and emperor.[108]

(There were some who said that the emperor had, of his own accord, plotted this infliction of the Tartars, and that *by this clever letter* he basely cloaked his nefarious crime). MS *B*, fol. 146^v, col. a; *CM*, IV, p. 119; *EH*, I, p. 348 (my italics).

104 'Redarguitur enim epistola, quasi continens falsitatem'. MS *B*, fol. 146^v, col. a; *CM*, IV, p. 119; *EH*, I, p. 348. Rudolf also considers this odd sentence in the context of the originality of the letter, Rudolf, 'Die Tartaren 1241/1242', p. 95.

105 Lewis, *The Art of Matthew Paris*, p. 15.

106 Reiterated in Hilpert, *Kaiser- und Papstbriefe*, p. 153. 'Matthaeus Paris hat von dort den "Länderkatalog" übernommen, ausgeschmückt und durch die Nennung von England, Wales, Irland, Schottland und Norwegen ergänzt, so daß der gesamte Text ab CM 4, S. 118 Z. 22 als nicht authentisch zu betrachten ist; der ganze letzte Teil, und nach Ficker auch die Datierung "Datum in recessu, post deditionem et depopulationem Faventiae, tertio die Julii" ist unecht'.

107 Hilpert, *Kaiser- und Papstbriefe*, p. 154.

108 On his biblical allusions, wordplay, and love of recurring phrases and similes, see Vaughan, *Matthew Paris*, pp. 127–28.

While the limited extent of tampering with the received text exonerates Matthew to some extent, it does not mean that the letter was indeed penned by the emperor. It is most likely an amalgamation of letters and reports sent from the Continent after the first worrying news of Hungary's devastation. Whether it was the emperor's court that produced the document to be disseminated in this form is questionable, but its elements seem to be bona fide reports about Central and Western European concerns triggered by the plight of their neighbours. The fact that it was material received from areas closer to the fire is immediately underpinned by wording and content — such as 'quorum vicinitas Ruthenos, ab eis non multum distantes' or 'percurrit Hungariam, Austriae finibus vicinandam' — unusual compared to Matthew Paris's generally more generic and vague geographical definitions.

Matthew's noted stylistic idiosyncrasies are absent in the text, except for the aforementioned quip about thrusting the Tartars back into Tartarus and the Church-critical phrase in which he states that the Mongols are a punishment from God, a concept that appears elsewhere repeatedly: 'quam diversis mundo contagiis inquinato, refrigescente caritate multorum [Matthew 24. 12], per quos fides praedicari et constare deberet, et pernicioso eorum exemplo mundum usuris et variis symoniae et ambitionis generibus maculante, divino judicio credimus emersisse' (which we believe to have arisen from a divine judgement, as the world is defiled by the infection of various sins, as charity begins to grow cold in many by whom the true faith ought to be preached and upheld, and their pernicious example pollutes the world with usury and diverse kinds of simony and ambition).[109] While not entirely unique among his contemporaries reporting about the cataclysm, this sentence about the Mongols being instruments of divine judgement indirectly addresses one of the red threads running through the main narrative of the *Chronica majora*: the pope's avarice.[110]

Although he subsequently probes its authenticity from various angles (the emperor wrote it under false pretence *vs* the emperor did not write it), Matthew used the 'emperor's letter' as the main bulk of this cluster. It needed but ever so slight additions to fit into the inspired account of

---

109 MS B, fol. 146ʳ, col. b; *CM*, IV, pp. 117–18; *EH*, I, p. 346. See, for example, Henry Raspe's wording in the previously discussed letter, 'peccatis nostris exigentibus' (*CM*, IV, p. 109), as well as in a letter copied into the *Additamenta*: 'credimus ipsos esse gladium furoris Domini propter peccata populi Christiani'. Hilpert, citing Oelrichs's original observation, points out that the phrase was inserted in order to prove a connection, i.e. Matthew changed the letter, and it was not the letter's wording repeated elsewhere in the chronicle. Hilpert, *Kaiser- und Papstbriefe*, p. 154. Citing Oelrichs, 'Untersuchung der Glaubwürdigkeit des Matthäus Parisiensis', p. 129. For the discussion of the pope's greed in an earlier letter in the *Chronica majora*, see Powell, 'Patriarch Gerold and Frederick II', p. 26.

110 Referred to as 'Matthaeus Paris' Standardrepertoire an Polemik' in Hilpert, *Kaiser- und Papstbriefe*, p. 154.

the variety of opinions about the cause of the Mongol campaign — or rather, of the variety of opinions about Frederick II. Juxtaposing various explanations regarding the cause of the Mongol irruption is one of the most important functions of this cluster. Matthew flutters from one speculation to another about various European powers or God himself using the Mongols as an *instrument*. The passage about the divine punishment brought on by the sinful ways of the Church, in a way, mirrors the allegations that Frederick brought the Mongol threat upon Christian Europe, recorded on the verso of the same folio.[111]

Frederick's letter takes up three folio pages of uninterrupted text in manuscript *B*. Similar to the previous letter, this one can also be divided into passages that reveal a diversity of sources, even though it is all written in Frederick's voice, without Matthew's commentary and explanation. After the usual greeting (*salutatio*), and in line with the previous emphasis on the emergency chain of information of Western powers, Frederick's letter reiterates that it is sent to convey intelligence that he had received from elsewhere:

> Frethericus imperator, etc. regi Angliae salutem. Rem quae tam Romanum imperium, velut ad praedicationem Evangelii praeparatum, quam cuncta mundi regna Christiano cultui dicata speciali zelo contingit, toti reipublicae universae Christianitatis excidium generale comminatur, et quanquam ad nostram rei gestae veritas sero pervenerit, quin ad vestram notitiam referamus, tacere non possumus.

> (Frederick, emperor, &c., to the king of England, greeting. We cannot be silent on a matter which concerns not only the Roman empire, whose office it is to propagate the Gospel, but also all the kingdoms of the world that practise Christian worship, and threatens general destruction to the whole of Christianity: we therefore hasten to bring it to your knowledge, although the true facts of the matter have but lately come to ours.)[112]

---

111 Later, in the *Historia Anglorum*, Matthew directly implicates the pope, suggesting that in his desperate fight to overcome the emperor, Gregory IX encouraged the Mongols' advance and joined forces with Baldwin II de Courtenay, the emperor of Constantinople, against him. [1248] 'Duo nuncii Tartarorum venerunt ad papam. Dicebatur quoque, quod domini pape propositum fuit, inde quoque tractatum fuit secretius, ut, si christianissimi titulo insigniretur rex ille Tartarorum, ipsum mitteret cum omnibus viris et viribus suis super vastigium Grecum, generum Fretherici, scismaticum christiane fidei, domino pape et imperatori Baldewino rebellem, et postea ipsum Frethericum contra Romanam curiam recalcitrantem'. *HA*, III, p. 39. For further examples of attempts to identify what or who brought on the Mongol attacks, see Menache, 'Tartars, Jews, Saracens and the Jewish-Mongol "Plot" of 1241', p. 324.

112 MS *B*, fol. 145ʳ, col. b, ll. 36–44; *CM*, IV, p. 112; *EH*, I, p. 341.

The letter loosely follows the rhetorical structure of similar epistles, although it is unusually long and a little disjointed — at times even slightly repetitive — a sign that materials have been added to it to inflate the content and message.[113] The *narratio* section is long because it contains two descriptions of the enemy and two distinct accounts of their military progress approaching imperial territories. There are two blocks of descriptive text about the Mongols in the letter: their emergence from the torrid zone of the South and their terrifying northbound advance, as well as a description of their appearance and way of life.

> Egressa enim dudum ex ultimis mundi finibus de regione Australi, quae diu sole sub torrida zona tosta latuerat, quae postea versus partes Boreales occupatis violenter regionibus diu manens ut brucus multiplicatur, gens barbarae nationis et vitae, quo nescimus a loco vel origine, Tartari nuncupata, non absque praeviso Dei judicio ad sui populi correptionem et correctionem, non utinam ad totius Christianitatis dispendium, ad haec novissima tempora reservatur. Secuta est igitur publica clades, communis regnorum desolatio, et terrae fertilis exterminium quam gens impia peragravit, ut sexui, stati, vel dignitati non parcat, et reliquum genus humanum delere confidat, dum ubique terrarum per immensam et incomparabilem eorum potentiam et numerum sola dominari satagat et regnare.

> (Some time since a people of a barbarous race and mode of life called (from what place or origin I know not) Tartars, has lately emerged from the regions of the south, where it had long lain hid, burnt up by the sun of the torrid zone, and, thence marching towards the northern parts, took forcible possession of the country there, and remaining for a time, multiplied like locusts, and has now come forth, not without the premeditated judgment of God, but not, I hope, reserved to these latter times for the ruin of the whole of Christianity. Their arrival was followed by a general slaughter, a universal desolation of kingdoms, and by utter ruin to the fertile territory, which this impious horde of people roved through, sparing neither sex, age, nor rank, whilst they confidently hope to destroy the rest of the human race, and are endeavouring

113 Richardson points out that the 'most frequent stylistic advice in medieval *artes dictandi* was for brevity, advice scrupulously followed in medieval non-literary letters'. Richardson, 'The Ars Dictaminis, the Formulary and Medieval Epistolary Practice', p. 56. See also in Constable, *Letters and Letter-Collections*, p. 19. The suggested five parts were (1) *salutatio* or formal greeting; (2) *captatio benevolentiae*, a section to win the receiver's sympathy and attention; (3) *narratio*, the background leading to the request; (4) *petitio*, the request or demand; (5) *conclusio*, formal ending, place, and date.

194   CHAPTER 4

to rule and lord it alone, trusting to their immense power and unlimited numbers.)[114]

As discussed previously, the description reiterates the history and character of the Mongols that can be found elsewhere in the chronicle. Providing an impressive catalogue of primary sources using similar phrasing, Peter Jackson briefly notes that some elements in the formulaic descriptions of the Mongols are shared in various documents and the decrees of the Lyon council.[115] Jackson also breaks down the 'usual' description of the Mongols — including that in Frederick's letter — into recurring characteristics, providing ample examples found in a variety of primary sources.[116] Although these are to give a general impression of the 'image of the Mongols' in Europe as described in texts loosely associated by their content rather than certifiable intertextual connections, Jackson's list of tropes suffices to show that the description of the Mongols in Frederick's letter not only repeats tropes found elsewhere in Matthew's text,[117] but is clearly a very compact summary of commonplace ideas prevailing in other unconnected sources:

Haec enim gens est feralis et exlex, humanitatis ignara. Sequitur tamen et dominum habet, quem obedienter colit et veneratur et nuncupat deum terrae. *Homines parvae ac brevis staturae sunt, quantum ad longitudinem, sed solidi, lati, et propaginati; rigidi, ac fortes, et animosi, ad nutum sui ducis ad quaelibet ambigua proruentes; vultus amplos, aspectus torvos,* clamores horribiles habent, cordibus consonantes; *cruda gestant coria, bovina, asinina, vel equina; insutis laminis ferreis pro armis muniuntur, quibus hactenus usi sunt.* Sed, quod non sine suspiriis dicere possumus, jamjam de victorum spoliis Christianorum

---

114 Altogether twenty-four lines: MS *B*, fol. 145^r, col. b, l. 44–145^v, col. a, l. 15; *CM*, IV, p. 112; *EH*, I, p. 341. See the textual similarities with other descriptions of the Mongols in the *Chronica majora* in Appendix 8, available online, <https://doi.org/10.1484/A.14453112>.

115 'They slaughtered Christians without mercy and with no regard for rank, age or sex (a detail which echoes more official pronouncements, like papal encyclicals and the decree of the Lyons Council)'. Jackson, *The Mongols and the West*, p. 142. This needs a bit of clarification: the most detailed text of the council resolutions is reconstructed on the basis of Matthew Paris's version in the *Chronica majora*, thus the similarity between Matthew's text and the official decrees published by Tanner arises from the fact that the latter was compiled out of the former, rather than the other way around. Besides the 'emperor's letter', Jackson cites many primary sources using the same trope. Jackson, *The Mongols and the West*, p. 157, n. 67.

116 Not restricted to those found in Frederick's letter, Jackson lists recurring characteristics including their express purpose to annihilate Christians; showing no respect for any religious Order; the aforementioned slaughter of Christians without with no regard for rank, age, or sex; association with the Antichrist (e.g. the khan branding captured children resembles the Antichrist in Revelation 13. 16); being accompanied by Amazons, cannibals, heretics, or bogus/renegade Christians. Jackson, *The Mongols and the West*, p. 142, and pp. 156–57, nn. 65–70.

117 Rudolf reiterates Schnith's argument that Matthew may have used the emperor's letter as a basis for self-authored descriptions of the Mongols: Rudolf, 'Die Tartaren 1241/1242', p. 93.

armis decentioribus elegantius muniuntur, ut propriis armis irato Deo turpius et anxius trucidemur. Insuper equis melioribus instaurantur, epulis lautioribus reficiuntur, vestibus pulchrioribus adornantur. *Ipsi autem Tartari, sagittarii incomparabiles, utres ferunt artificialiter factos, quibus flumina transmeant indempnes rapacissima et paludes.* Deficiente vero cibo, corticibus arborum et foliis et herbarum radicibus dicuntur esse contenti equi eorum, quos adducunt, quos tamen velocissimos inveniunt et fortissimos, in articulo necessitatis.

> (for this race of people is wild, outlawed, and ignorant of the laws of humanity; they follow and have for their lord one, whom they worship and reverence with all obedience, and whom they call the god of earth. *The men themselves are small and of short stature, as far as regards height, but compact, stout, and bulky, resolute, strong, and courageous, and ready at the nod of their leader to rush into any undertaking of difficulty; they have large faces, scowling looks,* and utter horrible shouts, suited to their hearts; *they wear raw hides of bullocks, asses, and horses; and for armour, they are protected by pieces of iron stitched to them, which they have made use of till now.* But, and we cannot say it without sorrow, they are now, from the spoils of the conquered Christians, providing themselves with more suitable weapons, that we may, through God's anger, be the more basely slain with our own arms. Besides, they are supplied with better horses, they live on richer food, and adorn themselves with more handsome clothes, than formerly. *They are incomparable archers, and carry skins artificially made, in which they cross lakes and the most rapid rivers without danger.* When fodder fails them, their horses are said to be satisfied with the bark and leaves of trees, and the roots of herbs, which the men bring to them; and yet, they always find them to be very swift and strong in a case of necessity.)[118]

The generic nature of the descriptive passages makes it impossible to pin down their origin, connections, or approximate time of writing. It is clear, however, that the distinguishing features of the Mongols were catalogued quite similarly in continental sources, some written close to the fire, for example, Thomas of Spalato's account:

> Terrificum valde exhibent faciei aspectum, breves habent tibias, sed vasta pectora, lata est facies et cutis alba, imberbis gena et naris adunca, breves oculi spatio longiori disiuncti. *Arma eorum sunt quedam tegmina ex taurinis coriis laminarum more compacta, impenetrabilia tamen et*

---

118 MS *B*, fol. 145ᵛ, col. b. ll. 29–51; *CM*, IV, pp. 115–16; *EH*, I, p. 344. See the textual similarities with other descriptions of the Mongols in the *Chronica majora* in Appendix 8, available online, <https://doi.org/10.1484/A.14453112>.

valde secura. Cassides gerunt ferreas et ex coriis factas, falcatos enses, faretras et arcus militariter cingunt. Sagitte eorum nostris sunt quattuor digitis longiores, ferrea, ossea et cornea cuspide conspicate. Teni vero sagittarum ita stricti sunt, ut cordas nostrorum arcuum minime capiant. Vexilla brevia, nigro alboque colore distincta, quendam lane globum in summitate habentia. *Equos breves sed fortes, patientes inedie ac laboris* more equitant rusticano, per rupes vero et lapides absque ferramentis ita discurrunt, ac si capre forent silvestres, *tribus enim continuis diebus labore quassati parvo stipularum pabulo sunt contenti.* [...] Nulla pene rapidorum fluminum eis aqua obsistit, quominus equis transeant insidendo. *Si qua vero immeabilis unda occurrit, continuo in modum lemborum ex viminibus cistas intexunt superducentes crudas animalium cutes, quibus sarcinas inferentes intrant et transeunt absque metu.* Tentoriis utuntur filtrinis et ex coriis factis. Equos ita bene habent edomitos, ut quotcumque unus habeat homo, omnes ipsum tamquam canes secuntur.

(Their countenances have a truly dreadful aspect: their thighs are short but their chests are huge; their faces are broad and their skin white, their cheeks beardless, their noses hooked, their eyes narrow and set rather far apart. *As armor they use coverings made out of bull hide and fitted together like plates, which are nevertheless impenetrable and quite secure.* They wear helmets of iron or leather, their swords are curved, and they wear at the waist quivers and bows in military style. Their arrows are four digits longer than ours, and pointed with a tip of iron, bone or horn. The slit tips of the arrows are so narrow that our bowstrings do not fit them. Their banners are short, colored black and white, and have a sort of woolen ball on the top. *Their horses are short but sturdy, able to tolerate hunger and toil,* and they ride upon them in the manner in which country people do. They race over rocks and stones like mountain goats, without the use of metal shoes. *Even after being ridden for three days on end they are satisfied with a small meal of chaff.* [...] The waters of rapid rivers are almost never an obstacle to them, and they cross them riding on the backs of their horses. *If they do encounter a stream that they cannot cross, they at once weave together wicker crates to act like little boats, cover the frame with raw hides, and then putting their belongings on board they climb in and cross without trepidation.* Their tents are made of felt or leather, and their horses are so well trained that however many a man has they all follow him like dogs.)[119]

---

119 Thomas of Spalato, *Historia Salonitanorum atque Spalatinorum pontificum*, pp. 282–85.

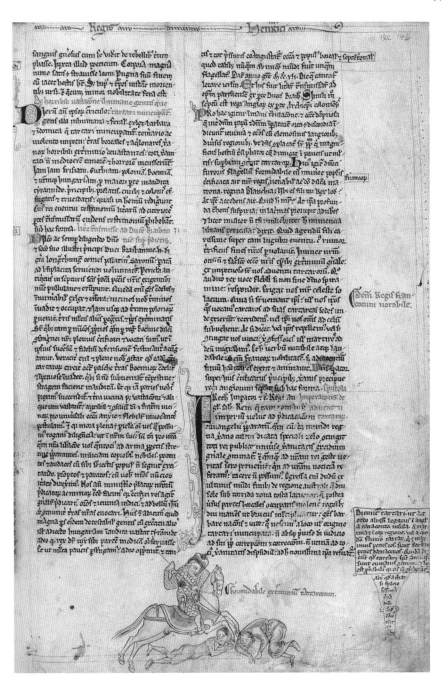

Figure 6. Mongol warrior, MS *B*, fol. 145[r]. By permission of the Parker Library, Corpus Christi College, Cambridge.

198   CHAPTER 4

This passage is all the more important because there is also a base-de-page illustration on fol. 145ʳ, which clearly intended to illustrate either the letter (starting at the very bottom of col. b) or the preceding text. In this, the aim is to depict the otherness and cruelty of the Mongols against the non-specific community of European Christians (see Fig. 6). It is a rather generic illustration of a Mongol warrior — indicated by the pointy 'oriental' hat and scaly armour, which is clearly the main point of interest in the picture as the cruel lancing is not unlike the few other warrior images in the *Chronica majora*.[120] As will be discussed below, this is only one of the two famous representations of Mongol cruelty in the *Chronica majora*; the other one also illustrates a letter — that of Ivo of Narbonne copied under the year 1243, on fol. 167ʳ (see Fig. 7, below). The images testify that the letters were inserted to be part of a multilayered narrative. Matthew's conscious interaction with the contents, editing, and curating of received materials is also reflected in his efforts to illustrate them. Being an inherent part of the text, this drawing makes 'Frederick's letter' Matthew's own production: adding such a specific image and engaging with the visual aspects of the content — in a way, translating the text into image — the scribe is not a mere copyist but an attentive reader and interpreter of the received text. This will be even more conspicuous in the other illustration of the Mongols: a 'catalogue image' of the identifiable features addressed in the text it accompanies.

The aforementioned rubric about Legate Otto and the origin of the Mongols in the bottom right corner demonstrates that Matthew revisited this easily identifiable landmark in his Mongol story. The rubric's odd shape and the colouring may suggest that it was added later to the image of a Mongol horseman which already carried the label 'formidabile exterminium Tartarorum':

> Dicuntur Tartari, ut ait Otto aliquando legatus in Anglia, a Taraconta insula, quae maxima est in eorum regione, vel a quodam fluvio Tartar, qui est maximos penes eos, sicut Farfar penes Damascenos. Quidam dicunt quod Tartari sunt Sicii, qui sunt Cumanis contermini; et hoc est probabilius, quia eis jam confoederantur. / Alii quod a Tharsi spatiosissima terra dicuntur / secundum alios Tattari dicuntur.
>
> (They are called Tartars, according to Otto the onetime legate in England, from Taraconta Island, which is the largest in their country, or from a certain Tartar River, which is the greatest one in their hands, just as the Orontes is in the hands of the Damascenes. Some say that the Mongols are the Sicii, who are neighbours of the Cumans, and this is probable, because they are presently allies.

---

120 See, for example, the image of the 'fight of Mareschal at Monmouth' at the bottom of MS *B*, fol. 88ʳ, or the flight of the French at Damascus in 1240 on fol. 134ᵛ.

Others that they are called Tartars from the spacious land of Tars; according to others they are called Tatars.)[121]

Despite the absence of the usual metadiscourse in Matthew's voice, the difference between the style and content of the constituent passages is sharp and easily visible. As Figure 5 shows in detail, sandwiched between the vivid descriptions of the exotic and cruel foe, a sixty-six-line-long passage is devoted to military intelligence: the actual progress of the Mongol invasion from Ruthenia and Kiev (*Cleva*) to Hungary, obviously and admittedly merged from different sources. The plight of the Hungarians, led by an 'idle and careless' king, is described in harrowing detail as a summary of the intelligence received from the bishop of Vác.[122] The language is active and chronologically ordered rather than timeless and descriptive, and the text is interspersed with phrases evoking a military analysis and precise local place names.[123] These nuggets of geographical information about the region are clearly borrowed from different sources

---

121 *CM*, IV, p. 109, n. 2. Caesurae marking the tripartite articulation of the rubric are mine. Translation from Dickens, 'Tarsā', p. 22. Dickens, summarizing analogies to similar etymological explanations from the thirteenth century and beyond, lists sources that are very similar to Matthew's, but all come from a couple of years later: John of Plano Carpini, Simon of Kéza, Phillippe Mousket, the chronicle of Salimbene of Parma, the *Annales Mantuani*, the *Annales capitula Posnaniensis*, the Armenian Het'um's *Flos historiarum terre orientalis*, and later chronicles. Dickens, 'Tarsā', pp. 22–25. See also Monneret de Villard, *Le leggende orientali sui magi evangelici*. It is notable that the other Mongol illustration in the chronicle (fol. 167ʳ) also stresses the existence of two names in a rubric 'nephandi Tartari vel Tattari humanis carnibus vescentes'. More on Otto's role in the chronicle in Chapter 2 ('Northern Connections') and Chapter 3 ('1237: Chaldeans, Medes, Persians, and Armenians').

122 This section takes up forty-four lines: MS B, fol. 145ᵛ, col. a, l. 15–col. b, l. 8.

123 Sentences redolent of military intelligence include 'cum lanceis missilibus et sagittis, quarum usus apud eos est continuus, et fortius aliis exerta habent brachia, ipsos penitus dissipatos devicerunt' (with their arrows and other missile weapons, which they are in continual use of, and by which their arms are more exercised and strengthened than other people's, they entirely dispersed and subdued that people [Cumans]); 'totum illud nobile regnum, caesis suis habitatoribus, in desolationem cecidit devastatum, quod, cum contermino regno Hungarorum dedisse debuit ad cautelam robur et munimen, sprevit negligenter' (the whole of that noble kingdom, which ought to have united itself with that of Hungary, for its defence and protection, but which it carelessly neglected to do, was, after its inhabitants were slain, reduced to a state of utter destruction and desolation); 'Sed hostium contemptores elati vel nescii, dum inimico vicinante segnes dormitarent, loci nativo munimine confidentes, ipsi more turbinis intrantes eos undique circumdabant repentini' (But, whilst these elated or ignorant people, despising their enemies, were idly sleeping with the enemy in their immediate neighbourhood, and trusting to the natural strength of the place, the Tartars made their way into the kingdom like a whirlwind, and suddenly surrounded them on all sides). Place names and peoples: 'Cumanorum coloniam' (colony of the Cumanians); 'Ruthenos, ab eis non multum distantes' (Ruthenians who dwell near them), 'Cleva civitatum maxima' (Kiev); 'majorem et nobiliorem Hungariae partem ultra Danubium fluvium' (the largest and finest part of Hungary, beyond the river Danube);

200   CHAPTER 4

and contexts and do not correspond with references to them elsewhere in Matthew's texts.[124]

It is notable that the king and the Hungarians are described as inept and unprepared. In a way, this motive is found in Roger of Várad's eye-witness description of the battle, albeit the emphasis in the *Carmen* is on the reluctance of the barons to go to battle upon Béla's summon.[125] The description of the battle concludes with the following end credits, suggesting that the attribution of intelligence to the bishop of Vác applies to the whole battle description, casting a shadow over the leadership and character of the Hungarian king and his followers:

> Victores igitur castris et spoliis victorum insederunt exultantes. Jam jamque majorem et nobiliorem Hungariae partem ultra Danubium fluvium et incolas ejus ferro et flamma feraliter vastantes, caetera confundere minantur procaciter, prout per venerabilem Vatiensem episcopum, dicti Hungariae regis legatum, ad nostrum curiam, postea ad Romanam didicimus destinatum. Hic per nos primo transitum faciens, his testimonium perhibuit quae vidit, et testimonium ejus nimis verus est.
>
> (The victors, exulting in the spoil, then took up their quarters in the camp of the conquered Hungarians; and at this very moment they are ravaging the largest and finest part of Hungary, beyond the river Danube, harassing the inhabitants with fire and sword, and

---

'venerabilem Vatiensem episcopum' (the venerable bishop of Vác). MS *B*, fol. 145ᵛ, cols a–b; *CM*, IV, pp. 113–14; *EH*, I, pp. 341–43.

124 For example, although not expressly referring to cardinal directions in this particular letter, on account of its association with the Rutheni and their capital, Kiev, the existence of a 'populosa Cumanorum colonia' is clearly a northern location here and does not correspond to the southern 'Cumani and Blacti' found in Matthew's Map of Palestine. 'Dum ad populosam Cumanorum coloniam pervenissent dicti Tartari [...]. Quorum vicinitas Ruthenos, ab eis non multam distantes, vix cautos efficit et munitos [...] intenderent praecavere'. *CM*, IV, p. 113. For the note found next to Matthew Paris's Map of Palestine see Chapter 1 ('The North by the North-west').

125 According to Master Roger, unwilling nobles either ignored the call to muster or managed to escape before the battle. Bishop Benedict of Várad and his troops, for example, escaped before the battle, while Count Ladislaus of Somogy, who originally obeyed the call, fled with his men when he received the news of the defeat. Roger of Várad [Master Roger], 'Epistle to the Sorrowful Lament', pp. 184–87. In contrast with Roger's detailed examination of the internal strife that caused the downfall of the king, clearly blaming his misguided policies for the catastrophe, the harsh judgement in the emperor's letter is different in tone: here the king is more than misguided, he is an indolent (*deses*) ruler. The condemnation is probably not entirely fair: recent archaeological studies and the revision of charter evidence show that the level of resistance put up by the king, and probably independently of him by the local population as well, appears to have been greater than what is suggested in the narrative sources including Roger and Thomas of Spalato. Laszlovszky and others, 'Contextualizing the Mongol Invasion of Hungary', pp. 429–31.

threaten to involve the rest in the same destruction, as we have
been informed by the venerable bishop of Vatzen, the said king
of Hungary's ambassador to our court [István Báncsa], afterwards
sent to that of Rome, who, passing through our territory first, bore
testimony to what he had seen; and his evidence is but too true.)[126]

Although the bishop's personal feelings towards his king are not known,
this kind of characterization would be — at a glance — highly unexpected
from István Báncsa whose steep upward mobility would have been impossible without Béla's support. Their close bond is also attested to by the
fact that Béla entrusted the safety of his fleeing family in Báncsa's hands
before appointing him to become his personal envoy to the pope.[127] It
is, however, not insignificant here that for various reasons the privileged
prelate turned against his patron later in his career.[128] The disgruntled
cleric's views, as recorded in Frederick's letter, were comparable to Thomas
of Spalato's damning views of the unprepared and haughty nobles of the
Hungarian camp and Roger of Várad's even more incriminatory account.[129]
Naming the informants so precisely, especially the bishop of Vác, suggests
that the accounts of the campaign, including both Báncsa's (above) and
Conrad's passages (below), may indeed have been collated and formulated
in a well-appointed chancery, maybe even — as the letter suggests —
during Frederick's sojourn at Faenza, where these accounts may have been
received and disseminated.[130]

---

126 MS *B*, fol. 145^v, col. b; *CM*, IV, p. 114; *EH*, I, p. 343.

127 Almási and Koszta, 'Báncsa István bíboros', p. 10.

128 Although indirectly, this animosity towards the Hungarian king suggests that Báncsa's
description of the battle was not formulated right after the Mongol campaign when he was
still on friendly terms with the king but after 1245, when their differences were becoming
more bitter. Kiss suggests that the first conflict over royal competence in episcopal elections
(known from a papal decree issued on 28 February 1245) was short-lived, and István
had a good rapport with the king during his episcopacy. Kiss, *Dél-Magyarországtól Itáliáig*,
pp. 28–29. Almási and Koszta suggest that the hostilities culminated in open conflicts over
unauthorized chapter elections and other ecclesiastical issues in the early 1250s. Almási and
Koszta, 'Báncsa István bíboros', pp. 11, 13.

129 István Báncsa is mentioned by Thomas of Spalato, as 'alter Stephanus Vacciensis et idem in
Strigoniensem archiepiscopum postulatus' where Thomas lists the nobles that accompanied
the king upon his entry into Split. This, however, does not prove a personal encounter
between the two since Thomas did not draw up his list from his memory of the event: most
of the prelates and barons are mentioned in the dignitary list of King Béla's privilege to the
Tragurins issued on 18 March 1242 — Thomas's source, according to Damir and Sweeney.
Thomas of Spalato, *Historia Salonitanorum atque Spalatinorum pontificum*, pp. 290–92.

130 Outside this letter, there is scarce evidence for Báncsa's presence at Frederick's court at
Faenza. The line 'Audito veruntamen per venerabilem episcopum Wacziensem, legatum ad
nos regis Ungarie' in Frederick's so-called *Encyclica contra Tartaros*, a letter which survived
in two versions: one addressed to the Roman Senate in Peter of Vinea's letter collection
(no. 235 in *Constitutiones et acta publica imperatorum et regum*, pp. 322–25), and Letter 4,
addressed to the people of Swabia in the Ottobeuren Collection (MS *OB*, fol. 4^v). Further

202   CHAPTER 4

The letter continues with a brief military-focused explanation of the whereabouts and direction of the tripartite Mongol army, which is attributed to Frederick's son, Conrad, as well as the king of Bohemia and the dukes of Austria and Bavaria by way of messengers.[131]

> Necnon et haec per literas dilecti filii nostri Conradi, in regem Romanorum electi, semper Augusti et regni Jerosolimitani haeredis, regisque Boemiae, Austriae et Bavariae ducum, ipsis quoque nuntiorum verbis, qui de vicinitate hostium experimento sunt edocti, plenius certificamur; nec haec sine magna animi perturbatione potuimus didicisse. Sane sicut innotuit et praeambula fama gestorum proclamat, indeterminatus exercitus eorum in tres partes infelices ex indultu Domini dampnandis consiliis divisus processit. Nam una ad Pructenos transmissa et ingrediente Poloniam, princeps et dux terrae illius ab eorum insequenti exterminio cecidit, et dein tota fuit per eos illa regio devastata. Secunda Boemiae fines ingressa est et aggressa substitit, rege illius terrae cum suis conatibus viriliter occurrente. Tertia percurrit Hungariam, Austriae finibus vicinandam.

> (We have also been fully informed of these events, by letters from our beloved son Conrad, king elect of the Romans, heir to the kingdom of Jerusalem, and king of Bohemia, and from the dukes of Austria and Bohemia, as also by the word of mouth of messengers, who have been practically made certain of the proximity of the enemy. And we have heard all this with great perturbation of mind. As we have been informed, and as the rumour of their proceedings, going in advance of them, declares, their innumerable army is divided into three ill-omened portions, and, owing to the Lord's indulging them in their damnable plans, has proceeded thus divided. One of these has been sent through the Pructenian territory and entered Poland, where the prince and duke of that country have fallen victims to their exterminating pursuers, and afterwards the whole of that country has been devastated by them. A second portion has entered the Bohemian territory, where it is brought to a stand, having been attacked by the king of that country, who has bravely met it with all the forces at his command;

---

evidence for Báncsa's visit in Faenza comes from the third continuation of the *St Pantaleon Annals* (1238–1249) from Cologne. *Chronica regia Coloniensis*. It is notable here that in early summer 1241, Frederick left Faenza and was travelling to 'the Roman countryside' in order to find new allies and intimidate the pope. Abulafia, *Frederick II*, p. 348. The Hungarian king's letter of appointment as royal emissary to the pope was issued in Zagreb on 18 May 1241 but does not mention other stops scheduled on his way to Rome: *Codex diplomaticus Hungariae ecclesiasticus ac civilis*, IV.1, p. 214.

131 Altogether twenty-two lines in length: MS *B*, fol. 145ᵛ, col. b, ll. 8–29.

and the third portion of it is overrunning Hungary, adjoining to the Austrian territories.)[132]

The identity of the emperor's sources, particularly the duke of Austria, against whom the Hungarian king was waging a war at the time, deserves a brief digression here to provide a glimpse into the highly convoluted networks of political alliances in these distraught times. Frederick II the Quarrelsome (Friedrich der Streitbare) was actively eroding peace with his neighbours. He not only quarrelled with his own Austrian nobility when he ascended the ducal throne in 1230 but was also embroiled in serious clashes and conflicts with King Wenceslas of Bohemia and King Andrew II (and later Béla IV) of Hungary. Although by the time of this letter their conflict was resolved, it is also notable that the Austrian duke was formerly banned from Vienna by Emperor Frederick II.[133] After the Battle of Muhi, Béla first fled to Pozsony (now Bratislava, Slovakia) and then to Frederick II of Austria who, foregoing the unwritten rules of royal hospitality, took him prisoner and only released him when Béla handed over the gold he carried and pledged three much coveted border provinces of his kingdom (probably Moson and Sopron, and the castle estate of Lutzmansburg (Locsmánd)). If Master Roger of Várad is to be believed, the ignominious deed was conducted much like a ransom situation:[134]

> Rex manus illius evader nequivit, quousque partem eiusdem pecunie in prompto, partem in vasis aureis et argenteis illi persolvit, pro parte autem tres comitatus sui regni illius terre contiguos illi obligavit. Et, licet ipsa vasa aurea et argentea maioris fuerint estimationis, tamen dux illa solum in duobus milibus marcarum simul cum lapidibus pretiosis recepit. Dux autem illico castrorum illorum comitatus corporali possessione est adeptus et illa ex propriis pecuniis contra Tartaros fecit reparare.
>
>> (The king could not escape from him until he had paid that money, partly in cash, partly in gold and silver vessels, and pledged him three counties of his country, adjacent to his land. Although the gold and silver vessels were worth much more, the duke accepted

---

132 MS B, fol. 145ᵛ, col. b; *CM*, IV, pp. 114–15; *EH*, I, p. 343.

133 Szende, 'Harc a Babenberg örökségért', pp. 290–99.

134 This issue later culminated in several clashes of arms after 1242, when Frederick II attacked Pozsony but King Béla IV's troops managed to avert the attack and marched into Austria to reconquer his lands. Laszlovszky and others suggest that the fact that he managed to do so despite the immense impact of the Mongol attacks is evidence that the devastation was on a smaller scale in the Western territories of Hungary and that the king could rely on forces whose military powers were not diminished because they did not participate in the Battle of Muhi a few years beforehand. Laszlovszky and others, 'Contextualizing the Mongol Invasion of Hungary', p. 429.

them for a mere two thousand marks, including the precious stones. Then the duke at once took actual possession of the castles of the counties and had them fortified from his own money against the Tatars.)[135]

This portion, again, is different in tone and content to the previous passage. The repetition of Conrad's titles suggests that it is a *rescriptum* of a letter received by the emperor. Here, the invasion of the Kingdom of Hungary is placed in a wider European context by providing an account of events taking place shortly before the attack on Hungary. The passage, seemingly unchronological, is a prequel to the Hungarian atrocities discussed above, which is designed to draw attention to the fact that the Mongol troops are not confined to a single attack on a remote kingdom, but their military manoeuvres constitute a three-pronged attack closer to home.[136] The story of the destruction of the Kingdom of Hungary and the rest of the campaign is an account that corresponds to the known history of the invasion of Hungary so faithfully that it came to be not only an obligatory part in source collections about the Mongols in Europe but also suggested to many scholars that Matthew Paris was intimately familiar with the events taking place in Hungary.[137] However, the part more important in Matthew's Mongol cluster — and the Mongol story at large — is the essence of the letter, the *petitio*: a long passage about Frederick's own conflict with the pope written by one king to another, asking for support and alliance against both threats.

Nos autem horum omnium quodammodo providi et praesagi frequenter per literas et nuntios regalem excellentiam vestram, necnon et aliorum principum Christianorum, meminimus requisisse, sollicitantes attentius et monentes, ut vigeret inter eos qui tribunalibus praesunt potestatibus unanimitas dilectionis et pacis, et sedatis dissentionibus quae reipublicae Christi saepius inferunt nocumenta, concorditer ad eorum obstacula, qui nuper emerserunt, alacrius consurgentes, cum praevisa jacula minus soleant sauciare, et ut nec communes hostes, ad viarum suarum praeparationes, gauderent tanta inter principes Christianos discidia pullulare. Ha Deus! quantum et

---

135 Roger of Várad [Master Roger], 'Epistle to the Sorrowful Lament', pp. 194–95. As the editors of the text note, Thomas of Spalato is curiously silent here about Béla's unfortunate sojourn in Austria: 'At vero Bela rex auxilio protectus divino, tantum evadens excidium cum paucis secessit in Austriam'. Thomas of Spalato, *Historia Salonitanorum atque Spalatinorum pontificum*, p. 272, n. 1.

136 The three-pronged attack is also mentioned in other sources; an odd example is the letter of Otto II to Bishop Siboto of Augsburg, which is found in the Ottobeuren Collection: 'Exercitus autem hostium antedictorum protenditur in tres partes; primus videlicet versus Norwagiam, secundus Boemiam, tercius in Hungariam'. MS *OB*, fol. 7^v.

137 See discussion in Chapter 7.

quotiens nos humiliare voluimus, omnem benivolentiam exponentes, ut Romanus Pontifex ab effuso per orbem contra nos dissensionis scandalo destitisset, et ab inconsultae voluntatis impetu motus suos temperantius revocasset, ut ad sedandum nostros jure subditos praevaleremus et quietius regeremus, nec eos, quorum adhuc per eum non minima pars fovetur, protegeret recalcitrantes; ut sedatis rebus, rebellibusque reformatis adversus quos multarum copiam opum effudimus et virium conatus exhausimus, potentia nostra major consurgeret et insurgeret in communiter adversantes. Sed cum voluntas ei pro jure fuerit, linguae lubricum discursum non regenti, et a multiplici genere discidii, quod attemptavit, dedignatus est abstinere, per legatos et nuntios suos crucem quam adversus tyrannidem Tartarorum vel Sarracenorum, Terram Sanctam invadentium et occupantium, exercuisse debuit et decebat, jussit contra me brachium et ecclesiae advocatum publicari, rebellibus nostris graviter contra honorem nostrum et famam exultando conspirantibus. Et cum maxima nobis immineat [cura] nos a domesticis et familiaribus hostibus expedire, qualiter et barbaros repellemus?

(We have, however, by some means or other, been forewarned of and foreseen all these events, and have by letters and messengers frequently requested of your majesty, as well as other Christian princes, and earnestly advised and entreated of you, to allow unanimity, affection, and peace, to flourish among those who hold supreme authority; to settle all dissensions, which frequently bring harm on the commonwealth of Christ; and to rise with alacrity, and unanimously to oppose those lately emerged savages, inasmuch as weapons foreseen are less apt to wound; that so the common enemies of us all may not have cause to rejoice, in furtherance of their progress, that discord is shooting forth amongst the Christian chiefs. O God! how much and how often have we been willing to humiliate ourselves, giving vent to every kind of good feeling, in order to prevail on the Roman pontiff to desist from giving cause of scandal throughout the world, by his enmity against us, and place the bounds of moderation upon his ill-advised violence, in order that we might be able to pacify our lawful subjects, and govern them in a state of peace, and not to protect those who kick against our authority, a large portion of whom are still favoured and assisted by him. Thus, by peaceably settling matters, and by reforming our rebellious subjects, against whom we have expended a large amount of money, and exhausted our strength, our power would increase and rise in greater force against the common enemy. But as will is law with him, for he does not rule the deceitful discourse of his tongue, and he has refused to abstain from the manifold quarrels which he has sought against us; and has ordered

206   CHAPTER 4

a crusade to be published against me, who am an arm and advocate of the Church, which it was his duty, and would have become him better to have put in practice against the tyranny of the Tartars, or the Saracens invading and occupying the Holy Land, and he exults in the rebellion of our subjects, who are conspiring against our honour and fame, and as it is our most urgent business to free ourselves from enemies at home, how shall we repel these barbarians as well?)[138]

While the anthropological detail of the enemy in previous parts is rather out of place in a royal letter (or at least over-long), the military intelligence above and the next lengthy passage is more in line with the usual rhetoric of such missives. This type of text was familiar in thirteenth-century diplomatic correspondence: the *littere exhortatorie* were 'concerned with admonitions, urging foreign rulers to settle their differences amicably, to strive for the unity of the Church and so on'.[139] And the real enemy here is not the Mongols but the *domestici et familiares hostes* who not only allow the tyranny of the Mongols and Saracens to increase, but also actively conspire against Frederick and, through him, against the commonwealth of Christ.

In the context of the chronicle narrative, the letter — devoid of any extradiegetic text or commentary — conveys a sense of real-time narration. Despite the narrative accounts embedded about the prehistory of the Mongols and the recent history of their invasion in Central Europe, the actual body of the epistle is a forward-looking text but with no hint of knowing the future. In fact, this uncertainty is what moves the story ahead. The letter shows a ruler who is the opposite of the 'idle and careless' Hungarian king: he is forewarned, well-informed, and ready to fight against the lawless pagans as 'an arm and advocate of the Church'. As before, this is not to be understood as 'the advocate of the pope': quite the contrary, Frederick here is seen as everything the pope should be but is not. Rather than the historiographical value that came to be attached to the description of the battle and the Mongol campaign threatening the heartlands of Christian Europe, the imperial *petitio* was the real motive behind including the long epistolary text in this cluster.

The *petitio* continues with Frederick's proactive model behaviour to be emulated by his kin and allies, such as the addressee of the letter, the English king:

Serenitatem etiam vestram, pro communi necessitate, per auctorem fidei nostrae Christianae, Dominum nostrum Jesum Christum, praecordialiter adjuramus, quatinus vobis et regno vestro, quem Deus

---

138 MS *B*, fols 145ᵛ, col. b–146ʳ, col. a; *CM*, IV, pp. 116–17; *EH*, I, pp. 344–45.

139 Chaplais, *English Diplomatic Practice in the Middle Ages*, p. 94.

in statu prosperitatis conservet, instantissima sollicitudine et provida deliberatione praecaventes, maturata militum strenuorum et aliorum armatorum et armorum subsidia non segniter praeparetis; hoc in aspersione sanguinis Christi et affinitatis foedere, quo connectimur, postulamus.

> (And we most sincerely adjure your majesty, in the name of the Lord Jesus Christ, the author of our Christian faith, with the most careful solicitude, and by prudent deliberation, to take precautions for the protection of yourself and your kingdom, which may God keep in a state of prosperity, and to prepare as soon as possible a complete force of brave knights and soldiers, and a good supply of arms; and this we beg of you, by the blood of Christ shed for us, and by the ties of relationship, by which we are connected.)[140]

Whether anyone even for a moment seriously entertained the idea that the Mongols' European progress westwards directly threatened the British Isles remains unknown — no written record suggests the news fomenting such fears in the English kingdom. This lack of direct threat may suggest that Matthew filled in the header of a template letter with his king's name to make it relevant for his English history,[141] but the rhetoric of kinship (*affinitatis foedere, quo connectimur*) and the request for troops to send them against the enemy at the 'boundaries of Germany', which is, as it were, 'the gate of Christendom', suggests a very real call to urge one's brother-in-law to send military aid for a crusade in preparation.[142]

The letter thus zooms in on Germany's borders as the theatre of imminent war. Like that of Henry Raspe, Frederick's information comes from the territories adjacent to the invasion and envisages rapid westward expansion: the Mongols are about to encroach upon the West, starting at the *fines Germaniae* and continuing with the conquest of the Occident. Hungary was just the antechamber of the Christian oecumene, whose example amply demonstrates the horrors that await: 'Nam si, quod absit, Germaniae fines invadant, nec inveniant obstaculorum repagula, pro foribus expectent caeteri venientis subito fulgura tempestatis' (For if, which God forbid, they invade the German territory, and meet with no opposition, the rest of the world will then feel the thunder of the suddenly-coming tempest). Without missing a beat, the letter here returns to the real

---

140 MS *B*, fol. 146ʳ, cols a–b; *CM*, IV, p. 117; *EH*, I, pp. 345–46.

141 In the postscript after the letter, Matthew himself describes this practice as 'mutatis tantum titulis et verborum raro sermone' (with only a change of titled headings, and of a few words therein). MS *B*, fol. 146ᵛ, col. a; *CM*, IV, p. 119; *EH*, I, p. 347.

142 'Germaniae terminos jam ingredi proponentes, velut Christianorum janam'. MS *B*, fol. 146ʳ, col. b; *CM*, IV, p. 117; *EH*, I, p. 346.

208   CHAPTER 4

root of the problem, in which the Mongol threat is just an instrument of divine judgement:

> quam diversis mundo contagiis inquinato, refrigescente caritate multorum, per quos fides praedicari et constare deberet, et pernicioso eorum exemplo mundum usuris et variis symoniae et ambitionis generibus maculante, divino judicio credimus emersisse. Provideat igitur excellentia vestra, et dum communes inimici in vicinis regionibus debacchantur, ad resistendum eis maturatis auxiliis vobis consulatis.

>> (which we believe to have arisen from a divine judgement, as the world is defiled by the infection of various sins, as charity begins to grow cold in many by whom the true faith ought to be preached and upheld, and their pernicious example pollutes the world with usury and diverse kinds of simony and ambition. May it please your majesty, therefore to provide for this emergency, and whilst these enemies of us all in common are venting their fury in the neighbouring countries, do you by prudent counsels make preparations to resist them.)[143]

Revisiting Hilpert's suggestion for potential interpolations by Matthew,[144] the most obvious addition to the letter is the last paragraph which Matthew certainly styled after what Hilpert calls the *Saladinbrief*, a letter allegedly sent by Frederick Barbarossa to Saladin.[145] It is prefaced by a familiar sentence, which rhymes with Matthew's previous entry suggesting that it was his addition to create a sense of coherence within his cluster of entries. Although the phrase 'ad sua Tartara Tartari detrudentur' (thrust them back to their Tartarus) may just be a witticism too appealing to use only once, it is more than just that. It is a link to Louis IX's words 'ad suas Tartareas sedes unde exierunt, retrudemus' at the end of the previous entry. Regardless whether the phrase was added to Frederick's letter to echo Louis's words or vice versa, this is almost certainly Matthew's own

---

143 MS *B*, fol. 146ʳ, col. b; *CM*, IV, pp. 117–18; *EH*, I, p. 346.

144 Hans-Eberhard Hilpert suggested that Matthew added no more than two passages to the original letter: the so-called 'Saladin-letter' and possibly the previously cited passage criticizing the Church. Hilpert, *Kaiser- und Papstbriefe*, p. 154. See also note 107 above.

145 Under the year 1188, i.e. in the portion authored by Roger of Wendover and revised by Matthew Paris: 'Et tu quidem, auctore Deo, intelliges, quid nostrae victrices aquilae, quid cohortes diversarum nationum, quid furor Theutonicus etiam in pace arma movens, quid caput indomitum Hreni, qui[d] Juventus [Histri] quae nunquam novit fugam, quid procerus Bavarus, quid Suevus astutus, quid Franconia circumspecta, quid in gladio ludens Saxonia, quid Turingia, quid Westfalkia, quid agilis Brebantia, quid nescia pacis Lotharingia, quid inquieta Burgundia, quid Alpini salices, quid Frisonia in amento pervolans, quid Boemia ultro mori gaudens, quid Bolemia suis feris ferior, quid Austria, quid Stiria, quid Bugresia, quid partes Illiricae, quid Leonardia, quid Tuscia, quid Archarictana, quid Ve[ne]tus proretha, quid Spinacius nauclerus'. *CM*, II, p. 332.

effort to connect them by attributing the same thoughts to them. What follows is certainly a text recycled from earlier history:

> Nec gloriabuntur tot impune peragrasse provincias, tot populos devicisse, tot facinora perpetrasse, cum ad victrices aquilas praepotentis imperialis Europae sors incauta, immo Sathan, ipsos traxerit morituros, ubi ultro furens ac fervens ad arma Germania, strenuae militiae genitrix et alumpna Francia, bellicosa et audax Hispania, virtuosa viris et classe munita fertilis Anglia, impetuosis bellatoribus referta Alemannia, navalis Dacia, indomita Ytalia, pacis ignara Burgundia, inquieta Apulia, cum maris Graeci, Adriatici, et Tyreni insulis piraticis et invictis, Creta, Cypro, Sicilia, cum oceano conterminis insulis et regionibus, cruenta Hybernia, cum agili Wallia, palustris Scotia, glacialis Norwegia, et quaecunque jacet nobilis et famosa sub occiduo cardine regio, suam electam militiam, praevio vivificae crucis vexillo, quod non tantum homines rebelles, immo daemones adversantes reformidant, alacriter destinabunt. Datum in recessu, post deditionem et depopulationem Faventiae, tertio die Julii.

> (Nor will they have to boast of having roved with impunity through so many provinces, subdued so many nations, and perpetrated so many wickednesses, when their own incautious destiny, or rather, Satan himself, has dragged them hither to die, before the victorious eagles of the potent European empire. When Germany, rising with rage and zeal to battle, and France, that mother and nurse of chivalry; the warlike and bold Spain, with fertile England, valorous in its men, and protected by its fleet; Almaine, full of impetuous warriors; the maritime Dacia; untameable Italy; Burgundy, that never knows peace; restless Apulia, with the piratical and unconquered islands of the Grecian, Adriatic, and Tyrrhene seas; Crete, Cyprus, and Sicily, with the islands and districts adjacent to the ocean; when bloody Ireland, with active Wales; Scotland, abounding in lakes, icy Norway, and every noble and renowned country lying under the royal star of the West, shall send forth their chosen ornaments preceded by the symbol of the life-giving cross, at which, not only rebellious subjects, but even opposing demons, are struck with dismay and awe. Given on our retreat, after the surrender and depopulation of Faenza, on the third day of July.)[146]

Matthew knew where to look for a great closing sentence for an epistle that is ultimately a charge against the pope rather than its subject, the Mongol threat. As Heather Blurton picks up on Matthew's suggestive

---

146 MS *B*, fol. 146ʳ, col. b; *CM*, IV, pp. 118–19; *EH*, I, p. 347.

210 CHAPTER 4

'homines rebelles / daemones adversantes' couplet, 'the neat comparison between "rebellious subjects" and "opposing demons" draws a clear analogy between the respective dangers of each. Matthew's own response to this idealism, however, is to pessimistically emphasize the aspect of internal dissension rather than that of the possibility of European unity'.[147] Originally serving as rhetoric uniting the fragmented Central European region, Barbarossa's adapted text here calls for the unity of the entirety of Europe, also evoking Isidorean geographical gazetteers. The 'catalogue of nations' frames the letter in the powerful rhetoric of European unity — the very thing that, as Matthew argues, does not exist outside Frederick's noble but wishful thinking.

Finally, as the exchange between Louis IX and Queen Blanche introduced Frederick's letter, the passage following it closes the French bracket. Here, the emperor turns directly to Louis IX:

> Publicatur haec epistola missa pluribus principibus. Sub harum tenore literarum scripsit dominus imperator, mutatis tantum titulis et verborum raro sermone, reipublicae sedulus procurator. Veruntamen regem Francorum sic scribens commovit vehementius; ait enim; 'Admiramur super Francorum prudentia, quod non subtilius caeteris Papales astutias consideratis, vel non attenditis cupiditates. Proponit enim ipsius ambitio insatiabilis omnia fidelium regna suo subicere dominatui, ab Anglorum conculcata corona sumens exemplariter consequentiam, et ut culmen imperii suis inclinet nutibus, ausa est praesumptuoso conatu et ausu temerario protervius inhiare'.
>
> > (The publication of the foregoing letter. Letters to the same effect, with only a change of titled headings, and of a few words therein, were written by that sedulous defender of the public weal, the emperor; but by adding the following words to the French king, he aroused him the most effectually; for, said he, 'We are, moreover, astonished, knowing the wisdom of the French, that you do not take more minute notice of the papal craft and avarice than all the others. For, in his insatiable ambition, he is now purposing to bring all Christian kingdoms into subjection to him, drawing an instance from his having trodden under-foot the crown of England; and now he dares, with greater rashness and presumption, aspire to bend the majesty of the empire at his nod'.)[148]

The letter contains no clues regarding when Matthew received the texts, but placed in its immediate textual context, the colligation of the news about Faenza's submission to Frederick II and the Hungarian defeat in the

---

147 Blurton, *Cannibalism in High Medieval English Literature*, p. 99.
148 MS B, fol. 146ᵛ, col. a; *CM*, IV, p. 119; *EH*, I, p. 347.

Battle of Muhi is impressively accurate as they did indeed take place very close in time. As for 'Frederick's letter', Hans-Eberhard Hilpert suggests that, similar to the 'Länderkatalog' quoted above, both the date and place of issue are spurious.[149] While the letter is dated to 3 July 1241 (Faenza surrendered on 14 April), the events described suggest that parts of the text were originally written *after* the Battle of Muhi (11 April 1241) and István Báncsa's visit at Faenza, but before the Mongol's withdrawal from Hungary a year after.[150]

In the next short entry, 'Oritur mala super his suspicio', Matthew Paris is playing his favourite game: the game of opposites in a story where there is no black and white. Frederick's cruelty at Faenza is placed side by side with the Mongol onslaught, his ultimate magnanimity with their ultimate mercilessness. Right after Frederick's letter, Matthew in his own voice refers to him as the 'sedulous defender of the public weal, the emperor', then inserts a curious entry about his alleged alliance with the Mongols.[151] The pope's inability to unite Christendom, where dissent and discord prevail, is juxtaposed with Frederick's efforts to unite the secular powers under one banner to protect Christendom. Oscillating in this way between mercy and mercilessness, unity and dissension, just war and depredation, enemies within and without, Matthew weaves an intricate story of right and wrong. The readers are often left to their own devices to make their mind up as Matthew creates moral tension by presenting together the questionable — and downright questioned — deeds of his protagonists.

This particular entry is indeed a thorny issue, a story of deception and incredulity: 'Orta est igitur discordia sententialis inter multos, diversis diversa super his sentientibus' (a difference of opinion arose amongst many, different people entertaining different thoughts on these matters), that is, the machinations of the emperor.[152] What is important regarding the narrative progress here, however, is the last sentence which leaves behind the contrived pars pro toto argumentation positing that if the letter contains falsehoods about the southern origin of the Mongols, then the rest must be questionable as well. On the one hand, this sentence harkens back to the pre-invasion entries by describing the pagan attackers as the markedly northern 'Hyrcanians and Scythians';[153] on the other hand, it

---

149 Hilpert, *Kaiser- und Papstbriefe*, pp. 153–54.

150 For more on Báncsa's visit at Faenza, see note 130.

151 MS B, fol. 146ᵛ, col. a; CM, IV, p. 119; EH, I, pp. 347–48. Note Matthew's poetic play with words: 'sententialis' *vs* 'sentientibus', 'diversis diversa'.

152 See in notes 103 and 104.

153 See Matthew's maps in Fig. 3 and Fig. 4, where, at the most extreme north of Europe, Scythia's (*Sicia*) immediate neighbours to the west are *Maior Hungaria*, *Minor Hungaria*, and the legend *Meodes paludes inferiores*.

212 CHAPTER 4

foreshadows the 1244 entries that mark the end of the Mongol subplot within Frederick's story.[154]

> Sunt igitur, ut inquiunt, Hircani et Sicii, humanam caedem avide sitientes, montes et salebras Boreales inhabitantes, qui feralem vitam ducentes, deos colunt montium, et praevisa in die; qui etiam cum Cumanis sibi conterminis et jam confoederatis, machinante imperatore, regem Hungariae cum quibusdam aliis magnatibus expugnarunt, ut fatigatus rex ad alas imperatoris avolaret, homagium ei pro succursu impendendo facturus. Unde cum haec fierent, ipsi hostes sunt regressi. Sed absit, ut in uno corpore mortali tanta sceleris immanitas latitaret.
>
> > (There are, also, as they say, Hyrcanians and Scythians, who thirst eagerly for human blood, inhabiting the mountainous and rugged regions of the north, leading the life of wild beasts, worshipping the gods of the mountains on appointed days; and these people, by the machinations of the emperor, have, together with their neighbours, the Cumanians, who have now entered into an alliance with them, *made war on the king of Hungary and some other nobles, in order that the harassed king may fly to the wings of the emperor for protection, and do homage to him for affording him assistance*; and as these things have been effected, the enemies have retreated. But God forbid that so much wickedness should be lurking in any mortal body.)[155]

Matthew's text shows that he was aware of conflicting views regarding Frederick's political game and had access to anti-imperial propaganda. The passage does echo surviving pro-papal texts, for example, the *Continuatio Sancrucensis Secunda*, whose author charges Frederick with blocking assistance to the king of Hungary in the hope that the Mongol threat would force the king to perform homage and become his vassal.[156] In another version of the rumours, Master Roger of Várad asserts that the vengeful and hostile barons 'sent a letter with specific contractual conditions to the duke of Austria and promised in it to hand over the crown of the realm and Hungary to Frederick, the Roman emperor'.[157] In the same vein but turning the accusations against Frederick around, in his *Historia Anglorum* Matthew argues that Pope Gregory IX together with Baldwin II de Courte-

---

154 See Chapter 5 ('1244: Frederick's Triumph'), and Appendix 5 below.

155 MS *B*, fol. 146ᵛ, col. a; *CM*, IV, p. 120; *EH*, I, pp. 348–49 (my italics). Matthew revisits this theme in 1244; see Chapter 5 ('1244: Frederick's Triumph'), and Appendix 5.

156 'Continuatio Sancrucensis II: a. 1234–1266', p. 640.

157 'Duci Austrie litteras cum certis pactis et conditionibus destinando domino Frederico Romanorum imperatori coronam regni et Hungariam dare promittebant'. Roger of Várad [Master Roger], 'Epistle to the Sorrowful Lament', pp. 149–51.

nay, the emperor of Constantinople, had encouraged the Mongol advance against Germany.[158]

In this particularly varied storm of conjecture, hearsay, and sinister conspiracy theories, hindsight is, again, an important issue as regards the building of the narrative. As Whalen notes about contemporary chroniclers' perspective about Frederick's arrogance and Innocent's flight to Lyon, 'These history writers, however, clearly collapse the circumstances of the pope's election and later events, anticipating the failed negotiations between the two sides, Innocent's flight to Lyons, and his eventual deposition of the emperor'.[159] Comparably, Matthew develops the conspiracy theory presented here into reality in 1244, the emperor's successful intervention — a fact also clearly supported by the eventual disappearance of the Mongols in Europe. This governs the entire story of crusading mobilization, the language of military manoeuvres, and the involvement of other members of the Hohenstaufen family. All these, and especially the latter, provide the momentum to carry on with the story of imperial troops, defending imperial lands and the whole of Christendom. What is more, the second 1241 cluster in the *Chronica majora* also has room to introduce a familiar Other, the Jews, whose alleged conspiracy adds to the image of the unfairly

---

158 'Duo nuncii Tartarorum venerunt ad papam. Dicebatur quoque, quod domini pape propositum fuit, inde quoque tractatum fuit secrecius, ut, si christianissimi titulo insigniretur rex ille Tartarorum, ipsum mitteret cum omnibus viris et viribus suis super vastigium Grecum, generum Fretherici, cismaticum christiane fidei, domino pape et imperatori Baldewino rebellem, et postea ipsum Frethericum contra Romanam curiam recalcitrantem', *HA*, III, p. 39. Although somewhat tenuous at this stage of research, these texts may be connected to a circle of familiar characters. If James Chambers is correct, Frederick was accused of such plotting in Philip of Pistoia's letter written and widely disseminated by Philip himself in 1241. Chambers, *The Devil's Horsemen*, p. 106. This statement is not supported by any primary source evidence, and to date I was unable to locate Philip's poison pen letter. More research is necessary to ascertain this connection. Philip, the bishop of Ferrara at the time (but soon to join the legatine network as legate in Germany, and later in Lombardy), was not only present at the Council of Lyon but also had an active relationship with Conrad of Hochstaden and Henry Raspe in the second half of the 1240s when he worked on the latter's election as anti-king. This contact is tenuous, but it seems reasonable to suggest that Raspe's circles in the mid-1240s were acutely aware of and probably disseminated such accusations. As the bishop of Ferrara, Philip was bishop of the pro-papal heartland in the so-called 'war of chanceries' between Frederick II and Gregory IX, ending in the 1239 excommunication of the emperor. Raccagni, 'The Crusade against Frederick II'. Philip was also a close friend of Salimbene de Adam, Franciscan chronicler and man of letters, who also waged the pope's war against the emperor with ink and parchment. More on Philip's later life and career in Canz, *Philipp Fontana im Dienste der Kurie*; Torre, 'La data della morte di Filippo Arcivescovo di Ravenna'; Petersen, *Prämonstratensische Wege nach Rom*, pp. 218–19, 281. For the other famous slanderer of the emperor, Cardinal Capocci, see note 169.

159 Whalen, *The Two Powers*, p. 134.

214   CHAPTER 4

treated Frederick II, who has to manoeuvre a political power game where ill will and sheer demonic *sceleritas* sabotage his fight for Christendom on a regular basis.

The Second 1241 Cluster

The second self-contained sequence under the year 1241 concerns the involvement of Frederick — through his sons — written in a tone and context that evokes contemporary crusading narratives. As Heather Blurton points out about the apocalyptic descriptions of cannibalistic Mongols, Matthew's 'contemporaries knew to read symbolically for contemporary relevance [...]. In other words, behind the apocalyptic symbolism of the Mongols lies a subtext of criticism directed at the leaders of Christendom'.[160] In front of this dark backdrop of discord and corruption in Christendom, and despite rumours and allegations, Frederick's crusading figure emerges triumphantly. Frederick's son Conrad may be appointed to stop the Mongol approach, but Matthew's entries are meant to be part of Frederick's story.[161]

After the first cluster, Matthew continues to interlace the continental progress of the war between pope and emperor with the Mongol story, and the interweaving subplots are tied to the separate strand of the history of England by Frederick's acknowledgement of the English king's alliance and unity with his own most Christian cause, which incidentally entailed kidnapping prelates: 'Et nos praedictorum principes successuum nostrorum participes, et vos praecipue, fieri gratulamur, quos in omni successurae felicitatis eventu ex unanimitate qua unimur cupimus esse consortes' (and we congratulate other princes, and you in particular, as being partakers in these aforesaid successes of ours, and whom we wish, by the unanimity

---

160 Blurton, *Cannibalism in High Medieval English Literature*, p. 86.

161 Henry and Conrad were Frederick II's sons: Henry (VII), king of the Romans, that is, king of Germany and co-ruler with his father between 1220 and 1235; and Conrad IV, who was crowned as king of the Romans and king of Italy in 1237 after Frederick II had dethroned Henry in 1235. Although it is clear that Matthew consistently refers to Enzio as Henry (e.g. as king of Tunis (Torres) and Gallura in *CM*, III, p. 587; in the Battle of Giglio: *CM*, IV, pp. 124–25), it is unlikely that Enzio was involved in any military manoeuvres in Central Europe since in July 1239 he was assigned as imperial vicar general in Lombardy and general-legate in Romagna, and on 3 May 1241, he participated in the capture of a papal fleet at the Battle of Giglio. See also note 18. Matthew drew the galleys of the Pisan and Genoese troops clashing on the bottom of fol. 147ᵛ in MS B. Enzio (Henry) is seated at the helm of the Pisan boat (Fig. 9). In 1242, he was mainly engaged in looting the territories of the Lombard Guelph Municipalities: he raided the Milanese area, besieged and took the Piacenza castle of Roncarello, and destroyed Treviglio and other localities on the left of the Adda until, wounded in the thigh by a dart near Palazzolo, in the Brescia area, he was forced to retire to Cremona. Pini, 'Enzo di Svevia, re di Sardegna'.

of feeling by which we are united, to participate in the occurrence of any future good fortune).[162] As ever, Matthew records that this news was duly disseminated, and the crowned heads of Europe were not unanimously pleased. Well, if not his victories over the pope's obedient servants — including Cardinal Otto of Montferrat, the bishop of Praeneste[163] — perhaps the emperor's victory over an equally formidable foe of Christendom, the Tartars, should please them:

> Completo igitur voto domini imperatoris, Domino permittente, misit idem imperator Henricum filium suum, qui de praelatis et eorum ducibus, ut dictum, triumpharat, ad fratrem Conradum, qui cum innumerabili exercitu ex diversis finibus imperii collecto, Tartarorum et Cumanorum [impetum] repellere magnifice parabatur, ut alter alterius fratris solatio mutuo roboraretur, et milite copiosiore stiparetur. Duxit autem secum quatuor milia equitantium jussu patris, et peditum manum non minimam, qui, cum aliis adjuncti fuissent quibus venerant in subsidium, incomparabilem exercitum conflaverunt. Quo comperto, hostium siluit jactantia, et arrogantia tepuit refraenata. Facta namque quadam congressione cruentissima juxta ripam fluvii Delpheos, non multum a Danubio distantis, multis utrobique cadentibus, tandem Deo propitio repulsus est hostilis exercitus, licet nullo numero posset comprehendi.

> (The emperor then, having, with the Lord's permission, effected his purpose, sent his son Henry, who had, as has been stated, conquered the prelates and their convoy, to join his brother Conrad, who was prepared with an innumerable army, raised from the various provinces of the empire to check the violence of the Tartars and Cumanians, in order that the brothers might mutually comfort and assist one another, and be surrounded by a larger force. The said Henry, by his father's orders, took with him four thousand cavalry and a large body of foot-soldiers, who, when united to the others to whose assistance they had come, composed an immense army; and when this was discovered by the enemy, their boastings were stilled, and their arrogance was checked and grew cold. For a most bloody battle took place near the banks of the river Delpheos, not far from the Danube, and after many had fallen

---

162 MS B, fol. 147ᵛ, col. b; *CM*, IV, p. 129; *EH*, I, pp. 355–56.

163 James of Pecorari (1231–1244), who was followed by István Báncsa (1251–1270) in his office. He also has a strong connection to intelligence about the Mongols at the time: Master Roger wrote the *Carmen miserabile* for him. Roger of Várad [Master Roger], 'Epistle to the Sorrowful Lament'.

216   CHAPTER 4

on both sides, the hostile army, although almost innumerable, was repulsed.)[164]

Matthew Paris is not the only English author that preserved this story in an imperial context. The *Tewkesbury Annals*, for example, notes the participation and victory of the duke of Bavaria in a riverside battle against the Mongols, in the last entry under the year 1240:[165]

> Obiit quaedam gens quae dicuntur Tartari, filii Ismael, egressi de cavernis ad xxx. milia milium et amplius. Vastaverunt omnes provincias per quas transitum faciebant. Sed dux Baverensis multos interfecit et in fluminis rivo praecipitavit.

> (Some people called Tartars, the sons of Ismael, having broken forth from caves, thirty thousand thousand and more. They had devastated all the provinces they had crossed. But the duke of Bavaria killed many of them in a small stream of a river.)[166]

Matthew's entry on the Hohenstaufens' involvement ends in the retreat of the immense Mongol army, 'Sed antequam retrocessit, quoddam, quod de Judaeorum fraude processit, existimantium ipsos hostes esse de Judaeis inclusis in montibus Caspiorum, et venientium in eorum subsidium et Christianorum subversionem, scelus immanissimum huic operi duxi breviter inserendum' (but before it retreated, a circumstance occurred, which proceeded from the trickery of the Jews, who thought that these enemies of ours were a portion of their Jewish race, who had been shut up in the Caspian mountains, and had therefore come to assist them, for the subversion of Christianity; and this enormous wickedness we have thought proper to insert in this work).[167]

At this point, in the second entry of the cluster, the story of kings and princes fighting the just war descends into an anecdotal account of an episode involving unnamed commoners and Jews, somewhere in Germany. Perhaps it is not surprising that the treachery of the Jews would

---

164 MS *B*, fol. 148ʳ, col. a; *CM*, IV, p. 131; *EH*, I, pp. 356–57.

165 A similar version of the story about the 'dus de Baiwière' is found in verses 30963–65 in Mousket, *Chronique rimée*, II, p. 681. For the discussion of the historical context and veracity of this passage, see note 17 in this chapter.

166 'Annales de Theokesberia', p. 118. The relatively rare term 'milia milium' also crops up in the *Chronica majora*, in Ivo of Narbonne's letter: 'nec possunt tamen milia milium computari'. *CM*, IV, p. 276. More on this letter in Chapter 5 ('1243: The Tartar Khan's Englishman'). Cf. 'Quem omnipotentis dei uirtute ut ceteros rebelles palam dimicando deuicimus et de suis computando *duo milia milium* pugnatorum necauimus, exceptis aliis quorum innumerabilis erat multitudo' in Hülegü's letter to the king of France in 1262 (Vienna, Österreichische Nationalbibliothek, MS 339, pp. 339–40). Meyvaert, 'An Unknown Letter of Hülegü' (my italics).

167 MS *B*, fol. 148ʳ, col. a; *CM*, IV, p. 131; *EH*, I, p. 356.

appear in Frederick's story. Almost blatantly so, Frederick was less hostile towards the Jews than, for example, the counts of Toulouse and Poitou, or the English king with a proven track record of discrimination and persecution of the worst kind, such as the harsh *Statute of Jewry* issued in 1253. For example, Frederick II commissioned thorough investigations to find if there were any truth in the rumours about their rituals and issued a privilege in July 1236 'describing the accusations against the Jews and their refutation, forbidding others from repeating the libel, and stating that the Jews were under the special supervision of the emperor as *servi camere nostre*'.[168] His sympathies for the Jewry, aggravated by his alleged atheism and ostentatious interest in all matters Muslim, were part and parcel of the poison pen letters and rhetoric circulated at the time, primarily by Raniero di Capocci (also known as Raynerius de Viterbo) and his circles.[169] This account of a nefarious plot straight from Germany is the last we hear about the Mongols until 1243. It begins by explaining the natural alliance between Mongols and Jews, the widespread belief of their ancient association:

> Labentibus autem illorum dierum curriculis, multi Judaeorum de partibus transmarinis, praecipue autem de imperio, credentes quod plebs Tartarorum et Cumanorum essent de genere eorum, quos Dominus in montibus Caspiis precibus magni Alexandri quondam inclusit, convenerunt in loco secretissimo ex communi condicto. Quos, qui sapientissimus eorum et potentissimus videbatur, sic alloquitur, dicens, 'Fratres, qui estis semen Abrahae praeclari, vinea Domini Sabaoth, Deus noster Adonay nos diu sub potestate Christianorum permisit affligi. Sed nunc venit tempus quo liberamur, ut nos vice versa Dei judicio et ipsos opprimamus, ut salvi fiant reliquiae Israel. Exierunt namque fratres nostri, tribus scilicet Israel, quondam inclusae, ut subdant sibi et nobis mundum universum. Et quanto praecessit

---

168 Abulafia, 'Ethnic Variety and its Implications', p. 219.

169 Cardinal Capocci was the pope's right-hand man, and the most vehement adversary of Frederick II in the papal court. Interestingly, in the 1220s, he is known to have maintained excellent relations with the English court, frequently exchanging letters and messengers with high prelates of the court. In 1217 he offered King Henry III his personal intervention with the pope; the British ambassadors to the Curia visited him regularly. In conflicts between England and France brought before the pope, Capocci almost always supported the English ambassadors as 'amicus regis Anglie'. This nexus was eroded when Frederick became Henry III's brother-in-law. He fought the emperor both with sword and ink. From 1236 onwards, culminating in 1245, he was a prolific author of vitriolic pamphlets such as *Ascendit de mare* (1236) and *Aspidis nova, Iuxta vaticinium Ysaie, and Eger cui lenia* (1245) about Frederick's godlessness, which contributed to his excommunication in 1245. Kamp, 'Capocci, Raniero di'. His letter to the pope about the execution of the bishop of Arezzo by Frederick II is copied in the *Chronica majora*. MS B, fol. 227^r, col. a; *CM*, v, p. 66; *EH*, II, p. 303. For the other famous slanderer of the emperor, Philip of Pistoia, see note 158.

durior et diuturnior tribulatio, tanto major nobis gloria subsequetur. Occurramus ergo eis in muneribus pretiosis, ipsos cum summo honore suscipientes. Vino, armis indigent, et frumento'.

> (During all this time, numbers of the Jews on the continent, and especially those belonging to the empire, thinking that these Tartars and Cumanians were a portion of their race, whom God had, at the prayers of Alexander the Great, shut up in the Caspian mountains, assembled on a general summons in a secret place, where one of their number, who seemed to be the wisest and most influential amongst them, thus addressed them: 'My brothers, seed of the illustrious Abraham, vineyard of the Lord of Sabaoth, whom our God Adonai has permitted to be so long oppressed under Christian rule, now the time has arrived for us to liberate ourselves, and by the judgment of God to oppress them in our turn, that the remnant of Israel may be saved. For our brethren of the tribes of Israel, who were formerly shut up, have gone forth to bring the whole world to subjection to them and to us. And the more severe and more lasting that our former suffering has been, the greater will be the glory that will ensue to us. Let us therefore go to meet them with valuable gifts and receive them with the highest honour: they are in need of corn, wine, and arms'.)[170]

In the *Chronica majora*, the connection between the Mongols and the Jews remains blurry at best.[171] While in an entry *s.a.* 1240, Matthew explains that the Mongols are believed to be one of the ten tribes who 'abandoned the law of Moses',[172] in the *Liber Additamentorum*, one letter lists the Jews as the victims of the Mongols: 'They have destroyed cities, castles, and even municipal towns, and spared neither Christians, pagans, nor Jews, putting to death all alike without mercy, except only the children, that their king Zingiton marks on the forehead with his seal'.[173] Judaism emerges in yet another context in the Mongol story in the letter of a Hungarian bishop who, relating the words of his Mongol prisoners, explains that the Mongols use Hebrew script (*literas Judaeorum*) taught to them by pale bearded foreigners who harm no one.[174]

---

170 MS *B*, fol. 148ʳ, col. a; *CM*, IV, pp. 131–32; *EH*, I, pp. 356–57.
171 Sophia Menache suggests that the earliest evidence for this later widespread belief is Peter Comestor's *Historia scholastica*. Menache, 'Tartars, Jews, Saracens and the Jewish-Mongol "Plot" of 1241', p. 332.
172 MS *B*, fol. 141ʳ, col. a; *CM*, IV, p. 77; *EH*, I, p. 313.
173 'Civitates, castra, immo et municipia destruendo, non solum Christianos, immo Paganos, Judaeos, nemini parcentes, omnibus indifferenter sine misericordia mortem inferentes, praeterquam parvulis tantum, quibus rex eorum, Zingiton vocatus, signa in frontibus imponit'. MS *LA*, fol. 86ʳ, col. a; *CM*, VI, p. 77; *EH*, III, p. 451.
174 MS *LA*, fol. 85ᵛ, col. b; *CM*, VI, p. 75; *EH*, III, p. 449.

While it has been suggested that this story reflects Matthew Paris's stereotyped image of the Jews, the convoluted double deception does not sound like Matthew's own creation.[175] The omniscient narrator of the Jewish episode formulates the entry by embedding a passage in direct speech by the *Judaeorum de partibus transmarinis*, which is worded in first person plural, from the subjective viewpoint of the Jews 'long oppressed under Christian rule'.

Quod verbum cum omnes gratanter accepissent, ut secretius fraudem suam occultarent, gladios et cultellos atque loricas quascunque poterant venales invenire emerunt, et in doliis ordinate reposuerunt. Dixeruntque palam principibus Christianis, quorum potestati subjacebant, quod *illi quos vulgus Tartaros dicebat, Judaei erant, nec bibebant vinum nisi a Judaeis vindemiatum, et hoc nobis significaverunt, magna instantia quasi a fratribus suis sibi dari talia vina, a nobis scilicet vindemiata, postulantes. Nos autem ipsos inhumanos et hostes publicos auferre de medio cupientes, et vos Christianos ab imminenti eorum tyrannica depopulatione liberare, paravimus circiter triginta dolia vino letaliter intoxicate referta, ipsis quantocius deferenda.* Toleraverunt igitur Christiani, ut ipsi Judaei tale xenium scelerati sceleratis optulissent. Sed cum in remotas partes Alemanniae pervenissent, et cum doliis suis quendam pontem transire pararentur, dominus pontis, ut moris erat, paagium pro transit sibi reddi postulavit. Ipsi autem frontose respondentes, et postulata reddere renuentes, dixerunt, quod pro utilitate imperii, immo totius Christianitatis, his negotiis sollicitarentur, directi ad Tartaros, ipsos vino suo cautius potionaturi. Gustos vero pontis suspectam habens Judaeorum assertionem, unum doliorum terebrando perforavit, nec inde ullus liquor eliquatus distillavit. Inde certior de fraude effectus, circulis ejectis illud dolium confregit, et apparuit armis diversis refertum.

(The whole assembly heard speech with pleasure, and at once bought all the swords, daggers, and armour, they could find for sale anywhere, and, in order to conceal their treachery, securely stowed them away in casks. They then openly told the Christian chiefs, under whose dominion they were, that *these people, commonly called Tartars, were Jews, and would not drink wine unless made by Jews, and of this they have informed us, and with great earnestness have*

---

175 'Matthew's accounts of Jews [...] were probably fairly typical of his mid-thirteenth-century milieu, and it is precisely for this reason that they are so interesting [...]. It is the justificatory purpose of Matthew's fictional constructions which makes them so particularly striking and potentially so dangerous'. Hyams, 'The Jewish Minority in Medieval England', pp. 282–83. Cited in Menache, 'Tartars, Jews, Saracens and the Jewish-Mongol "Plot" of 1241', p. 320.

begged to be supplied with some wine made by us, their brethren. We, however, desiring to remove from amongst us these our inhuman public enemies, and to release you Christians from their impending tyrannical devastation, have prepared about thirty casks full of deadly intoxicating wine, to be carried to them as soon as possible. The Christians therefore permitted these wicked Jews to make this wicked present to their wicked enemies. When, however, these said Jews had reached a distant part of Germany, and were about to cross a certain bridge with their casks, the master of the bridge, according to custom demanded payment of the toll for their passage: the Jews, however, replied insolently, refusing to satisfy his demands, saying that they were employed in this business for the advantage of the empire, indeed of all Christendom having been sent to the Tartars secretly to poison them with their wine. The keeper of the bridge, however, doubting the assertion of these Jews, bored a hole through one of the casks; but no liquor flowed there from; and becoming certain of their treachery, he took off the hoops of the cask, and, breaking it open, discovered that it was full of arms.)[176]

The Jews' direct speech in this entry does resemble actual letters relaying the news about the 'enclosed tribes' in the context of messianic expectations that were exchanged among Jewish communities in Spain, Sicily, and Germany. In these, the Mongols were seen as warriors 'sent by Providence to save the sons of Israel from the lengthy tyranny of the gentiles'.[177] Whether true or not, some German chronicles at the time recorded that Jews were celebrating the news of the Mongol onslaught; for example, Menache cites their Messianic exultation recorded in the *Annales Marbacenses* and the *Gestorum Treverorum Continuatio*.[178] Versions of or commentaries on these misguided speculations and letters were certainly available in Latin at the time and potentially lent themselves to speculations about schemes to exact vengeance on Christians.

Tying it to the rest of Frederick's story, the entry at one point obliquely refers to the emperor, when the Jews say that they were employed in this business '*pro utilitate imperii*, immo totius Christianitati' (*for the advantage of the empire*, indeed of all Christendom; my italics). It is also notable that the episode takes place somewhere where the Jews could meet with

---

176 MS B, fol. 148ʳ, cols a–b; *CM*, IV, pp. 131–33; *EH*, I, pp. 357–59 (my italics).

177 Menache, 'Tartars, Jews, Saracens and the Jewish-Mongol "Plot" of 1241', p. 334. James Chambers claims that some communities actually collected money to help the Mongols in their fight against Christendom but provides no evidence in support of this claim. Chambers, *The Devil's Horsemen*, pp. 35–36. Cited in Menache, 'Tartars, Jews, Saracens and the Jewish-Mongol "Plot" of 1241', p. 337.

178 Menache, 'Tartars, Jews, Saracens and the Jewish-Mongol "Plot" of 1241', p. 337. Also noted in Bradács, 'A tatárjárás osztrák elbeszélő forrásainak kritikája', p. 14.

'their brethren' to hand over their wine. This place is a 'distant part of Germany', but Germany nevertheless. The Mongols may be approaching the heartland of Christendom, but the other enemy, the Jews, are living in their midst. It is the latter discomfort that the German bridge-keeper articulates, evoking the previous and subsequent efforts of Christian rulers to distinguish Jews from the Christian majority, or make them disappear either by forced baptism or expulsion from their communities:

> Exclamans igitur ait; 'O proditio inaudita! ut quid tales inter nos patimur conversari?' Et statim ipse et alii, quos stupor convocavit, alia omnia dolia, quae protinus confregerunt, plena gladiis Coloniensibus sine capulis et cultellis sine manubriis, ordinate et conferte repositis, invenientes, omnibus in propatulo monstraverunt fraudis inauditae laqueos absconditos Judaeorum, qui publicis mundi hostibus, qui, ut dicebatur, armis maxime indigebant, maluerunt subvenire, quam Christianis, qui inter se ipsos tolerant conversari et in venalibus communicare, cum immo etiam cum Christianis liceat eis ea de causa foenerari. Legitur enim, 'Non foenerabis Egiptio', et subditur causa, 'quia colonum te et advenam in terra sua te Egiptii receperunt'. Traditi igitur sunt ipsi Judaei tortoribus, vel perpetuo carceri merito mancipandi, vel ipsis suis gladiis trucidandi.

> > (At this sight he cried out, 'Oh, unheard-of treachery, why do we allow such people to live amongst us?' And at once he and others, whom his astonishment had collected round him, broke open all the other casks, which, as soon as they had done, they found them also filled with Cologne swords and daggers, without hilts, closely and compactly stowed away; they then at once openly showed forth the hidden treachery and extraordinary deceit of the Jews, who chose rather to assist these, open enemies of the world in general, who, they said, were very much in need of arms to aid the Christians, who allowed them to live amongst them and communicate with them in the way of traffic. [It is to be read (Deut. 23. 7) that 'you shall not loathe an Egyptian', and the reason is given 'because Egyptians had received you as a settler and you as a stranger in their country'.][179] They were therefore at once handed over to the executioners, to be either consigned to perpetual imprisonment, or to be slain with their own swords.)[180]

---

179 This is missing from the translation in *EH*. Note the wordplay of adding the word 'colonus' (settler, farmer) to the biblical passage, to rhyme with the Latin name of the city where the episode is suggested to have taken place: Cologne. Though never specified where the 'in remotas partes Alemanniae' may be, the Jews' possession of 'gladiis Coloniensibus' may be another clue for the location.

180 MS *B*, fol. 148ʳ, col. b; *CM*, IV, p. 133; *EH*, I, p. 358.

222   CHAPTER 4

Both Mongol clusters under the year 1241 — the core of Frederick's story — are concluded with entries about double deception. On the one hand, in Frederick's case, 'deception about deception' in the imperial letter, which was thought by many — admittedly not by Matthew himself — to have been written under false pretences, as part of Frederick's ploy to conceal his wicked machinations with the Mongols. On the other hand, the Jews' ploy to deceive the Christians' by telling them that they were about to deceive the Mongols. In both cases Frederick's triumph over the Mongols is tainted by dark and twisting stories of *scelus*.[181] Previously, I noted the use of direct speech embedded into the Jewish story, creating the impression of an omniscient narrator. Here Matthew uses reported speech to situate the uncertainty outside his scriptorium — 'there were some *who said that* the emperor had, of his own accord, plotted this infliction of the Tartars' and 'the Jews, *who thought that* these enemies of ours were a portion of their Jewish race' — retaining his authority and distance from hearsay and common people's confusion.

These reports, although wrought out of received material, show Matthew the historiographer at work, his way of constructing a narrative using familiar methods of alternating and embedding. The further deconstruction of the clusters reveals the nature of the materials he worked from. While it is now clear that Matthew wrote from an anti-papal stance, understanding the layers of Matthew's received material also shows the powerful influence of the network of chanceries and monastic scriptoria all over Europe, which is important, since, needless to say, chronicles are innately ideological. As John Arnold formulates, they 'were often direct repositories of certain kinds of power, as kings, princes, popes, and bishops ensured that important documents were circulated to chronicle-writing centres in order that they be copied into the narrative, and thus preserved and disseminated'.[182]

Who exactly delivered these texts to Matthew and how they obtained them in the first place may never be established with full certainty. David Knowles writes that 'public men realized that their share in events could best be preserved for posterity by judicious conversations at St Albans'.[183] But a more robust and extensive network glimmers through Matthew's text

---

181 The repeated use of the word 'scelus' (crime) in both episodes also ties them together. Frederick's letter was thought to be a means to cover up crime ('per hanc elegantem epistolam scelus tam nepharium nequiter palliasse'), and the entry on the Jewish-Mongol plot, containing 'scelus immanissimum' in both its introduction and title, piles even more of it into the entry: 'Toleraverunt igitur Christiani, ut ipsi Judaei tale xenium scelerati sceleratis optulissent'.

182 Arnold, *What Is Medieval History?*, p. 37. Arnold, citing Gabrielle Spiegel, states that the chronicle is an innately ideological form, 'all the while dissimulating its status *as* ideology under the guise of a mere accounting of "what was"'. Spiegel, *Romancing the Past*, p. 2.

183 Knowles, *The Religious Orders in England*, p. 294.

than judicious conversations: there was a great deal of written documents forwarded to his scriptorium. As a result, Matthew Paris's chronicle deals with the issue of Frederick's relations with the kings within and outside his realm in such detail that his English chronicle has become a one-stop shop for sources about thirteenth-century imperial history.[184] And it is this imperial history where one can find the origins of the Mongol subplot.

The chapter began with an often misquoted saying, commonly attributed to Goethe. But the truth of the matter is that Goethe never said that; in fact, what he said was vaguely the opposite, *man sieht nur das, was man weiß,* 'one sees only what one knows'.[185] In this part of Matthew's Mongol story, what Matthew sees is what he knows from texts he receives from pro-Hohenstaufen networks of power and information. As was noted at the beginning, this material was heavily mediated through a chain of transmitters before reaching Matthew's desk, but it seems that what he noticed — *erblickte* — in this was what he was looking for: materials underpinning his continental history of pope and emperor.

---

184 Hubert Houben goes as far as calling Frederick one of the protagonists of the *Chronica majora*: 'Mehr über die Person Friedrichs erzählen dagegen zwei geistliche Chronisten, in deren Geschichtswerken der Kaiser die Rolle des Protagonisten spielt: der englische Benediktiner Matthäus Paris (1200–1259) aus der Abtei St Albans (norwestlich von London) und der italianische Franziskaner Salimbene de Adam (1221–1288/89) aus Parma'. Houben, *Kaiser Friedrich II*, p. 14. It is also notable that the nineteenth-century Monumenta Germaniae Historica series devoted nearly a whole volume to excerpting Matthew's account of 'German' history: Paris, 'Ex Mathei Parisiensis operibus'. This excerpted edition of Matthew's chronicle remains a staple in German historiography; even recent German-language scholarship cites Matthew's text using the Liebermann edition of German-related passages of the *Chronica majora*, primarily those which concern Frederick II. See, for example, the previously cited Gramsch-Stehfest, 'Entangled Powers', p. 378.

185 For precision's sake, according to the *Lexikon der Goethe-Zitate*, there are two known instances where Goethe formulated this thought, in both cases much more precisely than the popular commonplace: 'Was man weiß, sieht man erst!' appeared in a preface to Goethe's art journal *Propyläen*, and 'Man erblickt nur, was man schon weiß und versteht' is known from a letter to an F. von Müller on 24 April 1819. Goethe, *Lexikon der Goethe-Zitate*; Goethe, *Gedenksausgabe der Werke, Briefe und Gespräche*, XIII, p. 142, XXIII, p. 52.

CHAPTER 5

Flight

Rivalling Stories of Retreat (1243–1248)

> Behold, where the billowy clouds flow by,
> And leave us alone in the clear gray sky!
> Our horses are ready and steady, — So, ho!
> I'm gone like a dart from the Tartar's bow.[1]

Echoing the earliest Mongol-related entries, the post-1241 story of the Mongols is once again governed by materials coming from the nebulous network of information exchange that converged at Lyon in 1245. The Council of Lyon finally becomes reality in the narrative, and Matthew finds himself giving a full account of the proceedings in his chronicle. The Mongol-related entries under the years 1243–1245 contain themes similar to the pre-invasion account (see Chapter 3), but that is not the only thing that ties them together. The commonalities between the pre-invasion entries and the story afterwards emerge more sharply against the backdrop of Frederick's German military operations (by proxy) described in the 1241 entries wedged in between them.

The year 1241 in the *Chronica majora*, between fols 141ᵛ col. a and 154ʳ col. b, was dominated by Frederick II, and the Mongol story therein takes up a considerable amount of space. On the eight folios between 140ᵛ (1240) and 148ʳ (1241) there is something written about the Mongols on every other folio page, often massive contiguous clusters, as shown in Chapter 4. After the last entry in 1241, the hiatus in the story is conspicuously long: two years pass by — thirty-four busy folio pages filled with *historia* — but no more mention of the Mongol threat until suddenly a letter brings back the 'detestable memory' of Eastern Europe's invasion by the Mongol army. On the whole, it is indeed the *memory* of the Mongol invasion that is dealt with in this next phase, and episodes like the seemingly misplaced and spurious entry about Frederick liberating the kingdom of Hungary further corroborate this development.[2]

The post-invasion Mongol episodes open with Ivo of Narbonne's long and rambling 1243 letter, incorporating embedded accounts as usual. After

---

1 Proctor, 'Hunter's Song', in Woods, ed., *English Poetry and Prose*, p. 1169.
2 MS B, fol. 170ᵛ, cols a–b: *CM*, IV, p. 298; *EH*, I, pp. 489–90.

226   CHAPTER 5

this complex bundle of narratives, the Mongol story becomes increasingly fragmented and tapers off into short references and brief entries: an assemblage of disparate pieces of intelligence about the old/new foe of Christendom moving to where it hurts the most: the Holy Land during Louis IX's crusade. This marks the transposition of the Mongol story back where it seemingly came from — the East. It is here that the 1238 quip of Peter des Roches can be picked up again, history (at least Matthew's) proving the Butterfly Bishop wrong.[3] In the last fifteen years of the chronicle, the increasingly sporadic and remote references to the Mongols finally come full circle: the last ever Mongol-related entry in 1257 briefly puts an end to the story of Mongol ravages with a curt sentence: 'Around this year, the detestable Tartars destroyed the Assassins, a race still more detestable, who are called dagger-bearers'.[4] Matthew knew this was the last, as in the same entry — breaking the fourth wall and talking to his reader — he closes the story once and for all.[5] But the last chapter covering the *Chronica majora*'s story of the Mongol invasion in East Central Europe stops short much earlier, in 1248.[6] In the five years between Ivo of Narbonne's account and 1248, the references to Eastern Europe (some of them chronologically misplaced) oscillate between Mongols in the 'North' and Mongols in the East:

North:	1243 Ivo of Narbonne[7]
	1244 Frederick liberates Hungary[8]
North to East:	1244 Tartars disperse towards the East[9]
East:	1244 Letter of prelates in the Holy Land[10]
North:	1244 Archbishop Peter[11]
East:	1244 Demands of the Mongols from the prince of Antioch[12]
	1245 The Council of Lyon (four references)[13]
North:	1246 New irruption in Hungary[14]
	1246 Cardinal notes the Mongols in Hungary[15]
	1246 Cistercian cardinal lists the Mongols in Hungary in his criticism of the pope[16]
East:	1247 French king receives Mongol threatening letter[17]

---

3 See the discussion of the 1238 entry in Chapter 3 ('1237: Chaldeans, Medes, Persians, and Armenians').

4 'Circulo ejusdem anni Tartari detestabiles Assessinos detestabiliores, quos cultelliferos appellamus, destruxerunt'. MS *R*, fol. 202ᵛ, col. b; *CM*, v, p. 655; *EH*, iii, p. 251 (my translation).

5 See note 171.

6 The last truly Eastern European reference in the Mongol story comes even earlier, in 1246 in which a Cistercian cardinal lists the Mongols in Hungary in his criticism of the pope: MS *B*, fol. 208ʳ, col. a; *CM*, iv, pp. 578–79; *EH*, ii, p. 190.

North: 1247 Conrad's flight from Germany[18]

1248 Messengers from the Tartars to the pope to attack Frederick's cousin[19]

Swinging back and forth across these years, Matthew essentially dovetails two Mongol stories together, establishing the logical connection between them. The last stage in the chronicle of the Mongol invasion in Eastern Europe starts (1243) and ends (1246) in the Kingdom of Hungary, with a bit of the Orient thrown in the middle.

1243: The Tartar Khan's Englishman

Deeply personal, written from the perspective of a rank-and-file outcast, illustrated with gory images, and containing another adventurer's participatory story, Ivo of Narbonne's eyewitness testimony borders on confessions and, as such, is one of the most popular parts of the *Chronica majora*.[20] The text 'greatly alarm[ing] even the most undaunted men' is a true outlier in every sense. The letter is no doubt intended to be part of the chronicle's Mongol story, and Matthew anchors it in the narrative of the conflict between pope and emperor in many ways. For example, in the entry directly preceding it, he notes that some (unnamed) 'nobilibus et profundi consilii personis' (noblemen, and persons of profound wisdom) attempted to curb the renewed erosion of the peace process between pope and emperor — to no avail.[21] Ivo, in turn, describes how 'totus ille nephandus exercitus repente disparuit, omnesque illi cursores in miserabilem Hungariam sunt

---

7 MS B, fols 166[v], col. b–167[v], col. b; *CM*, IV, pp. 270–77; *EH*, I, pp. 467–73.
8 MS B, fol. 170[v], cols a–b; *CM*, IV, p. 298; *EH*, I, pp. 489–90.
9 MS B, fol. 170[v], col. b; *CM*, IV, pp. 299–300; *EH*, I, p. 491.
10 MS B, fols 175[v], col. b–176[v], col. b; *CM*, IV, pp. 337–47; *EH*, I, pp. 522–28.
11 MS B, fol. 182[r], cols a–b; *CM*, IV, pp. 386–89; *EH*, II, pp. 28–31.
12 MS B, fol. 182[r], col. b; *CM*, IV, pp. 389–90; *EH*, II, p. 31.
13 MS B, fols 187[v]–193[v]; *CM*, IV, pp. 430–73; *EH*, II, pp. 64–86.
14 MS B, fol. 203[r], col. b–203[v], col. a; *CM*, IV, p. 547; *EH*, II, p. 165.
15 MS B, fol. 208[r], col. a; *CM*, IV, pp. 578–79; *EH*, II, p. 190.
16 MS B, fol. 208[r], col. a; *CM*, IV, pp. 578–79; *EH*, II, p. 190.
17 MS B, fol. 212[r], col. a; *CM*, IV, pp. 607–08; *EH*, II, p. 214.
18 MS B, fol. 215[v], col. a; *CM*, IV, pp. 634–35; *EH*, II, pp. 235–36.
19 MS B, fol. 223[r], col. a; *CM*, V, pp. 37–38; *EH*, II, p. 280.
20 MS B, fols 166[v], col. b–167[v], col. b; *CM*, IV, pp. 270–77; *EH*, I, pp. 467–73. Base-de-page drawing on fol. 167[r].
21 In the entry entitled 'Humiliatus est imperator', MS B, fol. 166[v], col. a; *CM*, IV, p. 269; *EH*, I, p. 466.

reversi' (In a moment, all that execrable race vanished, all those riders returned into wretched Hungary).[22] Although the disappearing act of the Mongol army seems to connect nicely to what comes after — Frederick delivering Hungary from the grasp of the Mongols in 1244 — it does not quite fit. The perspective, the voice, the protagonists, and the locations make it unique and self-standing within the narrative of the chronicle at large.

First and foremost, Ivo's letter is unique because of its narrator. As opposed to others to whom Matthew gave a voice in his chronicle either by copying their letters or quoting their utterances, as far as we can tell, Ivo seems to be a man of no import whatsoever. What is more, he is an outcast and a drifter. His letter is one of those Matryoshka dolls that contain another letter, this time by a man even more of an outcast and a drifter than himself, the man who came to be known as the 'khan's Englishman'.[23] Both their life stories and eyewitness accounts about the Mongols have been the subject of tangential speculations, used chiefly as much-needed primary sources for the history of European religious dissent as well as intercultural connections and diplomacy.[24]

The structure of the letter is similar to the ones already discussed, albeit somewhat less complex (see Table 2). Peter Biller summarizes the letter as 'a conversation between a renegade Englishman, who had served the Tartars, and had been one of their emissaries to the Hungarian royal court, [that] was used in a letter written by Ivo, a renegade cleric from Narbonne who saw the Tartars retreating from Vienna'.[25] If Biller's summary sentence sounds confusing, it is because of the usual mise-en-abîme depth of the serially embedded material, which, in this instance, is not as easy to separate as in other similar entries.

---

22 MS B, fol. 167ʳ, col. b; *CM*, IV, p. 273; *EH*, I, p. 470.

23 The book that gave him this epithet is the semi-fictitious swashbuckler in which journalist-author Gabriel Ronay boldly identifies the anonymous *anglicus* with Robert Fitzwalter, the leader of the Barons' Revolt against King John. Ronay, *The Tartar Khan's Englishman*.

24 While Ivo's letter is most frequently cited in scholarship concerning the Mongol invasion in East Central Europe, many scholars picked up on its unique source value in researching Catharism in thirteenth-century Europe. Zbíral, 'Date of the "De Heresi Catharorum"'; Biller, 'Northern Cathars and Higher Learning'; Jackson, 'The Crusade against the Mongols (1241)'; Segl, *Ketzer in Österreich*.

25 Biller, *The Measure of Multitude*, p. 229.

Table 2. The structure of Ivo of Narbonne's letter with Matthew Paris's preface and commentary (MP: Matthew Paris; IN: Ivo of Narbonne; ?: descriptive/ unidentifiable voice).

1	2	3
MP: Matthew's preface to Ivo's letter		
	IN: *Salutatio*	
	IN: Preface to Confessions	
	IN: Confessions	
		IN: The Englishman's story
		IN: The Englishman's description of the Mongols (religion, appearance, weaponry)
	?: Military aims	
	?: Deception	
	?: State and response of Church	
	IN: *Exhortatio*	
MP: Commentary		

The similarity to other letters, though not their structure, is not lost on Matthew who prefaces it in his own words about 'other letters to the same effect'. The function of this brief foreword is not so much to tie it to the narrative flow of entries preceding and following it, as tying it to the rest of the pieces of the Mongol story inserted elsewhere in the chronicle, especially Frederick's:

Eisdem diebus, haec epistola archiepiscopo Burdegalensi transmissa, quae in multis consonat epistolae imperiali, regibus multis Christianis directa, de horribili vastatione inhumanae gentis, quam Tartaros vocant (sed in hac Tattari, vel Tatari) nuncupantur, multos etiam constantes viros vehementer perterruit.

(At the same time, the following letter, sent to the archbishop of Bordeaux, very greatly alarmed even the most undaunted men. The letter agrees in many things with the imperial letter directed to many Christian kings, concerning the horrible devastations of this inhuman people whom they call Tartars, but in this letter they are called Tattars, or Tatars.)[26]

After Matthew's introduction, Ivo's letter starts with a warning for Christians who, unlike what Matthew said in the foreword, were most undaunted and not at all greatly alarmed in the face of the gravest danger of Christians' impending extermination. More than just an introduction to Ivo's long personal life story leading up to the cataclysm which he witnessed in Austria decades later, this passage is the counterpart of the *exhortatio* at the very end of the letter. In this way, rhetorically flanked by Ivo's words addressed to the bishop and other potentates, the epistle also serves as a frame for another story, a report about another renegade's encounter with the Mongols, written in third person singular. The recursive embedding and the play with the grammatical person of the narrator (third person singular narrator-historian, first person singular storyteller, third person singular embedded story) creates extradiegetic, intradiegetic, and metadiegetic layers, or stories within stories (narrative levels are shown in the numbered columns of Table 2).

The letter itself is enclosed between Ivo's own introduction clarifying his aims and the *exhortatio* proper at the end, which both urge the bishop to take heed of the Mongol story and see the danger in the context of the disunity of the Church. Following Matthew's and his own introduction, Ivo's letter describes his own trials and tribulations being persecuted by the powerful Robert of Courçon, and for years — perhaps even decades — travelling on a kind of underground railroad of Patarenians to Wiener Neustadt.[27] His adventures provide a unique insight into the network of dissent across Europe — in fact, this letter is one of the most valuable sources that attest to their existence in Lombardy and Austria.[28] In Neustadt he witnesses a huge Mongol army ransacking and pillaging the city until the allied European forces appear on the horizon.[29] Ivo's description of the Mongols' conduct is perhaps the most graphic in all the

---

26 MS *B*, fol. 166ᵛ, col. b; *CM*, IV, p. 270; *EH*, I, p. 467.

27 Robert of Courçon (or Curzon) was canon of the cathedral chapter of Paris (title of S. Stefano al Monte Celio). He was appointed as legate in France to preach the crusade against the Albigensians and to prepare for the general council in 1213 and again in 1214. He died in 1219. Eubel, *Hierarchia catholica medii aevi*, pp. 5, 47, 205. This means that Ivo's rambling across Europe, summarized roughly in one folio, lasted for about twenty years.

28 Peter Segl devotes an entire chapter to Ivo's ramblings in his comprehensive monograph on heretic movements in Austria. Segl, *Ketzer in Österreich*.

29 An examination of the historical events at Neustadt based on this letter in Gießauf, 'Herzog Friedrich II. von Österreich und die Mongolengefahr'; Segl, *Ketzer in Österreich*, pp. 93–100. More recently Pow, 'The Historicity of Ivo of Narbonne's Account'.

Chronica majora, echoing the most gruesome passages in contemporary eyewitness accounts.[30]

> Quorum cadaveribus principes cum suis cenofaris aliisque lotofagis, quasi pane vescentes, nihil praeter ossa vulturibus relinquebant. Sed quod mirum est, famelici et edaces vultures, quae forte supererant, reliquiis vesci minime dignabantur. Mulieres autem vetulas et deformes antropofagis, qui vulgo reputantur, in escam quasi pro diarrio dabant; nec formosis vescebantur, sed eas clamantes et ejulantes in multitudine coituum suffocabant. Virgines quoque usque ad exanimationem opprimebant, et tandem abscisis earum papillis, quas magistratibus pro deliciis reservabant, ipsis virgineis corporibus lautius epulabantur.

>> (The Tattar chiefs, with the houndish cannibals their followers, fed upon the flesh of the carcasses, as if they had been bread, and left nothing but bones for the vultures. But, wonderful to tell, the vultures, hungry and ravenous, would not condescend to eat the remnants of flesh, if any by chance were left. The old and ugly women were given to their dog-headed cannibals — anthropophagi, as they are called — to be their daily food; but those who were beautiful, were saved alive, to be stifled and overwhelmed by the number of their ravishers, in spite of all their cries and lamentations. Virgins were deflowered until they died of exhaustion; when their breasts were cut off to be kept as dainties for the chiefs, and their bodies furnished a jovial banquet for the savages.)[31]

Peter Segl argues that Ivo's claim that he personally encountered a Mongol attack during his stay in Austria must be taken seriously, even if the explicit details of their conduct are exaggerated in his eyewitness account.[32] For

---

30 The level of horrors in the description, however, is not at all unique among eyewitness accounts such as Thomas of Spalato, Roger of Várad, or John of Plano Carpini. For example, Thomas writes about corpses of children impaled on lances 'like fish on a spear'. As Johannes Gießauf writes, these descriptions cut the Mongols in standard apocalyptic or barbarian models 'down to size': 'In their reports dealing with the crushing defeats by the hitherto unknown enemies the authority of topos was undermined by the power of individual experience'. Gießauf, 'A Programme of Terror and Cruelty', p. 96.

31 MS B, fol. 167ʳ, col. a; *CM*, IV, p. 273; *EH*, I, pp. 469–70.

32 Segl argues that an attack on Vienna would have been noted by contemporary historiography, but for Wiener Neustadt, an *oppidum* rather than *civitas*, this need not be the case. Segl, *Ketzer in Österreich*, p. 97. Besides citing the chroniclers of Garsten, Heiligenkreuz, and Zwettl to confirm that the Mongols made inroads into the territory of Austria, Segl underpins the validity of Ivo's account by letters written by Duke Frederick II. On 13 June 1241, he wrote from Vienna to King Conrad IV that the Tatars had invaded his country but remained only for a short time because they were afraid of him. They killed about a hundred people and lost three hundred, but since they had withdrawn only two days' march away from the border of Austria, a new incursion was to be expected any day. Segl also notes that

232 CHAPTER 5

others, this particular description of violence has also raised questions about the authenticity of the passage and Ivo's letter in general. Adding gruesome details is usually attributed to Matthew's own authorship, and the degree of his fabrication is approached in various ways in scholarship. Heather Blurton, for example, emphasizes the narrative elements used to construct an apocalyptic siege scene at an allegorically named *Civitas Nova* and analyses the text as Matthew's own (at least partly): 'if there was an original, Matthew has clearly embroidered upon it to create his most grotesque and most overtly literary representation of cannibalism.'[33]

A great deal has been written about European sources associating the Mongol invaders with rape, indiscriminate killing, and cannibalism, and due to its grisly detail, this particular episode in the *Chronica majora* is one of the most frequently cited examples for the Western view of the Mongols, drawing together a number of topoi found in their description. Comparing contemporary sources Gian Andri Bezzola argues that the image of defiling Christian women is a topos that is also to be found independently of the Tartar image that prevailed in the Western imagination.[34] Likewise, cannibalism is a topos found in other well-known sources such as the Dominican Simon of Saint-Quentin and many others.[35] Even in the *Secret History of the Mongols*, there is a line of generous poetic licence briefly noting that the 'Four Hounds' (generals) of Chinggis Khan customarily ate human flesh on the day of battle.[36] The tenacity and uniformity of this characterization of the Mongols in Christian Europe

---

nine days later, on 22 June 1241, he informed Henry of Tanne, bishop of Constance, about the Mongol incursions into his territory, during which his troops annihilated seven hundred men or more. Segl, *Ketzer in Österreich*, pp. 97–99. Though Segl's interpretation seems correct, note that the phrase 'ex ipsis per exercitia nostre milicię septingenti vel amplius ceciderunt' is translated as *seventy* men in Bradács, 'A tatárjárás osztrák elbeszélő forrásainak kritikája', p. 9. Both of these letters can be found in the so-called Ottobeuren manuscript, MS *OB*, fols 6[r–v], 7[r].

33 'Matthew overlays a classic Gog and Magog apocalyptic narrative with a selection of elements from other genres: from the Marvels of the East, dog-headed cannibals; from hagiography, the nipples of virgins; and perhaps even echoes of the giant of Mont-St-Michel of Arthurian romance'. Blurton, *Cannibalism in High Medieval English Literature*, p. 95. Very early on, Gustav Strakosch-Grassmann also suggests that it is 'ganz unwahrscheinlich, dass diese von Yvo behauptete Thatsache wirklich stattgefunden hat'. Strakosch-Grassmann, *Der Einfall der Mongolen in Mitteleuropa*, p. 146.

34 Bezzola, *Die Mongolen in abendländischer Sicht*, p. 84.

35 'They devour the flesh of men like lions, either roasted with fire or boiled, sometimes out of necessity, sometimes for the pleasure of it, and other times in order to incite fear and horror in people who will hear about it'; Simon of Saint-Quentin, 'History of the Tartars', xxx. 77. John of Plano Carpini writes, 'Their food consists of everything that can be eaten, they feed on dogs, wolves, foxes, and horses and, in times of emergency, on human flesh'. Bk IV, ch. 7 in Gießauf, *Die Mongolengeschichte des Johannes von Piano Carpine*, p. 93.

36 *The Secret History of the Mongols*, p. 119. Cited in Simon of Saint-Quentin, 'History of the Tartars', n. 1 on xxx. 77.

invited modern scholars to consider perceptions and their sources regarding the inhuman nature of the Other. Specifically about this description, Blurton, for instance, suggests that Matthew used the trope of Mongol cannibalism as a textual locus for the consideration of the internal threats to Christendom, whereby 'in their cannibalism the Mongols threaten to consume a Christendom that is, in any case, devouring itself from within'.[37]

More importantly, detecting the metaphorical depths of the entry, Blurton points out that internal dissent is equated with the external threat — perhaps not coincidentally evoking the 'five pains of Christendom' discussed at the Council of Lyon at length — when the letter 'uses the Tartar threat to draw attention to the problem he identifies of internal divisions within the body of the church itself. [...] The story within a story that he relates takes the theme of heresy as its crucial subtext'.[38] Continuing this thought about the role of the cannibalism topos, it is hard to miss that the very person enumerating the plagues upon Christendom is often described in the *Chronica majora* as a parasitic threat to the integrity of Christendom's body politic. While the cannibalistic Mongols should act as a foil to the Christian pope who is shown to be preaching resistance and defence against them, in view of the recurring theme of Innocent IV's extortions, avaricious schemes, and failure to attain Christian unity, they are in fact very similar: Christendom is indeed being devoured from within — partially by the pope himself.

The letter is also well known for another reason: Matthew's illustration found on fol. 167[r] is used in a myriad of readers, books, and textbooks to illustrate the Mongol atrocities in general (Fig. 7). In the chronicle, it seems to serve as an illustration for the description of cannibalism in Ivo's letter, but it is also more than that. On the one hand, by evoking images of the monstrous races and odd beasts in contemporary *mappae mundi* it visually connects the story to northern barbarians, Scythian Essedones.[39] On the other hand, Ivo's letter has descriptive parts that correspond to various elements of the drawing; some minute detail evokes other textual descriptions elsewhere in the chronicle.[40] In fact, it can be considered a so-called 'catalogue illustration' for a bunch of different descriptions, including Ivo's own words and the one found in the letter by Frederick II.[41]

The caption over the cannibal feast on the left reads 'Nephandi tartari vel tattari humani carnibus vescentes'; this adjective for the Mongols is

---

37 Blurton, *Cannibalism in High Medieval English Literature*, p. 95.
38 Blurton, *Cannibalism in High Medieval English Literature*, p. 96.
39 See note 57.
40 See Appendix 8 available online at <https://brepols.figshare.com>, from the link <https://doi.org/10.1484/A.14453112>.
41 MS B, fol. 145[r]; see Fig. 6.

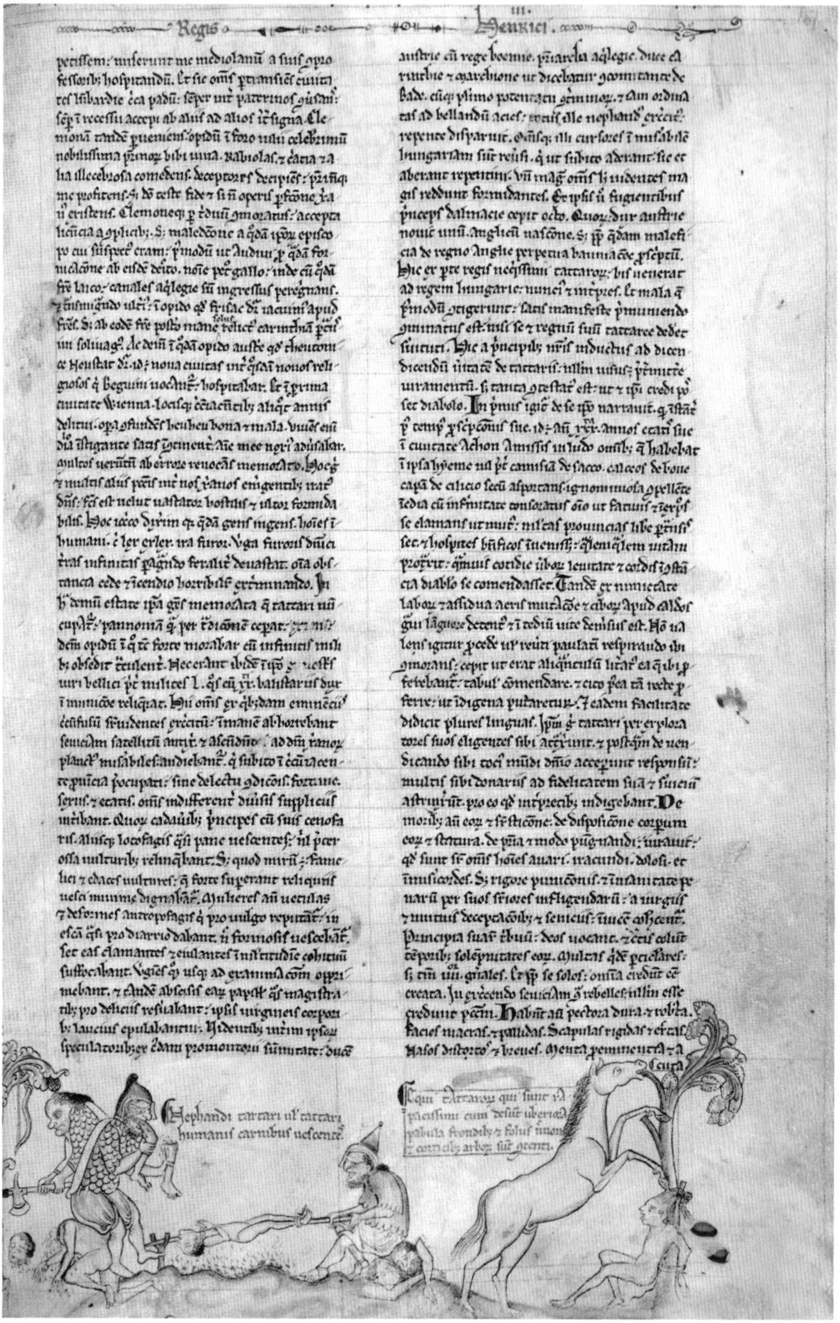

Figure 7. Cannibal feast, MS *B*, fol. 167[r]. By permission of the Parker Library, Corpus Christi College, Cambridge.

unique for this particular letter.[42] On the right, above the figure of the horse, the wording of the caption 'Equi Tattarorum qui sunt rapacissimi cum desunt uberiora pabula, frondibus et foliis necnon et corticibus arborum sunt contenti' corresponds to the letter's descriptions and, quite precisely, the unique name for the Mongols, rarely used in the chronicle. The variant spelling of the ethnonym in the rubric (*Tattari vel Tartari*) repeats the note in the preamble of Ivo's letter,[43] and the long-haired individual tied to the tree on the right refers to 'virgines quoque usque ad exanimationem opprimebant, et tandem abscisis earum papillis, quas magistratibus pro deliciis reservabant, ipsis virgineis corporibus lautius epulabantur' (virgins were deflowered until they died of exhaustion; when their breasts were cut off to be kept as dainties for the chiefs, and their bodies furnished a jovial banquet for the savages).[44]

Other features echo Frederick II's letter and other descriptions. For example, the image and rubric of the horse are more detailed than Ivo's 'solent autem non maximis, sed fortissimis equis, et parvo pabulo contentis' in the text.[45] Lewis suggests that it refers to the description under 1240 containing 'equos habentes magnos et fortes qui frondes et etiam arbores comedant',[46] but it is no less similar to Frederick II's line 'deficiente vero cibo, corticibus arborum et foliis et herbarum radicibus dicuntur esse contenti equi eorum'.[47] This description of strong horses that can find themselves food in harsh conditions was becoming common knowledge around this time; for instance, a similar description (albeit with no reference to trees) also appears in John of Plano Carpini's description which was not available for Western audiences until he returned to Lyon in 1247: 'Qui responderunt nobis quod si duceremus in Tartariam equos illos quos habebamus, cum nives essent magne et nescirent fodere erbam sub nive, sicut equi Tartarorum, nec inveniri posset aliquid aliud ad manducandum pro ipsis, cum Tartari nec stramina nec fenum nec pabulum habeant, morerentur omnes' (They [the *millenarius* and other local nobles] told us that all of our horses would perish on the proposed trip to *Tartaria*. Because

---

42 E.g. 'cujus ut vobis ritus nefandos breviter prosequar'; 'ille nephandus exercitus', *CM*, IV, pp. 270, 273. Interestingly, it is used for 'Conradus filius Fretherici, nefandus nefandi', in another Mongol-related passage later. *CM*, IV, p. 634. See also the discussion of the rubric in relation to Legate Otto's information about the names of the Tartars in Chapter 4, esp. note 121.

43 *CM*, IV, p. 270; *EH*, I, p. 467.

44 *CM*, IV, p. 273; *EH*, I, p. 470.

45 The rubric says 'Equi Tattarorum qui sunt rapacissimi cum desunt uberiora pabula, frondibus et foliis necnon et corticibus arborum sunt contenti'. The short note in the text is on the next page, the verso of the folio with the image: MS *B*, fol. 167ᵛ, col. a; *CM*, IV, p. 275; *EH*, I, p. 471.

46 MS *B*, fol. 140ᵛ, col. b; *CM*, IV, p. 77; *EH*, I, p. 313.

47 MS *B*, fol. 145ᵛ, col. b; *CM*, IV, p. 115; *EH*, I, p. 344.

of the large amount of snow, they could not scrape out the grass from under the blanket of snow, as the Tartar horses do. Since the Tartars had no straw, hay, or fodder, we could not find any other fodder for them.)[48] Even more striking is the similarity of the phrase to Thomas of Spalato's 'parvo stipularum pabulo sunt contenti'.[49]

The oriental-looking bow hanging from the tree on the left refers to their superior bowsmanship, which is a recurrent distinguishing feature of the Mongols in nearly all descriptions: while Ivo phrases this as 'sed prerogativam habent in arcubus et argutam industriam pugnandi',[50] elsewhere they appear as 'sagittarii incomparabiles' or 'sagittarii mirabiles'.[51] The bow itself looks like a recurving bow. While Matthew's penchant for close-up mounted combat scenes means there is more lance action in general, some drawings do feature archers, whose bows are generally drawn as a single arch.[52] The unusual looking Mongol bow, although strikingly similar to the actual Mongolian composite bows used in battle, may have been a generic indication of the differently shaped weapon of the Other.[53]

As opposed to the lack of textual references to the bow's shape, the armour worn by the warriors chopping up and devouring people appears both in Ivo's letter and elsewhere in the chronicle. Ivo writes 'de coriis earundem bullitis sibi arma levia quidem, sed tamen impenetrabilia, coaptarunt [...]. A tergo debilius armati, ne fugiant, non prius a conflictu recedunt' (out of the tanned hides of these animals [lions, bears, and other beasts] they made for themselves armour of a light description but impenetrable [...] their back armour is thin, that they may not be tempted to run away).[54] The warrior's strange smooth back and scaly mail shirt also have textual equivalents elsewhere, a little more in the way of explanation as for the scales, for example, 'cruda gestant coria, bovina, asinina, vel equina; insutis laminis ferreis pro armis muniuntur' (they wear raw hides

---

48 Bk IX, ch. 5 of the *Ystoria*. Gießauf, *Die Mongolengeschichte des Johannes von Piano Carpine*, p. 112.

49 Thomas of Spalato, *Historia Salonitanorum atque Spalatinorum pontificum*, p. 284. The 'criteria' for Mongol descriptions, citing similarities between Matthew Paris and Thomas of Spalato, in Strah, 'Die Mongolen und das Heilige Land', p. 30.

50 MS B, fol. 167ᵛ, col. a; *CM*, IV, p. 275; *EH*, I, p. 471.

51 See side by side citations in Appendix 8, available online, <https://doi.org/10.1484/A.14453112>.

52 Philip of France being shot at on fol. 41ʳ; the Siege of Lincoln on fol. 55ᵛ; the Siege of Damietta on fol. 59ᵛ, etc.

53 For a brief overview of Mongol equipment, suggesting that it was, in fact, probably sub-par compared to armies equipped by professional and standard-issue weaponry and armour, see Smith, "Ayn Jālūt', p. 316, n. 28.

54 MS B, fol. 167ᵛ, col. a; *CM*, IV, p. 275; *EH*, I, pp. 471–72.

of bullocks, asses and horses, and for armour they are protected by pieces of iron stitched to them).[55]

Suzanne Lewis suggests that 'Matthew's gory representation of the Mongols' cannibalistic atrocities may have been inspired by contemporary depictions of Gog and Magog similar to those in a copy of the *Romance of Alexander* in which hideous hairy men devour human arms and legs'.[56] However, the similarity between Matthew Paris's drawing and the huddling *Essedones* on the Hereford Map is even more striking.[57] Heather Blurton's suggestion (after Hans-Eberhard Hilpert) that Matthew's source about cannibalism was not a contemporary source but Pliny's *Natural History*, a copy of which was available for him in the St Albans library, seems to be at least partially confirmed by this pictorial similarity, as is her observation that 'textual representations of the Mongols were almost instantaneously integrated within the representational program of the Marvels of the East tradition'.[58]

The image, thus, is more than an illustration for this page in Ivo's letter; it is a synthesis of all descriptions Matthew had at his disposal composed into a scene inspired by Ivo's eyewitness account of the depravities after battle.[59] After concluding the description of the atrocities, Ivo relates how the sheer sight of the Christian army was enough to make the Mongols disappear into thin air.[60] The prince of Dalmatia, pursuing the retreating Mongols, captures eight prisoners, one of whom the duke of Austria is acquainted with: an English envoy and interpreter in the service of the khan, who had been sent to the court of the Hungarian king twice before the ultimate invasion of the kingdom. This is where the above-mentioned

---

55 MS *B*, fol. 145[v], col. b; *CM*, IV, p. 115, *EH*, I, p. 344. More variants in Appendix 8, available online, <https://doi.org/10.1484/A.14453112>.

56 Cambridge, Trinity College, MS O.9.34, fol. 23[v]; Lewis, *The Art of Matthew Paris*, p. 283.

57 In the *mappa mundi*, the rubric next to them says 'Essedones Sithe hic habitant, quorum mos est parentum funera cantibus prosequi et, congregatis amicorum, cetibus corpora ipsa dentibus laniare ac pecudum mixtis carnibus dapes facere, pulcrius a se quam a tineis hec absumi credentes'. Number 212, Section 4 in *The Hereford Map*, p. 101.

58 Blurton, *Cannibalism in High Medieval English Literature*, p. 83.

59 Increasing archaeological evidence shows that descriptions of the indiscriminate mass execution of women and children, executed with extreme violence, are not exaggerated. For example, Szabolcs Rosta's findings in the large-scale excavation project of Pétermonostora, a village near Bugac that was depopulated and razed to the ground during the Mongol invasion. More on these developments in Rosta, 'Pétermonostora pusztulása'; Laszlovszky and others, 'Contextualizing the Mongol Invasion of Hungary'; Gyucha and Rózsa, '"Egyesek darabokra vágva, egyesek egészben"'.

60 Bezzola, *Die Mongolen in abendländischer Sicht*, p. 85. The united forces of Dukes Frederick II of Austria and Bernhard II of Carinthia, King Wenceslas I of Bohemia, Patriarch Berthold of Aquileia, and Margrave Hermann V of Baden. Segl admits that not a single other source reports on their joint enterprise but suggests — *argumentum in silencio* — that nothing can be found in any of the relevant itineraries of these individuals that would not contradict the possibility. Segl, *Ketzer in Österreich*, p. 100.

238 CHAPTER 5

'story within the story' gains yet another layer. The prisoner not only describes the Mongols for the Christian audience but also embarks on his own biography embedded into Ivo's own — the difference is that it is written in Ivo's voice, in reported speech.

The Englishman's calamities after being banished from England thirty-two years before equal those of Ivo's in vivacity and adventure. The passage 'ut erat aliquantulum literatus, ea quae ibi proferebantur, tabulis commendare, et cito postea tam recte proferre, ut indigena putaretur; et eadem facilitate didicit plures linguas' (Being somewhat acquainted with letters, he began to put down in writing the words which were there spoken, and afterwards pronounced them so correctly that he was taken for a native, and he learnt several languages with the same facility) may seem unrealistic, but it needs to be borne in mind that the Englishman is chronicling several decades of wandering and learning here.[61] Scholars have also pointed out that similar individuals are documented in the service of the khans in various written sources. Proving the feasibility of the Englishman's account, for example, his person is compared to Hülegü's Latin scribe in a letter of 1268.[62] A similarly loquacious and multilingual interpreter is also described in Riccardus's report on Friar Julian's first journey to Asia, which suggests that talented vagrants like the Englishman existed and the Mongol leadership was keen to seek and employ such skilled communicators.[63]

---

61 MS B, fol. 167ʳ, col. b; CM, IV, p. 274; EH, I, p. 471.

62 Meyvaert, 'An Unknown Letter of Hülegü', p. 251.

63 Note the similarities between the descriptions of the Mongols which both interpreters feel necessary to share with their audience — at least according to the Western clerics reporting about them. 'In hac Ungarorum terra, dictus frater invenit Thartaros et nuntium ducis Thartarorum, qui sciebat Ungaricum Ruthenicum Cumanicum Theotonicum Sarracenicum et Thartaricum. Qui dixit, quod exercitus Thatarorum, qui tunc ibidem ad quinque dietas vicinus erat, contra Alemaniam vellet ire; set alium exercitum, quem ad destructionem Persarum miserant, expectabant. Dixit etiam idem, quod ultra terram Thartarorum esset gens multa nimis omnibus hominibus altior et maior, cum capitibus adeo magnis, quod nullo modo videntur suis corporibus convenire, et quod eadem gens de terra sua exire proponit, pugnaturi cum omnibus, qui eis resistere voluerint, et vastaturi omnia regna quecumque poterunt subiugare'. (Brother Julian found Tartars in this land of the Hungarians and the messenger of the chief of the Tartars who knew Hungarian, Ruthenian, Cumanian, Teutonic, Sarracenic, and Tartar. This messenger said that the army of the Tartars which was about fifteen days distant from there wished to go against Alemania and that they were expecting another army which they had sent for the destruction of the Persians. He also said that beyond the land of the Tartars there was a race much more numerous in which all the men were taller and larger with heads so great that they did not seem to fit their bodies, and that these people intended to go out of their country to fight with all who should resist them and to devastate all the lands which they could subjugate.) Hautala, Ot 'Davida, carja Indij' do 'nenavistnogo plebsa satany', p. 362; Dienes, 'Eastern Missions of the Hungarian Dominicans', p. 239.

It is perhaps no coincidence that the story of persecution contains another: more than simply a story-in-story, it is one of flight-in-flight. Compared to the Englishman who sold his soul to a king no less diabolical than Satan in return for his survival, Ivo's dalliance with the Patarenians seems like the innocent games of a misguided youth. While he is shown to be wined and dined by various hospitable heretics and recalls memories of culinary delights during his years of exile,[64] the Englishman is depicted roaming foreign lands in sackcloth on the verge of insanity just to end up with a people who feast on carcasses. The narrative abyss here is an abyss of depravity, moving closer to hell by each degree from one story to the next — from dallying with Christian dissent (Ivo),[65] through losing one's Christian faith (the Englishman),[66] to never having any in the first place (the Mongols).[67]

Besides their commonality in theme, both Ivo and the Englishman describe the Mongols. Compared to the frenzied killing and depravity so painstakingly visualized by Ivo, the statements of the English interpreter look like an encyclopaedia entry.

> De moribus autem eorum et superstitione, de dispositione corporum eorum et statura, de patria, et modo pugnandi, juravit, quod sunt super omnes homines avari, iracundi, dolosi, et immisericordes; sed rigore punitionis et immanitate poenarum, per suos superiores infligendarum, a jurgiis et mutuis deceptationibus et saevitiis invicem cohercentur. Principia suarum tribuum deos vocant, et certis colunt temporibus solempnitates eorum; multas quidem particulares, sed tantum quatuor generales. Et propter se solos omnia credunt esse creata. In exercendo saevitiam contra rebelles nullum esse credunt peccatum.

---

64 'nobilissima Paterinorum bibi vina, rabiolas, et ceratia, et alia illecebrosa comedens'; translated as 'I drank the most noble wines of the Patarenians, ate their preserved raisins, cherries, and other exciting meat' by Giles. MS B, fol. 167ʳ, col. a; CM, IV, p. 272; EH, I, p. 468. Segl at some point translates *rabiolas* as *schmalznudeln*, and — though dismissing the question as irrelevant — he goes on discuss the probable meaning of the word at some length. Oddly never explicitly mentioning *ravioli*, he speculates that the word refers to 'pasta or cakes filled with herbs and cheese, even fish patties or some other meatless dish'. Segl, *Ketzer in Österreich*, pp. 78, 91.

65 Ivo: 'et multos cotidie errores, immo potius horrores, quos contra fidem Apostolicam asserebant, audiens subticebam' (and every day listened in silence to the many errors — ay, horrors — which they uttered against the apostolic faith). CM, IV, p. 271; EH, I, p. 468.

66 The Englishman: 'quamvis cotidie verborum levitate et cordis inconstantia diabolo se commendasset' (he daily, in the levity of his tongue and the foolishness of his heart, had wished himself at the devil). CM, IV, p. 274; EH, I, p. 470.

67 The Mongols: 'Satellitum Antichristi' (Satellites of the Antichrist); and 'Principia suarum tribuum deos vocant, et certis colunt temporibus solempnitates eorum; multas quidem particulares, sed tantum quatuor generales' (The founders of their tribes are called gods, and they celebrate their solemnities at certain seasons; they have many especial celebrations, but only four regular ones). CM, IV, pp. 273, 275; EH, I, pp. 469, 471.

(Concerning their manners and their superstitions, the disposition and dimensions of their persons, their country, and mode of fighting, he swore that they are greedy, passionate, deceitful, and merciless beyond all other men. The vigour and ferocity of the punishments which were inflicted on them by their chiefs, is that which restrains them from quarrels, or from mutually cheating and injuring one another. The founders of their tribes are called gods, and they celebrate their solemnities at certain seasons; they have many especial celebrations, but only four regular ones. They think that everything was made for them alone, and they think that there is no cruelty in practising every kind of severity on those who rebel against them.)[68]

In his description, they are not so much the man-eating Antichrist but a terrible and ugly people, nevertheless quite ordinary.[69] Much like the Russian archbishop's account (to be discussed shortly), the appearance and character traits of the Mongols are described soberly and objectively, their ability and bravery in war — *infatigabiliter ac fortiter* — are emphasized, and concise information is provided about their origin and their religious ideas. About ten folios down, the Russian archbishop's thematic description enlarges on the exact same questions as the ones that the Englishman succinctly listed.[70] This passage continues with the various stories the Mongols spread about the cause of their appearance in Europe:

Omnes populos et principes regionum, secundum non causam, ut causam, tempore quietis decipiunt. Nunc se propter Magos reges, quorum sacris corporibus ornatur Colonia, in patriam suam reportandos; nunc propter avaritiam et superbiam Romanorum, qui eos antiquitus oppresserunt, relidendam; nunc propter subdendas sibi barbaras tantum et Hyperboreas nationes; nunc propter furorem Theutonicum sua modestia temperandum; nunc propter militiam a Gallis addiscendam; nunc propter terrae fertilitatem, quae suae multitudini sufficere possit, adquirendam; nunc propter peregrinationem ad Sanctum Jacobum in Galicia.

(In time of peace they deceive the people and the princes of the countries, on reasons which are no reasons. At one time they say they left their country to bring back the sacred bodies of the magi kings, which adorn the city of Cologne; at another time they say it

---

68 MS *B*, fol. 167ʳ, col. b; *CM*, IV, p. 275; *EH*, I, p. 471.

69 Segl, *Ketzer in Österreich*, p. 101.

70 For an excellent overview on what exactly classifies as 'eyewitness account' in medieval historiography as well as the 'default expectation of veracity and accuracy' on the part of the critic and historian — and as such 'somewhat resistant to the "linguistic turn" as a primary source': Bull, 'Eyewitness and the Medieval Historical Narrative'.

was to check the avarice and pride of the Romans, who oppressed them of old; another reason was, only to subdue under their dominion the barbarous Hyperborean nations and tribes; then they said it was their intention to temper the fury of the Teutonics with their own moderation; now it was to learn warfare from the French; now to gain a sufficiency of fertile land on which to maintain their multitudes and, lastly, they said it was to terminate their pilgrimage at St James's, in Gallicia.)[71]

The Mongol stratagems raise another important feature of the letter: deception. While in Ivo's account of his life among the Patarenians he repeatedly professes that he 'deceived the deceivers', the Englishman was less steadfast, serving the Mongols who deceived 'people and princes of countries'.[72] Heather Blurton connects this theme to various degrees of dissent in the letter: 'The message here, perhaps, is that, like an English Tartar, the new religious orders are not what they seem to be'.[73] The descriptive tone obfuscates the lines; it is not possible to tell who is speaking here. As no distinctive paragraph signs or initials are used to separate the various blocks within the letter, it is uncertain whether this passage is Ivo's or still the Englishman speaking — in fact, it looks like an interpolation that is connected to other nearby passages mentioning Cologne.

Both this passage and the next one about the internal poison eating Christendom from within (the new orders, mainly) stand out in Ivo's Mongol letter. Although the story of deception in peacetime follows smoothly from the description of Mongol military tactics and the logic of the threat (Mongol and mendicant), and the consequent exhortation in the letter is explained in Ivo's voice, the tone and theme suggest an interpolation here, which blurs the line between the end of the embedded story of the Englishman and Ivo resuming his own voice in his letter.

---

71 MS B, fol. 167ᵛ, col. a; CM, IV, p. 276; EH, I, p. 472. Interestingly, the threat to Cologne is found in none of the known sources coming from Cologne or its diocese. Peter Segl suggests two analogies for the rumours about Cologne relics: the continuation of the *Marbach Annals* written around 1240, which *s.a.* 1222 reports about a fearful people emerging in Persia, whose aim was to get hold of the relic which the Jews were immensely pleased about in hope of their imminent liberation. However, this people quickly returned to their homeland without ever appearing in Cologne. Also independent of Matthew Paris, Phillippe Mousket reports in his rhymed chronicle about the plan of the Tatars to fetch the relics. Segl, *Ketzer in Österreich*, p. 102.

72 'deceptores decipiens'. MS B, fol. 167ʳ, col. a; CM, IV, p. 272; EH, I, p. 468.

73 Blurton, *Cannibalism in High Medieval English Literature*, p. 98. Importantly, this passage not only connects issues within the letter, but also to a number of subsequent passages about new orders, some of which suggest a Cologne affiliation, to be discussed here shortly; see notes 92 and 93.

242 CHAPTER 5

Tantis igitur emergentibus toti Christianissimo populo periculis, quid rudium religionum, et adhuc fornacis, ex qua prodierunt, igne flagrantium, faciunt sancti fratres, qui credi volunt viam se perfectionis prae caeteris elegisse? Confessionibus siquidem et aliis familiaritatibus principum et magnatum sibi favorem conciliantes, in auribus eorum contra Tattaros instanter et importune clamare deberent; male faciunt, si non clamant; pejus, se si simulant; pessime, si succurrant. Quid monachi nigri et albi, et canonici Norbertini, qui mundo mortui credi volunt, quare haec videntes imminere pericula, contra Tattaros crucem non praedicant bajulandam? O regum stulta consilia! Episcoporum et abbatum taciturnitas supina!

> (Seeing, then, that such dangers are arising to the whole of Christendom, what are these holy brothers doing, with their new religious rites, and fresh from the fire of the furnace out of which they have been fashioned, who wish it to be believed that they alone have found out the way of perfection beyond all others? By confession, and other intimacies, they should gain the favour of the princes and nobles, and earnestly and importunately cry into their ears against the Tattars: they do badly, if they do not so cry; they do worse, if they only make pretences; but worst of all, if they assist the enemy. What are the Black and White friars doing? And the Norbertine canons, who wish to be thought dead unto the world? Why do they not preach a crusade against the Tattars, when they see all these perils approaching? Oh the foolish counsels of kings! The supine silence of bishops and abbots!)[74]

The tone and the accusations of 'supine silence of bishops' begs the question how Ivo, a persecuted heretic who himself admits having entertained the false beliefs of the Patarenians for some time, feels at liberty to address the archbishop of Bordeaux in such an accusatory tone. In view of this incongruent passage, it is worthwhile to consider Jean Duvernoy's opinion that the letter is fabricated as an attempt by Frederick's allies to bounce the accusation of heresy back on his enemies in the cities of the Lombard League.[75] This suggestion supports my impression that although he no doubt edited it to fit his narrative (and even illustrated it, which is definitely his own work), the fabrication was not entirely Matthew's doing.

---

74 It is also notable that Ivo suggests that the archbishop knows about his unfortunate accusations of heresy: 'Having formerly been accused, as you know [*ut nostis*], by my rivals, on account of heretical depravity'. MS B, fol. 167ᵛ, cols a–b; *CM*, IV, pp. 276–77; *EH*, I, pp. 472–73.

75 Duvernoy, *La Catharisme*, pp. 184–85. Other scholars of Catharism, however, accept the letter as an authentic witness to the spread of Catharism in Europe: Segl, *Ketzer in Österreich*; Borst, *Die Katharer*, p. 104.

FLIGHT   243

Unlike this blurred division, the next passage in the letter is certainly written in Ivo's voice, when his less aggressive *exhortatio* for the archbishop of Bordeaux is inserted after this crescendo of reproachful questions. As usual, Ivo's letter is followed by Matthew's commentary, which he places in the next entry.

Deconstructing the seemingly simple structure of the letter thus reveals a plurality of voices. With so many clues and even more uncertainties, the authenticity of the letter(s) remains an open question. The same way in which deception has many faces in the epistle, the issue of authenticity can be and is raised regarding the claim that the narrators are indeed eyewitnesses or whether the letter was written by a French cleric indeed. And if not him, then who? Matthew's sole authorship is improbable, and the adventures of the two men on the run — Ivo and the Englishman — are obviously not his work. Especially Ivo's itinerary teems with personal names and place names,[76] even in the vernacular, which is uncharacteristic for Matthew's usual style. As is the case of many other letters in the chronicle, the letter is wrought out of various sources. Although he probably did not write the passages himself, his intervention went beyond embroidering the prose for a more dramatic effect.[77] The familiar mise-en-abîme pattern suggests that it not only contains passages borrowed from elsewhere but also conscious attempts to tie the letter into the chronicle narrative. On the one hand, this is done by Matthew explicitly explaining the historical logic between the issues addressed in various parts of the letter and other entries; on the other hand, by the textual environment of the letter in the chronicle, where he continued some of the themes addressed therein. As other letters above, Ivo's letter can be contextualized as part of a subplot within the Frederick story and is made up of various closely associated entries inserted into the narrative at intervals (alternation). As will be shown, parts of Ivo's letter belong to a specific group of entries, which reveal their Cologne origin, and also provide clues for the information network that relayed them to Matthew's desk at St Albans, pointing to the Lyon Council as the place where these texts were gathered and disseminated.

First, the time of writing this portion of the chronicle can be inferred from a slip-up: on the same folio, the entries preceding the letter detail the treachery and desertion of Frederick's allies, among others the marquis

---

76 For example, the disgraced Cather leader Petrus Gallus, whom Segl identifies with the Petrus mentioned in *Tractatus de hereticis* by Anselm of Alexandria. Segl, *Ketzer in Österreich*, p. 90.

77 Segl argues that since Matthew is more interested in the Mongol material, the first part of Ivo's letter underwent many fewer stylistic changes than the Mongol-related passages where Matthew may have manipulated the text to have more impact. Segl, *Ketzer in Österreich*, p. 109.

244   CHAPTER 5

of Montferrat and Henry Raspe, resulting in the election of Henry as anti-king:[78]

> In Alemannia etiam multi abierunt retrorsum, et nolentes amplius stare cum eo, alium sibi in regem elegerunt vel imperatorem, videlicet Andegravium de [Duringia], virum elegantem et strenuum; cui Germaniae et Italiae pars potissima consilium et auxilium, usque ad capitum expositionem, spopondit indefessum.
>
>> (In Germany, too, many abandoned his cause, and not wishing longer to be his liege subjects, chose for themselves another king, or emperor, namely the landgrave [of Thuringia], a brave and well-favoured man, to whom Germany, and the most powerful part of Italy, promised both aid and counsel, unwearying, even to exposing their lives in his service.)[79]

In reality, this event did not take place until Raspe changed sides in 1245 — rather reluctantly, if Matthew is to be believed — and was elected anti-king in opposition to Conrad on 22 May 1246.[80] This makes 1246 the terminus post quem for writing down this entry. Although unnamed in MS *B* at this point, the 'brave and well-favoured man' unquestionably refers to Henry Raspe.[81]

---

78 The marquis of Montferrat at this time was Boniface II of Montferrat. Legate Otto, Matthew's recurring character on the papal side of the story, was his brother. Though occasionally changing sides — for example, his dalliance with the Guelphs in 1243 — Boniface belonged to Frederick's sphere of interest more often than not.

79 MS *B*, fol. 166ᵛ, col. a; *CM*, IV, p. 268; *EH*, I, p. 465. Why Raspe's title remains unfinished (*andegravium de*) in MS *B*, and added by a later hand in MS *C* is puzzling. It is probably a simple scribal error, easy to do at the end of the line, which was rectified in *C*, but left uncorrected in *B*.

80 The terminus post quem of entering the news of the election in the chronicle is May 1246 or later when Matthew received the news. The fact that Matthew inserts this piece of news under 1246 again also shows that the chronology was mixed up by writing in hindsight. 'Dominus igitur Papa vigilanti sollicitudine causam suam cupiens promovere, et partem suam justificare, et memoratum Frethericum irremediabiliter conterere, procuravit ut Andegravius Duringiae in imperatorem eligeretur, et electus ab omni ecclesia promoveretur' (The pope, then, in his watchful endeavours to promote his cause, justify his side of the question, and irreparably to crash the said Frederick, procured the election to the imperial dignity of the landgrave of Thuringia, and the acknowledgment of his election from all churches). MS *B*, fol. 203ʳ, col. a; *CM*, IV, pp. 544–45; *EH*, II, p. 163. Also note the proximity of a marginal note about the Mongols at the bottom of the facing page MS *B*, fol. 202ᵛ, see note 158 below.

81 In the entry entitled 'Recedunt ab imperatore multi nobiles': 'Recesserunt igitur ab imperatore multi nobiles et graves ac potentes, videlicet marchisii de Monteferrato, et de Malaspina; Vercellae, Alexandria, et multae nobiles civitates' (Therefore, many wise and powerful nobles left the emperor; viz., the Marquis de Montferrat, the Marquis de Malaspina, Vercelli, Alessandria, and many noble cities). MS *B*, fol. 166ᵛ, col. a; *CM*, IV, p. 268; *EH*, I, p. 465.

Tracking the possible journey of the entry from the addressee of the letter, Bishop Gerald (Géraud) of Malemort, Peter Segl suggests that Matthew Paris's source in England was none other than Henry III of England.[82] Dating the arrival of the letter at St Albans only a year after the date under which it is inserted, he suggests that it was handed over by the king either in June or December 1244 when he visited St Albans for a few days.[83] Although Segl admits that Matthew may have received the letter through less prestigious messengers, his general drift is that the letter was moved between the French bishop and the English king, who then directly relayed it to St Albans.[84] Indeed, Henry III (or someone in his entourage) may have learned of Ivo's letter directly from the archbishop (or someone in his entourage) sometime between mid-December 1242 and the beginning of September 1243, when he stayed mostly in Bordeaux, with the exception of a few short detours into the surroundings. And he is known to have been back in Winchester on 30 September and Westminster on 12 October 1243. However, as various examples bear it out in this present book, the journey of the Mongol-related material that reached St Albans was rarely that direct: most of the texts came from widely disseminated compilations, and some entries were wrought out of disparate texts — in some cases by Matthew, in some others by previous editors.

After the previous analyses of the chronicle's inevitably vicarious Mongol material, it seems justifiable to assume a similar dynamic of information acquisition at work here too. Matthew's own commentary following the letter also suggests that Ivo's letter arrived at his scriptorium as part of a circular, disseminated more openly than Segl's interpretation allows. Matthew writes, 'Haec igitur terribilis epistola regum et magnatum corda, ad quos pervenit, vehementer sollicitasset, et ad injuriam Christi et universalis ecclesiae et totius Christianismi ulciscendam efficaciter erexisset nisi Papae et imperatoris mutuum discidium totius mundi latitudinem perturbasset' (This terrible letter would have greatly disquieted the hearts of the kings and nobles to whom it came, and would have effectually excited

---

82 Ignoring the explicit aim of the letter and the signs suggesting that both the narrative and its author were quite the subversive types, Segl suggests that the praise of the French martial prowess and the disparaging emphasis on the *furor theutonicus* which the Tatars supposedly wanted to tame, point to France as the country of origin where Ivo heard the rumours upon his return from Austria. Segl, *Ketzer in Österreich*, p. 106.

83 Segl, *Ketzer in Österreich*, p. 104. For a careful and in-depth evaluation of Segl's arguments, see Lerner, 'Review of *Ketzer in Österreich*'.

84 Knowing the close nexus between the French bishop and the English king, this assumption is not at all far-fetched: the Bordeaux archbishops are historically known to have been agents of English policy in Aquitaine in the thirteenth century: Guillaume Amanieu (1207–1226), for example, was appointed by Henry III as seneschal of all his lands overseas; Gerald of Malemort (1227–1260) acted as mediator between Louis and Henry III and, later, defended Gascony against Simon de Montfort. Fisquet, *La France pontificale*, I, pp. 143–56.

them to avenge the injury offered to Christ, to the Catholic Church, and all Christendom, if the mutual dissensions of the pope and the emperor had not spread trouble over all the world).[85] This makes it clear that the letter addressed to Gerald reached Matthew as a *rescriptum*; it was more or less openly disseminated, probably collated together with other, thematically associated texts. Some of the issues addressed in these loosely connected texts point to information whose wide dissemination was in the interest of the legatine information network, and there are a few strong reasons why the letter should be seen as part of their wholesale information exchange at the First Council of Lyon, rather than through the personal mediation of the bishop himself.[86]

The better part of Chapter 2 above was devoted to discussing the role of the Council of Lyon in the dissemination of the materials and intelligence about the Mongols, so there is no need to duplicate the arguments for its role in connecting St Albans to information accessible for the highest ecclesiastical and political echelons at the time. It is, however, significant here that the French bishop in question was in fact in Lyon where he was kept busy indeed: 'Géraud de Malemort fut du nombre des évêques qui s'y trouvèrent et y prononcèrent la condamnation l'excommunication et la déposition de l'empereur Frédéric, pour crime d'hérésie, de sacrilège et de félonie'.[87] Although not directly concerned with the emperor, the letter about such abundant and varied cases of godlessness as Ivo of Narbonne's was an extremely valuable piece of evidence in his line of work, let alone its other subject which covered at length one of the other issues on the council's agenda, the Mongols.

And Gerald is not the only prelate who can be associated with Ivo's letter, suggesting other channels of information behind the interrelated series of passages here. The familiar figure of Legate Otto, also at Lyon at

---

85 MS *B*, fol. 167ᵛ, col. b; *CM*, IV, p. 277; *EH*, I, p. 473.

86 Since the archbishop is the only identifiable person in the letter itself, his figure has been used to get closer to the content of this mysterious letter. For example, knowing the archbishop's contempt for Franciscans in general, Victor Le Clerc quite astutely — despite his disparaging comment about the chaotic presentation of the missive — detected the hint of irony at the end: 'La lettre se termine par quelques traits satiriques contre les deux nouveaux ordres religieux, qui aiment mieux s'emparer de l'oreille des princes que de secourir les peuples. Ces reproches, déjà mérités, ne pouvaient déplaire à l'archevêque Gérald, qui, dans les statuts de ses conciles provinciaux, essaya plus d'une fois de racheter, par ses efforts pour réprimer les entreprises des frères, l'imprudence qu'il avait commise en admettant à Bordeaux, dè l'année 1227, l'ordre de Saint-François. Matthieu Paris, après avoir transcrit cette lettre, dit qu'elle fit une vive impression sur les rois et les grands, et qu'elle eut pu être utile à l'Église, si la rivalité du pape et d'empereur n'eut mis alors le désordre dans le monde entier. Ce document, vrai ou faux, inspirerait aujourd'hui plus d'intérêt, s'il était écrit avec moins d'emphase et de confusion'. Le Clerc, ed., *Histoire littéraire de la France*, p. 794.

87 Fisquet, *La France pontificale*, I, p. 149.

the time, is once again lurking nearby.[88] At the very bottom of the first column on fol. 166^v Matthew Paris reports that Cardinal Otto was made bishop of Portugal in 1243, and at the top of the next column begins Ivo's letter. As discussed earlier and demonstrated across a number of entries, the physical proximity of entries about Legate Otto and those about the Mongols suggests more association between the two than simple coincidence. Notably, this piece of information made the entry much longer than the space Matthew had originally dedicated to it, and instead of carrying it over to the next column where a new story with Ivo's letter begins, he crams Otto's news into a triangular shape at the bottom of the page, accompanied by a mitre and staff to make it into an elegant rectangle, cut diagonally like a party per bend shield (see Fig. 8). This is consistent with Matthew's general treatment of the writing grid, striving to fill available space where necessary to avoid orphan lines running onto the next column or page and compromising the visual cogency of the manuscript.

The news of Otto's episcopal election, tagged at the end of the entry about 'the humiliation of the emperor', appears rather prematurely in the chronicle, as the former papal legate to England was not appointed to the suburbicarian see of Porto e S. Rufina until the Consistory of 28 May 1244. The last time the reader may have seen him in the *Chronica majora* was in Frederick II's 1241 letter to Henry III, where he was seen gathering with other illustrious prelates to oppose Frederick's progress in Genoa, just to end up as Frederick's hostages soon thereafter (Fig. 9).[89] In the drawing, Otto is featured alongside the archbishop of Bordeaux, the addressee of Ivo's letter.

While their proximity to Ivo's account on the page could suggest that Otto and Gerald had something to do with the transmission of the text, it is quite likely that placing them on the same page was a consequence of their known real-life association, rather than evidence for their involvement in the physical dissemination of the texts. Instead, another prelate can be associated with Ivo's letter, although the connection is not as immediately obvious as in the case of Bishop Gerald and Legate Otto, who are named in or near the letter. Similarly to Gerald's mission at Lyon, Conrad of Hochstaden, archbishop of Cologne, together with Archbishop Sigfried of Mainz, was visiting in Innocent IV's new court in Lyon right before the pope announced the call for the Council of Lyon in December 1244. Their mission was to convince the pope, if he was still in doubt, to excommunicate Frederick II for the second time

---

88 See the discussion about alternating Otto's adventures in England with continental history in Chapter 3 ('1237: Chaldeans, Medes, Persians, and Armenians'), esp. Table 1.

89 MS *B*, fol. 147^r, col. a; *CM*, IV, p. 125; *EH*, I, p. 352. Giles incorrectly identifies him as Otto of Thuringia. About this incident, see also Chapter 4 ('Holy War on the Mongols' and 'The Second 1241 Cluster').

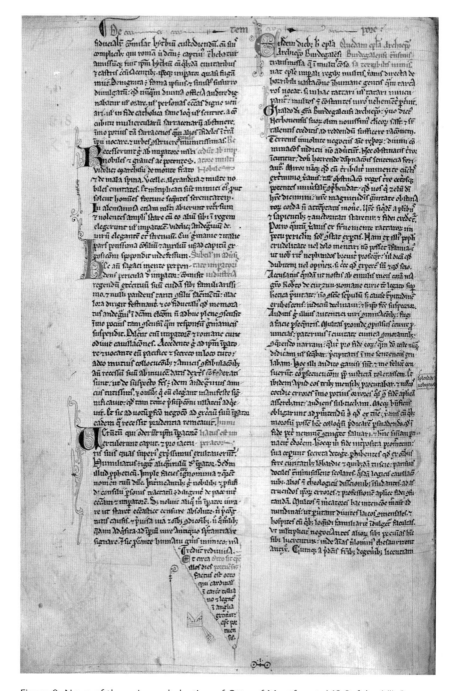

Figure 8. News of the episcopal election of Otto of Montferrat, MS *B*, fol. 166[v]. By permission of the Parker Library, Corpus Christi College, Cambridge.

Figure 9. Drawing of the Pisan and Genoese galleys, MS B, fol. 147ʳ. By permission of the Parker Library, Corpus Christi College, Cambridge. The names in the Genoese galley are 'Rothomagensis, Burdegalensis, Rothomagensis [sic] et alii archiepiscopi et episcopi; Praenestinus episcopus, Otto cardinalis, Gregorius de Romagna, legati; Cluniacensis, Cisterciensis, Clerevallensis, Pontiniacensis et alii abbates capti'.

250   CHAPTER 5

and depose him.[90] Internal evidence strongly suggests that the end-of-year entries under 1243, including Ivo's letter to the French bishop, all contain information from the Cologne archbishop's circles, carefully blended into the narratives of heterodoxy and dissent that are home to the Mongol story in this part of the chronicle. This internal evidence is the emergence of two conspicuous themes, namely the rise of the Beguine movement and the controversy between the Preachers and Minorites, both acutely associated with Cologne at the time. The amount and frequency of similar passages around Ivo's letter indicate that the Cologne archbishop's chancery may have been instrumental in collating and transmitting a number of texts about current problems of heresy and mendicant expansion in his neck of the woods, including Ivo's letter.

To sum up the Cologne passage very briefly, the Beguine movement is expressly mentioned both in Ivo's letter and in the entry 'De Beguinorum muliplicatione' afterwards:

> Ivo's letter:
> in quodam oppido Austriae, quod Theutonice Neustat dicitur, id est, nova civitas, inter quosdam novos religiosos, qui Beguini vocantur, hospitabar.
>
> Eiusdem temporibus quidam in Alemannia praecipue, se asserentes religiosos, in utroque sexu, sed maxime in muliebri, habitum religionis, sed levem, susceperunt, continentiam et vitae simplicitatem privato voto profitentes, sub nullius tamen sancti regula coarctatae, nec adhuc ullo claustro contenti. Earumque numerus in brevi adeo multiplicabatur, ut in civitate Coloniae et partibus adjacentibus duo milia invenirentur.

---

90 Huffman, 'Potens et Pauper', p. 119. Sigfried, archbishop of Mainz, is known to have been embroiled in anti-Mongol preparations as late as 1243. A letter from Henry, bishop of Constance, to Anselm, warden of the Franciscans at Uberlingen, contains King Conrad's and Sigfried's decrees issued at their Erfurt council on 25 April 1243. *Historia diplomatica Friderici Secundi*, v.2, pp. 1209–13; also printed in whole in Bernet, 'Beiträge zur Geschichte der Kreuzzüge gegen die Mongolen'. This is the same Henry of Tanne whose letter about the Mongols breaking into the Babenbergs' territory in 1241 is preserved in the Ottobeuren Collection (see '1243: The Tartar Khan's Englishman' above in the present chapter), and who is also the purported recipient of a letter entitled 'Nova pestis contra ecclesiam' (A fresh affliction confronting the Church). In the version of 'Nova Pestis' found in a manuscript in private possession in Florence, it purports to be addressed to the pope by the patriarch of Jerusalem and to have been forwarded to Henry of Tanne by the papal legate in Germany. This also found its way into the Courtenay Compendium, discussed in '1244: The Man from Russia' below in the present chapter. Jackson, 'The Testimony of the Russian "Archbishop" Peter', pp. 68–69.

(at a town called in the Teutonic tongue Neustadt, i.e. New-city, where I was hospitably entertained by some religious of a new order, called the Beguines.)[91]

(At the same time, chiefly in Germany, certain persons of both sexes, but principally women, declaring themselves religionists, took a religious habit, though not a very heavy one, and made profession of continence and simplicity of life by a private vow, without, however, being straitened by the rules of any saint, nor as yet shut up within the precincts of any cloister. In short, their number was increased to such an extent, that in the city of Cologne and neighbourhood, two thousand of them were found.)[92]

And the references to Cologne do not stop here: Ivo also notes that Cologne is a dangerous place; even the Mongols are reported to have told people that 'Nunc se propter Magos reges, quorum sacris corporibus ornatur Colonia, in patriam suam reportandos' (they left their country to bring back the sacred bodies of the magi kings, which adorn the city of Cologne).[93]

The mendicants' strife, lacking any direct reference to geography, may not seem so closely connected. However, whether it was Matthew or a gifted clerk in Conrad of Hochstaden's chancery, the collator of the bundle uses the power of association to paint the image of the Church and the new orders that serve it as being as bad as the enemies of Christendom proper. First, Ivo does not mince his words when it comes to the mendicant orders:

> Tantis igitur emergentibus toti Christianissimo populo periculis, quid rudium religionum, et adhuc fornacis, ex qua prodierunt, igne flagrantium, faciunt sancti fratres, qui credi volunt viam se perfectionis prae caeteris elegisse? Confessionibus siquidem et aliis familiaritatibus principum et magnatum sibi favorem conciliantes, in auribus eorum contra Tattaros instanter et importune clamare deberent; male faciunt, si non clamant; pejus, se si simulant; pessime, si succurrant.

> (Seeing, then, that such dangers are arising to the whole of Christendom, what are these holy brothers doing, with their new religious rites, and fresh from the fire of the furnace out of which they have been fashioned, who wish it to be believed that they alone have found out the way of perfection beyond all others? By confession, and other intimacies, they should gain the favour of the princes and nobles, and earnestly and importunately cry into their

---

91 MS B, fol. 167ʳ, col. a; *CM*, IV, p. 272; *EH*, I, p. 469.
92 MS B, fols 167ᵛ, col. b–168ʳ, col. a; *CM*, IV, p. 278; *EH*, I, p. 474.
93 MS B, fol. 167ᵛ, col. a; *CM*, IV, p. 276; *EH*, I, p. 472.

252   CHAPTER 5

ears against the Tattars: they do badly, if they do not so cry; they do worse, if they only make pretences; but worst of all, if they assist the enemy.)[94]

Then the story of the mendicants and their reprehensible master, the pope, continues with the description of an imperial response that befits their crimes and high treason. One entry down, still on the same page, Frederick II's son Conrad is seen tightening security in his territory, specifically looking out for individuals who carried money for the pope, and mendicants in general.[95] The previously quoted long exposé about just how deplorable the mendicant orders can get[96] is also closely associated with the entry about the controversy of the Minorites inserted after the Beguine entry:

> Hi jam sunt, qui in sumptuosis et diatim ampliatis aedificiis et celsis muralibus thesauros exponunt impreciabiles, paupertatis limites et basim suae professionis, juxta prophetiam Hyldegardis Alemanniae, impudenter transgredientes.

> (These are they who daily expose to view their inestimable treasures, in enlarging their sumptuous edifices, and erecting lofty walls, thereby impudently transgressing the limits of their original poverty, and violating the basis of their religion, according to the prophecy of the German Hildegarde.)[97]

The key to the connection with Ivo's letter and the passages discussing other threats facing Christendom is, once again, Cologne. There is no room here to go into the intricacies of the dissemination of *Pentachron seu speculum futurorum temporum sive de quinque temporibus*, a compilation of St Hildegard's prophecies made by Gebeno of Eberbach around the year 1220, let alone parts circulated separately; suffice it to note that the association of Hildegard's name and a few of her genuine writings with the tradition of anti-mendicant propaganda peaked in Cologne of all places.

---

94 MS *B*, fol. 167ᵛ, col. a; *CM*, IV, pp. 276–77; *EH*, I, pp. 472–73.

95 'Filius autem ejus Conradus, huic operi operam impendens diligentem, adeo vigilanter tam per mare quam per terras transire volentibus aditus praeclusit, ut nec fratribus Minoribus vel Praedicatoribus, vel alicui alii transfigurato, quem deprehendere posset, pepercisset, quin comprehensum usque ad animae exhalationem torqueret' (His son Conrad diligently applied himself to this work, and stopped with such vigilance the roads, both by sea and land, for all travellers, that he spared not the fraternity of Minorites, or Preachers, or any one disguised, whom he could seize, but tortured whom he caught till they died). MS *B*, fol. 167ᵛ, col. b; *CM*, IV, p. 278; *EH*, I, p. 472.

96 See note 74.

97 MS *B*, fol. 168ʳ, col. a; *CM*, IV, p. 280; *EH*, I, p. 475. The text was probably deemed too insulting at some point as the last part of the letter, including this sentence, was simply erased. The missing text was replaced by a hand from Archbishop Parker's time, copying from MS *C*, fol. 324ᵛ.

As Kathryn Kerby-Fulton explains, Gebeno 'gives special prominence to Hildegard's letter of warning to the clergy of Cologne, which was to become the single most popular extract from her works, circulating independently in numerous manuscripts throughout the later Middle Ages'.[98] In this letter, Hildegard chastises both the clergy and the people of Cologne for allowing the unchecked growth of the Cathar heretics to persist, but around the 1220s the clergy of Cologne also thought they were seeing a fulfilment of Hildegard's prophecy in another group of newcomers, the Dominicans, which gave a new impetus to the reconsideration of Hildegard's words.[99]

These snippets, all associated with Cologne in one way or another, bring together the Tartars, the mendicants, the Patarenes, and the Beguines and mark the perceived crisis in the Church. If Ivo's letter was not originally part of this bundle, someone — perhaps Matthew — certainly recognized the potential of fitting it together with the entries from Cologne, covering seemingly disparate topics affecting other parts of Europe but in reality all tightly connected by the same thread. The Patarene Frenchman's story about the Mongols serves as a link to connect questions of heterodoxy on a surprising number of levels. While the thought of uncloistered men and women and their vows of simplicity (Beguines) may not sound alarming in itself, wedged between the (faux-)Patarene Ivo's letter about the Mongols and the subsequent entries detailing the dangers of uncloistered mendicants and their (faux-)vows of simplicity and poverty, their *multiplicatio* assumes a threatening tenor. One can only imagine a cloistered monk's alarm and concern about the seemingly relentless changes and new developments that were so malignant that they began to mutually amplify each other. This is the same dynamic as the cause for distress in Ivo's letter: 'Unde discordia eorum longe lateque per orbem ventilata, utpote quibus non sunt majores, immo nec eis pares, in tota Christianitate, corda Tattarorum, immo omnium paganorum, necnon et universorum Christi inimicorum, exhilaravit et in spem erexit tutiorem' (the strife of the pope and the emperor pervaded all of Christendom, and exhilarated the hearts of the Tartars, ay, and of all pagans, and, moreover, of all the enemies of Christ, and made them increase their hopes).[100]

---

98 Kerby-Fulton, 'Hildegard of Bingen and Anti-Mendicant Propaganda', p. 388. Kerby-Fulton also notes that Hildegard wrote to the clergy of Mainz on the same subject, which may suggest another — admittedly, rather delicate — invisible thread connecting the two German archbishops' visit to Lyon and the curiously interconnected bunch of entries in the *Chronica majora*.

99 Kerby-Fulton, 'Hildegard of Bingen and Anti-Mendicant Propaganda', p. 388. More on Hildegard and the emergence of anti-fraternalism in Hoskin, 'Matthew Paris's *Chronica Majora* and the Franciscans in England', pp. 52–53.

100 MS *B*, fol. 167ᵛ, col. b; *CM*, IV, pp. 277–78; *EH*, I, p. 473.

254   CHAPTER 5

The clearly emerging thematic in this part of the chronicle reflects the emergence of intense doctrinal and theological debates, which were intimately tied to contemporary anxieties of dissent. Ivo's letter is an up-close-and-personal embodiment of these dogmatic questions. Followed by a number of shorter entries revisiting a variety of loosely associated topics, they form a mini cluster in the flow of the narrative in 1243, and before Matthew concludes the year, he closes the cluster with an important document. In 1241 the regent masters in theology at the University of Paris gathered together under their chancellor, Odo of Châteauroux, mandated by their bishop, William of Auvergne, to condemn ten propositions against theological truth and to affirm the true doctrine. The articles were issued a number of times, the surviving manuscripts variously dating to 1241 and 1244. It is no coincidence that the Jewish Moses ben Abraham includes the text of a 'testimony of a Tartar' in his apologetic text presented to William of Auvergne, at the time deeply involved in both drafting the *Condemnations* and the Parisian trial of the Talmud (1240–1248). As Maria Teresa Rachetta notes, Moses 'emphasises the special connection between Christians and Jews on moral grounds and the universality of the divine truths revealed by the "donated" books, which is not diminished by the fact that Albigensian heretics (a major topic in 1244, the year of the siege of Montségur), the Tartars, and the Saracens also find the basis for their faiths in them'.[101]

There are two reasons why the condemnations are worth a brief digression here. First, because many Mongol entries in the *Chronica majora*, primarily Ivo's letter and its textual environment, appear in a framework of dissent and threats to the Church, the paradigm that reached its apex in the First Council of Lyon where many of Matthew's informants gathered and disseminated pertinent texts. Secondly, and not unimportantly, because William of Auvergne, the bishop of Paris, the very person who orchestrated the condemnations at the university, appears in a very peculiar Mongol-related entry in the *Chronica majora*, the letter of a Hungar-

---

101 Rachetta, 'Paris 1244', pp. 247–48. The articles of the *Condemnation* were issued a number of times, the surviving manuscripts variously dating to 1241 and 1244. There is no properly edited text of the condemnation. The *Cartularium Universitatis Parisiensis* contains the commonly accepted version, including the order of articles that Matthew Paris cites under the year 1243. The fact that it was extremely influential at the time is underpinned by the fact that the complete list is found in important contemporary accounts, including the *Chronica majora*, and later in Bonaventure's commentary on Peter Lombard's *Sententiae*, and in the 1256 record of the Dominican Provincial Chapter of Provence. It is also referred to in numerous texts, for example, by Roger Bacon and Odo Rigaud, and in the records of the 1243 and 1256 Dominican General Chapters at Paris. It is also included alongside those of 1277 and others in collections of condemnations, such as the *Collectio errorum in Anglia et Parisius condempnatorum*. Grice, *Church, Society and University*, p. 7.

ian bishop to William in the *Additamenta*.[102] Though not immediately obvious, the parallels of these texts with the thematics of the Ivo cluster in the *Chronica majora* are remarkable. Studying the doctrinal influences and theological context of the articles, Deborah Grice suggests that the condemnations reflect on issues arising from the new anxieties of the 1240s: threats facing the Latin Church. Besides the internal disagreements within the bosom of the Church, these mainly concerned the Greeks and emerging dualistic heresies, such as Ivo's Patarenian error. Other threats also included the Jews — both William and Odo were heavily involved in controlling the books of the Jews in the 1230s. Fitting in this paradigm, the Muslim and Mongol threat, although external to the doctrine and carrying the promise of conversion, was also in the forefront of contemporary thinking. Lastly, the conflict between the papacy and the Holy Roman Empire was the ultimate discord which hampered effective response to these threats. These issues together continued to be intertwined until the 1245 Council of Lyon, which expressly made the 'five pains of the Church' its agenda.

All the threats facing Christendom, encapsulated by the 'five pains', are manifest in the intensive intellectual work on dogma published in the form of articles of condemnation at universities, specifically the University of Paris.[103] At the time when these urgent concerns emerged and blended into a coherent discourse, one of the threats was undergoing a significant reconfiguration. The memory of the apocalyptic Mongol attacks still lingered, but the Mongol military campaigns were moving on, creating a new situation in European foreign policy. Looking at the Mongol story from a

---

102 See Chapter 6, below. William of Auvergne is known to have been informed about the Mongols through many channels. Perhaps the most interesting document associated with him is The Hague, Koninklijke Bibliotheek, MS 131 A 3, the aforementioned *Livre* by Moses ben Abraham, an original, unfinished French historical and prophetic compilation based on Hebrew sources. Maria Teresa Rachetta argues that Moses ben Abraham composed it in 1244 and subsequently presented it to William of Auvergne, who was involved in the Parisian trial of the Talmud (1240–1248) and had received reports from Hungary in which the Tartars were described as people of Jewish customs. Moses's text claims to contain 'the testimony of a Tartar who had been sent by the King of Hungary and the King of the Rus' to the Duke of Brabant'. Rachetta, 'Paris 1244', p. 254.

103 As Grice explains, the condemnations were a theological response to the increasing anxieties that Matthew Paris covered in great historical detail after the Council of Lyon. 'More indirect concerns contributing to insecurity included the dispute with Frederick II, with Frederick's openly aggressive actions in 1240 taking this to a new level. There was a threat from the Mongols, at its peak with their invasion of Hungary in 1241, and concerns over other groups, including the Muslims. Latin territories in the east, and Constantinople itself, remained at risk, and crusades, such as the failed fifth crusade in 1217–1221 and the disastrous 1239 Syrian expedition, continued. Apocalyptic speculation was rife, including on the possible role of some groups, in particular Jews, Muslims and Mongols, with Frederick II himself painted by Gregory IX as the forerunner of the Antichrist'. Grice, *Church, Society and University*, p. 47.

1244: Frederick's Triumph

The summary of the year 1243 explains the unusually figurative initial of the new year which shows an innocently reclining naked figure, seemingly oblivious of the lion observing him while perched on the branches of a tree overhead. The future is dangerous, but if the readers want to see what happens when the lion pounces, they might just have to keep turning the pages.

> transiit igitur annus ille ecclesiae periculosus et procellosus, frugifer satis et fructifer, multos nobiles in Christianitate perimens et perturbans; regno et regi Angliae probrosus et dampnosus, Ytalicis praeliosus et hostilis, Terrae Sanctae suspectus, Templariis et Hospitalariis scismatis et scandali generativus.

> (This year [1243], therefore, passed over, threatening danger and trouble to the Church, plentiful enough in vegetables and fruits, bringing death and annoyance to many nobles in Christendom, reproachful and prejudicial to the kingdom and king of England, bringing battles and hostilities for the Italians, and mistrust for

---

104 The entry is intimately tied to the next one, in which Baldwin II, emperor of Constantinople, applies for Frederick's assistance, and Frederick's alliance with John III Doukas Vatatzes, emperor of Nicaea, further deteriorates his relationship with the pope. Frederick's bond with Vatatzes was not simply contractual; they were family through marriage. Matthew Paris is also correctly informed that Frederick became Vatatzes' father-in-law when his illegitimate daughter Anna (born Constance) II of Hohenstaufen married Vatatzes and became empress of Nicaea. 'Imperator Constantinipolitanus victus a Graecis confugit ad imperatorem F[rethericum] postulans ab eodem auxilium'. MS *B*, fol. 170ᵛ, col. b; *CM*, IV, p. 299; *EH*, I, pp. 490–91.

105 For a detailed discussion about the cloistered Benedictines' discomfort about the new orders and prevalent views about their poverty ideals, see Schnith, *England in einer sich wandelnden Welt*, pp. 179, 183–84.

the Holy Land, and generating schism and scandal between the Templars and Hospitallers.)[106]

Leaving both fruits and annoyances of 1243 behind, 1244 starts with a markedly English-focused content, but the patterns of configuring the news into a chronicle narrative remain consistent and the reader can expect stories from overseas shortly. The entry that first breaks the series of domestic issues is the letter of the grand master of the Knights Templar, Hermann of Perigold (Herman Petragorius or Armand de Périgord), which allows the outside world to seep back into the chronicle in the form of a long account of the 'condition of the Holy Land'.[107] As with Frederick's letter before this, Matthew appends an explanation about the debated authenticity of the missive. From this point on, the English events are peppered with international news at regular intervals, some in the form of letters that embed further letters, for example, the letter of Cardinal-Deacon Geoffrey of Trani sharing a letter by a familiar character, Legate Otto, who by this time was the freshly appointed bishop of Porto e Santa Rufina.[108] Familiar patterns with familiar faces then: besides Otto, we once again encounter John Mansel, too.[109]

The next mini-cluster bringing Mongol-related news to the chronicle in 1244 starts with Frederick II's immense army driving the Mongols beyond the limits of the Hungarian kingdom. Immediately after this emerges the first Mongol-related entry that concerns their appearance in the East: Matthew simply reports that they 'disperse towards the east', ravaging the Persians and causing the Khwarezmians to flee their own lands. It is spelled out explicitly that this 'dispersal' marks the end of the Mongol military manoeuvres in the north, that is, Eastern Europe. Immediately after this, Frederick's letter to Richard of Cornwall repeats the same story in more personal detail and opens a whole long cluster of various entries dedicated entirely to the Latin losses in the Holy Land.

> Ex omnibus terrae baronibus et regni Jerosolimitani militibus, toto conventu militiae Templi, trecentis videlicet fratribus, et ducentis Hospitalariis Sancti Johannis, ac toto posse domus Sanctae Mariae Theutonicorum, non nisi patriarcha praefatus, et dominus de Monteforti qui regni vexillifer fuerat et antesignatus, quatuor milites et paucissimi servientes Templarii, Hospitalarii vero decem et novem, et de fratribus Theutonicorum tres tantummodo servientes, fortunae vel fugae subsidio.

---

106 MS B, fol. 168ᵛ, col. a; *CM*, IV, p. 283; *EH*, I, p. 478.
107 MS B, fol. 169ʳ, col. b; *CM*, IV, p. 288; *EH*, I, p. 484.
108 MS B, fol. 169ʳ, col. b; *CM*, IV, pp. 291–94; *EH*, I, pp. 484–86.
109 MS B, fol. 169ʳ, col. b; *CM*, IV, p. 294; *EH*, I, pp. 486–87.

(Out of all the barons of the Holy Land, and the soldiers of the kingdom of Jerusalem; out of all the convent of the Temple militia, which had sent three hundred brothers; of the Hospitallers of St John, which had sent two hundred; of the whole they were able to muster of the Teutonic brothers of St Mary, not one, except the aforesaid patriarch, and the Lord Simon de Montfort (who was the standard-bearer of the kingdom and commander of the advanced guard), four chevaliers and a very few servants of the Temple, and nineteen Hospitallers and three servants only of the Teutonic brothers, returned, and these only through good luck or by flight.)[110]

Twenty-two short lines. In stark contrast to the staggering amount and interconnectedness of the 1241 clusters building up quite a momentum, Frederick's story is brought to an end by an entry that seems to be disproportionately little, and somewhat late. Matthew closes the sweep of Mongol episodes by briefly recounting how the king of Hungary asked for Frederick's help and how his country was freed by the intervention of the powerful emperor. While this entry about Frederick's liberation of King Béla's long-suffering kingdom contradicts not only historical facts but also Matthew's own entries about the Mongol ravages in later parts of the chronicle, there is archival evidence testifying that this plan seemed viable in the papal court in the early 1240s. Béla IV at some point made an oath of fealty to Frederick II, which he then requested to waive some time before or in 1245, owing to the fact that the emperor had failed to live up to the conditions of overlordship. The only document attesting to this deal is the pope's waiver issued in 1245.[111] Matthew's chronicle is oblivious of the Hungarian complaint of Frederick's failure to deliver.

As usual, it is a puzzling question whether he made this episode up or received the news from his usual sources and inserted it where he deemed it to fit. The most puzzling question is, however, why he deemed 1244 the best place to insert an entry which essentially reformulates and, to a limited extent, responds to some of the things he wrote under 1241. As Appendix 5 shows, the wording is entirely different, but the events and rumours covered are similar, except for the first and the last sentence of the 1244 entry, which develop the story towards a more finite end: Hungary's request for military assistance and the king's homage. While this in itself proves precious little, the repetition here seems more like a recap to jog the reader's memory and evoke the turbulent year of 1241.

---

110 MS *B*, fol. 171ʳ, col. a; *CM*, IV, p. 301; *EH*, I, pp. 492–93.

111 *CM*, IV, p. 298. Pauler, *A magyar nemzet története*, p. 176. The pope's response in a bull dated 21 August 1245: *Epistolae saeculi XIII e regestis pontificum Romanorum selectae*, I, 98–99. Also in Muldoon, *Popes, Lawyers, and Infidels*, p. 35; Whalen, *The Two Powers*, p. 181.

FLIGHT   259

And just like that, the Mongol invasion of Hungary was ended — at least for the time being. Considering its place and perceived relevance to the rest of the narrative in the chronicle, this entry is also interesting due to a marginal annotation in Matthew's hand: the disjointed rubric 'imperti' / 'nens Anglis usque huc' connected by a wavy red vertical line running downwards to a symbol at the bottom of the column marks the entry with a curious mixture of dismissal and highlighting (Fig. 10). This is not unique among the Mongol-related entries.[112] The symbol reappears in column a on fol. 172^v, next to the entry entitled 'Utilis sed nimis sera consideratio de reiciendo jugo multitiplicis servitutis in regno Angliae per Romanos subortae' where Matthew swerves the story back to the issue of papal money extortion in England.[113] The texts marked as 'impertinens' — that is, irrelevant — for English history cover the aforementioned closing episode of the Mongol campaign through a brief entry of transition transplanting the Mongol threat to the East ('Tartari exturbati versus partes Orientales discurrunt'), launching a domino-effect: fleeing from Hungary, they attack the Khwarezmians who, in turn, run to the sultan of Babylon who, instead of providing them with safe haven, sends them on to Jerusalem, which they ransack. Also marked as irrelevant is a letter by Frederick II to Richard of Cornwall about the developments in the Holy Land, and a letter from the master of the Hospitallers in Jerusalem.

The entry about the 'expelled Mongols' (*Tartari exturbati*) and their dispersal towards the East' starts as follows:

> Tartari interim exturbati nec potentes impetus imperiales sustinere, partes Boreales relinquentes, versus partes Orientales rapido cursu transmearunt. Et dum partes Persidae quasdam feraliter devastassent, quidam cruentissimi homines et inhumani confinia Rubri maris inhabitantes, et qui de potestate sunt pro majori parte Soldani Babiloniae, dicti Chorosmini, ab imminente fugerunt tempestate, Tartarorum vitantes irruptiones. Et venientes ad Soldanum Babiloniae, locum habitationis instanter et acriter postulabant.
>
> (Meanwhile the Tartars, being hunted about, and unable to sustain any longer the emperor's attacks, left the northern parts, and journeyed quickly eastward. While they were savagely ravaging some parts of Persia, certain extremely cruel and inhuman men

---

112 See other examples for the same mark-up next to Mongol-related entries in Fig. 10 as well as Chapter 3 ('1237: Chaldeans, Medes, Persians, and Armenians'), Chapter 4 ('Holy War on the Mongols'), and note 124 below.

113 MS *B*, fol. 172^v, col. a; *CM*, IV, p. 311; *EH*, I, p. 500. There are a number of 'impertinens' notations in the manuscript starting from fol. 53^v, where Matthew describes the Vera Icon. They include foreign troops (from Cologne and Frisia) in the Holy Land (fol. 56^v), an entry about priests' concubines (fol. 64^v), the Council of Bourges (fol. 66^v), Frederick II's preparations against the Milanese (fol. 104^{r-v}), and so on.

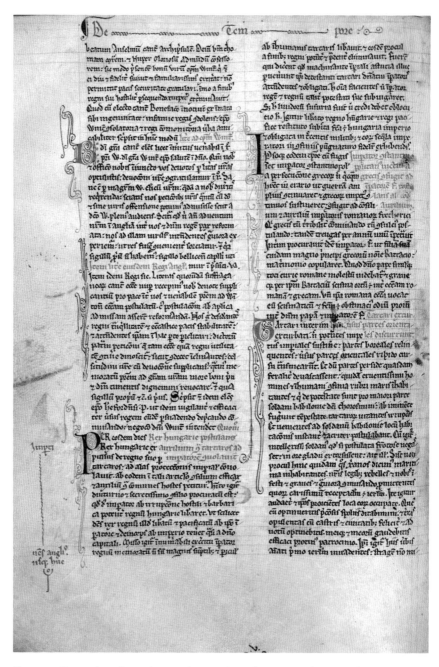

Figure 10. 'Impertinens' notation on the margin and arrows in the gutter between columns in MS *B*, fol. 170^v. By permission of the Parker Library, Corpus Christi College, Cambridge.

who dwell on the confines of the Red Sea, and who are for the most part subject to the sultan of Babylon, and called Choermians, fled from the threatening storm, by avoiding the irruptions of the Tartars; and they went to the sultan of Babylon, and demanded hastily and insolently a place wherein to dwell.)[114]

Although there is a brief excursion to Constantinople between the closing of the Mongol campaign in Eastern Europe by Frederick and this entry describing the new Mongol front in the Orient, between the columns a subtle row of arrowheads connects the two passages (see Fig. 10). Even though he does not use these consistently, and they may have been added in the course of a later revision or as aids for redaction projects, Matthew's personal annotations — both those marking passages to be skipped and those connecting split entries — serve the purpose of visually connecting parts of the narrative that felt disjointed due to the alternation of entries belonging to different subplots.[115] Suzannne Lewis exposes that Matthew Paris appropriated and improved Diceto's late twelfth-century method of distinguishing the secular from the ecclesiastical notices in his historical works by inserting appropriate symbols in the margins. Importantly, Lewis connects this practice with the chroniclers' toolkit to navigate a linear and chronological narrative: 'Within the restrictions of his annalistic format, Diceto could then manage to keep the deeds of kings, records of battles, and church history quite separate from one another, while at the same time observing the chronological sequence of events'.[116] Besides the

---

114 MS B, fol. 170ᵛ, col. b; *CM*, IV, pp. 299–300; *EH*, I, p. 491.

115 Vaughan and Gransden suggest that these were Matthew's own markings to help Matthew abridge the text for his *Historia Anglorum*. Vaughan, *Matthew Paris*, p. 65; Gransden, *Historical Writing in England*, I, pp. 366–67. At a glance, these look like tie-marks (*signes-de-renvoi*), i.e. visual marks that link 'a location in a text to a corresponding correction, annotation, or cross-reference in the margin. The "return" refers to the reader's practice of leaving the primary text to read the annotation and then returning to the primary text'. Neudorf and Liu, 'Signes-de-Renvoi'. However, since in this case the reader (or redactor) is not expected to return to the starting point of the annotation, I will refer to these as 'skipping marks' or use the more generic term 'personal markings' after Teeuwen's fitting observation: 'annotating practices also took place, for example in the shape of personal markings which redacted, summarized and reorganized texts in order to make them ready for a transport to new contexts'. Teeuwen, 'Writing in the Blank Space of Manuscripts', p. 5. Besides the present discussion (especially notes 112, 113, 116, 117, and Fig. 10), for further examples of 'skipping marks', see Chapter 3 ('1237: Chaldeans, Medes, Persians, and Armenians') and Chapter 4 ('Holy War on the Mongols') above.

116 Lewis, *The Art of Matthew Paris*, pp. 44–45. It is also remarkable how Diceto himself associates his *signa* with importance and memorability — in this case their own significance and purpose within his book: 'Itaque si, tempus gratiae diligenter percurrens, quaedam signa repereris in margine posita, non hoc statim quais superfluum reprehendas. Ea namque sunt ad memoriam facilius excitandam non parum accommoda'. (You will find certain *signa* placed in the margin. Do not immediately conclude that this is in any way superfluous for

262   CHAPTER 5

Mongol-related passages discussed in the present volume, there is a good number of these 'skipping marks' across a variety of themes in the *Chronica majora*.[117]

Leaving behind the 'irrelevant events' unfolding in Frederick II's increasingly less important theatres of war, the chronicle continues with four long and busy folios with no more mention of the Mongols or the Holy Land. Matthew had plenty on his mind on the home front. It is not before another long cluster on Welsh affairs, then another on the struggle for St Edmund of Abingdon's canonization, that Matthew swerves back to the conflict (and peace efforts for a change) between pope and emperor — with the involvement of Legate Otto. Fol. 175ᵛ contains yet another note about Legate Otto, this time nefariously helping to block St Edmund's canonization, which, as usual, precedes the foreign affairs section: Frederick's fury and retraction from previously agreed terms of peace introduces a letter from the Holy Land.[118] The story is essentially another version of the traumatic Jerusalem events. Perpetually stuck in the binary of pursuit, the Mongols morph from persecuted into persecutor, as their previous flight from Europe is followed by raising havoc in the Middle East.

> Desaeviens siquidem rabies Tartarorum totam orientalem plagam flagello multiplici et terrore concussit, qui, dum persequentes aequaliter universos, nullam differentiam facerent inter incredulos et fideles, praedam ab extremis finibus fugaverunt, Christianum populum praedaturam. Ipsi etenim Tartari, universalem Persidem destruentes, in nequiores se spiritus praelium converterunt, venantes crudelissimos hominum Corasminos, quos, quasi dracones de cavernis eductos, de propriis partibus expulerunt. Qui cum certum habitaculum non habentes non possent propter eorum nequitias ab aliquibus Sarracenis receptaculum adipisci, solus Soldanus Babiloniae, Christi

---

they are there to jog the memory more easily and are very convenient.) Radulfus de Diceto, *Opera historica*, I, p. 3. Translation in Lewis, *The Art of Matthew Paris*, p. 45.

117 For example, the entry about Prince Conrad's escape to Italy and about Frederick II's rumoured intention to enlist Mongol or Saracen allies to subjugate Christendom on fol. 215ᵛ is marked up by a key symbol and the usual rubric 'impertinens usque huc' split between the beginning and the end of the marked up section to show the boundaries of the text to be disregarded. *CM*, IV, pp. 634–35; *EH*, II, pp. 235–36. The Mongol-related entries are not at all the only ones marked up like this. Examples include the legend of an avaricious priest and a miraculous storm against avaricious peasants on fol. 94 (*CM*, III, pp. 300–301), the whole of fol. 104ʳ⁻ᵛ discussing Frederick's preparations against the Milanese until the defeat of the duke of Austria (*CM*, III, pp. 374–78) or the varied passage on fol. 107ʳ⁻ᵛ, starting with the battle of the Templars and the Saracens and ending with the entry reporting that Frederick occupied nearly the whole of Italy (*CM*, III, pp. 404–10).

118 The pope and Otto plotting to block the canonization process: MS *B*, fol. 175ᵛ, col. b; *CM*, IV, pp. 336–37; *EH*, I, p. 522.

fidei persecutor, eisdem Corasminis hospitium in terra propria denegans, optulit alienum, eosdem incredulos ad inhabitandam Terram Promissionis advocans et invitans, quam in Se credentibus Altissimus promiserat et donavit.

> (Yes, the rage and fury of the Tartars have now shaken the whole of the eastern region with the terrors of a manifold calamity: persecuting all alike, and making no difference between Christians and infidels, but driving off their booty from the most remote quarters, even of those who would themselves have preyed upon the Christian people. These said Tartars, after ravaging the whole of Persia, have made war in a worse spirit, and hunting out those cruel Chorosmins have dragged them forth like snakes from their holes, and driven them from their own provinces. These latter, having no habitation, as they could not obtain a place of refuge amongst any of the Saracens, owing to their wickednesses, were only aided by the sultan of Babylon, that persecutor of the Christian faith, who, although he refused them a place of refuge in his own territory, offered them that which belonged to others, and summoned and invited these said infidels to inhabit the land of promise which the Most High had promised and has given to those who believe in him.)[119]

In this giant game of tag, the same Mongols whom Frederick expelled from Europe appear in the East. They are easily identified by their usual description stressing the indiscriminate killing of their enemies. But expanding the scope of killing different kinds of Christians indiscriminately (in Ivo's words, 'sine delectu conditionis, fortunae, sexus, et aetatis, omnes indifferenter diversis suppliciis interibant'; without distinction of rank, fortune, sex, or age, all perished alike, by different kinds of death), their wholesale murders at this stage apply to Christians *and* non-Christians ('nullam differentiam facerent inter incredulos et fideles').[120] Despite the retreat, their memory lingers, and their story, though becoming more and more fragmented, is not over yet. As Matthew's *historia* is catching up with history, and the text is heading towards the Council of Lyon, the influence of the council on the Mongol entries becomes ever so palpable.

---

119 *Epistola flebilis*, a circular to the Church in England and France from the patriarch of Jerusalem together with various prelates, priors, and abbots, reporting about the intrusion of the Choresmians, the sack of Jerusalem and the Battle of Gaza, *s.a.* 1244: MS B, fols 175ᵛ, col. b–176ʳ, col. a; *CM*, IV, p. 338; *EH*, I, p. 523.
120 The phrase in Ivo's letter is on MS B, fol. 167ʳ, col. a; *CM*, IV, p. 273; *EH*, I, pp. 469–70.

264   CHAPTER 5

1244: The Man from Russia

Once the reader is fully informed about the Mongols' new whereabouts in the East, the narrative continues in other directions, still weaving various strands together in the familiar pattern. After Frederick II's victory and the Mongols' 'dispersal', two 1244 entries confirm the Mongol story's location in the Holy Land: first, a few folios down, Matthew inserts the copy of a long letter of prelates in the Holy Land — *epistola flebilis* — reporting about the emergence of the Mongols and their persecution of the Khwarezmians.[121] Then, after a longer hiatus, he copies the Russian Archbishop Peter's *examinatio*, which is used as a preface to the subsequent entry detailing the demands of the Mongols from the prince of Antioch.[122] The well-known entry, entitled 'Petrus archiepiscopus Russiae fugiens a facie Tartarorum de vita corum requisitus haec ait', follows a long cluster on Welsh-English affairs rather abruptly and without much ado: 'Et dum haec fatalis alea mundi revolvisset, quidam archiepiscopus de Russcia, [...] a Tartaris exterminatus' (whilst the die of fate was thus revolving the affairs of the world, a certain archbishop [...] [was] driven from his territory).[123] Needless to say, a familiar marginal notation warns the reader or future redactor that the letter is 'impertinens'. Symbols are used to mark the beginning and the end of the extraneous text that takes up exactly one page from Archbishop Peter's introduction at the top of fol. 182^r, col. a, to the very end of the Mongol's demands from the prince of Antioch at the bottom of col. b. The next page, fol. 182^v, col. a, begins with the 'pertinens' domestic news of the bishop of Winchester lifting the interdict on his episcopal city.[124]

While Matthew's version *s.a.* 1244 does not mention the Lyon council, the Burton annalist, who recorded the same text *s.a.* 1245, expressly situates the discourse in the context of the Council of Lyon, which certifies that Peter's intelligence arrived in England through the mediation of the

---

121 MS *B*, fols 175^v, col. b–176^v, col. b; *CM*, IV, pp. 337–47; *EH*, I, pp. 522–28. Cf. 'Literae Corsominis', in 'Annales de Burton', pp. 257–63.

122 MS *B*, fol. 182^r, col. b; *CM*, IV, pp. 389–90; *EH*, II, p. 31. This is not the only time that the *Burton Annals* share texts with the *Chronica majora*: they also have texts in common about papal matters, such as the response of the Berkshire rectors to the pope's demands (in 1240 in the *Chronica majora*; in 1244 in the *Burton Annals*), *CM*, IV, pp. 38–43; 'Annales de Burton', pp. 265–67; and then by the English clergy on the same issue, *CM*, IV, pp. 531–43; 'Annales de Burton', pp. 278–84 (both *s.a.* 1246 but with significant textual differences). Long accounts of the Council of Lyon appear in both under 1245: *CM*, IV, pp. 430–37; *EH*, II, pp. 64–65; 'Annales de Burton', pp. 267–71.

123 MS *B*, fol. 182^r, cols a–b; *CM*, IV, pp. 386–89; *EH*, II, pp. 28–31.

124 'Ecclesia Wintoniensis et totus conventus et ipsa civitas episcopo reconciliatur'. MS *B*, fol. 182^v, col. a; *CM*, IV, p. 390; *EH*, II, p. 31.

synod.[125] Matthew and the Burton annalist were not the only ones to get hold of Peter's report: the text travelled separately to a number of places. For example, it is nearly identical to *Tractatus de ortu Tartarorum* bound in the so-called Courtenay Compendium collecting other texts pertinent to the Mongol story,[126] the closely related passages from the *Burton Annals* and the *Tractatus* in Cambridge,[127] and a slightly different variant in Linz.[128] This wide dissemination, with three known copies in England, also suggests that this was a text intended to be widely circulated, and the low degree of textual variance suggests that it reached the English relatively fast and without mediation. The Compendium and the Cambridge *Tractatus* are especially interesting here as they also both contain a letter from a Hungarian bishop concerning his interrogation of two Mongol prisoners, known from the *Waverley Annals* and (in a slightly different version) in Matthew Paris's *Additamenta*.[129]

The *Chronica majora* and the *Burton Annals* share many documents received from and sent to Lyon.[130] The Burton annalist's collection is a contiguous record of a series of letters between the English (royal letters, barons' petitions to the pope) and the pope in Lyon (mostly concerning taxation). Some are in the form of *rescripta*, for example, the exemption of royal chapels, which contains the pertinent papal bull in its entirety.[131] Matthew Paris seems to have cherry-picked from the same collection and inserted the selected documents into his narrative where he deemed

---

125 'Examinatio facta de Tartaris apud Lugdunum per dominum Papam. Inter caeteros mundi praelatos venit ad concilium apud Lugdunum archiepiscopus Ruthenus, nomine Petrus, qui, prout quidam asserebant de concilio venientes, neque Latinam neque Graecam neque Hebraicam novit linguam, et tamen per interpretem peroptime coram domino Papa exposuit evangelium'. 'Annales de Burton', p. 271.

126 The Courtenay Compendium, probably written in the Augustinian priory of Breamore in Hampshire, is now in the Royal Library in Copenhagen (Acc. 2011/5) (MS CC), a late fourteenth-century English decorated manuscript on vellum. It may have been assembled by an Augustinian monk to provide his house with a scholarly collection of important historical texts copied from sources in the library of Glastonbury Abbey. Available online: <http://www5.kb.dk/manus/vmanus/2011/dec/ha/object78526/en/>. The codex also contains Gildas's *De excidio et conquestu Britanniae*, the *Encomium Emmae Reginae*, *Gesta Francorum*, *De Machometo* by William of Tripoli, Pipino's early fourteenth-century Latin redaction of Marco Polo's *Il milione*, *De ritibus orientalium regionum* by Odoric of Pordenone, and miscellaneous prophetic texts.

127 MS *BA*, fol. 29[r-v]; printed in 'Annales de Burton', pp. 271–78; and Cambridge, Gonville and Caius College, MS 162/83, fols 106[rv] (MS *GC*).

128 Linz, Oberösterreichische Landesbibliothek (formerly the Studienbibliothek), MS 446, fol. 267[v] (MS *L*) Notably Peter in this manuscript is designated as *archiepiscopus de Belgrab*, which Ruotsala interprets as Belgorod, near Kiev. Ruotsala, *Europeans and Mongols*, p. 154.

129 See Chapter 6 below.

130 The *Burton Annals* were written at the Benedictine abbey of Burton-upon-Trent, Staffordshire, from the founding of the abbey in 1004 to 1263; they are preserved in MS *BA*.

131 'Annales de Burton', pp. 275–76.

266   CHAPTER 5

appropriate. For example, the English response to the pope's demands for more money, *s.a.* 1244 in the *Burton Annals*, is entered under the year 1240 in the *Chronica majora*.[132] Besides this Lyon cluster, which is a more or less contiguous block in the *Burton Annals* between 1244 and 1245 but scattered between 1240 and 1245 in the *Chronica majora*, other shared passages crop up every now and then until 1258.[133] As a substantial amount of these shared texts point to Lincoln, it is justifiable to suggest that most of them, including those from the Council of Lyon, were disseminated to the monasteries by Robert Grosseteste's chancery.[134] Robert Grosseteste died in 1253, but the Lincoln tradition of sending documents to Benedictine abbeys — at least these two — lived on after his passing.[135]

A number of studies have examined the possible identity of this Russian cleric. According to Matthew Paris, Peter had come to the West as a refugee with the aim of securing the support of the Roman Church and Western princes.[136] He was at one point identified as Peter Akherovich from the Holy Saviour Monastery in Berestovo,[137] which has since been refuted.[138] In line with Matthew's dating (1244), Jackson argues that the cleric was questioned by Innocent IV and the cardinals, in advance of the First Council of Lyon (1245) and hence his answers were available to the Curia prior to the pope's despatch of John of Plano Carpini as well as later envoys to the Mongols after the Council of Lyon.[139] It is unclear, however, where or what he was fleeing. Was he a refugee of the Mongol sack of Kiev in December 1240? Though Peter's information in the report is said to have come from a mysterious Mongol informant, Kalaladin,

---

132 'Annales de Burton', pp. 265–67; *CM*, IV, pp. 535–36.

133 These include the last will and testament of Emperor Frederick II in 1250, Robert Grosseteste reporting about the pope's decree about procurations, Grosseteste's rejection of the pope's nephew as a Lincoln canon, a letter by Innocent about provisions (relegated into the *Additamenta* by Matthew), accusation of murder of St Hugh by the Lincoln Jews, and resolutions of Boniface of Savoy's Merton council in 1258 (in the *Additamenta*).

134 Even the seemingly separate report from the Council of Merton is intimately connected to the person of Robert Grosseteste: When in 1244, Boniface clashed with the king over the election of Henry's clerk, Robert Passelewe, to the see of Chichester, it was Robert Grosseteste who examined Passelewe and found him unfit for episcopal office. Creamer, 'St Edmund of Canterbury and Henry III', p. 134.

135 In fact, he is even mentioned in the St Hugh of Lincoln entry posthumously as it is recorded that St Hugh's body was interred next to his in Lincoln Cathedral. *CM*, V, p. 518; 'Annales de Burton', p. 344. Both are inserted under 1255, but Matthew cuts the reference to Robert Grosseteste, while the Burton monk is very specific: 'juxta tumulum sanctissimi patris Roberti'.

136 *CM*, IV, p. 386.

137 Richard, *La papauté et les missions d'Orient au Moyen Âge*, p. 67, n. 10.

138 Ruotsala, *Europeans and Mongols*, pp. 153–55; Jackson, 'The Testimony of the Russian "Archbishop" Peter'.

139 Jackson, 'The Testimony of the Russian "Archbishop" Peter', p. 66.

who was a refugee running away from his own kin,[140] Jackson posits that the archbishop may have been on the khan's payroll, similar to Ivo of Narbonne's anonymous Englishman who accompanied two Mongol embassies to the Hungarian king.[141] This theory is based on the time lag between the fall of Kiev and the Council of Lyon, as well as Peter's opinions about the Mongols and their *mores*, milder in tone than the panic-stricken letters found elsewhere.[142]

The theme of flight persists throughout the entire page. It is not only the archbishop and Kalaladin who are both on the run (*fugiens*), but the Mongols and their victims too: Peter's account of the origins of the Mongols starts with a story of flight and continues — twenty-four years later — with designs on world domination.[143] Confirming Matthew's previous suggestion that the Mongols defeated by the emperor dispersed from 'north' to 'east', Peter explains a three-pronged plan to maximize their domination: Tesirchan marched against Babylon, Curhican against the Turks, and Bathatarcan stayed in Ernac (a city they had previously conquered) and sent his chiefs against Russia, Poland, and Hungary.[144] It is

---

140 This statement at the end of the archbishop's report is confirmed in the Linz manuscript: 'Hec multa alia narravit dicto archiepiscopo quidam magnus de tartaris nomine Chalaladan qui filiam Cirkan habuit in uxorem'. (The said archbishop was told these things, and many others, by a certain Tartar grandee named Chalaladan whose wife was Chirkan's daughter). Jackson, 'The Testimony of the Russian "Archbishop" Peter', p. 71.

141 Jackson, 'The Testimony of the Russian "Archbishop" Peter', p. 77. This is even more palpable in the text found in the *Burton Annals* which is written in a Q&A format between Peter and his interlocutors — this format, if known to Matthew, had to be done away with in the *Chronica majora* because the chronicler inserted it a year *before* the council.

142 Dörrie noted the contrast between the responses of the cleric in 1245 and the frenzied letters crying for help coming from the region a couple of years earlier. Dörrie, 'Drei Texte zur Geschichte der Ungarn und Mongolen', pp. 182–83. Bezzola interprets this text as testimony for a new approach to the Mongols in the West, going from fiends of the apocalypse to human-faced foes, even potential allies.

143 'Reliquias credo fuisse Madianitarum fugientium a facie Gedeonis usque ad remotissimas partes subsolani et boreae, et sese recipientium in loco horroris et vastissime solitudinis, qui Etreu dicitur' (I believe that they are the remains of the Madianites who fled from before the face of Gideon, to the most remote parts of the east and the north, and took refuge in that place of horror and vast solitude, which is called Etren). This refers to the Old Testament story of Gideon's victory over the Midianites who were driven into western Palestine, after which they largely disappeared from the biblical narrative. Judges 6–8. This interpretation also appears in Julian's account, who relates it on the authority of a certain Russian cleric, *quidam clericus Ruthenorum*. For the Pseudo-Methodian link between these descriptions, see Jackson, 'The Testimony of the Russian "Archbishop" Peter', p. 69.

144 It has been suggested that 'this may be a garbled reference to Chinggis Khan, who had four sons by his first wife. To Ögödei, who succeeded him as great khan, he gave his lands in eastern Asia including China, to Chagatai, Central Asia and northern Iran, and to his eldest son, Jochi, the newly conquered Russia and Ruthenia. Because Jochi predeceased his father, his lands were divided among his sons, among them Batu, who invaded Russia, Poland and Hungary'. Bird, Peters, and Powell, eds, *Crusade and Christendom*, p. 328, n. 18.

268 CHAPTER 5

these three that 'are now invading the neighbouring region of Syria' (*partes Syriae vicinas invadere praesumunt*).

For seasoned readers of the Mongol story in the *Chronica majora*, the archbishop's description of the Mongols — *rudes, exleges, et inhumani* — contains familiar nuggets of information (barbarous eating and drinking, including cannibalism in times of necessity, punishing crimes severely, leather armour, and so on; see Appendix 8) but some others indeed suggest more intimate knowledge of the steppe nomad lifestyle. The new additions include polygamy, xenophobia, their ability to pick up sticks and be on the move, and a unique description of their religion and rites.

> De modo credendi requisitus, respondit, quod unum dominatorem mundi credunt, et cum legationem mitterent ad Ruthenos, mandaverunt in haec verba; Deus, et filius eius in catelis, et Chiarchan in terris. [...] De ritu autem ac superstitione eorum ait; Quolibet mane manus ad caelum levant, Creatorem adorantes. Comedentes vero, primum morsellum in aera jaciunt; bibentes, prius partem in terram fundunt, in veneratione Creatoris. Et dicunt se habere sanctum Johannem Baptistam pro duce. In novilunio gaudent et celebrant.

> (The archbishop, when asked as to their mode of belief, replied, that they believed there was one ruler of the world; and when they sent a messenger to the Muscovites, they commenced it in these words, 'God and his Son in heaven, and Chiar Khan on Earth'. [...] With respect to their rites and superstitions, he said, 'Every morning they raise their hands towards heaven, worshipping their Creator; when they take their meals, they throw the first morsel into the air; and when about to drink, they first pour a portion of the liquor on the ground, in worship of the Creator. They say, also, that they have John the Baptist for a leader, and they rejoice and observe solemnities at the time of the new moon'.)[145]

They are strange, but not inhuman. Peter's note of the Mongols' hardy military style, weaponry, and siege engines is also exceptionally factual and informative:

> Fortiores et agiliores nobis sunt, et potentiores sufferre dura; similiter et equi eorum et pecudes. Mulieres bellatrices, praecipue sagittatrices optimae sunt. Arma de corio habent vix penetrabilia, ad muniendum; ferrea et intoxicata, ad impetendum. Machinas habent multiplices,

---

145 MS *B*, fol. 182ʳ, cols a–b; *CM*, IV, pp. 387–88; *EH*, II, pp. 29–30. For a detailed bibliography about questions of faith, tolerance, and interfaith relations during the medieval Mongol conquests, see Jackson, 'The Mongols and the Faith of the Conquered'. On Pre-Buddhist religion and statecraft, see Baumann, 'By the Power of Eternal Heaven'.

recte et fortiter jacientes. Sub divo quiescunt, non curantes de aeris inclementia.

> (They are stronger and more nimble than we are, and better able to endure hardships, as also are their horses, and flocks, and herds; the women are warlike, and, above all, are very skilful in the use of bows and arrows; they wear armour made of hides, for their protection, which is scarcely penetrable, and they use poisoned iron weapons of offence. They have a great variety of engines, which hurl missiles with great force, and straight to the mark. They take their rest in the open air, and care nothing for the inclemency of the weather.)[146]

The rest of the description is pure military intelligence, a brief analysis of the Christians' strengths, weaknesses, opportunities, and threats for future dealings with the Mongols. On the one hand, the weakness of the 'Latins' lies in the seemingly mutually accepted fact that God uses the Mongol conquests to purge the world of sin, as it happened with the Deluge in the Bible:

De omnibus nationibus et sectis jam ad se multos attraxerant. Intendunt autem totum mundum sibi subjugare, et quod insinuatum est eis divinitus, quod debent totum mundum per triginta novem annos exterminare, asserentes, quod olim animadversio divina per diluvium purgavit mundum, sic in praesenti generali depopulatione, quam exercebunt, mundus purgabitur.

> (They have already enticed numbers of all nations and sects to them, and intend to subjugate the whole world; and they say that it has been intimated to them from heaven that they are to ravage the whole world for thirty-nine years; asserting that the Divine vengeance formerly purged the world by a deluge, and now it will be purified by a general depopulation and devastation, which they themselves will put in execution.)[147]

Even after their expulsion from Eastern Europe they remain a threat: 'Quos si vincant, toti mundo se profecto asserunt dominaturos. […] Insurgentibus in eos vel jugum eorum spernentibus nullatenus parcunt, vel qui eos expectant'. (They declare that, if they can conquer them, they will at once become lords over the whole world. […] They show no mercy to those who rebel against them, reject the yoke of their domination, or oppose them in the field.) But not all is lost, as the Latins' strength is the Church that the Mongols seem to fear: 'Credunt se habere et

---

146 MS B, fol. 182ʳ, col. b; CM, IV, p. 388; EH, II, p. 30.
147 MS B, fol. 182ʳ, col. b; CM, IV, p. 388; EH, II, p. 30.

CHAPTER 5

dicunt durum congressum cum Romanis; appellant autem omnes Latinos, Romanos miracula formidantes, et sententiam ultionis futurae posse commutari' (They think, and even say, that they will have a severe struggle with the Romans, and they call all the Latins Romans; they fear the miracles wrought by the Church, and that sentence of future condemnation may be passed against them).[148]

Finally and importantly, the Mongol military and diplomatic conduct may open opportunities for cooperation:

> Satis observant foedera, se sponte illis tradentibus et servientibus; accipientes sibi de illis electos bellatores, quos semper praeliantes praeponunt. Artifices varios similiter sibi reservant. [...] Nuntios benigne admittunt, expediunt, et remittunt.
>
>> (They pay proper respect to treaties, in the cases of those who voluntarily give themselves up to them and serve them, selecting the best soldiers from amongst them, whom, when they are fighting, they always station in front of them. In the same way, also, they retain amongst them the various workmen. [...] They receive messengers with kindness, expedite their business, and send them back again.)[149]

The document is clearly the product of a complex programme of translation, interpretation, and editing by the time it arrives in England.[150] Jackson notes that it is primarily formulated along the questions posed to the archbishop by the Western prelates at the Council of Lyon which, in turn, was also 'a useful means of securing the Council's retrospective support' for the pope's policy that had begun by seeking contact with the Mongols in their own homeland months earlier than the council.[151] In the *Chronica majora*, where Frederick has been the positive hero, this approach to the Mongols is a new development. Importantly, it is reminiscent of the pre-invasion entries, which Matthew also created out of material coming from Lyon. It was partly due to the nature of the received materials that the portions before and after Frederick's Mongol story were similarly framed by the pope's discourse about the Mongols: *rudes, exleges, et inhumani* though they may be, in the mid-1240s they were increasingly seen as an

---

148 MS *B*, fol. 182ʳ, col. b; *CM*, IV, p. 389; *EH*, II, p. 30.

149 MS *B*, fol. 182ʳ, col. b; *CM*, IV, p. 389; *EH*, II, p. 30.

150 The daisy chain of translation is an interesting (and entirely untraceable) question, since the Mongol information was probably translated for the archbishop, which was again translated for the council delegates for, as the *Burton Annals* note, he 'neque latinam neque grecam neque hebraicam novit linguam' (knew neither Latin, nor Greek, nor Hebrew). 'Annales de Burton', p. 272.

151 Jackson, 'The Testimony of the Russian "Archbishop" Peter', p. 77.

acceptable power in the East to be utilized against the 'Saracens' — as long as their menacing presence remains distant.

Peter's descriptive report about the Mongols' previous history and their *mores* is background information for the next entry which reports historical developments in the Mongols' new theatre of war. Although short, it underpins the new location of the Mongols and, concomitantly, the need for a new strategy that reckons with their presence and power in the East — 'Eodemque anno, aestate declinante, praecipus rex Tartarorum significavit bis per diversos nuntios principi Antiochiae' (In the same year, at the decline of summer, the chief king of the Tartars twice sent a message by different messengers to the prince of Antioch) — citing outlandish demands to destroy fortifications and send exorbitant amounts of gold and three thousand virgins in tribute to the khan, which the beleaguered prince declined.[152] The entry also specifies other addressees of the same threatening letters, including the king of Armenia and 'some powerful Saracen sultans' stating that their answer is unknown.

The role which the incumbent powers envisaged for the Mongols may have been based on their sheer ability to displace populations and use them as a vanguard, as Peter's report explains. Whether the crusaders wanted to imitate this and use the Mongols as their drill bit in the Holy Land, or planned to embroil them in a more sophisticated stratagem as allies — even as Christian converts ultimately — is unclear but reading these texts with a military eye, they may have rightly felt that they could use the Mongols' martial skill for their benefit. That this never really amounted to anything was becoming clear towards the end of the decade, but here (and back in the earlier portions of the chronicle) Matthew seems to accept the basic idea, despite the Eastern European interlude between 1241 and 1244.[153]

---

152 MS B, fol. 182ʳ, col. b; *CM*, IV, p. 389; *EH*, II, p. 31.
153 As Paula Strah sums up the climate of the 1240s, 'Die ersten Kontaktaufnahmen in den 1240er Jahren hatten abgesehen vom übergreifenden Zweck der Einordnung der Tartaren ins eigene Weltbild und in das päpstliche Weltherrschaftskonzept, auch zukünftigen Abwehrmaßnahmen gegen diese neuen furchterregenden Barbaren gedient. Daher hatte man auch stets den Hintergedanken einer Bekehrung der Mongolen im Sinne, um sie dadurch kontrollierbar zu machen'. Strah, 'Die Mongolen und das Heilige Land', p. 72. It was, however, not until after Matthew's death that the Mongols came to be portrayed as 'non-believing apocalyptic friends' (for an analysis of prophecies that gave rise to this concept, see Schmieder, 'Nota sectam maometicam atterendam a tartaris et christianis') and direct diplomatic contacts were established, mainly between the il-khans of Persia and the Latins against the Mamluks, in which England was also deeply involved due to Edward's participation in Louis IX's crusade of 1270. For a core bibliography in this field, see Paviot, 'England and the Mongols', p. 306, n. 4.

272   CHAPTER 5

1245–1248: Endgame

At various junctures in the present volume, it has been stressed that the First Council of Lyon was an important hub of exchange, a clearing house of sources about the Mongols, and a platform where Western intelligence and foreign policy met. Matthew minutely recorded the progress and results of the council in the *Chronica majora*. What did he have to say about the discussions and resolutions about the Mongol issue, which was apparently one of the priority points on the agenda of the council? In comparison with the other materials that may have arrived through the mediation of delegates at the council, the brief notes about Mongol-related council documents seem positively anaemic.[154]

Within the vast amount of text documenting the proceedings and resolutions of the council, the Mongols appear in five minor instances. First, he states — probably incorrectly — that 'Veruntamen de regno Hungariae, quae pro multa sui parte per Tartaros est vastata, nulli' (from the Kingdom of Hungary, however, which had to a great extent, been laid waste by the Tartars, none came).[155] This, of course, also contradicts Matthew's 1244 entry in which he categorically states that Frederick II ousted the Mongols and brought peace to the kingdom. The Mongol threat is then briefly mentioned in the account of the pope's instruction on the first day of the Council of Lyon, which reveals instantly why the 1244 entry was important for Matthew. We encounter Thaddeus de Sessa, *gran giustiziere* of Sicily and Frederick's representative by proxy, whom Matthew draws at the bottom of the page in a state of distress.[156] Here, he is still in

---

154 As Tudor Sălăgean observes 'the Mongol issue was rather left aside in the conciliar debates. The main issues discussed focused on more pressing issues like the relationship with Frederick II, the general reform of the Church, the freeing of the Holy Land, and endorsing the Latin Empire. Consequently the 16th Canon of the Concilium, *De Tartaris*, does nothing more than incriminate the violent devastation of "Poland, Russia, Hungary and other Christian countries" and to recommend Christian princes to reinforce their frontiers with the Mongols, in order to be able to ward off a new invasion'. Sălăgean, *Transylvania in the Second Half of the Thirteenth Century*, p. 50.

155 MS B, fol. 187[v], col. a; *CM*, IV, pp. 430–31; *EH*, II, pp. 64–65. The whole Council of Lyon block: *CM*, IV, pp. 430–73; *EH*, II, pp. 64–86. See Chapter 2, esp. 'The Council of Lyon in 1245', for the discussion of the Hungarian attendance at the council.

156 Probably depicting the moment when the pope dismissed his claim that the kings of England and France would vouchsafe for Frederick to keep his promises, the illustration portrays the pope and the prelates seated, huddling close together, away from an isolated, lonely figure of Thaddeus on the right. The rubric over Thaddeus's head reads 'Thadeus de Suessa procurator Fretherici recedit confusus'; and he is holding a scroll with 'Dies ista dies irae' on it. About this illustration and its counterpart in the *Historia Anglorum*, see Lewis, *The Art of Matthew Paris*, p. 265. Michael Camille focuses on the figure of the evil advisor, Master Martin, whispering in the ear of the pope from behind, the same way as Plato's hand scrapes Socrates' back in the famous 'postcard from Matthew Paris'. Camille, 'The Dissenting Image', p. 127, and fig. 4.6. Luard suggests that the image illustrates the first dejection, but

the mood to negotiate, not long before his eloquent arguments were shot down by the pope:

> Pro cujus pace et pristinae amicitiae reformatione optulit pro domino suo confidenter ad unitatem Romanae ecclesiae totum Romaniae, id est, Graciae imperium, revocare; et quod sese Tartaris, et Chorosminis, Sarracenis, et aliis ecclesiae hostibus et contemptoribus, Christo fideliter militando, potenter opponet; et quod statum Terrae Sanctae discrimini magno jam patentis sumptibus propriis personaliter pro posse suo reformabit; et ablata Romanae ecclesiae restituendo, de injuriis satisfacere.

>> (To make peace with the pope, and to re-establish their former friendship, he confidently offered to recall the whole of Romania, that is, the empire of Greece, to the unity of the Roman church, and to oppose in person, as a faithful soldier of Christ, the Tartars, Chorosmins, Saracens, and other enemies and despisers of the Church; also that, as far as he was able, he would, at his own expense and in person, re-establish the condition of the Holy Land, now exposed to such great and imminent peril; and at the same time restore to the Roman church the possessions he had taken from it, and also give full satisfaction to it.)[157]

Promising to keep the Mongols under control in the Holy Land certainly sounded more convincing with recent recommendations in the field, such as the liberation of Hungary. That the fight against the Mongols and the Khwarezmians was a major card in Frederick's hand is also shown by a tiny rubric at the bottom of the page where Matthew copied Frederick II's letter against the pope in his own defence: 'Nota hic incomparabilem stragem. .xii. [milia] hominum interfecti sunt a Chorosminis Jerusalem. Rex Turcorum a Tartaris. Soldanus Babiloniae restitit Tartaris stipatus .ccc. armatis'. (Note here an incomparable massacre. Twelve thousand people were killed by the Choresmians in Jerusalem. The King of the Turks is fought against and taken by assault by the Tartars. The Sultan of Babylon surrounded by three hundred armed men resisted the Tartars.)[158] As if to show how things escalate quickly without Frederick's watchful eyes, this brief note enumerates the enemies of the enemies fighting among themselves.

---

the figure is clearly leaving and the scroll displays Thaddeus's parting words (see note 160 below), at the very end of the Council of Lyon sequence, which makes one wonder why Matthew placed the image here rather than on fol. 193ᵛ.

157 MS B, fol. 187ᵛ, col. b; CM, IV, pp. 432–33; EH, II, p. 66. Whole entry: MS B, fols 187ᵛ, col. a–188ʳ, col. a; CM, IV, pp. 431–33; EH, II, pp. 65–67.

158 MS B, fol. 202ᵛ. Though written in the same hand as the rest of the page, it is not found in MS C.

274   CHAPTER 5

Frederick's promises foreshadow the pope's conciliar speech about the five 'pains' of Christendom, out of which the first one was the Mongol danger: 'Unum de inhumanis et feraliter Christianitatem vastantibus Tartaris' — formulated rather vaguely and separate from the issues in the Holy Land (the fourth pain).[159] Finally, moving towards some resolution for the future, the Mongols are mentioned in the last sentence uttered at the council in Matthew's account, once again by Thaddeus, in a dejected speech. The weeping procurator bid farewell to peace with these words:

> Haec autem cum intellexisset Thadaeus, ab imo trahens suspiria, ait, 'Intelligo nullum remedium patere discrimini'. Ejulansque et flens subintulit, quasi 'Vere dies ista dies irae', sicut antea dixerat, cum ad concilium plenum omnes praelati candelas suas accensas inclinarent et extinguerent, excommunicatum Frethericum deponentes. Et in calce sermonis adjunxit, 'Ex hoc tempore cantabunt haeretici, regnabunt Chorosmini, et insurgent Tartari'. Et haec nuntiaturus ad dominum suum est reversus. Dominus autem Papa omnibus in propatulo ait, 'Quod meum est feci, faciat et prosequatur super his Deus quod voluerit'.

> > (Master Thaddeus, on hearing this, said with a sigh, 'I see that there is no remedy open for this peril'; and then added, with weeping and lamentation, 'Truly was that day a day of anger', as he had said before when all the prelates in full council had inverted their lighted tapers, and extinguished them when deposing the excommunicated emperor Frederick. At the end of his speech Master Thaddeus said, 'From this time forth heretics will sing, the Chorosmians will reign supreme, and the Tartars will rise in their strength and prevail'; and he then returned to tell all these proceedings to the emperor. The pope then publicly said to all, 'I have done my duty, now let God do what he pleases, and proceed as he wills in these matters'.)[160]

That the references to the Mongols during the Council of Lyon are so jejune is perhaps not a coincidence. Since much of the Mongol-related material received via Lyon concerned the Christians' previous experience with the Mongols, Matthew simply used them up for the earlier parts of his chronicle. This left him with brief notes about the council itself and about some plans of action.[161] He copied conciliar documents as they were:

---

159 MS B, fol. 188ʳ, col. a; CM, IV, p. 437; EH, II, p. 67. Whole entry: MS B, fol. 188ʳ, col. a–188ᵛ, col. b; CM, IV, pp. 437–40; EH, II, pp. 67–73.

160 MS B, fol. 193ᵛ, col. a; CM, IV, p. 473; EH, II, p. 103.

161 Further travellers that were sent to the Mongols by Innocent IV before the council, mostly in the spring, included Lawrence of Portugal who was to have approached the Mongols in the south-west from the Levant. Nothing is known about his journey, if it ever had taken place at all. Guzman, 'Simon of Saint-Quentin and the Dominican Mission to the

FLIGHT   275

he kept the text formal and did not add any of the intelligence that was gathered there or materials that may have reached him afterwards. And the documents probably contained precious little about the Mongols, because (despite Thaddaeus's alarm) the council did not devote much attention to the question officially. Thus, the most important reason for the dearth of Mongol materials from the council itself is to be sought in the fact that not all pains are created equal: out of the five points of agenda — the Mongols, the Greeks, the European heresies, the Holy Land, and Frederick II — the latter was clearly the greatest cause for concern in the papal court in exile; everything else was subordinated to the emperor's excommunication.

Despite Frederick's triumph in 1244, despite the Mongols' move to the East, and despite the Church's increasingly open attitude towards their future 'non-believing Apocalyptic friends', the story of conquest was still not completely over in the *Chronica majora*. In fact, the post-synod continuation of Frederick's Mongol story shows that the Lyon material's references to the Mongols, including Peter's report, essentially have nothing to do with the Eastern European leg of Mongol military campaigns. The pope simply did not have the time or willingness to care, which, according to Matthew's account, was still the case in 1246. Two years after Frederick's alleged liberation of Hungary, the country is shown to reach out to the *pope*, just to be bitterly disappointed.

> Tartari debacchantes super Christianos magnam redivivam exercent tirannidem. Eodemque anno, amarissimae recordationis Tartari super Christianorum climata formidabilem facientes, impetum, cum sibi multos Sarracenorum principes violenter subjugassent, regem Armeniae et principem Antiochiae et alios multos nobiles Christianos, Deo mortalibus adversante, sibi sub tributo subegerunt. Et deinde sibi sperantes prosperiora, fines Hungariae, ut eis videbatur, sibi non prius subjugatos sed turpiter et probrose derelictos, iterato protervius invaserunt. Unde rex Hungariae non mediocriter perterritus, ab infirmioribus terrae suae cum habitatoribus suis secedens, et ad munitissima, quae tamen vix ei adhuc tuta videbantur, confugiens, nihil aliud quam bellum cruentissimum expectabat. Significavitque domino Papae, ut sollicite sibi totique Christianitati de tam formidabili peste provideret; sed nec sic tamen aversus est Papalis impetus imfrunitus, quin pecuniae colligendae totis rictibus inhiaret, ut in sequentibus enarrabitur.

> (Of the attacks made by the Tartars on the Christians. In this same year, the Tartars, of most hateful memory, made a formidable

---

Mongol Baiju', p. 234. John of Plano Carpini and Andrew of Lonjumeau were not back from their respective journeys until later, and the return Simon of Saint-Quentin and Ascelin of Lombardy (Ascelin of Cremona) was even further away in the future, in 1248.

incursion into the Christian countries, and after having subdued many of the Saracen princes, God being hostile to mankind, they made the king of Armenia, the prince of Antioch, and many other Christian nobles tributary to them. Afterwards, hoping for further good fortune, they again daringly invaded the provinces of Hungary, as it seemed to them that they were not previously subdued, although they were disgracefully abandoned by the inhabitants. The king of that country, greatly alarmed at their approach, withdrew with the inhabitants from the weaker portions of his territories, and fleeing to the most fortified places (and even they seemed to him to be scarcely safe), there awaited a bloody battle. He also sent word to the pope to use his anxious endeavours to protect him and all Christendom from such a fearful pest; but not even by this was the pope's sottish eagerness prevented from using all his exertions to collect money, as will be shown in the following pages.)[162]

It is unclear to what actual Mongol attacks this passage is alluding. Chronologically, it seems that this late reference to the Mongols in Eastern Europe refers to later military operations. When the Mongols made a repeated attack on Galicia (Halych), probably in 1243, Béla IV of Hungary informed his uncle, Berthold, the patriarch of Aquileia. The news made it to the pope fairly soon: in a letter dated to 21 July 1243, the newly elected Innocent IV commissioned Berthold to declare a crusade in the Holy Roman Empire against the Mongols in Hungary.[163]

The dry restraint characterizing Matthew's account of the Council of Lyon — save for Thaddeus's tears — is nowhere to be found in the last entries that refer to the Mongols in Eastern Europe. In these, Matthew's caustic commentary on the pope's greed is back in full force. The last mention of the Mongol threat is about the experience of a bitter encounter informing the future: the English-born Cistercian John of Toledo gives an impassioned speech urging the pope to edit his rapacious behaviour

---

162 MS *B*, fol. 203ʳ, col. b–203ᵛ, col. a; *CM*, v, p. 547; *EH*, ii, p. 165.

163 *Codex diplomaticus Hungariae ecclesiasticus ac civilis*, iv.1, pp. 299–301. Cited in Senga, 'IV Béla külpolitikája', p. 587. This was not a one-off attempt. In 1259, the year of Matthew's death, the Mongols were at Halych again, and it seems that they chose a new strategy to approach the Kingdom of Hungary: we know from a papal letter sent in response to the Hungarian king's report about the developments and request for help (a thousand archers rather than encouraging words) that a *princeps Tartarorum* offered to enter into dynastic ties with the king by the marriage of his son or daughter with one of theirs. In return they promised a tribute waiver and one fifth of war spoils collected. *Vetera monumenta historica Hungariam Sacram illustrantia*, i, pp. 239–41. Alexander's response was to caution the king about entering into alliances with pagans and letting him know that the archers will not be coming. A detailed examination of this letter, especially the debated dating issue, suggesting a terminus ante quem in 1248, in Senga, 'IV Béla külpolitikája'.

FLIGHT 277

in times so turbulent for European powers, including Hungary which 'cum suis terris sibi conterminis nihil aliud nisi a Tartaris expectat exterminium' (with its coterminous lands, expects nothing short of ruin from the Tartars).[164] This last brief reference to Hungary's rancorous experience with the Mongols describes Frederick as a man who 'non est potentior, immo nec par inter principes Christianorum' (has no superior, indeed no equal, amongst Christian princes), and revisits the pope's vengeance and 'expectations of gain'.[165] These two entries together continue the story of the conflict between the magnanimous Frederick II and the avaricious pope, and here ends the story of the Mongol invasion of Eastern Europe. It is remarkable that the anti-papal discourse that underlies all the Mongol entries, and indeed the entire second half of the *Chronica majora*, is often wrought out of information that Matthew received from and via the emperor's most powerful and vocal adversaries.

Although Matthew did not mention the European leg of the Mongol conquests again in the *Chronica majora*, the prospect of the Mongols returning was left open. This reflected contemporary realities: John of Plano Carpini, who was present in the khan's court in 1246, for example, reported about Mongol plans to invade Eastern Europe again. Returning in 1247, he recorded the following in his report:

> In predicta autem curia sunt bellatores et principes exercitus assignati. De decem hominibus mittunt tres cum famulis eorum, de omni terra potestatis eorum. Unus exercitus debet intrare per Hungariam, secundus per Poloniam, ut nobis dicebatur. Venient autem pugnaturi continue decem et octo annis: tempus est eis assignatum procedendi.
>
> > (The warriors and military commanders were appointed at the aforementioned imperial assembly. From each country under their rule, three out of ten men, together with their servants, are sent. As we have been told, one army is to march to Hungary, and a second to Poland. The Tartars will come and fight ceaselessly for eighteen years; that is the period of time assigned to them for the campaign.)[166]

Recurring Mongol danger also appears in Matthew Paris's *Additamenta*: in a letter to Peter of Savoy, the archbishop of Canterbury writes that

---

164 MS *B*, fol. 208ʳ, col. b; *CM*, ɪᴠ, p. 579; *EH*, ɪɪ, p. 190.
165 1246: MS *B*, fols 207ᵛ, col. b–208ʳ, col. a; *CM*, ɪᴠ, p. 579; *EH*, ɪɪ, pp. 189–90.
166 Bk ᴠɪɪɪ, ch. 4 of the *Ystoria*. Gießauf, *Die Mongolengeschichte des Johannes von Piano Carpine*, p. 108. See also the curious note about Béla's legates in Bibliothèque nationale de Luxembourg, MS 110: 'Quo intronizato in die iam dicto statim fuit vexillum erectum et expeditio edicta per .xix. annos contra occidentales populos. Bellatores autem sunt electi ita, quod de .x. hominibus tres fortiores cum uxoribus et pueris et pectoribus et omni substancia debet ire'. See Chapter 2 ('The Council of Lyon in 1245') and Chapter 6.

the Mongols returned to Hungary: 'Dicitur etiam quod Tartari reversi sunt super regnum Hungariae'.[167] Whether or not the Mongol assembly's decision was a smokescreen for the Western legates, a misunderstanding, or a real plan, Guyuk khan died in 1248 and the campaign deescalated — if it had ever begun in the first place.

To sum up this complex stage in the story of the Mongols in Europe, the Mongol-related entries in the main text of the chronicle continue to show signs of arriving at different times and from different places. While Matthew keeps the narrative fairly coherent, conflicting information, chronological confusion, and perceptibly different perspectives occasionally reveal that he is fusing at least three different accounts of the Mongol story — received in instalments — if not more. Previously, the earliest Mongol-related entries in the chronicle were shown to come from Lyon or from circles who acquired their information from there, with a good measure of mysteriously disconnected 'Northern' material thrown in the mix.[168] In 1241, the Mongol invasion is presented as part of Frederick's story, which gradually tapers off in the last phase discussed in the present chapter. The last references to the Eastern European region in a Mongol context, written in a more annalistic style than the materials beforehand, are few and far between and less organically incorporated into their immediate textual context, so it is harder to infer Matthew's sources. It is not impossible that the pro-Hohenstaufen pieces arrived from Lyon as well, as did many other materials that criticized the pope's policies.[169]

The news from Lyon, primarily concerned with the Mongol invasion as a past experience to inform future plans in the Holy Land, continued to feed into Matthew's narrative. While the council itself was shown to be less invested in solving (or even addressing) the Mongol question, a large part of Matthew's Mongol material was shown to be potentially associated with the buzz of prelates, royal and baronial representatives, and assorted abbots, monks, and friars in Lyon. Matthew's entries concerning the agenda of the council are less interesting than the wealth of other materials to which he had access through his channels, including fellow monks and clerics who attended the council. The texts brought to St Albans from Lyon in 1245 and thereafter were quite likely more abundant and diverse than we can now reconstruct. Ivo's letter and Archbishop Peter's report, Matthew's two most frequently cited Mongol-related texts, for example,

---

167 MS *LA*, fol. 89ᵛ, cols a–b; *CM*, VI, pp. 131–33. Not in *EH*. Dated to 1247 in a contemporary hand on the margin.

168 See Chapter 3 above.

169 For example, the Lyon material to which both Matthew Paris and the *Burton Annals* had access contained a great deal of correspondence between the pope and the English barons and king.

are almost certainly part of the Lyon materials, which brought alive the dry husks of the synodal constitutions with fresh blood — in Ivo's case quite literally, and not in a nice way.

Despite the language describing a fast-moving army, directionality or movement is hardly ever expressed in the entries themselves. When the reader sees the Mongol threat moving, the sense of direction is not provided by the chronicler on the narrative level of entries but through a series of static snapshots recording the conflicts' current whereabouts. Through the entries during these five years, the Mongol problem migrated back to the East where it came from and became a problem for the pope, the French king, and the East, represented by Armenians and Assassins.[170] The Assassins are indeed important here. Providing a peek into a curious contemporary conceptualization which remains largely unarticulated in the chronicle, twinning Mongols and Assassins in their Otherness, they serve as brackets: the Mongol story, which started with the Assassins in 1238, ends with the Assassins in 1257. Matthew's words, directly addressing his readers, leave no doubt that he considers the case closed in the *Chronica majora*. If you want to know more, do your own research; there is more where all this came from:

> Assessini a Tartaris destruuntur. Circulo ejusdem anni Tartari detestabiles Assessinos detestabiliores, quos cultelliferos appellamus, destruxerunt. Ipsorum Tartarorum immunditias, vitam et mores si quis audire desiderat, necnon et Assessinorum furorem et superstitionem, apud Sanctum Albanum diligens indagator poterit reperire.
>
>> (In the course of this year, these detestable Tartars destroyed the Assassins, a race still more detestable, and who carry knives about them. If any one is desirous of learning the impurities of these Tartars, and their mode of life and customs, or to read of the superstitions and fury of the Assassins, he may obtain information by making diligent search at St Alban's.)[171]

The parallels between the emergence of the Mongols in the first phase of the Mongol story and the disintegration in the last have been shown to be the result of working from different sources than those on which the 1241 entries relied. The people and the networks connecting them were unquestionably closer to the papal court than Matthew may have found

---

170 The Mongols were mentioned in this context in the following entries: [1247] *CM*, IV, pp. 607–08, 634–35; *EH*, II, pp. 214, 235–36. [1248] *CM*, V, pp. 37–38; *EH*, II, p. 280. [1249] *CM*, V, pp. 80, 87–88; *EH*, II, pp. 314, 319–20. [1250] *CM*, V, pp. 116, 191; *EH*, II, pp. 342, 405. [1252] *CM*, V, pp. 552–53; *EH*, II, p. 340. [1257] *CM*, V, pp. 645–55, 655, 660–61; *EH*, III, pp. 250–51, 251, 255–56.

171 MS R, fol. 202ᵛ, col. b; *CM*, V, p. 655; *EH*, III, p. 251. See this passage discussed in more detail in the next chapter.

comfortable, yet letters and reports written and disseminated by them, bearing the hallmark of papal policies even after many stages of mediation, supplied him with the bulk of the sources that he used in these parts of his narrative. During the reign of Innocent IV, the papacy was clearly not the Church for Matthew Paris, which raises questions of loyalty for the historian and the monk.[172] When and how did Matthew decide to turn much of the second half of his chronicle into an acerbic invective against the pope? The pope's 'avarice', monies extorted from the English religious through Legate Otto and others, no doubt darkened Matthew Paris's views about the papacy and created a vacuum that Frederick's person filled in the narrative. The discrepancy of perspectives which Matthew does not make discernible efforts to synchronize may seem odd, but his way of negotiating the differing tone of various passages inserted into the chronicle, or the lack thereof, resembles the practice of the modern historian quoting their primary sources as they are. Despite the absence of a harmonized perspective on the level of individual entries or their components, his interpretive passages (even when edited or erased later) make sure that his personal convictions remain obvious throughout.

---

172 Similarly puzzling and requiring further research is the question of placing Frederick II on a pedestal despite recording criticism and condemnation at times. What we know is what he wrote *against*: 'But undoubtedly its principal unifying factor was its theme. From beginning to end Matthew has a consistent attitude to centralized authority in church and state. He opposes it. He criticizes the king and government and he criticizes the pope and any ecclesiastic who interfered with established privileges. Not since the days of William Rufus had a chronicler had such an implacable attitude to royal power. [...] Sometimes he seems to complain for the sake of complaining, so that his invective has a homiletic ring'. Gransden suggests Matthew inherited his hostility to king and pope from Roger of Wendover, which he merely took over and elaborated. Gransden, *Historical Writing in England*, I, pp. 367–68. But his sympathies are less clear; it is never entirely certain what or whom he wrote *for*. Gransden, summarizing the potential motivations of historiography in this era, notes unattributed but very real sponsorship and explicit patronage, which is definitely not the case here. Besides the tangential relevance of some kind of 'patriotism' and Matthew's appeal to 'the right of the community of the realm to act against bad Government', none of the factors in her otherwise comprehensive overview are fit to convincingly explain Matthew's stance. Gransden, 'The Chronicles of Medieval England and Scotland: Part 2', pp. 137–41.

CHAPTER 6

Letters from the Afflicted Lands in the *Additamenta*

> The most merciful thing in the world, I think, is
> the inability of the human mind to correlate all its
> contents. We live on a placid island of ignorance in the
> midst of black seas of the infinity, and it was not meant
> that we should voyage far.[1]

Matthew Paris's original intention was to finish his chronicle in 1250, and to this effect there is even a colophon on fol. 146[r]:

Terminantur hic Mathaei
Cronica; nam jubilaei
Anni dispensatio
Tempus spondet requiei.
Detur ergo quies ei,
Hic, et caeli solio.
[...]
Siste tui metas studii, Mathaee, quietas,
Nec ventura petas quae postera proferet aetas.

> (Matthew's chronicle here ends
> and the jubilee year sends
> repose down from the skies.
> May repose to him be given
> here on Earth and up in Heaven
> when he there shall rise.
> [...]
> Matthew, here your toils are o'er
> stop your pen and toil no more.
> Seek not what the future brings
> another age has other things.)[2]

---

1 Lovecraft, 'The Call of Cthulhu', p. 159.

2 MS *B*, fol. 246[r], col. b; *CM*, v, pp. 197–98. Translation is Vaughan's in Paris, *The Illustrated Chronicles*, p. 203, based on *EH*, II, p. 411.

282   CHAPTER 6

However, he then decided to continue his narrative, thus physically separating the *Additamenta* from MS *B* in *c.* 1252, and continuing the chronicle (later in MS *R*) until 1259, where the well-known drawing of Matthew in his deathbed signals the end of his part of the *Chronica majora*.[3]

The *Liber Additamentorum* (or *Additamenta;*) was originally part of MS *AB* (that is, both MS *A* and MS *B*, which were a single manuscript).[4] The *Additamenta* is a miscellany, in which contemporary reports as well as shorter historical works, records of interest, maps, and drawings were collected by the community of St Albans.[5] In addition to the *Additamenta*, the tome contains other substantial pieces of text, including the *Vitae duorum Offarum* and the *Gesta Abbatum*, and smaller pieces such as an itinerary from London to Naples or the collection of arms of English nobility, and the obituaries of St Albans (see List of Manuscripts in Appendix 6). The *Additamenta* gained in length and importance from 1247 and was continuously added to until Matthew's death. The variety of documents in the *Additamenta* reflects the variety of the items making up the codex, and is one of the few English historical works that contain copies of documents originating in Eastern Europe.

The British Library's catalogue dates the section on fols 85–100 as documents of 1242–1250, copied in or before 1250.[6] Muñoz Garcia, using digital tools to reconstruct the scribal stints and chronology of Matthew Paris's texts, however, suggests that the manuscript received materials over a number of years and was written down between 1255 and 1259, the time when Matthew was already working on the manuscript that now contains the *Historia Anglorum* and the third volume of the *Chronica majora*. In either case, it is certain that the Mongol-related letters arrived relatively late, in or around 1250, and were probably written down even later. This partly explains why the letters remain outside the narrative of Matthew Paris's history.

Within this variety of the *Additamenta*, the contiguous text, referred to as the Mongol bundle here, is wedged between testimonies from various writers that the end of the world was approaching[7] and the record of

---

3 Muñoz García, 'The Script of Matthew Paris and his Collaborators', pp. 15, 18.

4 MS *LA*, now London, BL, MS Cotton Nero D I. See detailed contents in Appendix 6.

5 The *Additamenta* continued to be used for recording such material after Paris's death. There are documents from the reign of Edward I and some as late as from the fifteenth century.

6 Probably based on Vaughan, *Matthew Paris*, p. 82.

7 Under the heading 'Harum assertione auctoritatum et subscriptarum testimonio literarum praesumitur quod in fine sumus saeculorum', this contiguous entry contains the texts incipit (1) 'Prophetia Metodii episcopi et martiris de ultimis temporibus. Dicit sanctus Methodius de filiis Ysmael. Futurum est autem ut exeant adhuc semel, [...]'; (2) 'Item de eodem. Itaque cum venisset Alexander ad montes Caspios, miserunt ad eum filii captivitatis x. tribuum' [...]; (3) 'De libro etici philosophi ad idem. In insulis Taracontis contra ubera Aquilonis habitat gens ignominiosa'. MS *LA*, fol. 85^v, col. a; *CM*, VI, p. 497, n. 1.

LETTERS FROM THE AFFLICTED LANDS IN THE *ADDITAMENTA*   283

Robert Passelewe's inquisition held in the royal forests in 1244–1245.[8] The bundle is a contiguous compilation of six letters connected by their shared subject, the Mongol invasion of Eastern Europe.[9] The letters were very likely copied in the order they were received, as a collection of *rescripta* after a long chain of copying. But the placement of the cluster may be telling about the date of receipt at St Albans — or at least of the time of copying them into the *Additamenta*. The collation of the folios within the current arrangement of the codex is now jumbled, but originally may have been chronological.[10] Contrary to Luard's editorial decision to mark them as 1242, the letters are undated in the *Additamenta*. Luard also edits them as separate numbered units, although the Mongol-related letters are written contiguously with the text before and after, in the same hand and same ink. Vaughan, noting the ageing of the script in an evolution towards the 'coarse and untidy' hand found in Matthew's last documents in the *Additamenta*, divides all of his production into three distinct phases (up until *c.* 1250, 1250–1255, and 1256–1259).[11] The folios with the Mongol-related letters clearly fall in the second phase.

The Mongol letters written in the same hand contiguously extend over four folios. The red header marking the beginning of the first letter (*Epistula cujusdam episcopi Ungariensis ad episcopum Parisiensem*, on fol. 85[v]) after the page-and-a-half-long prophetic passage does not repeat for each subsequent letter. The next time Matthew inserts a red header is at the end of the last letter in this epistolary cluster on fol. 87[r], so the five letters comprise a unit on their own: Matthew either received them already in this form or treated them as a single document despite the various senders and addressees indicated. Although an integral part of the *Additamenta*'s flow of various documents in *scripta continua*, the 'Mongol bundle' is a coherent body of 'local' letters that seems self-standing and isolated within the wider context of the *Additamenta* and the *Chronica majora*. The sequence starts with two more substantial texts: the letter known as that of 'a Hungarian bishop to the bishop of Paris concerning the Mongols', which, as noted,

---

8 MS *LA*, fol. 87[r]: 'Inquisitiones de forisfactis diversis super foresta domini regis'. 'The commissioners were to investigate the injuries done to the king by the inhabitants of the Forest, who had enlarged their fields at the expense of the vert, put up buildings, made parks and warrens, sold wood and charcoal, pastured cattle and horses, and all without any legal authorisation'. Petit-Dutaillis and Lefebvre, *Studies and Notes Supplementary to Stubbs' Constitutional History*, p. 199.

9 The six letters in the *Additamenta* are in MS *LA*, fols 85[v], col. b–87[r], col b; letter nos. 46–51 in *CM*, VI, pp. 75–84; *EH*, III, pp. 449–55.

10 The quires were later rearranged in the fourteenth century (with later additions) and then by Sir Robert Cotton (1571–1631). More on the quire structure in Vaughan, *Matthew Paris*, pp. 78–80. The manuscript is digitized: <http://www.bl.uk/manuscripts/FullDisplay.aspx?ref=Cotton_MS_Nero_D_I>.

11 Vaughan, 'The Handwriting of Matthew Paris', pp. 388–89.

284   CHAPTER 6

can also be found in the *Waverley Annals*;[12] and a letter of the landgrave of Thuringia and Saxony to the duke of Brabant and Boulogne concerning the Mongols.[13] These first two letters are followed by four more generic missives, all of them coming from mendicant circles: a certain Jordan, Minorite vicar of Poland,[14] a 'Hungarian abbot of St Mary's',[15] R. and J., Dominican and Franciscan friars,[16] and a short double-decker: G., warden of the Cologne Franciscans, enclosing a letter of Jordan and A., warden of *Prangensis*.[17]

Even though the *Additamenta* seem like a record of various documents inserted in the order of their arrival at St Albans, the textual environment, more precisely the document preceding the letter collection, reveals Matthew's reasons for inserting them the way he did. In this case, the preceding text provides a quasi preamble for the Mongol bundle, and at the same time it establishes a connection with the *Chronica majora* too. The latter is a simple repetition of some lines of prophecy inserted under Roger of Wendover's text of the Nativity, where the so-called Sibylline prophecies in MS *A*, fol. 15^r end in an account of Antichrist who releases Gog and Magog, the peoples enclosed by Alexander.[18] According to Suzanne Lewis, this insertion at the beginning of the chronicle is in Matthew's late, more uneven hand, and was added to the bottom of the page hastily probably after the Mongol conquests in Europe — once it made sense in the context of the Mongol threat.[19] The same lines appear at the end of one of the Mongol-related *Additamenta* letters saying 'In these times also, on account

---

12 MS *LA*, fols 85^v, col. b–86^r, col. a; letter no. 46 in *CM*, VI, pp. 75–76; *EH*, III, p. 449.

13 MS *LA*, fol. 86^r, cols a–b; letter no. 47 in *CM*, VI, pp. 76–78; *EH*, III, pp. 450–51.

14 MS *LA*, fol. 86^r, col. b–86^v, col. a; letter no. 49 in *CM*, VI, pp. 80–81; *EH*, III, pp. 452–53.

15 MS *LA*, fol. 86^v, cols a–b; letter no. 48 in *CM*, VI, pp. 78–80; *EH*, III, pp. 453–54.

16 MS *LA*, fols 86^v, col. b–87^r, col. a; letter no. 50 in *CM*, VI, pp. 81–83; *EH*, III, pp. 454–55. Translation incomplete.

17 MS *LA*, fol. 87^r, cols a–b; letter no. 51 in *CM*, VI, pp. 83–84. Not translated.

18 About Matthew's use of the Sibyl, Weiler explains that it was first referenced in Antiquity, but the text copied by Matthew originated in the thirteenth century. It related the sayings of Sibyl, daughter of Priamos and Hecuba, when asked to explain a dream experienced by several Roman senators. It had not been part of Roger of Wendover's *Flores*, and its inclusion was therefore an editorial decision of Matthew's, as was its placement early on in the narrative, in sections dealing with Roman history. Yet only once did Matthew draw on the Sibyl to interpret contemporary events. In 1241, he reported that the imprisonment, at the hands of Emperor Frederick II, of prelates planning to attend a papal council proved true the Sibyl, and proceeded to cite the relevant passage. However, Hilpert has shown that the Sibylline reference was probably borrowed from a papal letter also copied into the *Chronica*. Weiler, 'History, Prophecy and the Apocalypse in the Chronicles of Matthew Paris', citing Hilpert, 'Zu den Prophetien im Geschichtswerk des Matthew Paris'. More on the Sibyl: Holdenried, *The Sibyl and her Scribes*, pp. 147–63. For the incarceration of the prelates, see Chapter 4 ('The Second 1241 Cluster') and Fig. 9.

19 Lewis, *The Art of Matthew Paris*, p. 103.

LETTERS FROM THE AFFLICTED LANDS IN THE *ADDITAMENTA*   285

of the terrible rumours of this kind, the following verses, declaring the coming of Antichrist, were spread'.[20]

Besides these short references to prophecies, the main collection of 'testimonies', which all pertain to the threat of an imminent Apocalypse, is inserted right before the letters of the Mongol bundle. Importantly, although not yet naming the Mongols as the 'Ishmaelites', the text contains excerpts from the Pseudo-Methodius prophecy:

> [Superscript in a later hand] Quae scriptae sunt suo loco, scilicet m.cc.xl.v.
> [Red header] Harum assertione auctoritatum et subscriptarum testimonio literarum praesumitur quod in fine sumus saeculorum Prophetia Metodii episcopi et martiris de ultimis temporibus.
> [black ink] Dicit sanctus Methodius de filiis Ysmael. Futurum est autem ut exeant adhuc semel, et obtinebunt orbem terre per .viii. ebdomadas annorum et uocabitur iter eorum uia angustie. Quia patrem eorum Ysmael uocauit dominus onagrum. In sacris locis interficient sacerdotes. Ibidem cum mulieribus dormient. Ad sepulcra sanctorum ligabunt iumenta. Et hoc pro nequitia Christianorum qui tunc erunt. De quibus dicitur. In novissimis diebus erunt homines sese amantes, etc. et tunc implebitur quod dictum est per Ezechielem. 'Fili hominis uoca bestias agri et exhortare eas dicens. "Congregamini et venite eo quod sacrificium magnum immolo nobis. Manducate carnes fortium et bibite sanguinem excelsorum"'.

> (Which is written in its place, namely under the year 1245.
> By assertion of these authorities and by evidence of letters written below it is anticipated in the prophecy of bishop Methodius and martyr about the end of times that we are at the end of times.
> Saint Methodius says about the sons of Ysmael. It will come to pass that they will come out once again and prevail over the whole world in eight times seven years and their path is called the way of hardship. Because the lord called their father Ysmael a wild ass. They shall slay priests in sacred places. There they shall also sleep with women. They shall tie tombs of saints to beasts of burden. And thereupon they shall be so for the idleness of the Christians. It is said of them. In the last days men will be lovers of themselves, etc. and there will be fulfilled what was said through Ezekiel. 'Son of

---

20 These verses were of Joachite origin, and they circulated in many copies in thirteenth-century England giving the year of the coming of Antichrist either as 1250 or 1260. Lewis, *The Art of Matthew Paris*, p. 103. About the relationship between Methodius and the Joachites, Benjamin Garstad writes that 'Joachim of Fiore, the great apocalyptic voice of the Middle Ages, may have neglected Pseudo-Methodius, but his followers read and adapted the Apocalypse with great enthusiasm'. [Pseudo]-Methodius, *Apocalypse*, p. xi.

man, call the beasts of the field and urge them on, saying, "Gather yourselves together and come, since I will offer a great sacrifice for you. Eat the flesh of the mighty and drink the blood of the lofty".)[21]

The placement of these prophetic passages makes it abundantly clear that they are intimately tied to the letters about the Mongol invasion that follow. The text seems to come specifically from the version found in Peter Comestor's *Historia scholastica*, and Matthew Paris (or a later contributor) seemingly had access to Comestor's text.[22] However, the mise-an-page reveals that the red header on top of fol. 85[r], col. a, 'Harum assertione auctoritatum et subscriptarum testimonio literarum praesumitur quod in fine sumus saeculorum Prophetia Metodii episcopi et martiris de ultimis temporibus', encompasses both the prophetic testimonies and the subsequent Mongol letters, which is redolent of a previously described collection of letters: the Ottobeuren Collection.[23] Within this larger unit, the letters are separated by alternating red and blue initials.[24] Textual connections also bear out that they belong together, for example, the above-mentioned reference to the Ishmael-onager theme is invoked in the second letter in the bundle, written by Henry Raspe. In this way, the two texts make sense together, and the originally vague Methodius text is specifically applied to the Mongol threat in Europe: 'teste beato Metodio qui istos Tartaros vocat Ysmaelitas et onagros, silvestres asinos, &c.'[25]

---

21 MS *LA*, fol. 85[r], col. a. Charlotte D'Evelyn's 1918 article is a treasure trove of the various English manuscripts containing the text. She also notes that Matthew Paris, and many others before and after him, borrowed from Peter Comestor's *Historia scholastica*. D'Evelyn, 'The Middle-English Metrical Version of the Revelations of Methodius', p. 145. Referring to Ezekiel 39. 17–18; cf. Apocalypse 19. 17–18.

22 This passage is found in Ch. 49: 'De fuga Agar, et ortu Ismaelis', in Comestor, 'Historia scholastica', col. 1097a. Matthew Paris was certifiably familiar with Comestor's work: London, BL, MS Royal 4 D VII, a copy of the *Historia* commissioned by Raymond, prior of St Albans Abbey from 1195 to 1214, was annotated by Matthew Paris. His distinctive hand, for example, can be recognized in the rubric in the middle of the right-hand margin of fol. 32[r]. Also note Thomas of Spalato's words: 'Tunc plerique litterati viri veteres scrutantes scripturas, coniciebant maxime ex dictis Methodii martiris, has fore illas gentes, que precedere debent Antichristi adventum' (Then many learned men, turning the pages of ancient scriptures, concluded, especially from the words of the martyr Methodius, that these were the peoples who were to precede the coming of the Antichrist). Thomas of Spalato, *Historia Salonitanorum atque Spalatinorum pontificum*, pp. 286–87.

23 Luard's edition of the *Additamenta* suggests that this document was inserted after Paris's death. According to Luard's Appendix III to the *Additamenta* (the full table of contents of the text of MS *LA*), fol. 85[r] contains 'testimonies' from various writers that the end of the world was approaching, including a 'Prophetia Metodii episcope et martiriis'. *CM*, VI, p. 497.

24 Only the letter of the Hungarian bishop has a short red header separating it from the prophetic material, but it is not on the same level as the title for the whole unit on the previous folio, boasting a larger initial and small decorative patterns in blue.

25 The last line refers to the *Revelations* by Pseudo-Methodius, which was translated into Latin relatively early and was widely disseminated by Peter of Comestor's twelfth-century *Historia*

There are two small aspects of the *Additamenta* bundle that are reminiscent of the Ottobeuren Collection. On the one hand, both collections contain references to the Ishmaelite theory which enjoyed limited dissemination at this time, as evidenced in other texts by various annalists: the English *Tewkesbury Annals*, the continental *Gestorum Treverorum Continuatio*, *Annales Scheftlarienses maiores*, and *Chronicon S. Medardi*, as well as sermons and the *memorabilia* authored by Albert Behaim of Passau.[26] The same is also found in the Ottobeuren Collection, in a dialogue between Alexander and Aristotle about the future trials to be brought by the Mongols.[27] On the other hand, they both have a similar arrangement in the sense that the Cedar of Lebanon prophecy directly precedes Friar Julian's account of the imminent Mongol threat providing a description of the Mongols, which is then followed by shorter circulars and letters of local importance.[28] The same order and focus can be found in the *Additamenta*, starting with the prophecy, continuing with two descriptive letters about the Mongols, which are then followed by shorter letters by refugees and eyewitnesses.

As for the internal structure of the series of letters following the prophetic preamble, the first two letters, one by 'a Hungarian bishop to the bishop of Paris concerning the Mongols' that is also found in the *Waverley Annals*,[29] and another by the landgrave of Thuringia and Saxony to the duke of Brabant concerning the Mongols, are set apart from the others by their length and their illustrious senders, the latter already familiar from the *Chronica majora*.[30] Moving these illustrious and detailed letters to the top was no doubt the result of conscious editorial decisions privileging intelligence from identifiable and consequential sources. Looking at the

---

Scholastica. Aerts and Kortekaas, *Die Apokalypse des Pseudo-Methodius.* See also Chapter 7 ('The *Flores historiarum*').

26 'Gesta Treverorum Continuata', p. 403; 'Annales Scheftlarienses maiores, a. 1092–1247', p. 341; 'Chronicon S. Medardi Suessionensis', p. 491; *FH*, II, p. 267. Klopprogge, *Ursprung und Ausprägung des abendländischen Mongolenbildes*, p. 174. See also vv. 1183–1201 in Maerlant and Snellaert, *Alexanders geesten*, p. 85. Jackson, *The Mongols and the West*, p. 144. Jackson lists, among others, Albert Behaim, the archdeacon of Passau, who is known to have copied a text of Pseudo-Methodius's work into his book of *memorabilia*. In Behaim, *Das Brief- und Memorialbuch*, pp. 134–78, no. 43; the onager reference is on p. 165. Notably, Albert was in attendance at the Council of Lyon after he had fled Bavaria in 1241–1242 and became an exile at the Curia. While at Lyon he negotiated an accord between Bishop Rüdiger of Passau and Innocent IV. Englberger, 'Verschwieg Hermann von Niederalteich in seinen Annalen die Tätigkeit Albert Behaims?'. I am very grateful to Matthew Coulter for this reference.

27 MS *OB*, fol. 8ʳ⁻ᵛ: '*incipit* Alexander Macedo quesivit ab Aristotile magistro suo, dicens "Dic michi quod erit in futuro tempore"'. Lerner, *The Powers of Prophecy*, p. 12.

28 For the documentary contents in this manuscript (fols 2ʳ–8ʳ) see Chapter 3 ('1238: Northbound to *Hungaria major*').

29 MS *LA*, fols 85ᵛ, col. a–86ʳ, col. a; *CM*, VI, pp. 75–76; *EH*, III, p. 449.

30 MS *LA*, fol. 86ʳ, cols a–b; *CM*, VI, pp. 76–78; *EH*, III, pp. 450–51.

288   CHAPTER 6

way *rescripta* are organized elsewhere in the chronicle, the arrangement also gives the distinct impression that the letters of the illustrious authors serve the purpose of framing the intelligence of their subordinates — abbots, monks, and friars — whose local details inform and authenticate their own fuller and more elevated synthesis of the situation described.

In the first letter, the identity of the addressee is intriguing, especially considering that the letter, explicitly addressed to *episcopum Pari[si]ensem* in Matthew's version, is vaguer in the Waverley version where a passage that ends the letter (missing in Matthew's version) is obviously truncated at the beginning:

> Caveant omnes qui hoc audierint, et pro certo hoc habeant; et hoc videbitur, et oculis probabitur; ut credo, ego dico, episcopus Hungariae, infra v. annos. Et ut hoc sciatur Parisius, et consilium bonum apponatur, si fieri potest, gratia Dei permittente, cuidam archidiacono meo qui erat scholaris Parisius, transcriptum istud misi sigillatum.[31]

>> (Let all who will hear this beware and uphold it as truth, and I, a bishop of Hungary, say that I believe it will be seen and attested by eyes five years after. And so that it is known in Paris, if possible and God permitting, I sent that good counsel to be put forth transcribed and sealed to my archdeacon who was a Paris scholar.)

Following Sándor Fest's interpretation, it is normally taken to be addressed to a 'former fellow student of the Hungarian bishop', but as Dániel Bácsatyai points out, a closer look at the phrase suggests otherwise.[32] Bácsatyai, partly based on this, speculates that the archdeacon in the address was Albert of Parma, a protégé of the future Innocent IV, who was archdeacon of Bars, Hungary, but probably resided in Paris at the time of the Mongol invasion as a papal notary and a canon of the Notre Dame. Albert was later constantly on the move between the royals of Europe, working on putting Richard of Cornwall on the throne of Sicily.[33] The sender, according to Bácsatyai, was 'certainly' Matthew, archbishop of

---

31 'Annales de Waverleia', p. 325.

32 Fest, 'Egy magyar püspök levele'. Most translations cite Matthew's version without the closing paragraph: Nagy, ed., *Tatárjárás*, p. 163; Katona, ed., *A tatárjárás emlékezete*, pp. 289–90; Makkai and Mezey, eds, *Árpád-kori és Anjou-kori levelek: XI–XIV. század*, pp. 147–48. For Fest's interpretation to be correct, *meo* (dative or ablative masculine singular of *meus*) and *scholaris Parisius* (nominative or genitive singular noun) should be in the same case, but *meo* here clearly belongs to *archidiacono*, and the subclause 'qui erat scholaris Parisius' simply refers to the Parisian education of the addressee rather than a connection between sender and recipient. Bácsatyai, 'Személyi összeköttetések a Curia Romana és a magyar egyház között', p. 305, n. 27.

33 Albert of Parma met Henry III of England on his diplomatic mission in Gascogne in 1254. Bácsatyai, 'Személyi összeköttetések a Curia Romana és a magyar egyház között', p. 305.

Esztergom, who died in the 1241 Battle of Muhi, and according to Master Roger, his body was never found.[34] However, it seems to me that rather than Archbishop Matthew, our *episcopus Hungariae* may be István Báncsa, then bishop of Vác, who was heavily involved in the communication of the Mongol invasion as is described elsewhere in the present volume, and also maintained a close familial and professional connection with Albert of Parma.[35] Báncsa's authorship also explains how the Hungarian bishop's letter in the *Additamenta* evokes the thematic of the description of the Mongols in the 1238 entry, as well as the other interrelated descriptions, including those contained in Frederick II's letter, in which he is named as an informant.[36]

The letter's question-and-answer format is reminiscent of the Russian archbishop's report. The fact that they address the same distinguishing features shows a relatively well-established pattern (description of face and physique, ability to cross rivers, arms and armour, and so on) in which Western Christian writers presented the Mongols. But the letter is not limited to the formulaic description of the Mongols' customs: it is a text more embedded in Eastern European realities than repeating mere commonplaces. It starts with the origin of the intelligence that the Hungarian bishop shares upon the request of his colleague in Paris: 'De facto Tartareorum vobis rescribo quod ipsi venerant prope confinium Ungariae per quinque dietas, et venerunt ad aquam quae vocatur Deinphir, quam transire non poterant in aestate. Volentes autem expectare hyemem, miserunt ante se quosdam exploratores in Russyam, ex quibus capti fuerunt duo et missi domino regi Ungariae, quos ego habui in defensu meo; et ab ipsis didici nova quae vobis mando'. (I write back to you about the Tartars, how they came near the frontiers of Hungary in five days' march, near to some water named Deinphir which they could not cross in the summer. But being willing to wait for the winter, they sent before them, into Russia, some spies, two of whom were taken, and sent to our lord the king of Hungary. I had these in my custody, and learned from them some new

---

34 Bácsatyai, 'Személyi összeköttetések a Curia Romana és a magyar egyház között', p. 305. Following the death of Matthew, archbishop of Esztergom, István Báncsa was elected. His election was confirmed on 7 July 1243. Little is known about his years as bishop; for a summary of surviving evidence, see Figure 5 in Kiss, *Dél-Magyarországtól Itáliáig*, pp. 133–34.

35 On 22 January 1253, Albert is referred to as István Báncsa's chaplain: 'dilectum filium magistrum Gerardum canonicum Strigoniensem, consobrinum dilecti filii magistri Alberti notarii nostri et venerabilis fratris nostri [...] episcopi Prenestini capellani'. *Vetera monumenta historica Hungariam Sacram illustrantia*, I, p. 216. Cited in Bácsatyai, 'Személyi összeköttetések a Curia Romana és a magyar egyház között', p. 306, n. 28. This hypothesis and a comprehensive overview of previous suggestions can also be found in Fried, 'Auf der Suche nach der Wirklichkeit', pp. 299–300, n. 55.

36 See Chapter 3. Text in Appendix 8, available online at <https://brepols.figshare.com>, from the link <https://doi.org/10.1484/A.14453112>.

290 CHAPTER 6

things, which I forward to you.)[37] It is not the first time that the Russian borderland appears in the context of transmitting intelligence about the Mongols: as seen in the previous chapter, a certain archbishop (of Russia), 'driven from his territory', is also associated with a similar report in the familiar question-and-answer format.[38]

While the Mongol-related material in the main chronicle text and these letters in the *Additamenta* are connected by similarities in themes and character, regarding the accumulation of these materials, their differences are more telling than their similarities. As opposed to the royal and noble letters exchanged between Western dignitaries in the main text, the letters in the *Additamenta* seem to be connected to ecclesiastic and mendicant information channels from Eastern Europe. As noted above, the first two letters are organically connected to *rescripta* circulated by mendicants, which is attested to by textual connections between them. The bishop's letter, for example, ends with a sombre note about the friars, intended as an update (*nova de ipsis*) after the description of the Mongols:

> Nova de ipsis certa audire non possumus; quia praecedunt eos quaedam gentes quae Mordani vocantur, qui interficiunt omnes homines indifferenter; et nullus de eis audet calciare pedes suos, donec interficiat hominem; et per illos credo esse interfectos Praedicatores et Fratres Minores, et alios nuntios, quos miserat rex Ungariae ad explorandum. Sine dubietate devastaverunt omnes terras, et destruxerunt quas invenerunt, usque ad aquam supradictam.
>
> > (We are not able to hear anything fresh about them that can be relied on for certain; for they are preceded by certain people called Mordani, who slay all without distinction; and none of them dare put on their shoes until they have slain their man. I believe it was they who slew the Preachers, Minorites, and other messengers, whom the king of Hungary had sent to explore. Without doubt, they have devastated and destroyed all the lands which they came to, as far as the river aforesaid.)[39]

Henry Raspe's letter, which ends with the Methodius prophecy, is likewise followed by a note of the Preachers and Minorites in a crusader context: 'Nos vero, de superni Judicis bonitate et misericordia confisi, humiliter sanctos viros Praedicatores et Minores [precamur], ut toti populo Christiano ducatui subdito crucem, orationes, afflictiones, et jejunia praedicent' (But we, trusting in the goodness and mercy of the Supreme Judge, have

---

37 MS *LA*, fols 85ᵛ, col. b–86ʳ, col. a; *CM*, VI, p. 75; *EH*, III, p. 449.
38 MS *B*, fol. 182ʳ, cols a–b; *CM*, IV, pp. 386–89; *EH*, II, pp. 28–31. Also in 'Annales de Burton', p. 271.
39 MS *LA*, fol. 86ʳ, col. a; *CM*, VI, p. 76; *EH*, III, p. 450.

humbly prayed those holy men, the Preachers and the Minorites, to preach a crusade, with prayers, mortifications, and fasts, to all the people of Christendom).[40] Later, another sentence was appended after the farewell of this mendicant postscript, referring to a certain Friar Robert de Theles's information that seven convents of the friars were reported to have been destroyed.[41]

References to the Deinphir (Dnepr) and the demise of the Hungarian kings' explorers place the original of the letter among the earliest Hungarian reports describing the Mongol military manoeuvres, prior to entering Hungarian territory through the Verecke Pass in early 1241. The letter clearly reflects the perceptions and information available to the mendicant networks and the royal court in Hungary on the eve of the Mongol attacks. For example, the last passage echoes Friar Julian's information, who, during his last journey to Suzdal, prior to returning home, received the news that two of his confreres may have been killed by the *Morducani*:

> Duobus autem fratribus ibi relictis ex ipsis, conductis interpretibus in festo Apostolorum Petri et Pauli proximo transacto venerunt ad ducem Morducanorum alterum, qui eodem die egressus quo isti venerant, cum toto populo et familia, sicut superius diximus, Tartaris se subiecit. De cetero, quid de duobus fratribus illis factum sit, utrum mortui sint vel a duce iam dicto ad Tartaros deducti, penitus ignoratur. Duo fratres relicti, admirantes de mora eorundem circa festum Michaelis proximo celebratum miserunt quendam interpretem, de eorum vita cupientes certificari; quem etiam Morducani invadentes occiderunt.

>> (They [four friars sent to the Mongols] left two friars behind and led by interpreters, reached the other Mordvin ruler on the feast of Sts Peter and Paul, who in the same day departed with their whole family where they had come from, and as said before, submitted themselves to the Tartars. What happened to these two friars, whether they died or the ruler took them to the Tartars, no one knows. The friars who stayed behind, wondering at their [the Tartar's] request, sent an interpreter around the feast of St Michael, to find out about their survival, but he was killed by the Mordvins.)[42]

---

40 MS *LA*, fol. 86ʳ, col. b; *CM*, VI, p. 78; *EH*, III, p. 451. By using a small red initial and starting in a new line, Matthew's manuscript indicates that this was appended to Henry's letter, originally ending with the reference to the pseudo-Methodius prophecy.

41 'Audivi a fratre Roberto de Theles quod sine dubio ipsi Tartari destruxerunt septem conventus fratrum suorum' (I have heard from Brother Robert de Theles, that those Tartars have actually destroyed seven convents of the brethren). MS *LA*, fol. 86ʳ, col. b; *CM*, VI, p. 78; *EH*, III, p. 451.

42 Hautala, *Ot 'Davida, carja Indij' do 'nenavistnogo plebsa satany'*, p. 381.

292   CHAPTER 6

Chronologically speaking, the second letter written in Thuringia is well placed to continue the story: the report on the Mongol invasion leaps ahead to the time by which 'the Tartars aforesaid have wholly destroyed all Russia, and Poland as far as the confines of the kingdom of Bohemia, and the middle part of Hungary'. The language evoking the image of Europe as neighbouring city homes is reminiscent of the emperor's letter alarming Western Europe to the fact that the Mongols are very much *ante portas*.

> Et quia jam *paries nobis proximus succenditur, et terra vicina patet vastationi*, et aliquae jam vastantur, auxilium et consilium Dei et fratrum vicinorum pro universali ecclesia anxie et flebiliter invocantes postulamus.
>
> Et si clipeus noster qui prima jacula sentiet conteratur, nostro pariete succenso et terra devastata, *vicini parietes et vicinae provinciae* formidabunt.

>> (And as *the house adjoining our own is already on fire, and as the neighbouring country is open to devastation*, whilst some countries are even now being ravaged, we, on behalf of the Church universal, anxiously invoke and beg assistance and advice from God and our neighbouring brother princes.)[43]
>>
>> (And if our shield shall be broken under the first discharge of javelins, our walls and our land devastated, *the neighbouring houses and the neighbouring provinces* will be alarmed.)[44]

The first two letters have one more thing in common that sets them apart from other Mongol-related texts in the *Chronica majora* and the *Additamenta*: unusually informed accounts about the Mongol khan that to my knowledge exist in no other source. Besides the usual descriptions of the Mongols as a people, the Mongol khan is named as Zingiton (Churchitan in the *Waverley Annals*), and both letters recount the tradition of marking captive children's foreheads with his seal.

> [Hungarian bishop]: Quocunque modo intrant terram, interficiunt habitatores terrae, praeter parvulos, quibus Zingiton, qui est dominus eorum, qui interpretatur rex regum, signum suum imponit comburendo in facie ipsorum. Quadraginta duo consiliarii sunt quibus Zingiton sigillum suum committit.
>
> [Henry Raspe] civitates, castra, immo et municipia destruendo, non solum Christianos, immo Paganos, Judaeos, nemini parcentes,

---

43 The 'emperor's letter': MS *B*, fol. 145ᵛ, col. a; *CM*, ɪv, p. 110; *EH*, ɪ, p. 339 (my italics).

44 MS *LA*, fol. 86ᵛ, col b; *CM*, vɪ, p. 78; *EH*, ɪɪɪ, p. 451 (my italics). Giles, perhaps sensing the text's similarity with that of Frederick's letter, got a little carried away by the metaphor evoked by the word *parietes* (house walls) and added 'when our house is on fire', which is not in the original text.

LETTERS FROM THE AFFLICTED LANDS IN THE *ADDITAMENTA*

omnibus indifferenter sine misericordia mortem inferentes, praeterquam parvulis tantum, quibus rex eorum, Zingiton vocatus, signa in frontibus imponit.

> (In whatever manner they invade a country, they slay the inhabitants, except the children, whom Zingiton, their lord, which is interpreted king of kings, marks with his seal, burning them on the face. Zingiton has forty-two counsellors, to whom he commits his seal.)[45]
>
> (They have destroyed cities, castles, and even municipal towns, and spared neither Christians, pagans, nor Jews, putting to death all alike without mercy, except only the children, that their king Zingiton marks on the forehead with his seal.)[46]

Although rendered nearly unintelligible by incorrect initials and garbled spelling — no doubt the result of serial copying of *rescripta* — the second letter explicitly names the sender and addressee: 'J. Dei gratia duci Barbaniae et Bononiae, N. Dei gratia Langd[?]n[u]s Turrigisi et Saxonie Comes Paletinus'.[47] It is not the first time that Mongol material is associated with the duke of Brabant, who received letters both from Henry Raspe and from Cologne, and who was certainly in possession of genuine eye-witness texts about the Mongol threat in Eastern Europe, which later crop up in the context of the *Condemnations* of Paris.[48] It is not certifiable whether the chronicler and his readers realized that the people in the *salutatio* of the *Additamenta* letter are the same as 'illustri principi Duci Braibannie, h. Dei gratia Longrathungie comes, palatinus saxonum' in the main text of

---

45 MS *LA*, fol. 85ᵛ, col. b; *CM*, VI, p. 76; *EH*, III, p. 450.

46 MS *LA*, fol. 86ʳ, cols a–b; *CM*, VI, p. 77; *EH*, III, p. 451.

47 MS *LA*, fol. 86ʳ, col. a; *CM*, VI, p. 76; *EH*, III, p. 450. 'J' is no doubt misspelled, it must be Henry II, duke of Brabant, who did not hold the title of Boulogne, but his mother was Matilda, countess of Boulogne. Though the landgrave's initial seems to be N. here, it is notable that in this hand the letters N and H are nearly identical: this is definitely Henry Raspe.

48 Letter concerning the Mongols, containing a dialogue between Louis IX and his mother, a letter of Frederick II to Henry III, and an illustration of a Mongol warrior on horseback; MS *B*, fols 145ʳ, col. a–146ᵛ, col. a; *CM*, IV, pp. 109–19; *EH*, III, pp. 339–47. See Chapter 4. The *Additamenta* letter from Friar G. in Cologne also refers to him, MS *LA*, fol. 87ʳ, col. a: 'Noverit caritas vestra, me recepisse literas directas a fratribus nostris duci Brabantiae, sub hac forma'. *CM*, VI, p. 83. Not translated in Giles. This is not the last time to hear from him: on MS *LA*, fol. 89ᵛ, col. b, Matthew Paris inserts a letter in the *Additamenta* in which he mentions the return of the Mongols to Hungary right after the news of Henry Raspe's death. The information, contained at the end of the letter of Archbishop Boniface to Peter of Savoy, 'Praeterea versus partes Germaniae nullus stat pro ecclesia nec cum ecclesia post mortem Landegravii, sed omnia cedunt voluntati regis Conradi. Dicitur etiam quod Tartari reversi sunt super regnum Hungariae'. *CM*, VI, pp. 132–33. Moses ben Abraham's *Livre*, containing a 'testimony of a Tartar' is studied in detail in Rachetta, 'Paris 1244'.

294   CHAPTER 6

the chronicle.[49] It is, however, indicative of the previous observation that the courts of the landgrave and the duke were central to disseminating Mongol-related information. This letter, relayed to England as a *rescriptum*, is another piece of evidence for this kind of epistolary activity. The *rescripta* Matthew received was a product of their efforts to collect and transmit information about the progress of the Mongol invasion in Europe.

The central role of Henry Raspe's circles in pulling together Franciscan (and Dominican) information — attested by the composition of this bundle and other passages connected to him in the *Chronica majora* — is also conspicuous in his efforts to launch a crusade against the Mongols through the efforts of the mendicant order.[50] The postscript to Henry's letter directly references the crusade: 'Nos vero, de superni Judicis bonitate et misericordia confisi, humiliter sanctos viros Praedicatores et Minores [precamur], ut toti populo Christiano ducatui subdito crucem, orationes, afflictiones, et jejunia praedicent' (But we, trusting in the goodness and mercy of the Supreme Judge, have humbly prayed those holy men, the Preachers and the Minorites, to preach a crusade, with prayers, mortifications, and fasts, to all the people of Christendom).[51] This corresponds to both the pope's bull ordering the Viennese mendicants to proclaim the crusade,[52] and the records of the Monastery of St Pantaleon in Cologne:

> Rex itaque profugus ad ducem Austrie se contulit et postmodum per Waciensem episcopum ab imperatore auxilium postulavit, sponsa illi perpetua subiectione, si per operam suam contingeret ipsum regnum recuperare. Ex hoc conflictu et ante conflictum tam Polonie quam Hungarie multi fratres Predicatores et Minores evaserunt, qui signo crucis per totam fere Teuthoniam clericos et laicos adversus predictos barbaros armaverunt. Imperator etiam scripsit magnatibus Teuthonie, ut se in adiutorium ipsius prepararent, eo quod ipse vellet afferre auxilium populo Christiano contra truculentiam barbarorum. Ipse etiam rex filius imperatoris, archiepiscopus Coloniensis et plurimi nobiles Teuthonie signum crucis vivifice assumpserunt.

> (Therefore the fleeing king brought himself to the duke of Austria and requested help from the emperor through the bishop of Vác, having pledged eternal submission to him should it come to pass that through his [the emperor's] works his kingdom is recovered.

---

49 The term *landegravius Thuringiae* appears in various forms throughout: in MS *B*, fol. 166ᵛ, col. a, Henry appears as *Andeg[ra]vium de*, but 'Thuringia' is missing; on fol. 203ᵛ, col. b, he is *Andeg[ra]vius H. de Duringe*. The other letter in the *Additamenta*, cited above, simply refers to *post mortem landeg[ra]vii*. MS *LA*, fol. 89ᵛ, col. b.

50 See more on the 'Holy War on the Mongols' in Chapter 4.

51 MS *LA*, fol. 86ʳ, col. b; *CM*, vi, p. 78; *EH*, iii, p. 451.

52 See Chapter 4 ('Holy War on the Mongols').

LETTERS FROM THE AFFLICTED LANDS IN THE *ADDITAMENTA*   295

Many Dominican and Minorite brothers fled from the conflict both in Poland and in Hungary, and even beforehand, who, by the sign of the cross, recruited clerics and laypeople against the aforementioned barbarians in nearly all of Germany. The emperor also wrote to the nobles of Germany to prepare themselves to help him, because he also wants to bring assistance to the Christian people against the cruelty of the barbarians. The son of the emperor, the king, as well as the archbishop of Cologne and many German nobles rapidly took the sign of the cross.)[53]

The letters, or rather, descriptions of the Mongols, by the Hungarian bishop and Henry Raspe are followed by letters from the horse's mouth: monasteries and abbeys in the afflicted region. As noted above, Matthew's bundle of *rescripta* and the Ottobeuren Collection reveal interconnected circles that were preoccupied with collecting and circulating information about the Mongols.[54] Though there are only a handful of clues to identify them with certainty, from the *salutationes* of the letters in the *Additamenta* emerges a specific intellectual circle whose affiliation with the German mendicant scene in the mid-thirteenth century as well as their professed interest and knowledge in the affairs of the Mongols across decades had a profound effect on the European communications and knowledge production about the subject.[55] The first of the four 'mendicant' letters is by a certain Jordan, Minorite vicar of Poland and the 'convent of *Pring*'.[56]

Carissimis Christi fidelibus universis, ad quos praesens scriptum pervenerit, frater Jordanus ordinis fratrum Minorum, vicarius provinciae Polemiae, Pringensis conventus, cum caeteris fratribus, salutem.

---

53 'Annales Monasterii Sancti Pantaleonis Coloniae: 1238–1249', pp. 476–77 (my translation).

54 Also note the lesser-known letter of Hungarian clerics that was originally part of an undelivered bundle stuck in Siena en route to the pope. The surviving letter is published in full in Schneider, 'Ein Schreiben der Ungarn an die Kurie'. See Chapter 2 ('Northern Connections').

55 Citing Jordan's letter, Joseph Huffman identifies Cologne mendicants' central role in disseminating the news about the threat: 'The initiative, however, appears to have originated among the Franciscans via Cologne [...]. Therefore, the call [Conrad of Hochstaden's letter to Henry III] was a general one to Christian princes to come and defend Central Europe against the Tartars, not an isolated request from Conrad to the English'. Huffman, *The Social Politics of Medieval Diplomacy*, p. 269, n. 211.

56 MS *LA*, fols 86[r], col. b–86[v], col. a; no. 49 in *CM*, VI, pp. 80–81; *EH*, III, pp. 452–53. Both Luard and Giles suggest Pinsk, in Lithuania, or *perhaps* Prague; Boehmer only Prague. *CM*, VI, pp. 80, 83; *EH*, III, p. 452; Jordan of Giano, *Chronica*, p. 72. A Friar Jordan in Pinsk seems to be the less convincing interpretation, and we would be hard pressed to prove the existence of a convent there in the 1240s. Amid the struggle for supremacy between the Kievan Rus' and the pagan (and in opportune times, Christian) Mindaugas's expansion, the Grand Duchy of Lithuania was still nascent at the time of writing these letters.

(To all Christ's dear and faithful sons to whom this present letter shall come, Brother Jordan, of the order of the Minorite brethren, vicar of the Province of Poland, and the convent of Pring with the rest of the brethren, Health!)[57]

The affiliation in *Pringensis* would be difficult to solve was there not another letter in the bundle, the last letter by G., warden of Cologne, which enclosed another by 'Jordanus viceminister fratrum Minorum regni Boemiae et Poloniae et frater A. custos Prangensis et gardianus ejusdem loci'.[58] For both *Pringensis* and *Prangensis*, Prague, seat of the brand new Bohemian-Polish Franciscan province (founded 1239), is a likely contender with its large Franciscan convent which, by this time, was a double monastery.[59]

Considering the now established fact that these letters were collected by Franciscans in Germany, two Jordans associated with *Prangesis* and *Pringensis* seem more than simple coincidence. But who is this Jordan who authored the letter and quite possibly co-authored another one in the bundle?[60] Gloria Allaire suggests that he is none other than Franciscan chronicler Jordan of Giano, and she uses this particular letter to argue that he had become vicar of Poland and vice-minister of the provinces of Bohemia and Poland sometime before 1241.[61] While this suggestion is tenuous (and circular) — based on Heinrich Boehmer's edition and a now largely forgotten dissertation by Edwin J. Auweiler — it is indeed noteworthy that Jordan of Giano was for many years in Erfurt as *custos* of Thuringia, and as the vicar of Gottfried, provincial minister of Saxony in 1242–1247, he was also colleague and successor of John of Plano Carpini (provincial minister of Saxony in 1232–1239).[62]

---

57 MS *LA*, fol. 86ʳ, col. b; *CM*, VI, p. 80; *EH*, III, p. 452.

58 MS *LA*, fol. 87ʳ, cols a–b; *CM*, VI, p. 83. Not translated by Giles.

59 It is not known when exactly the Franciscans arrived in Bohemia. 'Sometime before 1231, Agnes of Prague and King Wenceslaus I, children of the Bohemian King Premysl Ottokar I, established a house of Poor Clares in Prague, the first in Central Europe. The first nuns came from Italy, but shortly after (in 1234) some girls of noble families and Agnes herself joined the order. At first there had only been a female cloister connected with the hospital, but after 1237 a male cloister was added'. Pajor, 'The Poverty and the Power', p. 108. Before the Prague foundation, the *Analecta* mentions Myza in Bohemia under the year 1232. *Analecta Franciscana*, II, p. 56.

60 The other letter that may be attributed to Jordan is one that mentions a certain Franciscan friar, initialled as 'J': 'Fratribus universis frater R. de ordine Praedicatorum, et J. de ordine fratrum Minorum, salutem'. MS *LA*, fols 86ᵛ, col. b–87ʳ, col. a; *CM*, VI, pp. 81–83; *EH*, III, pp. 454–55.

61 'Jordan of Giano', in Friedman and Figg, eds, *Trade, Travel, and Exploration in the Middle Ages*, p. 312.

62 John of Plano Carpini was *custos* of Saxony in 1223, provincial minister of Teutonia in 1228–1230 and of Saxony in 1232–1239. The province of *Saxonia* was created in 1230 as a result of the division of the province of *Teutonia* into the Rhenish and Saxon provinces.

LETTERS FROM THE AFFLICTED LANDS IN THE *ADDITAMENTA*   297

Briefly noting the absence of sources, Auweiler furnishes the biographic data with philological analysis to suggest that three of the letters in the *Additamenta* were in fact written by Jordan, and received and presumably collected in the court of Henry of Brabant, and furthermore that Jordan served as Henry Raspe's special ambassador to Brabant. He also alludes to the possibility that his superiors and Henry Raspe caused Jordan's mission on account of the Mongol threat: the landgrave sending him as a preacher of a crusade against the Mongols, and his order appointing him as a *custos* in Poland 'to further the alliance against the savages, for which all well-wishers of Christian civilization, the Emperor Frederic II for once included were laboring at that time'.[63] While Auweiler's reconstruction of the events feels as satisfying as placing the last piece into a challenging puzzle, there are, admittedly, very strong arguments against this identification. For one thing, Jordan, an eloquent and detail-oriented chronicler, never once addresses anything vaguely connected to these affairs in his otherwise informative chronicle.[64] The value of Auweiler's bold hypothesis in the present discussion is that it does bring together letters and texts that otherwise seem disparate and unconnected. While there is a good deal of obscure details that remain unresolved, detecting Jordan behind these letters — whether *a* Jordan or Jordan of Giano himself — does indeed bring together Henry Raspe's Thuringia, Henry of Brabant, Prague, and Cologne in a complex network of highly mobile and literate friars, who were extremely well informed in all matters Mongol.

The next letter in the manuscript is the one by a 'Hungarian abbot of St Mary's', which also contains information that has been a subject of speculation.[65]

> Religiosis viris et universis sanctae matris Ecclesiae fidelibus, praesens scriptum visuris vel audituris, F. Dei gratia humilis abbas Sanctae Mariae, totusque conventus ejusdem loci, ordinis Sancti Benedicti, in Hungaria commorantes, consolationem Paracliti cum salute quam promeruit Sanctus Benedictus, et gloriam sempiternam. Latores praesentium fratres B. et I. sacerdotes, domus nostrae monachos, vestrae commendamus caritati, quos de claustro Sanctae Mariae in Ruscia in Hyberniam transmittimus, gratia commorandi.

Honemann, *Provinzialminister und -vikare bis zum Ende der Provinz(en der) Saxonia*; Gießauf, *Die Mongolengeschichte des Johannes von Piano Carpine*, p. 76.

63 Auweiler, *The 'Chronica Fratris Jordani a Giano'*, pp. 34–35. Before Auweiler's detailed discussion of the subject, Boehmer had published the two letters in the *Additamenta* attributed to Jordan. Jordan of Giano, *Chronica*, pp. lxxxii, 72–75.

64 Jordan of Giano, *Chronica*.

65 MS *LA*, fol. 86ᵛ, cols a–b; no. 48 in *CM*, VI, pp. 78–80; *EH*, III, pp. 453–54.

298   CHAPTER 6

(To all the religious and faithful community of the holy universal church, who shall see or hear the present letter. F., by the grace of God, the lowly abbot of St Mary's, and all the convent of the same place, of the order of St Benedict, dwelling in Hungary — the consolation of the Paraclete, with the health due to the merits of St Benedict, and glory for ever! — We recommend to your charity the bearers of these presents, brothers B. and J., priests and monks of our house, whom we have sent from the cloister of St Mary's in Russia, to reside in Ireland.)[66]

Accepting Luard's suggestion that this was written by the abbot of St Mary's in Hungary, there would be a number of candidates for the Hungarian Benedictine abbey ranging from the ancient foundations of Bakonybél and Tihany to Esztergom, but the affiliation of the abbot and the monks is more complicated than that.[67] As is suggested in a more recent edition, however, the letter is written by Felix, abbot of the Schottenkloster (Schottenstift) in Vienna.[68] Considering that the letter is addressed to 'all the religious' in general, it may seem odd that the line after Felix's *salutatio* is recommending to the charity of a specific person (*vestrae caritati*) two monks from St Mary's in Rus', who had been sent bearing gifts 'to stay in Ireland' (*in Hyberniam transmittimus, gratia commorandi*). This is because Felix's *salutatio* is merely an introduction to an embedded letter (and gifts) brought by the refugee brothers B. and J., asking the abbot to open his monastery's doors to refugees.

Mikhail Alekseyev uses this letter for his argument that there was an Irish cloister in Kiev, whose monks were forced to flee by the

---

66 MS *LA*, fol. 86ᵛ, col. a; *CM*, VI, p. 78; *EH*, III, pp. 453–54. Here, too, Giles names the priests 'B.' and 'J.' as Benedict and John, for no apparent reason.

67 Known Benedictine foundations dedicated to St Mary that were certifiably extant in Hungary in the mid-thirteenth century include Ákosmonostora, Almád, Bakonybél, Bény, Bizere (Bisztra), Csatár, Deáki (Diakovce, Sellye), Dömölk, Esztergom-Sziget, Iván, Kolos, Kolozsmonostor, Kompolt, Németújvár (Kőszín), Ohatmonostora, Pankota, Pécsvárad, Poroszló, Pozsony (Pressburg, Bratislava, St Mary Magdalene, affiliation uncertain), (Monostoros-)Sáp (uncertain), Sár (Abasár), Százd, Szentjobb, Széplak, (Ópuszta-)Szer, Tereske, Tihany, Ugramonostora, and Visegrád (dedication uncertain), Romhányi, *Kolostorok és társaskáptalanok*, pp. 8, 12, 13, 18, 20, 21, 24, 32, 37, 38, 47, 48, 49, 50, 52, 53, 56, 60, 63, 64, 67, 69, 73.

68 Nagy, ed., *Tatárjárás*, p. 175. The Schottenkloster or Schottenstift (Benediktinerabtei unserer Lieben Frau zu den Schotten) was founded in Vienna by Henry II (Jasomirgott) of Austria in 1158, for the *Iroschotten*, i.e. Irish Benedictines coming from Regensburg. It is notable that the so-called *Chronicon rhythmicum Austriacum*, written around 1270 in the Augustinian priory of Klosterneuburg, was partly based on the *Heiligenkreuz Annals* and the annals of the Vienna Schottenkloster. The institutional memorialization of the Mongol invasion was particularly long-standing here: in the mid-fifteenth century, Abbot Martin of Leibiz also included the death of Duke Henry, son of St Hedwig, in his *Senatorium sive dialogus historicus*. Bradács, 'A tatárjárás osztrák elbeszélő forrásainak kritikája', pp. 6, 8.

LETTERS FROM THE AFFLICTED LANDS IN THE *ADDITAMENTA*   299

Mongol onslaught via Vilnius.[69] More recently, Alexandr Nazarenko, based on Berthold Altaner's earlier research, also suggests the existence of a Hiberno-Scottish monastery in Kiev.[70] Accepting their suggestion, the Schottenstift in Vienna may have been one of the stops on the monks' long westward journey from Russia to Ireland. The letter from Vienna, containing another one carried by monks on the run, fits the overall spatial and temporal scope of the letter collection.

The next letter in the collection is signed off by a Dominican and a Franciscan friar, with names abbreviated to R. and J., respectively.[71] The content takes the reader to the eastern parts of the Empire: Saxony, where the refugees are spreading news of terror and impending doom, so much so that the populace is ready to take up the cross and fight the Mongols. By the time of writing, the campaign in Hungary was over and the king fled his country.

> Narraverunt nobis profugi de terra illa, in Saxonia praecipue, quod terram illam cum castris triginta duabus machinis impugnaverunt. Et Ruscenos impugnaverunt, viginti annis. Isto autem anno venientes ante Pascha in Poloniam, bonas civitates plurimis interfectis optinuerunt; quibus cum occurreret dux Henricus Poloniae cum exercitu suo, ipsum et, ut dicitur, fere decem milia de suis occiderunt. Procedentes de Polonia, fines Theutonicae attigerunt; deinde declinantes in Moraviam et illam bonam terram vastantes, alii exercitui venienti per Hungariam occurrerunt; et praevalentes dicuntur modo potissimam partem Hungariae, expulso rege possidere.

---

69 Regensburg also features in the purported foundation story of the Kiev cloister. Alekseyev writes that a certain Maurice, centuries before the Mongol invasion, had been given fur worth a hundred pounds of silver by a prince, presumably Vladimir Monomakh, which he then sold in Regensburg to construct a monastery dedicated to St Jacob and Gertrude there. Alekseyev, '"Anglo-saksonskaya parallel" k Poucheniyu Vladimira Monomakha', p. 57. As Michele Colucci stresses, because of the geographical location of these territories, Poland, Hungary, and the Holy Roman Empire continuously interfered in local events, and their western influences were felt in Kievan Rus' ranging from trade relations linking Kiev and Central Europe or Novgorod with the Germanic and Scandinavian worlds to the marriage agreements establishing ties between the house of Rjurik and the reigning families of Hungary, Bohemia, Poland, France, England, and the Empire. This also meant that Western Christianity encroached upon the ecclesiastical foundations and jurisdiction: from the role of cultural and religious mediation of the Bohemian monastery of Sázava; or the presence of western colonies in Novgorod or of Benedictine monks in Kiev. Colucci, 'The Image of Western Christianity in the Culture of Kievan Rus'', p. 585.

70 Nazarenko, 'Die Regensburger Ruzarii', p. 29, n. 33. Citing Altaner, *Die Dominikanermissionen des 13. Jahrhunderts*, pp. 214–25.

71 MS *LA*, fols 86ᵛ, col. b–87ʳ, col. a; letter no. 50 in *CM*, VI, pp. 81–83; *EH*, III, pp. 454–55. Giles's translation is incomplete. For some reason, Giles interprets R. and J. as Brother Richard and Friar John without any explanation.

(We have learned from those who have escaped out of that land, principally in Saxony, that they assailed that city and its towers with thirty-two engines. They have made war for twenty years against the Russians. But this year they came before Easter into Poland, where they slew numbers of persons and got possession of some good cities. Henry, duke of Poland, met them with his army, but was slain, together with almost ten thousand of his men. Proceeding from Poland, they touched on the frontiers of Germany, whence they turned aside into Moravia, and ravaged all that good land. Others of these met an army that was coming against them through Hungary, and getting the better of them, are said to be in occupation of the greater part of Hungary, from which they have expelled its king.)[72]

While the letters in the *Additamenta* cannot be said to form a narrative per se, they are carefully arranged into an order starting from the Mongols preparing to attack, held up by a river less than a week's march away from the borders of Hungary (the Hungarian bishop), and continuing with the image of a spreading city fire threatening Bohemia, Germany, and the whole of Christianity (Henry Raspe), fleeing Hungary at the end of 1241 (Brothers B. and J. in Abbot Felix's letter, signed 4 January 1242, in Vienna), and finishing with their victories over the Kingdom of Hungary (Friars R. and J.). The second half of the latter reveals a strong German connection recounting the response to the Mongol news in the eastern ends of German lands. Although the Germans are referred to as 'them' in third person plural, the writer of the letter is familiar with the event spurred by the Mongol threat, primarily in Saxony, and specifically Merseburg:

> Et modo audivimus quod denuo sex exercitus Tartarorum convenerunt, et iccirco, ut creditur, ut potenter intrent Theutoniam, cujus incolas sciunt esse bellicosos. Ideo tota Theutonia se ad praelium praeparat, crucem assumendo; studentque urbes firmare cum castris; summopere igitur necesse est pro statu ecclesiae instanter orare. Quia si fuerint Theutonici devicti, quod absit, non credimus aliquem Christianorum eis posse resistere. Rex Theutonicorum et filius imperatoris in festo Sancti Jacobi nunc instanti cum maxima militia proponunt proficisci contra eos, et quamvis dicantur Tartari, multi sunt cum eorum exercitu pessimi Christiani et Comani, quos Theutonice Values appellamus. Convenerant autem in civitate Merseburg; ibi audierunt quod rex Hungariae scripserat regi Boemiae, quod viribus receptis et maximo exercitu congregato occurrere voluisset. Sed non

---

72 MS *LA*, fol. 86ᵛ, col. b; *CM*, VI, p. 82; *EH*, III, pp. 454–55.

praesumpsit propter fortitudinem Tartarorum; sed tamen dixit se velle in aliquem locum munitum juxta mare cedere. Valete.

> (We have heard recently that six Tartar armies joined again, so that, as is believed, they would enter with more might into Germany, whose people they know to be belligerent. Therefore, all of Germany is preparing for battle, taking the cross, making efforts to strengthen their cities with fortifications. It is thus extremely crucial to incessantly pray for the preservation of the Church. For if the Germans are prevailed upon, may that never happen, we do not believe that anyone of the Christians could withstand them. The king of the Germans, son of the emperor, is now preparing to march against them with a great army on the Feast of Saint James [25 July], and although they are said to be Tartars, many people in their army are the worst Christians and Cumans whom we call *Valves* [Falben, Valwen][73] in the Theutonic language. They [the Germans] thus gathered in the city of Merseburg; there they heard what the king of Hungary wrote to the king of Bohemia, that, receiving forces, he wished to attack with a large army to be gathered. But on account of the strength of the Tartars he did not expect this, and said that he wished to retreat in some fortified place by the sea. Farewell.)[74]

Though not verbatim, this account is similar to the Cologne annals — in fact, it sounds as if the account of the German news in the friars' letter was a continuation of or response to the events recorded in the Monastery of St Pantaleon. The annalist uses the same phrases to describe the deficiency of the Hungarians — 'Rex vero Hungarorum fuga elapsus cum paucis vix evasit. [...] Nec mirum, cum totum regnum Hungarie fere *nullam civitatem muris munitam habuerit et castra firma.* [...] Ipse etiam rex filius imperatoris, archiepiscopus Coloniensis et plurimi nobiles Teuthonie signum crucis vivifice assumpserunt' (But the fleeing king of the Hungarians barely escaped with only a few men. [...] No wonder when, for the most part, there is no city in the entire Kingdom of Hungary that has *fortified walls or reinforced fortresses.* [...] The king himself, son of the emperor, the archbishop of Cologne, and many nobles of Teuthonia assumed the sign of the cross in a life-giving way) — as those in the Minorites' letter describing the German preparations.[75] The rapidly responding king is identified with the same phrase, 'rex filius imperatoris',

---

73 For the various vernacular names for the Cumans, see Pálóczi-Horváth, *Pechenegs, Cumans, Iasians*, p. 43.

74 MS *LA*, fols 86ᵛ, col. b–87ʳ, col. a; letter no. 50 in *CM*, VI, p. 82 (my translation; my italics).

75 'Annales Monasterii Sancti Pantaleonis Coloniae: 1238–1249', pp. 476–77 (my translation; my italics).

as well. The faint Cologne resonance of this letter turns into certifiable fact in the next. The last Mongol letter in the *Additamenta* is by G., warden of the Cologne Franciscans, enclosing a letter of Jordan and A., warden of *Prangensis*:

> Frater G. in Colonia gardianus indignus, salutem. Noverit caritas vestra, me recepisse literas directas a fratribus nostris duci Brabantiae, sub hac forma: Illustri principi domino H[enrico] duci Brabantiae frater Jordanus viceminister fratrum Minorum regni Boemiae et Polemiae et frater A. custos Prangensis, et gardianus ejusdem loci, una cum conventu, orationes humiles et devotas.
>
> > (Friar G., lowly warden in Cologne, greetings. Let it be known by your highness, that I have received letters sent to the duke of Brabant by our brothers, which goes as follows. To the illustrious prince, Lord Henry, duke of Brabant, friar Jordan vice-minister of the Minorite friars in the kingdoms of Bohemia and Poland, as well as friar A., the custodian of Prague and the warden of the same, together with the convent, with humble and devoted prayers.)[76]

Henry of Brabant is, of course, the same Henry II who was recipient of the second letter and others in the main text of the chronicle, but the transmitter of the letter is a Cologne cleric. Even if we assume the two Jordans are the same Franciscan friar with links to both Prague and Brabant — whether Jordan of Giano or not — there are, of course, plenty of details that remain unresolved regarding the ultimate authors of the accounts, for example, the person of A., *custos Prangensis*, who is shrouded in mystery.

A bull of Gregory IX from 1234 is addressed to Brother John of Plano Carpini, minister of Saxony, and Brother Thomas, *custos* (warden) in Bohemia, bidding them to appoint Agnes of Bohemia as the abbess of the Prague convent.[77] A. is most likely Thomas's successor as *custos*. Even more so than this warden, Agnes of Bohemia — albeit never mentioned in the letters — is a key person behind these opaque texts. The Franciscan complex that grew out of her mantle in Prague was connected to complex European power and information networks through her dynastic connections. Agnes, the founder and later the abbess of the Franciscan nunnery in Prague, was at one time asked in marriage both by Henry III of England and by Emperor Frederick II. She was intimately tied to European dignitaries through her family connections to her sister, Anne of Bohemia, the wife of the very Henry of Silesia who was killed by the Mongols in

---

76 MS *LA*, fol. 87ʳ, col. a; letter no. 51 in *CM*, VI, p. 83. Not translated in *EH*.
77 Seton, *Some New Sources for the Life of Blessed Agnes of Bohemia*, p. 50.

LETTERS FROM THE AFFLICTED LANDS IN THE *ADDITAMENTA*   303

the Battle of Legnica, and to her first cousin, St Elizabeth of Hungary in Thuringia. In fact, she seems to have arrived in Prague from Thuringia.

Both Agnes's spiritual and temporal power networks fit into those identified in the information network transmitting news about the Mongols. In an odd 1254 entry in the *Chronica majora*, where Matthew lists the parties that suffered from the war in Flanders, 'all Christianity' here happens to cover this very specific slice of Europe:

> A qua jam rediens, propter hoc discrimen revocatur ad dampnum totius Christianitatis. Et multi de Franciae regno primates. Dux Bavariae, qui centum milia marcarum Coloniensium ab antiquo tempore redditus annui habet, de novo autem plus incrementi, qui totum thesaurum suum in hac guerra exposuit. Dux Saxonum, eo non minor, similiter, domini regis Angliae consanguineus, dux Brunewik qui et consanguineus est regis ejusdem, dux Braibantiae qui et Lovaniae, qui se vocat ducem Lotharingiae, dux de Lemburg, dux Suaviae, dux Austriae, dux de Limburc; quaedam Landegravia potentissima, dicta Sopha, quae domina est Duringiae pro magna parte; duo Marchiones, unus versus Sclavoniam, alter versus Boemiam, Boemiae rex est. Dux Polemiae a Tartaris interemptus est. Landegravius de Duringe, sancta Elizabeth Landegravia de Duringe et filia regis Hungariae.

>> (and his [the French king's] return from that country — being recalled on account of this calamity — tended to the injury of all Christianity. Of the chief men of France, too, many were sufferers. The duke of Bavaria, who from times of old had received a hundred thousand Cologne marks of revenue yearly, and of late more than that, expended all his money in this war. Amongst the sufferers, too, were the duke of Saxony, as high in station as the last-named duke, and a blood relation of the king of England; the duke of Brunswick, also a relation of the same king; the duke of Brabant and Louvain, who also styles himself duke of Lorraine; the duke of Limbourg, the duke of Suabia, the duke of Austria, and the duke of Lomeburg; a certain landgravine of great power, named Sophia, who was mistress of a large portion of Thuringia; two marquises, one on the side of Sclavonia, the other on that of Bohemia, who was also king of Bohemia; the duke of Poland, who was slain by the Tartars; the landgrave of Thuringia; St Elizabeth, landgravine of Thuringia; and the daughter of the king of Hungary.)[78]

---

78 MS R, fol. 160ʳ, col. b–160ᵛ, col. a; *CM*, v, pp. 438–39; *EH*, iii, pp. 73–74. Obviously, St Elizabeth was no longer alive at this time, rendering the well-informed list seemingly unreliable, but besides this error, the connections are very real.

304   CHAPTER 6

Similar to this chronologically garbled family album, digging deeper than the surface of the Mongol bundle in the *Additamenta* reveals a diverse and expansive but finite network, which furnished the collator of the collection with multifariously connected materials about the Mongol progress. Although Agnes, daughter of King Ottokar I of Bohemia and Constance of Hungary, is not mentioned by name here either, the same circles glimmer through the text as those detected in many other previously mentioned Mongol entries, of which the Prague abbess was an active member.[79] No doubt, Matthew is privy to the details of this war through his usual channels, hence the overlaps with the reports about the Mongols and the European preparations.

The English chronicler's access to such material may seem serendipitous, so it is worthwhile to examine the channels which may have transmitted it across the Channel. None of the Mongol letters preserved in the *Additamenta* are addressed to anyone in England and — with one exception — are not known to other contemporary English historiographers: Matthew Paris seems to have received copies second-hand from the network of the original addressees, already selected and assembled by someone else. One of the letters can be found in another English chronicle which did not use Matthew's work as a source, which indicates that the collection or parts of it were disseminated to various religious houses, but seemingly the whole series was recorded in its entirety only in St Albans.[80]

While the Ottobeuren Collection is certainly similar, there are other collections of texts closer to St Albans that may provide useful insights into the type of materials Matthew worked with, and at some point he himself provides a clue about his access to 'local' information about the Mongol invasion in Europe. The previous chapter ended with the last reference to the Mongols in the *Chronica majora* under the year 1257, which he is to repeat in his English history as well:

> Ipsorum Tartarorum immunditias, vitam et mores si quis audire desiderat, necnon et Assessinorum furorem et superstitionem, apud Sanctum Albanum diligens indagator poterit reperire.
> Terra Sancta languit desolata, et formidine Tartarorum; habebat enim rex Tartarorum in comitatu suo armatorum pugnatorum quadragies centena milia, et ut accepimus a peritis et fide dignis, jam dominatui suo dimidium mundi feraliter subdiderunt; quorum vita[m]

---

79 The familiar figures include Henry II, duke of Brabant; his wife Sophie of Thuringia, Henry Raspe's niece and St Elizabeth's daughter. More on their family relations in Chapter 2 ('Northern Connections'). The 'king of Bohemia' is Wenceslas I of Bohemia, Agnes of Bohemia's brother, and at one time Henry Raspe's co-regent for Conrad. The 'duke of Poland' is Henry of Silesia, Agnes's brother-in-law, who was killed fighting the Mongols.

80 The Cistercian *Waverley Annals* contains the letter of a Hungarian bishop to the bishop of Paris under the year 1239. 'Annales de Waverleia', pp. 324–25.

LETTERS FROM THE AFFLICTED LANDS IN THE *ADDITAMENTA*   305

spurcissima[m] apud Sanctum Albanum poterit indag[at]or sedulus reperire.

> (If any one is desirous of learning the impurities of these Tartars, and their mode of life and customs, or to read of the superstitions and fury of the Assassins, he may obtain information by making diligent search at St Alban's.)[81]
>
> (The Holy Land languished in desolation and in fear of the Tartars; for the king of the latter had four million of fighting men in his train; and, as we have heard from learned and credible persons, they had already reduced half the world to subjection to them by their ferocity. Any one making a careful search and inquiry at St Alban's, may find there an account of their most filthy mode of life.)[82]

Matthew's emphasis in these passages is clearly on his own monastery's collection of materials, but as Jacques Paviot points out, there is a version of this note in the Benedictine John of Oxnead's *Chronica* under the year 1258 which seems more forthcoming about the source and current location of information.[83] But the passage, in fact, is closer to home than Paviot suggests: Oxnead borrowed this sentence from John of Wallingford's chronicle at St Albans, who refers to some materials received in the form of a commissioned text (*mandatum scriptum*) sent to Simon de Montfort:[84]

> Eodem etiam anno venit mandatum scriptum, quod tantum continet littere quantum continere creditur unum psalterium, de vita et moribus Tartarorum, ad comitem Legecestrie Simonem de Monte-forti, et eorum fortitudine et guerra et de adquisicionibus. Quod qui inspicere desiderat, apud Sanctum Albanum in Libro additamentorum poterit reperire.

---

81 MS R, fol. 202ᵛ, col. b; *CM*, v, p. 655; *EH*, III, p. 251. Note that Matthew Paris makes no attempt to connect this sentence to any documents in the *Additamenta* by way of marginal signs or otherwise.

82 MS R, fol. 203ᵛ, col. b; *CM*, v, p. 661; *EH*, III, p. 256. No marginal signs refer to any of the texts in the *Additamenta*.

83 Paviot, 'England and the Mongols', p. 305. 'Venit etiam mandatum scriptum quod tantum continet litterae quantum continere creditur unum Psalterium, de vita et moribus Tartarorum ad Comitem Legecestriae Simonem de Monteforti et de eorum fortitudine et guerra et de adquisitionibus, quod qui inspicere desiderat apud Sanctum Albanum in libro *Additamentorum* poterit reperire'. John of Oxnead, *Chronica*, p. 217.

84 John was a close friend and associate of Matthew Paris and had access to all Matthew Paris's historical material, including, it seems, his rough drafts. Much of his chronicle has found its way into the Norwich chronicle underlying that of Bartholomew Cotton, and into John of Oxnead's. Vaughan, 'The Chronicle of John of Wallingford', pp. 68–69.

> (In the same year a commissioned text came to Simon de Monfort, earl of Leicester, which contains as many letters as a psalter is known to contain, about the life and customs of the Tartars, and about their strength in war and their conquests. Which, whoever wishes to inspect can find in the *Liber additamentorum* in St Albans.)[85]

According to this passage, the Mongol material is not only located in St Albans, but specifically in the *Additamenta*, which Peter Jackson dismisses as a confusion.[86] Considering the size of a psalterium, for example the 204 folios of the St Albans Psalter (twelfth century, now in Hildesheim Dombibliothek), there is indeed a discrepancy between the size of the Mongol material in the *Additamenta* and the purported compendium. Although Jackson — understandably cautiously — suggests that Roger Bacon's *Itinerarium* written after Rubruck's report may be a likely contender for this text, there are other possibilities for such texts at the disposal of the monks working at the St Albans scriptorium. The existence of a letter collection, which was ultimately (though perhaps partially) copied into the *Additamenta*, is not wholly out of the question.[87]

If the surviving Mongol bundle is indeed the remnant of a lost larger collection from Simon de Monfort's chancery, another group of manuscripts — very much in existence — may be examined for possible connections. As noted, letters appearing separately or in pairs in various configurations across a number of English monastic manuscripts suggest that chroniclers may have cherry-picked from the same larger collection. For example, the previously mentioned Courtenay Compendium (MS CC) and its Cambridge version (MS GC) both contain letters that Matthew Paris recorded. For example, the letter entitled 'Anno domini millessimo ccmo xliv transmissa est haec prelato parisius de adventu Tartarorum' (In the year of the Lord 1244 this [letter] concerning the advent of the Tartars was sent to a prelate in Paris) is a version of the Hungarian bishop's letter inserted in the *Additamenta* and the *Waverley Annals*.[88] In the Compendium, this is followed by a similar text, entitled 'Nova pestis contra ecclesiam' (A fresh affliction confronting the Church), which Jackson surmises to have been written around 1244.[89] But, as described in

---

85 John of Wallingford, 'Ex chronicis', pp. 510–11.

86 While Davide Bigalli assumes that the passage refers to the *Additamenta*, Jackson argues that the chroniclers' claim that the book could be found in the *Liber Additamentorum* at St Albans was based on a confusion with the documents gathered by Matthew Paris. Jackson, *The Mongols and the West*, p. 154, n. 18; Bigalli, *I tartari e l'Apocalisse*, p. 25, n. 54.

87 Jackson, *The Mongols and the West*, p. 138.

88 MS CC, pp. 316b–317b; MS GC, fols 106ᵛ–107ᵛ. Cf. 'Annales de Waverleia', p. 324.

89 This letter, also known to have been circulated and copied into various manuscripts, is entitled 'Nova pestis contra ecclesiam' in MS CC, pp. 317b–318b, and MS GC, fols 107ᵛ–

the previous chapter, the report of Archbishop Peter, which came down to us in five known versions, provides a clue — specifically the wording in the *Burton Annals* — that these texts may have been brought from Lyon after 1245.[90]

Wallingford's clues about Simon de Montfort's involvement in commissioning and depositing letters about the Mongols are plausible. As discussed in more detail in Chapter 2, Simon was very close to his 'spiritual director', Adam Marsh (Adam de Marisco), lecturer of the Franciscan house at Oxford. And both were frequently corresponding friends of Robert Grosseteste, bishop of Lincoln, whose chancery was a veritable hub of information both plugged into international networks of information exchange and closely connected to St Albans.[91] As shown with previous passages with a Cologne connection in Chapters 2 and 5, the possibility of the dissemination of such collections through the conduit of networks meeting at Lyon always looms on the horizon. The person of the mediator is perhaps immaterial, since the extremely wide-reaching dissemination of documents back and forth makes the Council of Lyon — or rather the cloud of literacy around it — more than a physical hub of communication. Viewing the council as a meeting point, focused in space but protracted in time, is more conducive to understanding its role in the spread of the Mongol story and its impact on contemporary political communication. Matthew's materials that arrived at St Albans through the filter of the pope's assembly at Lyon bear the mark of the highest echelons of ecclesiastical society, even without direct connections.

Thus, although the actual mediators (and even the existence) of such a compendium remains speculative, the fact remains that the 'Mongol bundle' in the *Additamenta* is a collection of *rescripta*, not unlike the Ottobeuren Collection, and its *salutationes* and content point to a compiler

---

108[v]. Jackson suggests the 1244 date, since the Mongols are said to be already at 'our borders' and menacing Latin Christians, which fits best with the brief Mongol incursion into northern Syria in that year. Jackson, 'The Testimony of the Russian "Archbishop" Peter', p. 67.

90 There are four manuscript copies of the *Tractatus* currently in existence not counting the version supplied by Matthew Paris (MSS *L*, *GC*, *CC*, and *BA*, see also in Chapter 5 ('1244: The Man from Russia'), notes 126, 127, and 128). Other versions of the archbishop's report, e.g. that in the *Chronica majora* or the 'Tractatus de ortu Tartarorum' (MS CC, pp. 315a–316b), do not contain the *Burton Annals*' reference to Lyon. Other similar Mongol-related treatises are known to have circulated at the time, for example, the mysterious description of the world on fols 3[r] and 4[v] in Dublin, Trinity College, IS TCD MS 347, clearly a chapter out of a longer work on the Tartars, which starts with an explicit reference to their origin, progress, and customs: 'Ad sciendum ortum progressum consuetudines gentis que Tartari nuncupatur' and ends with 'Ceterum iam Tartari et qualiter exorti fuerunt breviter declarabo' (And now I shall briefly relate how the Tartars originated). Colker, 'America Rediscovered in the Thirteenth Century?', pp. 720, 726.

91 For more on their connections, see Chapter 2 ('The Scriptorium in England').

308   CHAPTER 6

with access to documents circulated by German mendicant networks. While the grand concerns of the network circulating these texts point to the prestigious ecclesiastical circles who dictated the agenda at Lyon and in the Church, the content of the letters brings us closer to the informants who supplied their policies with intelligence on the ground. This is how it happened that coming into the possession of these texts in a roundabout way, despite his well-known and explicitly negative attitude towards the growing importance of the Franciscans, Matthew Paris was one of the earliest Benedictine chroniclers in England to embrace materials arriving from the intrepid mendicants.

It has been suggested that Matthew received the bundle some time *after* the other documents had been written up for the *Chronica majora* about the same event.[92] While this seems intuitive enough, as has been demonstrated previously, the Mongol material in the *Chronica majora* was also written after the Council of Lyon, so the separation of materials into chronicle and appendix may have been Matthew's editorial decision rather than simple chronology. But despite their differences and physical separation, the documents collected in the *Additamenta* are connected to the main text of the *Chronica majora* by a number of invisible and explicit threads. The purpose of such collections of letters in the appendix was not limited to illustrating the chronicle; they also proved the veracity of the text and added to the prestige of the St Albans chronicle and chronicler. In the following, however, the most important aspect to consider is why certain letters are in the main text and others are in the *Additamenta* — and what this meant for the construction and use of the Mongol story. Besides the absence of textual correspondence but the presence of an interplay between the texts' perspective and direction, there is another type of nexus between the two volumes, which is more technical in nature. Matthew provides cross references to its contents in the course of both his *Chronica majora* and the *Historia Anglorum*.[93] In some cases, the documents he referenced ended up in the main narrative of the *Chronica majora*, while some were lost altogether.[94]

Björn Weiler suggests that 'much of the documentation on the Mongols, for example, is cited in summary in the *Chronica*, with the fuller versions reserved for the *Liber*. Text and documentary appendix were

---

92 J. J. Saunders, for example, suggests that he received them together with a 'mass of information' from his correspondents in Lyon and never got around to incorporating them in his narrative. Saunders, *The History of the Mongol Conquests*, p. 131.

93 See for example: 'Quae compositio plenius scribitur in libro additamentorum videlicet ad tale signum [image resembling a fish or pen nib]', referring to a 'composition' between the bishop of Lincoln and the abbey of St Albans concerning the vicarage of *Luton*. *CM*, III, p. 44. The referenced document can be found on fol. 63ʳ in the *Additamenta* (MS *LA*).

94 Luard enumerates the eight references that have no counterparts in the *Liber Additamentorum* in *CM*, VI, p. viii, n. 1.

mutually reinforced parts of a wider narrative.[95] While the latter was certainly Matthew's intention, the parallels between the chronicle and the *Additamenta*, however, are not necessarily manifested in directly corresponding passages; the ties between the two bodies of texts are more subtle than that. Matthew had at his disposal various ways of establishing the relevance of certain texts for the intended scope of the chronicle (or lack thereof). For example, as previously shown, following in Ralph of Diceto's footsteps, Matthew Paris used *signes-de-renvoi* to link corrections, commentary, annotations, and other marginal content to the main text, as well as their polar opposite: signs instructing to skip certain passages (e.g. Fig. 10). Whether meant to instruct the reader or to serve as a mark-up for himself or later copyists labouring on more focused English histories (such as his own *Historia Anglorum*), such signs appear more frequently towards the end of the *Chronica majora*, some hardly more than just a squiggly line or circle.[96]

While skipping marks were used as a visual means of lifting texts out of the *Chronica majora*'s narrative, there were also ones that marked physical separation. For example, an entry about one of Matthew's favourite topics, the pope's accumulation of money, is followed by 'How they prevaricated in fulfilling this business [the mendicant orders collecting money for the pope] will be found in the book of *Additamenta* at this sign ←○→'.[97] Indeed, Matthew could have his cake and eat it: exclude a text and keep it. While none of the Mongol-related texts have such signs next to them, their use in general indicates that the documents in the *Additamenta* were important and organic parts of the chronicle. Their separate placement was partly governed by chronological reasons (for example, receiving documents after completing the relevant passage in the main text of the chronicle) but primarily by narrative reasons, for example, important documents containing too many specific and uncontextualized details that would disrupt the text.[98]

---

95 Weiler, 'Matthew Paris on the Writing of History', p. 265. Citing my own Papp [Reed], 'Tartars on the Frontiers of Europe', which is here updated by more recent research.

96 One of the earlier ones is next to Prior Philip's letter recorded under 1237, discussed in Chapter 3 above. MS *B*, fol. 106ᵛ, col. b; *CM*, III, p. 397; *EH*, I, p. 56.

97 'Quod quam argumentose complere studuerint in libro Additamentorum poterit reperiri ad tale signum ←○→', MS *B*, fol. 215ᵛ, col. a; *CM*, IV, pp. 634–35; *EH*, II, pp. 235–36. The respective symbol is found next to 'Litterae generales directae per singulos episcopatus, super collectione decimarum et redemptione votorum crucesignatorum et aliorum, comiti Ricardo concessorum', MS *LA*, fol. 90ʳ, col. b; no. 71 in *CM*, VI, p. 134.

98 For example, Matthew makes notes of papal letters in the body of the chronicle and provides the full letter in the *Additamenta* twice: in 1252 (*CM*, V, p. 317) and in 1254 (*CM*, V, p. 428). In both cases he explains the location and provides a symbol corresponding to the text of the letters in the *Additamenta*.

The sequence discussed here is written from the perspective of German dignitaries — and of the mendicants who were not only their eyes and ears, but also the ones to experience the Mongols in real life. Like turning a telescope around, the letters show a miniature but sharp version of the Mongol story in the *Chronica majora*. As noted above, the *Additamenta* letters about the Mongols are at once more condensed and more detailed than the pertaining stories across the narrative of the chronicle, which ties the two bodies of text even more closely together. Revisiting the question of narrative space and literary devices, the *Additamenta* shows that where there is a narrative space, there are boundaries; and where there are boundaries, there is also liminality. In this case, by way of the traditional *signes-de-renvoi* and their opposite, the *impertinens* marks, certain elements of history were moved outside the narrative itself — into a separate volume even. Although the collection of *Additamenta* fills a separate volume by itself, the texts therein are part of the *Chronica majora* while resolutely remaining outside it at the same time. This liminality, however, is not some kind of marginalization: the *Additamenta*'s contents are important, especially for verification and authority; they are just not necessary to move the plot forward in the narrative.

With such a close connection between main text and appendix, the liminality of the materials in the *Additamenta* is an interesting question. Effectively, the text of the *Additamenta* can be seen as scholarly apparatus, endnotes. Talking about the referentiality of perigraphic apparatus in her tri-level model of historical narrative (reference — story — discourse), Dorrit Cohn explains that the presence of an entire 'perigraphic' apparatus, be they footnotes, endnotes, prefatory, or appended, 'constitute[s] a textual zone intermediating between the narrative text itself and its extratextual documentary base'.[99] In the case of the *Chronica majora*, the *Additamenta* is a link between the chronicle world and the extrabibliographic reality — this is where the real eyewitnesses dwell. One caveat is notable here: Cohn's historians arrange their narrative and referential materials into their respective spaces within a book that is finalized at a given point in time as a single product. In contrast, for the *Chronica majora*, a story accumulated and written across some time, the time of receipt of various sources did sometimes play a role in certain materials ending up as *additamenta*, though not as markedly as previously thought.

Observing the *Additamenta* as the intermediate zone where the narrative text and its extratextual documentary meet, an 'isograph' of voices emerges

---

99 Cohn adapts the term 'périgraphie' from Philippe Carrard's 1986 case study of French historical writing on World War I, in which he looks at the discursive norms of narrative history. Cohn, *The Distinction of Fiction*, p. 115; Carrard, 'Récit historique et fonction testimoniale'.

setting apart those that belong in the chronicle narrative and those which remain outside it. To simplify Cohn's observation, those who remain outside, residing in the liminal space of the *Additamenta*, have more to do with the actual reality of the Mongol invasion on the ground than the Mongol story in the chronicle. This manifests in the pool of sources used for these two bodies of texts: while Frederick II, the bishop of Winchester, Queen Blanche, and the Mongols themselves feature in the chronicle, letters circulated by mendicant friars from the region are in the appendix, a separate volume with no plot. This becomes significant in view of the afterlife of the chronicle in the following chapter, where the implications of placing certain texts in the *Additamenta* become palpable: the nearly complete absence of certifiable evidence for their later use suggests that for a long time anything recorded in the *Additamenta* remained outside of the Mongol story that was reused in later works.

The letters of the *Chronica majora* and the *Additamenta* together draw attention to an important hiatus in Matthew's coverage of the Mongol events, which largely rely on these epistolary sources. While the papacy is one of the main moving forces in the chronicle, neither the *Chronica majora* nor the *Additamenta* contains any letters by Gregory IX or Innocent IV regarding the Mongol invasion — rendering them silent antagonists rather than protagonist in the Mongol story.[100] The inherent bias of such unilateral representation of the events is primarily caused by Matthew's access to papal and legatine correspondence being limited to letters sent to English recipients, which results in a kind of (spontaneous) narrative subversion, stripping powerful men of their voice and agency in a story moved forward by the real powerful men whose power, among others, manifests in their ability to speak to posterity. Through their own words reported in direct or indirect speech and, more importantly, copying letters attributed to them, men like Frederick II, Henry III, or Henry Raspe — and eyewitnesses such as the Russian archbishop and Ivo of Narbonne caught in the act of informing distinguished prelates, legates, and other eminences — contribute to the narrative they inhabit, in a way becoming a co-author of their deeds in the chronicle.

---

100 In contrast with thirty-four letters by Innocent IV in the *Additamenta*, there are sixteen, quoted in full or in part, in the *Chronica majora*, none of which concerns the Mongol invasion. It is conspicuous that most of the sixteen papal letters inserted in the text typically concern Robert Grosseteste, bishop of Lincoln (e.g. *CM*, IV, pp. 258, 497–501; V, p. 300), the bishop of Winchester (*CM*, IV, p. 347), the archbishop(ric) of Canterbury (*CM*, IV, pp. 369, 507–09), specific abbots and abbeys (including St Albans in *CM*, V, p. 232), or prelates/councils in general, showing a clear pattern of the type of papal letters that were accessible for Matthew Paris through their recipients.

CHAPTER 7

The Afterlife of Matthew's Mongol Story

> It was, now I am trying to understand, as if — just
> as the whole universe is surely like a book written
> by the finger of God, in which everything speaks to
> us of the immense goodness of its Creator, in which
> every creature is description and mirror of life and
> death, in which the humblest rose becomes a gloss of
> our terrestrial progress — everything, in other words,
> spoke to me only of the face I had hardly glimpsed in
> the aromatic shadows of the kitchen.[1]

Understanding the history of the sources that gave us the history of an event is vital. In this vein, Peter Jackson draws attention to the potential pitfalls of using various types of sources in any reconstruction of the Mongols' role in European history: 'In the first place, to attempt a systematic exposition of Western views about the Mongols risks lending a spurious coherence to ideas that may in fact have been half-formed, transient and mutually contradictory. And secondly, we cannot be sure how much impact any particular letter or chronicle had.'[2] His warning is key to the understanding of the history of the Mongol invasion in Europe, and it points at an acute hiatus in the historiography of this momentous episode of the thirteenth century. The *Chronica majora* is undoubtedly one of the most frequently used texts with regard to the Mongol military movements in Eastern Europe. While the larger part of the present study concentrates on the conception of the text and the texts that had been received and processed before the clean copy froze them in time, heeding Peter Jackson's words, a brief outlook at the final version's impact and afterlife is in order.

Intertextuality works in two directions. Once again, Gide's concept of the mise-en-abîme can be used as a helpful tool to analyse the depth

---

1 Eco, *The Name of the Rose*, p. 164.
2 Jackson, *The Mongols and the West*, p. 136.

that a text can acquire both *during* and *after* its production.[3] The previous chapters were devoted to intertextual connections created during the construction of the chronicle by identifying Matthew's ways of creating depth in his narrative using serially embedded received materials. But, as the present chapter will unpick selected strands of its afterlife, the text does not stop evolving there. A self-portrait of Matthew Paris, kneeling in front of the image of the Virgin Mary, is a particularly striking example for this implicit understanding (MS R, fol. 6^r, see Fig. 11). Judith Collard notes that the image 'is both a dedication of the book and the author to the Virgin Mary and a statement of authorial presence, disguised as an act of humble devotion'.[4] Alexa Sand also touches upon the image representing Matthew's relationship with his book suggesting that he 'depicts himself, as a maker of pictures, as engaged in a form of Christomimesis, piously assimilating self to deity through the very act of representation'.[5]

The image of the creator of the Virgin's likeness is placed outside the frame of his devotional painting, doing what he may expect from the observer of such an image: kneel and pray. The rubric at his feet reads 'O felicia oscula lactentis labiis impressa cum inter crebra indicia reptantis infancie, utpote verus ex te filius [matri] alluderet cum verus ex patre deus dei genitus imperaret' (Oh happy kiss with milky lips impressed, abundant evidence along with the infant crawling and gambolling about you that you are truly the mother of his son, verily the only begotten son of God), a line from a sermon by Augustine.[6] But the monk's gaze is not directed at the virgin. His eyes are fixed on the text: Augustine's words that he reproduced and is holding in his hands. Continuing the recursivity and emulating his behaviour, Matthew's future readers are expected to hold his book with the same reverence and reuse his words in their own texts wisely.

The vision of past and future authorities takes us to another illustration. Matthew Paris's portrait on his deathbed — though not executed in his own hand — also shows the implicit understanding of this depth and recursivity (see Fig. 1, above). Besides the everyday process of creating their own texts, medieval chroniclers no doubt understood the place of their labours in the grand scheme of things: the textual mise-en-abîme continued by the afterlife of their *historiae*, of which they — being excerpters and users of previous texts themselves — were acutely aware in their physical and intellectual practice. Throughout its existence, there

---

3 As Matthew Fisher saliently observes, 'Matthew was deeply embedded in history as a textualized phenomenon. [...] Matthew wrote with an awareness that his texts existed as books'. Fisher, *Scribal Authorship*, p. 93.

4 Collard, 'Matthew Paris's "Self-Portrait with the Virgin Mary"', p. 177.

5 Sand, *Vision, Devotion, and Self-Representation*, p. 49.

6 Translation in Sand, *Vision, Devotion, and Self-Representation*, p. 47. Originally in Augustine of Hippo, *Opera omnia*, col. 2131.

Figure 11. Matthew Paris, 'Self-Portrait with the Virgin Mary', *Historia Anglorum*, MS R, fol. 6ʳ. By permission of the Parker Library, Corpus Christi College, Cambridge.

316   CHAPTER 7

were plenty of people who held the book in their hands after Matthew, thus becoming part of the abyss-like sequence. If they decided to reproduce any of the texts contained therein, their text became a container of Matthew's, itself made up of a dazzling variety of received material.

The Mongol story is essentially all received text, and as such is a particularly rich subject for traditional intertextual inquiries, identifying allusions to or citations from other texts. However, it immediately becomes a more complicated issue if one looks up from the text and considers the chronicle's extrabibliographic life *after* its completion. Literary criticism, especially after Julia Kristeva's work in the field (and Roland Barthes's thoughts about textuality and readers), takes a synchronic view that deals with texts as interconnected bodies of literature.[7] Acknowledging this phenomenon multiplies a thousandfold the mirrors of the author–reader interaction, no matter how limited the length of the text itself or its afterlife may be. The present chapter, thus, can only give a brief overview of the vicissitudes and some milestones in the metahistory of Matthew's Mongol story, with the primary aim to understand how modern scholarship knows and understands this text as historical evidence.

Concerning medieval readers and creators of this interconnected textual web, an ever-growing body of scholarship, including Rosamond McKitterick, C. P. Wormald, Brian Stock, Michael Clanchy, and many others, has shown that literacy is a 'fluid constellation of beliefs, practices, and habits', and includes multimodal skills such as visual literacy, numeracy, and others.[8] Allusions and citations primarily concern the readers because, instead of the author's intention or knowledge, the interpretation of the text is always hinged upon whether the readers can recognize and interpret the intertextual connections. With this in mind, while such connections between the *Chronica majora* and other medieval works reconstructed in Luard's and Vaughan's spirit are certainly informative in establishing the sources of the Mongol story, the later use and interpretation of the text offers further inspiring ways to think about intertextuality in the present volume.

Chronicles and their Afterlife

By now it is clear that the *Chronica majora* is not the origo of the historiographical mise-en-abîme it inhabits: a large part of it is, in fact, an edited version of an earlier historical work, Roger of Wendover's *Flores historiarum* — itself made up of the interwoven narratives of earlier

---

7 See the brief overview in Martínez Alfaro, 'Intertextuality'.
8 Sand, *Vision, Devotion, and Self-Representation*, p. 103.

THE AFTERLIFE OF MATTHEW'S MONGOL STORY   317

chroniclers, for example, Robert of Torrigni and Sigebert of Gembloux.[9] Some of Matthew's other works, in turn, are edited, abridged versions of the *Chronica majora*. For medieval scholars who were in some ways still directly connected to Matthew Paris's oeuvre, this was more a question of historiographical training and practice than a conceptual issue. Dorothy Kim's study of the *Royal Itinerary*, for example, tangentially touches upon Matthew's role in the institutional historiographical legacy that situated him as a central figure in what she termed virtual presence in the 'Corporate Matthew Paris' created by the bookmakers of St Albans.[10] What happened to the chronicle after completing the text (more or less) is exactly what Matthew and the 'Corporate Matthew Paris' did to his predecessors': reuse and, in this case specifically, redaction and continuation. Throughout the history of the *Chronica majora*, scholars editing, quoting, or printing passages of Matthew's narrative are essentially stages in an endless process.

Who read the *Chronica majora*? Who read the story of the Mongols? Connolly argues that the intended readers of Matthew Paris's historiographical work were noble and royal audiences, but in reality, not much is known about the people who had a chance to read the manuscripts of either the *Chronica majora* or any of its redactions or continuations.[11] Regardless of their status and their interaction with the text, they left hardly any marks on the manuscripts that would inform us about their perceptions or opinions about the events described in Matthew's text. The person who did so was Matthew Paris himself, readying and multiplying the text for future use, and primarily creating an abridged version called *Flores historiarum* — either in reference to its genre, or as an homage to the work of Roger of Wendover, who was his predecessor, and perhaps teacher in the St Albans scriptorium.

---

9 See more in *CM*, I, p. xxxiv.

10 'Furthermore, although Connolly argues convincingly that the Royal itinerary was produced after Matthew Paris's death as part of a specific royal call for documents, I do not think that Matthew Paris's virtual presence can be discounted, even if he was not directly involved in the construction of this prefatory material. He is present in the lingering effects of his collaborations with and training of those constructing it; he is present in their invocation of his visual auctoritas in portraits at the volume's beginning and end. From this presence, the bookmakers of St Albans created a "Corporate Matthew Paris" in which they participated and from which they drew for both inspiration and worldly currency'. Kim, 'Matthew Paris, Visual Exegesis, and Apocalyptic Birds', p. 4. Kim's concept is especially apposite to the authorship challenge of derivate textuality, presented in many works, notably by Alistair Minnis, which Fisher sums up succinctly: 'Derivative textuality and vernacular historiography fit poorly with theories of medieval authorship that have largely been shaped by Latin theological texts or the great vernacular poetry of the late fourteenth century'. Fisher, *Scribal Authorship*, p. 7.

11 Connolly, *The Maps of Matthew Paris*.

318   CHAPTER 7

So, after its completion, one of the *Chronica majora*'s first and most prolific redactors was Matthew Paris and his team, picking the 'flowers of history' out of the massive monolith of the *Chronica majora*. That he was aware of the importance of preserving some flowers and removing others is shown by his own words about the story of Egwin in his *Gesta abbatum*, not found in Wendover's records and elsewhere: 'Hujus historialis eventus seriem ego, frater Matthaeus Parisiensis duxi litteris commendare, ne iterum, incuria vel vetustate, a memoria hominum deleatur' (I, Brother Matthew Paris, thought it right to put down in writing the series of events of this story, so that they should not again be blotted out from human memory through lack of care or the passage of time).[12] The contemporary success and afterlife of his *Flores historiarum* and other abridged works and the eclipse of the *Chronica majora* is an important phase in the metahistory of Matthew's Mongol story, which had an indirect impact on the later memorialization of the Mongol invasion in Eastern Europe.

The Flores historiarum

Observing historiography as a longitudinal narrative is indebted to Iwona Irwin-Zarecka's model of the cultural recall of the past, which is particularly useful in the context of the development of medieval historical narratives. In this, she stresses the role of *relevance* in creating priorities that ensure the survival of certain aspects of the past and sideline others.[13] Sidelining is exactly what Matthew did to the Mongol story in his redaction of the *Chronica majora*. Its creation was a major consolidation programme: it resulted in a standardized and condensed historical narrative, essentially made out of the *Chronica majora* alone. This redaction, the *Flores historiarum*, was to become the most widely disseminated Benedictine history at the turn of the thirteenth century and afterwards, so Matthew's choices had far-reaching implications. Importantly for the subject of the present volume, this process entailed significant loss in the non-English material, including the Mongol-related entries which had formed a more or less coherent narrative in the *Chronica*. Once completed and disseminated, the many copies of the *Flores* began their own lives. As Judith Collard notes, 'A study of the *Flores* manuscripts shows how a monastic text can develop independently of its instigator' — and indeed, since most

---

12 Later he adds 'Veterum tamen negligentia ac simplicitate, nec ille memorabilis eventus, nec multi alii, etiam majores, litteris minime commendantur' (But through the negligence and lack of thought of our predecessors there has not been the slightest attempt to record in writing either of these memorable events or many others still more important). Walsingham, *Deeds of the Abbots of St Albans*, p. 67; Walsingham and Paris, *Gesta abbatum monasterii Sancti Albani*, p. 19.

13 Irwin-Zarecka, *Frames of Remembrance*.

THE AFTERLIFE OF MATTHEW'S MONGOL STORY 319

of the surviving copies have nothing to do with Matthew Paris or the monastery of St Albans, the concept of the 'Corporate Matthew Paris' is no longer tenable for this increasingly abstruse cloud of transmission and continuation.[14]

The authorship of Matthew Paris's *Flores historiarum* was for quite some time a matter of fierce debate, albeit often in the sphere of speculation. For example, Thomas Duffus Hardy eloquently argued against Frederick Madden's suggestion in 1871: 'Against my conclusions it may be urged that no positive proof can be given that a copy of [librarian] Walter of St Albans's compilation had found its way to Westminster, or that there ever was a Matthew a monk of Westminster. I freely admit both objections; but it does not follow, as a necessary consequence, because I cannot produce mathematical proof of an occurrence, that therefore no such occurrence ever took place; and it is certainly illogical to assert that a man never existed because you cannot prove that he lived. Although I am unable to demonstrate that at the beginning of the fourteenth century there was a monk named Matthew in the abbey of Westminster who compiled the "Flores Historiarum", yet I can demonstrate that in the middle of the fourteenth century there was a work so entitled ascribed to Matthew a monk of Westminster.'[15] After the initial fog of manuscripts, the authorship of the original is now firmly established as Matthew Paris's work, and based on the manuscript evidence, the location and relationship of the surviving copies and continuations is more or less clear.

The manuscript copies/continuations of the *Flores historiarum* are essentially divided into two groups: those that are based on the Chetham manuscript (*Ch*) and a smaller group of manuscripts continuing the Merton manuscript (*E*).[16] Luard drew attention to the fact that MS *E*

---

14 Collard, '"Flores Historiarum" Manuscripts', p. 442.
15 *Descriptive Catalogue of Materials Relating to the History of Great Britain and Ireland*, p. 325.
16 MS *Ch*: Manchester, Chetham Library, MS 6712, and MS *E*: Eton College Library, MS 123. Surviving manuscripts based on the Chetham manuscript (*Ch*) are MS *Ad* (Latin, fifteenth-century fragment, not found); MS *Ar* (to 1284, no additions to MS *Ch*, probable provenance: Christ Church Canterbury); MS *Bd* (to 1306, illustrated, bound with le Clerc's bestiary and other annals to 1356); MS *Ca* (*Chronicle of English History* (Adam Murimuth?), 1199–1368, incl. 'Westminster' continuation of *Flores historiarum* for 1298–1306); MS *Cl* (fifteenth-century copy of *Ch*, with many additions executed at Norwich); MS *F* (fourteenth-century fragment, to AD 635, written at Norwich); MS *H* (to 1307; a full table of contents and some illustrations added); MS *Ld* (to 1296; St Swithun's, Winchester); MS *Lm* (to 1341, copy with many omissions, few insertions, own continuation from 1307 to 1341, scribal errors e.g. *Coloniae ducatum for Polloniae ducatum* under 1289); MS *Lp* ('Westminster' continuation to 1306, copy with many omissions, a few insertions, incl. notes on St Paul's, London, between 1140 and 1303); MS *M* (to 1306, few additions from Higden, first part is an indirect copy from *Ch*, from 1298 it corresponds with *E*); MS *N* (to 1306, first part is copy of MS *Ar*, from 1284 probably copied from MS *M*, written in Rochester Priory, additions of local history); MS *O* (damaged in fire, many years wanting, from 1301 it

has much in common with *Ch* but does not directly derive from it.[17] MS *Ch*, the earliest surviving manuscript of this text, is a copy of the original *Flores historiarum* made in St Albans especially for the use of the monks at Westminster around 1250, possibly under Matthew Paris's personal supervision. One of the main theories for its production is that it was a presentation copy intended for Westminster Abbey.[18] This seems probable from the standard of production on the St Albans section where the scribal quality is high, decoration is regular, and the marking-up of the parchment is neat, unobtrusive, and consistent. It was produced in three different phases: up to the year 1249 it was written at St Albans Abbey, it was then continued up to 1265 at Pershore Abbey, before it arrived at Westminster Abbey and was brought up to date.[19] There, another continuation was added covering the years 1265–1307. This portion of the manuscript was to become the basis for the large number of manuscripts called the 'Westminster group'. The last phase of the continuation of the *Flores historiarum* in MS *Ch* covers 1307–1327, composed by Benedictine monks at Westminster, one of whom was possibly Robert of Reading (d. 1317).[20] MS *E* is a fair copy of the *Flores historiarum* written by a single scribe at the priory of Merton around the turn of the thirteenth century.[21]

---

follows Trivet and MS *Cl*); MS *Re* (written in St Benet Holme to 1304, continued in Tintern to 1323, lengthy omissions, additions on Norfolk history, many extracts from the so-called *Wroxham Chronicle*); MS *Rf* (to 1305 compilation from the *Flores*, probably MS *M*, and other sources, written at St Mary's, Southwark); MS *T* (to 1327, probably copied from MS *M*, from 1298 it is closer to MS *E*, many additions from Higden); MS *Wf* (to 1306, first part is an indirect copy from *Ch* with many additions, from 1265 it is closer to *E*). Sigla as given in Luard except *Ar* (Luard's *A*) and *Wf* (Luard's *W*), and *F, Ld, Lm, O, Rf*, which are mine. For shelf marks, see List of Manuscripts in Appendix 6.

17 *FH*, I, p. xvi. Based on the arguments of Luard and Liebermann, Richard Vaughan suggested that this is due to the two manuscripts sharing a common exemplar, which he calls MS *ChE*. Vaughan, *Matthew Paris*, p. 93.

18 Gransden, *Historical Writing in England*, I, p. 420.

19 Carpenter, 'The Pershore *Flores Historiarum*', pp. 1355–56.

20 This continuation is not included in the text disseminated in the manuscripts of the Westminster group. Gransden, 'The Continuations of the *Flores Historiarum* from 1265 to 1327', p. 248; Tout, 'The Westminster Chronicle Attributed to Robert of Reading'.

21 The first part of MS *E* is very different from MS *Ch*; the years 1245–1265 seem to be abridged directly from the *Chronica majora*. The last part follows MS *Ch* more closely with numerous additions, e.g. a detailed account of the Barons' War. Surviving manuscripts stemming from MS *E*: MS *As* (to 1307, fourteenth-/fifteenth-century copy of *E*, also known as John Rochfort's chronicle in earlier scholarship); MS *Be* (begins imperfectly in 1058 and contains continuations to 1327); MS *Hr* (fourteenth-century manuscript from St Augustine's, Canterbury, with medieval note attributing the work to John Bevere, monk of Westminster); MS *P* (to 1306, some alterations and omissions, provenance unknown); MS *Ra* (manuscript descriptions in *FH*, I, pp. xii–xxix; Gransden, 'The Continuations of the *Flores Historiarum* from 1265 to 1327'). Summaries of *Flores* manuscripts do not mention MS *Hu* (1066–1306, twenty-eight (?) missing leaves); MS *Lt* (Merton *Flores* attributed to Matthew of Westminster bound together with Martinus Polonus's *Chronicon pontificum et*

THE AFTERLIFE OF MATTHEW'S MONGOL STORY   321

This text ends in 1294. After 1294, it is continued in various hands up to 1306 where the chronicle stops abruptly due to a loss of leaves.

Fascinating as the continuations may be, what is relevant here, however, is not these but the fate of the *Chronica majora*'s Mongol story *s.a.* 1238–1248 in the abridgement project. The *Flores historiarum* was created for wide circulation and thus written along different principles than the larger chronicle. The folios for the years 1241–1249 in MS *Ch* are Matthew's autograph, so the selection of materials under these years reflects his editorial choices in drawing up the *Flores*.[22] Even within the MS *Ch* group there are considerable differences as to what was copied into further versions.[23] The Mongol story was handed down in this diminished form in subsequent copies of the *Flores*. There are some unabridged copies, for example, the neat and nearly unmarked MS *Ar* of the Chetham group, containing text that is identical with MS *Ch* without addition or deletions until 1284, and a continuation down to 1286.[24]

Later versions of the *Flores* reveal a more intensive use, as well as scribal and compiler interference with the text, and some have continuations to as late as the end of the fourteenth century. It is true for the whole volume, however, that the majority of the Eastern European material is omitted altogether. Adam Murimuth, one of the better known continuators of the *Flores*, aptly encapsulates the principle behind producing flowers of history, dismissing entries with curt notes such as 'in Anglia vero pauca notabilia contigerunt' or 'nihil acto quod meruit scribii'.[25] For example, being an integral part of British history, all three passages concerning the exile of Edmund Ironside's sons to Hungary remained in the text

---

imperatorum with continuations for 1277–1285, and other historical and prophetic texts); MS *U* (in unknown private collection, main text with 'Merton' continuation for 1066–1306). Sigla MSS *E* and *Ra* are as given in Luard; *As, Be, Hr, Hu, Lt, P,* and *U* are mine. For shelf marks, see List of Manuscripts in Appendix 6.

22 Gransden, 'The Continuations of the *Flores Historiarum* from 1265 to 1327', p. 246.

23 In the following, the passages are identified in four manuscripts of the *Ch* group to show how uneven was the rate of copying 'non-essential' entries across various versions: MS *Ar*, probably from Christ Church, Canterbury; MS *Re*, probably from St Benet Holme; MS *N*, probably a copy of MS *M* written in Rochester; as well as MS *J*, which is not a *Flores* manuscript per se, but an independent history of England in a compilation made by John of Wallingford in St Albans, which also contains a number of pages with Matthew Paris autographs.

24 Luard speculates that it is probably from 1284 (or shortly after) and may have belonged to Christ Church, Canterbury, but there is no certifiable evidence for this. *FH*, I, p. xvii. The manuscript is incomplete, and the text of the *Flores* is copied in two parts by different hands, whereby the continuation (down to 1286) is preceded by an inserted passage of the *De mirabilibus Anglie* (fol. 71^r).

25 Murimuth and Robert of Avesbury, *Continuatio chronicarum; De gestis mirabilibus regis Edwardi tertii*, pp. 29, 37. See also Matthew's own 'skipping marks' indicating certain passages' pertinence within his *Chronica majora* in Chapter 5 ('1244: Frederick's Triumph'), including Fig. 10.

322   CHAPTER 7

without textual variation.[26] At the same time, other references to the Eastern European region — such as crusading episodes in 1096 and 1215–1217 or recurring mentions of Saint Elizabeth of Hungary — which were originally in the *Chronica majora*, are omitted in the *Flores*.[27] In the same way, contrary to the *Chronica majora*'s sweeping story of an active Mongol military campaign in (mostly) identifiable European locations, in the *Flores* the Mongol-related passages are short and (except for one fleeting mention of Hungary) lack almost all geographical references to Eastern Europe.[28] Instead of forming a solid subplot in the emperor's story, they seem to be picked only to introduce and lead up to the Mongol presence in the Near East. They are presented in the voice of the chronicler, and there is no room for lengthy description or embedded letters or dialogues. The first short mention comes from 1238:

> Eo tempore, quaedam gens barbara et innumerabilis, dicta Tartari, partes Aquilonares Orientis miro vastarunt exterminio, magno pavore omnium Christianorum principes et populos concutientes.
>
> (About this time [1238], a certain barbarian nation of incalculable number, called the Tartars, devastated the northern countries of the East, spreading great destruction, and striking all the Christian princes with great fear.)[29]

Although Matthew removed the bulky Mongol invasion narrative which originally served as a subplot within the larger framework of European history, there are minor additions originally not included in the *Chronica majora*. The first such passage concerns the Mongols, entered under the year 1243.

---

26 These were originally in Roger of Wendover's *Flores*, which Matthew Paris copied as the beginning of his *Chronica majora*. *FH*, I, pp. 547, 575; II, p. 2. Originally in *CM*, I, pp. 501–02, 525–26; II, pp. 1–2.

27 Crusades: *CM*, II, pp. 53–54, 54–55, 55–56, 630–33; III, pp. 9–11, 13–14. St Elizabeth: *CM*, III, p. 51; IV, pp. 82–83. The only mention of her person is taken over from the summary of the year 1250 in the *Abbreviatio Chronicorum* where her appellation is simply 'andegravia duringia' with no reference to her relationship to the Hungarian royal family. *FH*, II, p. 373; *HA*, III, p. 318.

28 Two out of the five references to the Mongols in Europe mention the Kingdom of Hungary as the victim of the invasion, but none of these passages take over the references to *Hungaria major*, Poland, Russia, Bohemia, or Moravia. *FH*, II, pp. 292, 311. Entries on Eastern Europe and the Mongols, not in the *Flores*: *CM*, III, p. 639; *CM*, IV, pp. 9, 76–78, 106–07, 109–20, 270–77, 298, 386–89. Entries about Mongols only, not in the *Flores*: *CM*, IV, pp. 131–33, 337–44, 389–90, 544, 607–08, 634–35; V, pp. 37–38, 80, 87–88, 116, 191–97, 340, 654–55, 655, 660–61. No entries containing Mongol and Eastern European references in the *Additamenta* are copied in the *Flores*.

29 *FH*, II, p. 229; *FOH*, II, pp. 187–88. Corresponds to *s.a.* 1238 in *CM*, III, p. 488. This entry is universally copied into *Flores* manuscripts; for example, it is found in MS *J*, fol. 92ʳ; MS *Re*, fol. 203ᵛ, col. a; MS *Ar*, fol. 95ʳ; and MS *N*, fols 140ᵛ, col. b–141ʳ, col. a.

Temporibus etiam sub eisdem, non tantum partes Orientalium, immo jam Mediterraneorum et etiam Occidentalium, concussit et vehementer perterrit rumor, qui de Tartaris inhumanis et eorum exterminio ventilatus, omnia climate mundi pervolavit; ita ut videretur beati Metodii martiris prophetia effectum veritas evidenter sortiri.

> (At about the same time [1243], a rumour about the inhuman Tartars and of their destruction, which had reached all the regions of the world, violently shook and terrified not only the lands of the East, but indeed those of the West and the inland regions,[30] and, so that the prophecy of the blessed Methodius seemed to have been fulfilled.)[31]

Relinquishing Frederick's story as a conspicuous thread in the perspective and the function of the *Chronica majora*'s narrative, the distribution and proportions of the story of the Mongol invasion in Europe are different in the *Flores historiarum*. While the Mongol story in the *Chronica majora* was markedly Central European, especially the entries until 1246, the received portions of the *Flores* show a different picture. For example, although it is not made clear which regions are meant by these designations, the brief report above summarizes how *the fear* of the Mongol invasion moved on from Asia to Europe in the early 1240s.

Judging from the context in the *Flores*, specifically the passage about the Beguines following it, the text is intended as an abbreviated summary of the Mongol content of Ivo of Narbonne's letter to the archbishop of Bordeaux (*s.a.* 1243), which concerns the Mongols and is also closely followed by the entry on *De Beguinorum multiplicatione*.[32] Ivo's entry, however, is only used as a placeholder for the Methodius prophecy in the chronology of the redaction.[33] This confirms the suggestion in the previous

---

30 Before the term came to mean the region of the Mediterranean Sea (e.g. Isidore refers to it as 'Mare magnum' in the *De Origines*, 14.2), according to Lewis and Short it was simply used to designate landlocked, interior parts of a country. Lewis and Short, *A Latin Dictionary*, p. 1124b. Latham quotes a British example from *c.* 1400 using this term in a similar sense applied to the British Isles: 'mediterranei' designating the landlocked Mercians. See Latham, ed., *Revised Medieval Latin World-List*, p. 293.

31 *FH*, II, p. 267. My translation above is different than that in *FOH*, II, p. 220. This is an entry that was omitted from several *Flores* manuscripts. Found in MS *Ar*, fol. 99ʳ; omitted from MSS *J*, *Re*, and *N*.

32 *CM*, IV, pp. 270–77, 278.

33 As shown in the previous chapters, the Methodius prophecy appears elsewhere in the *Chronica majora*: at the beginning of MS *A* of the *Chronica majora* (fol. 15ʳ) in Matthew's late, more uneven hand, the actual prophecy in the *Additamenta* (MS *LA*, fol. 85ʳ), then noted (but not quoted) in Henry Raspe's subsequent letter: 'unde credimus ipsos esse gladium furoris Domini propter peccata populi Christiani, teste beato Metodio qui istos Tartaros vocat Ysmaelitas et onagros, silvestres asinos, &c.' (Wherefore we believe that they are the sword of the Lord's anger for the sins of the Christian people, as witness Saint

324   CHAPTER 7

chapter that the prophecy arrived after the clean copy of the chronicle was produced, and it was interpolated into the *Chronica majora* and the *Additamenta* later in the writing process (in Matthew's more aged hand), then integrated into the *Flores* narrative in place of Ivo's long rambling text. As a result, the 1243 *Flores* passage referring to these prophetic insertions in the chronicle has more to do with the apocalyptic expectations in the second half of the century than the Mongol military manoeuvres on the Continent.

Out of the Mongol-related accounts of the *Flores*, the last three concern the *memory* of their presence in Europe. After the first two entries under 1238 and 1243, the Mongols appear in an Eastern context under 1244 in an entry rephrasing the *Chronica majora*.[34] From 1245 onwards the Mongol-related passages, choppily abbreviating the original text (1245 and 1246), mention the Mongols in the context of their former exploits in Hungary:

> [1245] De Hungaria vel de Terra Sancta, propter Tartarorum et Chorosminum vastationem et propter regionum distantiam, nullus advenire valuit aut voluit.
> [1246] Anno quoque sub eodem amarissimae recordationis gens Tartarorum, exterminatis multis per eos regionibus orientalibus, reversa est hostiliter super regem Hungariae ut terram ipsius generali exterminio devastarent.

Methodias, who calls these Tartars 'Ishmaelites and wild asses', &c.). *CM*, VI, p. 78; *EH*, III, p. 451. See more in Chapter 6.

34 '[1244] Soldanus enim Babilonae, quem Templarii, rupto treugarum foedere per comites Ricardum inito, expugnarunt, in tantae injuriae vindictam Chorosminos in eorum direxit exterminium. Veruntamen Tartari memoratos Chorosminos a finibus suis in ore gladii prius propulsaverant, et sic miseri Christiani praeda praedae et praedonum, peccatis suis exigentibus, facti sunt'. (For the sultan of Babylon, whom the Templars had attacked, having broken the treaty of truce which had been entered into by Earl Richard, in revenge for an injury, urged on the Chorosmines to their extermination. But the Tartars had previously repelled the aforesaid Chorosmines from their territories with the edge of the sword, and so the miserable Christians became, as their sins had well deserved, the prey of robbers and plunderers.) *FH*, II, pp. 272–73; *FOH*, II, p. 226. Roughly corresponds to *s.a.* 1244 in *CM*, IV, pp. 299–300. The collapse of the Khwarezmian empire began with Ghinggis Khan's multipronged attack in the 1220s. Khwarazmshah Muhammad II fled and died soon thereafter. His successor, Jalal ad-Din Mingburnu, spent the rest of his life struggling against the Mongols and the Seljuks of Rum. After his death in 1231, a mercenary group called Khwarezmiyyas, consisting of former emirs of Jalal al-Din, emerged, followed by the emergence of other independent groups called Khwarezmiyyas, ranging from Anatolia to the Indian subcontinent. The 'Chorosmines' of the *Chronica majora* are these self-governing groups, who defeated the Frankish Kingdom of Jerusalem in 1244 and besieged Damascus in 1246.

(And no one was either able or desirous to come from Hungary, or from the Holy Land, on account of the devastations of the Tartars and Corosmines, and the distance of those countries.)[35]

(The same year, too, the nation of Tartars of the most bitter memory, after many of the kingdoms of the east had already been destroyed by them, returned in a hostile manner to attack the king of Hungary, with the intention of devastating and spreading general destruction through his territories.)[36]

And there is also new material in the continuation under the year 1261. A much lengthier passage on a renewed attack on Hungary finally shows the papacy in action, the lack of which was a leitmotif in the *Chronica majora*:

> Circa idem tempus dominus Papa cum nuper decrevisset Concilium suum generale in quindena Paschae Romae celebrare, archiepiscopo super hoc Cantuariensi, ut dicebatur, praemunito, audito tandem viciniore incursu Tartarorum in Christianos, praedictum tunc distulit decretum, et fratrem Walterum de Reigate in Angliam misit, super hoc et alia salubriter provisurum. Postea vero audiens idem Papa praedictos Tartaros usque ad lii. milia in Hungaria trucidatos, timensque residuos sibi caeterisque Christianis in brevi nocituros, summoneri fecit omnes praelatos transalpinos et viciniores; ut citra festum Apostolorum Petri et Pauli Romae conveniant, provisuri qualiter praedictis cautius inimicis resistant.

> (About the same time, though the lord the pope had lately determined to hold his general council at Rome, in the fortnight after Easter, having (as it was said) already informed the archbishop of Canterbury of this intention, afterwards, when he heard of the invasion of Christendom, by the Tartars coming nearer, he postponed the fulfilment of this decree, and sent brother Walter de Reigate into England, to make wise arrangements as to this and other matters. But afterwards, when the pope heard that fifty-two thousand of these Tartars above mentioned had been slain in Hungary, fearing that the remainder would soon do him and

---

35 *FH*, II, p. 292; *FOH*, II, p. 245. Corresponds to *s.a.* 1245 in *CM*, IV, p. 430. This is omitted from some manuscripts, for example, MS *J*, but it is copied in MS *Re*, fol. 214ᵛ, col. b; MS *Ar*, 102ʳ; and MS *N*, fol. 150ᵛ, col. b. Although there are mentions of them in relation to the Tartars' devastation prior to the European invasion (*s.a.* 1244, *CM*, IV, pp. 299–300), the emergence of the Khwarezmians in the *Chronica majora* dates to 1245, as a recurring theme in the text about the Council of Lyon.

36 *FH*, II, p. 311. *FOH*, II, p. 264 (Yonge's translation amended here). Paraphrase of *s.a.* 1246 in *CM*, IV, p. 547. This is omitted from several *Flores* manuscripts, for example, MSS *J*, *Re*, and *N*. It is, however, copied over into MS *Ar*, fol. 102ʳ.

the rest of the Christians much injury, he caused the Transalpine prelates, and all, too, who were nearer Rome, to be summoned to meet at Rome before the feast of the Apostles Peter and Paul to consider how they might offer the most effectual resistance to the aforementioned enemies.)[37]

Where the news of fifty-two thousand slain came from remains a mystery, but the entry clearly refers to the time when Pope Alexander IV wrote letters calling for provincial councils to address ways of dealing with the renewed Mongol threat. In England, the archbishop of Canterbury and the papal legate Walter de Rogatis convened a provincial council in London in the spring of 1261 and sent proctors to Rome with the council's proposals for aid. Henry III objected to legislating in the absence of royal representatives in the council and wrote a letter intended for Alexander IV to that effect.[38] The news appears in narrative sources on account of the scandal that broke out between Henry III and the pope, but the concomitant Mongol information is no doubt important — especially considering how precious little we know about the history of Mongol incursions into Eastern Europe after the Mongol campaign of 1241–1242.

To delve deeper into the mirror maze in the present longitudinal discussion of the Mongol-related texts, a brief overview of the afterlife of the *Flores historiarum* also merits a short digression here despite the paucity of Mongol-related texts therein. While the *Flores* slowly faded out of use and was superseded by newer productions, it would be once again in the limelight in the middle of the fourteenth century: continuations, especially those associated with London, resuscitated the old narrative by complementing it with a new batch of information and collating it with eminent works of different historical traditions. For example, John of Tynemouth certifiably used both the St Albans chronicles and Higden's innovative *Polychronicon*, one of the major historical narratives developed in the course of the fourteenth century.[39] Even though he devotes nearly a whole folio to St Elizabeth 'filia regis hungarie' and her husband, as

---

37 *FH*, II, p. 465. *FOH*, II, p. 393. This entry is omitted from some *Flores* manuscripts, for example, it is not found in MSS *J* and *Re*. It is copied over into MS *Ar*, fol. 120ʳ; and MS *N*, fol. 170ᵛ, col. b.

38 Bird, Peters, and Powell, eds, *Crusade and Christendom*, p. 332.

39 The *Historia Aurea*, a world history down to 1347, survives in a number of manuscripts. As Sally Harper notes, John of Tynemouth's association with St Albans is unclear as there is no direct evidence that he was a monk there. Fourteenth-century Thomas Gray and Henry of Kirkestede refer to him as a secular cleric: John, vicar of Tynemouth. John Taylor, based on a note in the Durham manuscript of the *Historia Aurea*, argues that he may have been identical with John Whetely (Wheatley, Yorkshire), vicar of Tynemouth after the 1350s. Harper, 'Traces of Lost Late Medieval Offices?', p. 7. Harper cites Taylor, *English Historical Literature in the Fourteenth Century*, pp. 60, 104–05. For the Sibylline prophecies in the *Historia Aurea*, see Spence, *Reimagining History in Anglo-Norman Prose Chronicles*, pp. 37–38.

THE AFTERLIFE OF MATTHEW'S MONGOL STORY   327

well as a lengthy account of the conflict between Mongali/Tartari and the 'Sultan of Babylon', his *Historia Aurea* (*c.* 1350) does not contain Matthew's Mongol-related entries.[40] In turn, his work later influenced Thomas Walsingham's continuation of the St Albans chronicle.[41] Walsingham was one of the few continuators who had access to and used the *Additamenta* at St Albans but picked up no references to the Mongols in Eastern Europe.[42] The continuation by Thomas Wykes, an Augustinian canon and an important user of the St Albans narrative, does not contain any references to the Mongols in Eastern Europe either.[43]

In sporadic snapshots found in later chronicles, the Kingdom of Hungary remained a zone of conflict and co-mingling with the Other, even when the texts describing the thirteenth-century Mongol onslaught had fallen out of use. A unique entry about the Hungarian king and his dalliance with 'Saracens' appears in in MS *E*, the primary exemplar of the Merton branch of the *Flores* afterlife. It is also found in MS *N*, a compilation of various historical sources, which contains the *Flores* (Item 1) and its continuation to 1306. While this entry on Saracens and Hungarians cannot have been seen as part of the Mongol story by any reader of the chronicle, the fictitious account may have roots in various discourses

---

40 Cambridge, Corpus Christi College, MS 6 (probably owned and perhaps even commissioned by William Wintershill (d. *c.* 1435) the almoner of the Benedictine Abbey of St Albans), for example, has a large amount of material about 'Mongali'/'Tartari' in the 1290s portions, including an unfinished drawing of a Mongol man on the margin of fol. 256ʳ. John of Tynemouth's *Historia Aurea* manuscripts: London, Lambeth Palace Library, MSS 10, 11, 12; the oldest copy from Bury St Edmunds (Part II only, abbreviated, and with many additions), Oxford, Bodleian Library, MS Bodley 240; as well as abbreviated fifteenth-century copies probably associated with St Albans, Cambridge, Corpus Christi College, MSS 5 and 6, and London, BL, MS Harley 655; brief fourteenth-century summaries, London, BL, Cotton Rolls and Charters, Cotton Ch XIII 2, and MS Royal 13 E IX; and a five-book abridgment of the second half of the chronicle, Cambridge, Cambridge University Library, Dd X 22. Taylor, *Medieval Historical Writing in Yorkshire*, p. 32. More on CUL, Dd X 22 and other northern copies in Friedman, *Northern English Books, Owners, and Makers*, pp. 90–99.
41 Galbraith, 'The "Historia Aurea" of John, Vicar of Tynemouth'; Gransden, *Historical Writing in England*, II, p. 56. Walsingham's *Chronicon Angliae*, a continuation of the St Albans narrative, was also intimately tied to Ranulf Higden's *Polychronicon*. This is corroborated by the fact that some copies of Walsingham's continuation contain maps similar to the 'Evesham-type' maps originally found in copies of the *Polychronicon*. Barber, 'The Evesham World Map', p. 19.
42 Walsingham's manuscript of the *Gesta Abbatum* is London, BL, MS Cotton Nero D VII. 'The *Gesta Abbatum* set a model for future works, and it was continued up to the end of the fourteenth century by Thomas Walsingham, who used some of Paris's documents transcribed in the *Liber Additamentorum* to enlarge the original text'. Muñoz García, 'The Script of Matthew Paris and his Collaborators', p. 19.
43 Wykes's *Chronicon* has come down to us in one manuscript: London, BL, MS Cotton Titus A XIV, printed in Wykes, 'Chronicon vulgo dictum Chronicon Thomae Wykes'.

about the apostasy of the king that emerged before and after the Mongol invasion:

> [1287] Rex hungariae in tanta cordis cecidit caecitate, ut, fide christianorum relicta, se ad errorem sarracenorum transferret, magis eligens machometo servire, quam christo. Qui tanta calliditate est usus, ut convocatis fraudulenter quasi ad parlamentum in quadam insula potentioribus terrae suae ipsisque ad mensam sedentibus gratia comedendi Miramomelimus sarracenorum potentissimus supervenit cum viginti milibus bellatorum regem una cum omnibus christianis congregates ibidem in vigilia sancti Johannis baptistae secum violenter abducens. Itinerantibus namque christianis, tempus clarum in nubilum est conversum, subitoque grandinosa tempestas multa milia incredulae et perfide comitivae occidit, et christiani ad propria sunt reversi, cum sarracenis solo rege apostota gradiente. Hungari igitur, ipsius filium coronantes, in fide catholica permanserunt.

> (The King of Hungary sank into such darkness of heart, that relinquishing the faith of Christians, he converted into the errors of the Saracens, choosing to serve Muhammad instead of Christ. He used such cunning, that as the potentates of his land gathered in some island, deceitfully as if for a parliament, and as the same sat at the table to eat, Miramolinus,[44] the most powerful leader of the Saracens came upon them with twenty thousand fighting knights, violently abducting the king together with all the Christians that gathered there on the eve of St John the Baptist. In fact, the Christians having departed, a storm gathered fast and, turning the clear weather into clouds, killed many thousands of the faithless and perfidious retinue, and the Christians returned to their home, leaving only the apostate king behind with the Saracens. Then, the Hungarians, crowning his son, remained in the Catholic faith.)[45]

This episode entered under year 1261 in the *Flores*, miraculous and fictitious as it may be, is certainly a response to a very real problem: the Curia's growing dissatisfaction with the Hungarians' tolerance of Muslim rite and other 'pagan' peoples and with the unnerving proximity of the enemies of

---

44 Miramolinus is a Latinized version of amir al-Mu'minin, an Arabic title that is usually translated 'Commander of the Faithful', a generic term that may refer to one of several rulers. Already in 1199, Pope Innocent III wrote a letter addressed 'to the illustrious Miramolinus king of Morocco and his subjects, praying that they may attain knowledge of the truth and abide therein to their advantage'. Cheney, 'The Letters of Pope Innocent III', p. 24; Flannery, 'The Trinitarian Order and the Ransom of Christian Captives', pp. 140–41.

45 MS N, fol. 183^{r-v}; FH, III, pp. 67–68; FOH, II, pp. 483–84. Cf. Rishanger, *Chronica et annales*, p. 115.

THE AFTERLIFE OF MATTHEW'S MONGOL STORY   329

the Church in the middle of Europe.[46] Although it is tempting to look for a historical event that inspired this story, it is not very likely that it can be tied to a Hungarian king's person; as Nora Berend ascertains, 'mass, or even individual, conversion to Islam in thirteenth-century Hungary is a far-fetched idea; no documentation of any such case exists'.[47] However, while they may have been conflated with 'Saracens', the real danger to the Church in Hungary was the increasing influence of another non-Christian community: the Cumans. At a time of growing strife and anarchy among the nobility, Hungarian kings sought to turn the Cumans into the military basis for royal power within the kingdom. King Béla and his son Stephen (István), and even more so King Ladislaus (László) IV (1272–1290) and his Cuman mother Queen Elizabeth (Erzsébet), attempted to rely on Cuman military power.[48] This did not go unnoticed in the West, especially that the Hungarian prelates and papal legates were on the case.[49] The Salzburg annalist, for example, seems to be well informed about the

----

46 See, for example, the pope's letter to the archbishop of Kalocsa on 23 August 1225: 'Honorius III Papa Ugrino Archiepiscopo Colocensi. Audivimus insuper, quod Sarraceni per dissimulationem vestram multa in partibus vestris habent mancipia christiana, que cum emant libere quando volunt, pro arbitrio suo dominantur eisdem secundum ritum ipsorum ea vivere compellentes. Preterea, quod est plurimum miserabile, nonnulli rustici christiani sponte se transferentes ad ipsos, et eorum ritum sectantes, Sarracenos se publice profitentur, ex eo quod in plurimis levior Sarracenorum condicio, quam christianorum existit'. (We have heard that, because of your negligence, Saracens in your region own Christian slaves, whom they trade freely at will, and compel to live according to their own [Muslim] rites. Furthermore, most deplorably, some Christian peasants are spontaneously joining them [Saracens], following their religious rites and publicly declaring themselves to be Saracens. This is happening because in many ways the lot of the Saracens is easier than that of Christians.) Štilrajterová, 'Convivenza, Convenienza and Conversion', p. 194, n. 59. Citing *Codex Diplomaticus et Epistolaris Slovaciae*, I, pp. 221–22, n. 304.

47 Berend, *At the Gate of Christendom*, p. 86.

48 'The king spent much time in the company of the Cumans, adopted their attire and hairstyle, and was excommunicated and accused of becoming "pagan". Ultimately Cuman discontent brought about László's end; he was assassinated by the Cumans'. This and more on the Cuman influence in Hungary in Berend, 'Cuman Integration in Hungary', pp. 110–11.

49 For example, Legate Philip arrived in Buda to work on the conversion of Patarenes and Cumans. During his stay in Hungary between 1279 and 1281, the young king demonstrated an astonishingly inconsistent attitude and intentions regarding his Cuman subjects. During these years, the four-sided strife with constantly shifting allegiances between legate, king, barons, and Cumans resulted in a series of abduction cases, including that of Legate Philip by Ladislaus, then of the king by his own *comes* followed by a baronial rebellion against the king. Finally, the Cuman uprising was ended in the Battle of Lake Hód, where the heavy rain soaked the Cuman bows and arrows so the Hungarians overcame them easier. After the battle the king confirmed his wish to keep his country on the straight and narrow, as the Salzburg annalist phrases: 'et disponit se ad resistendum fidei christiane'. The story of the battle and the events leading up to it were known to Latin chroniclers to some extent, but their narration is patchy and unreliable; see for example, 'Annales Sancti Rudberti Salisburgensis a. 1–1286', pp. 806–08. For the most recent analysis of the events and the battle, based on the king's itinerary and charter evidence, see Zsoldos, 'Téténytől a Hód-tóig'.

330   CHAPTER 7

Cuman troubles in the kingdom of Hungary and revisits the situation regularly in the 1280s. At one point the story shows up in particularly striking proximity to another conversion theme circulating in European Latinity at the time: the conversion of the Tartars.[50] The story enjoyed a little more attention, repeated in Rishanger's chronicle, who increased the number of Muslim fighters to thirty thousand.[51]

The continuations of the *Flores* and their afterlife show the same diminishing pattern as Matthew's Mongol story fell into oblivion. Besides the (probably two) anonymous canons who produced a continuation of the *Flores historiarum* running from 1306 to 1341, more is known about a third one who was the author of a later continuation, starting in 1338. This was Adam Murimuth, canon of St Paul's Cathedral, prebendary in Eald Street and Neasdon, Hereford, and envoy to the king and other dignitaries frequently crossing the Channel to Avignon and Rome.[52] To 1303 Murimuth used a copy of the *Flores* he found in Westminster Abbey, and it is certain that for events beyond that date he used other Westminster sources too.[53] The last entry in his chronicle is from 1347. Murimuth's work survives in several copies to different extent.[54] While the popularity of Murimuth's chronicle ensured that the text of the *Flores* lived on in

---

50 'Annales Sancti Rudberti Salisburgenses a. 1–1286', p. 806. Significantly, the Tartar king's conversion also features in the Merton continuation of the *Flores historiarum s.a.* 1299, which (along with the *Reimchronic* and others) has been shown to contain analogies with the baptismal miracle in the medieval English chivalric romance *King of Tars*. *FH*, III, pp. 300–301; Perryman, ed., *The King of Tars*.

51 *S.a.* 1287 in Rishanger, *Chronica et annales*, p. 115.

52 *Chronicles of the Reigns of Edward I and Edward II*, pp. 255–370. His life and career are well documented by both autobiographical details in his own works and official documents. Gransden, *Historical Writing in England*, II, pp. 29–30.

53 Gransden, *Historical Writing in England*, II, p. 30. Murimuth himself explains that the chronicles he uses do not go beyond 1302, except some in Westminster, which run until 1305. Murimuth and Robert of Avesbury, *Continuatio chronicarum; De gestis mirabilibus regis Edwardi tertii*, p. 3.

54 Edward Maunde Thompson argues that London, BL, MS Harley 3836 (full text) was transcribed from London, BL, Add. MS 32167 (damaged and incomplete copy running to 1346). Other known manuscripts include London, College of Arms, MS Arundel 18 (ending in 1337, contains the continuation of Trivet); Oxford, Queen's College, MS 304 (contains Ickham, Boston's *Speculum Coenobitarum*, Trivet's *Annales*, and a further continuation to 1380); MS *Cl* (to the year 1341 followed by various documents, written for Henry Spenser, bishop of Norwich, around 1400); London, BL, MS Royal 13 A XVIII (contains Henry of Huntingdon's work too, compiled in fifteenth century out of mid-fourteenth-century manuscripts); Oxford, Magdalen College, MS 53 (fifteenth-century MS, contains Hemingburgh's chronicle and many of the documents in Claudius E VIII); London, BL, MS Harley 1729 (imperfect copy of Higden's *Polychronicon* with part of Murimuth's chronicle incorporated, to 1339); MS *Ca* (sixteenth-century miscellany containing Robert of Reading to 1325, continued by Adam Murimuth to 1345, and then John of R(?) in Westminster to 1367). Murimuth and Robert of Avesbury, *Continuatio chronicarum; De gestis mirabilibus regis Edwardi tertii*, pp. xvii–xxi.

various other compilations, the Mongol story, even the later episodes, was gone entirely.

The copies of Adam Murimuth's work are intimately intertwined with other fourteenth-century chronicles: it was a popular component in historical writing until the early fifteenth century, usually copied together with the *Flores*, and often appearing alongside the Dominican Nicholas Trivet's *Annales* and various documents concerning the wars it relates.[55] Trivet, born a year before Matthew Paris died, was a truly eminent representative of the next and last generation of thirteenth-century English historical writing. His Dominican narrative is infused with hagiographical episodes, miracles of mendicant saints in locations that for Matthew Paris, cloistered in Hertfordshire, were not yet visible (or relevant) half a century before.[56] What was lost in the *Flores* and its continuations was restarted elsewhere with Trivet's brief notes. For example, the Prester John–Mongol connection, a latecomer in the *Chronica majora*, was inserted at the beginning of the Mongol story as their *origo gens*, and Trivet's first note about the Mongol threat under the year 1202 (!) is furnished with this piece of information.

> Hoc anno, ut a plerisque traditur, coepit Tartarorum dominium; qui sub montibus Indiae in regione Tartara constituti, dominum suum regem Indiae David nomine, filium Joannis presbyteri, occidentes, ad depraedationem processerunt aliarum terrarum.

> (In this year [1202], as related by many, the dominion of the Tartars, who had settled in the Tartar region under the mountains of India, having murdered their lord, the king of India called David, son of Prester John, went on to plunder other lands.)[57]

---

55 For example, London, BL, MS Cotton Nero D X is a miscellany of various manuscripts, which claims to be Trivet's *Annales* continued by Murimuth, but in fact is a compilation of Trivet's *Annales* and an unidentified continuation of the *Flores*. Smith, 'Further Manuscripts of Matthew Paris', p. 6, n. 4. The damaged MS *O* also contains the *Flores*, continued by a version of Trivet, and then continued by Murimuth's text. This is the text that was probably used by Walsingham. Other manuscripts that contain both a copy of the *Flores historiarum* and versions of Murimuth's continuation are MSS *Cl*, *Lm*, *Lt*. See List of Manuscripts in Appendix 6. The first printed edition of the text was based on Oxford, Queen's College, MS 304, a very rich early fifteenth-century manuscript containing a wide range of chronicle sources, for example, Peter of Ickham, Henry of Kirkestede, Nicholas Trivet, and others, mostly written by the same hand. Consequently, the eighteenth-century edition contained Murimuth's *Continuatio* as the continuation of the annals of Nicholas Trivet, and other materials from the codex such as John of Boston's *Speculum coenobitarum*. Trivet, *Annales sex Regum Angli*.

56 For example, St Elizabeth's posthumous miracle 'in Praga vero, quae est metropolis Boemiae' related in the entry on Blessed Jordanes, OP. Trivet, *Annales sex regum Angliae*, p. 223.

57 Trivet, *Annales sex regum Angliae*, p. 171. The figure of David was also a fluid element of this nebulous story. When the news of his existence first emerged, he was still identical with

332 CHAPTER 7

While Matthew Paris did write about Prester John before and after the Eastern European cataclysm, only the later entries link the mysterious priest-king to the Mongol story.[58] A lengthy letter by the Dominican Prior Philip, inserted under 1237, notes that his dominions are filled with Nestorian heresy.[59] While this is the first instance in Matthew's chronicle that briefly mentions the progress of the Mongols (still in the East), Prester John's figure is not yet fused into the Mongol story through so many details as it was later.[60] This association arrived to St Albans much later than the writing of the bulk of the Mongol story. In fact, it is the Dominican's letter that connects the priest to the Mongol story but — copied into the *Additamenta* much later — it never made into the narrative proper of the *Chronica majora*.[61]

Trivet's other Mongol episode under 1241 is similarly anecdotal, bringing to mind Rubruck's brief note that the Mongol soothsayers 'prescribe the days which are auspicious or otherwise for undertaking every transaction, and for this reason they [the Mo'als] never gather their forces or make war without them giving the word: they would long since have

---

John: 'In 1220 the army of the Fifth Crusade was ensconced in the Nile delta, where after a protracted siege it had captured the city of Damietta. It was after this victory, and in the course of the arduous struggle with the Muslims who were endeavouring to recover the city, that rumours reached the crusade concerning a Christian King David, "commonly called Prester John", who had overthrown the Muslim sovereigns in Iran and was advancing to the aid of his co-religionists'. Rubruquis, *The Mission of Friar William of Rubruck*, p. 6. Later — when the longevity of the priest-king became untenable — David was dubbed as his son, as is seen in Trivet's passage.

58 The first mention is that of the famous letter of Prester John to Pope Alexander III (1181). *CM*, II, p. 316.

59 *CM*, III, p. 398; *EH*, I, p. 56. See the letter in the context of the Mongol story in Chapter 3 ('1237: Chaldeans, Medes, Persians, and Armenians') above.

60 For example, while the Franciscan William Rubruck in the mid-thirteenth century refers to the priest-king's letter to the pope, he explains that John was a 'mighty herdsman' who lived in a plain surrounded by great mountains and took control of the khan's kingdom when he died. 'The Nestorians called him King John, and only a tenth of what they said about him was true'; and thus, because the Tartars generally gave credit to what the Christians said, the fame of 'King John' spread through Asia. Rubruquis, *The Mission of Friar William of Rubruck*, p. 122. Half a century later, Marco Polo described him as a Christian prince to whom the Mongols paid tribute and whom they called 'in their own language' Un-Khan. When Prester John tried to divide the Mongol tribes to reduce their power, they rebelled and elected Chinggis Khan as their king — who, after conquering the Un-Khan's territory, married his daughter. By Marco's time, Prester John's descendant was a king and a Christian priest named George who, under the Great Khan, governed an oriental province (Tenduk) where Christians, Muslims, and idolaters lived side by side. Ramos, *Essays in Christian Mythology*, pp. 105–06.

61 *CM*, VI, p. 115. In Andrew's account, Prester John is slain by the Mongols, his daughter marries the 'king of the Tartars', and his monk — very much in line with Matthew's general concern about the discord between pope and emperor — exhorts the pope and Frederick II to be at peace. *CM*, VI, pp. 115–16.

reappeared in Hungary, but the soothsayers will not allow it'. This is a story that evolved and was added to the knowledge circulating in Latin writings about the history of the Mongol invasion not long after Matthew Paris had stopped writing the *Chronica majora* and the *Flores*.[62]

> Tartari, subactis Georgia, India, Armenia majore, ac Turkia, per unum de principibus Poloniam et Hungariam sunt aggressi; cum vero timerent intrare Hungariam, consulentes idola, dum hostias immolarent, tale accepisse feruntur responsum, 'Ite secure, quia spiritus infidelitatis et discordie vos praecedent, quibus inter se turbati Hungari vobis minime praevalebunt'. Nec fefellit eos augurium; nam ante Tartarorum introitum, rex et principes, clerus et populus, tanta inter se dissidebant discordia, quod dum neglecto apparatu belli, fugam coguntur inire, usque ad multa millia occiduntur.

>> (The Tartars, having subjugated Georgia, India, Armenia majora, and Turkia, were led against Poland and Hungary by one of the princes but being too afraid to enter Hungary, they consulted idols and sacrificed animals to be given a response as follows: 'Go safely, because the spirit of infidelity and discord will go before you, by which the Hungarians thus confused will not prevail over you'. The prophecy did not deceive them, for prior to the coming of the Tartars, the king and the princes, the clergy and the people, were warring in such discord that having neglected preparations for war, they were forced to flee until many thousands were killed.)[63]

The generation of English chroniclers flourishing only a few years after Matthew's death produced new histories that soon came to enjoy more traction than the version produced by Matthew and his successors. Their tone, their sources and anecdotes, and the context are all alien to the Mongol story taking place in Matthew's chronicle world, very simply because they operated in and described a vastly different oecumene than that of Matthew.

After the fourteenth century, English historiography was for centuries largely reliant on Ranulf Higden's *Polychronicon*, a handy compilation of older histories, and its successors. While older perennial favourites such as

---

62 Rubruquis, *The Mission of Friar William of Rubruck*, p. 241.

63 Trivet, *Annales sex regum Angliae*, p. 232. First published in print: *Spicilegium sive collectio veterum aliquot scriptorum*, p. 589. Tudor Sâlâgean cites this passage as evidence that the Mongols were intimidated by an 'attack on the Mongols led by "one of the Polish or Hungarian princes"', which is a rather tenuous interpretation considering 'Poloniam et Hungariam' are in the accusative agreeing with 'aggressi' (*aggredior, aggredieris, aggredii, aggressus sum* (Dep.) 'approach', 'advance', or 'attack') here. Sâlâgean, *Transylvania in the Second Half of the Thirteenth Century*, p. 15. A version of the story appears in William of Nangis's chronicle: Guillaume de Nangis, *Chronique latine*, I, pp. 195–96.

Bede's *Ecclesiastical History*, Henry of Huntingdon's *Historia Anglorum*, and William of Malmesbury's *Gesta regum Anglorum* were still in use to some extent, the *Chronica majora* fell into disuse. Matthew felt the prescient tremors of a changing world. Several years mentioning reports about earthquakes, solar eclipses, and other portents at an intensifying regularity are followed by his summary description of the signs in the middle of the century foretelling the end of the world. As it was written long after 1250 when the apocalypse was supposed to happen, obviously the passage is not about Matthew's own mid-century apocalyptic fears. Still, the portents are fearful and important:

> Maris ascensus insolitus et dampnosus, qualis non est praevisus. Una noctium visae sunt stellae infinitae cadere de caelo, ita quod simul et semel decem vel duodecim, hae in Oriente, hae in Occidente, Austro, et Aquilone, et in medio firmamenti, volitare viderentur, quae si essent verae stellae, nec una in caelo remansisset, nec potest inde in libro metheororum ratio reperiri manifesta, sed ut Christi commination mortalibus immineret, Erunt signa in sole, etc.

>> (An unusual and destructive rise of the sea took place, such as had never been seen before. During one night immense numbers of stars were seen to fall from the heavens, so that at one and the same time ten or twelve seemed to be flitting about in the midst of the sky, some in the east, some in the west, in the south and the north, which if they had been real stars, not one would have remained in the sky: and no evident reason could be found for this event in the book on Meteors, except that Christ's threat was impending over men.)[64]

Matthew was not writing about the end of the world, but the end of the world as he knew it; not the end of history, but the end of his *historia* and its fallen stars. As Antonia Gransden explains, a strong bias is a means of imposing unity on a history. In the case of the *Chronica majora*, this bias was his persistent and carefully considered hostility, partly derived from his predecessor at St Albans, Roger of Wendover, a bitter critic of King John.[65] In Matthew's polarized world dominated by a pervasive opposition on the grandest scale, the death of Frederick II and the subsequent

---

64 *CM*, v, pp. 192–93; *EH*, ii, p. 406.

65 Gransden, *Historical Writing in England*, ii, p. 456. By this time, the emergence of new orders, threatening monastic stability and interfering in secular matters, also proved to be permanent, which further aggravated the feelings of fragmentation and the hostility towards realigning the existing mindset about religious life and monasticism. For Matthew's antifraternalism and attitudes about the new orders in general, see Gransden, *Historical Writing in England*, i, pp. 372–73; Hoskin, 'Matthew Paris's *Chronica Majora* and the Franciscans in England'; the emergence of the new orders as the sign of the apocalypse, at p. 54.

uncertainty and chaos scrambled the lines. This poetic and terrifying description of the beginning of the end in Matthew's lived world presages the last decade of his chronicle world, which was quickly becoming increasingly unchartable after its true axis — the conflict between papacy and empire — became a thing of the past. The popularity of the abridged *Flores*, which more or less discarded this plotline, eclipsed the *Chronica majora*. Parallel to this, the next generation of chronicles emerged, which represented and talked to a new world, born on the day when the emperor died.

An Elizabethan Bestseller

As explained in the previous chapter, the *Flores* flourished — as *flores* should — for a long time before its significance waned, but where was the *Chronica majora* all this time? As Vaughan notes 'only a handful of later writers knew anything of the other works [i.e. other than the *Flores*], and it is indeed extraordinary that the *Chronica majora*, the fullest and most detailed of all medieval English chronicles, was virtually unknown outside St Albans during the latter part of the Middle Ages'.[66] With a surprising twist of fate, after some lurking in the dark, it was Matthew's pronounced anti-papal rhetoric that sixteenth-century apologists of the Reformation discovered and adopted to their purposes.[67]

The two autograph copies of the *Chronica majora* (parts 1 and 2 in MSS *A* and *B*) are now in Cambridge. Their previous owner was the avid book collector Matthew Parker (1504–1575), archbishop of Canterbury and vice-chancellor of Cambridge University, who devoted his life to salvaging medieval manuscripts after the dissolution of monasteries. He entrusted his collection to Corpus Christi College in 1574.[68] Prior to his ownership MS *B* is known to have been in the possession of Sir Henry Sidney, but its previous provenance is unknown.[69] MSS *C* and *LA*, the clean copy of the *Chronica majora* and the *Liber Additamentorum*, respectively, once belonged to statesman and antiquarian Sir Robert Bruce Cotton (1571–1631), whose grandson donated the whole 'Cotton Library' to trustees 'for Publick Use and Advantage' in the mid-eighteenth century. Little is known about the provenance of MS *C* before Sir Robert Cotton's

---

66 Vaughan, *Matthew Paris*, p. 154.
67 Phillpott, 'The Compilation of a Sixteenth-Century Ecclesiastical History', pp. 208–09.
68 As M. R. James notes, compared to the potentially large size and rich holdings of the St Albans library, it is curious that only five volumes in Parker's library are known to have come from there. James, *The Sources of Archbishop Parker's Collection*, p. 13.
69 Garnett, *The Norman Conquest in English History*, p. 310, n. 155.

336   CHAPTER 7

acquisition, other than the names of Robert Glover (d. 1588),[70] John Stow (d. 1605),[71] and Henry Savile of Banke (d. 1617).[72] What is significant regarding the afterlife of the text is that before Cotton's collection, John Stow is known to have provided Archbishop Matthew Parker copies of Matthew Paris's books to be printed. In his words 'this reuerend father making diligent search for the antiquities of the Brytons, and English Saxons, to the end those monuments might carefully be kept, he caused them to be well bound and trimly couered, and such wereof he knew very few examples to be extant (among the which was Matthew Paris, Matthew Florilegus, Thomas Walsingham & other, *all which he received of my hands*) he caused to be printed'.[73]

In the *Additamenta*, various continuations and additions prove that it remained in St Albans until the late fifteenth century. A hundred years later, antiquaries Edward Ferrers (d. 1564) and Henry Ferrers (d. 1633) may have been the next owners of the volume, but apart from some notes on Frederick II's will (fol. 202^{r-v}) they do not seem to have interfered with the manuscript. Cotton's ownership (his signature is on fol. 161^r) was more invasive than modern library practice: the original volume is known to have been rearranged first in the fourteenth century (when extra material was added), and then by Sir Robert himself. It took Richard Vaughan's meticulous work to reconstruct the original quire order of MS *LA* and separate the documents that were added to the volume much later than Matthew Paris's lifetime.[74]

As shown, manuscripts of the *Chronica majora* were with Archbishop Parker at various times in their history. Indeed, the archbishop had an instrumental role in the afterlife of the text, particularly in launching

---

70 Glover, a king of arms and antiquarian, probably acquired the chronicle for professional reasons: he was responsible for heraldic visitations in the North under the reign of Elizabeth I.

71 Historian and antiquarian, John Stow also had professional interests in the volume, and although the catalogue of the British Library lists his name in the provenance of the manuscript, it is unlikely that he ever owned it. He wrote a series of chronicles of English history, for example, *The Summarie of Englyshe Chronicles*, *The Chronicles of England*, *The Annales of England*, and *A Survey of London*. See Gadd and Gillespie, *John Stow (1525–1605) and the Making of the English Past*.

72 The volume is listed as part of Henry Savile of Banke's collection (no. 21 in London, BL, MS Add. 35213, fol. 5), and it has marginalia in Savile's hand on fols 9 and 20. Watson, *The Manuscripts of Henry Savile of Banke*, p. 21. Based on bibliographical research, it is inferred that most of the items on the list ended up in six large collections after his death in 1617, one of them being the then incipient Cotton library. Watson, *The Manuscripts of Henry Savile of Banke*, p. 12.

73 Gadd and Gillespie, *John Stow (1525–1605) and the Making of the English Past*, p. 22 (my italics).

74 Chapter 5 in Vaughan, *Matthew Paris*, pp. 78–91.

the career of the long-dormant codices in print.[75] Parker was not only a collector of manuscripts, he also identified their author and often provided notes about them on end leaves. His antiquarian process of collecting and preserving the manuscripts acquired occasionally affected their textual content, especially in cases when manuscripts reached him in an incomplete state. While he himself is known to have written into the manuscripts copiously, he also employed practiced scribes to restore the manuscripts by inserting leaves containing transcriptions of the missing texts, imitating the original script. 'Parkerian supply leaves' containing transcriptions of lost portions of text can be found in MS B, the first part of the *Chronica majora*, where Parker inserted seven leaves at the front.[76] One of the better-known secretaries who worked on Parker's manuscript projects was John Joscelyn, who often annotated the manuscripts he or Parker owned.[77]

In addition to collecting, and at times amending, the original manuscripts, he launched an extensive 'publishing programme', a sequence of editions of major English historians based partly on his own manuscripts, partly on others borrowed from fellow collectors. Besides the *Flores historiarum* (first published in 1567, then reissued in a much expanded edition in 1570)[78] and the *Chronica majora* (1571), the sequence included Joscelyn's edition of Gildas's *De excidio et conquestu Britanniae* (1567), Asser's *De rebus gestis Ælfredi regis* (1574), and Thomas Walsingham's *Ypodigma Neustriæ* and *Historia Anglicana* (1574).[79] Frederick Madden, particularly irate about Archbishop Parker's 'mischievous habit of supplying deficiencies', was a harsh critic of the publication: 'it is obvious that a text made up with this unbounded license (even if it gained somewhat in point of Latinity) can be of no authority or value, and it is to be regretted that some recent editors of historical works have taken the trouble to give various readings from the printed edition of Matthew Paris, which in many instances represent only the arbitrary corrections of Parker, his editor, or his printer. So far indeed, did this license extend, that occasionally several

---

75 His duty was bestowed upon him by Queen Elizabeth's council: in July 1568 the Privy Council issued letters authorizing his agents to search throughout the realm for 'auncient recordes or monuments written' to preserve those particularly because writings formerly kept in the monasteries 'are nowe come to the possession of sundry priuate persons, and so partly remayne obscure and vnknowne'. Cited in Graham, 'Matthew Parker's Manuscripts', p. 326.

76 Graham, 'Matthew Parker's Manuscripts', p. 326.

77 For example, the so-called D manuscript of the *Anglo-Saxon Chronicle*, which was probably in his possession before ending up in the collection of Robert Cotton. Graham, 'Glosses and Notes in Anglo-Saxon Manuscripts', p. 198.

78 *MW (1567)* and *MW (1570)*.

79 Graham, 'Matthew Parker's Manuscripts', p. 336; Robinson, '"Darke Speech"', p. 1062.

lines, or even an entire paragraph, are inserted, which will be sought for in vain in the manuscripts'.[80]

As for the passages comprising the Mongol story, Parker did not send readers on a wild goose chase as Madden found the case to be in other sections.[81] On the contrary, examining the afterlife of the Mongol passages, his contribution is more important than exasperating. Matthew Paris's works were truly rediscovered and reanimated by Archbishop Parker's circles: many other extremely important and prolific Elizabethan authors collaborating with Parker either gained access to or provided Parker with texts by Matthew Paris, whose oeuvre was clearly brought into the limelight in the sixteenth century — and not only in England. One of the most important historians who published Matthew Paris's text in the sixteenth century was John Bale (1495–1563), an ex-Carmelite friar turned evangelical reformer, whose *Catalogus* as well as other works included extracts from Matthew Paris's *Historia Anglorum*.[82]

Based on Bale's recommendation, Matthew's text was then used in the *Catalogus testium veritatis* by the Lutheran Matthias Illyricus Flacius in Germany, and various volumes of the *Magdeburg Centuries* compiled by the so-called Magdeburg Centuriators.[83] Bale is known to have spent some time in Frankfurt and Basel, when he was in exile during the Marian restoration in England. Later Flacius's rapport with Bale, in fact, resulted in the Lutheran associates' direct request to Queen Elizabeth to let them borrow English codices to help their work, and the index of the works required from England included 'Chronica Matthei Parys'.[84] Timothy Graham suggests that Bale's letter, 'if not a symptom that Parker was already attempting to locate manuscripts on his own account at this early stage of his archiepiscopate, nevertheless seems to have had an important impact on Parker's activity as a manuscript collector. It surely helped to alert him

---

80 *HA*, I, p. xxxv.

81 For his added note about the Mongols *s.a.* 1237, see notes 89 and 91.

82 Although John Bale is thought to never have read the *Chronica majora*, Philpott cites Thomas S. Freeman's opinion that later in his life he may have gained access to a copy. Phillpott, 'The Compilation of a Sixteenth-Century Ecclesiastical History', p. 217, n. 4.

83 The *Magdeburg Centuries* (1559–1574) is an ecclesiastical history of thirteen hundred years, divided into thirteen 'centuries' down to the end of the thirteenth century. Each century was systematically treated under sixteen uniform headings in all the volumes. It was compiled by Lutheran scholars, the 'Centuriators of Magdeburg', led by the Croatian-born theologian Matthias Flacius (Vlacich). A staunch critic of the papacy, his *Catalogus testium veritatis, qui ante nostram aetatem reclamarunt Papae* (1556) is a catalogue of anti-papal witnesses. Lyon, 'Baudouin, Flacius, and the Plan for the Magdeburg Centuries'.

84 The letter is now in Cambridge University Library, Add. MS 7489. Transcribed in Bale, 'A Letter from Bishop Bale to Archbishop Parker'. More about their co-operation in Jones, 'Matthew Parker, John Bale, and the Magdeburg Centuriators', p. 39.

to the need to seek actively for manuscripts before they were lost for ever'.[85]

The exchanges between the impoverished and 'bilious' Bale, the powerful Archbishop Matthew Parker, and the Centuriators are invaluable sources for the sixteenth-century history of medieval books and antiquarianism, and, more pertinent to the present subject, they also reveal that Matthew Paris's chronicle was available on the Continent at some point. Whether it was the *Chronica majora* or the *Flores*, or some other codex, is unclear. What is known is that the Centuriators sent a certain Bernard Niger (Schwarz) to Parker, and he arrived via Antwerp near the end of June 1561. Though Schwarz was commissioned to conduct research and collect sources for his Magdeburg collaborators, he did not arrive empty handed. He bore books by Flacius (*Disputatio de originali peccato et libero arbitrio* and *De Fide*) to serve as an exemplar for the quality of their doctrine and scholarship for the archbishop. Importantly, 'when Niger rode into Canterbury, he delivered some 60 leaves copied from those portions of Matthew Paris' *Chronicon* that the archbishop had been unable to obtain in England. Flacius opined that these excerpts would be especially useful to English men of law. Along with this gift he sent a list of English books he was willing to send to the queen if she desired them'.[86] Since the manuscript disappeared from sight after an unsuccessful Sotheby's sale by Nan Ino Cooper, the Baroness Lucas, in 1922, it is not possible to ascertain which Matthew Paris chronicle travelled to Germany — to be copied and returned to England in the sixteenth century.

The work of Archbishop Parker eventually captured and fossilized a uniquely Elizabethan version of Matthew Paris's chronicles.[87] Sometimes

---

85 Graham, 'Matthew Parker's Manuscripts', p. 324.

86 Jones, 'Matthew Parker, John Bale, and the Magdeburg Centuriators', p. 45.

87 There is no need to duplicate here the excellent research of George Garnett, who — similar to the present project — traced the historiography of a historical event (the Norman Conquest) across English chronicles. It suffices to quote the most relevant information about Parker's edition of the manuscripts of Matthew Paris: 'For the main text of the *Chronica majora*, or as Parker confusingly titled it, *Historia major*, he used the partial autograph to which he had gained access, split between Cambridge, Corpus Christi College, MSS 26 and 16. This St Albans manuscript had already been divided into two before Parker's day: the first part, from Creation to 1188, was then owned by Edward Aglionby of Balsall Temple, Warwickshire, and the Middle Temple; the second from 1189 to 1253, by Sir Henry Sidney, the putative owner of a witness of Quadripartitus which has since been lost. Parker treated both parts of the divided partial autograph as a copy text for his printed edition; indeed, he marked it up for the printer [...] the witness of Matthew Paris was not a sixteenth-century transcript, but a thirteenth-century original. In the case of Matthew Paris's autograph [...] the printer's inky thumb prints are sometimes visible in the margins. [...] Parker consulted a number of other manuscripts, including, for the text of the continuation of *Chronica majora* for the years 1254–1259, that from the king's library currently in the possession of the earl of Arundel, to which Bale had drawn his attention.

odd passages appear in the familiar story through Archbishop Parker's aforementioned efforts to complement missing passages, and they reverberate down the textual tradition through subsequent editions and translations. One such example, pertinent to the transmission of the Mongol story, ended up in Giles's nineteenth-century translation making Matthew's copy of Prior Philip's 1237 letter — the first entry to mention the Mongol threat in the *Chronica majora* — look more invested in later Mongol events than Matthew's text originally was.[88] In his edition, Giles appends a sentence to the letter:

> All these things this neophyte did through fear of the Tartars, dreading their violence, and not being able to obtain assistance from those whose protection he hoped for, he fled to the sacrament of the Christians, and thus received effectual and speedy assistance; and in time of prosperity, by compulsion of his nobles, he basely departed from the faith.[89]

Although Giles does indicate that the sentence is an interpolation, the reality is that it is not found in any of Matthew Paris's original manuscripts. In fact, a whole folio is missing from MS B at this point, so the text continues with 'The slaughter of the Knights of the Temple, near Damietta'. The end of Philip's letter and the text about the Nestorians is only found in the 'fair copy' in MS C. There is a Latin note in MS B, fol. 106[v] in a much later hand, perhaps that of Archbishop Parker or his associate, advising that 'hic deest unum folium sed in libro impresso suppletur ex alio exemplari' (Fig. 12). But the sentence about the 'fear of the Tartars' is not in MS C either; it has only 'Haec omnia' run through with a pen. Since both Parker and William Watts include the additional sentence without any indication of interpolation, it seems, as Luard suggests too, that it is Parker's late sixteenth-century invention:[90]

> Haec omnia fecit Neophytus ille timore Tartarorum, quorum impetum formidans, auxilium Machometi et eorum quorum speravit habere patrocinium, nec habere potuit, ad Christianorum sacramentum convolavit, et sic efficax et sestinum senserunt auxilium. Tempore autem prosperitatis, coactus per magnates suos, a fide turpiter resilivit.[91]

The resulting printed edition of 1571 was a composite text, which drew on both the *Chronica Majora* and the *Historia Anglorum*'. Garnett, *The Norman Conquest in English History*, p. 328.

88 See the discussion of Philip's letter in Chapter 3 above.

89 *EH*, I, p. 58.

90 *CM*, III, p. 399.

91 First edition in London: *HM* (1571), p. 590. Same in the Zurich edition: *HM* (1589), p. 426. Watts's seventeenth-century edition: *HM* (1640), p. 372.

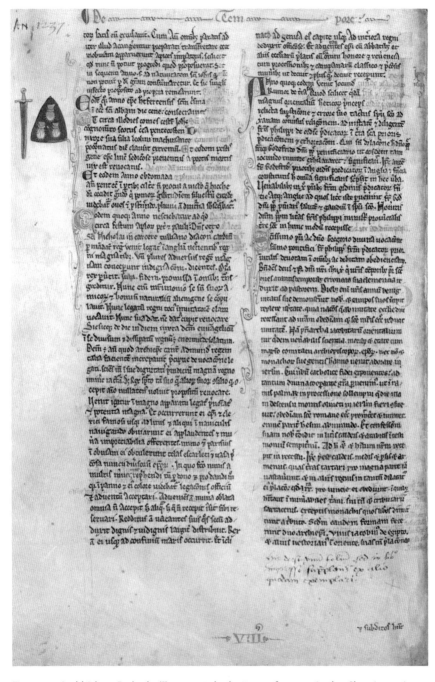

Figure 12. Archbishop Parker's (?) note at the bottom of a page in the *Chronica majora*. MS *B*, fol. 106ᵛ, col. b. The next leaf is torn from MS *B*. By permission of the Parker Library, Corpus Christi College, Cambridge.

342   CHAPTER 7

As demonstrated above, the *Flores historiarum* was continued in various manuscripts after Matthew Paris's death, and Parker printed it too. Despite attributing the *Flores* to a single scribe, a certain Matthew of Westminster, Archbishop Parker obviously collated his edition from more than one source. As a result, regardless of the paucity of materials in the actual manuscripts of the *Flores*, the printed version of the *Flores historiarum* by 'Matthew of Westminster' contains all the Mongol-related entries nearly verbatim, starting with 1239 (originally *s.a.* 1238),[92] through the reference to the Methodius prophecy in 1244,[93] to the first mention of them together with the 'Chorosmians' in 1244,[94] and in the context of the Council of Lyon in 1245.[95] He also faithfully copies the return of the Tartars to Hungary in 1246, although either by oversight or consciously, the Tartars here appear as simple 'barbarians'.[96] Mongols are briefly mentioned in 1260,[97] also taken from the continuation of the *Flores* word by word. The later

92 'Eo tempore, quaedam gens barbara et innumerabilis, dicta Tartari, partes Aquilonares Orientis miro vastarunt exterminio, magno pavore omnium Christianorum principes et populos concutientes'. *MW (1570)*, p. 150. Note that the pagination restarts after the first section ending at p. 440. Corresponds verbatim to *FH*, II, p. 229. This entry is universally copied into *Flores* manuscripts, for example, it is found in MS *J*, fol. 92^r; MS *Re*, fol. 203^v, col. a; MS *A*, fol. 95^r; and MS *N*, fols 140^v, col. b–141^r, col. a.

93 'Temporibus etiam [1244] sub eisdem, non tantum partes Orientalium, immo jam Mediterraneorum et etiam Occidentalium, conclusit ["concussit" in *Flores*] et vehementer perterruit rumor, qui de Tartaris inhumanis et eorum exterminio ventilatus, omnia climata mundi pervolavit; ita ut videretur beati Metodii ["martiris" in *Flores*] prophetia effectum veritatis evidenter sortiri'. *MW (1570)*, p. 176. Corresponds verbatim to *FH*, II, p. 267. This is an entry that was omitted from several *Flores* manuscripts, but found in MS *A*, fol. 99^r.

94 'Soldanus enim Babiloniae, quem Templarii, rupto treugarum foedere per comitem Ricardum inito, expugnarunt, in tantae injuriae vindictam Chorosminos in eorum direxit exterminium. Veruntamen Tartari memoratos Chorosminos a finibus suis in ore gladii prius propulsaverant, et sic miseri Christiani praeda praedae et praedonum, peccatis suis exigentibus, facti sunt'. *MW (1570)*, p. 180. Corresponds to *FH*, II, pp. 272–73. Roughly corresponds to *s.a.* 1244 in *CM*, IV, pp. 299–300.

95 'De Hungaria vel de Terra Sancta, propter Tartarorum et Corosminorum vastationem et propter regionum distantiam, nullus advenire valuit aut voluit'. *MW (1570)*, p. 294. Corresponds to *FH*, II, p. 292, and *s.a.* 1245 in *CM*, IV, p. 430. This is omitted from some manuscripts, for example, MS *J*, but it is copied in MS *Re*, fol. 214^v, col. b; MS *A*, fol. 102^r; and MS *N*, fol. 150^v, col. b. Although there are mentions of them in relation to the Tartars' devastation prior to the European invasion (*s.a.* 1244, *CM*, IV, pp. 299–300), the emergence of Khwarezmians in the *Chronica majora* dates to 1245, as a recurring theme in the text about the Council of Lyon.

96 'Anno quoque sub eodem amarissimae recordationis gens barbarorum ["Tartarorum" in the *FH*], exterminatis multis per eos regionibus orientalibus, reversa est hostiliter super regem Hungariae ut terram ipsius generali exterminio devastarent'. *MW (1570)*, p. 208. Corresponds nearly verbatim to *FH*, II, p. 311. Paraphrase of *s.a.* 1246 in *CM*, IV, p. 547. This is omitted from several *Flores* manuscripts, for example, MSS *J*, *Re*, and *N*. It is, however, copied over into MS *A*, fol. 102^r.

97 'Nunciatum enim fuit quod Tartari cum innumerabili procedentes potentia'. *MW (1570)*, p. 297; *FH*, II, p. 452.

THE AFTERLIFE OF MATTHEW'S MONGOL STORY   343

years, when the scribe begins to call the Tartars 'Moalli' in the continuation of the *Flores*, include 1274,[98] 1278,[99] 1289,[100] and 1299.[101] These are nearly all verbatim copies from the *Flores*, but not from one single copy.[102] And there are entries that do not correspond to the manuscripts surveyed by Luard for his well-known nineteenth-century transcription.[103] Matthew Parker's exemplar was fuller than the manuscripts Luard used: only one passage *s.a.* 1261 can be found in the continuation of the *Flores*; the rest of the Mongol-related passages in a long account of the Council of London and its role in what Jessalyn Bird and others termed the 'Mongol Crusades' are not included.[104]

---

98 'His diebus, cum Eadwardus in ciuitate Acon diutius expectasset Christianorum et Tartarorum auxilium, eo quod proposuisset per manum validam Saracenos delere, videns se ab utrisque delusum, quia Christiani ad propria recesserunt, et Tartari, qui et Moalli, intestina tyrannide perierunt, dimissis in Acon stipendaris, mare transit, applicans in regno Siciliae'. *MW (1570)*, pp. 352–53.

99 'Tartari Moalli Terram sanctam adquisierunt'. *MW (1570)*, p. 366. Also found in MS E (the so-called Merton manuscript) under 1261(!). *FH*, III, p. 249.

100 'Tartari, qui et Moalli, Poloniae Ducatum ingressi, ab eo in captiuitatem abduxerunt plusquam sexcenta millia personatim, paucis videlicet Christianis, septem vel octo admodum interfectis, et ut fertur Tartarorum cosideratio [*sic*] talis fuit, quod terras suas steriles redigerent in culturam'. *MW (1570)*, p. 376. Corresponds verbatim to *FH*, III, p. 69.

101 'Horum autem Tartarorum, ut fertur, miraculosa conuersionis extitit causa. Regis Tartarorum magni Cassani frater, Paganus, adamauit filiam regis Armeniae Christianam'. *MW (1570)*, p. 414. Corresponds verbatim to *FH*, III, p. 107.

102 For example, under the year 1288, Parker's edition contains the only Hungarian entry in the whole text where the kingdom is not mentioned in the context of the Mongol campaigns. This is not found in all of the *Flores* manuscripts. Parker may have used the Merton manuscript or MS M (the first part of which is an indirect copy from *Ch*, from 1298 it corresponds with *E*), MS N, or cognates to complement his text. *MW (1570)*, p. 375. This is the story of the apostasy of the Hungarian king, not related to the history of the Mongol invasion but found in MS N of the *Flores historiarum*, *FH*, III, pp. 67–68, and in Rishanger's chronicle. See note 45.

103 [1261] 'Annus etiam iste licet Terrae sanctae fuerit maxime pro Tartarorum incursione ut minabantur, formidabilis: Anglis tamen et Francis mortalitate excepta, bene dinoscitur tollerabilis'; 'Super his autem et aliis maxime ad resistendum Tartaris communiter provisis, nuntios discretos et generals prouiderunt Romam dirigere qui communi eorum bursa victuri, dominum papam possent super eorum responsis in Concilio praedicto, Romae celebrando, certificare'; 'Consilio praesulum provinciae suae, super executione praefati mandati apostolici contra Tartaros, qui iam orbem terrae maxima ex parte grauiter oppresserant, prout superius plenius demonstratur'. *MW (1570)*, pp. 303, 308, 309. MS E also has 'Ungari interfecerunt quinquaginta duo milia Tartarorum. Terram namque Ungariae suae ditioni sicut alias nationes, subdere nitebantur' under this year, but Matthew Parker's edition does not contain this passage. *FH*, III, p. 250.

104 This is the incident in which Matthew Paris's successor (at least in MSS *A* and *N*), relates how Pope Alexander IV wrote letters about the Tartar's intentions in the East and called for provincial councils to be arranged to dispute the potential countermeasures. Previously quoted at note 37. The letter is copied into the *Burton Annals* in full. 'Annales de Burton', pp. 495–99.

344   CHAPTER 7

Through important works like Parker's, each editing, adding, and subtracting a little or not-so-little, Matthew Paris's works continued to influence publications that embedded portions of his text or even publications of the original text transcribed and 'completed' where necessary. After Archbishop Parker's work, the transmission and dissemination are impossible to follow in their entirety due to the proliferation of works that used his edition in their own chronicles, primarily on account of the compatibility of Matthew's anti-papal sentiments with the prevailing historical ethos at the time. As Garnett points out, 'what made Matthew Paris an especially attractive prospect to Bale, to Flacius, and to Parker was that "no chronycle paynteth out the byshopp of Rome in more lyuely colours, nor more lyuely declareth hys execrable procedynges, than it doth".[105] In the same vein, William Stanley and Thomas Staveley, in their critical evaluation of politically biased historians, explain the sudden popularity of Matthew Paris, affectionately called 'an angry nibler', without mincing their words:

> Of the Historians which we have made use of in these discoveries, and Collections, you see we have been much beholden to Matt. Paris, who seldom spares to cry out, with great resolution, upon the corruptions of the Church in his time, and particularly upon the cruel exactions, and extorsions of the Popes, and their Creatures [...]. Thus, having set our honest Author rectus in Curia, upon the testimonies of so many creditable Witnesses, we may well conclude, That the Times, the Popes, and the Court of Rome were corrupted, and not the Historian: and that what we have of Matt. Paris is but the Eccho of the People's complaints, and groans, in those times, which sounding so harsh in the Romanists ears, it is no wonder they are so displeased to hear it.[106]

---

105 Garnett, *The Norman Conquest in English History*, p. 327, n. 275. Also cited in Phillpott, 'The Compilation of a Sixteenth-Century Ecclesiastical History', p. 206.

106 Ch. 23. 'Matthew Paris Vindicated', in Stanley and Staveley, *The Roman Horseleech*, pp. 180, 185. William Stanley (1647–1731) was master of Corpus Christi College, Cambridge, archdeacon of London, and dean of St Asaph. His co-author was Thomas Staveley (1626–1684), Cambridge-trained Church historian and antiquarian, famous for his anti-papist 'historical essays'. Their bitter invective against those who criticized Matthew Paris's reliability mentions by name John Pitz and Brian Twine: 'Which aspersions upon the credit of our Historian, induces me to make a little enquiry into his quality, and reputation: and that the rather, in regard I find two of our own Countrymen endeavouring also to throw some blots upon his credit, viz. John Pitz, a Collector of our English Writers, insinuating his discoveries of the corruptions of the Church in his time, *non ab ipso sic scripta, sed ab aliis illi falso ascripta fuisse*. And Brian Twine the Oxford Advocate, suspecting the fidelity of Archbishop Parker, in his Edition of Matt. Paris, could not vent, without endeavouring to blast the memory of a most reverend, learned, and faithful Prelate, whose great integrity, and fame, will ever stand impenetrable to the teeth of this angry nibler'. Stanley and Staveley, *The Roman Horseleech*, pp. 184–85.

THE AFTERLIFE OF MATTHEW'S MONGOL STORY 345

Martyrologist John Foxe (1516/17–1587) was certainly of this school, never too tired to chastise 'those wallowing continually in a most filthy puddle of pestilent error, not much vnlike to the Romish Synagogue in this our age'.[107] Both Foxe and Matthew Parker essentially developed Bale's ideas regarding Matthew Paris's relevance in their own time.[108] Foxe's *Acts and Monuments of Matters Most Speciall and Memorable*, enshrining Matthew's chronicle, was regularly republished in full and abridged versions until Samuel Maitland's works superseded it in the nineteenth century. His first edition of the *Acts and Monuments* was still using excerpts from the *Historia Anglorum* and contained but a brief summary of the medieval period, but the second edition, ending in the year 1260, was much more enlarged by the fact that he was able to consult and reframe Matthew's text.

The early reign of Henry III in the *Acts and Monuments* was almost entirely based on the *Chronica majora*, and Foxe cited folio references to Parker's manuscripts, held in the library of Corpus Christi College, Cambridge, to prove that he consulted original copies rather than lifting passages from Parker's edition of the text.[109] One of the major differences between Matthew's original and Foxe's narrative is that while Matthew embedded a variety of other speeches, documents, and dialogues to weave his story, Foxe flattened the narrative levels, which required stylistic intervention. Otherwise, he seldom changed the text in his translation, but he was highly selective about what he included and often added his own commentary.[110] Because of Foxe's agenda, the text is hinged upon the leitmotif of the pope's avarice and England's poverty. The events of the 1240s are summarized in the chapter entitled 'A brief table or declaration of the pope's unreasonable gathering, enactions, and oppressions' — Matthew's very own hobby horse — and even though he does rely on Matthew Paris heavily, the Mongol episodes are outside its purview entirely.[111]

In the seventeenth century, the *Chronica majora*'s Latin text was republished in its entirety with minor changes by William Watts (1640), which remained the definitive edition until Luard's transcription for the *Rerum Britannicarum Medii Aevi Scriptores* (Rolls Series). Watts worked from original manuscripts; it is known, for example, that the polymath lawyer,

---

107 Comparing the errors of papacy and Judaism in Foxe, *A Sermon Preached at the Christening of a Certaine Iew*, n.p.

108 Phillpott, 'The Compilation of a Sixteenth-Century Ecclesiastical History', p. 206.

109 Phillpott, 'The Compilation of a Sixteenth-Century Ecclesiastical History', p. 215.

110 Phillpott gives as an example Foxe's characterization of Legate Otto placing 'papal extortion and infringement of English rites and customs' in a teleological, historical context highly instructive and relevant for Elizabethan audiences. Otto's story in the *Chronica majora*, especially its imbrication with the Mongol story, is discussed in detail in Chapter 2. Phillpott, 'The Compilation of a Sixteenth-Century Ecclesiastical History', p. 210.

111 Foxe, *The Acts and Monuments*, p. 420.

346   CHAPTER 7

scholar, and parliamentarian John Selden (1584–1654) lent his own manuscript to him for his edition.[112] Watts's edition reproduces the history of the Mongol invasion across the narrative faithfully. Starting with the Dominican Friar Philip's letter *s.a.* 1237 (containing the previously mentioned note about the neophytes),[113] the history of the Mongol invasion follows Matthew's original. In a 1238 entry entitled 'Tartari terras Septentrionalis devastant', the whole episode with the bishop of Winchester is recounted verbatim.[114] Entries under the years 1240 and 1241 also saved a great deal of Matthew Paris's Mongol story. For example, Matthew's first lengthy description of the Mongols, originally entitled by Matthew Paris as 'Quomodo Tartari resumptis viribus de montibus suis prorumpentes, Orientalium multis finibus vastatis, etiam Christianos jam perterruerunt' (here simply as *Erupta Tartarorum*),[115] is copied without any alteration besides unpacking the medieval abbreviations and ligatures.[116] Frederick's letter to the English king about the Mongols enclosed in Henry Raspe's letter dated to 1241,[117] the Hungarian king's request for Frederick's help under the year 1244,[118] and so on, everything found in the *Chronica majora* about the Mongols is faithfully reproduced in Watts's edition. Even the bundle of Mongol-related letters in the *Additamenta* are all found verbatim diligently cross-referenced to passages in the main text.[119]

The sixteenth- and seventeenth-century preoccupation with Matthew Paris's histories was not restricted to producing text editions. Along other expansive medieval histories, such as Geoffrey of Monmouth or the twelfth-century *Chronicon ex chronicis* attributed to Florence of Worcester, it was a much-respected primary source for historians who began to depend on these critical editions rather than the less accessible manuscripts. For example, lesser known histories by the aforementioned John Stowe, as well as William Camden (1551–1623) and William Prynne (d. 1669), also embraced portions of the *Chronica majora*. After the hiatus of the *Chronica majora*'s Mongol story in the later Middle Ages, Matthew Paris's Elizabethan revival and the subsequent editions brought his texts back into the limelight. But the fame was waning again: as the historians' libraries

---

112 Toomer, *John Selden*, I, p. 104.

113 *HM (1640)*, p. 441. See notes 89 and 90.

114 *HM (1640)*, p. 471; *HM (1684)*, pp. 398–99. This entry is copied verbatim from MS B, fols 116ᵛ, col. b–117ʳ, col. a; *CM*, III, p. 488; *EH*, I, p. 131.

115 MS B, fol. 140ᵛ, col. b; *CM*, IV, pp. 76–78; *EH*, I, pp. 312–13.

116 *HM (1640)*, pp. 546–47; *HM (1684)*, p. 487.

117 *HM (1640)*, pp. 558–60; *HM (1684)*, pp. 497–98.

118 *HM (1640)*, p. 618.

119 *HM (1640)*, pp. 211–14. The *Chronica majora* is continued until 1273 (p. 1009) and the *Additamenta* documents are found at the end of the volume, after concordances, variant readings, indices, and the *Vita Offarum*. The page numbering restarts at each additional item.

THE AFTERLIFE OF MATTHEW'S MONGOL STORY   347

swelled at a hitherto unparalleled pace,[120] they picked fewer and fewer references from Matthew Paris.

Although no longer invested in retelling the Mongol story in any lengthy way, historical treatises did pick up on interesting titbits from it. The popular *Hakluytus Posthumus or, Purchas his Pilgrimes* by Samuel Purchas, for example, contains Ivo of Narbonne's letter.[121] At the same time, others still preferred going *ad fontes*. The previously mentioned John Selden, who lent Watts his copy of the manuscript, furnishes his own text with precise references to the original source in notes like this:

> But in the manuscript copy of Matthew Paris, which I use, in a very antient hand, these words are noted in the upper margin over the year MLXX. *Hoc anno seruitium baroniae imponitur Ramesiae.* It seems that the volume belonged to the abbey of Ramsey, and so some monk of the house noted that in the margin touching his own abbey, which equally concerned the rest of the abbeys that were meant in relation.[122]

Selden's works on English medieval history, including Eadmer and his contributions to Matthew Paris and Twysden's *Decem Scriptores*, are unduly neglected in modern scholarship where the importance of his antiquarianism is dwarfed by his immense oeuvre in natural law and treatises discussing political/moral issues prevalent in the discourse of his age. But in Rosenblatt's words, Selden had 'a humanist's respect for historical investigation and an antiquarian's interest in the documents of the past simply because they exist'.[123] For example, one significant milestone in English history on which seventeenth-century authors turned to Matthew Paris's authority is the Magna Carta.[124] As David Carpenter points out, Selden wrote about the Magna Carta in his *England's Epinomis* (1610), where he contrasted the Matthew Paris text of the 1215 charter with the printed text of the charter of 1225.[125]

---

120 Jurist and politician Sir Edward Coke's library at Holkham, for example, contained a staggering amount of history books, including all the volumes Archbishop Parker ever published. Boyer, *Sir Edward Coke and the Elizabethan Age*, p. 140.

121 Purchas and Hakluyt, *Hakluytus Posthumus*, pp. 183–87. Original edition Purchas, *Purchas his Pilgrimage, Or, Relations of the Vvorld*.

122 Selden, *Joannis Seldeni jurisconsulti opera omnia*, III, col. 728.

123 Rosenblatt, *Renaissance England's Chief Rabbi*, pp. 160–61, n. 10.

124 The Magna Carta, of course, was most often studied by jurists and political theorists. Judge Edward Coke who used Matthew's version, for example, owned at least three different versions of the Magna Carta but does not seem to have recognized that it existed in variant editions. Boyer, *Sir Edward Coke and the Elizabethan Age*, p. 141. More on the entanglement between the study of law and history in Styles, 'Politics and Historical Research in the Early Seventeenth Century'.

125 Selden did not yet know that Paris's text was a hybrid of the Charters of 1215, 1217, and 1225. Thompson, *Magna Carta*, pp. 239–42. Cited in Carpenter's brief study of the copy of

348   CHAPTER 7

Similar to the way in which Matthew Paris was plundered for anti-papist passages in the previous century, his works for Selden (and other well-known scholars of his age such as Samuel Purchas and Thomas Barlow) were becoming interesting for another topic: the Jews. While Rosenblatt argues that it was his respect for the 'documents' that overcame Selden's healthy scepticism when he borrowed Matthew's stories of Jewish ritual murders in his brief *Treatise on the Jews in England* (1617), the horrific medieval accounts were at this time beginning to be cited with a more thoughtful and critical approach than Matthew's original.[126] Thomas Barlow, for example, who (since Selden spoke Hebrew) relied heavily on John Selden's relevant writings, puts forward general arguments that were rather sympathetic. He cites examples from Matthew Paris and others to suggest that the Jews' 'readmission' — hence the subtitle *De Judaeis in Reipublica Christiana tolerandis, vel de novo admittendis* — would 'constitute moral reparations for past suffering':

> It appears by our Story that the Jews (at their Expulsion, and many times before) were not only Unchristianly, but Inhumanely and Barbarously used; and then seeing Commonwealths and Societies never die (though particular Persons do) it may be a Question whether the Common-wealth of *England* now are not bound in Conscience and Equity to make some Satisfaction by real Kindness and Civility to the present *Jews* for the Injuries the same Common-wealth did to their Progenitors then?[127]

What is relevant for the present discussion, however, is how much of Matthew's Mongol story seeped into the works of an erudite Englishman who was both very familiar with Matthew Paris's works and seemingly

---

Magna Carta 1215 is Selden's volume, London, Lincoln's Inn, MS Hale XII, fols 184^r–188^v: Carpenter, 'A Lost Engrossment of the 1215 Magna Carta?'.

126 Gerald J. Toomer argues that Selden's position on the matter is not at all straightforward. His history of the Jews appears in the third edition of Samuel Purchas's *Pilgrimage* (1617), and parts of it — such as a reference to 'one cruell and (to speake the properest phrase) Jewish crime […] usuall amongst them' — sound like Purchas rather than Selden. In fact, Toomer proposes that Selden, reproducing his sources in a mostly straightforward narrative, 'was already too much of a skeptic to endorse the stories of Matthew Paris as is done in Purchas's rendering'. There is also evidence in a thoroughly anti-Jewish William Prynne passage suggesting that Purchas meddled with Selden's text. Toomer also brings as evidence a copy of the *Treatise* that seems to derive directly from an archival source and is accompanied by one of Selden's characteristic learned notes suggesting that the episode was not about an accusation of ritual murder but rather of forced circumcision in Norwich. Toomer, *John Selden*, I, pp. 168–70, 384–85; Rosenblatt, *Renaissance England's Chief Rabbi*, pp. 160–61, n. 10; Haivry, *John Selden and the Western Political Tradition*, p. 347. Seldon's ambiguous two-page piece is in Purchas, *Purchas his Pilgrimage, Or, Relations of the Vvorld*.

127 Barlow, *Several Miscellaneous and Weighty Cases of Conscience*, p. 37. Cited in Rosenblatt, *Renaissance England's Chief Rabbi*, p. 174.

also interested in the world of the Tartars. Selden, for instance, refers to Matthew as 'an old monk, speaking of the Tartars' victories over the Saracens, Arabians, and the rest of Asia' quoting the line 'factisque sunt eisdem Tartaris multitudo gentium in tributum, soldani videlicet, admirabiles, et principes, etiam caliphi'.[128]

Here, it is notable that Selden had first-hand information and plenty of more up-to-date literature about Tartary and matters *Asiatick* in general. One eminent piece of evidence for the latter is the so-called Selden Map of China, an early seventeenth-century map showing the maritime trade routes in Asia. The map, which looks like a landscape painting with detailed annotations in Chinese of administrative seats in Ming dynasty China as well as cities and ports in Asia, was in John Selden's possession, and he donated it to the Bodleian Library, Oxford, in his bequest of 1654.[129] And indeed, a brief glance at Selden's impressively informed passages on *Tartar* matters shows that though he was aware of Matthew's authority on the Mongol invasions of the thirteenth century, he chose to rely on fresher, more relevant material; for example, his discussion of the forms and designations (titles of honour) of lordship in Asia shows a wealth of references he consulted — ancient, medieval, and very recent alike.[130] Matthew's Mongol story is reduced to 'those great irruptions of the Tartars' citing in the footnotes the Russian 'Archbishop' Peter's testimony, or in Selden's words, *epist[ola] Petr[i] arch[iepiscopi] Russiae ap[ud] Matth[aei] Paris[iensis]*. The 'old monk, speaking of the Tartars' victories over the Saracens, Arabians, and the rest of Asia' was becoming outdated and fell out of use, despite — or rather, because of — the West's steady thirst for knowledge and exoticism regarding the Mongols, whose history and presence on the Continent was gaining new depths through

---

128 Selden, *Joannis Seldeni jurisconsulti opera omnia*, III, col. 954.

129 The 'rediscovery' of the map in 2008 by the historian Robert Batchelor with the help of the Bodleian librarian David Helliwell has initiated a burst of research interest in the history and interpretation of the map. Since 2008, a number of books have been written about the map, and the Bodleian Library has launched a special exhibition devoted to it. See references in Kogou and others, 'The Origins of the Selden Map of China', p. 1.

130 Selden cites an impressive list of authorities who informed his work on Mongol titles in the volume: Odoric of Pordenone, John of Plano Carpini, Het'um of Armenia, Vincent of Beauvais, and his near contemporary Martinus Broniovius (Marcin Broniewski) who was Stephen Bathory's ambassador to the Crimean khan, Mehmed Giray, in 1578–1579. Broniewski's *Tartariae descriptio* (Cologne, 1595) is a travel diary describing towns and castles in Crimea and the way of life of Crimean Tatars. Selden, *Joannis Seldeni jurisconsulti opera omnia*, III, cols 185–87.

350 CHAPTER 7

ethnographic accounts, diplomacy,[131] literature,[132] marvels (see Fig. 13), and even people exhibited in freak shows.[133]

The Mongol story written by chroniclers and travellers in the Middle Ages enjoyed a rare longevity, and with the rise of a nascent form of Orientalist discourse, the English perception of the Mongols and their contact with Europe was at once becoming conceptually cemented and textually fragmented. As Eric Song reminds us of Edward Said's concept of 'the reservoir of accredited knowledge, the codes of Orientalist orthodoxy', 'certain orthodoxies about the Tartars established in medieval narratives remain firmly in place in early modern writings'.[134] And so they remained despite the fact that eclipsing the old historical accounts, new, original materials were gaining widespread popularity among the men of letters in England, for example, the aforementioned Selden map or Giles Fletcher's description of the Tartars in his report on Russia (c. 1589).[135]

Going further, observing that the 'Tartars are consistently described not as a unified political entity but as a teeming menace to the very concept of stability' despite the enormous cultural and geopolitical shifts between travel accounts of the thirteenth century and descriptions of Tartary in the sixteenth, Eric Song refers to medieval images of the Mongols in William of Rubruck's travelogue.[136] This image, the concept of swarming, unbridled, and amorphous alienage, however, goes a little further back

---

131 Besides the aforementioned Broniewski's travels available in Latin, examples include Scottish translator, impresario, and cartographer John Ogilby's contributions to the field, who translated Nieuhof, *An Embassy from the East-India Company*; and Arnoldus Montanus and Olfert Dapper, *Atlas Chinensis*. The anonymous English translation of *Historia de la conquista de la China por el Tartaro* in Palafox y Mendoza, *The History of the Tartars*.

132 Perhaps the most well-known English literary reference is Cambinskan's (Chinggis Khan) appearance in Chaucer's *Canterbury Tales* (Squire's Tale), and Milton's version in the *Il Penseroso*: Cambuscan, the 'Tartar king' riding a horse of brass that would take him wherever he wished to go. *The King of Tars* is relevant here on account of its analogies with the *Flores historiarum*, specifically its continuation in the Merton group where the chronicler's account of the defeat of the Saracens at Aleppo (1299) has been shown to contain analogies with the story. *FH*, III, pp. 300–301; Perryman, ed., *The King of Tars*; Herlands Hornstein, 'The Historical Background of the King of Tars'.

133 A number of giants and prodigies were exhibited in London in the seventeenth century, for example, Samuel Pepys's clerk, James Paris du Plessis, records in his *History of Human Prodigies* that he has seen the 'Prodigious Tartar' on display in London. Thompson, *The History and Lore of Freaks*, p. 149. Du Plessis's manuscripts (c. 1730–1733) are in London, BL, MSS Sloane 5246 (1730) and 3253 (1732).

134 Song, 'Nation, Empire, and the Strange Fire of the Tartars', p. 120.

135 The latter was extensively used by John Milton in his own *Brief History of Moscovia*, in which the poet described it as 'judicious and exact'. For his account 'unhampered by any eyewitnessing of his own', Milton plundered Hakluyt and Purchas, and made occasional references to Giles Fletcher's *Of the Russe Common Wealth* (1591), and to various other accounts of the experiences of travellers. Bedford, 'Milton's Journeys North', p. 80.

136 Song, 'Nation, Empire, and the Strange Fire of the Tartars', p. 120.

THE AFTERLIFE OF MATTHEW'S MONGOL STORY   351

Figure 13. The Croatian-Hungarian Count Nicholas Zrinyi's victories over the Ottomans were transformed into curious Tartar-themed materials, such as this printed sheet. Anon., *The Exact Effigies of a Monstrous Tartar Taken in Hungary by the Valour of the Noble Count Serini February, 1664*. London, printed for W. Gilbertson at the [...]; and H. Marsh at the Princes Armes in Chancery Lane, 1664. Retrieved from <https://search.proquest.com/books/exact-effigies-monstrous-tartar-taken-hungary/docview/2240930862/se-2?accountid = 15607>.

352 CHAPTER 7

than Rubruck and other travellers' accounts: the resilient image of the Mongols in England certainly has its roots in the 'accredited knowledge' of eyewitness accounts and documents moulded into the *Chronica majora*'s complex narrative about the first encounters with the Mongols in Europe.

Back to the Future: Modern Historiography

Once again acknowledging that it is beyond the scope of the present volume to address all the antiquarians and scholars of history (and everything in between) who used Matthew Paris's Mongol passages, I will now leave behind the deliciously garbled Carolean image of the 'monstrous Tartar' and leap ahead to more recent developments.[137] Perhaps the single most momentous event in the biography of a manuscript is when it becomes available in a printed edition with critical apparatus in the modern sense. For over two hundred years, the definitive edition available for scholars was that of Watts, which was conscientiously reprinted over the years. Along with Matthew Parker's even older print edition, it remained the accessible gateway to Matthew Paris's world until the publication of the — hitherto most recent — critical editions in the *Rerum Britannicarum Medii Aevi Scriptores* (Rolls Series) and, about a decade later, excerpts in the Monumenta Germaniae Historica.[138]

Nineteenth-century scholars working on manuscripts from St Albans faced a vast number of very similar texts across dozens of libraries and had to piece together the story of Matthew Paris through painstaking work lasting nearly a century — started by Luard and Madden roughly in the 1860s, and culminating in Richard Vaughan's seminal volume on Matthew Paris in 1958. To provide a glimpse into the manuscript chaos in the first half of the nineteenth century, Archbishop Parker attributed the *Flores*

---

137 The leap in the development of English historiography is huge (see the many-faceted transformation of the discipline, e.g. in Woolf, 'From Hystories to the Historical') and there is certainly no room to address all of the ever-proliferating material in this brief overview. Similarly, the chapter cannot go in detail about the equally fascinating German and French scholarly reception of Matthew's Mongol materials. The European reception and translations of Matthew Paris's historiography merits further in-depth research, which the present dicussion can only hope to inspire. The metahistory of the Mongol story becoming unmappable in the space of the present short chapter, I leave the Western European evolution of the story to future research and focus on the milestones that eventually brought Matthew's continental sources home to Central Eastern Europe.

138 The well-known Rolls Series, published between 1858 and 1911, remains the most often used major collection of British and Irish historical materials and primary sources. The *Chronica majora*, published in 1872–1883 occupies seven volumes (six volumes + index). Liebermann's edition (1888): Paris, 'Ex Mathei Parisiensis operibus'. Notably, the French translation of the whole chronicle by Alphonse Huillard-Bréholles was published before these editions in 1840–1841: Paris, *Grande chronique*.

historiarum to a Matthew of Westminster, and C. D. Yonge maintained the same argument of authorship in his translation three hundred years later.[139] The fact that Matthew of Westminster was a fabricated name for the author was first noted in 1826 by Francis Turner Palgrave (Cohen), who said that Matthew was 'a phantom who never existed',[140] which was later proven and elaborated by Henry Richards Luard who used internal evidence to prove that the *Flores* was compiled and composed by a number of writers at St Albans and Westminster.[141]

Besides the resolution of the Matthew of Westminster conundrum by Henry Richards Luard, every little detail had to be slotted into its place one by one. John Allen Giles translating from Watts's text, for example, believed that Matthew Paris lived until 1273, which was refuted in Frederick Madden's foundational first attempt to draw together the available evidence for Matthew's life in the third volume of his edition of the *Historia Anglorum* for the Rolls Series.[142] Many important historical works, including those of Matthew Paris, have not received newer critical editions since the Rolls Series, which means that most modern historians using these texts as primary evidence rely on the transcription and critical apparatus prepared by Luard and Madden, which (before digital access) was rarely checked against the manuscripts. It is rather fortunate that they did a stellar job for the most part.[143]

---

139 Matthew of Westminster, *Flores historiarum* (*MW*); Matthew of Westminster, *Flowers of History* (*FOH*).

140 In this anonymously published review, Palgrave criticizes David Hume's uncritical use of authorities, including Matthew of Westminster. Palgrave, 'The History of England from the Invasion of Julius Caesar to the Revolution of 1688 by David Hume', p. 250.

141 *FH*, I, pp. x–xi.

142 *EH*, I, p. iii; *HA*, III, pp. vii–xxii. Maurice Powicke challenged the suggestions that Matthew lived longer than 1259, but this was refuted by both Vivian Galbraith and Richard Vaughan. Powicke, 'Compilation of the *Chronica Majora*', pp. 157–58; Galbraith, 'Roger Wendover and Mathew Paris', pp. 29–31; Vaughan, *Matthew Paris*, pp. 7–11.

143 For instance, nineteenth-century historian Henry H. Howorth's description of the Mongol history during Frederick II's time is obviously a summary based on nothing but Matthew Paris's Mongol entries for these years. Howorth, *History of the Mongols*, II, pp. 53–56. Using letters and other sources originally in the *Chronica majora* but citing them by the alleged sender is common because of modern edited letter collections which often take them out of the chronicle context and present them as correspondence. Examples for this can be easily found everywhere in modern scholarship; for example, Gergely Kiss's reconstruction of István Báncsa's career also cites 'Frederick's letter' from Fejér, without noting the context of its preservation; Kiss, *Dél-Magyarországtól Itáliáig*, p. 23, citing *Codex diplomaticus Hungariae ecclesiasticus ac civilis*, VI.1, pp. 220–26. Denis Sinor also quotes Frederick II's opinion straight from 'Frederick's letter': 'Hungary's collapse came as a shock to the pope, to the Emperor Frederick and to all other potentates of the west, all ready to blame Bela (to use Frederick's words "the idle and careless" king [note 28: *rex deses et nimis securus*, in a letter addressed to king Henry III of England, dated 3 July 1241. Cf. *Chronica majora*, VI, 113]), none willing to provide effective help in preventing the further advance of the Mongols.' Sinor, 'The Mongols in the West', p. 11.

354   CHAPTER 7

Matthew's chronicle was also edited and excerpted by Felix Lieber-mann, a scholar of Old English and Norman law and constitution.[144] Liebermann's edition for the Monumenta Germaniae Historica is particularly interesting because — although it was an excerpted edition spanning less than 350 pages — to this day many continental scholars use it as the go-to critical edition of Matthew Paris's chronicles.[145] Under the motto *Sanctus amor patriae dat animum,* the remit of the *Societas aperiendis fontibus rerum Germanicarum medii aevii* was to publish documents pertaining to the history of Germany and other areas subjected to the influence of Germanic tribes or rulers, including Britain, Czech lands, Poland, Austria, France, Low Countries, Italy, Spain, and so on. The organizing principle is absolute chronology and historical utility, so, for example, the *Additamenta* is not part of Liebermann's purview but the Mongol bundle originally found there is inserted in the form of massive footnotes, far exceeding the size of mine in the present volume, under the 1241 letter of Henry Raspe to the duke of Brabant.[146] Because much of the Mongol story in the *Chronica majora* appears as part of Emperor Frederick's history, the Mongol-related entries did in fact make it into Liebermann's excerpts.

A similar agenda drove the editors of another publishing program, Josef Kalousek and Adolf Bachmann, who set out to gather letters and documents related to the history of the Czech state, specifically the Czech-Moravian lands until 1310, following Sickel's model of editing the MGH. Organizing pertinent documents in strict chronology between 1241 and 1242, the *diplomatae* (nos 297–323) contain some of the letters found

---

144 Knowles, 'Presidential Address'. As Muñoz García warns, fragments of the *Flores Historiarum, Chronica Majora, Gesta Abbatum,* and *Vita Stephani archiepiscopi Cantuariensis* were edited by Liebermann, who still ascribed the *Flores Historiarum* to Matthew of Westminster: 'Luard and other authors like Liebermann refused to believe in Paris's intellectual authorship of these texts due to the textual errors found in them, an aspect that was contested by Galbraith when he showed a number of textual common phrases and words common to other Paris texts like the *Chronica Majora*'. Muñoz García, 'The Script of Matthew Paris and his Collaborators', pp. 29, 35; Galbraith, 'Roger Wendover and Mathew Paris', p. 32.

145 While English-language publications refer to Luard's edition without exception, continental scholars do rely on Liebermann's edition regularly. To name a few random examples from various fields: Osten-Sacken, *Jakob von Vitrys Vita Mariae Oigniacensis*; Bleisteiner, 'Der Doppeladler von Kaiser und Reich im Mittelalter'; Heinisch, ed., *Kaiser Friedrich II*. Some scholars cite both, e.g. 'Auszüge aus seiner Chronik finden sich in der jüngeren Ausgabe der MGH. Da in den Auszügen der MGH nicht alle Stellen abgedruckt sind, zitiere ich nach der Gesamtausgabe Luards'. Bezzola, *Die Mongolen in abendländischer Sicht*, p. 63. Although using Luard's edition for the *Chronica majora,* Joseph Huffman cites the *Additamenta* letters via *Regesta imperii,* ed. by Böhmer, Ficker, and Winkelmann in 1881–1901. E.g. Huffman, *The Social Politics of Medieval Diplomacy,* p. 269, n. 211.

146 Paris, 'Ex Mathei Parisiensis operibus', pp. 207–09. Liebermann omits the letter of the Hungarian bishop to Paris and in another set of footnotes directs the reader to consult Luard's edition.

in the *Chronica majora* and the *Additamenta*: letters of the landgrave of Thuringia, the letter of Friar Jordanus to his confreres, Jordanus to the duke of Brabant, the emperor to the English king, the letters of 'Robert and Jordanus', and the letter of Ivo of Narbonne.[147] In the *Codex diplomaticus et epistolaris regni Bohemiae*, the source of the letters that are clearly from Matthew Paris's *Chronica majora* is invariably František Palacký's collection, who had reproduced them from Watts's edition.[148]

Curiously, Watts's edition also had a long afterlife in the Hungarian scholarship of the Mongol invasion, which for one reason or another sidestepped the straightforward sequence of increasingly precise critical editions. While the Monumenta and the Rolls editions became the most important access points to Matthew's Mongol-related material, teaching and scholarship in Hungary continued to use derivative collections of *diplomatae* using Watts's edition from 1684. Tracing the ultimate sources of the most recent and frequently used source reader on the Mongol invasion, a representative tome published in Hungarian translation in the series Nation and Memory (*Nemzet és emlékezet*) in 2003, yields surprising results.[149] Similar to František Palacký's publication, the fact that the *Chronica majora*'s letters appear as royal and papal correspondence in the chapter devoted to 'Letters from the Age of the Mongol Invasion' somewhat obscures the real nature of these epistles, although this is remedied by thorough modern footnotes. The 2003 volume shows how the distance between manuscript and modern translation can be surprisingly long and winding. To take the example of Henry Raspe's letter, it appears in the beautifully flowing Hungarian translation of Izabella G. Ruitz, which — as is clearly stated in the references — is reprinted from a previous Mongol invasion reader published in 1981.[150] But the editor of that reader, Tamás Katona, cites neither the MGH nor the Rolls Series as his source; the basis for the translation was Albin Gombos's *Catalogus fontium*,[151] and for other letters taken from the *Chronica majora*, he uses the *Codex diplomaticus* published by György Fejér in 1829.[152] Fejér, in turn, clearly used Watt's seventeenth-century edition.[153] In the end, a letter known to modern students of history in the West from Luard's edition and Giles's translation as the 'letter of the Count of Lorraine' is known to their Hungarian peers as

---

147 *Codex diplomaticus et epistolaris regni Bohemiae*, IV.1, pp. 493–508.

148 Palacký, *Der Mongolen Einfall im Jahre 1241*.

149 Nagy, ed., *Tatárjárás*.

150 Nagy, ed., *Tatárjárás*, p. 164; Katona, ed., *A tatárjárás emlékezete*, pp. 290–91.

151 Gombos, *Catalogus fontium historiae Hungaricae*, pp. 1581–82.

152 *Codex diplomaticus Hungariae ecclesiasticus ac civilis*, IV.1, pp. 232–34.

153 Despite the scanty footnotes, this is certifiable because Fejér refers to his source as 'Apud Matth. Paris. Hist. Angl. p. m. 496. Litteras has Duci Brabantiae destinauit H. Lotharingiae Comes, Palatinus Saxonum', and the page number corresponds exactly with Watt's edition in *HM* (1684), p. 496.

the 'letter of Hermann, landgrave of Thuringia', through Ruitz's translation looking back on the mediation of Watts, Gombos, and Katona.[154]

While it is not entirely clear why Katona opted for using Matthew's letters from Fejér and Gombos, it may have had something to do with the fact that it was published in Hungary in the 1980s. Even if they were available for academics, these 'Western European' series were probably less accessible for the target audience of the Mongol invasion reader than the customary and familiar compilations that served generations of historians before them. This academic distance from the English edition was, however, a modern development. There was a time, not much earlier than Katona's compilation, when Luard's edition was very much present in Hungarian scholarship. Specifically, in one important field, which more or less began with the discovery of Matthew Paris's valuable materials about Hungary: the history of Anglo-Hungarian relations and Sándor Fest's historiographical enterprise in the 1930s and 1940s. The anglophile professor, whose work peaked exactly seven hundred years after the year of Matthew's first note about the Mongols in *Hungaria major* in his chronicle, worked from and copiously cited Luard's edition.

Matthew repeatedly reiterates that the *Chronica majora* is a *historia regni Angliae*, yet Hungary does indeed appear in it relatively frequently. This observation is what gave rise to much thinking about Matthew's reasons and motivation to devote so much ink and parchment to events taking place in faraway Eastern Europe. The chronicle's appreciation as a major source of Eastern European history at large is reflected in the statements in pre-war scholarship of Anglo-Hungarian relations, for example, Henrik Marczali and Sándor Fest, stressing the importance of Matthew Paris's contribution to medieval knowledge of the region. Their works offer a de-contextualized (or rather recontextualized) reading of the *Chronica majora* as a historical source and give the general impression that Matthew Paris's chronicle was a central collection of all things Eastern European, available for his contemporaries and generations of historians to come.

The implied conceptions about Matthew Paris's personal investment in recording Eastern European matters and the role of the *Chronica majora* in the dissemination of information was a product of its time.[155] A couple of years after the Great War, Henrik Marczali devoted a historical survey

---

154 Neither identification is correct, see Chapter 4 ('Henry Raspe's Letter'), note 102.

155 A generation later, Polish Anglicist Henryk Zins's oeuvre is rooted in a similar methodology and approach to cultural relations, but his interest was far broader and much less polemic than Fest's. He also published extensively on Anglo-Polish relations. Zins, 'Ze stosunków Polsko-Angielskich w pol. XV wieku'; Zins, *Mikołaj Kopernik w angielskiej kulturze umysłowej epoki Szekspira*; Zins, *England and the Baltic in the Elizabethan Era*; Zins, 'Echa odkryć Kopernika w literaturze angielskiej na początku XVII w.'; Zins, *Polska w oczach Anglików XIV–XVI w.* For a comprehensive overview of Zins's publications, see Korytko, 'Bibliografia Prac Prof. Henryka Zinsa'.

THE AFTERLIFE OF MATTHEW'S MONGOL STORY   357

from the eleventh century to his own time to proving that 'Hungary could always count on England's Platonic sympathies, but effective support was only received when it happened to coincide with English interests'.[156] After the territorial losses suffered at the Paris Peace Conference in 1920, a palpable rift appeared in the politics of the country, and by the mid-1930s, the Germanophile and Anglophile approaches within the Hungarian political elite permeated cultural and — as these examples show — academic matters as well.[157] It was in this era when sentiments of the bond between civilizer and civilizee appeared in Fest's efforts to portray the Hungarian kingdom as a recipient of ideas and ideologies arriving from England.[158]

In this atmosphere, Sándor Fest's interpretation of Matthew's descriptions of the Mongol ravages was, again, used as evidence for the chronicler's 'keen interest with which contemporary Hungarian history was followed in England at the time', which echoed an earlier writing by Henrik Marczali.[159] As was shown in the present volume, the reality, however, was at once simpler and more complicated than this. By definition, the story of the Mongol invasion in Hungary should lie at the intersection of

---

156 Marczali, 'Az angol-magyar érdekközösségről a múltban', p. 123.

157 Tibor Frank says the following about 'dissenting voices with different and alternative concepts in interwar Hungary. Its political élite included a group that expected support for Hungarian revisionist claims from the "Anglo-Saxon", the English-speaking Powers. For this group, Britain and the former British Empire rather than the United States held out the promise of Hungary's salvation, although there were some one and one-half million Hungarian-Americans not completely without political influence. The Anglophile élite, who spoke or understood English, cultivated an Anglophone culture and even British social contacts. Some studied at English or Scottish universities. Most belonged to the aristocracy, the world of money, the diplomatic corps, certain educated sections of the middle class, the professions, authors, artists, scholars, university professors, and a fair number with a Jewish background'. Frank, 'The "Anglo-Saxon" Orientation of Wartime Hungarian Foreign Policy', p. 592. More on this in Bán, *Hungarian-British Diplomacy, 1938–1941*, pp. 147–48.

158 'However, we [Hungarians] had other — direct — connections with medieval England — connections dating from periods when the caprice of history bridged over the wide gulf dividing these two countries from one another. The intermarriages of dynasties, common political aims and ideals, now and then tightened the bonds of intercourse between Hungary and England which appeared to be about to slacken or to break asunder, and Latin — the common language to the educated and the refined — on occasion proved able to introduce into the intellectual world of far-distant Hungary ideas originating from England which found no recipient farther east'. Fest, 'Political and Cultural Connections between Hungary and England', p. 19. This discourse was, of course, far more complicated, but a full overview of the question is beyond the purview of the present chapter. For a more nuanced and sensitive understanding of Fest's scholarship in this context, see Dávidházi, '"A kérdés továbbgondolására késztet"'.

159 'The vivid descriptions of the Tartars' destruction in Hungary by Matthew Paris, the greatest thirteenth-century chronicler, prove how contemporary Hungarian events were observed with keen interest in England.' Fest, 'Párhuzam az angol és magyar alkotmány fejlődése között', p. 155 (my translation). Similar statement in Marczali, 'Az angol-magyar érdekközösségről a múltban', p. 114.

358   CHAPTER 7

texts about the Mongols and texts about Hungary within the narrative of the *Chronica majora*; however, the relationship of these two sets was not that of intersection: entries about Hungary are, in fact, a subset, almost invariably *contained in* texts about the Mongol invasion, which in turn is also a subset in the bigger story of the emperor's struggles with the pope. It is notable, however, that with eyewitness accounts such as Thomas of Spalato and Roger of Várad, as well as local charters and royal correspondence, Matthew Paris's Mongol story, regardless of its importance and bulk, constitutes but a sliver of written texts available for modern Hungarian scholarship in this field. Its continued significance is partly due to its relevance and partly because of the trends in twentieth-century national historiography. Other countries in the region have different stories. For example, modern scholarship about the Mongols in the Adriatic, the southern ends of the medieval Kingdom of Hungary and the furthest reach of the Mongol invasion of 1241–1242, seemingly belongs here, yet it shows a rather different scholarly landscape, using different sources.

Recent overviews of the historiography of this leg of the military operations provide a glimpse into particularly rich and diverse material, which I have no room to discuss in detail here, and Matthew Paris's Mongol story is of explicably little use for these inquiries.[160] While Thomas of Spalato's and Roger of Várad's narratives loom over both scholarly discourse and historical memory in the field, regional historiography grapples with similar issues as the Czech and Moravian cases discussed below. The ethos of Croatian lands as *antemurale Christianitatis*,[161] together with local nobility's legitimization efforts gave rise to famous forgeries whose disproval took concerted scholarly efforts.[162]

---

160 E.g. Sardelić, '"Quasi per aerem volans"'; Sophoulis, 'The Mongol Invasion of Croatia and Serbia in 1242'. The remit of Romanian scholarship in the field of Mongol military campaigns in the territory of Romania and Moldavia also covers a much longer period of complicated conflicts and contacts than the events discussed in the *Chronica majora*. Regarding 1241/42, scholarship has for long relied on the type of charter and narrative sources that were collected in Sacerdoțeanu, *Marea invazie tătară și Sud-Estul european*, although some of them have been proven to be forgeries and/or evidence for later Mongol activities. For recent historiography in Romanian literature, see Gemil, 'The Tatars in Romanian Historiography'; Papacostea, *Românii în secolul al XIII lea între cruciată și Imperiul mongol*; and Sălăgean, *Transylvania in the Second Half of the Thirteenth Century*.

161 For a late bloom of this, see Croatian-German Petar Preradovic's (1818–1872) Byron-inspired 'Na Grobniku' ('At Grobnik'): 'Hrvatskom se ovdje krvi | Spasi Zapad' (Croatia is bleeding here | saving all of Europe). Cited in Zivancevic-Sekerus, 'Croatian Writers in the Byronic Mould', p. 151.

162 For example, a forged privilege issued by King Béla IV in 1260, rewarding Feldricus and Bartholomeus Frankapan for their assistance during the Mongol invasion, and Franciscan chronicler Ivan Tomašić's sixteenth-century *Brevis chronologia Croatiae* commemorating the epic, albeit fabricated, story of the 1242 Battle of Grobnik (*Grobničko polje*), then in the hands of the Frankapan family. Klaić, 'Paški falsifikati'; Margetić, 'Izvještaj Ivana Tomašića o Grobničkoj bitci'.

THE AFTERLIFE OF MATTHEW'S MONGOL STORY   359

The Mongol story and Matthew Paris's role in constructing its modern historiography in Czech lands is also interesting. To this day, the go-to reference book of European sources about the Mongols is *Putování k Mongolům* (Travelling to the Mongols), essentially a light Czech counterpart of Katona's Hungarian *Tatárjárás* reader. Ignoring Matthew Paris completely, and focusing on Eastern encounters, this accessible and popular reader only contains the modern Czech translation of John of Plano Carpini, William Rubruck, and Ruy González de Clavijo — and is riddled with omissions and occasional mistranslation.[163] However, unreliability is one thing, falsification is another, and the latter can be seen to plague the national historiographies of Czech lands from their inception.

As for primary sources in the field beyond the MGH and Western European editions, national historiographical projects mainly concentrate on calendared forms of the letters preserved in the *Chronica majora* and the *Additamenta*, which were entered in the *Codex diplomaticus et epistolaris regni Bohemiae*[164] and the *Codex diplomaticus et epistolaris Moraviae*. Both were compromised by the insidious shadows of forging the past. From the seventeenth century onwards, the story of the Mongol invasion was very much about miracles and pilgrimage, as well as about continuing the sixteenth-century cult of Jaroslav of Sternberg, 'the hero who defeated the Mongols at Olomouc'. In 1817, Václav Hanka 'found' a 1247 fragment of a manuscript in a church in Dvůr Králové nad Labem (Königinhof an der Elbe) written in Czech, and thus boosting the self-confidence of the nascent Czech National Revival. This turned out to be a forgery.[165] The prevalent discourse about the Moravian leg of the Mongol campaign continues to be affected by the history of nineteenth-century forgeries, including the above-mentioned Sternberg case, and the earlier but more

---

163 Knobloch, ed., *Putování k Mongolům*. I am grateful to Jana Valtrová at Masaryk University, Brno, for her insights.

164 Nos 1017, 1018, 1021, 2024 in 'Regesta Bohemiae at Moraviae, pars 1, 600–1253', pp. 472–73, 476, 478–79. Erben reproduces the text of the selection of letters from a Paris reprint of Watts's edition: *HM (1644)*. The texts *s.a.* 1241 also include the Julianus report and some of the Ottobeuren Collection, reproduced from Hormayr's edition.

165 'The key part of this fragment, later called the Manuscript of Dvůr Králové (*Königinhofer Handschrift*), was the poem "Jaroslav", exalting Jaroslav of Sternberg and his heroic victory against the Tartars in 1241. It also mentioned the events in Hostýn. There was only one problem. This fragment (and the one found a year later, the Manuscript of Zelená Hora, dating to the turn of the 10th century) was an elaborate forgery by Václav Hanka, which was definitely proved [*sic*], after fierce discussions, only at the end of the 19th century. This "ancient" Czech poem about the epic victory over the Asian invaders re-invented the myth once again, only this time it was used to document the historical importance of the Czech nation'. Somer, 'Forging the Past', p. 247.

360   CHAPTER 7

extensive fraud of Antonín Boček.[166] The *Codex diplomaticus et epistolaris Moraviae* contained falsified documents related to the invasion, the destruction of particular places, and, of course, the brave opposition of the Moravian nobility.[167]

Celebrated Historian František Palacký, 'the father of the nation', believed in the authenticity of the Hanka manuscript, and prepared a lecture to commemorate the six hundredth anniversary of the epic victory. In this, he famously focused on King Wenceslas's role in averting an even greater catastrophe and stopping the onslaught in Europe altogether.[168] Using Watts's 1644 edition, Palacký quotes Frederick's letters, including those preserved in the *Chronica majora*,[169] and praises Wenceslas despite the prevailing views which he calls *Germanismus*: 'Dagegen verdiente König Wenzel I von Böhmen in vollem Masse jene Lobsprüche, welche derselbe Kaiser Freidrich II ihm ertheilte. Wir haben gesehen, dass er der einzige machtigere Fürst in diesem Theil Europa's gewesen, der, auf den natürlichen Schutz der Riesengebirgskette sich stützend, bei Zeiten eine plan- und zweckmässige Thätigkeit entwickelte, um jene Unholden von seinen Landen, und somit zugleich von Deutschland, fern zu halten'.[170] Although one of his major sources, the *Chronica majora*, is itself a monument to *Germanismus*, he is strongly of the opinion that the German-skewed approach is not valid in the reconstruction of the events precisely due to ignoring Wenceslas's role as the bastion of Christendom.[171] But

---

166 Nos 10–18, in *Codex diplomaticus et epistolaris Moraviae*, pp. 7–8. Boček probably used Watts's edition (referring to it as *Matthaeus Parisien.- Historia magna 496*), but did not provide the texts of the letters.

167 The falsification was exposed in the course of the nineteenth century, but the extent remains unknown, Bretholz, 'Die Tataren in Mähren und die moderne mährische Urkundenfälschung'; Šebánek, 'Moderní padělky v moravském diplomatáři Bočkově do in 1306'. For a recent overview of the Boček problem, see more in Rychterová, 'The Manuscripts of Grünberg and Könighof', pp. 25–26.

168 'Dagegen verdanken wir dem in noch weiterer Ferne lebenden Matthäus Paris, dem Mönche von St Alban in England, die schätzbarsten Nachrichten über diese Begebenheit; dieser im J. 1259 verstorbene Chronist hatte überhaupt damals nicht seines Gleichen in Europa. In allen diesen von uns angeführten Quellen ist von den Kämpfen der Böhmen und Mährer mit den Mongolen keine Meldung zu finden; ausser implicite, in den von Matthäus Paris uns erhaltenen und mitgetheilten Briefen'. Palacký, *Der Mongolen Einfall im Jahre 1241*, p. 390.

169 Palacký, *Der Mongolen Einfall im Jahre 1241*, p. 373.

170 Palacký, *Der Mongolen Einfall im Jahre 1241*, p. 408.

171 'Über die Verdienste des "Germanismus" bei Abwehrung der Mongolen ist in den letzten Jahren mehrfach geschrieben worden. Wie diese beschaffen waren, kann man aus der bisherigen Erörterung von selbst entnehmen. Trotz der Zwietracht, welche die Reichsstände wegen des ewigen Haders zwischen Kaiser und Papst beherrschte, ist nicht zu zweifeln, dass die Deutschen jenen Barbaren den tapfersten Widerstand würden geleistet haben — wenn es zum Kampfe mit ihnen gekommen wäre. Allein es kam nicht dazu — weil K. Wenzel I die Mongolen nicht bis nach Deutschland vordringen liess. Darin liegt die Lösung des grossen Räthsels nicht minder wesentlich, als im Tode Oktaj's'. Palacký, *Der Mongolen Einfall*

Germanismus carried on regardless, and it is found, among others, in the works of Otto Wolff, whose *Geschichte der Mongolen* was used even in Howorth's seminal English-language history of the Mongols.[172] Wolff refers to Palacký in his condemning description of Wenceslas's conduct, who chose to complain cowardly and idly about its devastation ('feig und unthätig über dessen Verwüstung zu jammern').[173]

The response to perceived *Germanismus*, often connected to the trope of 'the bastion of Christendom', is also detectable in the early Polish scholarship of the Mongol invasion of 1241, which assumed an entirely different scope and trajectory through the years than similar works in neighbouring countries. Earlier Polish works depict the Battle of Legnica (Liegnitz) as a Polish victory after which Batu, who was apparently present at it, withdrew to the steppe. For instance, Polish historian Oscar Halecki, although acknowledging the defeat of various European forces at Liegnitz, 'states that together with rumoured event in Asia the desperate resistance of Poland contributed to make the Mongolian hordes retreat. Europe was saved'.[174] Matthew Paris's material is certainly not replete with references to Poland, especially this angle, which may explain the silence about his

---

im Jahre 1241, p. 408. The bastion trope is common in regional historiographies. S. L. Tikhvinskii, for example, explains that Western Europe was 'saved from inevitable death at the hands of an opponent superior to them in both military strength and strategy [...] thanks to the heroic opposition of the neighboring peoples — Slavs and Hungarians — to the Tatar-Mongol domination'. Introduction to Tikhvinskii, *Tataro-Mongoly v Azii i Evrope*, p. 8. Cited in translation in Rogers, 'An Examination of Historians' Explanations for the Mongol Withdrawal from East Central Europe', p. 12. The idea was refuted by scholars such as Charles Halperin.

172 Wolff, *Geschichte der Mongolen oder Tataren*; Howorth, *History of the Mongols*.

173 'Daß Wenzel ihnen mit einem großen Heer entgegen ging, ist wahr, aber eben so wahr und von ihm selber eingestanden, daß er sie nicht angegriffen, sie nicht vor ihm flohen, sondern er ihnen erst nach Guben scheu auswich und sein Kriegsheer entlassend, sich auf den Königstein verbarg, wo er sich schon, wie urkundlich fest steht und Palacky selber zugestehen muß — am 7. Mai 1241 befand, da er doch seinem Lande Mähren hätte schützend zueilen sollen und können, statt feig und unthätig über dessen Verwüstung zu jammern'. Wolff, *Geschichte der Mongolen oder Tataren*, pp. 204–05.

174 Rogers, 'An Examination of Historians' Explanations for the Mongol Withdrawal from East Central Europe', p. 13. The aforementioned idea of bastion — *defensor* or *propugnaculum Christi* — already present in contemporary written sources and embraced by scholarship, also applies to the case of Hungary. Twentieth-century historian József Deér cites a letter written by King Béla to Innocent IV to add the trope of solitude, sentiments of being abandoned in time of danger. 'The letter contains all that the Hungarian king could say about the fate of his country: the faith in Christian, what is more, in European, unity, the passionate dedication to belonging together, and the clear awareness that due to its position the defence of this country is the defence of the whole of Christendom, and thus it is a universally Christian, universally European undertaking. And it also voices the solitude of Hungary: beyond kind words, serving the European-Christian interest [the country] can count on nothing but obstacles from its immediate neighbours'. Deér, *A magyar nemzeti öntudat kialakulása*, pp. 8–9.

few passages. The most frequently cited primary sources concerning the Mongol invasion are collected in the *Monumenta Poloniae historica*, which, as compared to its German, Hungarian, and Czech counterparts, mostly contains material written in Poland: relatively brief passages in local annals and chronicles, and none of the documents pertaining to Poland in the *Chronica majora* or the *Additamenta*.[175]

Rather than tinkering with Matthew's sporadic and vague references, the work of Jan Długosz looms large over Polish reconstructions of the historical events or debates about the possible sources.[176] The Mongol military campaign on Polish territories, then a number of constantly morphing principalities ruled by different branches of the Piast dynasty, was first summarized by Gustav Strakosch-Grassmann in the 1870s, who — using both Luard's edition and Liebermann's in the Monumenta Germaniae Historica — gave a prominent place to the letter of Frederick II to Henry III in his line of evidence for a three-pronged campaign.[177] While Strakosch-Grassmann's ideas were not received with great enthusiasm in German-language historiography, they were influential in Polish military history.[178] Stefan Krakowski criticized Strakosch-Grassmann's use of foreign sources such as Emperor Frederick's letter and Rashid-ad-Din's chronicle, and argued that Długosz's information is based on a lost thirteenth-century Ruthenian chronicle written in Slavic, thus proving to be a suitable primary source for the Polish leg of the three-pronged Mongol campaign.[179]

And it is indeed mostly the question of sources that has preoccupied the scholarship of the Mongol invasion in Poland. Józef Matuszewski brought another important text to the source base for Polish inquiries into the Mongol invasion, the *Historia Tatarorum* or 'Tartar Relation' by C. de Bridia, found in the late 1950s in manuscripts bound together with the world map and part of the *Speculum historiale* by Vincent of Beauvais.[180]

---

175 *Monumenta Poloniae historica* , ed. by Bielowski, II; III.

176 Długosz, *Ioannis Dlugossii Annales seu Cronicae*.

177 Strakosch-Grassmann, *Der Einfall der Mongolen in Mitteleuropa*, pp. 37–53.

178 Kukiel, *Zarys historii wojskowosci w Polsce*; Zatorski, 'Pierwszy najazd Mongołów na Polskę w roku 1240–41'. I am extremely grateful to Michał Machalski for his overview of the development of Polish historiography of the Mongol invasion. Also see a brief English overview of Polish historiography about the withdrawal of Mongol troops from Europe in the literature review of Pow, 'Conquest, Withdrawal, and Diplomatic Overture' and more recently, Lubocki, 'Mongol Invasion of Hungary in the Light of Polish Medieval Sources'.

179 Krakowski, *Polska w walce z najazdami tatarskimi w XIII wieku*, pp. 133–40, 144. Rashid-ad-Din's chronicle in Rashid al-Din Tabib, *Rashiduddin Fazlullah's Jami` ut-Tawarikh / Compendium of Chronicles*.

180 Matuszewski, *Relacja Dlugosza o najezdzie tatarskim w 1241 roku*; Labuda, *Zaginiona kronika z pierwszej polowy XIII wieku*; Matuszewski, 'Spór o zaginioną kronikę'. C. de Bridia's text is almost identical with John of Plano Carpini's *Ystoria Mongalorum*. Late copies in Lucerne, Zentral- und Hochschulbibliothek, MS P 13 fol. 4, and New Haven, Yale University,

THE AFTERLIFE OF MATTHEW'S MONGOL STORY   363

Gerard Labuda's criticism of Wacław Zatorski's and Stefan Krakowski's reliance on secondary sources, and his speculations about a hypothetical Dominican annal/chronicle tradition behind Długosz's text (*Rocznik-Kronika Dominikańska*), seems to have channelled the scholarship into a debate largely about the original sources and, thus, the credibility as a primary source of Jan Długosz's *Cronica*.[181] To the present day, the subsequent debate between Labuda and Józef Matuszewski continues to define and inform the Polish discourse about the Mongol military campaigns, so it is understandable, thus, how popular syntheses such as Jerzy Maroń's *Legnica 1241*, for example, contain no references to any of the relevant material found in Matthew Paris.[182]

Starting its career in English monasticism, through antiquarianism and its adoption by nascent Orientalism regarding 'the Tartar', Matthew's Mongol story crossed the Channel in the nineteenth and twentieth centuries, both in parts and in whole. In the end, the European texts that the English monk preserved at St Albans returned to their distant place of origin in more recent times, when the letters and texts preserved in the *Chronica majora* and the *Additamenta* were discovered as primary sources for Eastern and Central European history. As has been shown, the use of Matthew Paris's texts in national historiographies of the Mongol conquests is uneven, often unattributed, decontextualized. On the one hand, this is due to differences in the accessibility of the texts in respective 'national' source collections in Latin and translation. On the other hand, because the conveyance of Matthew's chronicle into national historiographies, often relying on a daisy-chain of editions going back to the seventeenth-century printed version, rendered it into monumenta of 'relevant' correspondence rather than a *historia*, and the authorship of texts was attributed to Matthew's named sources, the 'senders' of the letters. Parallel to this, however, a different approach to Matthew's text and the letters contained therein was also shown to have existed, specifically in the self-standing field of Anglo-Hungarian relations, whose subject was Matthew Paris, and through him English historiography, celebrated as a chronicle tradition informed of and interested in Eastern European history. Admittedly, the *Chronica majora* is only one of the surviving medieval witnesses to the Eastern European campaign of the Mongol armies, yet, in one way or another,

---

Beinecke Rare Book and Manuscript Library, MS 350A. Printed in C. de Bridia, *Hystoria Tartarorum*; Matuszewski, *Relacja Dlugosza o najezdzie tatarskim w 1241 roku*, pp. 118–24.

181 Gerard Labuda suspects lost near-contemporaneous texts behind Długosz's, e.g. a Friar Jan Iwanovic, mentioned as a survivor of the Battle of Liegnitz, and a common source also used by the *Annales Silesiaci compilati*. Labuda, 'Wojna z Tatarami w roku 1241', p. 206.

182 Maroń, *Legnica 1241*. More specialized publications, such as Aleksander Paroń's 2008 article in English, do not gloss over the *Chronica majora*: Paroń, 'The Battle of Legnica (9 April 1241) and its Legend', p. 102, n. 55.

364   CHAPTER 7

parts of Matthew's Mongol story — which nearly completely overlaps with the history of Eastern Europe in his work — have seeped into the knowledge and perceptions of the invasion in Central and Eastern European scholarship in the last century and a half.

Loco prologi

Compared to the world of scholarship, replete with debate and a drive to unearth and connect more sources, modern school textbooks used in countries which look back on episodes of Mongol violence in their history are strikingly similar to medieval chronicles. For example, evoking descriptions of the *Chronica majora* and other contemporary sources, Polish students learn that

> Czyngis-chan w dużej mierze zawdzięczal swoje sukcesy znakomicie zorganizowanej i niezwykle zdyscyplinowanej armii. Jej trzon stanowiła niemal wyłącznie kawaleria. Szacuje się, że w czasach panowania Temudżina siły mongolskie składały się z ok. 100 tys. Wojowników. Każdy najazd poprzedzano wyslaniem zwiadowców i szpiegów. Podczas ataku wyjątkowa ruchliwość niewielkich oddziałów mongolskich dawała złudzenie ich przewagi liczebnej. W trakcie bitew wojownicy nacierali z zaskoczenia, nagle zmieniali szyk oraz kirunek uderzenia, pozorowali ucieczki. Unikali bespośrednich starć — zasypyvali wrogów gradem strzał. W Chinach nauczyli się budować machiny oblężnicze oraz zdobywać obwarowane miasta i twierdze. Wykorzystywali także wynalezione przez Chińczyków trujące gazy. Świadomie stosowali okrucieństwo, które osłabiało u przeciwników wolę walki.
>
>> (Czyngis-chan [Chinggis Khan] owed his successes to an extremely well-organized and highly disciplined army. Its core was almost exclusively cavalry. During the reign of Temudżin [Temujin was Ghinggis Khan's given name], the Mongolian forces consisted of around a hundred thousand warriors. Each raid was preceded by the sending of scouts and spies. During attack, the mobility of small Mongol units gave the illusion of their numerical superiority. In battle, the warriors attacked by surprise, suddenly changed their order and direction, simulating escapes. They avoided direct combat; they showered their enemies with a barrage of arrows instead. In China, they learned how to build siege machines to conquer fortified cities and fortresses. They also used poisonous

gases invented by the Chinese. They demonstrated cruelty deliberately to weaken their enemies' morale.)[183]

The description of Mongol warfare, resembling the thematic of the khan's Englishman or the Russian archbishop and their ultimate sources, also evokes a chronicle page; at the bottom of the text a mounted warrior in peaked helmet illustrates the narrative description, with the explanatory 'rubric': 'Wojownicy mongolscy najczęściej byli ubrani w filcowe kubraki, sprodnie oraz futrzane czapy. Tylko bogatsi dysponowali zbrojami wyko-nanymi z metalowych lub skózanych płytek nasztych na wełniane kubraki. Ich podstawową broń stanowił łuk. Oprócz nich używali włóczni oraz charakterystycznych zakrzywionych szabli'. (Mongol warriors were most often dressed in felt coats, trousers, and fur hats. Only the richer ones had armour made of metal or leather plates sewn onto woollen doublets. Their primary weapon was the bow. Besides that, they used spears and distinc-tive curved sabres.) With the spear and iron-enforced armour (but sans the bodies of the victims), the aspect and the appearance of the horseman in this modern rendering is nearly identical with Matthew Paris's Mongol warrior, at the bottom of MS *B*, fol. 145[r] (see Fig. 6). A Russian textbook of history for sixth graders similarly evokes the brief entries of medieval annals, summarizing the events as follows: 'Hungary: In 1241–1242 Hun-gary faced a horrible affliction in the form of the Mongol-Tatar armies, that is, conquerors from the east. They ravaged the land: cities and villages were destroyed and burned to the ground, harvests were devastated, and livestock was driven away. The Mongol invasion was followed by terrible famine which led to the death of a large part of the population'.[184]

A Hungarian textbook offers a much longer account, focusing on the military movements and the period of reconstruction and repopulation by Béla IV, known as the Second Foundation of the Homeland (*Második*

---

183 Kulesza and Kowalewski, *Zrozumieć przeszłość*, 389. I am grateful to Justyna Baron, Instytut Archeologii Uniwersytet Wrocławski, for her invaluable help with modern Polish textbooks.

184 Iskrovskaya, Fedorov, and Gur'yanova, *Istorija Srednih vekov*, p. 225 (my translation). See also Thomas of Spalato's text seeping through the text of the Croatian textbook: 'During the reign of Andrew's successor Béla IV, Tatars (Mongols) from Asia invaded Europe. In 1241 Béla IV suffered a catastrophic defeat in battle at the river Šajo, so he was forced to flee to the fortified coastal towns. After ravaging Hungary, the Tatars crossed Croatia over the frozen rivers in the winter. On their way to the sea, they also devastated Zagreb, and when they reached the coast and began to lay siege on Trogir, Béla took refuge on the nearby islands. The news of the death of their khan, Ogotaj, made the Tatars return to southern Russia. After their withdrawal, Béla IV decided to pay more attention to the defence of the country. The king realized that the Tatars could be effectively withstood by well-fortified cities, because their cavalry could not overcome solid city walls. He therefore began to encourage the construction of such cities by giving them privileges'. Posavec and Medic, *Povijest 2*, p. 91 (my translation). Texts accessed through the National Textbook Project: <http://archiv.nationaltextbook.hu/index/1241/>.

Honalapítás). Though the mise-en-page is different, the practice of quoting sources at length resembles the *Chronica majora*; in this case, relevant parts of the *Carmen miserabile* by Master Roger of Várad are added to illustrate the linear narrative and causality explained in the text by the authors.[185] Although they (ideally) rely on critical historiography, these brief summaries in schoolbooks are, of course, the tip of the iceberg made up of scholarship, source interpretation, and a healthy dose of the traditional discourse of historical and national identity. Through inter- and intralingual translation, their ancient sources are enshrined in their recurrent themes, familiar wording and images, as well as their simplicity operating with memorable statements and a distinct lack of source references. Their solid causality and familiar stories of plundering mounted warriors, frozen rivers, as well as the flight and plight of locals and kings lay bare how the European discourse about the Mongol invasion in Europe is as old as the first reports about it in Latin reports and chronicles.

These potted histories of the Mongol invasion and their resemblance to various types of medieval records accentuate that Matthew Paris's chronicle, and the Mongol story in it, was infinitely more complex than simple annals or schoolbooks: it was historiography proper. Framed by the overarching theme of Christian fragility and vulnerability, Matthew's Mongol story was shown to be both part and product of the contemporary discourse about anxieties of internal heterodoxy and external threats to the Church and her fold. In the *Chronica majora*, similarly to other contemporary Western chronicles (and their humble latter-day successors, the textbooks), the Mongols are often described but rarely speak. They are, however, important players in the chronicle world designed and built by Matthew. Mute and cruel, the Mongols are represented as an instrument in the hands of God for the sins of Christians. Revisiting the imagery of the personal mise-en-abîme of creation, in the way God in his world used Mongol arrows to punish Christian guilt, Matthew is the creator of his own world and uses the Mongols to his own ends.[186] The Mongols are his instrument to mete out justice in his microcosm, where the sins of Christians seem to be packed into the head of all Christians sitting on Peter's throne.

---

185 The main themes addressed vaguely follow Roger's account: the three-pronged attack, the reluctance of baronial powers to come to the aid of the king, the Battle of Muhi and the king's flight, the importance of fortification during defence, and the royal resettlement policies of depopulated areas. Száray, *Történelem 9*, pp. 194–95.

186 Recently and citing fresh interpretive frameworks, Robert Rouse sums up and places in historical context the previous explorations of the recursivity of the historian as creator: 'For the ancient Greeks, the storyteller was the "midwife of worlds", prefiguring in narrative form the true nature of the *oikoumene*'. Rouse, 'Chronicle and Romance', p. 402. See also in Westphal, *Geocriticism*, p. 77.

THE AFTERLIFE OF MATTHEW'S MONGOL STORY   367

Presenting the Mongol invasion as a sweeping story which Matthew built out of postcards from the edge, and which was, in turn, gradually transformed, dismantled, and sometimes lost in transmission and translation, this book is about historical texts in constant movement and reuse. It is about the staggering amount of contemporary correspondence that Matthew's prose provides glimpses into; about the changes of meanings through loss and addition of texts in the process; about the role of chance, opportunity, and tradition in historiography; and about a historian's vision and duty. Firmly planted in England, the analysis of the *Chronica majora*'s Mongol story exposes Matthew Paris and his informants as both isolated from and connected to European networks of information. The image of a solitary, sequestered monk is irrevocably undone by these explorations of intertextuality, information exchange, and teamwork across space and time.

At the same time, his personal vision and skill as a trained historian was indispensable in this process. The present analysis probed the interplay between the chronicler's accumulation of received texts, and his methods of colligating, interpreting, and commenting on this material *to make sense of it all*. Indeed, the texts describing and contextualizing the Mongol invasion show a historian at work: 'an eloquent and famous man full of innumerable virtues; a magnificent historian and chronicler; an excellent author (*dictator*), who frequently revolved in his heart the saying: "Laziness is the enemy of the soul", and whom widespread fame commended in remote parts where he had never been. Diligently compiling his chronicle from the earliest times up to the end of his life, he fully recorded the deeds of magnates, both lay and ecclesiastical, as well as various and wonderful events; and left for the notice of posterity a marvellous record of the past'.[187] Among others, Matthew's agency, sources, historiographical practice, and narrative style were examined as factors that shaped his 'marvellous record' of the Mongol story and the world around it. As for the present chronological survey of his peculiarly English corpus of

---

187 'vir quidem eloquens et famosus, innumeris virtutibus plenus, historiographus ac chronographus magnificus, dictator egregius, corde frequenter revolvens, "Otiositas inimica est animae". Quem quidem, ubi nunquam fecerat praesentia cognitum, partibus remotis fama reddiderat divulgata commendatum. Hic vero, a multis retroactis temporibus usque ad finem vitae suae Chronica diligenter colligens, gesta magnatum, tam saecularium quam ecclesiasticorum, necnon casus et eventus, varios et mirabiles, in scriptis plenarie redegit, mirabilemque ad posterorum notitiam praeteritorum reliquit certificationem'. Walsingham and Paris, *Gesta abbatum monasterii Sancti Albani*, pp. 394–95. Vaughan's translation in Vaughan, *Matthew Paris*, pp. 19–20. Another translation in Walsingham, *Deeds of the Abbots of St Albans*, p. 496. Note that 'the word for composition in the Middle Ages was *dictare* — to dictate, whereas *scribere* was generally indicative of the slavish copying of script on to parchment'. Camille, 'The Dissenting Image', p. 136.

documents, letters, and chronicle entries, it is hoped that the readers —
Matthew's readers — will make good use of it: a diligently compiled and
annotated meta-chronicle of the first encounter between Christian Europe
and the Mongols.

APPENDIX 1 _____

Alternating Storylines: Europe, Britain, and the Holy Land in 1237

Interweaving the stories of Frederick II, domestic affairs in England mainly in relation to Legate Otto, and news from the Holy Land under the year 1237.

FREDERICK II	ENGLAND / LEGATE OTTO	HOLY LAND
Quomodo imperator Frethericus reversus est ab Italia impeditus a proposito (The cause of the emperor's return from Italy)[a]		
Quomodo imperator vocavit omnes magnates Christianitatis (The emperor summons all the princes of Christendom)[b]		
	Confectum est crisma in ecclesia Sancti Albani (The holy unction in the church of St Albans is consecrated)[c]	
	De morte J[ohannis] comitis Cestriae (The death of John of Chester)[d]	
	De quodam mirabili grandine et pluvia diuturna (Hailstorm in Chiltern)[e]	
	De adventu O[ttonis] legati in Anglia (Arrival in England of Otto the legate)[f]	
		De jocundo mandato fratris Philippi de ordine

APPENDIX 1

FREDERICK II	ENGLAND / LEGATE OTTO	HOLY LAND
		Praedicatorum (Letter of Philip, a brother of the order of Preachers, to the pope) [enclosing *Literae ad dominum Papam*][g]
		De haeresi Nestorianorum (The heresy of the Nestorians)[h]
	Quomodo legatus moderate se habebat (Of the legate's modesty)[i]	
	Pacificati sunt magnates (Pacification of the nobles)[j]	
		De strage militum Templi circa partes Anthiochenas (The slaughter of the Knights of the Temple, near Damietta)[k]
		Theodoricus prior Hospitalis mittitur in succursum Terrae Sanctae (Theodoric, prior of the Hospitallers, is sent to the assistance of the Holy Land)[l]
Quomodo reversus est dominus imperator in Ytaliam in manu hostili (The emperor returns into Italy with a large army)[m]		
De bello commisso inter imperatorem et Mediolanenses (The war between the emperor and the Milanese)[n]		
	Quomodo cum magna cordium amaritudine et quanta difficultate concessa fuerit regi tricesima et collecta (The indignation of the nobles	

FREDERICK II	ENGLAND / LEGATE OTTO	HOLY LAND
	of England against the King)[o]	
	Quomodo comes Ricardus frater regis regem increpaverit (Earl Richard reproaches the king)[p]	
	Quomodo legatus saginatus est bonis Angliae (The legate fattens himself on the good things of England)[q]	

[a] MS *B*, fol. 106[r], col. b; *CM*, III, p. 392; *EH*, I, p. 53.　[b] MS *B*, fol. 106[r], col. b; *CM*, III, p. 393; *EH*, I, p. 53.　[c] MS *B*, fol. 106[v], col. a; *CM*, III, p. 394; *EH*, I, p. 54.　[d] MS *B*, fol. 106[v], col. a; *CM*, III, p. 394; *EH*, I, p. 54. Also notes the attempt on the life of Robert Grosseteste, bishop of Lincoln. [e] MS *B*, fol. 106[v], col. a; *CM*, III, p. 394; *EH*, I, p. 54.　[f] MS *B*, fol. 106[v], col. a; *CM*, III, p. 395; *EH*, I, p. 54.　[g] MS *B*, fol. 106[v], col. b; *CM*, III, p. 396; *EH*, I, p. 55. Around halfway, a leaf is torn in MS *B*. Luard supplied the missing text from MS *C*, fol. 264[v].　[h] MS *C*, fol. 264[v]; *CM*, III, p. 403; *EH*, I, p. 58.　[i] MS *C*, fol. 264[v]; *CM*, III, p. 403; *EH*, I, p. 61.　[j] MS *C*, fol. 264[v]; *CM*, III, p. 403; *EH*, I, p. 61. [l] MS *B*, fol. 107[r], col. a; *CM*, III, p. 406; *EH*, I, p. 63.　[m] MS *B*, fol. 107[r], col. b; *CM*, III, p. 406; *EH*, I, p. 64.　[n] MS *B*, fol. 107[r], col. b; *CM*, III, p. 407; *EH*, I, p. 64.　[o] MS *B*, fol. 107[v], col. b; *CM*, III, p. 410; *EH*, I, p. 67.　[p] MS *B*, fol. 108[r], col. a; *CM*, III, p. 411; *EH*, I, p. 68.　[q] MS *B*, fol. 108[r], col. a; *CM*, III, p. 412; *EH*, I, p. 69.

APPENDIX 2 _____

Comparison of Phrases

Comparison of phrases used to describe the Mongols in three self-contained descriptions.

DESCRIPTIVE FEATURE	[1238] *CM*, III, PP. 488–89	[1240] *CM*, IV, PP. 75–78 (NOT IN THIS ORDER)	[1241 'FREDERICK'S LETTER'] *CM*, IV, PP. 112–16 (NOT IN THIS ORDER)
Body	Hi quoque capita habentes, magna nimis et nequaquam corporibus proportionata	statura curti et grossi, corpore compacti, viribus integri	Homines parvae ac brevis staturae sunt, quantum ad longitudinem, sed solidi, lati, et propaginati
Food	carnibus crudis et etiam humanis vescuntur	Viri enim sunt inhumani et bestiales, potius monstra dicendi quam homines, sanguinem sitientes et bibentes, carnes caninas et humanas laniantes et devorantes	
Archers	**sagittarii incomparabiles**	sagittarii mirabiles	**sagittarii incomparabiles**
Leather boats	flumina quaevis cimbis de **corio factis** et portatilibus transeuntes	naves ex **coriis** boum **factas** secum deni vel duodeni in communi habentes	utres ferunt artificialiter **factos**,
Crossing water		natare et navigare docti, unde flumina maxima et rapidissima sine mora et difficultate transeunt	Quibus [utres] flumina transmeant indempnes rapacissima et paludes.

APPENDIX 2

DESCRIPTIVE FEATURE	[1238] *CM*, III, PP. 488–89	[1240] *CM*, IV, PP. 75–78 (NOT IN THIS ORDER)	[1241 'FREDERICK'S LETTER'] *CM*, IV, PP. 112–16 (NOT IN THIS ORDER)
Strength	robusti viribus, corporibus propagati		rigidi, ac fortes
Faith	**impii**		**gens impia**
Laws		humanis legibus* carentes	Haec enim gens est feralis et exlex, humanitatis ignara.
Indiscriminate		**sexui, aetati, vel dignitati non** parcentes	**ut sexui, aetati, vel dignitati non** parcat
Inexorable	inexorabiles	bello invicti, laboribus infatigabiles	
Language, writing	quorum lingua incognita omnibus quos nostra attingit notitia	nullius alterius linguam noscentes praeter suam, quam ignorant omnes alii. Non enim usque ad haec tempora patebat ad eos accessus, nec ipsi exierunt, ut habetur de moribus aut personis eorum per commune hominum commercium notitia	
Herds	gregibus, armentis, et equitiis abundantes	armenta sua [cum uxoribus suis, quae ad bella ut viri sunt edoctae], secum ducentes	
Women warriors		[armenta sua] cum uxoribus suis, quae ad bella ut viri sunt edoctae, secum ducentes	
Horse descriptions	equos vero habentes **velocissimos**		Quos tamen **velocissimos** inveniunt et

COMPARISON OF PHRASES 375

DESCRIPTIVE FEATURE	[1238] *CM*, III, PP. 488–89	[1240] *CM*, IV, PP. 75–78 (NOT IN THIS ORDER)	[1241 'FREDERICK'S LETTER'] *CM*, IV, PP. 112–16 (NOT IN THIS ORDER)
			fortissimos, in articulo necessitatis.
Horses eating		equos habentes magnos et fortes qui frondes et etiam arbores comedant	Deficiente vero cibo, corticibus arborum et foliis et herbarum radicibus dicuntur esse contenti equi eorum, quos adducunt
Leather/iron armour		**coriis** taurinis vestiti, **laminis ferreis** armati	cruda gestant **coria**, bovina, asinina, vel equina; insutis **laminis ferreis** pro armis muniuntur, quibus hactenus usi sunt.
Weapons		Gladios et sicas una parte secantes habent	
Front armour only	ante, non retro, bene armati, ne fugam ineant	parte posteriori corporis inermes, anteriori tamen armis protecti	
Their leader	ducem habentes ferocissimum, nomine Caan		Sequitur tamen et dominum habet, quem obedienter colit et veneratur et nuncupat deum terrae.
Break forth from behind rocks	Hi borealem plagam inhabitantes, vel ex Caspiis montibus vel ex vicinis,	eodem anno plebs Sathanae detestanda, Tartarorum scilicet exercitus infinitus, a regione sua montibus circumvallata prorupit; et saxorum immeabilium soliditate penetrata	
Two versions of their name		ut bene **Tartari**, quasi **tartarei**	dicti **Tartari**, immo **Tartarei**,
Tar/Tartarus River	dicti Tartari, a Tar flumine	Dicuntur autem Tartari a quodam	

APPENDIX 2

DESCRIPTIVE FEATURE	[1238] *CM*, III, PP. 488–89	[1240] *CM*, IV, PP. 75–78 (NOT IN THIS ORDER)	[1241 'FREDERICK'S LETTER'] *CM*, IV, PP. 112–16 (NOT IN THIS ORDER)
		flumine per montes eorum, quos jam penetraverant, decurrente, quod dicitur Tartar; sicut flumen Damasci Farfar nuncupatur	
Plague, pest	in pestem hominum creduntur ebullire	et quasi locustae terrae superficiem cooperientes	manens ut brucus multiplicatur, gens […] non absque praeviso Dei judicio ad sui populi correptionem et correctionem, non utinam ad totius Christianitatis dispendium, ad haec novissima tempora reservatur.

APPENDIX 3

Alternating Frederick's Story

Alternating Frederick's story (grey cells) with English history (white cells) leading up to the Mongol clusters.

	ENGLISH HISTORY	IMPERIAL-PAPAL HISTORY
De quadam visione cuidam presbytero facta Londoniis mirabili.[a]	A wondrous vision at night in London The king deprives the mayor of London of his income	
Quomodo imperator mutato consilio praelatos praemunivit ne ad concilium celebrandum convenirent.[b]		The emperor forbids his prelates to assemble at the council that Gregory IX convoked Speech by Frederick (embedded)
Epistola consolatoria Papae admonens praelatos, ut spretis minis imperialibus ad concilium properare minime formidarent.[c]		The letter of the pope to Frederick
Continuatio.[d]	The outcome of the exchange with special emphasis on the bishop of Norwich	
De miseria Foegiae (supralinear gloss: vel Favenciae) civitatis Ytalicae jam diu obsessae.[e]		Frederick's speech to the women of Faenza (embedded dialogue) The sufferings of the city of Faenza
Quam venalis facta est eo tempore curia Romana, et inhians et confidens in pecunia consimilis facta est meretrici prostanti.[f]		The Roman court likened to a harlot

ENGLISH HISTORY		IMPERIAL-PAPAL HISTORY
Dominus Papa petiit a monachis de Burgo annuum redditum centum marcarum de aliqua ecclesia.[g]	The pope demands a hundred marks from the monks of Peterborough	
	Miracles at Catesby	
De gloriosa fama signipotentissimi Aedmundi Cantuariensis archiepiscopi et confessoris.[h]	St Edmund becomes distinguished by miracles	
Quomodo monachi Cantuariae beneficium absolutionis a domino Papa impetrarunt, et quomodo Bonefacium electum Ballay avunculum reginae secundum regis desiderium et preces elegerunt.[i]	The monks of Canterbury obtain absolution from the pope, and elect Boniface as their archbishop	
	The king's plan to secure Boniface's acceptance by the pope	
De oppressione comitis Provinciae.[j]	Richard of Cornwall's successful efforts to bring peace to Provence	
Veneti pro nece Potestatis Mediolanensis filii ducis Venetorum guerram continuant contra imperatorem.[k]		Venetian attacks on Frederick
De captione Foegiae civitatis Ytaliae et de multiformi sollicitudine imperatoris ut se defenderet contra multos rebelles.[l]		The capture of Faenza and Frederick's six wars

[a] MS B, fol. 142ᵛ, col. b; CM, IV, p. 93; EH, I, p. 326. The two units of the entry are separated with a medium-sized red initial.   [b] MS B, fol. 143ʳ, col. b; CM, IV, p. 95; EH, I, p. 327. Contiguous script, the embedded text is not marked.   [c] MS B, fol. 143ʳ, col. b; CM, IV, p. 96; EH, I, p. 329.   [d] MS B, fol. 143ᵛ, col. a; CM, IV, p. 98; EH, I, p. 330. Short addendum to fill the end of the column, slightly overruns the allocated space.   [e] MS B, fol. 143ᵛ, col. b; CM, IV, p. 98; EH, I, p. 331. Contiguous script, the embedded text is not marked.   [f] MS B, fol. 143ᵛ, col. b; CM, IV, p. 100; EH, I, p. 332. [g] MS B, fol. 144ʳ, col. a; CM, IV, p. 101; EH, I, p. 332. The two units of the entry are separated with a medium-sized red initial.   [h] MS B, fol. 144ʳ, col. a; CM, IV, p. 102; EH, I, p. 334.   [i] MS B, fol. 144ʳ, col. a; CM, IV, p. 103; EH, I, p. 334. The two units of the entry are separated with a medium-sized red initial.   [j] MS B, fol. 144ᵛ, col. a; CM, IV, p. 105; EH, I, p. 336.   [k] MS B, fol. 144ᵛ, col. a; CM, IV, p. 106; EH, I, p. 336.   [l] MS B, fol. 144ᵛ, col. a; CM, IV, p. 106; EH, I, p. 336.

APPENDIX 4 —————————————

Mongol-Related Entries and Clusters: 1241

Mongol-related entries and clusters *s.a.* 1241 (grey cells: Mongol-related entries within imperial history).

TITLE OF ENTRY IN *CM*	ENGLISH HISTORY	IMPERIAL HISTORY	
		MONGOL RELATED	OTHER
De captione Foegiae civitatis Ytaliae et de multiformi sollicitudine imperatoris ut se defenderet contra multos rebelles.[a]		The six wars in which Frederick is involved: The emperor's diligence in defending himself against his various enemies (including the Mongols)	
De constantia et oppressionibus monachorum Wintoniensium.[b]	The firmness of the monks of Winchester, and the oppression exercised against them		
Quomodo capta civitate Foegiae imperator civibus pepercit.[c]			The emperor takes the city of Faenza and shows mercy to the inhabitants
Mongol cluster 1: (a) De horribili vastatione inhumanae gentis quae Tartari nuncupantur.[d]		Of the dreadful ravages committed by the Tartars	
Mongol cluster 1: (b) Literae transmissae ad ducem Braibanniae super praedictis.[e]		The letter to the duke of Brabant concerning the Mongols	
		Dialogue between Louis IX and his mother (embedded)	

APPENDIX 4

Title of entry in *CM*	English history	Imperial history	
		Mongol related	**Other**
Mongol cluster 1: (c) Epistola imperatoris de adventu Tartarorum.[f]		The letter of the emperor	
Mongol cluster 1: (d) Publicatur haec epistola missa pluribus principibus.[g]		The publication of the foregoing letter	
Mongol cluster 1: (e) Oritur mala super his suspicio.[h]		Suspicions of Frederick II's plot to bring on the Mongol invasion	
Cluster: Frederick and the pope (a) Admonitio Papae ut legati et praelati ad concilium, spreto imperatoris consilio, convenient.[i]			The pope admonishes prelates to spurn the advice of the emperor (*Dominus Sathanae*), and to come to the council
Cluster: Frederick and the pope (b) Quomodo imperator omnibus modis procuravit ut praelati non navigarent, si irrefra[ga]hiliter ad concilium venire vellent, quod tamen ipsi contempserunt.[j]			The emperor asks the prelates to travel through his territory to the council
Cluster: Frederick and the pope (c) Causa quare dominus imperator non poterat ad praelatos in propria persona venire et cum eis colloqui.[k]			The emperor's reasons for not coming to the prelates
Cluster: Frederick and the pope (d) Quomodo Iegati			The legates refuse to go through his

Title of entry in *CM*	English history	Imperial history	
		Mongol related	Other
nullo modo voluerunt a proposito suo resilire quin navigando ad concilium convenirent.[l]			territory to the council
Cluster: Frederick and the pope (e) Quomodo jam provocatus ad iram imperator praecepit omnes praelatos sine misericordia capi et sibi praesentari, quod sic evenit.[m]			The emperor orders the prelates to be captured
Cluster: Frederick and the pope (f) De captione praelatorum et legatorum.[n]			The capture of the legates and prelates
Cluster: Frederick and the pope (g) Epistola imperatoris ad regem Angliae missa de captione Faventiae et de captione praelatorum in mari.[o]			The emperor's letter concerning the capture of the city of Faenza, and the prelates by sea
Cluster: Frederick and the pope (h) Quomodo jussu imperatoris ducti sunt praelati Neapolim incarcerandi.[p]			How the prelates were taken to Naples to be imprisoned
Cluster: Frederick and the pope (i) Nota praelatorum miseriam.[q]			Note the misery of the prelates
Cluster: Frederick and the pope (j) Prophetia Sibillae magnae super hoc sic prophetavit.[r]			The prediction of the great Sybil, in which she prophesied in this way

382 APPENDIX 4

Title of entry in *CM*	English history	Imperial history	
		Mongol related	Other
Mongol cluster 2: (a) Quomodo captis et incarceratis legatis et praelatis et qui cum ipsis fuerunt, Henricus filius imperatoris ad Conradum mittitur in adjutorium contra Tartaros et Cumanos.[s]		Henry is sent to assist his brother Conrad against the Tartars	
Mongol cluster 2: (b) De quodam immani scelere Judaeorum.[t]		Stratagem of the Jews to bear arms to the Tartars	

[a] MS *B*, fol. 144ᵛ, col. a; *CM*, IV, p. 106; *EH*, I, p. 336. [b] MS *B*, fol. 144ᵛ, col. b; *CM*, IV, pp. 107–08; *EH*, I, pp. 337–38. [c] MS *B*, fol. 144ᵛ, col. b; *CM*, IV, pp. 108–09; *EH*, I, p. 338. [d] MS *B*, fol. 145ʳ, col. a; *CM*, IV, p. 109; *EH*, I, pp. 338–39. (See the internal structure of the cluster in detail in Figure 5.) [e] MS *B*, fol. 145ʳ, cols a–b; *CM*, IV, pp. 109–12; *EH*, I, pp. 339–41. Contiguous script, the embedded text is not in the text, but a separate red rubric — 'Dictum regis Francorum notabile' — draws attention to it on the margin. [f] MS *B*, fols 145ʳ, col. b–146ʳ, col. b; *CM*, IV, pp. 112–19; *EH*, I, pp. 341–47. Contiguous script, no paragraph marks. [g] MS *B*, fol. 146ᵛ, col. a; *CM*, IV, p. 119; *EH*, I, p. 347. [h] MS *B*, fol. 146ᵛ, col. a; *CM*, IV, pp. 119–20; *EH*, I, pp. 347–48. [i] MS *B*, fol. 146ᵛ, col. a; *CM*, IV, pp. 120–21; *EH*, I, pp. 349–51. [j] MS *B*, fols 146ᵛ, col. b–147ʳ, col. a; *CM*, IV, pp. 121–23; *EH*, I, pp. 351–52. [k] MS *B*, fol. 147ʳ, col. a; *CM*, IV, p. 123; *EH*, I, p. 351. [l] MS *B*, fol. 147ʳ, col. a; *CM*, IV, p. 124; *EH*, I, pp. 351–52. [m] MS *B*, fol. 147ʳ, col. b; *CM*, IV, p. 124; *EH*, I, p. 352. [n] MS *B*, fol. 147ʳ, col. b; *CM*, IV, p. 125; *EH*, I, pp. 352–53. [o] MS *B*, fol. 147ʳ, col. b–147ᵛ, col. b; *CM*, IV, pp. 126–29; *EH*, I, pp. 353–56. [p] MS *B*, fol. 147ᵛ, col. b; *CM*, IV, pp. 129–30; *EH*, I, p. 356. [q] MS *B*, fol. 147ᵛ, col. a, separate bottom rubric; *CM*, IV, p. 130; not in *EH*. [r] MS *B*, fol. 147ᵛ, col. b, separate bottom rubric; *CM*, IV, p. 130; not in *EH*. [s] MS *B*, fol. 148ʳ, col. a; *CM*, IV, p. 131; *EH*, I, pp. 356–57. [t] MS *B*, fol. 148ʳ, cols a–b; *CM*, IV, p. 131; *EH*, I, pp. 357–58.

APPENDIX 5

Events and Rumours: 1241 vs 1244

Events and rumours covered in both 1241 and 1244.

1241	1244[A]
-	Per eosdem dies, rex Hungariae, expulsus de regno suo per Tartaros, ad alas protectionis imperialis convolavit, ab eodem in tali articulo consilium efficax et auxilium contra communes hostes petiturus. (About this time the king of Hungary, having been expelled from his kingdom by the Tartars, applied to the court of the emperor for protection, and asked for effectual advice and assistance against the common enemy.)
qui etiam cum Cumanis sibi conterminis et jam confoederatis, machinante imperatore, regem Hungariae cum quibusdam aliis magnatibus expugnarunt, ut fatigatus rex ad alas imperatoris avolaret, homagium ei pro succursu irapendendo facturus. (and these people, by the machinations of the emperor, have, together with their neighbours, the Cumanians, who have now entered into an alliance with them, made war on the king of Hungary and some other nobles, in order that the harassed king may fly to the wings of the emperor for protection, and do homage to him for affording him assistance.[b])	Habito igitur diuturno et secretissimo consilio, procuratum est, quod dominus imperator ab irruptione hostili et barbarica potenter regnum Hungariae liberaret, ut scilicet dictus rex regnum illud liberatum et pacificatum ab ipso imperatore et deinceps ab imperio teneret, quasi a domino capitali. (Long and secret deliberation was then held, and it was determined that the emperor should, with a strong hand, free the kingdom of Hungary from the hostile irruption of the barbarians, on condition, forsooth, that the said king should receive back his kingdom, when restored to freedom and to peace, from the emperor, and should hold it of the empire as of a lord paramount.)
misit idem imperator Henricum filium suum, qui de praelatis et eorum ducibus, ut dictum, triumpharat, ad fratrem Conradum, qui cum innumerabili exercitu ex diversis finibus imperii collecto,	Misso igitur innumerabili exercitu, imperator regnum memoratum, non sine magnis sumptibus et periculis, ab inhumanis Tartaris liberavit, et eosdem procul a finibus regni potenter et prudenter

1241	1244[A]

Tartarorum et Cumanorum [impetum] repellere magnifice parabatur, ut alter alterius fratris solatio mutuo roboraretur, et milite copiosiore stiparetur. Duxit autem secum quatuor milia equitantium jussu patris, et peditum manum non minimam, qui, cum aliis adjuncti fuissent quibus venerant in subsidium, incomparabilem exercitum conflaverunt. [...] tandem Deo propitio repulsus est hostilis exercitus, licet nullo numero posset comprehendi. (The emperor then [...] sent his son Henry, who had, as has been stated, conquered the prelates and their convoy, to join his brother Conrad, who was prepared with an innumerable army, raised from the various provinces of the empire, to check the violence of the Tartars and Cumanians, in order that the brothers might mutually comfort and assist one another, and be surrounded by a larger force. The said Henry, by his father's orders, took with him four thousand cavalry and a large body of foot-soldiers, who, when united to the others to whose assistance they had come, composed an immense army; [...] and after many had fallen on both sides, the hostile army, although almost innumerable, was repulsed.[c]) Unde cum haec fierent, ipsi hostes sunt regressi. (and as these things have been effected, the enemies have retreated.[d])

eliminavit. (An immense army was therefore sent, and the emperor, not without great outlay of money and danger, freed the abovenamed kingdom from the inhuman Tartars, and powerfully and ably drove them beyond the limits of that kingdom.)

Fuerunt namque qui dicerent, imperatorem hanc Tartarorum pestem sponte fuisse machinatum, et per hanc elegantem epistolam scelus tam nepharium nequiter palliasse, et ad totius mundi monarchiam, in fidei Christianae subversionem, ad instar Luciferi vel Antichristi, hiatu protervo conspirare. (There were some who said that the emperor had, of his own accord, plotted this infliction of the Tartars, and that by this clever letter he basely cloaked his nefarious crime, and that in his grasping ambition he was, like Lucifer, or Antichrist, conspiring against the monarchy of the

Fuerunt qui dicerent, quod machinante imperiali astutia illuc pervenerunt ipsi detestandi Tartari, dominatui imperatoris attendentes et obligati, haec omnia facientes, ut imperator regem et regnum taliter potestati suae subjugaret. (There were some who said that those detested Tartars came there from the first by the cunning machinations of the emperor; that they only awaited his bidding, and were bound to fulfil his commands, acting in such a way that the emperor might reduce that king and his kingdom under his own dominion.)

1241	1244[A]
whole world, to the utter ruin of the Christian faith.[e])	
Sed absit, ut in uno corpore mortali tanta sceleris immanitas latitaret. (But God forbid that so much wickedness should be lurking in any one mortal body.[f])	Sed haec lividorum susurra fuit, nec credi debet oblocutio haec. (But this is what was whispered by those who were jealous of him, and such calumny ought not to be believed.)
-	Igitur liberato regno Hungariae et regi pacifice restituto, subjecta facta est Hungaria imperio, et obligata in trecentis militibus et eorum sequela, imperatori in confiniis pugnaturo fideliter exhibendis. (When the kingdom of Hungary, therefore, was freed, and its king restored in peace, Hungary became subject to the empire, and was bound to supply three hundred knights, and their followers, to fight on the borders for the emperor, loyally and faithfully.)

[a] MS B, fol. 170[v], cols a–b; CM, IV, p. 298; EH, I, pp. 489–90.   [b] MS B, fol. 146[v], col. a; CM, IV, p. 120; EH, I, p. 348. See also Chapter 4 ('Frederick II's Letter').   [c] MS B, fol. 148[r], col. a; CM, IV, p. 131; EH, I, pp. 356–57. See also Chapter 4 ('The Second 1241 Cluster').   [d] MS B, fol. 146[v], col. a; CM, IV, p. 120; EH, I, pp. 348–49.   [e] MS B, fol. 146[v], col. a; CM, IV, p. 119; EH, I, p. 348.   [f] MS B, fol. 146[v], col. a; CM, IV, p. 120; EH, I, p. 349.

APPENDIX 6 ────────────────

List of Manuscripts

Manuscripts Containing the *Chronica majora* and its Fragments / Continuations

A: Cambridge, Corpus Christi College, MS 26
Latin and French, *c.* 1200–1299, ii+vi+140+ii+i fols
Available at <https://parker.stanford.edu/parker/catalog/rf352tc5448>

fols i^r–vi^v: Preliminary matter: itinerary from London to the Holy Land (i^r–iv^r), table of Concurrentes, etc. from 1116 to 1620 (iv^v)
fols 1^r–141^v: Matthew Paris, *Chronica majora*, part 1
fols vii^r–viii^v: drawing of Virgin with child and faces of Christ (vii^r), *mappa mundi* (vii^v) genealogy of Anglo-Saxon kings (viii^{r-v})
fol. ix^r: flyleaf with notes (*Cronica ab origine mundi usque ad a. d. millesimum … simum videlicet usque ad mortem henrici (II) Regis anglie // iiii marce auri dedit … de … pro pacevii marce dabantur comiti legr S. pro carta quam habuit a rege de custodia Wascon //* S. Patrick prophesies greatness of the unborn S. David // *Circa carleolum patria est dicta aluedele. Hic. uersus austrum cocormue villa. patria. complem. Aqua dorecte et currit (?) per cocormue //* Edwarde Aglionby of Balsall Temple (sixteenth-century hand) // IhesusmariaJohnes (fifteenth-century hand) // note on dispersion of Apostles and division of the world, list of Saxon kings, etc.

B: Cambridge, Corpus Christi College, MS 16II
Latin and French, *c.* 1200–1299, 284 fols
Available at <https://parker.stanford.edu/parker/catalog/qt808nj0703>

fols 1^r–284^r: Matthew Paris, *Chronica majora*, part 2 (1189–1253)
(fols 4^r–11^r: early modern insertion, 284^v crossed out)

BI: Cambridge, Corpus Christi College, MS 16I
Latin and French, *c.* 1200–1299, 5 fols
Available at <https://parker.stanford.edu/parker/catalog/rb378fk5493>

388   APPENDIX 6

fols i^r–v^v (originally preliminary matter in MS 16): Matthew Paris: lists and genealogies of kings, a diagram of the winds, itineraries, maps, and the picture of the elephant given by Louis IX to Henry III

C: London, BL, MS Cotton Nero D V

Latin, Middle English, mid-thirteenth and mid-fourteenth century, i+395+i fols

fol. 1^v: *Mappa terrae habitabilis*
fols 2r–393r: Matthew Paris, *Chronica majora* ('the fair copy')
fol. 150^v: St Godric's hymn to the Blessed Virgin Mary
fols 393^r–395^r: *De gestis regis Arthuri* from Geoffrey of Monmouth's *Historia regum Britannniae*

LA: London, BL, MS Cotton Nero D I

Latin and Anglo-Norman, mid-thirteenth and early fourteenth century, ii+ii+202+ii fols
Available at <http://www.bl.uk/manuscripts/FullDisplay.aspx?ref = Cotton_MS_Nero_D_I>

fol. 1^r: Notes related to the contents of the manuscript (seventeenth century)
fol. 1^v: Table of contents by Richard James (d. 1638)
fols 2^r–25^r: Matthew Paris, *Vita Offarum*
fols 25^v–26^v: Matthew Paris, *Cum Danorum rabies*: 'Cum danorum rabies in anglia feralius grassaretur ... litteris minime commendatur'.
fols 27^r–29^v: Matthew Paris, Tracts on St Alban
fols 30^r–63^v: Matthew Paris, *Gesta abbatum monasterii sancti Albani*, part I, with attached documents
fols 64^r–73^v: Matthew Paris, *Gesta abbatum monasterii sancti Albani*, part II, followed by documents of 1255–1257, in roughly chronological order
fols 74^r–84^v: *Additamenta* of 1256–1259
fols 85^r–100^v: *Additamenta* of 1242–1250, copied in or before 1250; fols 168–69 were probably placed originally before fol. 85.
fols 101^r–105^v: Miscellaneous documents of 1250 and 1256–1257
fols 106r–120v: *Additamenta*, mainly of 1252–1254, used in the *Chronica maiora*
fols 121^r–129^v: Miscellaneous documents, including many of 1254
fols 130^r–137^v: Miscellaneous material of 1257, together with later material added after Matthew's death
fols 138^v–144^v: Later material added after Matthew's death, incl. 'Provisiones novae baronum', *De passibus custodiendis et corrigendis*, miscellaneous agreements and charters relating to property at St Alban's

fols 145^r–148^v: Miscellaneous documents, including Matthew Paris's tract on the St Albans gems. Formerly, fols 145–47 followed fol. 63; moved to this location when part II of the *Gesta abbatum* was inserted into its present position

fols 149^r–161^r: 'Antiqua et primitiua munimenta ecclesie sancti Albani': St Albans charters and papal privileges, copied from a lost twelfth-century St Albans cartulary

fols 162^r–167^v: *List of Popes* from Peter to Gregory IX, continued in several hands to Paul II; *Liber provincialis*; obituary of St Albans from 1216 to 1253; *List of Kings of England from Ine to Henry III*, with a long note on John (probably added by Robert Cotton)

fols 168^r–169^r: Charges against Hubert de Burgh: 'Responsiones magistri laurentii de sancto Albano pro comite kancie Huberto de Burgo contra quem mouit dominus rex grauissimas questiones'

fols 169^v–170^v: Drawing and account of the elephant sent to Henry III by Louis IX of France as a gift in 1255

fols 171^{r-v}: Coloured drawings of coats of arms of the English nobility

fols 172^r–175^v: St Albans tenants, with copies of charters (fourteenth century)

fols 176^r–183^r: Pleas from St Albans (fourteenth century), including list of lands owned by St Albans, '*Iste sunt firme pertinentes tam ad quoquinam monachorum sancti Albani quam abbatis*', in Matthew Paris's hand, with fourteenth-century *placita* added (fols 181^v–182^r)

fols 183^v–184^r: Matthew Paris, mapped itinerary from London to Naples

fol. 184^v: Accounts of the children of Thomas of Savoy and Eleanor of Aquitaine, genealogical trees in the margin

fol. 185^r: Note on King Offa; note of the different winds with a diagram, with a drawing of a bird

fol. 185^v: Circular diagram of the winds with the names in Latin and Anglo-Norman linked to the elements; verses about the winds, 'Frater matheus de ventis'

fol. 186^r: Diagram showing the *parhelion* (bright spots appearing on either side of the sun) seen in the sky over England on April 1233; notes on ecclesiastical affairs, heraldic device of the count of Flanders, count of Brabant, and Peter of Savoy; some Latin verses

fol. 186^v: List of saints from a martyrology

fol. 187^r: Note of the defeat of Louis IX; a receipt; extracts from Gregory

fol. 187^v: Map of Britain, showing four Roman military roads, with notes on St Albans lands

fols 188^r–193^v: Statutes of St Julian's Hospital (near St Albans), its foundation charter, and other charters and papal privileges (fourteenth century)

fols 194^{r-v}: Monastic rules of the nunnery of Sopwell (fourteenth century)

fols 194^v–195^r: Rules of St Julian's Abbey (fourteenth century) fols 196^{r-v}: Letters of John, abbot of St Albans (fourteenth century)

fol. 197^r: Fragment of a *Life of Stephen Langton*

fol. 197^v: Charter of St Albans documenting a loan from Florentine merchants in London

fol. 198^r: Fragment of a *Life of Stephen Langton*

fol. 199^r: Note on the death of Emperor Frederick II followed by a rough drawing of a coat of arms and a signature 'Symons Thomas' on the upper margin; a letter from Pope Innocent IV to the bishop of Ely (fourteenth century)

fol. 199^v: Copy of Magna Carta with an account of a letter of Innocent IV dated to 1253 and an account of the Battle of Walcheren, 1253 (fourteenth century)

fol. 200^r: Drawings of coats of arms

fol. 200^v: Pen trials, including several names of monks

fols 201^{r-v}: 'Compositio facta inter infirmarium sancti albani et vicarium sancti petri', with a brief list of expenses (fifteenth century)

fol. 202^r: Note regarding the will of Frederick II (seventeenth century)

R: London, BL, MS Royal 14 C VII

Latin and Anglo-Norman, mid-thirteenth century, fols ii+i+232+iii (fols 2–5: parchment leaves mounted separately)

Available at <http://www.bl.uk/manuscripts/FullDisplay.aspx?ref = Royal_MS_14_C_VII&index = 126>

fols 1^v–8^r: Maps and other prefatory material including a diagram of winds, the *Itinerary from London to the Holy Land*, Easter tables, and a calendar. Maps in colours and gold of an itinerary from London to Apulia (fols 2^r–4^r), and to the Holy Land (fols 4^v–5^r), now mounted separately.

fols 10^r–156^v: Matthew Paris, *Historia Anglorum* prefaced with images of English kings (fols 8^v–9^r)

fols 157^r–218^v: Matthew Paris, *Chronica Majora*, part 3, with the continuation written after Paris's death (from 1254)

Manuscripts Containing Matthew Paris's *Flores historiarum* and its Fragments / Continuations

1. 'Westminster' Continuation (Chetham Group)

Where necessary Luard's sigla are modified to differentiate them from *Chronica majora* manuscripts (e.g. Luard's MS *A* = *Ar*, MS *W* = *Wf*). Manuscripts identified and added by Trevor Russel Smith, Antonia Gransden, and myself are assigned new sigla here.[1]

Ch: Manchester, Chetham Library, MS 6712 [A.6.89]
Latin, fourteenth century, 301 fols

fols 1^r–3^v: fifteenth-century notes
fols 4^r–6^v: incomplete liturgical calendar: *Calendarium cum notis obituorum, Liber Ecclesiae Petri Westmonasterii*
fols 7^r–298^r: [Matthaei Westmonasteriensis], *Flores historiarum* cum continuatio ad a. 1326 (pt 1: Creation to 1066, based on Wendover's *Flores*; from 1066 to its 1327 abbreviated from the *Chronica majora* and others)

Ad: Oxford, Bodleian Library, MS Add. C. 22 [SC 28782]
Latin, fifteenth-century fragment, purchased at Sotheby's 21 Jan. 1861, lot 787.
Not found.[2]

[Matthew of Westminster], *Flores historiarum, a.* 1187–1204

Ar: London, BL, MS Arundel 96
Latin, fourteenth century, no additions to MS *Ch*, probable provenance: Christ Church Canterbury), iii+128 fols

[Mathai Westmonasteriensis], *Flores Historiarum usque ad an. 1284: deinde sequuntur gestis per annos 1285, 1286*

Bd: Oxford, Bodleian Library, MS Bodley 912 [SC 30434], part 2 (cf. MS *H* and *Ld*)
French, English, and Latin, fourteenth century, part 1+2 (23+207 fols)

Part 1.
fols 1^r–15^v: Guillaume le Clerk, *Bestiaire* and rules of health in English (fol. 15)

Part 2.
fols 16^r–22^v: Contents of the *Flores historiarum*
fols 24^r–224^v: [Matthew of Westminster], *Flores historiarum* (to 1306), three leaves missing compared to table of contents. Illustrated

---

1 *FH*, I, pp. xvii–xxix.
2 Hunt, Madan, and Douglas, eds, *A Summary Catalogue of Western Manuscripts in the Bodleian Library*, p. 506.

fols 225ᵛ–228ᵛ: John Bevere, *Commendatio lamentabilis in transitu magni Edwardi regis*

fols 229ʳ–230ᵛ: Abbreviated *Annals*, 1307–1356

Ca: London, BL, MS Cotton Cleopatra A XVI

Latin, late fourteenth and fifteenth century, 197 fols = ii+66 (fols 3–68)+129 (fols 69–197)

fols 3ʳ–68ʳ: Treatises relating to the Exchequer, including *Leges Edwardi regis* (fols 56ʳ–61ᵛ)

fols 69ʳ–197ʳ: *Chronicle of English History*, AD 1199–1368, incl. 'Westminster' continuation of *Flores historiarum* for 1298–1306 (fols 69ʳ–85ʳ)[3]

Cl: London, BL, MS Cotton Claudius E VIII (cf. MS *F* and *Re*)

Latin and French, mid-fourteenth and fifteenth century, 273 fols

Found in medieval library catalogue.[4]

fol. 1ʳ⁻ᵛ: Psalter leaf (*c.* 1350–1360)

fol. 3ʳ⁻ᵛ: unidentified Anglo-Norman text

fols 5ʳ: *De fundatoribus ecclesiarum per Angliam*

fols 5ᵛ: Prophecies

fols 10ʳ–11ʳ: Description of Rome

fols 13ᵛ–14ʳ: *De uiris illustribus quo tempore scripserunt*

fols 18ʳ–26ᵛ: Index to the *Flores historiarum*

fols 26ᵛ: List of the priors of Norwich Cathedral Priory

fol. 27ʳ⁻ᵛ: Prophecies

fols 27ᵛ–240ʳ: *Flores historiarum* to 1307, copy of MS *Ch*, with many additions executed at Benedictine cathedral priory of Holy Trinity, Norwich

fols 242ʳ–253ᵛ: Adam Murimuth, *Chronicon*, AD 1303–1340

fols 253ᵛ–254ʳ, 256ʳ–259ᵛ, 261ʳ–262ᵛ: Anglo-Norman texts

fols 268ʳ–272ᵛ: Ecclesiastical lists, end of fourteenth century

---

3 Added by Smith, 'Further Manuscripts of Matthew Paris', p. 6, n. 3; Gransden, 'The Continuations of the *Flores Historiarum* from 1265 to 1327'. Also noted in Tout, 'The Westminster Chronicle Attributed to Robert of Reading'.

4 No. B61.6, in 'Benedictines: The Shorter Catalogues: Norwich; B61. Bale, *c.* 1550'.

LIST OF MANUSCRIPTS   393

F: Oxford, Bodleian Library, MS Fairfax 20 [SC 3900] (cf. MS *Cl* and *Re*)

Latin, mid-fourteenth century, i+82 fols
Found in medieval library catalogue.[5]

fol. 1^r: Description of Rome

fol. 3^r: Description of England

fol. 4^r: Description of an inexpugnable castle in Armenia and the seven wonders of the world

fol. 4^v: Ralph of Diceto, *De mirabilibus Angliae*

fol. 5^v: Ralph of Diceto, *De viris illustribus quo tempore scripserunt*

fol. 6^v: *De denario sancti Petri que Romescot dicitur*

fol. 7^r: Weights, measures, Old English legal terms

fol. 7^v: *De modo coronationis regis Ricardi*

fol. 8^r: Henry of Huntingdon, Prophecy of the Norman conquest

fol. 8^v: letter of Hugh, bishop of Coventry concerning the election of the bishop of Ely

fol. 10^r: *De primo adventu Yberniam*, composite text from Gerald of Wales and Hoveden

fols 11r–70v: *Flores historiarum* from Creation to AD 635, based on MS *Ch*, written at Benedictine cathedral priory of Holy Trinity Norwich before 1352

fol. 71^r: Letters patent of Edward III to Yarmouth (1333)

fol. 72^r: Extract from the Domesday Book and fourteenth-century liberties relating to Yarmouth

fol. 73^r: fragment from Roger of Wendover's *Flores historiarum*

fol. 73^v: list of the priors of Norwich ad a. 1344

fol. 74^r: index of persons and things beginning with *E*

fol. 81^r: a passage on early English history

fol. 81^v: historical prophecies in verse

H: Oxford, Bodleian Library, MS Hatton 53 [SC 4122] (cf. MS *Bd* and *Ld*)

Latin, early fourteenth century, ii+248 fols

fol. 1^r: table of contents

fol. 9^r–135^v: *Liber qui Flores hystoriarum intitulatur*, to 1307

fols 243^r–246^v: John of Bevere, *Commendacio lamentabilis in transit Regis Edwardi quarti*

fols 247^r–248^v: notes in sixteenth-century hand

---

5 No. B58.27 = B60.1, in 'Benedictines: The Shorter Catalogues: Norwich; B58. Books owned by Simon Bozoun, 14th cent.' Also note marginal notation '*Liber fratris Symonis Bozoun prioris Norwic*' (fol. 13^r).

394   APPENDIX 6

Ld: Oxford, Bodleian Library, MS Laud 572 (cf. MS *Bd* and *H*)
English, Latin, *c.* 1300, probably from Winchester, 220 fols

fol. i: sixteenth-century lawsuit writ
fols 1–217ʳ: Matthaei Westmonasteriensis *Chronicon* quod dicitur *Flores historiarum*
fols 217ᵛ–220ʳ: John Bevere, *Commendatio lamentabilis in transitu magni Edwardi regis* (9 items)

Lm: London, Lambeth Palace Library, MS 188
Latin, thirteenth to mid-fourteenth century, 213+ii fols, pagination according to original folio numbers written.[6]

fols 1ʳ–165ʳ: ***Flores historiarum*, 'Westminster' continuation from Creation ad a. 1306**
fol. 165ʳ: *Flores* continued by Adam Murimuth, *Chronicon* without a break
fol. 165ᵛ: blank except for note at the bottom
fol. 166ʳ: diagrammatic genealogy (Latin) of French kings from St Louis to Edward, king of England
fol. 166ᵛ: blank
fols 168ʳ–173ᵛ: Inc. '*Quoto anno ab incarnatione Domini Britanni qui primum Britanniam incolebant*' (hand *c.* 1200)
fol. 174ʳ: continuation in fourteenth-century hand
fols 174ᵛ–175ʳ: blank, notes in early modern hand
fols 176ʳ–177ᵛ: list of bishops of Norwich until 1299 (fourteenth-century hand), with a continuation until 1356 in secretary hand
fols 178ᵛ–179ʳ: inc. '*Sequenti vero die Alexander prior conuocato capitulo*'
fols 180ʳ–210ᵛ: Geoffrey of Monmouth, *Historia Regum Brittanie*
fols 211ʳ–213ᵛ: recto ruled, blank

Lp: London, Lambeth Palace Library, MS 1106
Latin, late thirteenth to fourteenth century, 2 + 120 + 2 fols

fols 1–93ʳ: *Flores historiarum*, 'Westminster' continuation from Creation ad a. 1306, copy with many omissions, a few insertions, various notes touching on the history of St Paul's, London between 1140 and 1303
fols 93ʳ–110ᵛ: the so-called *Annales Paulini*, scribe's own continuation of the *Flores* from 1307 to 1341
fols 111ʳ–120ᵛ: *Annals of Elias of Trickingham, monk of Peterborough, AD 626–1268*

---

6 Added by Smith, 'Further Manuscripts of Matthew Paris', p. 6, n. 5.

M: Oxford, Bodleian Library, MS e. Musaeo 149 [SC 3659]
Latin, early fourteenth century, iii+387 fols

fols 1ʳ–387ʳ: *Flores historiarum* (indirect copy from MS *Ch*; from 1298 to 1303 it corresponds with MS *E*, with additions to 1306 from Higden, etc.)

N: London, BL, MS Cotton Nero D II
Latin, Anglo-Norman, and French, between *c.* 1100–*c.* 1650, composite, containing 11 items, i+ 314 fols: (parchment 213+2+21+4+10+14+11) + (paper 20) + (parchment 9+8) + (paper 1)

fol. 1ᵛ: Cottonian list of contents
fols 2ʳ–214ʳ: Chronicle of Rochester Cathedral Priory to 1377; including a list of the rulers of the eight kingdoms of England (fol. 80ᵛ). It is a version of the *Flores Historiarum* with material relating to Rochester probably added by Edmund of Hadenham, monk of Rochester (*c.* 1300).
fols 215ʳ–216ᵛ: Annalistic chronicle to 1089 (imperfect)
fols 217ʳ⁻ᵛ: List of donations to Holme St Benets Priory, imperfect
fols 218ʳ–237ʳ: John of Oxnead, Chronicle to 1293
fols 238ʳ–241ʳ: Chronicle of Battle Abbey to 1206
fols 242ʳ–251ᵛ: Miscellaneous historical texts, including *De mirabilibus Anglie* (fols 245ᵛ–246ᵛ)
fols 252ʳ–265ᵛ: Heraldic miscellany, including *La livre de la ffoundacion et ordonnance de l'ordre et compaignie de la Iartier* (fols 252ʳ–254ʳ) and *Le livre de la creacion et foundacion des heraulx* (fols 254ᵛ–256ᵛ)
fols 266ʳ–276ʳ: Robert Grosseteste, *Constitutiones*
fols 277ʳ–296ᵛ: Continuation of Walter of Guisborough's *Chronicle*, 1327–1346
fols 297ʳ–305ʳ: Index to the Rochester *Chronicle* on fols 2–214
fols 306ʳ–313ᵛ: Jean Froissart, *Chroniques* (imperfect)
fol. 314ʳ: Drawing of an unidentified church
(fols 2–214, 242–51 and 297–305 are from the same manuscript)

O: London, BL, MS Cotton Otho C II
Latin, end of fourteenth century, damaged in fire, many years wanting, 1 item, 138 fols

fols 1–138: *Flores historiarum*, with a continuation from Adam Murimuth from 1301 it follows Trivet and MS *Cl*

396   APPENDIX 6

***Re*:**   **London, BL, MS Royal 14 C VI** (cf. MS *Cl* and *F*)
Latin, the main portion probably *c.* 1304, at Hulme Abbey (the Tintern addition only occupies five leaves), 1 item, i+259 fols

fols 1–7^v: prefatory matter, cf. MS *Cl* (fols 6–14)

fol. 1^r: Description of Rome, beg. 'Habet autem urbs Rome'

fol. 2^v: Description of England, dioceses, shires, principal roads, languages, and kingdoms of England, incl. a passage in English on weights

fol. 3^v: Paragraph *'De castellis Armenie'*, inc. *'In Armenia minori est quoddam castellum'* continued by *De septem miraculis mundi*

fol. 4^r: 'De mirabilibus Anglie' from Ralph de Diceto, *Abbreviationes Chronicorum*

fol. 5^r: 'De uiris illustribus quo tempore scripserunt', from Ralph de Diceto, *Abbreviationes Chronicorum* with additions of William of Malmesbury and Henry of Huntingdon

fol. 5^v: 'De denario sancti Petri qui Romesscot dicitur'

fol. 6^r: 'Diversorum nominum interpretationes': explanations of certain English legal terms

fol. 6^r: 'De modo coronacionis regis et de coronacione regis Ricardi', from Hoveden's *Chronica*

fol. 7^r: Prophecy of the Norman Conquest, quoted from Henry of Huntingdon

fol. 7^r: 'De primo adventu in Yberniam', composite text from Gerald of Wales and Hoveden

fols 8–259: *Flores Historiarvm*, Creation to 1259, prepared at St Albans and continued there to 1265, and further continued at Westminster to 1326. Additions relating to the abbey of S. Benet Holme, Norfolk, down to 1304, and from 1305 to 1323 to Tintern Abbey.

***Rf*:**   **Oxford, Bodleian Library, MS Rawlinson B 177**
Latin, early fourteenth-century with fifteenth-century additions, 286 fols

fols 1^r–72^v: [Matthew of Westminster], *Flores historiarum* (probably from MS *M*)

fols 73^r–186^v: Martin (Polonus) of Troppau, *Chronicon pontificum et imperatorum usque ad a. 1284*

fols 187–90: blank

fol. 191^v: fifteenth-century notes

fols 192^r–286: *Annales Angliae usque ad a. 1305*, written at St Mary's, Southwark (cf. London, BL, MS Cotton Faustus B VIII)

LIST OF MANUSCRIPTS   397

T: Cambridge, Trinity College, MS R.4.2 (James no. 635)
Latin, fourteenth and fifteenth century, iv+260+ii fols, <https://mss-cat.trin.cam.ac.uk/Manuscript/R.4.2>

fols 1ʳ–132ʳ: *Liber qui flores historiarum intitulatur* **(probably copied from MS *M*)**
fol. 132ᵛ: blank
fols 133ʳ–240ʳ: *Liber secundus de coronacione regis Willelmi primi* (from 1298 it is closer to *E*, many additions from Higden)
fols 241ʳ–260ʳ: *Liber tertius ad a.* 1327

Wf: Westminster, Library of the Dean and Chapter, MS 24
Latin, fourteenth century, 1 item, 374 fols

fols 1ʳ–374: *Flores historiarum Matthei Westmonasteriensis ad a. 1306*
   (first part is an indirect copy from *Ch* with many additions, from 1265 it is closer to *E*)

2. Merton (Eton) Group

Sigla as given in Luard (MS *E* and *Ra*) except *As, Be, Hr, Hu,* and *P* (without sigla in Luard) which are mine.[7]

E: Eton College Library, MS 123. Also known as the Merton manuscript.
Latin, thirteenth and fourteenth century, written at the Priory of Merton, Surrey, formerly owned by Archbishop Matthew Parker, 1 item, 277 fols

fols 1ʳ–277: [**Matthaei Westmonasteriensis**] *Flores historiarum* **(ending in 1306)**

As: Oxford, All Souls, MS 37. Also known as John Rochfort's chronicle after his table of contents appended to the *Flores* and other historical works.
Latin, fourteenth and fifteenth century, 214 fols

fols 2–157: [**Matthaei Westmonasteriensis**] *Flores historiarum* **(copy of MS *E*, ending in 1307)**
fols 170–95: Nigel Wireker, *Brunellus sive Speculum Stultorum*
fols 196–205: Hugh of St Victor, *Hexameron in libris duobus*
fols 206–13: *Notabilia extracta per Johannem Rochefort militem*

---

7 *FH*, I, pp. xvii–xxix.

398 APPENDIX 6

Be: **New Haven, Yale University, Beinecke Rare Book and Manuscript Library, MS 426** (formerly Phillips MS 15732; Luard's siglum: *Tenison*)[8]
Latin, mid-fourteenth century, probably from Cluniac priory of St Saviour, Bermondsey, 1 item, iii+87+i+iii fols

fols 1ʳ–87ᵛ: *Historia Mathei Parisiensis; Manuscriptum Loftusianum*
(text begins imperfectly *s.a.* 1058 and contains continuations to 1327)

Hr: **London, BL, MS Harley 641** (under the name John Bevere, monk of Westminster, due to a medieval note of attribution (fol. 115ᵛ))
Latin, early fourteenth century, Canterbury, Kent. Benedictine abbey of St Augustine (originally of St Peter and St Paul), 1 item: fols ii + 206 (fol. 116 is an original blank leaf; fol. 117 is a later addition) + vi
Found in medieval library catalogue.[9]

Part 1 (fols 1ʳ–115ᵛ).
fols 1ʳ–8ʳ: Dares Phrygius, 'De bello troiano'
fols 9ʳ–19ᵛ: Miscellaneous historical texts
fols 24ᵛ–115ᵛ: 'Flores historiarum' attributed to John Bevere
Part 2 (fols 118ʳ–206ᵛ).
fols 118ʳ–174ᵛ: Martinus's 'Chronica pontificum et imperatorum'
fols 174ᵛ–186ᵛ: additions possibly by John Merelynch
fols 186ᵛ–206ᵛ: 'Proceedings against Dame Alice Kyteler'

Hu: **San Marino, Huntington Library, MS HM30319.** Formerly Phillipps 8517.
Latin, early fifteenth century, vi+108 fols, bound together by the time it was given to Battle Abbey by John Newton, cellarer, in mid-fifteenth century

fols i–iiiʳ: copied by Richard Aleyn, cellarer of Battle Abbey, 1459–1463:
1. Walter Map, *Dissuasio Valerii ad Ruffinum philosophum ne uxorem ducat*
2. *De Cacuvio [sic] et eius arbore capitulo 16*
3. John Ridevall, *Commentary on the Dissuasio Valerii*
fols iiiᵛ–ivʳ: Genealogy of Sir Hugh Halsham
fol. ivᵛ: blank

---

8 Phillipps, *Catalogus librorum manuscriptorum in bibliotheca*, p. 301; Shailor, *Catalogue of Medieval and Renaissance Manuscripts in the Beinecke Rare Book and Manuscript Library*, pp. 350–51.
9 No. 641 BA1.*926c ('cronica a conquestu Anglie et deinceps'), in 'Benedictines: Canterbury-St Augustine's; BA1. Catalogue, 15th cent.'.

fols v^r–vi^v: *Nomina sanctorum quorum reliquie hic in Bello continentur hec sunt* copied by Thomas Bryd, cellarer, 1436–1438

fols 1^r–94^r: Matthew Paris, *Flores Historiarum*

fol. 94^v: blank

fols 95^r–105^r: *Historia Apollonii Regis Tyri*

fols 105^v–106^v: Correspondence between the Emperor Lucius and King Arthur

fols 106^v–107^r: Notes on the history of England

fols 107^v–108^v: blank

Lt: **Oxford, Bodleian Library, MS Lat. hist. D IV (formerly Phillipps MS 11257)**

Sold in the 1965 Phillips manuscript auction in London (item 16), unknown to Ker and editors of the *Flores*.[10]

Latin, early fourteenth century, Abbey of Bury St Edmunds, 213+v fols

Part 1.

fol. 7^r: table of contents (fourteenth-century hand)

fol. 7^v: Martinus Polonus (Martin of Troppau), *Chronicon pontificum et imperatorum*

fol. 49^r: account of the missions of papal legates in England 1206–1317 (fourteenth-century hand, inserted later)

Part 2.

fols 50^r: summary of William of Malmesbury's *De gestis Pontificum Anglorum*

fols 50^v–51^r: Lists of the archbishops of Canterbury, the deans of St Paul's, London and the bishops of London

fols 59^r–65^r: *Leges sancti Edwardi per Willelmum Conquestorem regem Angliae approbate et confirmate*

fol. 62^v [inserted leaf in fourteenth-century hand]: Extracts from Geoffrey of Monmouth

fol. 65^{r-v}, Pseudo-Hildegard of Bingen, *Insurgent gentes*

fols 66^{r-v}: Extracts from Gildas, and description of Britain form another author

fol. 67^v: List of founders of English monasteries

fol. 70^{r-v} [inserted leaf in fourteenth-century hand]: list of papal bulls addressed to Kings of England

fol. 71^{r-v}: *Regnum Scotorum fuit inter cetera regna* (prophecy on Scotland in verse)

---

10 From the library of Rev. Taylor of Hereford Cathedral. Noted in Phillipps, *Catalogus librorum manuscriptorum in bibliotheca*, p. 190. In Sotheby & Co., *Catalogue of Thirty-Nine Manuscripts*, pp. 49–52. Also in Smith, 'Further Manuscripts of Matthew Paris', p. 7, n. 7.

fols 72^r–73^v [inserted leaf in fourteenth-century hand]: *Prophetia methodii et memoriale temporum* (cf. London, BL, MS Royal 8 F VIII, fol. 170^r)

fols 74^r–75^r: *Prognosticacio de futuris temporibus secundum fratrem Vincencius Belvacensem* (extracts from the *Speculum majus*)

fols 76^r–202^v: *Flores historiarum* (abridged main text with 'Merton' continuation for Creation–1306, perhaps by Ralph de Baldock [*Explic. Cronica Rad. Baldok*], closely related to MS *Lm*)

fols 76^{r-v} [inserted leaf in fourteenth-century hand]: List of papal bulls relating to England

fol. 202^v: *Annales Paulini*

fols 205^r–218^r: Continuation from 1309 to 1334: based on Adam Murimuth

fols 218^r–219^r: *Continuatio Chronicorum* 1335–1340, not by Murimuth

fols 219^r–224^v: *Annales* by Henry of Kirkestede 1341–1363

Part 3.

fols i^r–v^v: obits 1341–1361, miscellaneous philosophical texts (Commentary on Aristotle, *De generatione et corruptione*), list of historical events ad a. 1135

P: Paris, Bibliothèque nationale de France, MS Latin 6045
Latin, fourteenth century, 173 fols
<https://gallica.bnf.fr/ark:/12148/btv1b90779223>

fols 2^r–171^r: *Flores historiarum à creatione mundi ad annum 1306*

***Ra:*   Oxford, Bodleian Library, MS Rawlinson B 186 [SC 11547]**
Latin, fifteenth century, 1 item, 277 fols

fols 1–277: *Matthaei Westmonastriensis Flores historiarum ad a. 1307*

U: Unknown private collection (formerly A. Chester Beatty, MS W 70)
Latin, early fourteenth century, sold Sotheby's lot 18, 3 December 1968.

fols 9^r–140^v: *Matthaei Westmonastriensis Flores historiarum* (main text with 'Merton' continuation for 1066–1306)[11]

---

11 Added by Smith, 'Further Manuscripts of Matthew Paris', p. 7, n. 8.

3. *Unique / Uncategorized* Flores *Manuscripts*

London, Lambeth Palace Library, MS 419
Latin and English, fourteenth century, St Augustine's, Canterbury,
ii+161 fols
Found in medieval booklist.[12]

fols 3ʳ–95ʳ: *Cronica a tempore Willelmi bastardi et deinceps = Flores historiarum 1066–1306*
fols 95ʳ–99ʳ: continuation ad a. 1321 with frequent notices of Kentish affairs[13]
fols 99ʳ–102ᵛ: John Bevere, *Commendatio lamentabilis in transitu magni regis Edwardi*
fols 102ᵛ–103ʳ: *Litera consoliatoria Clementis papae regine Angliae directa super obitu regis*
fol. 103ᵛ: *Litera citatoria pro rge Scocie directa Boniface*
fols 104ᵛ–106ᵛ: *Declaracio Regis Angliae super negocio cum Scotiae 1301*
fol. 107ʳ: *Consideratio confederationis inter rehem Anglie et regem Alemannie*
fol. 108ᵛ: blank
fols 111ʳ–161ʳ: *Chronicon T. Sprot*, inc. 'Lux vera que illuminat omnem hominem'

W: Oxford, Bodleian Library, MS Douce 207 [SC 21781]
Latin, early fourteenth century, iv+244 fols

fols 1ʳ–213ᵛ: Roger of Wendover, *Flores historiarum*. Lacuna after fols 72 and 139 (a. 878–94, 1191–1192). This and London, BL, MS Cotton Otho B V are the only copies which extend from Creation to 1235.
fol. 214ʳ–230: Roger of Howden, *Chronica* (fragments, *s.a.* 1187–1191)
fols 231ʳ–234ʳ: short epitome of Matthew Paris's Flores historiarum, and short account of early British history based on Geoffrey of Monmouth
fol. 235ᵛ–237ʳ: Henry Kirkstead (?), *Speculum coenobitarum* (part)

London, BL, MS Cotton Nero D X
Latin, Anglo-Norman, French, mid-fourteenth century and seventeenth century, composite manuscript: i + 198 fols, 8 items; paper: (i+2+100+2) + parchment: 33+2+58+1)

---

12 No. BA1.*929a ('cronica a tempore Willelmi bastardi et deinceps'), in 'Benedictines: Canterbury- St Augustine's; Catalogue; fifteenth century'.
13 *Descriptive Catalogue of Materials Relating to the History of Great Britain and Ireland*, no. 618.

402   APPENDIX 6

fols 3^r–102^v: Gelasius of Cyzicus, *Liber de rebus gestis in sancto concilio Niceno*

fols 103^r–104^v: List of Roman emperors from Claudius (II) Gothicus to Julian 'the Apostate'

fols 105^r–137^r: *Chronicle of English history*, AD 1287–1346 (imperfect), based on the works of Nicholas Trivet and Adam Murimuth, including a peculiar expanded unidentified continuation of the *Flores historiarum* for 1287–1323 (fols 105^r–113^r)[14]

fols 138^r–139^r: Record of the boundaries of Huntingdonshire, Northamptonshire, and Cambridgeshire, 1244

fols 140^r–197^r: Hugh of Wells, *Matriculus de omnibus ecclesiis in archidiaconatu Leycestrie*

fol. 198: Fifteenth-century notes on British history

4. Unidentified copy of the Flores historiarum

London, BL, MS Lansdowne 96

Noted by Luard as a *Flores historiarum* manuscript of the *Ch* group; however, Lansdowne 96 is a sixteenth-century compilation of letters which does not contain any reference to the *Flores historiarum*, Matthew Paris, or Matthew of Westminster.[15]

Perhaps refers to a compilation copied by the librarian of Westminster Abbey, Richard Widmore (1681–1764), now in London, BL, MS Lansdowne 791.[16]

Flores Manuscripts Listed in Medieval Catalogues[17]

No. B60.1 = B61.7, in 'Benedictines: The Shorter Catalogues: Norwich; B61. Bale, *c.* 1550': Norwich: Leland, *c.* 1536–1540

No. B61.7, in 'Benedictines: The Shorter Catalogues: Norwich; B61. Bale, *c.* 1550': Norwich: Bale, *c.* 1550

No. Ss1.640, in *Brigittines: Syon*; Registrum of the Library of the Brethren, *c.* 1500–*c.* 1524

---

14 Smith, 'Further Manuscripts of Matthew Paris', p. 6, n. 4.

15 *CM*, I, p. xvi; British Library, *Western Manuscripts Lansdowne Manuscripts*, pp. 2973–95.

16 Contents of this late copy described in *Chronicles of the Reigns of Edward I and Edward II*, I, p. lvi.

17 *Medieval Libraries of Great Britain*, <http://mlgb3.bodleian.ox.ac.uk/>.

No. Uo3.61, in (Anon.) *University and College Libraries of Oxford University*: Gift of books by Humfrey, duke of Gloucester, 25 February 1444

No. Uo6.*61, in *University and College Libraries of Oxford*: All Souls College: Inventory of the Library, *c.* 1443

Other Miscellaneous Manuscripts Referred to in this Volume

Bologna, Colegio de España, MS 275: *Brevis nota eorum quae in primo concilio Lugdunensi*

Budapest, Egyetemi Könyvtár, Coll. Hevenesi Kaprinay Pray, MS 10831: *De facto Hungariae Magnae a fratre Ricardo*

Cambridge
Cambridge University Library, MS Dd X 22: John of Tynemouth, *Historia aurea*
Cambridge University Library, MS Ee III 59: Matthew Paris, *Life of King Edward the Confessor*
Corpus Christi College, MSS 5 and 6: John of Tynemouth, *Historia Aurea*, 2 vols
Gonville and Caius College, MS 162/83: tracts on Muhammad and the 'Saracens'; Marco Polo's travels; Odoric of Pordenone's travels, history of the 'Tartars', Jacques de Vitry, *Historia Hierosolimitana* (= MS GC)
St John's College, MS 239: *Bible* and misc.
Trinity College, MS O.9.34: The Romance of Alexander (probably St Albans)

Copenhagen, Det Kgl. Bibliotek, Acc. 2011/5: Courtenay Compendium (= MS CC)

Dublin
Trinity College, IE TCD MS 177 (formerly MS E I 40): a manuscript containing a *Life of St Amphibalus*, and other works relating to the history St Albans Abbey
Trinity College, IE TCD MS 347: Misc. incl. French verses on the Death of Simon de Montfort, *Annales de Monte Fernandi* (Annals of Multifernan), sermons or materials for sermons, Gilbertus Minorita's *Distinctiones*, and *Descripciones terrarum*

Florence, Biblioteca Riccardiana, Riccardiano, MS Ricc. 228: *Liber censualis Romanae curiae*, incl. Riccardus, *De facto Ungarie Magne*

Ghent, Universiteitsbibliotheek, MS 92: Lambert of St Omer, *Liber Floridus*

The Hague, Koninklijke Bibliotheek, MS 131 A 3: *Livre* by Moses ben Abraham, unfinished French historical and prophetic compilation

Innsbruck, Universitäts- und Landesbibliothek Tirol, MS 187: Ottobeuren Collection (= MS *OB*)

Linz, Oberösterreichische Landesbibliothek (formerly the Studienbibliothek), MS 446: Thomas Aquinas, *Glossa in evang. s. Matthaei*, (Re)quisitus Petrus archiepiscopus super Tartarorum (= MS *L*)

London

BL, Add. MS 32167: Adam Murimuth, *Chronicon*, imperfect

BL, MS Arundel 157: Psalter, including a calendar, preceded by a prayer from St Albans

BL, MS Cotton Claudius D VI: Matthew Paris, *Abbreviatio chronicorum* (or *Historia minor*) (= MS *AC*)

BL, MS Cotton Julius D VII: *Chronica Joannis Wallingford* or *Chronicle of John of Wallingford* bound with with many autograph texts and drawings by Matthew Paris (= MS *J*)

BL, MS Cotton Nero D VII: The Benefactors' Book of St Albans Abbey (Golden Book of St Albans) by Thomas Walsingham and others

BL, MS Cotton Otho B V: Roger of Wendover, *Flores historiarum* (= MS *Ow*)

BL, MS Cotton Titus A XIV: Thomas Wykes (attributed), *Chronicle*, Transcript of Parliament rolls, 21–24 Henry VIII; William Camden, collections relating to continental history

BL, MS Cotton Vespasian E III: The annals of Burton Abbey, an account of the Council of Oxford of 1222; St Cyprian, Confessio; Pseudo-Basil, *Admonitio ad Filium Spiritualem*; Isidore of Seville, *Synonyma*; Pseudo-Methodius, *De Initio et Fine Saeculi*, etc. (= MS *BA*)

BL, Cotton Rolls and Charters, Cotton Ch XIII 2: John of Tynemouth, *Historia Aurea*, abridged

BL, MS Harley 655: Ranulf Higden, *Polychronicon* with additions from John of Tynemouth, *Historia aurea*; Geoffrey of Monmouth, *Vita Merlini*

BL, MS Harley 1729: Ranulf Higden, *Polychronicon*, vol. II, part of Adam Murimuth, *Chronicon* incorporated

BL, MS Harley 3836: Adam Murimuth, *Continuatio chronicarum*

BL, MS Royal 4 D VII: Petrus Comestor, Richard of Saint-Victor, *Historia scolastica*; Robert Grosseteste, *Translation of Testamenta duodecim patriarcharum, and Suidas De probatione Virginitatis Beate Marie*

BL, MS Royal 13 A XVIII: Chronicles of English history and miscellaneous tracts, incl. Adam Murimuth, *Chronicon*, Henry of Huntingdon, *Historia Anglorum*, etc.

BL, MS Royal 13 E IX: Historical and geographical works: *Des Grantz Geanz*, John Mandeville, Thomas Walsingham, *Chronica majora*, John of Tynemouth, *Historia Aurea*, abridged, etc.

BL, MSS Sloane 5246 and 3253: [James Paris] Du Plessis, *A Short History of Human Prodigious & Monstrous Births of Dwarfs, Sleepers, Giants, Strong Men, Hermaphrodies, Numerous Births, and Extream Old Age &c.* (1730 and 1732, respectively)

College of Arms, MS Arundel 18: Chronicle from death of Edward I to 1320, 'Annals of Adam Murymuth'

Lambeth Palace Library, MSS 10, 11, 12: John of Tynemouth, *Historia Aurea*, 3 vols

Luxemburg, Bibliothèque nationale de Luxembourg, MS 110: works by Solinus, Iulius Valerius, Ps.-Alexander Magnus, Iohannes de Alta Silva, John of Plano Carpini

Lucerne, Zentral- und Hochschulbibliothek, MS P 13 fol.:4: books 25–32 of the history of the world by Vincent of Beauvais; fols 372–78 contain an early copy of the *Historia Tartarorum* by C. de Bridia

Oxford

Bodleian Library, MS Ashmole 304: Matthew Paris, collection of fortune-telling tracts (*sortes*)

Bodleian Library, MS Bodley 240: John of Tynemouth, *Historia aurea*, pt 2; misc. lives of saints, local documents, and poetry

Bodleian Library, MS Lat. 68: 'Carinthian' *Ars dictaminis*

Corpus Christi College, MS CCC 2*: St Albans Bible (= MS CO)

Magdalen College, MS 53: misc., incl. *De electione priorum Wymondham*, with St Albans and Wymondham lists, William of St Albans, *Life of St Alban and St Amphibalus*, Adam Murimuth, *Chronicon*, Hemingburgh's chronicle, and copies of documents in London, BL, MS Cotton Claudius E VIII

Queen's College, MS 304: Chronicles, genealogies, etc., by English authors, incl. Peter of Ickham, Nicholas Trevet, *Annales sex regum Angliae*, Adam Murimuth, *Continuatio chronicarum*, etc.

Paris

Bibliothèque nationale de France, MS Clairambault 1021

Bibliothèque nationale de France, MS Latin 8990: *Transsumpta de Lyon* (de Barive copy)

Vatican

Archivio Apostolico Vaticano, Archivum Arcis, MS Arm. C. 398: *Transsumpta de Lyon*

Archivio Apostolico Vaticano, MS Miscell. Arm. XV. T. 1: *Liber censualis Romanae curiae*, incl. Riccardus, *De facto Ungarie Magne*

Archivio Apostolico Vaticano, MS Miscell. Arm. XV. T. 2: *Liber censualis Romanae curiae*, incl. Riccardus, *De facto Ungarie Magne*

BAV, MS Barb. Lat. 2514: *Liber censualis Romanae curiae*, incl. Riccardus, *De facto Ungarie Magne*

BAV, MS Ottobon. Lat. 2520: *Relatio de concilio Lugdunensi*

BAV, MS Ottobon. Lat. 2546: *Summarium (Transsumpta de Lyon)*

BAV, MS Pal. Lat. 443: *Misc.*, incl. *Epistula de vita Tartarorum*

BAV, MS Pal. Lat. 965: *Diversa ad historiam pertinentia*, incl. Riccardus, *De facto Ungarie Magne*

BAV, MS Vat. Lat. 1437: *Liber censualis Romanae curiae*, incl. Riccardus, *De facto Ungarie Magne*

BAV, MS Vat. Lat. 3822: Prophetic texts of Joachim de Fiore

BAV, MS Vat. Lat. 4161: *Misc.*, incl. *Epistula de vita Tartarorum*

BAV, MS Vat. Lat. 4734: *Relatio de concilio Lugdunensi*

BAV, MS Vat. Lat. 6223: *Liber censualis Romanae curiae*, incl. Riccardus, *De facto Ungarie Magne*

Vienna

Österreichische Nationalbibliothek, MS 339: *Vita prima sanctae Brigitae*, incl. a copy of Hülegü's letter to the king of France in 1262

Österreichische Nationalbibliothek, MS 590 (olim Philol. 305): letters from Thomas de Capua and Petrus de Vinea, *(Baumgartenberger) Formularius de modo prosandi.*, and others

Wilhering, Stiftsbibliothek, MS 60: Papal and State letters and others from the *(Baumgartenberger) Formularius de modo prosandi*, Transmundus, Riccardus de Pofis, Thomas de Capua, and others

Notes on Transcription

Where sufficient Matthew Paris's text is cited from Henry Richards Luard's edition, unless otherwise noted. For ease of reference, Giles's translation is referenced, although not followed in every instance due to errors and lacunae.

In my own manuscript transcriptions, I adhere to the orthography of the manuscript, except in writing 'v' for consonantal 'u'. I do not report minor orthographical variants unless significant, and punctuation and capitalization are modernized. Uncertain readings and obliterated or illegible passages are marked by ellipsis points or suggested readings in square brackets.

Further Appendices

Further appendices not printed here but referenced in the text:
Appendix 7: Mongol-related content in the *Chronica majora*
Appendix 8: Comparative table of various descriptions of Mongols in Matthew Paris's and Thomas of Spalato's texts

Appendices 7 and 8 are available online at <https://brepols.figshare.com>, from the link <https://doi.org/10.1484/A.14453112>.

Bibliography

Manuscripts

See Appendix 6, which contains a tabulated and detailed list of all known
manuscripts of the *Chronica majora* and the *Flores historiarium* (parts,
fragments, continuations) as well as a list of all other manuscripts referred to in
this volume (shelf marks, title, or relevant content).

Primary Sources

Adam of Eynsham, *The Life of St Hugh of Lincoln / Magna Vita Sancti Hugonis*,
ed. by Decima Langworthy Douie, 2 vols (Oxford: Clarendon Press, 1985)

Alberic of Trois-Fontaines, 'Chronica Albrici monachi Trium Fontium, a monacho
Novi Monasterii Hoiensis interpolata', ed. by Paul Scheffer-Boichorst, in
Chronica aevi Suevici, MGH, SS, 23 (Hannover: Hahn, 1874), pp. 631–950

*Analecta Franciscana: sive, Chronica aliaque varia documenta ad historiam Fratrum
Minorum spectantia*, 10 vols (Quaracchi: Typographia Collegii S.
Bonaventurae, 1885–1951)

Annales Cestrienses; or, Chronicle of the Abbey of S. Werburg, at Chester, ed. by
Richard Copley Christie, Record Society for the Publication of Original
Documents Relating to Lancashire and Cheshire, 14 (London: Wyman and
Sons for the Record Society, 1887)

'Annales de Burton', ed. by Henry Richards Luard, in *Annales monastici*, vol. I, RS,
36 (London: Longman, Green, Longman, Roberts, and Green, 1864),
pp. 183–500

'Annales de Prioratus de Wigornia', ed. by Henry Richards Luard, in *Annales
monastici*, vol. IV, RS, 36 (London: Longman, Green, Longman, Roberts and
Green, 1869), pp. 355–564

'Annales de Prioratus Dunstaplia', ed. by Henry Richards Luard, in *Annales
monastici*, vol. III, RS, 36 (London: Longman, Green, Longman, Roberts, and
Green, 1866), pp. 3–420

'Annales de Theokesberia', ed. by Henry Richards Luard, in *Annales monastici*,
vol. I, RS, 36 (London: Longman, Green, Longman, Roberts, and Green,
1864), pp. 43–180

'Annales de Waverleia', ed. by Henry Richards Luard, in *Annales monastici*, vol. II, RS, 36 (London: Longman, Green, Longman, Roberts, and Green, 1865), pp. 129–411

'Annales Monasterii Sancti Pantaleonis Coloniae: 1238–1249', ed. by Alfons Huber and Johann Friedrich Böhmer, in *Fontes rerum Germanicarum*, vol. IV: *Heinricus de Diessenhofen und andere Geschichtsquellen Deutschlands im späteren Mittelalter* (Stuttgart: J. G. Cotta, 1868), pp. 470–96

'Annales Sancti Pantaleonis Coloniensis', ed. by Hermann Cardauns, in *Historici Germaniae saec. XII.*, MGH, SS, 22 (Hannover: Hahn, 1872), pp. 529–47

'Annales Sancti Rudberti Salisburgenses a. 1–1286', ed. by Georg H. Pertz, in *Chronica et annales aevi Salici*, MGH, SS, 9 (Hannover: Hahn, 1851), pp. 758–810

'Annales Sancti Trudperti', ed. by Georg H. Pertz, in *Annales aevi Suevici*, vol. II, MGH, SS, 17 (Hannover: Hahn, 1861), pp. 283–94

'Annales Scheftlarienses maiores, a. 1092–1247', ed. by Georg H. Pertz, in *Annales aevi Suevici*, vol. II, MGH, SS, 17 (Hannover: Hahn, 1861), pp. 335–43

'Annales Wormatienses, 873–1360', ed. by Georg H. Pertz, in *Annales aevi Suevici*, vol. II, MGH, SS, 17 (Hannover: Hahn, 1861), pp. 34–73

'The Annals of Lewes Priory', ed. by Felix Liebermann, *English Historical Review*, 17.65 (1902), 88–89

Anonymus and Master Roger, *The Deeds of the Hungarians / Anonymi Bele Regis Notarii Gesta Hungarorum and Epistle to the Sorrowful Lament upon the Destruction of the Kingdom of Hungary by the Tatars / Magistri Rogerii Epistola in miserabile carmen super destructione Regni Hungarie per tartaros facta*, trans. by János Bak, Martyn Rady, and László Veszprémy, Central European Medieval Texts, 5 (Budapest: Central European University Press, 2010)

'Appendix 1: Relatio de concilio Lugdunensi', ed. by Ludwig Weiland, in *Constitutiones et acta publica imperatorum et regum*, vol. II: *Inde ab a. MCXCVIII usqve ad a. MCCLXXII (1198–1272)*, ed. by Ludwig Weiland, MGH, Const. (Hannover: Hahn, 1896), pp. 505–39

Arnoldus Montanus and Olfert Dapper, *Atlas Chinensis Being a Second Part of A Relation of Remarkable Passages in Two Embassies from the East-India Company of the United Provinces to the Vice-Roy Singlamong and General Taising Lipovi and to Konchi, Emperor of China and East-Tartary : With a Relation of the Netherlanders Assisting the Tarter against Coxinga and the Chinese Fleet, Etc; Collected out of Their Several Writings and Journals by Arnoldus Montanus*, trans. by John Ogilby (London: Thomas Johnson, 1671)

Árpádkori új okmánytár: Codex diplomaticus Arpadianus continuatus, vol. II: 1234–1260, ed. by Gusztáv Wenzel (Pest: Eggenberger, 1861)

Augustine of Hippo, *Opera omnia Augustini Hipponensis*, vol. V: *S. Aurelii Augustini Hipponensis episcopi sermones ad populum*, ed. by J.-P. Migne, Patrologia Latina, 39 (Paris: J.-P. Migne, 1846)

Bacon, Roger, *Opus majus*, ed. by John Henry Bridges, 3 vols (Frankfurt a. M: Minerva, 1964)

Bale, John, 'A Letter from Bishop Bale to Archbishop Parker', ed. by Henry Richards Luard, *Cambridge Antiquarian Communications*, 3 (1879), 157–73

Bartholomew of Lucca [Ptolemaeus], *Die Annalen des Tholomeus von Lucca in doppelter Fassung: (Tholomei Lucensis Annales): nebst Teilen der Gesta Florentinorum und Gesta Lucanorum*, ed. by Bernhard Schmeidler (Berlin: Weidmann, 1930)

———, *Historia ecclesiastica nova: nebst Fortsetzungen bis 1329*, ed. by Ottavio Clavuot and Ludwig Schmugge, MGH, SS, 39 (Hannover: Hahn, 2009)

Das Baumgartenberger Formelbuch: Eine Quelle zur Geschichte des 13ten Jahrhundert, ed. by Hermann Baerwald, Fontes rerum Austriacarum, Abteilung 2: Diplomataria et Acta, 25 (Vienna: K. K. Hof- und Staats-Druckerei, 1866)

Behaim, Albert, *Das Brief- und Memorialbuch des Albert Behaim*, ed. by Thomas Frenz and Peter Herde, MGH, Briefe des späten Mittelalters, 1 (Munich: Monumenta Germaniae Historica, 2000)

'Benedictines: Canterbury-St Augustine's; BA1. Catalogue, 15th cent.', *Medieval Libraries of Great Britain*, ed. by Richard Sharpe and James E. Willoughby, funded by grants from the Andrew W. Mellon Foundation and Neil F. Ker Memorial Fund, <http://mlgb3.bodleian.ox.ac.uk/authortitle/medieval_catalogues/BA1/>

'Benedictines: The Shorter Catalogues: Norwich; B58. Books owned by Simon Bozoun, 14th cent.', *Medieval Libraries of Great Britain*, ed. by Richard Sharpe and James E. Willoughby, funded by grants from the Andrew W. Mellon Foundation and Neil F. Ker Memorial Fund, <http://mlgb3.bodleian.ox.ac.uk/authortitle/medieval_catalogues/B58/>

'Benedictines: The Shorter Catalogues: Norwich; B61. Bale, *c.* 1550', *Medieval Libraries of Great Britain*, ed. by Richard Sharpe and James E. Willoughby, funded by grants from the Andrew W. Mellon Foundation and Neil F. Ker Memorial Fund, <http://mlgb3.bodleian.ox.ac.uk/authortitle/medieval_catalogues/B61/>

Blomefield, Francis, *An Essay towards a Topographical History of the County of Norfolk: Containing a Description of the Towns, Villages, and Hamlets, with the Foundations of Monasteries, Churches, Chapels, Chanteries, and Other Religious Buildings. […] Collected out of Ledger-Books, Registers, Records, Evidences, Deeds, Court-Rolls, and Other Authentic Memorials by Francis Blomefield, Rector of Fersfield*, ed. by Charles Parkin, 11 vols (London: William Miller, 1805–1810)

Calendar of Patent Rolls, Henry III, vol. IV: *1247–1258*, ed. by H. C. Maxwell Lyte (London: Mackie and Co., for His Majesty's Stationery Office, 1908)

Carroll, Lewis, *Sylvie and Bruno Concluded* (London: Macmillan, 1893)

———, *Through the Looking-Glass: And What Alice Found There* (London: Macmillan, 1872)

C. de Bridia, *Hystoria Tartarorum C. de Bridia monachi*, ed. by Alf Önnerfors (Berlin: De Gruyter, 1967)

Chronica de Mailros, e codice unico in Bibliotheca Cottoniana servato, nunc iterum in lucem edita, ed. by Joseph Stevenson (Edinburgh: Bannatyne Club, 1835)

Chronica regia Coloniensis: Annales maximi Colonienses, ed. by Georg Waitz, MGH, SS. rer. Germ., 18 (Hannover: Hahn, 1880)

Chronicles of the Reigns of Edward I and Edward II: Annales Londonienses and Annales Paulini, ed. by William Stubbs, RS, 76 (London: Longman, 1882), vol. I

Chronicon de Lanercost: 1201–1346, ed. by Joseph Stevenson (Edinburgh: Edinburgh Printing Company for the Bannatyne Club, 1839)

'Chronicon S. Medardi Suessionensis', ed. by Luc D'Achéry, in *Spicilegium sive collectio veterum aliquot scriptorum qui in Galliae Bibliothecis delituerant*, 3 vols (Paris: PP. Augustinianorum, 1723), II, pp. 486–92

Close Rolls of the Reign of Henry III, 1254–1256 (London: H. M. Stationery Office, 1931)

Codex diplomaticus et epistolaris Moraviae, vol. III: *ab annis 1241–1267*, ed. by Antonín Boček (Olomouc: Aloysius Skarnitzl, 1841)

Codex diplomaticus et epistolaris regni Bohemiae, ed. by Jindřich Šebánek and Saša Dušková, 3 vols (Prague: Československé Akademie Věd, 1962)

Codex Diplomaticus et Epistolaris Slovaciae, ed. by Richard Marsina, 2 vols (Bratislava: Obzor, 1971)

Codex diplomaticus Hungariae ecclesiasticus ac civilis, ed. by Georgius Fejér, 11 vols in 44 (Buda: Typis Typogr. Regiae Universitatis Ungaricae, 1829–1844)

Comestor, Petrus, 'Historia scholastica eruditissimi viri Magistri Petri Comestoris', in *Saeculum XII: Adamus Scotus canonicus regularis Ordinis Praemonstratensis; Petrus Comestor; Godefridus Viterbiensis*, ed. by J.-P. Migne, Patrologia Latina, 198 (Paris: J.-P. Migne, 1855), cols 1045–1720

Constitutiones et acta publica imperatorum et regum, vol. II: *Inde ab a. MCXCVIII usqve ad a. MCCLXXII (1198–1272)*, ed. by Ludwig Weiland, MGH, Const. (Hannover: Hahn, 1896)

'Continuatio Garstenses, a. 1182–1257', ed. by Georg H. Pertz, in *Chronica et annales aevi Salici*, MGH, SS, 9 (Hannover: Hahn, 1851), pp. 594–601

'Continuatio Sancrucensis II: a. 1234–1266', ed. by Georg H. Pertz, in *Chronica et annales aevi Salici*, MGH, SS, 9 (Hannover: Hahn, 1851), pp. 637–46

Descriptive Catalogue of Materials Relating to the History of Great Britain and Ireland to the End of the Reign of Henry VII, vol. III: *From A.D. 1200 to A.D. 1327*, ed. by Thomas Duffus Hardy, RS, 26 (London: Longman & Trübner, 1871)

Diplomatarium Norvegicum: Oldbreve til Kundskab om Norges Indre og Ydre Forholde, Sprog, Slaegter, Saeder, Lovgivning og Retterhand i Midelalderen, ed. by Christian C. A. Lange and Carl R. Unger, 22 vols (Christiana: P. T. Mallings Forlagshandel, 1847)

Długosz, Jan, *Ioannis Dlugossii Annales seu Cronicae incliti regni Poloniae*, 3 vols (Warsaw: Państwowe Wydawnictwo Naukowe, 1975)

Documente privind istoria României, C, Transilvania, Veacurile XI, XII, XIII, vol. I: *1075–1250* (Bucharest: Editura Academiei Republicii Populare Române, 1951)

Epistolae saeculi XIII e regestis pontificum Romanorum selectae, ed. by Georg H. Pertz, MGH, Epp., 3 vols (Berlin: Weidmann, 1883)

Eubel, Konrad, *Hierarchia catholica medii aevi, sive Summorum pontificum, S.R.E. cardinalium, ecclesiarum antistitum series [...] e documentis tabularii praesertim vaticani collecta, digesta, edita* (Regensburg: Monasterii Sumptibus et typis librariae Regensbergianae, 1913), vol. I

Fasti Ecclesiae Anglicanae, 1066–1300, vol. III: *Lincoln*, ed. by Diana E. Greenway (London: Institute of Historical Research, 1977)

Foedera, conventiones, litterae, et cujuscunque generis acta publica, inter reges Angliae et alios quosvis impeatores, reges, pontifices, principes, vel communitates: ab ingressu Gulielmi I. in Angliam, A.D. 1066, ad nostra usque tempora habita aut tractata, ed. by Thomas Rymer, 4 vols in 7 (London: [n.pub.], 1816)

Foxe, John, *The Acts and Monuments of John Foxe: A New and Complete Edition*, ed. by Stephen Reed Cattley and George Townsend (London: R. B. Seeley and W. Burnside, 1837)

———, *A Sermon Preached at the Christening of a Certaine Iew at London by John Foxe: Conteining an Exposition of the xi. Chapter of S. Paul to the Romanes*, trans. by James Bell (London: Christopher Barker, 1578)

Gems from Petőfi and Other Hungarian Poets with a Memoir of the Former, and a Review of Hungary's Poetical Literature, ed. and trans. by William N. Loew (New York: Paul O. D'Esterhazy, 1881)

Gerald of Wales, *The Autobiography of Gerald of Wales*, trans. by Harold Edgeworth Butler (Rochester, NY: Boydell Press, 2005)

Gervase of Tilbury, *Otia Imperialia: Recreation for an Emperor*, trans. by S. E. Banks and J. W. Binns, Oxford Medieval Texts (Oxford: Clarendon Press, 2002)

'Gesta Domni Gaufridi de Loduno Episcopi', in *Actus pontificum Cenomannis in urbe degentium*, ed. by G. Busson and A. Ledru, Archives Historiques du Maine, 2 (Mans: Société des Archives Historiques du Maine, 1902), pp. 486–505

'Gesta Treverorum Continuata', ed. by Georg Waitz, in *Annales aevi Suevici (Supplementa tomorum XVI et XVII); Gesta saec. XII. XIII. (Supplementa tomorum XX–XXIII)*, MGH, SS, 24 (Hannover: Hahn, 1879), pp. 368–488

Godfrey of Viterbo, 'Memoria saeculorum', ed. by Georg Heinrich Pertz, in *Historici Germaniae saec. XII.*, MGH, SS, 22 (Hanover: Hahn, 1872), pp. 94–106

Goethe, Johann Wolfgang von, *Gedenksausgabe der Werke, Briefe und Gespräche*, ed. by Ernst Beutler and Wolfgang Baumgart (Zürich: Artemis, 1948), vol. XIII

———, *Gedenksausgabe der Werke, Briefe und Gespräche*, ed. by Ernst Beutler and Wolfgang Baumgart (Zürich: Artemis, 1948), vol. XXIII

———, *Lexikon der Goethe-Zitate*, ed. by Richard Dobel (Zürich: Artemis, 1968)

Gombos, Albin Ferenc, *Catalogus fontium historiae Hungaricae, aevo ducum et regum ex stirpe Arpad descendentium ab anno Christi DCCC usque ad annum MCCCI*, 4 vols (Budapest, 1937)

Grosseteste, Robert, *Letters of Robert Grosseteste*, trans. by Joseph Ward Goering and Frank Anthony Carl Mantello (Toronto: University of Toronto Press, 2010)

Guillaume de Nangis, *Chronique latine de Guillaume de Nangis, de 1113 à 1300, avec les continuations de cette chronique, de 1300 à 1368*, ed. by Jean de Venette and Géraud Hercule, 2 vols, Société de l'histoire de France, 33 and 35 (Paris: Crapelet, 1843)

Henry of Livonia [Henricus Lettus], *The Chronicle of Henry of Livonia*, trans. by James A. Brundage (Madison: University of Wisconsin Press, 1961)

———, *Heinrichs Livländische Chronik*, ed. by Leonid Arbusow and Albert Bauer, MGH, SS. rer. Germ., 31 (Hannover: Hahn, 1955)

The Hereford Map: A Transcription and Translation of the Legends; with Commentary, ed. and trans. by Scott D. Westrem, Terrarum Orbis, History of the Representation of Space in Text and Image, 1 (Turnhout: Brepols, 2001)

Historia diplomatica Friderici Secundi: sive, Constitutiones, privilegia, mandata, instrumenta quae supersunt istius imperatoris et filiorum ejus: accedunt epistolae paparum et documenta varia, ed. by Jean Louis Alfonse Huillard-Bréholles (Paris: Plon, 1861), vol. VI.2

Historia diplomatica Friderici Secundi: sive, Constitutiones, privilegia, mandata, instrumenta quae supersunt istius imperatoris et filiorum ejus: accedunt epistolae paparum et documenta varia, ed. by Jean Louis Alfonse Huillard-Bréholles and Honoré Théodoric Paul Joseph d'Albert Luynes (Paris: Plon, 1852), vol. V.2

Isidore of Seville, *Isidori Hispalensis Etymologiarum originum Libri XX*, ed. by W. M. Lindsay (Oxford: Clarendon Press, 1911), vol. II

John of Oxnead, *Chronica Johannis de Oxenedes*, ed. by Henry Ellis, RS, 13 (London: Longman, Brown, Green, Longmans, & Roberts, 1859)

John of Wallingford, *The Chronicle Attributed to John of Wallingford*, ed. by Richard Vaughan, Camden Third Series, 90 (London: Offices of the Royal Historical Society, 1958)

———, 'Ex chronicis Johannis de Wallingford', ed. by Felix Liebermann, in *Ex rerum Anglicarum scriptoribus saec. XIII.*, MGH, SS, 28 (Hannover: Hahn, 1888), pp. 505–11

Joinville, Jean, *Memoires de Jean sire de Joinville, ou, Histoire et chronique du très-chrétien roi Saint Louis*, ed. by Francisque Michel, Ambroise Firmin-Didot, and Paulin Paris (Paris: Firmin Didot frères, fils et cie, 1859)

Jordan of Giano, *Chronica fratris Iordani*, ed. by Heinrich Boehmer (Paris: Librairie Fischbacher, 1908)

Letters from the East: Crusaders, Pilgrims and Settlers in the 12th–13th Centuries, ed. by Malcolm Barber and A. K. Bate, Crusade Texts in Translation, 18 (Farnham: Ashgate, 2010)

Lovecraft, H. P., 'The Call of Cthulhu', *Weird Tales*, 11.2 (1928), 159–78

Map, Walter, *De nugis curialium*, ed. by Montague Rhodes James, Christopher Nugent Lawrence Brooke, and Roger Aubrey Baskerville Mynors (Oxford: Clarendon Press, 1983)

Marsh, Adam, *The Letters of Adam Marsh*, ed. by Clifford Hugh Lawrence, 2 vols (Oxford: Clarendon Press, 2006)

Martinus Polonus, 'Martini Oppaviensis Chronicon pontificum et imperatorum', ed. by Ludwig Weiland, in *Historici Germaniae saec. XII.*, MGH, SS, 22 (Hannover: Hahn, 1872), pp. 377–475

Matthew of Westminster, *Flores historiarum Matthaei Westmonasteriensis monachi*, ed. by Matthew Parker (London, 1567)

———, *Flores historiarum Matthaei Westmonasteriensis monachi*, ed. by Matthew Parker (London: Ex officina Thomæ Marshij, 1570)

———, *Flowers of History*, trans. by C. D. Yonge, 2 vols (London: Henry G. Bohn, 1853)

Medieval Libraries of Great Britain, ed. by Richard Sharpe and James E. Willoughby, funded by grants from the Andrew W. Mellon Foundation and Neil F. Ker Memorial Fund, <http://mlgb3.bodleian.ox.ac.uk/>

Monumenta Poloniae historica / Pomniki dziejowe Polski, ed. by August Bielowski, 6 vols (Lwów: Nakładem Własnym, 1864–1893)

Mousket, Philippe, *Chronique rimée de Philippe Mouskes*, ed. by Frédéric-Auguste-Ferdinand-Thomas Reiffenberg, 2 vols and supplement (Brussels: M. Hayez, Imprimeur de la Comission Royale d'Histoire, 1836–1845)

Murimuth, Adam, and Robert of Avesbury, *Adae Murimuth Continuatio chronicarum; Robertus de Avesbury De gestis mirabilibus regis Edwardi tertii*, ed. by Edward Maunde Thompson (London: HMSO; Eyre and Spottiswoode, 1889)

Otto of Freising and Rahewinus, *The Deeds of Frederick Barbarossa*, trans. by Charles Christopher Mierow and Richard Emery (New York: Columbia University Press, 2004)

Paris, Matthew [Matthieu Paris], 'Ex Abbreviatione cronicorum Angliae', ed. by Felix Liebermann, in *Ex rerum Anglicarum scriptoribus saeculi XIII.*, MGH, SS, 28 (Hannover: Hahn, 1888), pp. 443–55

———, 'Ex Mathei Parisiensis operibus', ed. by Felix Liebermann, in *Ex rerum Anglicarum scriptoribus saeculi XIII.*, MGH, SS 28 (Hannover: Hahn, 1888), pp. 74–443

———, *Flores historiarum*, ed. by Henry Richards Luard, RS, 95, 3 vols (London: HMSO, 1890)

———, *Grande chronique de Matthieu Paris*, trans. by Alphonse Huillard-Bréholles (Paris: Paulin, 1840–1841)

———, *The Illustrated Chronicles of Matthew Paris: Observations of Thirteenth-Century Life*, trans. by Richard Vaughan (Cambridge: Corpus Christi College, 1993)

———, *Matthaei Paris, monachi Albanensis, Angli, historia maior à Guilielmo Conquaestore, ad vltimum annum Henrici tertij*, ed. by Matthew Parker (London: Reginaldum Vuolfium [Reyner Wolfe], 1571)

—, *Matthaei Paris, monachi Albanensis, Angli, historia maior à Guilielmo Conquaestore, ad vltimum annum Henrici tertij,* ed. by Matthew Parker (Zurich [Tiguri]: Christoffel Froschauer, 1589)

—, *Matthæi Parisiensis, monachi Sancti Albani, Chronica majora,* ed. by Henry Richards Luard, RS, 57, 7 vols (London: Longman, 1872–1883)

—, *Matthæi Parisiensis, monachi Sancti Albani: Historia Anglorum, sive, ut vulgo dicitur, Historia Minor,* ed. by Frederick Madden, RS, 44, 3 vols (London: Longmans, Green, Reader, and Dyer, 1866–1869)

—, *Matthew Paris's English History, from 1235 to 1273,* trans. by J. A. Giles, 3 vols (London: Henry G. Bohn, 1852)

Paris, Matthew, William Rishanger, and Roger of Wendover, *Matthæi Paris monachi Albanensis Angli, historia major: Juxta exemplar Londinense 1571, verbatim recusa; et cum Rogeri Wendoveri, Willielmi Rishangeri, authorisque majori minorique historiis chronicisque MSS, in Bibliotheca Regia, Collegii Corporis Christi Cantabrigiæ, Cottoniáque, fidelitèr collata,* ed. by William Watts (London: Richard Hodgkinson, 1640)

—, *Matthaei Paris monachi Albanensis Angli, historia major: Juxta exemplar Londinense 1571, verbatim recusa; et cum Rogeri Wendoveri, Willielmi Rishangeri, authorisque majori minorique historiis chronicisque MSS, in Bibliotheca Regia, Collegii Corporis Christi Cantabrigiae, Cottoniaque, fideliter collata,* ed. by William Watts (Paris: Guillelmus Pele, 1644)

—, *Matthaei Paris monachi Albanensis Angli, historia major: Juxta exemplar Londinense 1571, verbatim recusa; et cum Rogeri Wendoveri, Willielmi Rishangeri, authorisque majori minorique historiis, chronicisque MSS, in Bibliotheca Regia, Collegii Corporis Christi Cantabrigiae, Cottoniáque, fidelitèr collata,* ed. by William Watts (London: A. Mearne, T. Dring, B. Tooke, T. Sawbridge, & G. Wells, 1684)

Phillipps, Thomas, *Catalogus librorum manuscriptorum in bibliotheca D. Thomae Phillipps, Bart., A.D. 1837* ([Middle Hill, Worcs.]: Typis Medio-Montanis, 1837)

Potthast, August, *Regesta Pontificum Romanorum,* vol. I: *inde ab a. post Christum natum 1198 ad a. 1304* (Berlin: Rudolf de Decker, 1874)

[Pseudo]-Methodius, *Apocalypse of Pseudo-Methodius: An Alexandrian World Chronicle,* ed. and trans. by Benjamin Garstad, Dumbarton Oaks Medieval Library, 14 (Cambridge, MA: Harvard University Press, 2012)

Purchas, Samuel, *Purchas his Pilgrimage, Or, Relations of the Vvorld and the Religions Obserued in al Ages and Places Discouered, from the Creation Vnto This Present: In Foure Parts* (London: William Stansby for Henry Fetherstone, 1617)

—, and Richard Hakluyt, *Hakluytus Posthumus,* vol. XI: *Or, Purchas his Pilgrimes: Contayning a History of the World in Sea Voyages and Lande Travells by Englishmen and Others* (Cambridge: Cambridge University Press, 2014)

Radulfus de Diceto, *Radulfi de Diceto decani Lundoniensis opera historica: The Historical Works of Master Ralph de Diceto, Dean of London*, ed. by William Stubbs, RS, 68, 2 vols (London: Longman, Trübner, 1876)

Rashid al-Din Tabib, *Rashiduddin Fazlullah's Jami`ut-Tawarikh / Compendium of Chronicles*, trans. by W. M. Thackston (Cambridge, MA: Harvard University, Dept. of Near Eastern Languages and Civilizations, 1998)

'Regesta Bohemiae at Moraviae, pars 1, 600–1253', ed. by Karel Jaromir Erben, *Abhandlungen der Böhmischen Gesellschaft der Wissenschaften*, 5th Ser., 8 (1854), 1–800

Regesta Imperii, vol. v: *Jüngere Staufer 1198–1272; Die Regesten des Kaiserreichs unter Philipp, Otto IV, Friedrich II, Heinrich (VII), Conrad IV, Heinrich Raspe, Wilhelm und Richard*, ed. by Johann Friedrich Böhmer, Julius Ficker, and Eduard Winkelmann, 3 vols in 5 (Innsbruck: Wagner'sche Universitäts-Buchdruckerei, 1881–1901)

Les registres d'Innocent IV, publiées ou analysées d'après les manuscrits originaux du Vatican et de la Bibliothéque Nationale, ed. by Élie Berger, 4 vols (Paris: Ernest Thorin, 1884)

The Registrum Antiquissimum of the Cathedral Church of Lincoln, vol. IV, ed. by Charles Wilmer Foster and Kathleen Major, Publications of the Lincoln Record Society, 32 (Hereford: Printed for the Lincoln Record Society by the Hereford Times, 1937)

The Registrum Antiquissimum of the Cathedral Church of Lincoln, vol. VII, ed. by Charles Wilmer Foster and Kathleen Major, Publications of the Lincoln Record Society, 46 (Hereford: Printed for the Lincoln Record Society by the Hereford Times, 1953)

'Richeri Gesta Senoniensis ecclesiae', ed. by Georg Waitz, in *Gesta saeculi XIII.*, MGH, SS, 25 (Hannover: Hahn, 1880), pp. 249–345

Rishanger, William, *Willelmi Rishanger quondam monachi S. Albani chronica et annales*, ed. by Henry Thomas Riley, RS, 28 (London: Longman, Green, Longman, Roberts and Green, 1865)

Roger of Várad [Master Roger], 'Epistle to the Sorrowful Lament upon the Destruction of the Kingdom of Hungary by the Tatars / Magistri Rogerii Epistole in miserabili carmen super destructione Regni Hungarie per tartaros facta', trans. by János Bak and Martyn Rady, in Anonymus and Master Roger, *The Deeds of the Hungarians / Anonymi Bele Regis Notarii Gesta Hungarorum and Epistle to the Sorrowful Lament upon the Destruction of the Kingdom of Hungary by the Tatars / Magistri Rogerii Epistola in miserabile carmen super destructione Regni Hungarie per tartaros facta*, Central European Medieval Texts, 5 (Budapest: Central European University Press, 2010), pp. 133–227

Roger of Wendover, *Flores Historiarum*, ed. by H. O. Coxe, 5 vols (London: English Historical Society, 1841)

——, *Liber qui dicitur Flores historiarum ab anno Domini MCLIV annoque Henrici Anglorum regis secundi primo*, ed. by H. G Hewlett, RS, 84, 3 vols (London: Longman, 1886)

Rubruquis, Guilelmus de [William Rubruck], *The Mission of Friar William of Rubruck: His Journey to the Court of the Great Khan Möngke, 1253–1255*, trans. by Peter Jackson, Works Issued by the Hakluyt Society, Ser. 2, 173 (London: Hakluyt Society, 1990; repr. Farnham: Ashgate, 2010)

Saxo Grammaticus, *Gesta Danorum / The History of the Danes*, trans. by Karsten Friis-Jensen and Peter Fisher (Oxford: Clarendon Press, 2015)

The Secret History of the Mongols: A Mongolian Epic Chronicle of the Thirteenth Century, ed. and trans. by Igor de Rachewiltz, Brill's Inner Asian Library, 7 (Leiden: Brill, 2004)

Selden, John, *Joannis Seldeni jurisconsulti opera omnia, tam edita quam inedita*, ed. by David Wilkins, 3 vols (London: William Bowyer, 1726)

Simon of Saint-Quentin, 'History of the Tartars', trans. by Stephen Pow, Flora Ghazaryan, Tamás Kiss, and Anna Romsics, <http://simonofstquentin.org>

Spicilegium sive collectio veterum aliquot scriptorum qui in Galliae Bibliothecis delituerant, ed. by Luc D'Achery (Paris: Charles Savreux, 1668)

Stanley, William, and Thomas Staveley, *The Roman Horseleech, or An Impartial Account of the Intolerable Charge of Popery to This Nation: To Which Is Annexed an Essay of the Supremacy of the King of England* (London: R. W. for Ralph Smith, 1674)

Statutes of Lincoln Cathedral, ed. by Henry Bradshaw and Christopher Wordsworth, 2 vols in 3 (Cambridge: Cambridge University Press, 1892)

Testamenta vetusta, Being Illustrations from Wills, of Manners, Customs, &c. as Well as of the Descents and Possessions of Many Distinguished Families: From the Reign of Henry the Second to the Accession of Queen Elizabeth, ed. by Nicholas Harris Nicolas, 2 vols (London: Nichols and Son, 1826)

Thomas of Spalato, *Thomae archidiaconi Spalatensis Historia Salonitanorum atque Spalatinorum pontificum = History of the Bishops of Salona and Split*, ed. by Damir Karbic, Mirjana Matijevic-Sokol, and James Ross Sweeney, Central European Medieval Texts, 4 (Budapest: Central European University Press, 2006)

Tiraboschi, Girolamo, *Vetera Humiliatorum Monumenta*, 3 vols (Milan: Galeatius, 1767)

Treaty Rolls, vol. I: *1234–1325*, ed. by Pierre Chaplais (London: H. M. Stationery Office, 1955)

Trivet, Nicholas, *F. Nicholai Triveti de ordine frat. praedicatorum Annales sex regum Angliae, qui a comitibus andegavensibus originem traxerunt (A.D. MCXXXVI–MCCCVII)*, ed. by Thomas Hog (London: English Historical Society, 1845)

——, *Nicolai Triveti, Dominicani, Annales sex Regum Angli: E praestantissimo codice Glastoniensi nunc primum emendate edidit Antonius Hall*, ed. by Anthony Hall (Oxford: Theatro Sheldoniano, 1719)

Urkundenbuch zur Geschichte der Deutschen in Siebenbürgen, vol. I: *1191–1342, Nr. 1–582*, ed. by Franz Zimmermann and Carl Werner (Cologne, 1892)

Vetera monumenta historica Hungariam Sacram illustrantia, ed. by Augustin Theiner, 2 vols (Rome: Typis Vaticanis, 1859–1860)

Walsingham, Thomas, *Deeds of the Abbots of St Albans: Gesta Abbatum Monasterii Sancti Albani*, ed. by David Preest, trans. by James Clark (Woodbridge: Boydell Press, 2018)

———, and Matthew Paris, *Gesta abbatum monasterii Sancti Albani, a Thoma Walsingham, regnante Ricardo Secundo, ejusdem ecclesiæ præcentore, compilata*, ed. by H. T. (Henry Thomas) Riley (London: Longmans, Green, 1867)

Wykes, Thomas, 'Chronicon vulgo dictum Chronicon Thomae Wykes', ed. by Henry Richards Luard, in *Annales monastici*, vol. IV, RS, 36 (London: Longmans, Green, Longman, Roberts, and Green, 1869), pp. 6–352

Secondary Studies

Aalto, Pentti, 'Swells of the Mongol-Storm around the Baltic', *Acta Orientalia Academiae Scientiarum Hungaricae*, 36.1/3 (1982), 5–15

Abulafia, David, 'Ethnic Variety and its Implications: Frederick II's Relations with Jews and Muslims', in 'Symposium Papers 24: Intellectual Life at the Court of Frederick II Hohenstaufen', special issue, *Studies in the History of Art*, 44 (1994), 213–24

———, *Frederick II: A Medieval Emperor* (New York: Oxford University Press, 1992)

Aerts, W. J., and G. A. A. Kortekaas, *Die Apokalypse des Pseudo-Methodius: Die ältesten griechischen und lateinischen Übersetzungen*, Corpus Scriptorium Orientalium, 569–70, 2 vols (Louvain: Peeters, 1998)

Agapētos, Panagiōtēs, and Lars Boje Mortensen, eds, *Medieval Narratives between History and Fiction: From the Centre to the Periphery of Europe, c. 1100–1400* (Copenhagen: Museum Tusculanum Press, 2012)

Alekseyev, Mikhail P. [Алексеев, Михаил П.], '"Anglo-saksonskaya parallel" k Poucheniyu Vladimira Monomakha' [Англо-саксонская параллель' к Поучению Владимира Мономаха; An 'Anglo-Saxon Parallel' of Vladimir Monomakh's Instruction], Trudy Otdela drevnerusskoy literatury [Труды Отдела древнерусскоы литературы; Proceedings of the Department of Old Russian Literature], 2 (1935), 39–80

Allen, Rosamund, ed., *Eastward Bound: Travel and Travellers, 1050–1550* (Manchester: Manchester University Press; New York: Palgrave, 2004)

Almási, Tibor, 'Egy rogeriusi motívumegyezés értelmezési lehetőségei' [Possible interpretations of a parallel Rogerian motif], in *Auxilium historiae: Tanulmányok a hetvenesztnedős Bertényi Iván tiszteletére*, ed. by Tamás Körmendi and Gábor Thoroczkay (Budapest: Eötvös Loránd Tudományegyetem Bölcsészettudományi Kara, 2009), pp. 11–19

BIBLIOGRAPHY

———, 'Forrásadatok és feltevések Rogerius életrajzi vázlatához' [Sources and suppositions about the biography of Master Roger], in *Nagyvárad és Bihar az Árpád-kor végén*, ed. by Attila Zsoldos, Tanulmányok Biharország történelméről, 3 (Nagyvárad: Varadinum Kulturális Alapítvány, 2016), pp. 55–82

Almási, Tibor, and László Koszta, 'Báncsa István bíboros (1205 k.–1270): Életrajzi vázlat' [Cardinal István Báncsa: Biographical outline], *Acta Historica: Különszám a III. Nemzetközi Hungarológiai Kongresszus tiszteletére*, 1991, 9–17

Altaner, Berthold, *Die Dominikanermissionen des 13. Jahrhunderts: Forschungen zur Geschichte der kirchlichen Unionen und der Mohammedaner- und Heidenmission des Mittelalters*, Breslauer Studien zur historischen Theologie (Habelschwerdt: Franke, 1924), vol. III

Ambler, Sophie, *The Song of Simon de Montfort: The Life and Death of a Medieval Revolutionary* (New York: Oxford University Press, 2019)

Arnold, John, *What Is Medieval History?*, What Is History? (Cambridge: Polity, 2008)

Artner, Edgár, Kornél Szovák, József Török, and Péter Tusor, eds, *Magyarország mint a nyugati keresztény művelődés védőbástyája: a Vatikáni Levéltárnak azok az okiratai, melyek őseinknek a Keletről Európát fenyegető veszedelmek ellen kifejtett erőfeszítéseire vonatkoznak (cca 1214–1606)* [Hungary as the *propugnaculum* of Western Christianity: Documents from the Vatican Secret Archives regarding our forebears' efforts against Eastern threats facing Europe], Bibliotheca Historiae Ecclesiasticae Universitatis Catholicae de Petro Pázmány Nuncupatae, Series I, Collectanea Vaticana Hungariae, Classis 1, 1 (Budapest: PPKE Egyháztörténeti Kutatócsoport, 2004)

Auweiler, Edwin J., *The 'Chronica Fratris Jordani a Giano'* (Washington, DC: [National capital press], 1917)

Avonds, Piet, 'The Duchy of Brabant', in *Medieval Germany: An Encyclopedia*, ed. by M. Frassetto, J. M. Jeep, and L. K. Smid (New York: Garland, 2001), pp. 72–76

Babinger, Francesco, 'Maestro Ruggiero delle Puglie relatore prepoliano sui Tartari', in *Nel VII centenario della nascita di Marco Polo*, ed. by Roberto Almagià (Venice: Palazzo Loredan, 1955), pp. 53–61

Bácsatyai, Dániel, 'Személyi összeköttetések a Curia Romana és a magyar egyház között a 13. század közepén: Pármai Albert és Báncsa István' [Personal relations between the Curia Romana and the Hungarian Church in the mid-thirteenth century: Albert of Parma and István Báncsa], *Történelmi Szemle*, no. 2 (2018), 299–323

Bainton, Henry, 'Epistolary Documents in High-Medieval History Writing', *Interfaces: A Journal of Medieval European Literature*, 4 (2017), 1–29

Bal, Mieke, 'Mise en abyme et iconicité', *Littérature*, 29.1 (1978), 116–28

———, *Narratology*, trans. by Christine van Boheemen (Toronto: University of Toronto Press, 1985)

Balogh, László, 'A mongol támadások a Volga-vidéki népek ellen, 1222–1236'
[Mongol attacks on peoples of the Volga region], in *Tanulmányok a
középkorról: A II. Medievisztikai PhD-konferencia (Szeged, 2001. április 3.)
előadásai (Studies on the Middle Ages: Papers Read at the Second Medievalist PhD
Conference Held in Szeged, 3 April, 2001)*, ed. by Gyula Kristó (Szeged: Szegedi
Középkorász Műhely, 2001), pp. 7–19

Bán, András, *Hungarian-British Diplomacy, 1938–1941: The Attempt to Maintain
Relations* (London: Frank Cass, 2004)

Bárány, Attila, 'A Tatárjárás híre Nyugat-Európában' [News and reports of the
Mongol invasion of 1241 in Western Europe], *Hadtörténeti Közlemények*, 133.3
(2020), 486–527

——, József Laszlovszky, and Zsuzsanna Papp [Reed], *Angol-magyar kapcsolatok
a középkorban* [Anglo-Hungarian relations in the Middle Ages] (Máriabesnyő:
Attraktor, 2008)

Barber, Peter, 'The Evesham World Map: A Late Medieval English View of God
and the World', *Imago Mundi*, 47 (1995), 13–33

Barlow, Thomas, *Several Miscellaneous and Weighty Cases of Conscience Learnedly
and Judiciously Resolved* (London: Mrs Davis, 1692)

Barrow, Julia, *The Clergy in the Medieval World: Secular Clerics, their Families and
Careers in North-Western Europe, c. 800–c. 1200* (Cambridge: Cambridge
University Press, 2015)

——, 'Education and the Recruitment of Cathedral Canons in England and
Germany, 1100–1225', *Viator*, 20 (1989), 117–38

Bate, A. K., 'Walter Map and Giraldus Cambrensis', *Latomus*, 31.3 (1972), 860–75

Battelli, Giulio, 'I Transunti di Lione del 1245', *Mitteilungen des Instituts für
Österreichische Geschichtsforschung*, 62 (1954), 336–64

Bauer, Charlotte, 'Picturing and Promoting New Identities: The Medieval
University at Paris and its "Nations"', in *Mobs: An Interdisciplinary Inquiry*,
ed. by Nancy Van Deusen and Leonard Michael Koff (Leiden: Brill, 2012),
pp. 117–40

Baumann, Brian, 'By the Power of Eternal Heaven: The Meaning of Tenggeri to the
Government of the Pre-Buddhist Mongols', *Extrême-Orient, Extrême-Occident*,
35 (2013), 233–84

Baylen, Joseph O., 'John Maunsell and the Castilian Treaty of 1254: A Study of the
Clerical Diplomat', *Traditio*, 17 (1961), 482–91

——, 'John Maunsell: The Royal Clerk and the King's Will in Thirteenth
Century England', *Journal of Public Law*, 2 (1953), 47–62

Bayley, C. C., 'The Diplomatic Preliminaries of the Double Election of 1257 in
Germany', *English Historical Review*, 62.245 (1947), 457–83

Beazley, C. Raymond, *The Dawn of Modern Geography* (London: J. Murray, 1897),
vol. II

Bedford, R. D., 'Milton's Journeys North: "A Brief History of Moscovia" and
"Paradise Lost"', *Renaissance Studies*, 7.1 (1993), 71–85

BIBLIOGRAPHY

Bendefy, László, *Az ismeretlen Juliánusz: A legelső magyar ázsiakutató életrajza és kritikai méltatása* [The unknown Julian: The biography and critical appraisal of the first Hungarian Asia explorer] (Budapest: Stephaneum, 1936)

——, *Magna Hungaria és a Liber Censuum* (Budapest: Szalay Sándor, 1943)

Benham, Jenny, *Peacemaking in the Middle Ages: Principles and Practice*, Manchester Medieval Studies (Manchester: Manchester University Press, 2011)

Berend, Nora, *At the Gate of Christendom: Jews, Muslims, and 'Pagans' in Medieval Hungary, c. 1000–c. 1300* (Cambridge: Cambridge University Press, 2001)

——, 'Cuman Integration in Hungary', in *Nomads in the Sedentary World*, ed. by Anatolij Michajlovič Chazanov and André Wink, Routledge-IIAS Asian Studies Series (London: Routledge, 2001), pp. 103–26

Bernet, Xaver, 'Beiträge zur Geschichte der Kreuzzüge gegen die Mongolen im XIII. Jahrhundert: Zunächst für das Bisthum Constanz', *Der Geschichtsfreund: Mitteilungen des Historischen Vereins der Fünf Orte Luzern, Uri, Schwyz, Unterwalden und Zug*, 1 (1844), 351–64

Bezzola, Gian Andri, *Die Mongolen in abendländischer Sicht* (Berlin: Francke Verlag, 1974)

Bigalli, Davide, *I tartari e l'Apocalisse* (Firenze: La nuova Italia, 1971)

Biller, Peter, *The Measure of Multitude: Population in Medieval Thought* (Oxford: Oxford University Press, 2001)

——, 'Northern Cathars and Higher Learning', *Studies in Church History. Subsidia*, 11 (1999), 25–53

Bird, Jessalynn, Edward Peters, and James M. Powell, eds, *Crusade and Christendom: Annotated Documents in Translation from Innocent III to the Fall of Acre, 1187–1291* (Philadelphia: University of Pennsylvania Press, 2013)

Bleisteiner, Claus D., 'Der Doppeladler von Kaiser und Reich im Mittelalter: Imagination und Realität', *Mitteilungen des Instituts für Österreichische Geschichtsforschung*, 109 (2001), 4–52

Blin, Léon, 'Du Brabant à Lyon et en Italie par la Champagne et la Bourgogne (XIIe et XIIIe siècles)', *Publications du Centre Européen d'Etudes Bourguignonnes*, 23 (1983), 105–22

Blurton, Heather, *Cannibalism in High Medieval English Literature* (New York: Palgrave Macmillan, 2007)

Boba, Imre, 'Vlachs in the History of Central Europe: A "Problemstellung"', in *Kelet És Nyugat Között: Történeti Tanulmányok Kristó Gyula Tiszteletére*, ed. by László Koszta (Szeged: Szegedi Középkorász Műhely, 1995), pp. 95–102

Boer, Dick de, '"He Proved to Be an Inseparable Travel Companion": Emo of Wittewierum and his Rome Journey in 1211–1212', in *Gender, Companionship, and Travel: Discourses in Pre-Modern and Modern Travel Literature*, ed. by Floris Meens and Tom Sintobin (London: Routledge, 2018), pp. 47–65

Borges, Jorge Luis, *A Universal History of Infamy*, trans. by Norman Thomas di Giovanni (Harmondsworth: Penguin Books, 1975)

Borst, Arno, *Die Katharer: mit einem Nachwort von Alexander Patschovsky* (Freiburg: Herder, 1995)

Boyer, Allen D., *Sir Edward Coke and the Elizabethan Age* (Stanford: Stanford University Press, 2003)

Bradács, Gábor, 'A tatárjárás osztrák elbeszélő forrásainak kritikája' [The critique of the medieval Austrian narrative sources on the Mongol invasion of Hungary]', *Hadtörténelmi Közlemények*, 124.1 (2014), 3–22

Brégaint, David, *Vox Regis: Royal Communication in High Medieval Norway* (Leiden: Brill, 2015)

Bretholz, Berthold, 'Die Tataren in Mähren und die moderne mährische Urkundenfälschung', *Zeitschrift des Vereins für Geschichte Mährens und Schlesiens*, 1.1 (1897), 1–64

British Library, *Western Manuscripts Lansdowne Manuscripts (c 1200–c 1700) (Lansdowne MS 1–1245)* (London: British Library, [n.d.][n.d.]), <http://hviewer.bl.uk/IamsHViewer/FindingAidHandler.ashx?recordid = 032–002060013>

Broun, Dauvit, 'Creating and Maintaining a Year-by-Year Chronicle: The Evidence of the Chronicle of Melrose', in *The Medieval Chronicle VI*, ed. by Erik Kooper (Amsterdam: Rodopi, 2009), pp. 141–52

——, and Julian Harrison, *The Chronicle of Melrose Abbey: A Stratigraphic Edition* (Aberdeen: Scottish History Society; Woodbridge: Boydell Press, 2007), vol. I

Bull, Marcus, 'Eyewitness and the Medieval Historical Narrative', in *Medieval Chronicle 11*, ed. by Erik Kooper and Sjoerd Levelt (Leiden: Brill, 2018), pp. 1–22

Bullón-Fernández, Maria, 'Introduction: Not All Roads Lead to Rome; Anglo-Iberian Exchanges in the Middle Ages', in *England and Iberia in the Middle Ages, 12th–15th Century: Cultural, Literary, and Political Exchanges*, ed. by María Bullón-Fernández, New Middle Ages (New York: Palgrave Macmillan, 2007), pp. 1–10

Burger, Michael, *Bishops, Clerks, and Diocesan Governance in Thirteenth-Century England: Reward and Punishment* (New York: Cambridge University Press, 2012)

Buzár, Ágota, and Zsolt Bernert, 'Bugac–Felsőmonostor-Csitári Tanya és Kiskunmajsa-Jonathermál tatárjárás kori lelőhelyek csontmaradványainak embertani vizsgálata' [Examination of the human bone remains of Bugac–Felsőmonostor-Csitári Tanya és Kiskunmajsa-Jonathermál sites from the time of the Mongol invasion], *Archaeologiai Értesítő*, 143.1 (2018), 203–13

Calvino, Italo, *Invisible Cities*, trans. by William Weaver (New York: Harcourt Brace Jovanovich, 1978)

Camille, Michael, 'The Dissenting Image: A Postcard from Matthew Paris', in *Criticism and Dissent in the Middle Ages*, ed. by Rita Copeland (Cambridge: Cambridge University Press, 1996), pp. 115–50

——, *Image on the Edge: The Margins of Medieval Art*, Essays in Art and Culture (London: Reaktion Books, 2010)

Canz, Oskar Wilhelm, *Philipp Fontana im Dienste der Kurie unter den Päpsten Gregor IX. und Innocenz IV.* (Leipzig: Quelle & Meyer, 1910)

Carpenter, David A., 'Chronology and Truth: Matthew Paris and the Chronica Majora', in *Matthew Paris: A Companion*, ed. by James Clark (Cambridge: Cambridge University Press, forthcoming)

———, 'King, Magnates, and Society: The Personal Rule of King Henry III, 1234–1258', *Speculum*, 60.1 (1985), 39–70

———, 'A Lost Engrossment of the 1215 Magna Carta?', *The Magna Carta Project*, Feature of the Month: June 2015, <https://magnacarta.cmp.uea.ac.uk/read/feature_of_the_month/Jun_2015_2>

———, *Magna Carta* (London: Penguin, 2015)

———, 'The Pershore *Flores Historiarum*: An Unrecognised Chronicle from the Period of Reform and Rebellion in England, 1258–65', *English Historical Review*, 127.529 (2012), 1343–66

Carrard, Philippe, 'Récit historique et fonction testimoniale', *Poétique*, 65 (1986), 47–61

Catto, J. I., *The Early Oxford Schools* (Oxford: Oxford University Press, 1984)

Chambers, James, *The Devil's Horsemen: The Mongol Invasion of Europe* (London: Phoenix Press, 2001)

Chaplais, Pierre, *English Diplomatic Practice in the Middle Ages* (London: Hambledon and London, 2003)

Chartier, Roger, *On the Edge of the Cliff: History, Language, and Practices* (Baltimore: John Hopkins University Press, 1997)

Chatman, Seymour, *Story and Discourse* (Ithaca, NY: Cornell University Press, 1978)

Cheney, Christopher Robert, *Episcopal Visitation of Monasteries in the Thirteenth Century* (Manchester: Manchester University Press, 1983)

———, 'The Letters of Pope Innocent III', *Bulletin of the John Rylands Library, Manchester*, 35.1 (1952), 23–43

———, 'Notes on the Making of the Dunstable Annals, AD 33 to 1242', in *Essays in Medieval History Presented to Bertie Wilkinson*, ed. by T. A. Sandquist and Maurice R. Powicke (Toronto: University of Toronto Press, 1969), pp. 79–98

Cohn, Dorrit, *The Distinction of Fiction* (Baltimore: Johns Hopkins University Press, 1999)

Coleman, Edward, 'Lombard City Annals and the Social and Cultural History of Northern Italy', in *Chronicling History: Chroniclers and Historians in Medieval and Renaissance Italy*, ed. by Sharon Dale, Alison Williams Lewin, and Duane J. Osheim (University Park: Pennsylvania State University Press, 2007), pp. 1–27

Colker, Marvin L., 'America Rediscovered in the Thirteenth Century?', *Speculum*, 54.4 (1979), 712–26

Collard, Judith, '"Flores Historiarum" Manuscripts: The Illumination of a Late Thirteenth-Century Chronicle Series', *Zeitschrift für Kunstgeschichte*, 71.4 (2008), 441–66

————, 'Matthew Paris, Brother William and the Franciscans', in *Interpreting Francis and Clare of Assisi: From the Middle Ages to the Present*, ed. by Constant J. Mews (Mulgrave: Broughton, 2010), pp. 92–110

————, 'Matthew Paris's "Self-Portrait with the Virgin Mary" in the Historia Anglorum', *Parergon*, 32.1 (2015), 151–82

Colledge, Edmund, 'The Capgrave Autographs', *Transactions of the Cambridge Bibliographical Society*, 6.3 (1974), 137–48

Colucci, Michele, 'The Image of Western Christianity in the Culture of Kievan Rus'', in 'Proceedings of the International Congress Commemorating the Millennium of Christianity in Rus'-Ukraine', special issue, *Harvard Ukrainian Studies*, 12/13 (1988), 576–86

Connolly, Daniel K., *The Maps of Matthew Paris: Medieval Journeys through Space, Time and Liturgy* (Woodbridge: Boydell & Brewer, 2009)

Constable, Giles, *Letters and Letter-Collections*, Typologie des Sources du Moyen Âge Occidental (Turnhout: Brepols, 1976)

Cosgrove, Peter, *Impartial Stranger: History and Intertextuality in Gibbon's Decline and Fall of the Roman Empire* (Newark: University of Delaware Press; London: Associated University Presses, 1999)

Coulter, Matthew, 'Patterns of Communication during the 1241 Mongol Invasion: Insights from the Ottobeuren Letter Collection', paper presented at 'The Mongols in Central Europe: The Profile and Impact of their Thirteenth-Century Invasions', online conference of The Mongol Invasion of Hungary and its Eurasian Context Project, 26–27 November 2020 [entitled 'Ulrich of Ulten and Other German Crusaders against the Mongols' in the published transactions of the conference]

Creamer, Joseph, 'St Edmund of Canterbury and Henry III in the Shadow of Thomas Beckett', in *Thirteenth Century England XIV : Proceedings of the Aberystwyth and Lampeter Conference, 2011*, ed. by Janet E. Burton, Phillipp R. Schofield, and Björn K. U. Weiler (Woodbridge: Boydell Press, 2013), pp. 129–39

Crombie, Alistair Cameron, *Robert Grosseteste and the Origins of Experimental Science, 1100–1700* (Oxford: Clarendon Press, 1971)

Csukovits, Enikő, 'A konstanzi zsinat mint könyvvásár és tudományos fórum', in *'Causa unionis, causa fidei, causa reformationis in capite et membris'*: *Tanulmányok a konstanzi zsinat 600. évfordulója alkalmából* (Debrecen: Printart Press, 2014), pp. 52–59

Dällenbach, Lucien, *The Mirror in the Text* (Chicago: University of Chicago Press, 1989)

————, *Le récit spéculaire: Essai sur la mise en abyme* (Paris: Editions du Seuil, 1977)

Davenport, Tony, *Medieval Narrative: An Introduction* (Oxford: Oxford University Press, 2004)

Dávidházi, Péter, '"A kérdés továbbgondolására késztet": Ruttkay irányjelzései a magyar anglisztika útkereséséhez' ["Fosters further consideration": Ruttkay's guiding lights in the period of reflection of English Studies in Hungary], in *Párbeszédben Ruttkay Kálmánnal: egy rejtőzködő életmű újraolvasása* [In dialogue with Kálmán Ruttkay: Rereading a hidden oeuvre], ed. by Zsolt Komáromy and Péter Dávidházi (Budapest: Reciti, 2015), pp. 51–77

Davies, A., 'The Appointment of Cardinal-Deacon Otto as Legate in Britain (1237)', in *Thirteenth-Century England XI: Proceedings of the Gregynog Conference 2005*, ed. by Björn Weiler, Janet Burton, Phillipp Schofield, and Karen Stöber (Woodbridge: Boydell, 2007), pp. 147–58

Davis, H. W. C., 'An Unpublished Life of Edmund Rich', *English Historical Review*, 22.85 (1907), 84–92

Deanesly, Margaret, *A History of the Medieval Church, 590–1500* (repr. London: Routledge, 1994)

Deér, József, *A magyar nemzeti öntudat kialakulása* (Budapest: Magyarságtudomány, 1936)

Denholm-Young, Noël, 'The Cursus in England', in *Oxford Essays in Medieval History Presented to Herbert Edward Salter*, ed. by Frederick Maurice Powicke (Oxford: Clarendon Press, 1934), pp. 68–103

D'Evelyn, Charlotte, 'The Middle-English Metrical Version of the Revelations of Methodius; with a Study of the Influence of Methodius in Middle-English Writings', *PMLA*, 33.2 (1918), 135–203

Dickens, Mark, 'Tarsā: Persian and Central Asian Christians in Extant Literature', in *Artifact, Text, Context: Studies on Syriac Christianity in China and Central Asia*, ed. by Li Tang and Dietmar W. Winkler, Orientalia - Patristica - Oecumenica, 17 (Zurich: Lit, 2020), pp. 9–42

Dickmann, Iddo, *The Little Crystalline Seed: The Ontological Significance of Mise en Abyme in Post-Heideggerian Thought* (Albany: State University of New York Press, 2019)

Dienes, Mary, 'Eastern Missions of the Hungarian Dominicans in the First Half of the Thirteenth Century', *Isis*, 27 (1937), 225–41

Dobenecker, Otto, ed., *Regesta diplomatica necnon epistolaria historiae Thuringiae* (Jena: Gustav Fischer, 1925), vol. III

D'Ohsson, Constantin Mouradgea, *Histoire des Mongols: Depuis Tchinguiz-Khan jusqu'à Timour Bey ou Tamerlan* (Amsterdam: Les Frères Van Cleef, 1834), vol. II

Donald, James, 'Metropolis: The City as Text', in *Social and Cultural Forms of Modernity*, ed. by Robert Bocock and Kenneth Thompson (Cambridge: Cambridge University Press, 1992), pp. 418–61

Döring, Johann Michael Heinrich, *Der Thüringer Chronik* (Erfurt: Expedition der Thüringer Chronic, 1841)

Dörrie, Heinrich, 'Drei Texte zur Geschichte der Ungarn und Mongolen: Die Missionsreisen des fr. Iulianus O.P. ins Ural-Gebiet (1234/5) und nach Rußland (1237) und der Bericht des Erzbischofs Peter über die Tartaren', *Nachrichten der Akademie der Wissenschaften in Göttingen, phil.-hist. Klasse*, 6 (1956), 125–202

Duarte, German A., *Fractal Narrative: About the Relationship between Geometries and Technology and its Impact on Narrative Spaces*, Media Studies (Bielefeld: transcript, 2014)

Dumville, David, 'What Is a Chronicle?', in *The Medieval Chronicle II: Proceedings of the 2nd International Conference on the Medieval Chronicle; Driebergen/Utrecht 16–21 July 1999*, ed. by Erik Kooper (Amsterdam: Rodopi, 2002), pp. 1–27

Dunning, Andrew, 'St Frideswide's Priory as a Centre of Learning in Early Oxford', 29 May 2019, https://andrewdunning.ca/st-frideswides-priory-learning-early-oxford [accessed 18 January 2021]

Düring, Marten, 'Should I Do Social Network Analysis?', *Digital Humanities LAB at CVCE Powered by Uni.Lu*, <https://cvcedhlab.hypotheses.org/125> [accessed 4 June 2019]

Duvernoy, Jean, *La Catharisme*, vol. II: *L'histoire des cathares* (Toulouse: Privat, 1979)

Eco, Umberto, *The Name of the Rose* (Boston: Houghton Mifflin, 1983)

Edson, Evelyn, *Mapping Time and Space: How Medieval Mapmakers Viewed their World*, The British Library Studies in Map History, 1 (London: British Library, 1997)

Englberger, Johann, 'Verschwieg Hermann von Niederalteich in seinen Annalen die Tätigkeit Albert Behaims? Zur Thematisierung unterschiedlicher Personengruppen in hochmittelalterlichen Geschichtswerken', in *Von 'Sacerdotium' und 'Regnum': Geistliche und weltliche Gewalt im frühen und hohen Mittelalter: Festschrift für Egon Boshof zum 65. Geburtstag*, ed. by Franz-Reiner Erkens and Harmut Wollf (Cologne: Böhlau, 2002), pp. 551–85

Fabre, Paul, and L[ouis] Duchesne, *Le Liber censuum de l'Église romaine* (Paris: Ernest Thorin, 1889)

Falk, Seb, *The Light Ages: The Surprising Story of Medieval Science* (New York: W. W. Norton, 2020)

Fest, Sándor, 'Egy magyar püspök levele volt párizsi iskolatársához a tatárokról' [A Hungarian bishop's letter to his former fellow student at Paris], *Levéltári Közlemények*, 12 (1934), 223–25

———, 'Párhuzam az angol és magyar alkotmány fejlődése között a XIII. században' [Parallels between the development of the English and Hungarian constitutions in the thirteenth century], in *Skóciai Szt. Margittól a walesi bárdokig: Magyar-angol történeti és irodalmi kapcsolatok* [From Saint Margaret of Scotland to the bards of Wales: Anglo-Hungarian literary connections], ed. by Lóránt Czigány and János H. Korompay (Budapest: Universitas, 2000), pp. 147–65

———, 'Political and Cultural Connections between Hungary and England in the Middle Ages', *Danubian Review*, 5 (1938), 18–28

Fisher, Matthew, *Scribal Authorship and the Writing of History in Medieval England*, Interventions: New Studies in Medieval Culture (Columbus: Ohio State University Press, 2012)

Fisquet, Honoré Jean P., *La France pontificale: Histoire chronologique et biographique des archevêques et évêques de tous les diocèses de France*, 21 vols (Paris: E. Repos, 1864–1874)

Flannery, John, 'The Trinitarian Order and the Ransom of Christian Captives', *Al-Masāq*, 23.2 (2011), 135–44

Fletcher, Stella, *The Popes and Britain: A History of Rule, Rupture and Reconciliation* (London: I. B. Tauris, 2019)

Foot, Sarah, 'Finding the Meaning of Form: Narrative in Annals and Chronicles', in *Writing Medieval History*, ed. by Nancy Partner (London: Hodder, 2005), pp. 88–103

Frank, Tibor, 'The "Anglo-Saxon" Orientation of Wartime Hungarian Foreign Policy: The Case of Antal Ullein-Reviczky', *Diplomacy & Statecraft*, 26.4 (2015), 591–613

Fried, Johannes, 'Auf der Suche nach der Wirklichkeit: Die Mongolen und die europäische Erfahrungswissenschaft im 13. Jahrhundert', *Historische Zeitschrift*, 243 (1986), 287–332

Friedman, John Block, *Northern English Books, Owners, and Makers in the Late Middle Ages* (Syracuse, NY: Syracuse University Press, 1995)

———, and Kristen Mossler Figg, eds, *Trade, Travel, and Exploration in the Middle Ages: An Encyclopedia* (New York: Routledge, 2014)

Gadd, Ian Anders, and Alexandra Gillespie, *John Stow (1525–1605) and the Making of the English Past: Studies in Early Modern Culture and the History of the Book* (London: British Library, 2004)

Gajewski, Alexandra, 'The Patronage Question under Review: Queen Blanche of Castile (1188–1252) and the Architecture of the Cistercian Abbeys at Royaumont, Maubuisson, and Le Lys', in *Reassessing the Roles of Women as 'Makers' of Medieval Art and Architecture*, ed. by Therese Martin, 2 vols, Visualising the Middle Ages, 7 (Leiden: Brill, 2012), I, 197–244

Galbraith, Vivian Hunter, 'The "Historia Aurea" of John, Vicar of Tynemouth, and the Sources of the St Albans Chronicle (1327–1377)', in *Essays in History Presented to Reginald Lane Poole*, ed. by H. W. C. Davis (Oxford: Clarendon Press, 1927), pp. 379–98

———, 'Roger Wendover and Mathew Paris', in *Kings and Chroniclers: Essays in English Medieval History.*, ed. by V. H. Galbraith, History Series (London: Hambledon, 1982), IV, Essay X: pp. 5–48

Garnett, George, *The Norman Conquest in English History*, vol. I, *A Broken Chain?* (Oxford: Oxford University Press, 2021)

Garrison, Mary, '"Send More Socks": On Mentality and the Preservation Context of Medieval Letters', in *New Approaches to Medieval Communication*, ed. by Marco Mostert, Utrecht Studies in Medieval Literacy, 1 (Turnhout: Brepols, 1999), pp. 69–99

Gaudio, Michael, 'Matthew Paris and the Cartography of the Margins', *Gesta*, 39.1 (2000), 50–57

Gelsinger, Bruce E., 'A Thirteenth-Century Norwegian-Castilian Alliance', *Medievalia et Humanistica*, n.s., 10 (1981), 55–80

Gemil, Tasin, 'The Tatars in Romanian Historiography', in *Ottomans—Crimea—Jochids: Studies in Honour of Mária Ivanics* (Szeged: University of Szeged, Department of Altaic Studies, 2020), pp. 111–22

Genette, Gérard, *Narrative Discourse*, trans. by Jane E. Lewin (Ithaca, NY: Cornell University Press, 1980)

——, *Narrative Discourse Revisited*, trans. by Jane E. Lewin (Ithaca, NY: Cornell University Press, 1988)

Gerry, Kathryn, 'Artistic Patronage and the Early Anglo-Norman Abbots of St Albans', in *Writing History in the Anglo-Norman World: Manuscripts, Makers and Readers, c. 1066–c. 1250*, ed. by Laura Cleaver and Andrea Worm, Writing History in the Middle Ages, 6 (Woodbridge: York Medieval Press, 2018), pp. 167–88

Gide, André, *Journal (1889–1939)* (Paris: Gallimard, 1948)

Gießauf, Johannes, 'Herzog Friedrich II. von Österreich und die Mongolengefahr 1241/42', in *Forschungen zur Geschichte des Alpen-Adria-Raumes: Festgabe für Othmar Pickl zum 70. Geburtstag*, ed. by Herwig Ebner and Othmar Pickl, Schriftenreihe des Instituts für Geschichte, 9 (Graz: Graz Institut für Geschichte, 1997), pp. 173–99

——, *Die Mongolengeschichte des Johannes von Piano Carpine: Einführung, Text, Übersetzung, Kommentar*, Schriftenreihe des Instituts für Geschichte, 6 (Graz: Institut für Geschichte der Karl-Franzens-Universität Graz, 1995)

——, 'A Programme of Terror and Cruelty: Aspects of Mongol Strategy in the Light of Western Sources', *Chronica*, 7–8 (2008), 85–96

Gillingham, John, 'Royal Newsletters, Forgeries and English Historians', in *La Cour Plantagenet (1154–1204)*, ed. by Martin Aurell, Civilisation Médiévale, 8 (Poitiers: Université de Poitiers, Centre d'études supérieures de civilisation médiévale, 2000), pp. 171–86

Ginzburg, Carlo, 'Our Words, and Theirs: A Reflection on the Historian's Craft, Today', in *Historical Knowledge: In Quest of Theory, Method and Evidence*, ed. by Susanna Fellman and Marjatta Rahikainen (Newcastle upon Tyne: Cambridge Scholars, 2012), pp. 97–119

Given-Wilson, Chris, *Chronicles: The Writing of History in Medieval England* (London: Hambledon and London, 2004)

Gladysz, Mikolaj, *The Forgotten Crusaders: Poland and the Crusader Movement in the Twelfth and Thirteenth Centuries* (Leiden: Brill, 2012)

Göckenjan, Hansgerd, 'Das Bild der Völker Osteuropas in den Reicheberichten ungarischen Dominikaner des 13. Jahrhunderts', in *Östliches Europa: Spiegel der Geschichte; Festschrift für Manfred Hellmann zum 65 Geburtstag*, ed. by Carsten Goehrke, D. O. Morgan, and Peter Jackson (Wiesbaden: Steiner, 1977), pp. 125–52

———, and James Ross Sweeney, eds, *Der Mongolensturm: Berichte von Augenzeugen und Zeitgenossen 1235–1250*, Ungarns Geschichtsschreiber, 3 (Graz: Styria, 1985)

Goering, Joseph, '"Notus in Iudea Deus": Robert Grosseteste's Confessional Formulary in Lambeth Palace MS 499', *Viator*, 18 (1987), 253–73

Graham, Timothy, 'Glosses and Notes in Anglo-Saxon Manuscripts', in *A Companion to Anglo-Saxon Literature*, ed. by Phillip Pulsiano and Elaine Treharne, Blackwell Companions to Literature and Culture, 11 (Malden, MA.: Blackwell, 2008), pp. 159–204

———, 'Matthew Parker's Manuscripts: An Elizabethan Library and its Use', in *The Cambridge History of Libraries in Britain and Ireland*, ed. by Elisabeth Leedham-Green and Teresa Webber (Cambridge: Cambridge University Press, 2006), pp. 322–42

Gramsch-Stehfest, Robert, 'Entangled Powers: Network Analytical Approaches to the History of the Holy Roman Empire during the Late Staufer Period', *German History*, 36.3 (2018), 365–80

Gransden, Antonia, 'The Chronicles of Medieval England and Scotland: Part 2', *Journal of Medieval History*, 16.2 (1990), 129–50

———, 'The Continuations of the *Flores Historiarum* from 1265 to 1327', *Mediaeval Studies*, 36 (1974), 472–92; repr. in Gransden, *Legends, Traditions and History in Medieval England* (London: Hambledon, 1992), pp. 245–65, 332–33 (references are to the latter edition)

———, *Historical Writing in England*, vol. I: *c. 550 to c. 1307* (Ithaca, NY: Cornell University Press, 1974)

———, *Historical Writing in England*, vol. II: *c. 1307 to the Early Sixteenth Century* (Ithaca, NY: Cornell University Press, 1982)

Grant, Lindy, *Blanche of Castile, Queen of France* (New Haven: Yale University Press, 2016)

———, 'The Queen and the Abbots: Blanche of Castile', in *Sur les pas de Lanfranc, du Bec à Caen: Recueil d'études en hommage à Véronique Gazeau*, ed. by Pierre Bauduin and Véronique Gazeau, Cahier des Annales de Normandie, 37 (Caen: Annales de Normandie, 2018), pp. 139–48

Greasley, Nathan, 'Matthew Paris's Networks of Information' (unpublished doctoral dissertation, University of Aberystwyth, forthcoming)

———, 'Revisiting the Compilation of Matthew Paris's *Chronica Majora*: New Textual and Manuscript Evidence', *Journal of Medieval History*, 47.2 (2021), 230–56

Grévin, Benoît, 'Writing Techniques in Thirteenth- and Fourteenth-Century England: The Role of the Sicilian and Papal Letter Collections as Practical Models for the Shaping of Royal Propaganda', in *Fourteenth Century England VII*, ed. by W. Mark Ormrod (Woodbridge: Boydell & Brewer, 2012), pp. 1–30

Grice, Deborah, *Church, Society and University: The Paris Condemnation of 1241/4* (London: Routledge, 2019)

Grillnberger, Otto, 'Die Handschriften der Stiftsbibliothek zu Wilhering', in *Die Handschriften-Verzeichnisse der Cistercienser-Stifte*, vol. II: *Wilhering, Schlierbach, Osegg, Hohenfurt, Stams*, Xenia Bernardina II, 2: Die Handschriften-Verzeichnisse der Cistercienser-Stifte, 2 (Vienna: Alfred Hölder, 1891), pp. 1–114

Gulyás, Gyöngyi, 'Egy elpusztult falu Cegléd határában (Pest M.)' [A vanished village in the outskirts of Cegléd], in *A tatárjárás* [The Mongol Invasion], ed. by Ágnes Ritoók and Éva Garam (Budapest: Magyar Nemzeti Múzeum, 2007), pp. 52–53

——, 'Egy elpusztult tatárjáráskori ház Cegléd határában' [A destroyed Mongol invasion-period house in the outskirts of Cegléd], in *Carmen miserabile: A tatárjárás magyarországi emlékei; Tanulmányok Pálóczi Horváth András 70. születésnapja tiszteletére* [Archaeological finds from the Mongol invasion in Hungary: Studies in honour of András Pálóczi Horváth on his seventieth birthday], ed. by Szabolcs Rosta and György V. Székely (Kecskemét: Kecskeméti Katona József Múzeum, 2014), pp. 29–56

Guzman, Gregory G., 'Simon of Saint-Quentin and the Dominican Mission to the Mongol Baiju: A Reappraisal', *Speculum*, 46.2 (1971), 232–49

Györffy, György, *Julianus barát és a napkelet fölfedezése* [Friar Julianus and the discovery of the East] (Budapest: Szépirodalmi Kiadó, 1984)

Gyucha, Attila, and Zoltán Rózsa, '"Egyesek darabokra vágva, egyesek egészben": A tatárjárás nyomainak azonosítási kísérlete egy dél-alföldi településen' ["Some cut to pieces, some as a whole": The identification of the Mongol invasion at a village in the southern Great Hungarian Plain], in *Carmen miserabile: A tatárjárás magyarországi emlékei; Tanulmányok Pálóczi Horváth András 70. születésnapja tiszteletére* [Archaeological finds from the Mongol invasion in Hungary: Studies in honour of András Pálóczi Horváth on his seventieth birthday], ed. by Szabolcs Rosta and György V. Székely (Kecskemét: Kecskeméti Katona József Múzeum, 2014), pp. 57–68

Hagger, Mark, 'A Pipe Roll for 25 Henry I', *English Historical Review*, 122.495 (2007), 133–40

Haivry, Ofir, *John Selden and the Western Political Tradition* (Cambridge: Cambridge University Press, 2017)

Hansen, Anne Mette, ed., *The Book as Artefact, Text and Border*, Variants, 4.2005 (Amsterdam: Rodopi, 2005)

Harper, Sally, 'Traces of Lost Late Medieval Offices? The Sanctimonium Angliae, Walliae, Scotiae, et Hiberniae of John Tynemouth (Fl. 1350)', in *Essays on the History of English Music in Honour of John Caldwell: Sources, Style, Performance, Historiography*, ed. by David Nicholas Maw, John Caldwell, and Emma Hornby (Woodbridge: Boydell, 2010), pp. 1–21

Hartog, Leo de, *Genghis Khan: Conqueror of the World* (London: Taurisparke, 2004)

Hautala, Roman [Хаутала, Роман], *Ot 'Davida, carja Indij' do 'nenavistnogo plebsa satany': Antologija rannich latinskich svedenij o tataro-mongolach* [От 'Давида, царя Индий' до 'ненавистного плебса сатаны': Антология ранних латинских сведений о татаро-монголах; From 'David, King of the Indies' to 'the detestable plebs of Satan': An anthology of early Latin reports about the Tatar-Mongols], Yazma miras: Pis'mennoe nasledie / Textual heritage, 2 (Kazan': Institut istorii im. Š. Mardžani AN RT, 2015)

Heinisch, Klaus J., ed., *Kaiser Friedrich II: sein Leben in zeitgenössischen Berichten*, dtv Dokumente, 2901, 4th edn (Munich: Dt. Taschenbuch-Verlag, 1994)

Helle, Knut, 'Anglo-Norwegian Relations in the Reign of Håkon Håkonsson, 1217–63', *Mediaeval Scandinavia*, 1 (1968), 101–14

———, Arnvid Lillehammer, and Stein-Morten Omre, *Aschehougs Norgeshistorie*, vol. III: *Under kirke og kongemakt: 1130–1350* (Oslo: Aschehoug, 1995)

Herlands Hornstein, Lilian, 'The Historical Background of the King of Tars', *Speculum*, 16.4 (1941), 404–14

Hilpert, Hans-Eberhard, *Kaiser- und Papstbriefe in den Chronica majora des Matthaeus Paris* (Stuttgart: Klett-Cotta, 1981)

———, 'Zu den Prophetien im Geschichtswerk des Matthew Paris', *Deutsches Archiv für Erforschung des Mittelalters*, 41 (1985), 175–91

Hinnebusch, William A., *The Early English Friars Preachers* (Rome: Istituto Storico Domenicano, 1951)

Hobbins, Daniel, *Authorship and Publicity before Print: Jean Gerson and the Transformation of Late Medieval Learning* (Philadelphia: University of Pennsylvania Press, 2009)

Holdenried, Anke, *The Sibyl and her Scribes: Manuscripts and Interpretation of the Latin Sibylla Tiburtina c. 1050–1500, Church, Faith, and Culture in the Medieval West* (Aldershot: Ashgate, 2006)

Hollahan, Eugene, 'Reviews: Dällenbach, Lucien, *The Mirror in the Text*, trans. by Jeremy Whiteley with Emma Hughes', *Studies in the Novel*, 22 (1990), 357–61

Holt, J. C., 'The St Albans Chroniclers and Magna Carta', *Transactions of the Royal Historical Society*, 14 (1964), 67–88

Honemann, Volker, *Provinzialminister und -vikare bis zum Ende der Provinz(en der) Saxonia im 16. Jahrhundert* (Leiden: Ferdinand Schöningh, 2015)

Hormayr zu Hortenburg, Joseph, *Die goldene Chronik von Hohenschwangau, der Burg der Welfen, der Hohenstauffen und der Scheyren* (Munich: Franz, 1842), vol. II

Hoskin, Philippa M., 'Matthew Paris's *Chronica Majora* and the Franciscans in England', in *The English Province of the Franciscans (1224–c. 1350)*, ed. by Michael J. P. Robson, The Medieval Franciscans, 14 (Leiden: Brill, 2017), pp. 46–62

———, *Robert Grosseteste and the 13th-Century Diocese of Lincoln: An English Bishop's Pastoral Vision* (Leiden: Brill, 2019)

Houben, Hubert, *Kaiser Friedrich II, 1194–1250: Herrscher, Mensch und Mythos* (Stuttgart: W. Kohlhammer, 2008)

Howorth, Henry H., *History of the Mongols: From the 9th to the 19th Century*, 4 vols (London: Longmans, Green, 1876–1888)

Huffman, Joseph P., *Family, Commerce, and Religion in London and Cologne: Anglo-German Emigrants, c. 1000–c. 1300* (Cambridge: Cambridge University Press, 2003)

———, 'Potens et Pauper: Charity and Authority in Jurisdictional Dispute over the Poor in Medieval Cologne', in *Plenitude of Power: The Doctrines and Exercise of Authority in the Middle Ages: Essays in Memory of Robert Louis Benson*, ed. by Robert C. Figueira (Oxford: Routledge, 2016), pp. 107–24

———, *The Social Politics of Medieval Diplomacy: Anglo-German Relations (1066–1307)* (Ann Arbor: University of Michigan Press, 2000)

Huillard-Bréholles, Jean Louis Alfonse, *Vie et correspondance de Pierre de la Vigne* (Paris: Henri Plon, 1864)

Hunt, Richard William, Falconer Madan, and Peter Douglas, eds, *A Summary Catalogue of Western Manuscripts in the Bodleian Library at Oxford*, vol. v: *Nos 24331–31000* (Oxford: Clarendon Press, 1905)

Hyams, Paul R., 'The Jewish Minority in Medieval England, 1066–1290', *Journal of Jewish Studies*, 25 (1974), 270–93

Iafrate, Allegra, 'The Workshop of Fortune: St Albans and the Sortes Manuscripts', *Scriptorium*, 66.1 (2012), 55–87

Irwin-Zarecka, Iwona, *Frames of Remembrance: The Dynamics of Collective Memory* (New Brunswick: Transaction Publishers, 1993)

Iskrovskaya, L. V., S. E. Fedorov, and Y. V. Gur'yanova [Искровская, Л. В., С. Е. Фёдоров, Ю. В. Гурьянова], *Istorija Srednih vekov: 6 klass* [История Средних веков: 6 класс; The history of the Middle Ages: Grade 6] (Moscow: Ventana-Graf, 2011)

Istványi, Géza, 'XIII. századi följegyzés IV Bélának 1246-ban a tatárokhoz küldött követségéről' [A thirteenth-century note about legates sent to the Tartars by Béla IV in 1246], *Századok*, 72 (1938), 270–72

Jackson, Peter, 'The Crusade against the Mongols (1241)', *Journal of Ecclesiastical History*, 42.1 (1991), 1–18

———, 'The Crusades of 1239–41 and their Aftermath', *Bulletin of the School of Oriental and African Studies, University of London*, 50.1 (1987), 32–60

——, 'Medieval Christendom's Encounter with the Alien', in *Travellers, Intellectuals, and the World beyond Medieval Europe*, ed. by James Muldoon, The Expansion of Latin Europe, 1000–1500, 10 (Aldershot: Ashgate, 2010), pp. 31–53

——, 'The Mongols and the Faith of the Conquered', in *Mongols, Turks, and Others: Eurasian Nomads and the Sedentary World*, ed. by Reuven Amitai and Michal Biran, Brill's Inner Asian Library, 11 (Leiden: Brill, 2005), pp. 245–90

——, *The Mongols and the West, 1221–1410* (New York: Routledge, 2014)

——, ed., *The Seventh Crusade, 1244–1254: Sources and Documents*, Crusade Texts in Translation, 16 (Aldershot: Ashgate, 2009)

——, 'The Testimony of the Russian "Archbishop" Peter Concerning the Mongols (1244/5): Precious Intelligence or Timely Disinformation?', *Journal of the Royal Asiatic Society*, 26.1–2 (2016), 65–77

Jacquart, Danielle, 'St Giles, John of (d. 1259/60), Dominican Friar and Physician', in *The Oxford Dictionary of National Biography*, ed. by H. C. G. Matthew and B. Harrison (Oxford: Oxford University Press, 2004), <10.1093/ref:odnb/14851>

James, M. R., *The Sources of Archbishop Parker's Collection of Mss. at Corpus Christi College, Cambridge with a Reprint of the Catalogue of Thomas Markaunt's Library* (Cambridge: Cambridge Antiquarian Society, 1899)

Jauss, Hans Robert, *Toward an Aesthetic of Reception*, trans. by Timothy Bahti, Theory and History of Literature, 2 (Minneapolis: University of Minnesota Press, 1982)

Jones, Norman L., 'Matthew Parker, John Bale, and the Magdeburg Centuriators', *Sixteenth Century Journal*, 12.3 (1981), 35–49

Kamp, Norbert, 'Capocci, Raniero di', in *Dizionario Biografico degli Italiani* (Rome: Istituto dell'Enciclopedia Italiana, 1975), XVIII, pp. 608–16

Katona, Tamás, ed., *A tatárjárás emlékezete* [The memory of the Mongol invasion] (Budapest: Magyar Helikon, 1981)

Kay, William, 'Living Stones: The Practice of Remembrance at Lincoln Cathedral' (unpublished doctoral dissertation, University of St Andrews, 2013)

——, 'Wendover's Last Annal', *English Historical Review*, 84.333 (1969), 779–85

Kerby-Fulton, Kathryn, 'Hildegard of Bingen and Anti-Mendicant Propaganda', *Traditio*, 43 (1987), 386–99

Kersken, Norbert, 'High and Late Medieval National Historiography', in *Historiography in the Middle Ages*, ed. by Debora Mauskopf Deliyannis (Leiden: Brill, 2003), pp. 181–215

Kim, Dorothy, 'Matthew Paris, Visual Exegesis, and Apocalyptic Birds in Royal MS 14 C. VII', *Electronic British Library Journal*, 2014, Article 5 (33 pages)

Kindt, Tom, and Hans-Harald Müller, eds, *What Is Narratology? Questions and Answers Regarding the Status of a Theory*, Narratologia, 1 (Berlin: Walter de Gruyter, 2003)

King, Archdale A., *The Rites of Eastern Christendom* (Piscataway, NJ: Gorgias Press, 2007)

Kiss, Gergely, *Dél-Magyarországtól Itáliáig: Báncsa nembeli István (1205 k.–1270) váci püspök, esztergomi érsek, az első magyarországi bíboros életpályája* [From Southern Hungary to Italy: The career of István of Báncsa Kindred, bishop of Vác, archbishop of Esztergom, and first Hungarian cardinal] (Pécs: Kronosz, 2015)

Kivimäe, Jüri, '"Henricus" the Ethnographer: Reflections on Ethnicity in the Chronicle of Livonia', in *Crusading and Chronicle Writing on the Medieval Baltic Frontier*, ed. by Marek Tamm, Carsten Selch Jensen, and Linda Kaljundi (Farnham: Ashgate, 2011), pp. 77–106

Kjær, Lars, 'Food, Drink and Ritualised Communication in the Household of Eleanor de Montfort, February to August 1265', *Journal of Medieval History*, 37.1 (2011), 75–89

———, 'Valdemar 2. Sejr, Matthew Paris og den engelske invasionsfrygt, 1240–41', *Historisk Tidsskrift*, 118.1 (2018), 21–50

Klaić, Nada, 'Paški falsifikati' [The Pag forgeries], *Radovi Filozofskog fakulteta: Odsjek za povijest*, 1 (1959), 15–63

Klaniczay, Gábor, *Holy Rulers and Blessed Princesses: Dynastic Cults in Medieval Central Europe*, Past and Present Publications (Cambridge: Cambridge University Press, 2002)

Kline, Naomi Reed, *Maps of Medieval Thought: The Hereford Paradigm* (Woodbridge: Boydell, 2003)

Klopprogge, Axel, *Ursprung und Ausprägung des abendländischen Mongolenbildes im 13. Jahrhundert: Ein Versuch zur Ideengeschichte des Mittelalters* (Wiesbaden: Harrassowitz, 1993)

Knobloch, Edgar, ed., *Putování k Mongolům* (Prague: Státní nakladatelství krásné literatury a umění, 1964)

Knowles, [Michael] David, 'Presidential Address: Great Historical Enterprises III. The Monumenta Germaniae Historica', *Transactions of the Royal Historical Society*, 10 (1960), 129–50

———, *The Religious Orders in England* (Cambridge: Cambridge University Press, 1979), vol. I

Koch, Hugo, *Richard von Cornwall*, vol. I: *1209–1257* (Strassburg: Universitäts-buckdr. von J. H. E. Heitz, 1887)

Kogou, Sotiria, and , 'The Origins of the Selden Map of China: Scientific Analysis of the Painting Materials and Techniques Using a Holistic Approach', *Heritage Science*, 4.1 (2016), 1–24

Korytko, Andrzej, 'Bibliografia Prac Prof. Henryka Zinsa' [The bibliography of the works of Prof. Henryk Zins], *Echa Przeszłości*, 2 (2001), 23–32

Krakowski, Stefan, *Polska w walce z najazdami tatarskimi w XIII wieku* [Poland in the struggle against the Tartar invasions in the thirteenth century], Prace Komisji Wojskowo-Historycznej Ministerstwa Obrony Narodowej, A (Warsaw: Wydawn: Ministerstwa Obrony Narodowej, 1956), vol. IV

Kristó, Gyula, 'Egy 1235 körüli Gesta Ungarorum körvonalairól' [About the outlines of a Gesta Ungarorum from around 1235]', in *Középkori kútfőink kritikus kérdései* [Critical questions of our medieval sources], ed. by János Horváth and György Székely (Budapest: Akadémiai Kiadó, 1974), pp. 229–38

Kukiel, Marian, *Zarys historii wojskowosci w Polsce* [An outline of the military history of Poland] (Poznan: Kurpisz, 2006)

Kulesza, Ryszard, and Krzysztof Kowalewski, *Zrozumieć przeszłość*, vol. I: *Podręcznik do historii dla liceum ogólnokształcącego i technikum; zakres rozszerzony* [Understanding the past, vol. I: Textbook of history for general and technical secondary schools; extended edition] (Warszawa: Nowa Era, 2019)

Labuda, Gerard, 'Wojna z Tatarami w roku 1241' [War with the Tartars in 1241], *Przegląd Historyczny*, 50.2 (1959), 189–224

——, *Zaginiona kronika z pierwszej polowy XIII wieku w Rocznikach Królestwa Polskiego Jana Długosza: Próba rekonstrukcji* [A lost chronicle from the first half of the thirteenth century in Długosz's Annals of the Kingdom of Poland: An attempt at reconstruction] (Poznan: Wydaw. Naukowe UAM, 1983)

Lämmert, Eberhard, *Bauformen des Erzählens*, 6th edn (Stuttgart: Metzler, 1975)

Laszlovszky, József, 'Tatárjárás és régészet' [The Mongol invasion and archaeology], in *Tatárjárás* [The Mongol invasion], ed. by Balázs Nagy, Nemzet és emlékezet (Budapest: Osiris, 2003), pp. 453–68

——, Stephen Pow, and Tamás Pusztai, 'Reconstructing the Battle of Muhi and the Mongol Invasion of Hungary in 1241: New Archaeological and Historical Approaches', *Hungarian Archaeology*, Winter (2016), 29–38

——, ——, Beatrix F. Romhányi, László Ferenczi, and Zsolt Pinke, 'Contextualizing the Mongol Invasion of Hungary in 1241–42: Short- and Long-Term Perspectives', *Hungarian Historical Review*, 7.3 (2018), 419–50

Latham, R. E., ed., *Revised Medieval Latin World-List from British and Irish Sources* (London: Oxford University Press, 1999)

Le Clerc, Victor, ed., *Histoire littéraire de la France; ouvrage commencé par des religieux Bénédictins de la Congrégation de Saint-Maur*, vol. XXI: *Suite du treizième siècle depuis l'année 1296* (Paris: H. Welter, 1895)

Le Goff, Jacques, *The Medieval Imagination* (Chicago: University of Chicago Press, 1988)

Leach, Henry Goddard, 'The Relations of the Norwegian with the English Church, 1066–1399, and their Importance to Comparative Literature', *Proceedings of the American Academy of Arts and Sciences*, 44.20 (1909), 531–60

Lerner, Robert E., *The Powers of Prophecy: The Cedar of Lebanon Vision from the Mongol Onslaught to the Dawn of the Enlightenment* (Ithaca: Cornell University Press, 2009)

——, 'Review of *Ketzer in Österreich: Untersuchungen über Häresie und Inquisition im Herzogtum Österreich im 13. und beginnenden 14. Jahrhundert* by Peter Segl', *Speculum*, 62.2 (1987), 472–74

————, 'The Uses of Heterodoxy: The French Monarchy and Unbelief in the Thirteenth Century', *French Historical Studies*, 4.2 (1965), 189–202

Lewis, Charlton T., and Charles Short, *A Latin Dictionary* (Oxford: Clarendon Press, 1969)

Lewis, Suzanne, *The Art of Matthew Paris in the Chronica Majora*, California Studies in the History of Art, 21 (Berkeley: University of California Press in collaboration with Corpus Christi College, Cambridge, 1987)

Leyser, Karl, *Communications and Power in Medieval Europe: The Carolingian and Ottonian Centuries*, ed. by Timothy Reuter (London: Hambledon Press, 1994)

————, *Communications and Power in Medieval Europe: The Gregorian Revolution and Beyond*, ed. by Timothy Reuter (London: Hambledon Press, 1994)

Linehan, Peter, 'La carrera del obispo Abril de Urgel: La Iglesia española en el siglo XIII', *Annuario de Estudios Medievales*, 8 (1972), 143–98

Lisini, Alessandro, *Inventario generale del R. Archivio di Stato in Siena*, vol. I: *Diplomatico, statuti, capitoli* (Siena: L. Lazzeri, 1899)

Liu, Hui, 'Matthew Paris and John Mansel', in *Thirteenth Century England XI: Proceedings of the Gregynog Conference, 2005*, ed. by Björn Weiler, Janet Burton, Phillipp Schofield, and Karen Stöber (Woodbridge: Boydell, 2007), pp. 159–73

Lubocki, Adam, 'Mongol Invasion of Hungary in the Light of Polish Medieval Sources', paper presented at 'The Mongols in Central Europe: The Profile and Impact of their Thirteenth-Century Invasions', online conference of The Mongol Invasion of Hungary and its Eurasian Context Project, 26–27 November 2020 [published transactions of the conference forthcoming]

Lunt, W. E., 'The Sources for the First Council of Lyons, 1245', *English Historical Review*, 33.129 (1918), 72–78

Lyon, Gregory B., 'Baudouin, Flacius, and the Plan for the Magdeburg Centuries', *Journal of the History of Ideas*, 64.2 (2003), 253–72

Macaulay, G. C., 'The Capture of a General Council, 1241', *English Historical Review* 6.21 (1891), 1–17

Maddicott, J. Robert., *Simon de Montfort* (Cambridge: Cambridge University Press, 1994)

Maerlant, Jacob van, and Ferdinand Augustijn Snellaert, *Alexanders geesten* (Brussel: Hayez, 1860)

Maier, Christoph T., *Preaching the Crusades: Mendicant Friars and the Cross in the Thirteenth Century* (Cambridge: Cambridge University Press, 1998)

Makkai, László, and László Mezey, eds, *Árpád-kori és Anjou-kori levelek: XI–XIV. század* [Árpád-era and Angevin letters: Eleventh to fourteenth centuries] (Budapest: Gondolat, 1960)

Mamachi, Tommaso Maria, and Vincenzo M. Ferretti, *Annales ordinis Praedicatorum*, vol. I (Rome: Typographia Palladis, 1756)

Mandelbrot, Benoit B., *The Fractal Geometry of Nature* (San Francisco: W. H. Freeman, 1982)

Marczali, Henrik, 'Az angol-magyar érdekközösségről a múltban' [About shared Anglo-Hungarian interests in the past], *Századok*, 53–54 (1919), 113–23

Margetić, Lujo, 'Izvještaj Ivana Tomašića o Grobničkoj bitci' [Ivan Tomašić on the Battle of Grobnik], *Grobnički zbornik*, 2 (1992), 28–34

Maroń, Jerzy, *Legnica 1241*, Historyczne Bitwy, 68 (Warsaw: Bellona, 1996)

Marrou, Henri-Irénée, 'Comment comprendre le métier d'historien', in *L'histoire et ses méthodes*, ed. by Charles Samaran, Encyclopédie de la Pléiade, 11 (Paris: Gallimard, 1986), pp. 1465–1540

Martin, Geoffrey, and Rodney M. Thomson, 'History and History Books', in *The Cambridge History of the Book in Britain*, vol. II: *1100–1400*, ed. by Nigel J. Morgan and Rodney M. Thomson (Cambridge: Cambridge University Press, 2008), pp. 397–415

Martínez Alfaro, María Jesús, 'Intertextuality: Origins and Development of the Concept', *Atlantis*, 18.1/2 (1996), 268–85

Matthews, Alastair, *The Kaiserchronik: A Medieval Narrative*, 1st edn (Oxford: Oxford University Press, 2012)

Matuszewski, Józef, *Relacja Długosza o najezdzie tatarskim w 1241 roku: Polskie zdania legnickie* [Długosz's account of the 1241 Tartar invasion: Polish opinions on Legnica] (Łódz: Łódzkie Towarzystwo Naukowe, 1980)

——, 'Spór o zaginioną kronikę' [The debate about a lost chronicle], *Czasopismo Prawno-Historyczne*, 37.1 (1985), 121–43

McEvoy, J. J., *Robert Grosseteste*, Great Medieval Thinkers (Oxford: Oxford University Press, 2000)

McGinn, Bernard, *Visions of the End: Apocalyptic Traditions in the Middle Ages* (New York: Columbia University Press, 1979)

Menache, Sophia, 'Tartars, Jews, Saracens and the Jewish-Mongol "Plot" of 1241', *History*, 81 (1996), 319–42

——, 'Written and Oral Testimonies in Medieval Chronicles: Matthew Paris and Giovanni Villani', in *The Medieval Chronicle VI*, ed. by Erik Kooper (Amsterdam: Rodopi, 2009), pp. 1–30

Meyvaert, Paul, 'An Unknown Letter of Hülegü Il-Khan of Persia to King Louis IX', *Viator*, 11 (1980), 245–61

Mink, Louis O., 'Narrative Form as a Cognitive Instrument', in *The Writing of History: Literary Form and Historical Understanding*, ed. by R. H. Canary and H. Kozicki (Madison: University of Wisconsin Press, 1978), pp. 129–49

Minois, Georges, *Blanche de Castille* (Paris: Perrin, 2018)

Miron, Paul, 'Die rumänische Sprachgemeinschaft', *Dacoromania: Jahrbuch für östliche Latinität*, 1 (1973), 183–88

Mittman, Asa Simon, 'Forking Paths? Matthew Paris, Jorge Luis Borges, and Maps of the Labyrinth', *Peregrinations*, 4.1 (2013), 134–60

——, *Maps and Monsters in Medieval England* (New York: Routledge, 2006)

Monneret de Villard, Ugo, *Le leggende orientali sui magi evangelici* (Vatican: Biblioteca apostolica vaticana, 1952)

Morgan, Mary S., 'Narrative Ordering and Explanation', *Studies in History and Philosophy of Science Part A*, 62 (2017), 86–97

Muldoon, James, *Popes, Lawyers, and Infidels: The Church and the Non-Christian World, 1250–1550*, The Middle Ages (Philadelphia: University of Pennsylvania Press, 1979)

Muñoz García, Manuel, 'The Script of Matthew Paris and his Collaborators: A Digital Approach' (unpublished doctoral dissertation, King's College London, 2017)

Muratova, Xenia, 'Bestiaries: An Aspect of Medieval Patronage', in *Art and Patronage in the English Romanesque*, ed. by Sarah Macready and F. H. Thompson, Occasional Paper, n.s., 8 (London: Society of Antiquaries, 1986), pp. 118–44

Nagy, Balázs, ed., *Tatárjárás* [The Mongol invasion], Nemzet és emlékezet (Budapest: Osiris, 2003)

Nazarenko, Alexandr V., 'Die Regensburger Ruzarii: Der bayerisch-russische Handel des Mittelalters', in *Bayern und Russland in vormoderner Zeit: Annäherungen bis in die Zeit Peters des Großen*, ed. by Alois Schmid (Munich: C. H. Beck, 2012), pp. 15–38

Neudorf, Benjamin, and Yin Liu, 'Signes-de-Renvoi', *ArchBook: Architectures of the Book*, <http://drc.usask.ca/projects/archbook/signes_de_renvoi.php> [accessed 20 January 2020]

Nieuhof, Johann, *An Embassy from the East-India Company of the United Provinces, to the Grand Tartar Cham, Emperour of China Delivered by Their Excell[en]cies, Peter de Goyer and Jacob de Keyzer, at His Imperial City of Peking; Also an Epistle of Father John Adams Concerning the Whole Negotiation*, trans. by John Ogilby (London: John Macock, 1669)

Nünning, Ansgar, 'Narratology or Narratologies? Taking Stock of Recent Developments, Critique, and Modest Proposals for Future Usages of the Term', in *What Is Narratology? Questions and Answers Regarding the Status of a Theory*, ed. by Tom Kindt and Hans-Harald Müller, Narratologia, 1 (Berlin: Walter de Gruyter, 2003), pp. 239–75

Oelrichs, Helga, 'Untersuchung der Glaubwürdigkeit des Matthäus Parisiensis für die Jahre 1236–1241 mit besonderer Berücksichtigung der Geschichte des Kaisertums' (unpublished doctoral dissertation, Thüringische Landesuniversität, 1922)

Osten-Sacken, Vera von der, *Jakob von Vitrys Vita Mariae Oigniacensis: Zu Herkunft und Eigenart der ersten Beginen* (Gottingen: Vandenhoeck & Ruprecht, 2010)

Otter, Monika C., *Inventiones: Fiction and Referentiality in Twelfth-Century English Historical Writing* (Chapel Hill: University of North Carolina Press, 1996)

Paja, László, 'Tatárjárás kori leletek vizsgálati lehetőségei a Szank határából előkerült embertani szérián' [The possibilities of research on the Mongol invasion-period anthropological assemblage discovered in the outskirts of Szank], in *Carmen miserabile: A tatárjárás magyarországi emlékei; Tanulmányok Pálóczi Horváth András 70. születésnapja tiszteletére* [Archaeological finds from the Mongol invasion in Hungary: Studies in honour of András Pálóczi Horváth on his seventieth birthday], ed. by Szabolcs Rosta and György V. Székely (Kecskemét: Kecskeméti Katona József Múzeum, 2014), pp. 111–26

Pajor, Piotr, 'The Poverty and the Power: Duke Boleslaus the Chaste's Patronage of the Franciscans in 13th-Century Lesser Poland', *Umění/Art*, 2 (2017), 106–22

Palacký, František, *Der Mongolen Einfall im Jahre 1241: Eine kritische Zusammenstellung und Sichtung aller darüber vorhanderen Quellennachrichten, mit besonderer Rücksicht auf die Niederlage der Mongolen bei Olmütz* (Prague: Kronberger und Řiwnač, 1842)

Palafox y Mendoza, Juan de, *The History of the Tartars Being an Account of their Religion, Manners, and Customs, and their Wars with, and Overthrow of the Chineses* (London: Thomas Mercer, 1679)

Palgrave, Francis Turner, 'The History of England from the Invasion of Julius Caesar to the Revolution of 1688 by David Hume', *Quarterly Review*, 34 (1926), 248–98

Pálóczi-Horváth, András, *Pechenegs, Cumans, Iasians: Steppe Peoples in Medieval Hungary* (Budapest: Corvina, 1989)

Papacostea, Şerban, *Românii în secolul al XIII lea între cruciată şi Imperiul mongol* (Bucharest: Editura Enciclopedic, 1993)

Papahagi, Adrian, 'Lost Libraries and Surviving Manuscripts: The Case of Medieval Transylvania', *Library & Information History*, 31.1 (2015), 35–53

Papp Reed, Zsuzsanna, 'Post It: Notes from Thirteenth-Century St Albans', in *Genius Loci: Laszlovszky 60*, ed. by Dóra Mérai, Kyra Lyublyanovics, Judith Rasson, András Vadas, Ágnes Drosztmér, and Zsuzsanna Papp Reed (Budapest: Archaeolingua, 2018), pp. 207–12, <http://www.archaeolingua.hu/book/genius-loci-laszlovszky-60>

Papp [Reed], Zsuzsanna, 'Tartars on the Frontiers of Europe: The English Perspective', *Annual of Medieval Studies at the CEU*, 11 (2005), 231–46

Parkes, M. B., 'Handwriting in English Books', in *The Cambridge History of the Book in Britain*, vol. II, *1100–1400*, ed. by Nigel J. Morgan and Rodney M. Thomson (Cambridge: Cambridge University Press, 2008), pp. 110–35

Paroń, Aleksander, 'The Battle of Legnica (9 April 1241) and its Legend', in *Meetings with Emotions: Human Past between Anthropology and History*, ed. by Przemyslaw Wiszewski (Wroclaw: Chronicon, 2008), pp. 89–108

Pauler, Gyula, *A magyar nemzet története az Árpádházi királyok alatt* [The history of the Hungarian nation in the age of the Árpáds], 2nd edn (Budapest: Athenaeum, 1899), vol. II

Paviot, Jacques, 'England and the Mongols (c. 1260–1330)', *Journal of the Royal Asiatic Society*, 10.3 (2000), 305–18

Perryman, J., ed., *The King of Tars: Edited from the Auchinleck Manuscript, Advocates 19.2.1*, Middle English Texts, 12 (Heidelberg: Winter, 1980)

Petersen, Stefan, *Prämonstratensische Wege nach Rom: Die Papsturkunden der fränkischen und swäbischen Stifte bis 1378* (Cologne: Böhlau, 2015)

Petit-Dutaillis, Charles, and Georges Lefebvre, *Studies and Notes Supplementary to Stubbs' Constitutional History*, vols I–III (Manchester: Manchester University Press, 1930; repr. 1968)

Phillpott, Matthew, 'The Compilation of a Sixteenth-Century Ecclesiastical History: The Use of Matthew Paris in John Foxe's Acts and Monuments', in *The Medieval Chronicle VII*, ed. by Juliana Dresvina and Nicholas Sparks (Amsterdam: Rodopi, 2011), pp. 205–22

Pier, John, 'Metalepsis', in *Handbook of Narratology*, ed. by Peter Hühn, Wolf Schmid, Jörg Schönert, and John Pier, Narratologia (Berlin: Walter de Gruyter, 2009), pp. 190–203

Pini, Antonio I., 'Enzo di Svevia, re di Sardegna', in *Dizionario Biografico degli Italiani* (Rome: Istituto dell'Enciclopedia Italiana, 1993), XLIII, <https://www.treccani.it/enciclopedia/enzo-di-svevia-re-di-sardegna_(Dizionario-Biografico)/>

Piron, Sylvain, 'La parole prophétique', in *Le pouvoir des mots au Moyen Âge*, ed. by N. Bériou, J.-P. Boudet, and I. Rosier-Catach (Turnhout: Brepols, 2014), pp. 255–86

Plehn, Hans, *Der politische Charakter von Matheus Parisiensis: Ein Beitrag zur Geschichte der englischen Verfassung und des Ständetums im 13. Jahrhundert*, Staats- und socialwissenschaftliche Forschungen, 14 (Leipzig: Duncker & Humblot, 1897), vol. III

Polak, Emil J., *Medieval and Renaissance Letter Treatises and Form Letters: A Census of Manuscripts Found in Part of Western Europe, Japan, and the United States of America*, Davis Medieval Texts and Studies, 9 (Leiden: Brill, 1994)

Poole, Reginald Lane, *Chronicles and Annals: A Brief Outline of their Origin and Growth* (Oxford: Clarendon Press, 1926)

Posavec, V., and T. Medic, *Povijest 2: udžbenik iz povijesti za II. razred gimnazije* (Zagreb: CIP, 2006)

Pow, Stephen Lindsey, 'Conquest, Withdrawal, and Diplomatic Overture: Understanding the Mongol Invasions of Europe in the Thirteenth Century' (unpublished doctoral dissertation, Central European University, 2020)

——, 'The Historicity of Ivo of Narbonne's Account of a Mongol Attack on "Neustat"', paper presented at 'The Mongols in Central Europe: The Profile and Impact of their Thirteenth-Century Invasions', online conference of The Mongol Invasion of Hungary and its Eurasian Context Project, 26–27 November 2020 [published transactions of the conference forthcoming]

Powell, James M., 'Matthew Paris, the Lives of Muhammad, and the Dominicans', in *Dei Gesta per Francos: Estudes sur les croisades dédiées à Jean Richard*, ed. by Michel Balard, Benjamin Z. Kedar, and Jonathan Riley-Smith (Aldershot: Ashgate, 2001), pp. 65–70

———, 'Patriarch Gerold and Frederick II: The Matthew Paris Letter', in *The Crusades, the Kingdom of Sicily, and the Mediterranean*, ed. by James M. Powell, Variorum Collected Studies Series, 871 (Aldershot: Ashgate, 2007), Essay VII: 19–26

Power, Amanda, *Roger Bacon and the Defence of Christendom* (Cambridge: Cambridge University Press, 2013)

Powicke, Maurice, 'Compilation of the *Chronica Majora*', *Proceedings of the British Academy*, 30 (1944), 147–60

———, 'Review of *Matthew Paris* by Richard Vaughan, Cambridge University Press, 1958', *English Historical Review*, 74.292 (1959), 482–85

Prestwich, Michael, 'Edward I and the Maid of Norway', *Scottish Historical Review*, 69.188 (1990), 157–74

Raccagni, Gianluca, 'The Crusade against Frederick II: A Neglected Piece of Evidence', *Journal of Ecclesiastical History*, 67.4 (2016), 721–40

Rachetta, Maria Teresa, 'Paris 1244: The Jews, the Christians, and the Tartars; The *Livre* of Moses Ben Abraham, a Little-Known Case of Jewish Apologetics in Medieval French', *Medium Ævum*, 89.2 (2020), 244–66

Ramos, Manuel João, *Essays in Christian Mythology: The Metamorphosis of Prester John* (Lanham, MD: University Press of America, 2006)

Rayfield, Donald, *Anton Chekhov: A Life* (New York: Henry Holt, 1998)

Richard, Jean, *La papauté et les missions d'Orient au Moyen Âge, 13e–15e siècles* (Rome: École française de Rome, 1977)

Richardson, Malcolm, 'The Ars Dictaminis, the Formulary and Medieval Epistolary Practice', in *Letter-Writing Manuals and Instruction from Antiquity to the Present: Historical and Bibliographic Studies*, ed. by Carol Poster and Linda C. Mitchell (Columbia: University of South Carolina Press, 2007), pp. 52–66

Rimányi, Áron, 'Closing the Steppe Highway: A New Perspective on the Travels of Friar Julian of Hungary', *Annual of Medieval Studies at CEU*, 24 (2018), 99–112

Rimmon-Kenan, Shlomith, *Narrative Fiction: Contemporary Poetics* (London: Routledge, 1983)

Robinson, Benedict Scott, '"Darke Speech": Matthew Parker and the Reforming of History', *Sixteenth Century Journal*, 29.4 (1998), 1061–83

Rockhill, William Woodville, *The Journey of William of Rubruck to the Eastern Parts of the World, 1253–55: As Narrated by Himself with Two Accounts of the Earlier Journey of John of Pian de Carpine* (London: Hakluyt Society, 2017)

Rogers, Greg S., 'An Examination of Historians' Explanations for the Mongol Withdrawal from East Central Europe', *East European Quarterly*, 30.1 (1996), 3–26

Romhányi, Beatrix F., *Kolostorok és társaskáptalanok a középkori Magyarországon: Katalógus* (Budapest: Pytheas, 2000)

Ron, Moshe, 'The Restricted Abyss: Nine Problems in the Theory of Mise en Abyme', *Poetics Today*, 8.2 (1987), 417–38

Ronay, Gabriel, *The Tartar Khan's Englishman* (London: Cassell, 1978)

Rorty, Richard, *The Linguistic Turn* (Chicago: University of Chicago Press, 1967)

Rosenblatt, Jason Philip, *Renaissance England's Chief Rabbi: John Selden* (Oxford: Oxford University Press, 2008)

Rosta, Szabolcs, 'Pétermonostora pusztulása' [The destruction of Pétermonostora], in *Carmen miserabile: A tatárjárás magyarországi emlékei; Tanulmányok Pálóczi Horváth András 70. születésnapja tiszteletére* [Archaeological finds from the Mongol invasion in Hungary: Studies in honour of András Pálóczi Horváth on his seventieth birthday], ed. by Szabolcs Rosta and György V. Székely (Kecskemét: Kecskeméti Katona József Múzeum, 2014), pp. 193–230

Rouse, Robert, 'Chronicle and Romance', in *Medieval Historical Writing*, ed. by Jennifer Jahner, Emily Steiner, and Elizabeth M. Tyler (Cambridge: Cambridge University Press, 2019), pp. 389–403

Rudolf, Karl, 'Die Tartaren 1241/1242: Nachrichten und Wiedergabe; Korrespondenz und Historiographie', *Römische Historische Mitteilungen*, 19 (1977), 79–107

———, 'Untersuchungen zur summa dictaminis "de scartabello fratris Hermanni": Eine ars dictaminis des beginnenden 14. Jahrhunderts' (Institut für Österreichische Geschichtsforschung, 1974)

Ruotsala, Antti, *Europeans and Mongols in the Middle of the Thirteenth Century: Encountering the Other* (Helsinki: Finnish Academy of Science and Letters, 2001)

Russell, Josiah Cox, 'Some Notes upon the Career of Robert Grosseteste', *Harvard Theological Review*, 48.3 (1955), 197–211

Rychterová, Pavlína, 'The Manuscripts of Grünberg and Könighof: Romantic Lies about the Glorious Past of the Czech Nation', in *Manufacturing a Past for the Present: Forgery and Authenticity in Medievalist Texts and Objects in Nineteenth-Century Europe*, ed. by János M. Bak and Gábor Klaniczay, National Cultivation of Culture, 7 (Leiden: Brill, 2015), pp. 3–30

Sacerdoțeanu, Aurelian, *Marea invazie tătară și Sud-Estul european* [The great Tartar invasion and South-Eastern Europe] (Bucharest: Tipografia 'Bucovina' I. E. Torouțiu, 1933)

Saenger, Paul, *Space between Words: The Origins of Silent Reading* (Stanford, CA: Stanford University Press, 2001)

Sălăgean, Tudor, *Transylvania in the Second Half of the Thirteenth Century: The Rise of the Congregational System*, East Central and Eastern Europe in the Middle Ages, 450–1450, 37 (Leiden: Brill, 2016)

Sand, Alexa, *Vision, Devotion, and Self-Representation in Late Medieval Art* (Cambridge: Cambridge University Press, 2014)

Santi, Mara, 'Performative Perspectives on Short Story Collections', in 'Cycles, Recueils, Macrotexts: The Short Story Collection in Theory and Practice', ed. by Elke D'Hoker and Bart Van Den Bossche, special issue, *Interférences Littéraires / Literaire Interferenties*, 12 (2014), 145–54

444 BIBLIOGRAPHY

Sardelić, Mirko, '"Quasi per aerem volans": The Mongols on the Adriatic Coast (AD 1242)', paper presented at the 'The Mongols in Central Europe: The Profile and Impact of their Thirteenth-Century Invasions', online conference of The Mongol Invasion of Hungary and its Eurasian Context Project, 26–27 November 2020 [published transactions of the conference forthcoming]

Saul, Nigel, 'England and Europe: Problems and Possibilities', in *England in Europe, 1066–1453*, ed. by Nigel Saul (New York: St Martin's Press, 1994), pp. 9–20

Saunders, J. J., *The History of the Mongol Conquests* (Philadelphia: University of Pennsylvania Press, 2001)

Sayers, Jane, 'Center and Locality: Aspects of Papal Administration in England in the Later Thirteenth Century', in *Authority and Power: Studies on Medieval Law and Government Presented to Walter Ullmann on his Seventieth Birthday*, ed. by B. Tierney and Peter Linehan (Cambridge: Cambridge University Press, 1980), pp. 115–26

Schmieder, Felicitas, 'Der Einfall der Mongolen nach Polen und Schlesien: Schreckensmeldungen, Hilferufe und die Reaktionen des Westens', in *Wahlstatt 1241: Beiträge zur Mongolenschlacht bei Liegnitz und zu ihren Nachwirkungen*, ed. by Ulrich Schmilewski (Würzburg: Bergstadtverlag Korn, 1991), pp. 77–86

—— , *Europa und die Fremden: Die Mongolen im Urteil des Abendlandes vom 13. bis in das 15. Jahrhundert*, Beiträge zur Geschichte und Quellenkunde des Mittelalters, 16 (Sigmaringen: Thorbecke, 1994)

—— , 'Nota sectam maometicam atterendam a tartaris et christianis: The Mongols as Non-believing Apocalyptic Friends around the Year 1260', *Journal of Millennial Studies*, 1.1 (1998), 1–11

Schmilewski, Ulrich, ed., *Wahlstatt 1241: Beiträge zur Mongolenschlacht bei Liegnitz und zu ihren Nachwirkungen* (Wurzburg: Bergstadtverlag Korn, 1991)

Schneider, Fedor, 'Ein Schreiben der Ungarn an die Kurie aus der letzten Zeit des Tatareneinfalles (2. Februar 1242)', *Mitteilungen des Instituts für Österreichische Geschichtsforschung*, 36 (1915), 661–70

Schnith, Karl, *England in einer sich wandelnden Welt (1189–1259): Studien zu Roger Wendover und Matthäus Paris*, Monographien zur Geschichte des Mittelalters, 7 (Stuttgart: Hiersemann, 1974)

Schwammel, Eduard Josef, *Der Antheil des österreichischen Herzogs Friedrich des Streitbaren an der Abwehr der Mongolen, und seine Stellung zu König Bela von Ungarn in der Zeit des Mongolensturmes* (Vienna: Druck und Verlag von Carl Gerold's Sohn, 1857)

Šebánek, Jindřich, 'Moderní padělky v moravském diplomatáři Bočkově do in 1306', *Časopis Moravského musea*, 60 (1936)

Sebestyén, István, 'A tatár népirtás nyomai a Kiskunságon' [Vestiges of Tartar genocide in the Kiskunság], *Félegyházi Közlöny*, 26 June 2016

Segl, Peter, *Ketzer in Österreich: Untersuchungen über Häresie und Inquisition im Herzogtum Österreich im 13. und beginnenden 14. Jahrhundert*, Quellen und Forschungen aus dem Gebiet der Geschichte, n.s., 5 (Paderborn: Schöningh, 1984)

Selart, Anti, and Fiona Robb, *Livonia, Rus' and the Baltic Crusades in the Thirteenth Century* (Boston: Brill, 2015)

Senga, Toru, 'IV Béla külpolitikája és IV Ince pápához intézett "tatár-levele"' [Béla IV's foreign policy and his "Tartar-Letter" to Pope Innocent IV], *Századok*, 121 (1987), 584–612

Seton, Walter W., *Some New Sources for the Life of Blessed Agnes of Bohemia* (New York: Cambridge University Press, 2010)

Shailor, Barbara A., *Catalogue of Medieval and Renaissance Manuscripts in the Beinecke Rare Book and Manuscript Library, Yale University*, vol. II: *MSS 251–500*, Medieval & Renaissance Texts & Studies, 48 (Binghamton, NY: Center for Medieval & Early Renaissance Studies, 1987)

Shen, Dan, and Dejin Xu, 'Intratextuality, Extratextuality, Intertextuality: Unreliability in Autobiography versus Fiction', *Poetics Today*, 28.1 (2007), 43–87

Silanos, Pietro, 'Ottone da Tonengo', in *Dizionario Biografico degli Italiani* (Rome: Istituto dell'Enciclopedia Italiana, 2014), LXXX, <https://www.treccani.it/enciclopedia/ottone-da-tonengo_%28Dizionario-Biografico%29/>

Sinor, Denis, 'The Mongols in the West', *Journal of Asian History*, 33 (1999), 1–44

——, 'Le rapport du Dominicain Julien écrit en 1238 sur le péril mongol', *Comptes rendus des séances de l'Académie des Inscriptions et Belles-Lettres*, 146.2 (2002), 1153–68

——, 'X: Les relations entre les Mongols et l'Europe jusqu'à la mort d'Arghoun et de Béla IV', in *Inner Asia and its Contacts with Medieval Europe*, Variorum Collected Studies Series, 57 (London: Variorum, 1977), pp. 39–62

Slater, Laura, 'Matthew Paris, Cecilia de Sanford and the Early Readership of the Vie de Seint Auban', in *Writing History in the Anglo-Norman World: Manuscripts, Makers and Readers, c. 1066–c. 1250*, ed. by Laura Cleaver and Andrea Worm, Writing History in the Middle Ages, 6 (Woodbridge: York Medieval Press, 2018), pp. 189–212

Smith, Arthur Lionel, *Church and State in the Middle Ages* (Oxford: Clarendon Press, 1913)

Smith, David M., and Vera C. M. London, *The Heads of Religious Houses: England and Wales*, vol. II: *1216–1377* (Cambridge University Press, 2001)

Smith, John Masson, ''Ayn Jālūt: Mamlūk Success or Mongol Failure?', *Harvard Journal of Asiatic Studies*, 44 (1984), 307–45

Smith, Trevor Russell, 'Further Manuscripts of Matthew Paris' "Flores Historiarum" and Continuations', *Notes and Queries*, 67.1 (2020), 6–7

Soja, Edward, *Thirdspace: Journeys to Los Angeles and Other Real-and-Imagined Places* (Oxford: Blackwell, 1996)

Somer, Tomáš, 'Forging the Past: Facts and Myths behind the Mongol Invasion of Moravia in 1241', *Golden Horde Review*, 6.2 (2018), 238–51

——, 'Sources on the Mongol Invasion of the Kingdom of Bohemia in 1241', paper presented at 'The Mongols in Central Europe: The Profile and Impact of their Thirteenth-Century Invasions', online conference of The Mongol Invasion of Hungary and its Eurasian Context Project, 26–27 November 2020) [published transactions of the conference forthcoming]

Song, Eric B., 'Nation, Empire, and the Strange Fire of the Tartars in Milton's Poetry and Prose', *Milton Studies*, 47 (2008), 118–44

Sotheby & Co., *Catalogue of Thirty-Nine Manuscripts of the Ninth to the Sixteenth Century to Be Sold by Auction by Messr Sotheby & Co.*, New Series: Medieval Manuscripts, 1: Bibliotheca Phillippica (London: Sotheby's, 1965)

Sophoulis, Panos, 'The Mongol Invasion of Croatia and Serbia in 1242', *Fragmenta Hellenoslavica*, 2 (2015), 251–77

Spence, John, *Reimagining History in Anglo-Norman Prose Chronicles* (Woodbridge: York Medieval Press, 2013)

Spiegel, Gabrielle M., *Romancing the Past: The Rise of Vernacular Prose Historiography in Thirteenth-Century France*, The New Historicism, 23 (Berkeley: University of California Press, 1993)

Stacey, Robert C., 'Kilkenny, William of', in *The Oxford Dictionary of National Biography*, ed. by H. C. G. Matthew and B. Harrison (Oxford: Oxford University Press, 2004), <10.1093/ref:odnb/15527>

——, 'Review: Receipt Rolls for the Fourth, Fifth and Sixth Years of the Reign of King Henry III, Easter 1220, 1221, 1222', *English Historical Review*, 120.485 (2005), 195–96

Stafford, Pauline, 'Noting Relations and Tracking Relationships in English Vernacular Chronicles, Late Ninth to Early Twelfth Century', in *The Medieval Chronicle X*, ed. by Ilya Afanasyev, Juliana Dresvina, and Erik S. Kooper (Leiden: Brill, 2015), pp. 23–48

Stallcup, Stephen, 'An Arthurian Excerpt from the "Historia Regum Britanniae" in British Library MS Cotton Nero D.v', *Arthuriana*, 8 (1998), 12–41

Staunton, Michael, *The Historians of Angevin England* (Oxford: Oxford University Press, 2017)

Stevenson, Francis Seymour, *Robert Grosseteste, Bishop of Lincoln, a Contribution to the Religious, Political and Intellectual History of the 13th Century* (London: Macmillan, 1899)

Štilrajterová, Katarína, 'Convivenza, Convenienza and Conversion: Islam in Medieval Hungary (1000–1400 C.E.)', *Journal of Islamic Studies*, 24.2 (2013), 175–98

Strah, Paula, 'Die Mongolen und das Heilige Land: Von Ängsten und Hoffnungen des Abendlandes im 13. Jahrhundert' (master's thesis, Universität Graz, Geisteswissenschaftliche Fakultät, Institut für Geschichte, 2014)

Strakosch-Grassmann, Gustav, *Der Einfall der Mongolen in Mitteleuropa in den Jahren 1241 und 1242* (Innsbruck: Wagner'sche Universitäts-Buchdruckerei, 1893)

Styles, Philip, 'Politics and Historical Research in the Early Seventeenth Century', in *English Historical Scholarship in the 16th and 17th Centuries*, ed. by Levi Fox, Dugdale Society (London: Oxford University Press, 1956), pp. 49–72

Suerbaum, Almut, '"Entrelacement"? Narrative Technique in Heinrich von Dem Türlin's *Diu Crône*', *Oxford German Studies*, 34.1 (2005), 5–18

Sweeney, James Ross, 'Thomas of Spalato and the Mongols: A Thirteenth-Century Dalmatian View of Mongol Customs', *Florilegium*, 4 (1982), 156–83

Sz. Wilhelm, Gábor, '"Akiket nem akartak karddal elpusztítani, tűzben elégették": az 1241. évi pusztítás nyomai Szank határában' ['Those who they did not want to kill with a sword, they burned': remains of the Mongol invasion of 1241 at the borders of Szank], in *Carmen miserabile: A tatárjárás magyarországi emlékei; Tanulmányok Pálóczi Horváth András 70. születésnapja tiszteletére* [Archaeological finds from the Mongol invasion in Hungary: Studies in honour of András Pálóczi Horváth on his seventieth birthday], ed. by Szabolcs Rosta and György V. Székely (Kecskemét: Kecskeméti Katona József Múzeum, 2014), pp. 81–110

Száray, Miklós, *Történelem 9* [History 9] (Eger: Eszterházy Károly Egyetem; Nemzedékek Tudása Tankönyvkiadó, 2013)

Szende, László, 'Harc a Babenberg örökségért (1246–1261)' [The struggle for the Babenberg inheritance], *Sic Itur ad Astra: Fiatal történészek folyóirata*, 11.2–4 (1999), 263–306

Szilágyi, Magdolna, 'Perished Árpádian-Age Village at Dunaföldvár', *Acta Archaeologica Academiae Scientiarum Hungaricae*, 63.1 (2012), 155–79

Tally, Robert T., Jr, 'Review of Bertrand Westphal, *La Géocritique: Réel, fiction, espace*', *L'Esprit Créateur: The International Quarterly of French and Francophone Studies*, 49.3 (2009), 134

Tangl, Michael, *Die päpstlichen Kanzleiordnungen von 1200–1500* (Innsbruck: Wagner, 1894)

———, 'Die sogenannte Brevis nota über das Lyoner Concil von 1245', *Mitteilungen des Instituts für Österreichische Geschichtsforschung*, 12 (1891), 247–49

Taylor, John, *English Historical Literature in the Fourteenth Century* (Oxford: Clarendon Press, 1987)

———, *Medieval Historical Writing in Yorkshire* (York: St Anthony's Press, 1961)

Teeuwen, Mariken, 'Writing in the Blank Space of Manuscripts: Evidence from the Ninth Century', in *Ars Edendi Lecture Series*, vol. IV, ed. by Barbara Crostini, Gunilla Iversen, and Brian M. Jensen, Studia Latina Stockholmiensia, 62 (Stockholm: Stockholm University Press, 2016), pp. 1–25

Thomas, Alfred, *A Blessed Shore: England and Bohemia from Chaucer to Shakespeare* (Ithaca: Cornell University Press, 2007)

Thomas, Hugh M., *The Secular Clergy in England, 1066–1216* (Oxford: Oxford University Press, 2014)

Thompson, C. J. S., *The History and Lore of Freaks* (London: Senate, 1996)

Thompson, F., *Magna Carta: Its Role in the Making of the English Constitution, 1300–1629* (Minneapolis: University of Minnesota Press, 1948)

Thomson, Rodney M., *Catalogue of the Manuscripts of Lincoln Cathedral Chapter Library* (Woodbridge: Brewer on behalf of the Dean and Chapter of Lincoln, 1989)

Tikhvinskii, S. L. [Тихвинский, С. Л.], *Tataro-Mongoly v Azii i Evrope: Sbornik Statej* [Татаро-монголы в Азии и Европе: сборник статей; The Tataro-Mongols in Asia and Europe: A collection of articles] (Moscow: Nauka, 1977)

Todorov, Tzvetan, 'Les catégories du récit littéraire', *Communications*, 8 (1966), 125–51

Toomer, G. J., *John Selden: A Life in Scholarship*, 2 vols (Oxford: Oxford University Press, 2009)

Torre, Augusto, 'La data della morte di Filippo Arcivescovo di Ravenna', *Archivio Storico Italiano*, 128.2 (466) (1970), 199–206

Tout, Thomas Frederick, 'Richard of Cornwall', in *Dictionary of National Biography*, ed. by Leslie Stephen and Sidney Lee, 63 vols (London: Smith, Elder, 1885–1900), XLVIII, pp. 165–75

——, 'The Westminster Chronicle Attributed to Robert of Reading', *English Historical Review*, 31.123 (1916), 450–64

Treharne, Elaine, *Perceptions of Medieval Manuscripts: The Phenomenal Book* (New York: Oxford University Press, 2021)

Tuan, Yi-Fu, *Space and Place: The Perspective of Experience* (Minneapolis: University of Minnesota Press, 2002)

Tyler, E. M., and Ross Balzaretti, eds, *Narrative and History in the Early Medieval West*, Studies in the Early Middle Ages, 16 (Turnhout: Brepols, 2006)

Vaughan, Richard, 'The Chronicle of John of Wallingford', *English Historical Review*, 73.286 (1958), 66–70

——, *Chronicles of Matthew Paris: Monastic Life in the Thirteenth Century* (repr. Gloucester: Sutton, 1986)

——, 'The Handwriting of Matthew Paris', *Transactions of the Cambridge Bibliographical Society*, 1.5 (1953), 376–94

——, *Matthew Paris* (Cambridge: Cambridge University Press, 1958)

Verbaal, Wim, 'Epistolary Voices and the Fiction of History', in *Medieval Letters: Between Fiction and Document*, ed. by Christian Høgel and Elisabetta Bartoli (Turnhout: Brepols, 2015), pp. 9–32

Veszprémy, László, 'A Tatárjárás: Magyarország ismét bekerül a nyugat-európai világképbe' [The Mongol invasion: Hungary's place in the contemporary medieval historiography], *Hadtörténeti Közlemények*, 133.3 (2020), 459–85

———, and Kornél Szovák, 'Pótlás 1999-ben', in *Scriptores Rerum Hungaricarum tempore ducum regumque stirpis Arpadianae gestarum*, ed. Emericus [Imre] Szentpétery, 2 vols (Budapest: Magyar Tudományos Akadémia, 1937; repr., Budapest: Nap Kiadó, 1999), II, pp. 683–799

Veyne, Paul, *Writing History: Essay on Epistemology*, trans. by Mina Moore-Rinvolucri (Manchester: Manchester University Press, 1984)

Vincent, Nicholas, '"Corruent Nobiles!": Prophecy and Parody in Burton Abbey's Flying Circus', in *Crusading Europe: Essays in Honour of Christopher Tyerman*, ed. by G. E. M. Lippiatt and Jessalynn L. Bird, Outremer, 8 (Turnhout: Brepols, 2019), pp. 249–90

———, *Peter des Roches: An Alien in English Politics, 1205–1238*, Cambridge Studies in Medieval Life and Thought, 4th ser., 31 (Cambridge: Cambridge University Press, 1996)

———, 'The Politics of Church and State as Reflected in the Winchester Pipe Rolls, 1208–1280', in *The Winchester Pipe Rolls and Medieval English Society*, ed. by Richard Britnell (Woodbridge: Boydell & Brewer, 2003), pp. 157–81

Wand, K., 'Die Englandpolitik der Stadt Köln und ihrer Erzbischöfe im 12. und 13. Jahrhundert', in *Aus Mittelalter und Neuzeit: Gerhard Kallen zum 70. Geburtstag.* (Bonn: P. Hanstein, 1957), pp. 77–95

Watson, Andrew G., *The Manuscripts of Henry Savile of Banke* (London: Bibliographical Society, 1969)

Weiler, Björn, 'Bishops and Kings in England, c. 1066–c. 1215', in *Religion und Politik im Mittelalter: Deutschland und England im Vergleich = Religion and Politics in the Middle Ages: Germany and England by Comparison*, ed. by Ludger Körntgen and Dominik Wassenhoven, Prinz-Albert-Studien, Prince Albert Studies, 29 (Berlin: De Gruyter, 2013), pp. 157–204

———, 'Henry III and the Sicilian Business: A Reinterpretation', *Historical Research*, 74.184 (2001), 127–50

———, *Henry III of England and the Staufen Empire, 1216–1272* (Woodbridge: Boydell & Brewer, 2006)

———, 'Historical Writing and the Experience of Europeanization: The View from St Albans', in *The Making of Europe: Essays in Honour of Robert Bartlett*, ed. by John Hudson and Sally Crumplin (Leiden: Brill, 2016), pp. 205–43

———, 'History, Prophecy and the Apocalypse in the Chronicles of Matthew Paris', *English Historical Review*, 133.561 (2018), 253–83

———, 'How Unusual Was Matthew Paris? The Writing of Universal History in Angevin England', in *Universal Chronicles in the High Middle Ages*, ed. by Michele Campopiano and Henry Bainton, Writing History in the Middle Ages (Woodbridge: York Medieval Press, 2017), IV, pp. 199–222

———, 'Image and Reality in Richard of Cornwall's German Career', *English Historical Review*, 113.454 (1998), 1111–1142

———, 'Matthew Paris in Norway', *Revue Bénédictine*, 122.1 (2012), 153–81

———, 'Matthew Paris on the Writing of History', *Journal of Medieval History*, 35.3 (2009), 254–78

———, 'Matthew Paris, Richard of Cornwall's Candidacy for the German Throne, and the Sicilian Business', *Journal of Medieval History*, 26.1 (2000), 71–92

Weiss, Miriam, *Die 'Chronica maiora' des Matthaeus Parisiensis*, Trierer historische Forschungen, 73 (Trier: Kliomedia, 2018)

———, 'M[athaeus] Parisiensis, hujus scriptor libelli: Die Konstruktion der Person des Matthaeus Parisiensis in den "Chronica maiora"', in *Sprechen, Schreiben, Handeln: Interdisziplinäre Beiträge zur Performativität mittelalterlicher Texte*, ed. by Annika Bostelmann (Münster: Waxmann, 2017), pp. 183–99

Weltecke, Dorothea, 'Contacts between Syriac Orthodox and Latin Military Orders', in *East and West in the Crusader States: Context, Contacts, Confrontations*, ed. by Krijna Nelly Ciggaar and Herman G. B. Teule (Leuven: Peeters, 2003), pp. 53–78

Werner, Matthias, *Heinrich Raspe, Landgraf von Thüringen und römischer König (1227–1247): Fürsten, König und Reich in spätstaufischer Zeit* (Frankfurt am Main: P. Lang, 2003)

Westphal, Bertrand, *Geocriticism: Real and Fictional Spaces* (New York: Palgrave Macmillan, 2011)

Whalen, Brett Edward, *The Two Powers: The Papacy, the Empire, and the Struggle for Sovereignty in the Thirteenth Century* (Philadelphia: University of Pennsylvania Press, 2019)

White, Hayden V., *The Content of the Form: Narrative Discourse and Historical Representation* (Baltimore: Johns Hopkins University Press, 1990)

———, 'The Historical Text as Literary Artifact', in *Tropics of Discourse: Essays in Cultural Criticism* (Baltimore: Johns Hopkins University Press, 1978), pp. 81–100

———, *Metahistory: The Historical Imagination in Nineteenth-Century Europe* (Baltimore: John Hopkins University Press, 1973)

Wild, Benjamin Linley, 'A Gift Inventory from the Reign of Henry III', *English Historical Review*, 125.514 (2010), 529–69

Williamson, Dorothy, 'Some Aspects of the Legation of Cardinal Otto in England 1237–41', *English Historical Review*, 64.251 (1949), 145–73

Wolff, Otto, *Geschichte der Mongolen oder Tataren: Besonders ihres Vordringens nach Europa, so wie ihrer Eroberungen und Einfälle in diesem Welttheile* (Bresslau: C. Dülfer, 1872)

Woods, George Benjamin, ed., *English Poetry and Prose of the Romantic Movement* (Chicago: Scott, Foresman, 1916)

Woolf, Daniel R., 'From Hystories to the Historical: Five Transitions in Thinking about the Past, 1500–1700', *Huntington Library Quarterly*, 68.1–2 (2005), 33–70

Ysebaert, Walter, 'Medieval Letters and Letter Collections as Historical Sources: Methodological Questions, Reflections, and Research Perspectives (Sixth–Fifteenth Centuries)', in *Medieval Letters: Between Fiction and Document*, ed. by Christian Høgel and Elisabetta Bartoli (Turnhout: Brepols, 2015), pp. 33–62

Zatorski, Wacław, 'Pierwszy najazd Mongołów na Polskę w roku 1240–41' [The first Mongol invasion of Poland in 1240–41], *Przegląd Historyczno-Wojskowy*, 9 (1937), 175–86

Zbíral, David, 'Date of the "De Heresi Catharorum"' <https://www.academia.edu/37741213/Date_of_the_De_heresi_catharorum?source = swp_share> [accessed 27 January 2020]

Zerubavel, Eviatar, *Time Maps: Collective Memory and the Social Shape of the Past* (Chicago: University of Chicago Press, 2003)

Zins, Henryk, 'Echa odkryć Kopernika w literaturze angielskiej na początku XVII w.' [Echoes of Copernicus's discoveries in English literature at the beginning of the seventeenth century], *Euhemer – Przegląd Religioznawczy*, 17 (1973), 45–57

——, *England and the Baltic in the Elizabethan Era*, trans. by H. C. Stevens (Manchester: Manchester University Press, 1972)

——, *Mikołaj Kopernik w angielskiej kulturze umysłowej epoki Szekspira* [Nicholas Copernicus in the English intellectual culture of Shakespeare's time] (Lublin: Wydawnictwo PAN, 1972)

——, *Polska w oczach Anglików XIV–XVI w* [Poland through English eyes in the fourteenth to sixteenth centuries] (Lublin: Wydawn. Uniwersytetu Marii Curie-Skłodowskiej, 2002)

——, 'Ze stosunków Polsko-Angielskich w poł. XV wieku: Sprawa Orderu Podwiązki dla Kazimierza Jagiellończyka' [Polish-English relations in the mid-fifteenth century: The case of the Order of the Garter for Casimir Jagiellon], *Zapiski Historyczne*, 33 (1968), 33–58

Zivancevic-Sekerus, Ivana, 'Croatian Writers in the Byronic Mould', *Modern Language Review*, 87.1 (1992), 143–56

Zsoldos, Attila, 'Ténytől a Hód-tóig: Az 1279 és 1282 közötti évek politikatörténetének vázlata' [From Tétény to Lake Hód: Outline of political history between 1279 and 1282], *Történelmi Szemle*, no. 1 (1997), 68–98

Zutshi, Patrick, 'The Dispersal of Scholars from Oxford and the Beginnings of a University at Cambridge: A Study of the Sources', *English Historical Review*, 127.528 (2012), 1041–62

Index

Entries in italics indicate that a person is referred to by their rank or royal title but not by name.

Abingdon, town: 67 (n. 51)

Acre, town: 44, 70

Adam of Eynsham, chronicler: 82

Adam of Murimuth, chronicler: 161, 319 (n. 16), 321, 321 (n. 25), 330, 330 (n. 53, 54), 331 (n. 55), 392, 394–95, 400, 402, 404–05

Adriatic: 48, 209, 358

Agnes of Bohemia, blessed, O.S.C foundress: 296 (n. 59), 302–04, 302 (n. 77), 304 (n. 79)

Alberic of Trois–Fontaines (Cistercian): 93 (n. 166), 142 (n. 62), 143–45, 143 (n. 63), 145 (n. 68, 69)

Albert (Albrecht) I, duke of Saxony: *170, 303*

Albert Behaim (Albertus Bohemus) of Passau, papal legate: 287, 287 (n. 26)

Albert of Parma, archdeacon of Bars: 288–89, 288 (n. 33)

Albertus Magnus, scholar, theologian: 88, 88 (n. 147)

Alemannia see Germany

Alexander the Great: 98 (n. 186), 137 (n. 42), 144, 218, 282 (n. 7), 284, 287, 287 (n. 27), 394
   see also Romance of Alexander

Alexander III, king of Scotland: 75

Alexander III, pope: 332 (n. 58)

Alexander IV, pope: 326, 343 (n. 104), 276 (n. 163)

Andrew II, king of Hungary: 152 (n. 95), 203, 303, 365 (n. 184)

Andrew of Longjumeau, missionary: 275 (n. 161), 332 (n. 61)

Anna (born Constance) II of Hohenstaufen, empress of Nicaea: 256 (n. 104)

Annales Cestrienses see Chester Monastery (Benedictine), annals of

Annales de Burton see Burton Abbey (Benedictine), annals of

Annales de Prioratus Dunstaplia see Dunstable Priory (Augustinian), annals of

Annales de Theokesberia see Tewkesbury Monastery (Benedictine), annals of

Annales de prioratus Wigornia see Worcester, annals of

Annales Garstenses see Garsten Monastery (Benedictine), annals of

Annales Marbacenses see Marbach Abbey, annals of

Annales monasterii de Waverleia see Waverley Monastery (Cistercian), annals of

Annales monasterii Sancti Pantaleonis Coloniaen see St Pantaleon Monastery (Benedictine), Cologne, annals of

Annales prioratus Lewensis see Lewes
Priory (Cluniac), annals of
Annales Sancrucenses see
Heiligenkreuz Monastery
(Cistercian), annals of
*Annales Sancti Rudberti Salisburgenses
see* St Rudbert Monastery,
Salzburg, annals of
Annales Scheftlarienses see Schäftlarn
Monastery (Benedictine), annals
of
Annales Zwetlenses see Zwettl
(Cistercian), annals of
Antichrist: 17, 17 (n. 9), 194 (n. 116),
239 (n. 67), 240, 255 (n. 103),
284–86, 285 (n. 20), 286 (n. 22),
384
archer(s), archery: 134, 147 (n. 77),
157, 195, 236, 276 (n. 163), 373
Arles, town: 70
Armenia, Armenian(s): 44, 126, 128,
132, 135, 271, 275–76, 279, 333,
343 (n. 101), 393, 396
armour: 157, 195, 198, 219, 236, 236
(n. 53), 237, 268–69, 289, 365,
375
Arnold of Holland, clerk of Richard of
Cornwall: 72
assassins: 108, 145, 226, 279, 305
Asser, monk, biographer of Alfred the
Great: 337
Augsburg, bishop of *see* Siboto
Augustine of Hippo, saint: 314, 314
(n. 6)
Augustinian order/houses: 39
(n. 46), 78, 81 (n. 112), 84, 99
(n. 190), 118, 265 (n. 126), 298
(n. 68), 327
Austria, Austrian(s): 97, 137 (n. 42),
166, 170, 181 (n. 76) 202, 203
(n. 134), 204 (n. 135), 208
(n. 145), 230, 230 (n. 28), 231,
231 (n. 32), 245 (n. 82), 354

Austria, duke of *see* Frederick II the
Quarrelsome, Henry II
(Jasomirgott), Leopold VI

Babylon: 259, 261, 263, 267, 273, 324
(n. 34), 327
Bacon, Robert, Dominican scholar:
85, 85 (n. 132)
Bacon, Roger, Franciscan scholar,
theologian: 85 (n. 132), 137, 137
(n. 42), 254 (n. 101), 306
Baldwin II, emperor of
Constantinople: 162, 164 (n. 17),
192 (n. 111), 212, 256 (n. 104)
Bale, John, antiquarian: 338–39, 338
(n. 82, 84), 339 (n. 86, 87), 344–
45
Barlow, Thomas, bishop of Lincoln:
348
Battle of Liegnitz *see* Legnica
(Liegnitz)
Battle of Muhi *see* Muhi
Batu, khan: 179 (n. 69), 264 (n. 144),
361
Baumgartenberger Formelbuch
(Baumgartenberg Formulary):
90, 98, 406
Bavaria: 98, 154, 166, 170, 202, 287
(n. 26)
Bavaria, duke of *see* Ludwig (Louis)
II, Otto II
Beaulieu Abbey (Cistercian): 72
Becket, Thomas, saint, archbishop of
Canterbury: 57
Bede: 334
Beguine(s): 250–52
Béla III, king of Hungary: 136 (n. 39)
Béla IV, king of Hungary: 26, 51, 94,
97, 98, 98 (n. 186), 107 (n. 221),
112, 113 *(n.* 237*),* 138, 141,142
(n. 58), *145, 153, 161,* 162, 166,
181 (n. 77), 200–04, 201 (n. 128),
201 (n. 128), 202 *(n. 130),* 203

(n. 134), 204 (n. 135), 212, 255
(n. 102), 258, 258, 276, 289, 290,
291, *301*, 303, 325, 327–29, *346*,
353 (n. 143), 357, 358 (n. 162),
361 (n. 174), *361 (n. 174)*, 365,
365 (n. 184), 383
Benedictine(s), order/monasteries:
17, 34 (n. 33), 48 (n. 68), 96, 98,
100, 190, 203, 206, 237, 256
(n. 105), 265 (n. 130), 266, 267,
276 (n. 163), 298, 298 (n. 67, 68),
299 (n. 69), 305, 308, 318, 320,
327 (n. 40), 392–93, 398, 402
Benedictus Polonus, traveller: 114,
114 (n. 244)
Bergen, town: 43, 102–03
Bernhard II, duke of Carinthia: 237
(n. 60)
Berthold, patriarch of Aquileia: 141,
237 (n. 60), 276
Bevere, John, monk at Westminster,
chronicler: 320 (n. 21), 392, 393,
394, 398, 401
Bigod, Roger, earl of Norfolk: 120,
120 (n. 266)
Black Sea: 48, 48 (n. 69), 139
Blanche, queen of France: 69–71, 70
(n. 59), 71 (n. 65), 73, 93
(n. 167), 173, 184, 184 (n. 84,
86), 185, 185 (n. 93), 187, 210,
311
boat(s): 44, 86 (n. 137), 105 (n. 214),
134, 147, 152, 154, 157, 196, 215
(n. 161), 373
Boček, Antonín, historian: 360, 360
(n. 166, 167)
Bohemia(ns), *Boemia*: 42, 43 (n. 54),
48, 53, 137 (n. 42), 150, 153, 154,
175–76, 177–78, 180, 180 (n. 74),
202, 204 (n. 136), 208 (n. 145),
292, 296, 296 (n. 59), 299 (n. 69),
300, 302, 303, 322 (n. 28), 331
(n. 56), 355, 359
see also Czech (lands)

Bohemia, king of *see* Ottokar I,
Wenceslas I
Bologna, city: 81, 85, 108
Boniface II, marquis of Montferrat:
244 (n. 78)
Boniface VIII, pope: 77 (n. 98), 111
(n. 229)
Boniface (of Savoy), archbishop of
Canterbury: 168 (n. 38), 266
(n. 133, 134), 293 (n. 48), 378
Bordeaux, archbishop of *see* Gerard of
Malemort
Brabant, *Brabantia*: 49, 77, 91–92, 92
(n. 163), 95, 154, 173 (n. 56),
186, 297, 302
Brabant, duke of *see* Henry I, Henry
II, John II the Peaceful
Brevis nota (Bologna, Colegio de
España, 275): 108–09, 108
(n. 223), 109 (n. 225) 140 (n. 51),
403
Buda, city: 99, 329 (n. 49)
Bulgaria, Bulgarian(s): 50 (n. 75), 51
(n. 80), 89 (n. 152), 112, 128, 138
(n. 46), 142 (n. 58), 152 (n. 94),
164 (n. 17)
Burton Abbey (Benedictine), annals
of (*Annales de Burton*): 264–67,
264 (n. 121, 22), 265 (n. 125, 127,
130, 131), 266 (n. 132, 135), 267
(n. 141), 276 (n. 150), 278
(n. 169), 290 (n. 38), 307, 307
(n. 90), 343 (n. 104), 404
Byarmians: 150, 150 (n. 49)

C. de Bridia, traveller: 362, 362
(n. 180), 405
Cambridge, city: 84, 85 (n. 131), 87,
265, 306, 335, 344 (n. 106), 345,
387, 404
Camden, William, antiquarian,
topographer: 346, 404

456 INDEX

cannibals, cannibalism: 157, 161, 214, 232–33, 232 (n. 33), 234 (Fig. 7), 237, 268

Canterbury, archbishop of *see* Becket, Thomas; Boniface; St Edmund of Abingdon; Langton, Stephen; Rich, Edmund; Parker, Matthew

Cantilupe, Thomas, bishop of Hereford: 80 (n. 108)

Cantilupe, William II, steward of Henry III: 120, 120 (n. 266)

Carinthia, duke of *see* Bernhard II

Carmelite, order: 84, 338

Cathars, Catharism: 228 (n. 24), 253; *see also* Patarene(s)

Cedar of Lebanon prophecy: 100, 142–45, 143 (n. 65), 144 (n. 69), 287

Chester Monastery (Benedictine), annals of (*Annales Cestrienses*): 120, 120 (n. 267)

Chester, town: 77 (n. 98)

Chetham, manuscript group: 56 (n. 3), 319, 319 (n. 16), 321, 390–97

China: 267 (n. 144), 349, 364

Chinggis, khan: 232, 267 (n. 144), 324 (n. 34), 332 (n. 60), 350 (n. 132), 364

Chorosmian(s) *see* Khwarezm, Khwarezmian(s)

Chronica de Mailros, Chronicle of Melrose Abbey *see* Melrose, chronicle of

Chronicon de Lanercost see Lanercost Priory (Augustinian), chronicle of

Chronicon S Medardi Suessionensis see St. Médard of Soissons (Benedictine), chronicle of

Cicero: 27

Cistercian(s), order/monasteries: 72, 73, 73 (n. 75), 86, 86 (n. 134,

137), 100, 125, 143, 144, 144 (n. 66), 145, 145 (n. 69), 163, 183, 185, 226, 276, 304 (n. 80)

Citeaux, town: 73 (n. 75), 105 (n. 214)

Cologne, city: 84, 87–88, 88 (n. 146, 47), 91, 95, 95 (n. 174, 177), 137 (n. 44), 138 (n. 45), 154, 221, 221 (n. 179), 240–41, 241 (n. 71, 73), 243, 250–53, 259, 284, 293, 293 (n. 48), 295–97, 302–03, 307

Cologne, archbishop of *see* Conrad of Hochstaden, Henry I of Müllenark

Comestor *see* Peter Comestor

Condemnations of Paris: 254–55, 254 (n. 101), 255 (n. 103), 293

Conrad of Hochstaden (Hochstadt, Hostade), archbishop of Cologne: 71, 76, 93, 95, 95 (n. 174), 96 (n. 181), 97, 117, 154, 181, 182, 213 (n. 158), 247, 250, 251, 295, 295 (n. 55), 301

Conrad IV, king of Germany (of Romans): 92, 98 (n. 186), 142 (n. 58), 160, 163–64, 164 (n. 18, 20), 166, 171, 176 (n. 62), 181, 184, 202, 214, 214 (n. 161), 215, 231 (n. 32), 244, 252, 252 (n. 95), 304 (n. 79), 381, 384

Constance of Hungary, queen of Bohemia: 304

Constance (Konstanz), town: 115 (249)

Constance (Konstanz), bishop of *see* Henry of Tanne

Constantinople, emperor of *see* Baldwin II

Continuatio Zwetlensis see Zwettl (Cistercian), annals of

Cotton, Robert, antiquarian: 283 (n. 10), 335–37, 336 (n. 72), 337 (n. 77), 389

Courtenay Compendium (MS CC): 250 (n. 90), 265, 265 (n. 126), 306, 306 (n. 88, 89), 307 (n. 90), 403

Cuman(s), (*Cumania, Comania, Valves*): 49–51, 49 (n. 75), 123–24, 128, 141–42, 142 (n. 58), 145, 150 (n. 85), 171, 198, 199 (n. 123), 212, 215, 218, 238 (n. 63), 300–01, 301 (n. 73), 329–30, 329 (n. 48, 49), 383–84

Czech (lands): 23, 114, 354, 358–59, 362
see also Bohemia (*Boemia*)

Dacia see Denmark

Dagmar (Margaret) of Bohemia, queen, wife of Valdemar II of Denmark: 154 (n. 104)

Dalmatia: 237

Damietta, town: 93 (n. 166), 131, 187 (n. 94), 236 (n. 52), 332 (n. 57), 340, 370

Danne, Nicholas, clerk of Richard of Cornwall: 71 (n. 68)

Danube, river: 48–49, 50 (n. 75), 51 (n. 80), 163, 163 (n. 17), 199 (n. 123), 200, 215

Deinphir see Dnepr, river

Denmark (*Dacia*): 100, 101, 104, 135, 148–55, 160, 209

Długosz, Jan, chronicler: 362, 362 (n. 176), 363

Dnepr, river (*Deinphir*): 163 (n. 17), 289, 291

Dominican Dossier: 68–69, 69 (n. 54), 89, 89 (n. 152)

Dominican order, Dominicans: 85, 87, 87 (n. 140), 88, 97, 99 (n. 190), 112, 114, 128, 129 (n. 19), 130, 138, 142, 166 (n. 30), 232, 254 (n. 101), 274

(n. 161), 284, 294, 295, 299, 331, 332, 346, 363

Don, river (*Tanais*): 49

Duns Scotus, John: 88

Dunstable Priory (Augustinian), annals of (*Annales Prioratus Dunstaplia*): 61 (n. 27), 142 (n. 61)

Edmund Ironside, king of England: 321

Edmund of Abingdon, saint, archbishop of Canterbury *see* Rich, Edmund

Edward I, king of England: 75, 75 (n. 91), 77 (n. 98), 120, 156, 271 (n. 153), 282 (n. 5), 394, 405

Elbe, river: 48, 359

Eleanor of Aquitaine, queen, wife of Henry II of England: 70 (n. 59), 389

Eleanor of Castile, queen, wife of Edward I of England: 75 (n. 91)

Eleanor of England, countess of Leicester, wife of Simon de Monfort: 74, 74 (80)

Eleanor of England, queen consort of Castile: 70 (n. 59)

Eleanor of Savoy, queen of England, wife of Henry III of England: 130 (25), 169 (n. 39)

Elizabeth of Thuringia (of Hungary), saint: 75 (n. 91), 93, 93 (n. 166), 94, 94 (n. 169), 180, 303–04, 303 (n. 78), 304 (n. 79), 322, 322 (n. 27), 326, 331 (n. 56)

Elizabeth, queen of England, Elizabethan: 335, 336 (n. 70), 337 (n. 75), 338–39, 346

Elizabeth the Cuman, queen consort of Stephen V, king of Hungary: 329

England, king of *see* Edmund Ironside, Edward I, Henry II, Henry III, John, Richard I, William II Rufus

Enzio *see* Henry, king of the Romans

Essedones: 233, 237, 237 (n. 57)

Esztergom, archbishop of, *see* Job, Lucas, Matthew

exhortatio: 229, 230, 243

Falben (Valwen) *see* Cuman

Fermo, bishop of *see* Philip

Ferrers, Edward and Henry, antiquarians: 336

Fest, Sándor, historian: 288, 288 (n. 32), 356–57, 356 (n. 155), 357 (n. 158, 59)

Flacius [Vlacic], Matthias Illyricus, historian: 338, 338 (n. 83), 339, 344

Flanders: 71, 78, 154, 154 (n. 104), 164, 186 (n. 93), 303, 389

Foigny, monastery (Cistercian): 144 (n. 66)

Foxe, John, antiquarian: 345, 345 (n. 107, 111)

fractals: 34, 34 (n. 34), 36

Franciscan order, Franciscans: 74, 85 (n. 132), 88, 114, 120 (n. 265), 123, 142, 213 (n. 158), 284, 294, 296, 296 (n. 60), 299, 302, 307, 332 (n. 60), 358 (n. 162)

Frederick I Barbarossa, Holy Roman emperor: 154, 190, 208

Frederick II the Quarrelsome, duke of Austria: 97, 165, 170, 202, 203, 212, 237, 237 (n. 60), 262 (n. 117), 294, 303

Frederick II, Holy Roman emperor, throughout the volume

Frederick Madden, paleographer, historian: 337–38, 352–53

Friesland (*Frisia*): 132–33, 148, 152–53, 153 (n. 98), 175, 259 (n. 113)

Garsten Monastery (Benedictine), annals of (*Annales Garstenses*): 166, 166 (n. 29–30), 231 (n. 32)

Genoa, Genoese: 86 (n. 134), 105 (n. 214), 110–11, 110 (n. 228), 111 (n. 229), 214 (n. 161), 247, 249 (Fig. 9)

Geoffrey of Trani, cardinal deacon: 257

Georgia, Georgians: 333, 128

Gerald (Gerard) of Malemort, archbishop of Bordeaux: 105–06, 105 (n. 214), 106 (n. 216), 229, 242–47, 244 (n. 89), 246 (n. 86), 323

Gerald of Wales, archdeacon of Brecon, historian: 81 (n. 114), 82, 85 (n. 129), 393, 396

Germany (*Alemannia*): 49, 170, 209, 244, 250

Germanismus: 360–61, 360 (n. 171)

Gerson, Jean, scholar: 115 (n. 249)

Gesta Abbatum: 29, 34 (n. 33), 57, 59, 101 (n. 193), 282, 318, 327 (n. 42), 354 (n. 144), 367 (n. 187), 388, 389

Gestorum Treverorum see Trier (Trèves), Deeds of the Trevians

Gide, André, writer: 32, 32 (n. 28, 30)

Gildas, chronicler: 265 (n. 126), 337, 399

Gloucester, earl of *see* Richard de Clare

Godfrey of Viterbo, chronicler: 136 (n. 40)

Godfrey, papal penitentiary: 129, 131, 177 (n. 64)

Gog and Magog: 232 (n. 33), 237, 284

Gothland (*Gothia*): 132–34, 148, 151–52, 152 (n. 94), 153, 176, 177

Gravesend, Richard, bishop of
 Lincoln: 73, 73 (n. 77), 86
Gray, Thomas, chronicler: 326 (n. 39)
Greater Hungary *see Hungaria major*
Greece, Greek(s): 48, 49, 51, 79, 109,
 128, 255, 270 (n. 150), 273, 275,
 366 (n. 186)
Gregory IX, pope: 86 (n. 134), 89
 (n. 152), 105, 112, 128, 128
 (n. 15), 139, 139 (n. 50), 159,
 163, 167 (n. 34), 171, 192
 (n. 111), 212, 213 (n. 158), 255
 (n. 103), 302, 311, 377, 389
Grosseteste, Robert, bishop of
 Lincoln: 73–75, 73 (n. 76, 77), 74
 (n. 78, 80), 75 (n. 87) 78–80, 78
 (n. 103), 79 (n. 103, 104, 107), 80
 (n. 108), 82, 85–88, 85 (n. 131,
 132, 133), 87 (n. 140), 88 (n. 148,
 151), 106, 106 (n. 217), 107, 117,
 119, 119 (n. 261, 262, 263, 264),
 266, 266 (n. 133, 134, 135), 307,
 311 (n. 100)
Guyuk, khan: 278
Győr, town: 99 (n. 190), 112

Hailes Monastery, (Cistercian): 69,
 69 (n. 55), 73
Håkon IV, king of Norway: 101–03,
 101 (n.195), 102 (n. 199), 103
 (n. 206), 150, 151 (n. 89), 153
Hákonar saga: 102, 150
Halych (*Galicia*): 112, 150, 240, 276,
 276 (n. 163)
Hardy, Thomas Duffus, antiquarian:
 319
Heiligenkreuz: 145 (n. 69), 163
Heiligenkreuz Monastery
 (Cistercian), annals of (*Annales
 Sancrucenses*): 212, 212 (n. 156),
 231 (n. 32), 298 (n.68)
Henry (Enzio), king of the Romans:
 160, 163, 164, 164 (n. 18), 171,
 214 (n. 161), 215, 381, 384

Henry I of Müllenark (Molenark),
 archbishop of Cologne: 95
Henry I, duke of Brabant: 77 (n. 97)
Henry II, duke of Brabant: 75, 75
 (n. 91), 76, 76 (*n. 92*), 91, 94, 94
 (*n. 172*), 95, 101, 135 (n. 36), 153,
 160, 173, 177, 180, 180 (n. 71),
 181, 181 (*n. 77*), 182, 186 (n. 93),
 255 (*n. 102*), 284, 287, 293, 293
 (n. 47), 297, 302, 303, 304
 (n. 79), 354–55, 379, 389
Henry II (Jasomirgott), duke of
 Austria: 298 (n. 68)
Henry II the Pious, duke of Silesia:
 178 (n. 66), 298 (*n. 68*), 300, 302,
 303, 304 (n. 79)
Henry II, king of England: 70 (n. 59),
 154 (n. 104), 353 (n. 143)
Henry III, king of England: 57
 (n. 12), 70 (n. 57–59), 71–75, 73
 (n. 76), 77 (n. 97), 78, 91
 (n. 159), 95–96, 101, 104, 110
 (n. 227), 120, 120 (n. 266, 268),
 130 (n. 25), 131, 131 (*n. 30*), 133,
 135, 146, 154, 160, 169 (n. 39),
 170 (n. 45), 171, 181, 184, 188,
 192, 216, 217 (n. 169), 245, 245
 (n. 84), 247, 256, 266 (n. 134),
 288 (n. 33), 293 (n. 48), 295
 (n. 55), 302, 303, 311, 326, 345,
 346, 353 (n. 143), 355, 362, 388,
 389
Henry IV, bishop of Brixen: 98
 (n. 186), 141
Henry of Hungary, clerk: 81 (n. 113),
 83, 83 (n. 122)
Henry of Huntingdon, chronicler:
 393, 396, 405
 see also Historia Anglorum
Henry of Lexington, bishop of
 Lincoln: 86 (n. 137)
Henry of Livonia (Henricus Lettus),
 chronicler: 15 (n. 86), 149

460 INDEX

Henry of Tanne, bishop of
Constance: 98 (n. 186), *165*
(n. 21), 232 (n. 32)

Henry Raspe, landgrave of Thuringia:
22, 51 (n. 78), 75 (n. 91), 76, 77,
91–95, 93 (n. 165), 94 (n. 170),
101, 160, 165, 173, 175–78, 176
(n. 62), 180–82, 180 (n. 71, 72,
74), 181 (n. 75), 187–89, 191
(n. 109), 207, 213 (n. 158), 244,
244 *(n. 80)*, 284, 286, 287, 290–
95, 291 (n. 40), 293 (n. 47, 48),
294 (n. 49), 295, 297, 300, 303,
304 (n. 79), 311, 323 (n. 33), 346,
354–56, 355–56, 356 (n. 154)

Henry Zundendorp, clerk: 96

Hereford Mappamundi: 45, 49, 49
(n. 71, 73), 152 (n. 94), 237, 237
(n. 57)

Hereford, bishop of *see* Cantilupe,
Thomas

Hermann II, landgrave of Thuringia:
93, 93 (n. 167), 180, 180 (n. 71)

Hermann of Perigold (Herman
Petragorius or Armand de
Périgord), grand master of the
Knights Templar: 257

Hildegard of Bingen, saint: 253, 253
(n. 98, 99), 399

Historia Anglorum by Matthew Paris:
35 (Fig. 1), 56, 58, 116, 192, 261,
272 (n. 156), 282, 308, 309, 315
(Fig. 11), 338, 340 (n. 87), 345,
353, 390: by Henry of
Huntingdon: 334, 405

Holy Land: 22, 26, 37, 44, 51, 56
(n. 6), 70, 108, 109, 124, 125
(n. 8), 129, 131, 132, 147, 151,
162, 165 (n. 23), 171, 185–87,
206, 226, 257–59, 259 (n. 113),
262, 264, 271, 272 (n. 154), 273–
75, 278, 305, 325, 369–71, 387,
390

Honorius III, pope: 112, 128, 329
(n. 46)

Honorius of Autun
(Augustodunensis), theologian,
scholar: 152 (n. 94)

horse(s)/horseman/men: 71 (n. 68),
76, 110, 110 (n. 226), 172 (n. 51),
225, 283 (n. 8)
Mongol horses, horseman/men:
38, 134, 147 (n. 77), 157, 160,
195–96, 198, 232 (n. 35),
235–37, 269, 293 (n. 48), 350
(n. 132), 365, 374

Hospitallers, Knights Hospitaller,
Knights of St John : 99 (n. 190),
109, 131, 257–58, 259, 370

Hugh (Hugh of Avalon), saint, bishop
of Lincoln: 80 n. 108, 82, 84, 266
(n. 135)

Hülegü, khan: 62

Hungaria major (Greater Hungary):
21, 25, 48, 132, 135–39, 141,
144–45, 147, 149, 149 (n. 83),
151, 160, 177, 322, (n. 28), 356

Hungary, *Hungaria (minor)*: 16 (n. 6,
7), 17, 20, 21, 23, 25, 25 (n. 2), 26,
42–44, 48–49, 53 (n. 88), 82
(n. 121), 85, 90, 94, 98, 105, 106
(n. 215), 111, 112–14, 112
(n. 234), 113 (n. 240, 242), 114
(n. 243), 124, 127, 135–41, 136
(n. 37, 38), 137 (n. 42), 138
(n. 45, 46), 144–45, 144 (n. 66),
145 (n. 69), 150–55, 150 (n. 85),
152 (n. 94), 159 (n. 1), 160, 162,
163, 165 (n. 24), 166, 176–81,
178 (n. 66), 181 (n. 76, 77), 189,
189 (n. 100), 191, 199, 199
(n. 123) 200, 201, 203, 203
(n. 134), 204, 207, 210–12, 218,
225–28, 226 (n. 6), 238 (n. 63),
254, 255 (n. 102, 103), 257–59,
265, 267, 267 (n. 144), 272, 272
(n. 154), 273, 275–78, 276

(n. 163), 283–84, 286 (n. 24),
287–89, 291–92, 293 (n. 48), 295,
295 (n. 54), 297–99, 298 (n. 67),
299 (n. 69), 300, 301, 304, 306,
321–22, 322 (n. 27, 28), 324–25,
327–30, 329 (n. 48, 49), 333, 333
(n. 63), 342, 343 (n. 101, 102),
351 (Fig. 13), 353 (n. 143), 354
(n. 146), 355–59, 357 (n. 157,
158, 59), 361 (n. 171, 174), 362–
63, 362 (n. 178), 365, 365
(n. 184)

Hungary, king of *see* Andrew II,
Andrew III, Béla III, Béla IV,
Ladislaus (László) IV

Illyria: 26
impertinens, marginal notation in
chronicles: 131, 259, 259
(n. 113), 260 (Fig. 10), 262
(n. 117), 264, 310
ink: 39, 41, 48, 116, 143 (n. 63), 170
(n. 44), 213 (n. 158), 217 (n. 69),
283, 285, 339 (n. 87), 356
Innocent IV, pope, throughout the
volume
Ireland: 104, 172 (n. 51), 209, 298–99
Isabella of England, wife of Emperor
Frederick II: 69, 70 (n. 57), 71, 87
Isidore of Seville, saint,
encyclopedist: 27, 27 (n. 5), 137
(n. 42), 323 (n. 30), 404
Islam, *see* Muslim
István (Stephen) Báncsa, bishop of
Vác: 97, 112, 113, *113*, 113
(n. 240), *199–201, 200 (n. 123)*,
201, 201 (n. 128, 129, 130), 211,
211 (n. 150), 215 (n. 163), 289,
289 (n. 34, 35), 294, 353 (n. 143)
Ivo of Narbonne: 106 (n. 216), 129
(n. 21), 161 (n. 8), 178 (n. 68),
198, 216 (n. 166), 225–26, 227–
56, 228 (n. 24), 229 (Table 2),
230 (n. 27, 28, 29, 30), 231 (32)

239 (n. 165), 242 (n. 74), 243
(n. 77), 245 (n. 82), 263, 263
(n. 120), 267, 278–79, 311, 323–
24, 347, 355

James of Hungary *see* Pastoreaux
James of Pecorari, bishop of
Palestrina: 86, 86 (n. 137), 105,
105 (n. 214), 215 (163)
Jaroslav of Sternberg, mythical
Moravian warrior: 359, 359
(n. 165)
Jean de Joinville, chronicler: 93
(n. 167)
Jerusalem, city: 70, 70 (n. 58), 89
(n. 152), 94 (n. 168), 108–09, 128
(n. 15), 170, 179–80, 202, 250,
258, 259, 262, 263 (n. 119), 273,
324 (n. 34)
Jew(s), Jewish: 37 (n. 42), 76 (n. 92),
160, 171, 175, 213, 216–22, 219
(n. 175), 220 (n. 177, 178), 221
(n. 179), 222 (n. 181), 241
(n. 71), 254–55, 255 (n. 103), 266
(n. 133), 293, 348, 348 (n. 126),
357 (n. 157), 382
Joachim of Fiore, Joachites: 285
(n. 20), 406
Job, archbishop of Esztergom: 112
John de Bulum, monk of St Albans:
118
John II the Peaceful, duke of Brabant :
77, 77 (n. 98)
John III Doukas Vatatzes, emperor of
Nicaea: 256 (n. 104)
John of Lexington, baron: 86 (n. 137)
John of Oxnead, chronicler: 305,
305 (n. 84), 395
John of Plano Carpini (Pian
Carpine), traveller: 107, 114, 123,
123 (n. 2), 124, 124 (n. 4), 137–
38 (n. 44), 145 (n. 69), 199
(n. 121), 231 (n. 30), 232 (n. 35),

235, 266, 275 (n. 161), 277, 296
(n. 62), 302, 349, 359, 362
(n. 180), 405

John of Schipton, prior or Newburgh:
68, 77, 78, 78 (n. 102)

John of St Albans, goldsmith: 66
(n. 50), 100, 154 (n. 101)

John of St Giles, theologian: 87, 87
(n. 139, 140, 141), 88, 88 (n. 147, 148)

John of Toledo, cardinal: 86, 113, 113
(n. 242), 276

John of Tynemouth, chronicler: 84,
326, 326 (n. 39), 327 (n. 40, 41),
403, 404, 405

John of Wallingford, chronicler: 44
(n. 59), 66 (n. 47), 305, 305
(n. 84), 404

John, king of England: 77 (n. 97), 96,
116, 118, 228 (n. 23), 321 (n. 23),
334, 389

Jordan of Giano, Franciscan
provincial of Germany: 295
(n. 56), 296, 297, 302

Jordan of Saxony, Dominican master
general: 87

Joscelyn, John, antiquarian: 337

Julian of Hungary, Dominican friar,
traveller: 137–42, 137 (n. 43),
138 (45, 46), 140 (n. 52), 238
(n. 63)

khan (*chayn*): 26, 134, 140, 147
(n. 77), 148, 194 (n. 116), 232,
237, 267 (n. 144), 268, 271, 278,
292, 332 (n. 60), 349 (n. 130),
350 (n. 132), 364, 365 (n. 184)

khan *see* Batu, Chinggis, Guyuk,
Hülegü, Zingiton (Churchitan)

Khwarezm, Khwarezmian(s): 94
(n. 168), 109, 128 (n. 15), 257,
259, 263–64, 273–74, 324, 324

(n. 34), 325 (n. 35), 342, 342
(n. 94, 95)

Kiev (*Cleva*), city: 107, 124, 149, 150,
199, 199 (n. 123), 200 (n. 124),
265 (n. 128), 266, 267, 295
(n. 56), 298, 299, 299 (n. 69)

King of Tars: 330 (n. 50), 350 (n. 132)

Knighton, Henry, chronicler: 161,
189, 266 (n. 135)

Knights Hospitaller *see* Hospitallers

Knights of St John *see* Hospitallers

Knights Templar: 99 (n. 190), 109,
131, 256–57, 262 (n. 117), 324
(n. 34), 342 (n. 94)

Knights Templar, grand master of
see Hermann of Perigold

Konstanz *see* Constance

Konrad *see* Conrad

Ladislaus (László) IV, king of
Hungary: 329, 329 (n. 49), 343
(*n. 102*)

Lanercost Priory (Augustinian),
chronicle of: 142 (n. 61), 146
(n. 75)

Langton, Stephen, archbishop of
Canterbury : 57, 80 (n. 108), 390

Legnica (Liegnitz), village: 94, 127,
163, 178 (n. 66), 303, 361, 363,
363 (n. 181, 182)

Leopold VI, duke of Austria: 152
(n. 95)

Lewes Priory (Cluniac), annals of
(*Annales prioratus Lewensis*): 142
(n. 61)

Liber censuum: 136 (n. 39), 139, 139
(n. 49), 140 (n. 51)

Liber provincialis: 140, 140 (n. 51)

Liegnitz *see* Legnica

Lincoln, town: 65, 68, 73, 78–88, 78
(n. 103), 80 (n. 108, 110), 82
(n. 121), 83 (n. 122), 84 (n. 126),
85 (n. 129), 86 (n. 137), 88

(n. 151), 95, 106. 107, 119, 119
(n. 260), 146 (n. 70), 236 (52),
266, 266 (n. 133, 135)

Lincoln, bishop of *see* Henry of
Lexington; Barlow, Thomas;
Gravesend, Richard; Robert
Grosseteste; St Hugh

Lithuania, Grand Duchy of: 295
(n. 56)

Lombardy: 109, 112, 213 (n. 158),
214 (n. 161), 230, 275 (n. 161)

London, city: 43, 49, 53, 56 (n. 6), 57
(n. 7), 70 (n. 58), 79, 82 (n. 121),
104, 156, 167, 223 (n. 184), 282,
319 (n. 16), 326, 343, 344
(n. 106), 350 (n. 133), 377, 387,
389, 390, 394, 399

Louis IX, king of France: 57 (n. 12),
69, 70–71, 73, 75, 93 (n. 167),
102, 160, 169 (n. 39), 173, 182–
87, 184 (n. 83), 186 (n. 93), 208,
210, 226, 245 (n. 84), 271
(n. 153), 293 (n. 48), 379, 388,
389, 394

Lucas (Lukács), archbishop of
Esztergom: 82 (n. 121)

Ludwig (Louis) II, duke of Bavaria :
75 (n. 91), 145, *303*

Ludwig (Louis) IV, landgrave of
Thuringia: 75 (n. 91), 93, 93
(n. 166), 180, 180 (n. 71)

Lyon(s), city: 21, 22, 70, 71, 90, 105,
107–21, 110 (n. 228), 111
(n. 229), 117 (n. 255) 119
(n. 261), 120 (n. 268), 126, 137
(n. 44), 139, 139 (n. 50), 213,
225, 235, 246, 247, 253 (n. 98),
265, 266, 270, 274, 275, 278, 278
(n. 169), 279, 287 (n. 26), 307-08,
307 (n. 90), 308 (n. 92)

Lyon(s), First Ecumenical Council of:
21, 22, 68, 79, 86, 104, 107–21,
125, 125 (n. 9), 126, 161 (n. 9),
189, 194, 194 (n. 115), 213

(n. 158), 225, 226, 233, 243, 246,
247, 254, 255, 255 (n. 103), 263,
264, 264 (n. 122), 266, 267, 270,
272, 272 (n. 155), 273 (n. 156),
274, 276, 287 (n. 26), 307, 308,
325 (n. 35), 342, 342 (n. 95)

Maeothian Marshes, *Meodes/
Meotidas paludes see* Sea of Azov

Magdeburg Centuries/Centuriators:
338, 338 (n. 83), 339

Magna Carta: 83 (n. 124), 347, 347
(n. 124), 348 (n. 125), 390

Magna Hungaria see Hungaria major

Mainz, city: 87, 88, 253 (98)

Mainz, archbishop of *see* Sigfried III

Mansel (Maunsel, Maunsell), John,
clerk: 68, 74, 75, 75 (n. 91), 76, 76
(n. 95), 77, 91, 95, 101, 113
(n. 240), 161, 257

Map, Walter, courtier, writer: 82
(n. 121), 85 (n. 129), 398

Marbach Abbey, annals of: 241
(n. 71)

Margaret of Bohemia, queen, wife of
Valdemar II of Denmark: *see*
Dagmar of Bohemia

Marsh (Marisco), Adam, scholar: 73,
73 (n. 77), 74, 74 (n. 78), 87, 88
(n. 151), 119, 120 (n. 265), 307

Marshall, Gilbert, 4th earl of
Pembroke: 126, 172, 172 (n. 51)

Marshall, Walter, 5th earl of
Pembroke: 126

Master Roger (Magister Rogerius) *see*
Roger of Várad (also of Torre
Maggiore, of Apulia)

Matthew of Westminster, *chronicler:
56, 56 (n. 4), 57 (n. 11), 320
(n. 21), 342, 353, 353 (n. 140),
354 (n. 144), 391, 396, 402

Matthew, archbishop of Esztergom:
288–89, 289 (n. 34)

Meinhard, count of Tyrol: 141

Melrose, monastery (Cistercian): 125

Melrose, chronicle of: 125 (n. 8), 127

Merseburg, town: 165, 165 (n. 24), 300–01

Methodius *see* Pseudo–Methodius

Milton, John, poet: 123 (n. 1), 350 (n. 132, 135)

mise–en–abîme: 23, 27, 32–39, 32 (28), 33 (n. 31), 34 (n. 33), 36 (n. 35), 39 (n. 45, 46), 42, 172, 172 (n. 52), 228, 243, 313, 314, 316, 366

Muhammad (Machomet): 127 (n. 13), 265 (n. 126), 328, 340, 403

Monumenta Germaniae Historica: 223 (n. 184), 352, 354, 355, 362

Moravia: 43, 142 (n. 58), 178 (n. 66), 179 (n. 69), 181 (n. 76), 299–300, 322 (n. 28), 354, 358

Mordvins, *mordani, morducani*: 290–91

Mousket, Philip, chronicler: 199 (n. 121), 216 (n. 165), 241 (n. 71)

Muhi, village: 25 (n. 2), 179 (n. 69), 189, 203, 203 (n. 134), 211, 289, 366 (n. 185)

Muslim(s), Saracen(s): 21, 42, 108, 109, 128, 128 (n. 16), 133, 134–35, 136, 136 (n. 38), 143, 143 (n. 65), 145–49, 143 (n. 65), 148 (n. 82), 151, 155, 160, 162, 187 (n. 94), 206, 217, 254, 255, 262 (n. 117), 263, 271, 273, 276, 327–30, 329 (n. 46), 332 (n. 57), 343 (n. 98), 349, 350 (n. 132), 403

Neckam (Nequam), Alexander, theologian, poet: 81

Nestorians: 128, 129, 132, 332 (n. 60), 340, 370

Neustadt *see* Wiener Neustadt

Nicaea, emperor of *see* John III Doukas Vatatzes

Nicaea, empress of *see* Anna II of Hohenstaufen

Niger (Schwartz), Bernard, antiquarian: 339

Norway: 43, 66 (n. 47), 91, 101–04, 102 (n. 201), 103 (n. 205, 206), 104 (n. 207), 150, 209

Odo of Châteauroux, papal legate, theologian: 254, 255

Ogilby, John, translator, cartographer: 350 (n. 131)

Old Man of the Mountain: 134, 135, 144, 145

Oliver of Paderborn (Cologne), Scholasticus, crusader, chronicler: 152 (n. 95)

Otto (Oddone) of Montferrat (Montefferrato), papal legate: 86, 86 (n. 137), 103–07, 104 (n. 207), 105 (n. 213, 214), 106 (Table 1), 126, 129–32, 129 (n. 21), 130 (n. 30), 156, 181, 198–99, 199 (n. 121), 215, 235 (n. 42), 244 (n. 78), 246–49, 247 (n. 88), 248 (Fig. 8), 249 (Fig. 9), 257, 262, 262 (n. 118), 280, 345 (n. 110), 369–71

Otto II, duke of Bavaria: 150, 216

Ottobeuren Collection, Innsbruck, Universitätsbibliothek, MS 187 (MS *OB*): 98–100, 98 (n. 186), 141, 141 (n. 55, 56, 57), 142, 142 (n. 62), 144, 144 (n. 66), 150, 150 (n. 87), 165 (n. 20), 201 (n. 130), 204 (n. 136), 232 (n. 32), 250 (n. 90), 286–87, 287 (n. 27), 295, 304, 307, 359 (n. 164)

Ottokar I, king of Bohemia: 154 (n. 104), 296 (n. 59), 304

Oxford, city: 39 (n. 46), 57, 65, 73, 74 (n. 78), 81–88, 81 (n. 112), 82 (n. 121), 84 (n. 126, 127, 128), 85 (n. 129, 131), 107, 119, 137, 307, 344 (n. 106), 349, 405

Palacký, František, historian: 360–61, 361 (n. 173)

Palestine: 43, 44 (n. 59), 49, 49 (n. 74), 51, 200 (n. 124), 267 (n. 143)

Pannonia: 48 (n. 69), 49, 136 (n. 40), 152 (n. 94)

Paris, city: 70, 80, 81–85, 81 (n. 111), 85 (n. 131), 87, 88, 95, 111, 137 (n. 42), 181, 181 (n. 77), 185 (n. 88), 230 (n. 27), 254–55, 254 (n. 101), 283, 287–89, 293, 304 (n. 80), 306, 357, 359 (n. 164), 405

Paris, bishop of *see* William of Auvergne

Paris, Matthew: throughout the volume

Parker, Matthew, archbishop of Canterbury: 56 (n. 4), 335–40, 339 (n. 87), 342–45, 343 (n. 102), 344 (n. 106), 347 (n. 120), 352, 397

Pastoreaux: 184, 184 (n. 84–85)

Patarenian(s), (Paterins): 109, 230, 239, 239 (n. 64), 241–42, 253

Pécs, town: 99 (190)

Peter Comestor, scholar: 38 (n. 44), 218 (n. 171), 286, 286 (n. 21, 22, 25), 404

Peter des Roches, bishop of Winchester: 73 (n. 76), *108 (n. 222), 130, 135, 146, 146, 146* (n. 70), 147, 147 (n. 76), *170, 186, 226, 264, 311, 311 (n. 100)*, 346

Peter II, count of Savoy: 277, 293 (n. 48), 389

Peter of Hungary, canon of Lincoln Cathedral: 81 (n. 113), 82, 83 (n. 122), 85

Peter of Vinea, chancellor: 70 (n. 57), 72 (n. 71), 98, 98 (n. 189), 201 (n. 130), 406

Peter, *igumen* (archbishop) of Russia: 115, 226, 264–68, 265 (n. 128), 264 (n. 141), 271, 275, 278, 307, 349

Philip II, king of France: 82

Philip, bishop of Fermo, papal legate to Hungary: 329 (n. 49)

Philip, prior of Terra Sancta province (Dominican): 128, 129, 309 (n. 96), 332, 340, 346, 369

Philip of Pistoia, bishop of Ferrara: 213 (n. 158)

Pinsk, town: 295 (n. 56)

Pliny, the Elder: 237

Poland (*Polonia*): 25, 42, 43 (n. 54), 98 (n. 186), 123, 124, 142 (n. 58), 150, 153, 166, 175, 176, 180, 181 (n. 176), 202, 267, 267 (n. 144), 272, (n. 154), 277, 284, 292, 295, 296, 297, 299, 299 (n. 69), 300, 302–04, 304 (n. 79), 322 (n. 28), 333, 333 (n. 63), 343, 354, 361, 362

Polo, Marco: 265 (n. 126), 332 (n. 60), 403

Prague, city: 295–97, 295 (n. 56), 296 (n. 59), 302–04

Premonstratensian order, Premonstratensians: 99 (n. 190)

Pres[by]ter John (Johannes sacerdotus): 129 (n. 19), 132 (n. 32), 331–32, 332 (n. 57, 58, 60, 61)

Prynne, William, writer, jurist: 346, 346 (n. 126)

Pseudo–Methodius, prophecy of: 282 (n. 7), 285–90, 285 (n. 20), 286

(n. 21, 22, 25), 287 (n. 26), 290–91, 291 (n. 40), 323, 323 (n. 33), 342, 404

Purchas, Samuel, cleric, traveller: 347–48, 348 (n. 126), 350 (n. 135)

Ranulf de Blondeville, 6th earl of Chester: 73 (n. 76)

Ranulf Higden, chronicler: 327 (41), 333, 404

Rashid–ad–Din Tabib, historian: 362, 362 (n. 179)

Regensburg, town: 298 (n. 68), 299 (n. 69)

rescriptum / rescripta: 34, 41, 98–99, 177 (n. 64), 188, 204, 246, 265, 283, 288, 290, 293–95, 307

Rerum Britannicarum Medii Aevi Scriptores *see* Rolls Series

Riccardus (Richardus), Dominican friar: 136–40, 138 (n. 45, 47), 139 (n. 49), 142

Rich, Edmund (of Abingdon), saint, archbishop of Canterbury: 57, 80 (n. 108), 85, 85 (n. 131), 119, 168 (n. 38), 262, 378

Richard de Clare, earl of Gloucester: 76, 120

Richard I, king of England: 66, 82, 154 (n. 104)

Richard, earl of Cornwall: 37, 37 (n. 41), 68–73, 69 (n. 53, 54, 55, 56), 70 (n. 57, 58, 59), 71 (n. 63, 65, 68), 72 (n. 71), 76, 89 (n. 152) 91, 96 (n. 182), 98, 98 (n. 189), 101, 102 (n. 198), 121, 121 (n. 271), 130 (n. 25), 161–62, 168, 169 (n. 39), 183, 185, 257, 259, 288, 324 (n. 34), 370, 378

Rishanger, William, chronicler: 74, 330, 343 (n. 102)

Robert of Courçon (Curzon), papal legate: 230, 230 (n. 27)

Robert of Reading, chronicler: 320, 330 (n. 27)

Robert of Theles, friar: 291, 291 (n. 41)

John de Rochford the Younger of Boston, baron, administrator: 320 (n. 21), 397

Roger de Holden, clerk: 118

Roger of Howden, chronicler: 99 (n. 191), 176 (n. 63), 401

Roger of Várad (also of Torre Maggiore, of Apulia), archdeacon of Várad: 86, 105, 106 (n. 215), 113, 189, 200–04, 200 (n. 125), 204 (n. 135), 212, 215 (n. 163), 231 (n. 30), 289, 358, 366, 366 (n. 185)

Rolls Series: 345, 352–53, 352 (n. 138), 353, 355

Romance of Alexander: 237, 403

Rubruqis/Rubruck, William *see* William of Rubruck

Rus' (*Ruscia, Ruthenia, Rutheni*): 43, 43 (n. 55), 49, 94, 123–24, 142 (n. 58), 149, 150 (n. 85), 152 (n. 94), 153 (n. 98), 255 (n. 102), 295 (n. 56), 297–99, 299 (n. 69)

Russia, archbishop (igumen) of *see* Peter, 'archbishop of Russia'

Salvius (de) Salvis, bishop of Perugia, papal legate: 141

Saracen *see* Muslim

Savoy, count of *see* Peter II, count of Savoy

Saxo Grammaticus, chronicler: 150 (n. 89)

Saxony (*Saxonia*): 87, 154, 165, 170, 177, 178, 180, 208 (n. 145), 284, 287, 293, 296, 296 (n. 62), 299, 300, 302–03, 355 (153)

scedula(e): 61, 61 (30)

Schäftlarn Monastery (Benedictine), annals of (*Annales*

Scheftlarienses): 166, 166 (n. 27), 287, 287 (n. 26)

Schottenkloster (Schottenstift), Vienna: 298, 298 (n. 68), 299

Schwartz, Bernard *see* Niger, Bernard

Sclavonia: 43, 303

Scotland: 44 (n. 59), 125, 209, 399

Scotland, king of *see* Alexander III, king of Scotland

Scythia (*Sicia*), Scythian(s): 48, 49, 49 (n. 71), 51, 153, 211 (n. 153), 212, 233

Sea of Azov (Maeothian Marshes, *Meodes/Meotidas paludes*): 48, 49, 49 (n. 71), 136 (n. 40), 211 (n. 153)

Selden Map of China: 349, 349 (n. 129), 350

Selden, John, jurist, scholar: 346–49, 348 (n. 126), 349 (n. 130)

Siboto, bishop of Augsburg: 98 (n. 186), 150, 204 (n. 136)

Siena, monastery of (Dominican): 99, 99 (n. 190), 295 (n. 54)

Sigfried III von Eppstein, archbishop of Mainz: 92, 93, 117, 247, 250

signes-de-renvoi: 261 (n. 115), 309–10

Simon de Montfort (Monfort), earl of Leicester: 68, 73, 73 (n. 76, 77), 74, 74 (n. 78, 80, 81), 77, 245 (n. 84), 258, 305, 305 (n. 83), 306–07, 403

Simon of Kéza, chronicler: 199 (n. 121)

Simon of Saint-Quentin, Dominican friar, traveller: 138 (n. 44), 142, 232, 275 (n. 161)

Simon of Sywell, canon lawyer: 84

Sophie of Thuringia, duchess of Brabant: 75 (n. 91), 94, 94 (n. 172), 304 (n. 99)

St Albans, monastery (Benedictine): 17, 23, 25 (n. 2), 30, 39 (n. 45), 43, 55, 57 (n. 8, 10, 11), 58–60, 58 (n. 16), 60 (n, 25), 63–67, 64 (n. 40), 65 (n. 42,45), 66, 67 (n. 51), 69–71, 69 (n. 54), 70 (n. 58), 71 (n. 63), 74, 76–79, 78 (n. 103), 79 (n. 107), 81 (n. 112), 83, 89, 89 (n. 152), 91, 93, 93 (n. 167), 99–101, 101 (n. 193), 116, 118–21,126, 130 (n. 24), 136–37, 140–41, 147, 154 (n. 101), 154-55, 157, 160, 169, 222, 223 (184), 237, 243, 245–46, 278, 282–84, 286 (n. 22), 304–08, 306 (n. 86), 308 (n. 93), 311 (100), 317–21, 317 (n. 10), 321 (n. 23), 326–27, 326 (n. 39), 327 (n. 40, 41), 332, 334–36, 335 (n. 68), 339 (n. 87), 352–53, 363, 369, 389–90, 396, 403, 404, 405

St Albans Bible: 44 (n. 59), 49, 405

St Médard of Soissons (Benedictine), chronicle of: 287

St Pantaleon Monastery (Benedictine), Cologne, annals of (*Annales monasterii Sancti Pantaleonis Coloniae*): 96, 138 (n. 44), 202 (n. 130), 294, 301

St Rudbert Monastery, Salzburg, annals of (*Annales Sancti Rudberti Salisburgenses*): 16 (n. 6), 329 (n. 49), 330 (n. 50)

Stams, Abbey of (Cistercian): 100

Stanley, William, historian: 344

Staveley, Thomas, historian: 344

Stephen of Bohemia, traveller: 114

Stow, John, historian and antiquarian: 336, 336 (71), 346

Sibyl(line), prophecy (Sybil): 143 (n. 63), 284, 284 (n. 18), 326 (n. 39), 381

Swereford, Alexander, administrator: 121 (n. 271), 65, 65 (n. 43)

Székesfehérvár, town: 99

Tanais, see Don

Tar(tar), river: 133–34, 147 (n. 77), 198, 375

Templars see Knights Templar

Teutonic Order: 261, 258

Tewkesbury Monastery (Benedictine), annals of (*Annales de Theokesberia*): 216, 216 (n. 61), 160 (n. 6), 287

Thaddeus de Sessa/Suessa, jurist: 272, 272 (n. 156), 274

Thomas, warden (*custos*) of Bohemia: 302

Thomas of Spalato, archdeacon, chronicler: 157, 189, 195, 200 (n. 125), 201, 201 (n. 129), 204 (n. 135), 231 (n. 30), 236, 236 (n. 49), 286 (n. 22), 358, 365 (n. 184), 407

Thuringia: 91, 92, 101, 165 (n. 25), 177 (n. 65), 178 (n. 66), 180, 180 (n. 74), 188, 292, 296, 297, 303

Thuringia, landgrave of see Ludwig (Louis) IV, Henry Raspe, Hermann II

Tonengo, Otto see Otto (Oddone) of Montferrat, legate

Tractatus de ortu Tartarorum: 265, 307 (n. 90)

Transsumpta de Lyon: 111, 119 (n. 262), 405, 406

Transylvania: 50 (n. 75), 113–14, 114 (n. 243)

Trier (Trèves), Deeds of the Trevians (*Gestorum Treverorum*): 220, 287, 287 (n. 26)

Trivet, Nicholas, chronicler: 129 (n. 19), 319 (n. 16), 330 (n. 54), 331–32, 331 (n. 55), 332 (n. 57), 395, 402

universities see Paris, Bologna, Toulouse, Oxford, Cambridge

Vác, bishop of see István (Stephen) Báncsa

Valdemar (Waldemar) II, king of Denmark: 101, 148, 152, 153–55, 153 (n. 98), 154 (n. 104)

Valves (Valwen) see Cuman

Vaucouleurs, town: 130

Verecke Pass: 291

Veszprém, town: 99 (n. 190)

Vienna, city: 165, 203, 228, 231 (n. 32), 298, 298 (n. 68), 299, 300, 406

Vincent of Beauvais, scholar: 137, 138 (n. 44), 349 (n. 130), 362, 405

Vitae durorum Offarum: 282, 346 (n. 119), 57 (n. 10), 388

Waldemar see Valdemar

Walsingham, Thomas, chronicler: 161, 327, 327 (n. 42), 331 (n. 55), 336, 337, 404, 405

Walter of Reigate (de Rogatis), papal legate: 325

Watts, William, hector of St Alban, antiquarian: 340, 345–47, 352–53, 355–56, 359 (n. 164), 360, 360 (n. 166)

Waverley Monastery (Cistercian), annals of (*Annales monasterii de Waverleia*): 147 (n. 80), 256, 284, 287–88, 288 (n. 31), 292, 304, 304 (n. 80), 306, 306 (n. 88)

Wenceslas I, king of Bohemia: 92, *111 (n. 232)*, 176 (n. 62), 178, 178 (n. 66), 179 (n. 69), 180, 202, 203, 237 (n. 60), *301, 303,* 304 (n. 79)

Wendover, Roger, chronicler: 32, 33, 56–60, 56 (n. 5), 57 (n. 11), 58 (n. 16), 59 (n. 22), 60 (23), 84

(n. 128), 85 (n. 132), 93, 93 (n. 166), 121 (n. 271), 146, 152, 190, 208 (n. 145), 280 (n. 172), 284, 284 (n. 181), 316–18, 322 (n. 26), 334, 391, 393, 401, 404

Westminster: 43, 45, 77, 96 (n. 179), 129, 245, 319, 320 (n. 20, 21), 330, 330 (n. 53, 54), 353, 390, 392, 394, 396, 397, 398, 402

Wiener Neustadt (Civitas Nova), town: 23 (n/ 32), 230, 230 (n. 29), 251

Wilhering, (Cistercian) Abbey of : 72 (n. 71), 406

William II Rufus, king of England: 280 (n. 172)

William de Montibus, scholar: 85 (n. 129)

William de Raleigh, bishop of Norwich, then Winchester: 85 (n. 132), 170 (n. 45)

William of Auvergne, bishop of Paris: 85, 85 (n. 133), 95, 181, 254, 255 (n. 102), 283, 287, 304 (n. 80)

William of Kilkenny, bishop of Ely: 78 (n. 102)

William of Malmesbury, chronicler: 62, 65, 334, 396, 399

William of Montferrat, Dominican monk: 132 (n. 32)

William of Nangis, chronicler: 333 (n. 63)

William of Powic(ke), clerk: 118, 120 (n. 266)

William of Rubruck, traveller: 137, 137 (n. 41), 332 (n. 57, 60), 350, 359

William of Sabina (William of Modena, Guglielmo de Chartreaux, or Guglielmus de Sabaudia [Savoy]): 101, 102–03, 103–04 (n. 207), 104, 106

William of Savoy, bishop of Valence: 130 (n. 25)

William of Tripoli, missionary and papal legate: 265 (n. 126)

William of Wintershill, almoner of St Albans: 327 (n. 40)

Winchester, bishop of *see* Peter des Roches

Worcester, annals of (*Annales de prioratus Wigornia*): 61, 61 (n. 27)

Wykes, Thomas, chronicler: 327, 404, 407

Yarmouth, town: 134, 145, 151, 152, 155, 393

York, city: 113 (n. 240)

York, archbishop of: *104*

Zingiton (Churchitan), khan: 218, 218 (n. 173), 292–93 *see also* Chinggis, khan

Zwettl (Cistercian), annals of (*Annales Zwetlenses*): 231 (n. 32)

Cultural Encounters in Late Antiquity and the Middle Ages

All volumes in this series are evaluated by an Editorial Board, strictly on academic grounds, based on reports prepared by referees who have been commissioned by virtue of their specialism in the appropriate field. The Board ensures that the screening is done independently and without conflicts of interest. The definitive texts supplied by authors are also subject to review by the Board before being approved for publication. Further, the volumes are copyedited to conform to the publisher's stylebook and to the best international academic standards in the field.

Titles in Series

De Sion exibit lex et verbum domini de Hierusalem: Essays on Medieval Law, Liturgy, and Literature in Honour of Amnon Linder, ed. by Yitzhak Hen (2001)

Amnon Linder, *Raising Arms: Liturgy in the Struggle to Liberate Jerusalem in the Late Middle Ages* (2003)

Thomas Deswarte, *De la destruction a la restauration: L'ideologie dans le royaume d'Oviedo-Leon (VIIIe-XIe siecles)* (2004)

The Jews of Europe in the Middle Ages (Tenth to Fifteenth Centuries): Proceedings of the International Symposium held at Speyer, 20–25 October 2002, ed. by Christoph Cluse (2004)

Christians and Christianity in the Holy Land: From the Origins to the Latin Kingdoms, ed. by Ora Limor and Guy G. Stroumsa (2006)

Carine van Rijn, *Shepherds of the Lord: Priests and Episcopal Statutes in the Carolingian Period* (2007)

Avicenna and his Legacy: A Golden Age of Science and Philosophy, ed. by Y. Tzvi Langermann (2010)

Writing 'True Stories': Historians and Hagiographers in the Late Antique and Medieval Near East, ed. by Arietta Papaconstantinou, Muriel Debié, and Hugh Kennedy (2010)

Carolingian Scholarship and Martianus Capella: Ninth-Century Commentary Traditions on 'De nuptiis' in Context, ed. by Mariken Teeuwen and Sinéad O'Sullivan (2011)

John-Henry Clay, *In the Shadow of Death: Saint Boniface and the Conversion of Hessia, 721–54* (2011)

Ehud Krinis, *God's Chosen People: Judah Halevi's 'Kuzari' and the Shī 'ī Imām Doctrine* (2013)

Strategies of Identification: Ethnicity and Religion in Early Medieval Europe, ed. by Walter Pohl and Gerda Heydemann (2013)

Post-Roman Transitions: Christian and Barbarian Identities in the Early Medieval West, ed. by Walter Pohl and Gerda Heydemann (2013)

Between Personal and Institutional Religion: Self, Doctrine, and Practice in Late Antique Eastern Christianity, ed. by Brouria Bitton-Ashkelony and Lorenzo Perrone (2013)

D' Orient en Occident: Les recueils de fables enchassees avant les Mille et une Nuits de Galland (Barlaam et Josaphat, Calila et Dimna, Disciplina clericalis, Roman des Sept Sages), ed. by Marion Uhlig and Yasmina Foehr-Janssens (2014)

Conflict and Religious Conversation in Latin Christendom: Studies in Honour of Ora Limor, ed. by Israel Jacob Yuval and Ram Ben-Shalom (2014)

Visual Constructs of Jerusalem, ed. by Bianca kühnel, Galit Noga-Banai, and Hanna Vorholt (2014)

The Introduction of Christianity into the Early Medieval Insular World: Converting the Isles I, ed. by Roy Flechner and Máire Ní Mhaonaigh (2016)

Motions of Late Antiquity: Essays on Religion, Politics, and Society in Honour of Peter Brown, ed. by Jamie kreiner and Helmut Reimitz (2016)

The Prague Sacramentary: Culture, Religion, and Politics in Late Eighth-Century Bavaria, ed. by Maximilian Diesenberger, Rob Meens, and Els Rose (2016)

The Capetian Century, 1214–1314, ed. by William Chester Jordan and Jenna Rebecca Phillips (2017)

Transforming Landscapes of Belief in the Early Medieval Insular World and Beyond: Converting the Isles II, ed. by Nancy Edwards, Máire Ní Mhaonaigh, and Roy Flechner (2017)

Historiography and Identity I: Ancient and Early Christian Narratives of Community, ed. by Walter Pohl and Veronika Wieser (2019)

Inclusion and Exclusion in Mediterranean Christianities, 400–800, ed. by Yaniv Fox and Erica Buchberger (2019)

Leadership and Community in Late Antiquity: Essays in Honour of Raymond Van Dam, ed. by Young Richard Kim and A. E. T. McLaughlin (2020)

Pnina Arad, *Christian Maps of the Holy Land: Images and Meanings* (2020)

Historiography and Identity II: Post-Roman Multiplicity and New Political Identities, ed. by Helmut Reimitz and Gerda Heydemann (2020)

Historiography and Identity III: Carolingian Approaches, ed. by Helmut Reimitz, Rutger Kramer, and Graeme Ward (2021)

Minorities in Contact in the Medieval Mediterranean, ed. by Clara Almagro Vidal, Jessica Tearney-Pearce, and Luke Yarbrough (2021)

Historiography and Identity IV: Writing History Across Medieval Eurasia, ed. by Walter Pohl and Daniel Mahoney (2021)

Historiography and Identity VI: Competing Narratives of the Past in Central and Eastern Europe, c. 1200–c. 1600, ed. by Pavlina Rychterová (2021)

Political Ritual and Practice in Capetian France: Essays in Honour of Elizabeth A. R. Brown, ed. by M. C. Gaposchkin and Jay Rubenstein (2021)

Yossi Maurey, *Liturgy and Sequences of the Sainte-Chapelle: Music, Relics, and Sacral Kingship in Thirteenth-Century France* (2022)

Les transferts culturels dans les mondes normands médiévaux (VIIIe–XIIe siècle): objets, acteurs et passeurs, ed. by Pierre Bauduin, Simon Lebouteiller, and Luc Bourgeois (2022)

Civic Identity and Civic Participation in Late Antiquity and the Early Middle Ages, ed. by Cédric Brélaz and Els Rose (2022)

In Preparation

Historiography and Identity V: The Emergence of New Peoples and Polities in Europe, 1000–1300, ed. by Walter Pohl, Francesco Borri, and Veronika Wieser

From Sun-Day to the Lord's Day: The Cultural History of Sunday in Late Antiquity and the Early Middle Ages, ed. by Uta Heil